ACTA CONVENTUS
NEO-LATINI SANCTANDREANI

medieval & renaissance texts & studies

VOLUME 38

ACTA CONVENTUS NEO-LATINI SANCTANDREANI

Proceedings of the Fifth International Congress of Neo-Latin Studies

St Andrews 24 August to 1 September 1982

EDITED BY

I. D. McFarlane

medieval & renaissance texts & studies
Binghamton, New York
1986

Library of Congress Cataloging-in-Publication Data

International Congress on Neo-Latin Studies (5th :
  1982 : University of St. Andrews)
  Acta Conventus Neo-Latini Sanctandreani.

  (Medieval & Renaissance texts & studies ; 38)
  Includes index.
  1. Latin literature, Medieval and modern—History and criticism—
Congresses.   2. Latin language, Medieval and modern—
Congresses.   3. Classicism—Congresses.   4. Learning and
scholarship—History—Congresses.   5. Humanists—Congresses.
6. Renaissance—Congresses. I. McFarlane, I. D. (Ian Dalrymple)
II. Title.   III. Series: Medieval & Renaissance texts & studies ; 38.
PA8002.I57 1982   940   85-28405
ISBN 0-86698-070-9 (alk. paper)

Contents

C: Humanists connected with the Low Countries and Germany

D: France

E: Great Britain

F: Poland

G: Miscellaneous

Foreword

The fifth Congress of the IANLS took place from 24th August to 1st September 1982 at the University of St Andrews, Scotland. The proceedings were divided into two sections: on the one hand there was the celebration of George Buchanan's death in 1582; it was particularly appropriate that the venue was St Andrews, since the humanist had been an undergraduate at the University and later became Principal of St Leonard's College. And on the other hand, papers of a wider range were given during the other days of the Congress. The *Acta* print a good number of the papers and lectures delivered, but as has happened before, a few have appeared or will appear in print in learned journals. Among these were those devoted to John Barclay whose quatercentenary was celebrated at the same time: these appeared in *Humanistica Lovaniensia.*

This time, more care has been taken to limit the length of the printed text of the papers; it has been necessary, more perhaps than in former *Acta*, to respect financial constrictions; any shortening has been carried out with the approval of those concerned. The Congress was a great success; and for this we must express our gratitude to the efforts of the local committee under the able chairmanship of Professor J. K. Cameron; and we record too the welcome extended to the Association by both the University and the City of St Andrews. The Renaissance resources of the University Library and the numerous attractions of the surrounding regions contributed in substantial measure to the enjoyment of those present; a special word of thanks must go to those who organised and took part in the memorable performance of Buchanan's *Jephthes*, in the elegant translation of Professor Peter Walsh (University of Glasgow); this was an experience that made a deep impression on the assembled company.

Finally, I thank Professor Mario A. Di Cesare for undertaking to publish this volume of Acta and for his help on the editorial side as well as in the technical matters of modern publication.

I. D. McFarlane

ACTA CONVENTUS
NEO-LATINI SANCTANDREANI

B U C H A N A N

The References to Classical Authors in Buchanan's
Rerum Scoticarum Historia
für J. Fleckenstein zum 65. Gebürtstag

C. J. Classen

Histories of English literature, even histories of British literature, often ignore George Buchanan, and when they take notice of him, they are content with a few brief remarks on his works.[1] This reveals a deficiency which one also meets with in the histories of other national literatures: the neglect of the products in Latin. One might, of course, argue that such works are not part of the vernacular literature; and yet they are part of the production of their authors. This raises the question whether one can do justice to a writer or, indeed, to an artist of any kind, when one considers part of his work only, Michelangelo as a painter only, but not as an architect, not as a sculptor; or Barlach as a sculptor, but not as a poet. Furthermore another problem arises; when an author feels free or even prefers to write some of his works in Latin, one is bound to ask when and why does he choose to do so, to what extent do his works in Latin differ from those in the vernacular (and *vice versa*); can one discern features which are common to all his works? Moreover, one asks what kind of education did the author enjoy, did he continue to read ancient authors (or even teach Classics), which role does his classical education play in his writing works in Latin, what kind of audience is he addressing.

With regard to the *Rerum Scoticarum Historia*[2] which the great Humanist, poet, pedagogue and politician G. Buchanan[3] wrote during the last years of his life, a work which may not be considered a piece of literature in the narrow sense, but which may yet tell us much about its author and its public, as it was reprinted at least twenty times, very special questions arise.

There is no need to ask which part the Classics played in Buchanan's education, nor whether he continued to study Latin and Greek literature. Both his position as a teacher or tutor and his writings, his poems, his tragedies, the *Sphaera* and his translations testify to his ability, his ambitions and his achievements, which were widely praised even during his lifetime.[4] The *Historia* makes us ask what the knowledge of the ancient literatures meant to Buchanan in writing it, whether it influenced his idea of historiography, his use of sources, his style, whether he referred to the ancients for his ideas, whether he used them as sources or whether he exploited them to embellish his style.

As is well known, Th. Ruddiman, the conscientious editor of Buchanan's *Opera omnia* questioned his reliability;[5] Father Th. Innes launched what seemed a fatal attack not only on his credibility, but even on his honesty.[6] While P. Hume Brown, in his biography, did not face the problem,[7] Hugh R. Trevor-Roper summarized the findings of his brief, penetrating study of the *Historia*, especially the attacks on the Welsh antiquarian Humphrey Lhuyd, and of the political writings of Buchanan's last years (including his possible contribution to a document presented to Queen Elizabeth by the Scottish commissioners to justify the deposition of Queen Mary) in the following manner: "What we see is a vain humanist, who, having plunged into revolutionary politics and become the propagandist of a revolutionary idea, easily believed his own arguments and then, when his errors were exposed, and he knew that they could not be defended, lost his faith but preferred to compromise with falsehood rather than disown it."[8] Much kinder than the verdict of the historian is the judgment of the professor of French literature who is thoroughly at home in the world of the Humanists and of Renaissance literature as well as scholarship: "Buchanan's critical sense obviously has very pronounced limits—in which he differs little from his contemporaries."[9] In the body of his paper, Trevor-Roper says of Buchanan that "he belonged to the clearly defined school of humanist historians," and he continues to say "The essential character of the humanist historians was that they believed in texts, and especially in literary texts. Provided they had an authoritative literary text, they clung to it, and the only originality in which they indulged was to purge their chosen text of barbarous solecisms."[10] What kind of text or texts does Buchanan use? Which of his statements does he support by references to ancient sources, and which are they? Does he apply his critical faculties when consulting them? Is there any evidence of deliberate omission or distortion? These are the questions which pose themselves, and in the course of our study one or two others will arise and will have to be answered.

Buchanan's *Rerum Scoticarum Historia* need not be introduced here at length. However, it may be helpful to remember that the author, like many earlier historians of Britain (and other countries),[11] begins with a description of the British Isles (*liber primus*) and of the tribes inhabiting them and of their origin (*liber secundus*), and that he adds excerpts from a number of ancient sources (*liber tertius*), before he starts with his narrative account from the earliest times. As it has been emphasized again recently that the first two books seem to have been written separately (together with the third), possibly later than the bulk of the work on the early Scottish history and probably in answer to the publication of Humphrey Lhuyd's *Fragmentum* and its attacks on Hector Boece and his *Scotorum Historia* (1526),[12] it is preferable to begin with what in the manuscript is labelled as Book I, i.e. Book IV.

Here the references to sources from classical antiquity are very rare, though

Buchanan first repeats a few facts "ea potissimum," as he emphasizes, "quae a fabularum vanitate abessent, et a vetustis rerum scriptoribus non dissentirent," namely that first some people went from Spain to Ireland, thence to Scotland, invited by the aeris salubritas et pabuli foecunditas. The only author cited for any detail is the Venerable Bede (arrival of a classis Germanica, vel (ut scribit Beda) Scythica), and except for a general remark that unnamed writers place the arrival of Fergus, the first elected king of the Scots, in Albion in the time, when Alexander the Great conquered Babylon,[13] no particular source is mentioned in the account of the first seventeen kings, no attempt is made to relate the events in Scotland to those in the rest of the world, while Boece several times refers to events or personalities in Greece or Rome.[14] Indeed, it is probably not an ancient, but a later source from which Buchanan derived the dating of Fergus's arrival.

Of the eighteenth king, Caratacus, Buchanan reports that he conquered the *Aebudae* (the Hebrides), adding that he does not believe the *nostri scriptores* who claim that during his reign the Oreades (Orkney Islands) were conquered by Claudius. Against Orosius, Eutropius and Bede, the sources allegedly cited by the *nostri scriptores*, he puts forward the authority of Tacitus's statement that before the arrival of Iulius Agricola that part of Britain was totally unknown to the Romans,[15] even though both Pomponius Mela and the Elder Pliny mention these islands in passages which Buchanan refers to in the first book (see below),[16] but does not seem to think of here. This is a clear indication that this was written independently of the first two books.

Buchanan refers to Tacitus again in introducing the twenty-first king, this time, as he says, because sunt qui hunc (i.e., Corbredum secundum cognomento Galdum) Galgacum a Tacito appellari existiment,[17] and again the reference is to Boece. However, he does not indicate whether he accepts the identification, although it would, if correct, provide the first piece of evidence from a Roman source for any of the early Scottish kings; he is content to explain the origin of the cognomen Galdus. Obviously, he is not particularly concerned to look for support for the early kings, whereas Boece from the time of Ederus, the fifteenth king, and Caesar's invasion of Britain relates the history of Scotland to that of the Romans (see note 14).

In Buchanan's account immediate contacts between Scots and Romans are mentioned first during the reign of Corbredus II (Galdus) at least as a possibility (*opinor*): the Roman expedition against the Brigantes and Silures makes it appear likely to Buchanan that these tribes received help from their Northern neighbours. But he registers the victories of Petilius Cerialis and Iulius Frontinus without explicit reference to Tacitus, although he clearly draws on his work,[18] as he also does for the following account of Agricola's activities, again without explicitly citing his source.[19] Interestingly, though Buchanan registers the identification of Corbredus Galdus with Tacitus's Calgacus (Galcagus) and is quite fond of adorning his history with speeches, he does not even hint at, let alone reproduce, the speech which Tacitus puts in his mouth, while Boece incorporates it in its entirety.[20]

Though with the Roman conquest of England and the attacks on Scotland, Buchanan has entered the period of permanent contacts between the Romans and the Scots, his explicit references to the Romans, let alone Roman sources, remain rare. In his account of Mogaldus's reign he criticizes Bede for not mentioning Hadrian's Wall, while both the Roman Aelius Spartianus in his life of the emperor and the Greek Herodian in his account of Severus speak of it;[21] but otherwise no source is appealed to, not even where he names individuals, though his historical account seems to owe a good deal not only to Livy for the general manner of presentation or to such models as the *Scriptores Historiae Augustae* for his gruesome picture of some of the Scottish kings, but also to several historians for factual details.[22] Only for the losses the Romans suffered during Severus's expedition he cites Cassius Dio;[23] and, a little later in the life of Donald I, he gives a quotation from Aelius Spartianus in describing Severus's *murus* to distinguish it clearly from Hadrian's *vallum*.[24] Obviously, Buchanan is anxious to make his own position clear in view of the archeological evidence that had come to light during his time and in view of what *nostrorum quidam* wrongly believed about Camulodunum. This passage again deserves special attention, because Buchanan had dealt with this problem also earlier, in his description of Britain, where he had stressed that the remains of a town discovered near the river Carron must be what Bede called Guidi, and that Camulodunum is not anywhere near the wall of Severus, but in the South and that the round building near the Carron is not the temple of Claudius Caesar.[25]

For some events during the reign of the following kings from Ethodius II to Fergus II ancient authorities are available (as Boece's history shows); yet Buchanan does not cite them, not even where he clearly relies on them heavily, as he does, e.g., on Eutropius for the section on Carausius.[26] Obviously, he sees no reason why he should confirm the details of the story as he unfolds it, except for a few controversial points where he calls the ancients (or some of them) to his aid.

Before we turn to the first two (or three) books, a few brief remarks may not be superfluous on the references to ancient authors or classical antiquity in general in the following books (i.e., V–XX). While Buchanan very rarely alludes to Greek or Roman names or words, institutions or particular habits, examples or parallels from antiquity,[27] there are hardly any quotations from ancient authors, and those which we do meet with, are cited not as source of information, but of general wisdom, often without the author's name.[28]

When we now turn to the first books, the picture we find there is very different indeed: a large number of texts referred to or even quoted from a long list of Greek and Roman authors. Some of them one would expect in an account of Britain and its inhabitants, especially as Buchanan does not confine his *descriptio* to Scotland, but gives some general information about the British Isles: Caesar and Tacitus, Pliny the Elder and Solinus, Claudian and Orosius, Strabo, Ptolemy and Stephanus of Byzantinum. These and others also occur in the medieval and late medieval historians of Britain (such as William of Malmesbury, Henry of Huntingdon, Geoffrey of Monmouth, Richard of Devizes, John of Fordun),[29] a good many more in the historical and antiquarian writers of the sixteenth century, e.g. John Major (Mair), Hector Boece, Polydore Vergil, John Leland, John Lesley or Humphrey Lhuyd as the following table shows:[30]

	Major	Boece	Vergil	Leland	Lesley	Lhuyd
Aelius Spartianus		x	x			x
Ammianus				x	x	x
Ps.-Aristoteles				x	x	x
Cassius Dio						x
Cicero	x			x		
Diodorus				x		x
Dionysius Afer	x					x
Dionysius Halic.		x	x			x
Eutropius		x	x		x	x
Festus		x				x
Flavius Vopiscus						x
Herodian		x	x		x	x
Horace	x		x	x		x
Juvenal	x		x	x		x
Itineraria Ant.					x	x
Iulius Capitolinus						x
Aelius Lampridius		x	x			x
Livius		x	x			x
Lucan	x	x		x		
Martial				x		x
Notitia Dignitatum						x
Panegyrici						x
Plato						x
Pomponius Mela		x				x
Plutarch						x
Suetonius		x	x			x
Virgil	x	x	x	x		

But while some whom one meets with in these earlier writers of the sixteenth century, are conspicuously absent from Buchanan's *Historia*, e.g., Appian and Aurelius Victor, Lucian and Pausanias, Sidonius Apollinaris and Valerius Maximus,[31] as indeed a number of the Fathers of the Church (Ambrose, Augustine, Eusebius, Jerome, Socrates and Tertullian),[32] from whose ranks Buchanan seems to mention Sozomenus and Theodoretus only,[33] several ancient authors are found in his work whom the earlier writers do not mention: Arrian, Cato, Ennius, Ephorus, the Etymologicum Magnum, Hyginus, Martianus Capella or rather Markianos, Philemo, Propertius, Seneca, Suidas, Terence, Theophrastus, and Varro. Even though I may well have overlooked some references, it will at once be obvious that Buchanan draws on a much wider selection than any of the earlier historians or antiquarians, except for Humphrey Lhuyd who even cites several authors one does not find in Buchanan's work (see note 31).

But how are we to explain the difference between the first two books of the *Rerum Scoticarum Historia* and the rest, how the difference between Buchanan and the other historians? Is Buchanan the more conscientious historian or has he enjoyed the better classical training? Is it his experience as tutor and teacher of the classical languages and literatures which makes him cite ancient authorities with greater frequency (and if so, why does he do it in the first two books, but not later), or is he merely parading his learning? The following considerations and observations will help to answer these questions.

Neither in the first two books nor in the later ones do we meet with more than a few classical quotations as a form of embellishment, woven into the text as *lumina* of the kind quite common in works of medieval historiography and not rare in later ones.[34] Even in Buchanan's *De iure regni* examples of this kind occur more frequently,[35] whereas the prose of the *Historia* owes its force and grace to the author's ability to reproduce the flow of classical prose such as Livy's, which would have been spoilt, if interrupted by the intrusion of longer classical quotations for the sake of raising its stylistic level; and only very rarely a particular word or phrase is deliberately filched from a classical author.[36]

As indicated above, references to the sources from classical antiquity are rare in Book IV, even where Buchanan relies on them heavily, while they abound in the first two books. Admittedly, some of the Greek and Latin authors he appeals to he knows second-hand only, as e.g., Ephorus (through Strabo) or the geographer Marcianus (Markianos through Stephanus of Byzantium), as he points out himself in both cases, or Varro and the geographer Philemo (through Pliny, without indicating this).[37] Occasionally, he lists a whole group of authors, though he does not seem to have consulted their works, but to have taken their names from a commentary such as that by Joachim Vadianus on Pomponius Mela, who, in his note on Mela's brief version of Hercules's fight with the sons of Neptunus in Liguria, collects much additional material, and for this refers to Cato, Aeschylus in Strabo, Hyginus, Pliny, Diodorus, and others.[38] As none of the authors mentioned by Buchanan (Diodorus, Strabo, Cato, Hyginus and Pomponius Mela) gives the whole story as he tells it, one can explain Buchanan's references to them most easily by a somewhat superficial use of such a secondary source as a commentary.[39]

Furthermore, as Buchanan in one of the passages just mentioned is not quite accurate in reproducing what Pliny makes Philemo say, and in another is wrong in attributing a particular view to Marcianus — whom he, moreover, confuses with

Martianus Capella[40] — one begins to ask how reliable Buchanan's references are, how exact his quotations, how faithfully he reproduces the sources on which he relies.

I begin with some observations on the names Buchanan cites, leaving aside misprints and orthographical matters,[41] though occasionally even they may be of interest. Sometimes Buchanan gives a name in a form which differs slightly from that used in his source, e.g., *Britannia* instead of *Britanni* (Lucr. 6. 1106) or *insulae Britannicae, Caledonii* instead of *Dicaledonii* or *Caledones*.[42]

At times Buchanan gives entirely new forms which are not found in any ancient text and clearly wrong, e.g., Apoceanitas, allegedly from Strabo, though it does not fit Buchanan's own context and explanation, possibly a mistake for Παρωκεανίτας, or *Moremarusa* from Pliny and Solinus instead of *Morimarusa*, clearly not a misprint, as only this form *Moremarusa* suits his etymological explanation — but both of these occur in a very special passage to which I shall have to return later[43] — or *Aestiones* instead of *Aestii* (Tacitus *Germ.* 45. 2), an error which seems due not to an old edition or Buchanan's own misreading of his source, but to his arch-enemy Humphrey Lhuyd who also uses this form.[44] However, it would be wrong to assume that Buchanan was simply negligent in these matters, as is shown by his critical remarks on the particular forms of names; more than once the correct form of a name which we read in our texts today seems to occur for the first time in Buchanan's *Historia*, a fact which classical scholars appear to be not aware of.

Sixteenth-century editions of Claudian have a variety of readings or conjectures for the name of Ireland in two passages, where it is found at the end of the line: *Hyberne, hybernae,* or *Hiberne* (8. 33) and *Ibernam, Hybernam, Hibernam, Ivernam* (22. 251). Buchanan, when citing these passages prints *Ierne* and *Iernam* respectively,[45] the latter of which is commonly attributed to J. J. Scaliger, the former tentatively to Cujas's manuscripts.[46] However, there is no indication of such a reading in Cujas's notes, which have been preserved in his copy of the 1534 edition (in Göttingen). J. Koch, therefore, assumed that Claverius, who in his commentary (1602) claims: "Duobus manuscr. haec fulcitur lectio," in fact owed the form to Greek authors, Stephanus of Byzantium and Strabo.[47] Indeed, it does occur long before Claverius in Latin translations, not of Strabo or Stephanus of Byzantium, but of Ps. Aristotle.[48] However, it was not Claverius who first introduced *Ierne* into the text of Claudian at 8. 33 (in his edition of 1602) nor Scaliger (in 1603) *Iernam* at 22. 251, as modern scholars assume; for we find both in Buchanan's *Historia* of 1582. But while his interest in the correct form of such names as well as his familiarity with their Greek equivalents and with the actual usage of his own time might well account for such an emendation, especially as Buchanan was not worried by paleographical scruples, he does not seem to have been responsible for it either. For in Lhuyd's *Fragmentum* on reads: "Unde multo melius eos fecisse qui eam Iverniam ut Mela et Iuvenalis Satyra 2. aut Ierna ut Claudianus et Dionysius, quam qui Hiberniam, scripsere reor."[49] Once more,

it looks as if Buchanan is dependent on his arch-enemy, this time for an emendation which one might otherwise have attributed to his ingenuity or scholarship,
but he may have taken this form from another source. For further investigation
shows that Hermolaus Barbarus already suggests *Iernae* as correct reading at 8. 33
in his *Castigationes* on Pliny's *naturalis historia* (Rome 1492).[50] In the first of these
two passages Buchanan also prints the correct genitive *Pictorum* (8. 32), where
the earlier editions of the sixteenth century had *Pictonum*.[51] But while Claverius
corrects this error with reference to a *vetus liber* and four spurious lines in Lucan's
first book (accepted by Cujas), Th. Pulmann had printed *Pictorum* already in 1571,
and the young M. A. Delrio had pointed out in his notes (1572) that this was
the correct form.[52] However, it seems less likely that Buchanan used the most
recent edition of Claudian, thus displaying the attitude of a conscientious scholar;
rather he relied here as elsewhere[53] on his better knowledge which prevented him
from confusing the *Pictones* and the *Picti*. At any rate we can register his concern
for the correct form of such names.

   That Buchanan did not hesitate to change a text is shown by such a remark
as one finds added to the name of one of the long list of cities ending in *-ica*: "Cor-
imbrica: Pli. in Lusi.; sed nisi fallor corrupte pro Conimbrica, cuius meminit
It. Ant. et quae suum vetus nomen adhuc servat ad Mundam amnem." He corrects what the editions of his time print with the help of another text (*Itin. Anton.
Aug.* 421. 4, where e.g., the edition 1526 reads *Conembrica*) and of the actual usage
of his time.[54] No less instructive is another example. In the third book Buchanan
prints a passage from Orosius (1. 2. 81–82), giving the name of the island there
mentioned as *Meuania*, where modern editors, in accordance with the manuscripts,
also read *Mevania*.[55] Admittedly, this is a mistake, but probably a mistake which
Orosius made like others who gave the island the name of a city in Umbria with
which he was more familiar. But as it is the editor's task to print what the author
(presumably) wrote, Buchanan goes too far when he alters the text in the first
book, and simply says "dicta ... a Paulo Orosio *Meuania* aut potius *Maenauia*."[56]
At the same time he leaves no doubt that he is familiar with the places he mentions and the names used for them by his contemporaries, and that he is concerned about their correct form. Thus he is prepared to alter the transmitted text
even against the authority of the manuscripts.

   In the list of cities ending in *-ica*, which I have already referred to, Buchanan
suggests, rather cautiously, that where Pliny mentions *Flaviobrica* (4. 110) instead
of *ad Amanum portum* one should read *Magnum*—in accordance with Ptolemy.[57]
Without caring about the manuscripts and without allowing for an error of the
author, he is prepared to change the text, merely because he believes he has found
the correct form in another author, which, in this case, happens to be a mistake
on his part, as Ptolemy mentions (Αὐτριγόνων) Φλαουιόβριγα without giving further information (2. 6. 7), while of Φλαούιον Βριγάντιον he says that it is ἐν τῷ
Μεγάλῳ λιμένι (2. 6. 4). However, there are instances where Buchanan registers
two different forms side by side: "Medubrica, cognomento Plumbaria, Pli., in

Lus. Haec ni fallor in Itinerario Ant. vocatur Mundobrica" or "Nertobrica alt. in Celtibe. Ptol., in It. Ant. Nitobrica."[58] Elsewhere he even changes the text, merely with reference to the usage of his time. Thus the name of *Dumnacus*, whom Hirtius mentions several times in the eighth book of the Gallic War, he proposes to alter "quod mihi ex Dunaco corruptum videtur. Dunach enim Dunanum, et Dunensem significare potest, ut Romach Romanum. Dunacus, sive potius Dunachus adhuc inter propria virorum nomina usurpatur, qůod nomen utrius- que linguae Latinae et Britannicae ignari perperam nunc Duncanum, nunc Donatum vertunt."[59] Similarly, he suggests to write in Ptolemy "pro mari Deucaledonio ... Duncaledonium: et apud Marcellinum pro Dicaledones, Dun- caledones," adding "et mari, et gente a Duncaledonio oppido cognominatis."[60] Here, he himself feels that he is very near, if not beyond the limits of what is permitted to a scholar, and he introduces his suggestion with the word "Et si adver- sus consensum omnium Ptolemaei codicum mihi aliquid permittere auderem." However, several pages later, where again he has occasion to refer to Ammianus, he repeats his suggestion: "... Dicaledones (sive ut ego legendum censeo Duncaledones)."

Clearly, Buchanan reads his texts carefully, and though his work is full of misprints, a good many of the divergences from the editions of his time are due not to negligence or error, but to deliberate alteration and correction which he felt justified in making in view of the forms of names he found in other authors or in the actual usage of his time.[61]

When we now turn to the passages Buchanan quotes from ancient authors, we find him again not infrequently differing from the texts we read today, sometimes because he merely paraphrases what his sources say,[62] more often because he, naturally, uses the editions available in his time. In some cases we can name the particular edition he consulted;[63] in others we can at least give a *terminus ante quem* or *post quem* for the edition used, as particular readings disappear, while others (or conjectures) appear for the first time.[64] Generally speaking — and this may be of some interest for the general development of Buchanan's studies — the editions consulted by him seem to have been published before 1550, and this corresponds exactly with what the list of books from his library teaches us.[65]

But to return to Buchanan's quotations, their accuracy and their function, one has to register several obvious mistakes (apart from misprints which abound, of course, not only in proper names).[66] In citing several epigrams of Ausonius, which Buchanan turns into one, he quite inexplicably prints

> Simplicior res est dicere Britto malus   instead of
> simplicior res est credite Britto malus   (ep. 111);

and in a quotation from Lucan (1. 488) he prints *diffunditis* instead of *dimittitis* (or *demittitis*), which may be due to *fudistis* in the following line.[67] But in a quota- tion from Pliny (3. 125) Buchanan has: "Unde Bergomates Cato dixit ortos, etiam nomine prodentes se altius, quam felicius sitos." While the editions of his time

disagree on *prodentes* or *prodente* and on the last word (*sitos*; *situm*; *siti*), no one has
felicius, and *nomine* is clearly introduced by Buchanan as a deliberate emendation,
as he says explicitly ostendit locus Plinij libro tertio, quem ita legendum conten-
do, to support his interpretation of this sentence.[68]

This raises the question, according to which standards Buchanan emended and
interpreted the texts to which he appeals from antiquity, and this in turn, raises
the wider question which function these references perform, when and for which
reasons ancient sources are adduced. But before we consider such more general
problems, a word need be said on the actual mistakes in Buchanan's references.

One may safely ignore, I think, such errors as the attribution of a *vita Alexandri*
to Arrian or the remark that Lucretius mentioned Britain before Caesar's birth;
this may be due to the original version being corrected here and the correction
either not being completely carried out or not being clearly written, as the
manuscript indicates.[69] And one need not worry overduly about the fact that
Buchanan is a little generous in calculating the years between various events in
the first century A.D. or later,[70] though one wonders how he would have reacted,
had he found something of that order in the writings of one of those he criticizes
or attacks. Nor need we spend much time over such slight misrepresentations,
as when he writes "Galli enim Caesare, et Germani Tacito authoribus a Dite patre
se oriundos ferebant";[71] for Tacitus (*Germ.* 2. 2) merely says "celebrant ...
Tuistonem deum terra editum. ei filium Mannum, originem gentis conditorem-
que, Manno tris filios adsignant etc." Similarly the statement "Attacottas ex
Marcellino apparet fuisse ex eis, qui aliquando vallo Adriani exclusi postea pro-
latis imperij finibus ad Seŭeri vallum vsque intra proŭinciam sint comprehensi"
does not correspond to what Ammianus says (26. 4. 5), who merely lists them
together with the Picts (divided into *Dicalydones* [s.a.] and *Verturiones* see 27. 8.
5) and others as those who "Britannos aerumnis vexavere continuis," and this implies, if anything, that they lived outside the province.

It is a little more irritating when Buchanan, so well known as a Greek scholar,
speaks of Martianus Capella when referring to the geographer Markianos and,
wrongly, attributes to him instead of Pliny (4. 103) the mention of seven *Acmodae*,
while Marcianus, according to Stephanus of Byzantium, like Ptolemy and Solinus,
speaks of five Αἰβοῦδαι.[72]

Strabo is misrepresented several times. Whereas he reports that the *Turditani*
were the wisest of the *Iberi* (3. 1. 6) and used their own art of writing, while the
others used one, but not their own, Buchanan credits him with the view that the
Turditani alone of the barbarians used letters. Later he refers to Strabo for the
statement that there were three hundred thousand Celts; but Strabo gives this
figure for the Belgians (4. 4. 3) in a passage dealing with the Celts.[73] However,
there are more serious mistakes.

In discussing the origin of the *Britanni*, Buchanan claims "Qui Britannos
Gallorum colonos esse contendunt, hi Herculem e Celto puella Gallica Britan-
num filium genuisse produnt: a quo gentem Britannam propagatam. Hanc na-

tionem Plinius vicinam Morinis, Atrebatibus, Gessoriacis collocat. Qui e Graecis haec confirment non desunt Grammatici, Soujdas, et qui Etymologicon magnum scripsit."[74] These odd remarks are again found in the passage which is not in the Edinburgh-manuscript; but it does not help much to point out that they may have been inserted later[75] or to assume that Buchanan here invokes the authority of the *Grammatici* only for the fact that the *Britanni* were the neighbours of *Morini*, *Atrebates* and *Gessoriaci* for which he appeals to Pliny (correctly: 4. 102 and 106); for neither Suda nor Etymologicum Magnum says anything like this, and Buchanan in the second book, again, remarks "Ab his non dissentiunt quidam Graecorum Grammatici, qui Britannos a Britanno Celtus filio nomen accepisse tradunt."[76] Whatever the explanation for this mistake may be, it would not be reasonable or fair to base our judgment on a few errors of the kind we have just discussed.

Instead we turn next to some examples of Buchanan's detailed interpretation of quotations from ancient authors and of his consideration of textual points. In discussing the earliest inhabitants of Scotland, Buchanan attacks the *audacia* and *stupor* of Lhuyd "qui, Attacottas fuisse Scotos, sed nullo prorsus auctore, aut con-iectura verisimili affirmet ... quod in loco Marcellini a se citato Scotos ab Attacot-tis separari non videat."[77] Indeed, the wording in Ammianus suggests (26. 4. 5; 27. 8. 5) that *Scotti* and *Attacotti* (this is the form which Ammianus uses, while Buchanan also has *Attacottae* cf. above p. 12) were different as were *Picti* and *Attacotti* (whom Buchanan throws together a little earlier). What Lhuyd in fact says is that the *Attacotti* were of Scottish origin according to Ammianus Marcellinus, and for such a statement there is little justification.[78] Immediately afterwards Buchanan criticizes Lhuyd's view that "Caledonios e Brittonum gente fuisse," because the author of the panegyricus for Constantinus uses the expression "Caledonum et aliorum Pictorum siluas."[79] Buchanan rightly takes this to mean that the *Caledones* were *Picti*, yet his attack is without foundation, as Lhuyd simp-ly lists the earliest passages which mention the Picts in Latin literature. Never-theless Buchanan repeats his attack later, after taking Lhuyd to task for using what he calls Mamertinus's panegyricus for Maximinianus to show "primum, solos tum Brittones insulam incoluisse: deinde, qui ibi dicuntur Hiberni, postea Scotos fuisse appellatos";[80] Buchanan, following the text of the editions of his time ("AD hoc natio et tum rudis, et soli Britanni Pictis modo et Hibernis assueta hostibus adhuc seminudis, facile Romanis armis, et signis cesserunt"),[81] takes *soli Britan-ni* as genitive, and, secondly, emphasizes that "omnes Hiberniae incolas ab anti-quissimis usque temporibus dictos fuisse Scotos," as he claims to have shown "ex Paulo Orosio Hispano et Beda Anglo."[82] But while his interpretation is acceptable—though, of course, the evidence from Orosius and Bede does not really help to decide what the words of the panegyricus mean[83]—it fails to affect Lhuyd's position who had adduced this passage as the first where the Picts are mentioned in antiquity.

In all these cases, no one will hesitate to accept Buchanan's interpretations, who thus proves his skill and competence; at the same time one cannot feel but irritated by his polemics — I do not mean the violent language which he uses to attack his adversary, as this is exactly the same as that which Lhuyd himself employs to attack Boece — but the fact that he misrepresents the views of his victim, and then attacks them.

There is one more passage to which we have to turn briefly, as Buchanan explains at some length why, in this case, he accepts a conjecture, proposed by the younger Scaliger in Seneca's *Apocolocyntosis: Scotobrigantes* instead of *Scutabrigantes*.[84] Joseph Justus Scaliger may have become known to Buchanan through his father;[85] certainly the two scholars were in touch during and after Buchanan's stay in France in the fifties (1552–61).[86] Though by the time of the publication of the *Historia* the younger Scaliger had long established his fame as an editor and textual critic, Buchanan first elaborately recommends him, before he advances several arguments to justify the conjecture (which incidentally was not published till 1577, a fact, which is important for the date of the composition or final revision of the first two books of the *Historia*), presumably because it had failed generally to carry conviction.[87] It was rejected by Camden in 1586 and by Delrio in his commentary on Seneca's tragedies in 1594; but it may well have been questioned more widely, not least because Scaliger had recommended it partly as a sign of his kindness towards his Scottish friends.[88] It may well be for this reason that Buchanan accepted it so enthusiastically, and indeed, if correct, it would provide the earliest reference to the Scots in ancient literature, several hundred years before the next one. But such a motive is hardly sufficient to justify a conjecture.

This particular passage as well as a good many other emendations and conjectures reveal Buchanan's concern in these first two books to provide as much and as early convincing evidence as possible for the Scots, the names of their tribes and their places, and to prove anyone wrong who would question this evidence. This leads us on to the problem of how Buchanan uses the evidence from ancient authors. Unfortunately, it will not be possible here to offer a full length discussion of Buchanan's views and principles of historiography;[89] only a few remarks on some selected aspects can be made here.

Generally speaking, Buchanan refers to ancient writers or even quotes their words verbatim in order to give a particular statement more authority and to add to its credibility. As our survey has shown, such references to the sources are rare in the historical account of the fourth book, though some events there narrated are mentioned or described at length in the Greek or Latin authors on whose accounts Buchanan even seems to rely in some cases, but without indicating this. In the following books events are related for which there are no longer sources from antiquity available; but there, too, references to parallels from antiquity and quotations from Greek or Latin writers for general views are very rare indeed. The first two books, on the other hand, abound in such references and quotations, and the third is nothing but a series of excerpts providing supporting evidence for what has been said before. This calls for an explanation.

Right at the beginning of his work Buchanan implies that the knowledge the Romans had of Britain was very limited, at least in the period of their first contacts with the British Isles — something similar he says of Strabo — and that it increased gradually, as they penetrated further;[90] at the same time he emphasizes again and again that the ancient writers were diligent and reliable,[91] and he is anxious to have their authority to appeal to for the period for which they are available as witnesses, when he is contradicting or trying to refute the view of another writer.[92] However, the argument "this or that cannot be correct or true, as the ancients do not know of it or record it" is not used indiscriminately. Indeed, it is explicitly rejected for the earliest period of Scottish history as the Greeks and Romans had no knowledge of it.[93] Thus what indigenous historians in the Middle Ages and the fifteenth and sixteenth centuries write about the origin and the early history of the peoples of the British Isles is accepted by Buchanan, but only in part.[94]

Though there is no trace of the earliest kings of Scotland in the writings of the Greeks and Romans, Buchanan, whom we have found so anxious to recover as much early evidence for the Scots from ancient writers as possible, retells their story, acquiescing in the fact that they precede in time the period of immediate contact between the Greeks and the Romans with the British Isles. He devotes the whole of the fourth book to paint a lively picture of the earliest kings of Scotland, as presupposed by John of Fordun[95] and as presented in a fantastic account by Hector Boece[96] and again — despite scepticism and criticism of Polydore Vergil and Humphrey Lhuyd and others — by John Lesley, whom Buchanan never mentions.[97] But he rejects as fictitious the stories about the Syrian king Diocletian and his wife Labana and their daughters etc., about Brutus, and about Gathelus,[98] partly, he says, because they are unlikely,[99] partly because they spring from a desire, also noticeable elsewhere, to trace the origin of one's people as far back as possible and to give it a noble ancestry,[100] partly because they have been invented clearly in accordance with patterns well known from antiquity, but also because e.g., the Syrian king Diocletian is not mentioned anywhere;[101] and in this Buchanan is inconsistent, as he accepts the early kings, as we have seen, though they, too, are not recorded in the Greek and Roman sources available.

But, as all our observations have shown, while Buchanan seems concerned to register as much early evidence for the British Isles from Greek and Roman writers as possible, it is not historical events for which he appeals to them, but geographical and ethnographical details, and especially names and what they may tell about people, their origin and their relationship with others. Correspondingly, he does not explicitly refer to the historiographical standards and criteria of the ancients, but to their methods of linguistic interpretation and even to the principles of the actual use of their languages.[102] In adducing references and parallels, Buchanan shows himself thoroughly familiar with all aspects of antiquity, the languages of the Greeks and Romans,[103] even the metrical conventions;[104] he knows stories and facts recorded only rarely,[105] and he uses the scholarly instruments developed

by the Humanists and their principles of textual criticism, relying as much on
ingenuity as on paleography; so that he deserves a place in the history of classical
scholarship.[106] As Buchanan is at home in the world of the ancients, he expects
his readers to be equally conversant with it, and to accept it as providing standards in many respects. Indeed, it is very rare that he criticizes an ancient author,
and where he does so, it is because he differs from several others of the ancients,
as e.g., Pliny: "cum ... interque tot scriptores vnum Plinium reperiam, qui ge-
nuinam nominis vim non videatur intellexisse."[107]

But while Buchanan accepts the standards and the learning of the ancients,
he is deeply suspicious of his contemporaries, especially one of them, Humphrey
Lhuyd; and whereas the general conception of the *Historia* as well as its execution
and language owes almost everything to the models of ancient historiography,
the actual references to particular ancient sources, I think it is fair to say, are
due to his anger and indignation with Lhuyd more than to his respect for the
Greeks and Romans. He cites some contemporary scholars and scholars of the
preceding generation with approval such as John Leland or Donald Monroe,[108]
he treats others with mild irony, ignores them or criticizes them without mentioning their names.[109] But Humphrey Lhuyd he attacks with all the acrimony
and venom scholars — and especially scholars of his time — seem to be have been
capable of; and it is in order to add force to his attacks, that he calls the ancients
to his aid in the first and second (and third) books. Thus these references are used
not to adorn the style, not to put the historical account on a firmer basis, but
to demolish his opponent's position.

This cannot be the place to consider at length the gradual growth of Buchanan's
Historia. Suffice it to say that while Buchanan was in the process of composing
it, Lhuyd's *Fragmentum* was published posthumously in 1572; thus part of what
Buchanan had (probably) written by that time was called in question. A counterattack was called for; and as little could be said in support of the story of the early
kings, the enemy had to be met on other grounds. He had to be silenced right
at the beginning and to be shown as totally untrustworthy and as an inventor
of lies. This is the spirit in which Buchanan seems to have written or revised the
first two (three) books. Thus our examination of the classical references confirms
what other observations have indicated, the special nature of the first books. They
may have been part of the original design or they may have been conceived of
later (which seems less likely, as such sections usually precede historical accounts);
their final form they owe to Buchanan's intention to nullify the influence of his
adversary, the scholar who had shaken the foundations of early Scottish "history,"
before he begins with his own historical account. This conclusion calls for a final
remark on Buchanan as a historian.

Professor Trevor-Roper classifies Buchanan as a typical humanist historian,
and in many respects everybody will readily agree with the characteristics he attributes to him;[110] but is it fair to say of him that he was "not critical or sceptical?" That he was one of those who "provided they had an authoritative literary

text, clung to it?" That his "purpose was not to understand the past but to polish the narratives of ancient authors?" Where Buchanan writes history, he does not follow an ancient writer; and where he turns to the texts of the ancients, he does not write history, but gives an introductory account of the country, of the origin of the peoples, of their prehistory; and he writes these books not only for their own sake, not only to show his readers the scenery, as it were, of the following narrative, but to put his own *Historia* on a firm basis by removing the adversary who had called it in doubt. Buchanan does not defend his predecessor Boece, he even criticizes him mildly, he does not mention Lesley or others who had also accepted the early history of Scotland, he does not explicitly justify his own position in retelling the story of the early kings for which there is no reliable evidence; he is content to counterattack Lhuyd, and he does so in exactly the same biting language which Lhuyd (and Polydore Vergil) had used against Boece, and he does so with the help of references to Greek and Roman authorities. However much Buchanan's *Historia* may owe to ancient historiography for its conception and execution or for its structure and language; the actual quotations and allusions serve as weapons in his fight to destroy his opponent and his position and thus to establish his own. It is hardly possible to approve of this practice, and the only redeeming feature seems to be that Buchanan does so in the interest of what he takes to be Scottish history, the history of his own country.

University of Göttingen

Notes

1. See e.g., C. S. Lewis, *English Literature in the Sixteenth Century* (Oxford, 1954) with the standard judgement: "Boece was a humanist, Major a scholastic" (p. 67); for F. P. Wilson, *The English Drama 1485–1585* (Oxford, 1969), pp. 88–90; 126, B. even belongs to the continental Humanists. A more substantial treatment may be found in *The Cambridge History of English Literature* ed. A. W. Ward and A. R. Waller, III (Cambridge, 1908), pp. 157–65 (by P. Hume Brown).

2. First published Edinburgh, 1582; a list of all editions is given by I. D. McFarlane (see note 3) pp. 513–14. The references here are first to the *editio princeps* of 1582 (quotations are from this edition), next to Ruddiman's edition of 1715 (see note 5) and finally to that of Utrecht, 1697. The manuscript of the *Historia* which has been preserved and is now in Edinburgh University Library differs in numerous details from the printed version of 1582 and, moreover, lacks several longer passages as well as the whole of Book III. I am most deeply grateful to Professor I. D. McFarlane (Oxford) for lending me a microfilm of the manuscript for several months.

3. I. D. McFarlane, *Buchanan* (London, 1981) (with bibliography: pp. XV–XVII and 544–52); see also P. Hume Brown, *George Buchanan. Humanist and Reformer* (Edinburgh, 1890).

4. Th. Ruddiman (see note 5) has collected a number of *testimonia*, pp. 13–24; see also his *praefatio*, p. X. On Buchanan's education see I. D. McFarlane, pp. 19–28, on his teaching at Ste. Barbe id. pp. 28–42, also J. Quicherat, *Histoire de Sainte-Barbe* (Paris, 1860–1864), 3 vols., I, pp. 150–64 (cf. also his verses ibid. pp. 356–57; on the earlier period of his study: pp. 122–39).

5. Georgii Buchanani Scoti ... *Opera Omnia* (Edinburgh, 1715), 2 vols. (the *Historia* with separate pagination: I, pp. 1–408, followed by *annotationes*: pp. 409–66, also *Index* and *Propriorum Nominum Interpretatio*, again with new pagination); R.'s adverse criticism: *praefatio*, p. XI, stressing B.'s old age and partiality for Moray, two points which he justified again in his *Animadversiones On a late Pamphlet, intituled A Vindication of Mr. George Buchanan* ... (Edinburgh, 1749); there were, of course, earlier critics, see Ruddiman, *praefatio*, pp. XI–XIV and e.g., W. A. Gatherer, *The Tyrannous Reign of Mary Stewart* ... (Edinburgh, 1958), pp. 6–10.

6. Th. Innes, *A Critical Essay on the Ancient Inhabitants of the Northern Parts of Britain or Scotland* (first published: London, 1729, also in:) *The Historians of Scotland*, VIII (Edinburgh, 1879), pp. 176–223, esp. pp. 206–23. On further earlier and later criticism of Buchanan's work see also I. D. McFarlane, pp. 436–40.

7. P. Hume Brown (see note 3), pp. 293–326, esp. pp. 326–28; an unprejudiced, yet fairly harsh verdict is given by E. Fueter, *Geschichte der Neueren Historiographie* (Handbuch der mittelalterlichen und neueren Geschichte, I, 3), Munich ³1936, pp. 172–74; cf. also W. A. Gatherer (see note 5), pp. 3–42. J. A. Balfour seeks to save Buchanan by calling him a chronicler, not a historian in: D. A. Millar (ed.), *George Buchanan. A Memorial 1506–1906* (St Andrews, 1907), p. 107.

8. H. R. Trevor-Roper, *George Buchanan and the Ancient Scottish Constitution*, EHR, Suppl. 3 (London, 1966), p. 38; he gives further details on the Edinburgh manuscript: pp. 51–53.

9. I. D. McFarlane, p. 440.

10. Loc. cit. p. 21, with justified criticism of J. E. Philipps, FHLQ, 12 (1948–49, pp. 23–45, esp. pp. 49–55.

11. Only some of the histories of Britain or Scotland can be mentioned here, all of which Buchanan was certainly familiar with: (J. Major), *Historia Maioris Britanniae* ... (Paris, 1521) (*descriptio* etc., I. 1–10, ff. Iʳ–XVIIIʳ); (H. Boece-Boethius), *Scotorum Historiae* ... (Paris, no year: 1526 or 1527); ... *libri XIX* (Paris, 1574) (second edition with additions by G. Ferrerio; *descriptio* etc. in both editions at the beginning with separate foliation); the work was translated early (in 1531?) by John Bellenden: *Heir beginnis the hystory and croniklis of Scotland* ... (Edinburgh, ?1538), again with the description separate (reprinted in: The Scottish Text Society, 3. ser. 10 and 15, Edinburgh, 1938 and 1941), and this was translated into English by W. Harrison in: R. Holinshed, *The First volume of the Chronicles of England, Scotlande, and Irelande* (London, 1577), 3 vols., vol. I second part: pp. 1–22 the description of Scotland, and with new pagination pp. 1–518 the history (there is in the first half also a description of Britain pp. 1–126, preceding the history with new pagination). An early metrical version (1531–35) of Boece's history by W. Stewart (*The Buik of the Cronicles of Scotland*) was not published till 1858 in: *Rerum Britannicarum medii aevi Scriptores* (Rolls Series), 6 (London, 1858) 3 vols., by W. B. Turnbull, another translation not till 1946: *The Mar Lodge Translation*, Scottish Text Society, 3. ser. 17, Edinburgh, (vol. I only); Polydore Vergil, *Anglicae Historiae l. XXVI* (Basle, 1534; ²1546); ... *l. XXVII*,(Basle, 1555) (edition here cited) with *descriptio*: pp. 3–15; J. Lesley, *De origine moribus, et rebus gestis Scotorum libri decem* ... (Rome, 1578), pp. 1–41 (*descriptio*, followed by book I).

12. I. D. McFarlane, pp. 419–21, see already Th. Ruddiman (cf. note 5), p. 413, modified by Th. Innes (note 6) who tries to argue "that these first books ... were composed ... before the history, and only revised and augmented by Buchanan with new observations" (p. 212); Ruddiman's views were rejected by J. Man, *A Censure and Examination Of Mr. Thomas Rud-*

diman's philological notes ... (Aberdeen, 1753), pp. 11–29; Th. Ruddiman replied: *Anticrisis: or, a Discussion of A scurrilous and malicious Libel* ... (Edinburgh, 1754), to be supplemented by *Audi alteram partem: or, a further vindication of Mr. Tho. Ruddiman's Edition* (Edinburgh, 1756). Lhuyd's work was published after his death by A. Ortelius: *Commentarioli Britannicae Descriptionis Fragmentum Auctore Humfredo Lhuyd* (Cologne, 1572) (edition here cited; reprinted London 1731) and translated: *The Breuiary of Britayne* ... *Englished by Thomas Twyne* (London, 1573) (reprinted in J. Lewis, *The History of Great-Britain*, London, 1729, with separate pagination).

13. 33ʳ/ 53/ 87; Bede: 33ʳ/ 53/ 88; arrival of Fergus: 34ʳ/ 54/ 90; the source may well be John of Fordun, *Chronica Gentis Scotorum*, ed. W. F. Skene, *The Historians of Scotland*, I (Edinburgh, 1871), p. 45 (I.12).

14. II, f. 20ᵛ: Ptolemaeus Philadelphus (rejected by Lhuyd, 34ᵛ); III ff. 31ʳ–34ʳ: Caesar; III ff. 34ᵛ–36ʳ: Augustus; III, f. 36ʳ: Tiberius — Roman authors of the time; Boece's remark that Claudian mentioned Euenus's or rather Cadallus's victory over Gillus (f. 28ᵛ) is rejected by Lhuyd, 35ʳ⁻ᵛ; Buchanan gives the same story in brief form (naming the general Caduallus), but without reference to Claudian (36ᵛ/ 59/ 98).

15. 37ᵛ/ 60/ 99–100; cf. Tacitus *Agricola* 10. 4; Orosius 7. 6. 10; Eutropius 7. 13. 3; Beda 1. 3 (pp. 22–24, Mynors). It is interesting to note that while Major mentions Claudius's conquest of the Orkney Islands without giving an authority (I.13, ff. XIXᵛ–XXᵛ; see also Polydore Vergil II, p. 33), Boece (III, f. 40ʳ) cites Suetonius, Eutropius and Bede, also John Campbell and Cornelius Hiber, though Suetonius does not speak of the Orkney Islands (but is referred to by Orosius 7. 6. 10 for another statement). Buchanan replaces Suetonius correctly by Orosius, after Lhuyd had referred to Suetonius, Eutropius and Orosius in attacking Boece (19ʳ) whom he also criticizes for misunderstanding Tacitus (25ʳ).

16. 8ᵛ/ 13/ 22, cf. Pomponius Mela 3. 6. 54 and Plin. *n.h.* 4. 103.

17. 38ʳ/ 61/ 101, cf. Boece IV., f. 57ᵛ and Tacitus *Agricola* 29. 4 where *Galgacus* is the reading of most editions of the sixteenth century (e.g., Basle, 1519; 1553; Lyon, 1539 etc.), while the early ones have *Calgacus* (e.g., Venice, 1512; Rome, 1515).

18. 38ʳ/ 61/ 101–02, cf. Tacitus *Agricola* 17. 1–2.

19. 38ʳ⁻ᵛ/ 62/ 101–02, cf. Tacitus *Agricola* 18–37; *Glota* (so also Lhuyd 40ʳ⁻ᵛ) not *Glotta* as Buchanan writes (Boece IV, f. 65ʳ (1526) *Clotta*; but in the locorum declaratio: *Glotta*, also in the edition of 1574: f. 62ᵛ) nor *Clota* as modern editors print (see also note 41), and *mons Grampius*, not *Graupius* are the forms printed in all sixteenth-century editions which I have checked. On Agricola's activities see now J. Kenworthy (ed.), *Agricola's campaigns in Scotland* (Edinburgh, 1981).

20. The long story (IV, ff. 60ᵛ–68ᵛ) includes the whole speech of Galdus Galcagus (ff. 65ᵛ–66ʳ = Tacitus *Agricola* 30–32).

21. 39ʳ/ 62/ 103; cf. Beda 1. 5 (p. 26, Mynors, see also n. 24 below); SHA Spartianus *Hadr.* 11. 2; Herodian 3. 14. 10.

22. 38ᵛ/ 62/ 103, cf. Dio C. 69. 13. 2 (Iulius Severus); 39ʳ/ 63/ 104, cf. SHA Capitolinus *Ant. Pius* 5. 4 (Lollius Urbicus); 40ᵛ/ 65/ 107, cf. SHA Capitolinus *Pert.* 3. 6 (Pertinax).

23. 40ᵛ/ 65/ 108, cf. Dio C. 76. 13. 7 (the whole chapter has been used by Buchanan).

24. 40ᵛ/ 65/ 109, cf. SHA Spartianus *Sept. Sev.* 18. 2; while Buchanan criticizes Bede here (1. 5), later he seems to follow his view (*vallum*): 47ᵛ/ 75/ 126, see also 63ʳ/ 97/ 164.

25. 40ᵛ–41ᵛ/ 65/ 108–09 and earlier 6ʳ/ 9–10/ 15–16, writing *Camelodunum*, like other sixteenth-century writers, though the ancient authors referred to at 6ʳ/ 9–10/ 15–16 have *Camulodanum* (Ptol. 2. 3. 11: 1482; *Camudolan*: 1513; Καμουλόδανον: 1533; 1546; *Camudolanum*: 1540; 1562), *Camoloduno* (*It. Anton. Aug.* 480. 3) and *Camulodunum* (Tac. *ann.* 12. 32. 2; 14. 31–32) cited by Buchanan himself from Tacitus 23ʳ/ 37/ 63 together with *Camŭlodŭnŭm in Brigantibus* from Ptolemy (2. 3. 10, where sixteenth-century editions read *Camŭnlodunum*). For *Giudi* see Beda 1. 12 (p. 40, Mynors). The views which Buchanan rejects here are

those of Boece (*Camelodunum*: I, f. 12ʳ; III, f. 45ʳ⁻ᵛ; round building, *templum Claudii*: III, f. 45ᵛ, see also X, ff. 198ᵛ-200).

26. 42ᵛ/ 68/ 113-14, cf. Eutropius 9. 21-22. 9.

27. Names: *sinus Rerigonius*: 79ᵛ/ 142/ 242 (cf. Ptol 3. 3. 1, see earlier: 5ᵛ/ 8/ 14 with note below); words: δορυδρέπανα for Bede's *uncinata tela* (1. 12 p. 44, Mynors): 48ʳ/ 75-76/ 126 (probably inspired by Strabo 4. 1.1, a passage frequently used by Buchanan for geographical and ethnographical information; this is an indication that Buchanan consulted Strabo in the Greek original and not in a Latin translation; see on this problem note 63 below); institutions: *Coss. a Caesaribus designatio*: 62ᵛ/ 97/ 163; titles: *Caesar* and *rex*: 68ʳ/ 105/ 178; habits: *mos Graecorum*: 74ᵛ/ 115/ 195-96; theatres: 51ᵛ/ 81/ 136 (similar, but different: *Milesiae fabulae*: 74ᵛ/ 115/ 195); examples and parallels (including negative ones): 86ᵛ/ 153/ 261 (*Cato, Brutus, Marius*); 243ʳ/ 398/ 681; 244ʳ/ 399-400/ 684. A remark such as *quam medici* ἀποπλεξίαν *vocant* need not point to knowledge of ancient writers, but it does show familiarity with Greek (242ʳ/ 396/ 677, see also χαμφός: 9ʳ/ 14/ 24).

28. Quotation without author: 132ᵛ/ 222/ 378; *dicta* of Trajan and Theodosius: 243ʳ/ 398/ 681. These lists do not pretend to be complete.

29. The editions of their works are listed by A. Gransden, *Historical Writing in England c. 550 to c. 1307* (London, 1974), who also has some remarks on their knowledge of and allusions to classical authors (see Index, e.g., s. vv. Cicero, Juvenal, Lucan, Ovid, Suetonius, Vergil), to be supplemented by the indices of the various editions. For John of Fordun see Johannis de Fordun, *Chronica Gentis Scotorum* (see note 13), also the translation in: *The Historians of Scotland*, IV (1872), where pp. 375-79 a list of authors referred to is given: Aelius Spartianus, Cicero, Eutropius, Herodian and others, see also notes 31 and 32.

30. For the editions of Major, Boece, Vergil and Lesley see note 11, for Lhuyd note 12. On Polydore Vergil see D. Hay, *Polydore Vergil, Renaissance Historian and Man of Letters* (Oxford, 1952), p. 105; he is, of course, familiar with many more authors as his *De inventoribus rerum* (published first Venice, 1499, often reprinted with additions, also abridged and translated) proves, and so is John Leland the antiquarian, most of whose works were not published till the eighteenth century (on him see T. D. Kendrick, *British Antiquity* (London, 1950), pp. 45-64). Boece, too, mentions quite a large number of Roman authors, some under the reign of each emperor.

31. Most of them in Lhuyd: e.g., Appian (45ᵛ), Aurelius Victor (34ʳ), Lucian (32ʳ), Pausanias (45ʳ⁻ᵛ), Sidonius Apollinaris (9ʳ⁻ᵛ; 10ᵛ-11ʳ), also Athenaeus (45ᵛ), Polybius (44ᵛ); in John of Fordun Valerius Maximus (I.32, p. 37) and Herodotus (II.8, p. 41).

32. They are all referred to by John of Fordun; Paulus Diaconus by Boece (VII, f. 112ᵛ; X, f. 191ʳ), Polydore Vergil (III, p. 50) and Lhuyd (74ᵛ), Jerome by Lhuyd (36ʳ), whereas Buchanan ignores him, probably because of his crude comment on the *Atticoti* (*adv. Iovin.* 2. 7), so cruelly exploited by Lhuyd (36ʳ).

33. 15ʳ/ 23/ 40, obviously wrongly, together with St Paul who, however, uses the Greek form Ἐπανία, while the Latin translations have *Hispania*; I have not been able to trace a Latin translation of the two historians in which the form *Spania* is used.

34. See, e.g., a quotation from Juvenal (13. 141-42): 25ʳ/ 40/ 68, a paraphrase of an expression in Horace (*sat.* 1. 1. 63-64): 2ᵛ/ 4/ 6, a single word or phrase (Hor. *epist.* 2. 3. 441): 3ʳ/ 4/ 7; further examples are listed by Th. Ruddiman (see note 5) in his *annotationes*; expressions like *illud tantum quaero* (16ʳ/ 25/ 43) are reminiscent of Cicero, others of Livy.

35. A good many quotations from classical authors are registered in the translation by Ch. F. Arrowood, *George Buchanan on the Powers of the Crown in Scotland* (Austin, 1949).

36. See note 34. On the imitation of Livy and other ancient historiographers see Th. Ruddiman *praefatio*, p. X and the authorities there cited, especially R. Rapin, *Les comparaisons des grands hommes de l'antiquité, II: Les réflexions sur l'éloquence, la poétique, l'histoire et*

la philosophie (Amsterdam, 1693), p. 306: "Bucanan est un trop servile imitateur de Tite
Live ...".

37. Ephorus 17ᵛ/ 27/ 47, cf. Strabo 4. 4. 6 (= FGrHist, 70, F 131); Marcianus (2ʳ/ 3/
4, cf. Stephanus Byz. s. v. 'Αλβίων and s.v. Βρεττία, cf. also 8ᵛ/ 13/ 22 and Stephanus
Byz. s. v. Αἰβοῦδαι); on Cato see below note 39. For Philemo see 18ʳ/ 28/ 48, cf. Plin.
n.h. 4. 95, for Varro 14ʳ/ 22/ 38, cf. Plin. *n.h.* 3. 8.

38. Cf. *Pomponii Melae de orbis situ libri tres, accuratissime emendati una cum commentariis Ioachimi
Vadiani* ... (Paris, 1540), p. 121 on Mela 2. 5. 78; the use of this edition is also likely because
Buchanan writes *Albionem* and *Bergiona*, not *Albiona* and *Bergion* as the earlier editions (e.g.,
Florence, 1526), see below note 64.

39. 4ᵛ/ 6–7/ 11, cf. Diodor. 4. 19. 3–4; Strab. 4. 1. 7 (with Aesch. F 326 a Mette); Ps.-
Hygin. *astr.* 2. 6; Cato is mentioned by Vadianus for the view *in Liguria locum fuisse ...
quo compluti a Iove lapides iacuerunt, in auxilium Herculis ...* which one may find almost verbatim in the expanded version of the *Origines* current at the time and printed, e.g., together
with Varro's *de Lingua Latina ... M. Portij Catonis Originum lib. I.*, (Basle, 1536), p. 239,
or in *Antiquitatum variarum autores* (Lyon, 1552), pp. 7–20 (18). Th. Ruddiman, p. 412,
lists several authors not mentioned by Buchanan for this story.

40. 18ʳ/ 28/ 48 and 8ᵛ/ 13/ 22.

41. A few examples of misprints in the 1582 printing may be registered here which are
not due to the readings of the sixteenth-century editions consulted by Buchanan (see also
note 63, and for inaccuracies note 42, for actual mistakes note 44): 4ᵛ/ 7/ 11: *Gerione* for
Geryone; 4ᵛ/ 7/ 11: *Albionia* for *Alpionia* (Strab. 4. 6. 1, Latin for 'Αλπιονία: see edition of
1549); 4ᵛ/ 7/ 11: *Albium Intimelium* for *Albium Intemelium* (Strab. 4. 6. 1); 22ʳ/ 36/ 61:
Pultobria for Πολτυμβρία, *Mesimbria* for Μεσημβρία, *Selimbria* for Εηλυμβρία (Steph. Byz. s.
vv. Βρουτοβρία 187. 1–3, Μεσημβρία 446. 15–19 and Εηλυμβρία 562. 9–11 Meineke); 22ᵛ/
36/ 61 *Amalobrica* for *Amallobriga* (*It. Ant. Aug.* 435. 1); 23ᵛ/ 37/ 63: *Segodunum* for *Segedunum*
(*Not. Dign.* 40. 33); 23ᵛ/ 38/ 64: *Corrodunum* (*in Sarmatia*) for *Carrodunum* (Ptol. 3. 5. 15);
23ᵛ/ 38/ 64: *Ebrodunum* (*in Alpibus*) for *Eborodunum* (Ptol. 3. 1. 35, so already in the edition of 1475, but the Ulm edition of 1482 has *Eburdunum*).

42. *Britannia* (1ᵛ/ 2/ 3) also for *insulae Britannicae* (νῆσοι Βρεττανιχαί) in Ps. Arist. *de mundo* 393 b 13–17; *Caledones aut Caledonii* (7ʳ/ 11/ 18) for *Dicaledones* (Amm. Marc. 27. 8. 5,
see Buchanan himself later 20ᵛ/ 32/ 54); *Caledonii* (20ʳ/ 31–32/ 54) for *Caledones* (Paneg.
6. 7. 2; in antiquity *Caledonius* was used almost exclusively as adjective; but the Greeks
had Καληδόνιος as noun, and this was translated by *Caledonius* so that in the sixteenth century it is quite common as noun in Latin also). *Brigantes* (23ʳ/ 37/ 62) for Βριγάντιον (Strab.
4. 1. 3). In addition there are several instances of inaccuracy, where a parallel or modern
usage seems to have caused confusion. From the *It. Ant. Aug.* 476. 1 Buchanan cites *Isobrigan-
tium* (23ʳ/ 37/ 62), while the reading there is *Isubrigantum* (the correct form being *Isurium
Brigantum*); but *Brigantium* is a familiar name and compounds with *Iso-* are common. Later
he lists *Lugdunum* (23ᵛ/ 38/ 64) as town in Germany (Ptol. 2. 11. 13) instead of *Lugidunum*,
clearly influenced by the common name of *Lugdunum* which he had mentioned earlier (23ʳ/
37/ 63, cf. Ptol. 2. 8. 12). The spelling of *Ocellum* for a *promontorium Britanniae* and two
places (Ptol. 2. 3. 4; 2. 5. 7 and Caes. 1. 10. 5) may well be due to the *Ocelli montes in
Scotia* (24ʳ/ 39/ 66); see also his *Ocellodurum* (23ᵛ/ 38/ 64) for which Buchanan refers to
Ptolemy, though he has Ὄχελον only (2. 5. 7), while it is the *It. Ant. Aug.* where it is called
Oceloduri (1512: 73ᵛ; 74ᵛ; ed. 1929: *Ocelo Duri*: 436. 6; 439. 10). When Buchanan lists *Brige
vicus ... ad Cottias Alpes* (22ᵛ/ 36/ 61) which he mentions again on the following page with
reference to Strabo (23ʳ/ 37/ 62), who has, however, only Βριγάντιον χώμη (4. 1. 3), he
may well be influenced by *Brige ... in Britannia* to which he refers in the preceding line
(22ᵛ/ 36/ 61, cf. *It. Ant. Aug.* 483. 3; 486. 12); for a *Briga mons* cited from Ptolemy (23ʳ/
37/ 62), there is no evidence from antiquity. This is not the only case where Buchanan

misrepresents his authorities: Ptolemy uses Ἰουερνία (2. 2. 1, in Latin *Ibernia*, *Hibernia* or *Iuernia*), not *Iuverna* (24ʳ/ 39/ 65) and Ταμάρα, not Τάμαρος (24ʳ/ 39/ 66) is the name he gives to the river (2. 6. 2), which Mela (3. 11) calls *Tamáris*, whereas he has Τάμαρος for a river in Britain (2. 3. 3). For *Iuliobrica* Buchanan refers (22ᵛ/ 36/ 61) to Pliny (correctly: *n.h.* 3. 21; 27; 4. 111) and the *Itinerarium Ant. Aug.*, though it does not occur there, but in Ptolemy (2. 6. 50) and in the *Notitia dignitatum* (*occ.* 42. 30).

43. It is one of the sections which are not in the Edinburgh manuscript and may have been added at a very late stage (see note 75).

44. For *Apoceanitas* (4ʳ/ 6/ 10) see Th. Ruddiman p. 411, who suggests Παρωκεανῖται (cf. Strab. 17. 3. 19; 24); I assume that Buchanan is rather thinking of a phrase like ἡ Κελτικὴ ἡ παρωκεανῖτις (Strab. 2. 1. 16). *Moremarusa* (3ʳ/ 4/ 7; see also 4ʳ/ 6/ 10; 21ʳ/ 33/ 57; 26ʳ/ 43/ 72) for *Morimarusa*, cf. Plin. *n.h.* 4. 95; sixteenth-century editions of Solinus have different forms, but none has *more*—; Lhuyd reads (42ᵛ) *Morimarussium*. *Aestiones* (18ʳ/ 28/ 48 and 26ᵛ/ 43/ 73 for *Aestii*, cf. Tac. *Germ.* 45, thus Buchanan himself correctly 19ᵛ/ 31/ 53), but see Lhuyd 43ʳ. Further errors are listed in the appendix.

45. *Ierne* (8. 33): 12ʳ/ 19/ 33 and 18ᵛ/ 29/ 50; *Iernam* (22. 251): 18ᵛ/ 29/ 50. At 8. 33 the following editions have *Hyberne* (1510; 1548; 1551, so also Lhuyd: 39ʳ), *hybernae* (1523), *Hybernae* (1530), *Hiberne* (1571; 1596; 1603; 1620), *Iuerne* (1571 *in margine*; 1596 *in mg.*), *Ierne* (1602); at 22. 251 one finds *Hibernam* in the editions of 1510; 1530; 1571; 1620, *hybernam* 1523, *Ibernam* 1548, *Hybernam* 1551; 1572 (as lemma in Delrio's notes; see also Lhuyd 39ʳ), *Iuernam* 1571 *in mg.*; 1596 *in mg.*, *Hybernen ci.* Delrio 1572, *Iernen* 1602, *Iernam* 1603 (Raph.).

46. See *Claudii Claudiani Carmina* ed. Th. Birt (Berlin, 1892), *in app. ad loc.* 8. 33, p. 151; 22. 251, p. 212.

47. *Cl. Claudiani Poetae ... Opera ... Cum Annotationibus perpetuis* St. Claverii ... (Paris, 1602), f. 147ʳ; cf. J. Koch, *De codicibus Cuiacianis quibus in edendo Claudiano Claverius usus est*, Diss. phil. (Marburg, 1889), p. 37; see also in general pp. 8–12; 12–21.

48. *De mundo Aristotelis lib. I*, Basle 1533, p. 10 (zuerst 1526): G. Budé, influenced not by the medieval translations of Aristotle (published in Venice, 1496), but perhaps by the conjecture in the Aldine edition of Apuleius (Venice, 1521, *de mundo*, f. 104ᵛ), suggested no doubt by the Greek form Ἰέρνη which occurs in this passage and also in Strabo for Ireland (1. 4. 3; 4; 2. 1. 13; 17; 18) and for a promontory in Spain (3. 1. 3, Latin translation: *Hierna* [edition of 1549]), but neither in Ptolemy nor in Stephanus of Byzantium; *Ierna* is also the reading of sixteenth-century editions of Mela at 3. 1. 10 for *Laeron*.

49. 41ʳ; already John Leland in his *Commentarii in Cygneam cantionem* printed with the ΚΥΚΝΕΙΟΝ ΑΣΜΑ, London, 1545) notes s. v. Iberi: "Poetae mentionem faciunt et Iuuernae, et Iernae, quae verba, ut ego interpretor, Hiberniam, de qua nunc tracto, denotant", and W. Camden prints *Ierne* when quoting Claudian 8. 33, though he retains *Hibernam* at 22. 251 (*Britannia*, London, 1586, p. 495).

50. "Pomponius Iuvenalis et fere vetus omnis familia Iuuernam tetrasyllabos non Hiberniam. Graeci quoque Ἰουέρναμ Strabo Ἰέρναμ Claudianus Scotorum cumulos flevit glacialis iernae."; the edition of Basle, 1534 adds "quamquam et Hybernae legitur," cf. G. Pozzi (ed.), *Hermolai Barbari Castigationes Plinianae ... (Padua 1973–79)* 4 vols., I p. 302. The emendation is accepted e.g., by J. Vadianus (see note 38) p. 171. On Pliny *n.h.* 4. 21 Barbarus points out that what Pliny and Mela call *Celticum*, is called *Ierna* and *Nerium* by Strabo and Ptolemy. For another instance of Buchanan anticipating modern editors in their choice of the correct reading see 23ᵛ/ 38/ 64 *Octodurum* at Ptol. 2. 12. 3 instead of Ἐκτόδουρον (all editions checked till 1562).

51. E.g., 1510; 1523; 1530; 1548; 1551, see also Lhuyd in citing this passage 38ᵛ; but the form *Picti* is known e.g., from Amm. Marc. 20. 1. 1 (see edition 1544) and used by sixteenth-century authors (but see note 53). Incidentally, Buchanan prints, of course, *cumulos*

in citing Claudian in accordance with the editions of this time.

52. St. Claverius (see note 47) f. 147^r; for Pullman's conjecture see his edition (Antwerp, 1571), p. 172, for Delrio's comment cf. his *Notae* (Antwerp, 1572), p. 30.

53. See also 20^r/ 31/ 54, where he prints *et aliorum Pictorum silvas*. Lhuyd uses the correct form *Pictorum* several times (33^r; 33^v; 35^r; 37^r), while citing the wrong genitive *Pictonum* from *Paneg.* 6. 7. 2 in accordance with the editions of his time (e.g., Basle, 1520), which he also has in introducing this quotation and later (37^v; see also note 51): 31^r he remarks qui Romanorum primi horum meminere non Pictos, sed Pictones eos appellabant.

54. 22^v/ 36/ 61, cf. Plin. *n.h.* 4. 113; of 21 editions of the sixteenth century which I have checked, all but one have *Conimbrica* (the earlier ones till 1516 and the later ones from 1553) or *Conibrica* (1518 to 1543) and only the edition Venice, 1559 has *Cornibrica* (20; its index of 1558 has *conibrica*), which Buchanan seems to have misread and corrected not from other editions of Pliny, but from *It. Ant. Aug.* 421. 4.

55. 30^r/ 48/ 81 (the whole of the third book is not contained in the Edinburgh manuscript). Zangemeister points out in his edition (CSEL Vienna, 1882, *in app. crit. ad loc.*, p. 30) that the same mistake is found in Iul. Honorius (see also Beda 2. 5; 9 pp. 148; 162, Mynors) and rejects rightly the conjecture *Menavia* which he attributes to Cellarius and Genthe, without mentioning Buchanan; for *Mevania* see W. Kroll, Pauly Wissowa R. E., 15 (1932), 1507-08.

56. 9^r/ 14/ 23; 1/ 1/ 1 he writes *Meneuia*.

57. 22^v/ 36/ 61: Flauiobrica, Pli. ad Amanum portum, Ptol. in Autrigonib. Magnum vocat: ac nescio an apud Plin. Magnum scribi debeat.

58. 22^v/ 36/ 62, cf. Plin. *n. h.* 4. 118 (*Medubrica*), *It. Ant. Aug.* 420. 4 (ed. 1929: *Montobrica*, ed. 1512, 70^v: *Mundobrica*); cf. Ptol. 2. 6. 57 (Νερτόβριγα), *It. Ant. Aug.* 437. 4 (ed. 1929: *Netorbriga*, ed. 1512, 74^r: *Nitobrica*) and 439. 2 (ed. 1929: *Nertobriga*, ed. 1512, 74^v: *Nertobrica*). A little later Buchanan is content to register two forms (22^v/ 36/ 61) which occur side by side in all sixteenth-century editions of the *Itinerarium Ant. Aug.*: Gerabrica (419. 9; ed. 1929: *Ierabrica*) and Ierabrica (421. 1; ed. 1929: *Ierabriga*); in case of *Brigantium in Rhaetis* (23^r/ 37/ 62) he refers to Ptolemy (2. 12. 3) and adds "opinor quod in lib. de notitia provinciarum Po. Ro. est Brecantia" (*occ.* 35. 32, so also ed. 1552).

59. 23^v/ 38/ 65 (The sentence is not in the Edinburgh manuscript), cf. Caes. *B. G.* 8. 26. 2; 3; 27. 2; 5; 29. 1; 31. 1; 2; 5.

60. 20^r/ 32/ 54 (see also 25^v/ 41/ 69), cf. Ptol. 2. 3. 1 ('Ωκεανὸς ... Δουηκαληδόνιος = *Oceanus Deucaledonius*, cf. 7. 5. 2; 8. 3. 2) and Amm. Marc. 27. 8. 5; elsewhere Buchanan speaks of the *mare Deucaledonium* (6^v-8^v/ 11-13/ 19-22 et saep.). W. Camden, *Britannia* (London, 1586), p. 33, suggests *Deucaledonios* for *Dicaledonios* in Ammianus.

61. Occasionally Buchanan's remarks are very puzzling, e.g., when he says (24^r/ 39/ 66): "Ocellum ultimum Galliae togatae oppidum, Caes. Uxellum oppidum Britanniae, forte pro Ocello. Nam et Marlianus in antiquis urbium Galliae nominibus explicandis id se nomen varie scriptum invenisse testatur, Ocellum, et Oscela et Oscellium. atque hinc fortasse Uxellodunum, quod et Uxellodurum solet scribi." For the suggestion that *Uxellum oppidum Britanniae* (cf. Ptol. 2. 3. 6) stands for *Ocelum* (found for a place in Gaul in Caes. *B. G.* 1. 10. 5) is difficult to understand and Marlianus's variants (his *Notae* reprinted e.g., in the edition of Caesar's works, Frankfurt, 1606, pp. 553-71, see p. 564: "Ocelum quod est Oscellum seu Oscela") do not support it (for *Oscela* see Ptol. 3. 1. 34 where the editions of 1482, 1513, 1540 and 1562 read *Oscela* [s. also O. Cuntz, *Die Geographie des Ptolemaeus* (Berlin, 1923), p. 191]; for *Oscellum*, not *Oscellium*, I find no evidence from antiquity) and Buchanan's further suggestion tells against it "atque hinc fortasse Uxellodunum" (cf. Caes., *B. G.* 8. 32. 2; 40. 1; 2, see also Buchanan 23^r/ 37/ 63 and *Not. dig. occ.* 40. 49 with *app. cr.*); there seems to be no evidence for the form *Uxellodurum*.

62. See e.g., 1^r/ 1/ 1: Caes. *B.G.* 5. 13. 6; 1^r/ 1/ 2: Caes. *B.G.* 5. 12. 6; 2^r/ 3/ 4: Plin.

n.h. 4. 102; 3ʳ/ 4/ 7: Plin. *n.h.* 3. 7 and 28; 3ᵛ/ 5/ 8: Claud. 26. 417; 18ʳ/ 28/ 49: Pomp. Mela 3. 52; 20ʳ/ 32/ 54: Tac. *Agr.* 11. 3.

63. See above note 54; the reading *Boemi* (17ᵛ/ 28/ 48) at Tac. *Germ.* 28. 3 seems to occur in the edition Florence (Iunt.) 1527 (p. 340) only; but *Boemi* is, of course, also the term current at the time. In case of Herodian Buchanan himself says that he used the translation of Poliziano (30ᵛ/ 49/ 82, see also 18ᵛ/ 30/ 51, where he reproduces Poliziano's version of 3. 14. 7, cf. the edition of 1535, p. 183); but the section from Cassius Dio (31ʳ⁻ᵛ/ 50-51/ 81-84) does not correspond to Xylander's translation (Basle, 1558, pp. 70-71); in places it looks more like a translation of the Italian version of M. N. Neonicenus (Venice, 1548, ff. 67-68). — When Buchanan says (15ʳ/ 23/ 40) that St Paul used the Latin form *Spania* for Spain, one wonders whether he relied on the Greek text (which has Ἐπανία at *Rom.* 15. 24 and 28); for most Latin translations read *Hispania* (but see the edition of the Vulgate ed. by J. Wordsworth, pt. II (Oxford 1913-1949), p. 143) and other Latin translations of Greek authors generally have *Hispania*. Of Stephanus of Byzantium he seems to have used the edition of 1568 (and not of 1521, though he possessed a copy of it, see McFarlane, p. 528), for his remark (2ʳ/ 3/ 4) "In voce ALBION ... eam esse insulam Brettanicam" corresponds to that edition only. But he may, of course, have taken his information from secondary sources; for in case of Ptolemy I have not been able to find any edition or translation which corresponds in all instances to the forms cited by Buchanan. It is important to remember that a good many readings which modern editors reject occur in all sixteenth-century editions and cannot, therefore, be used to determine the use of a particular one, see e.g., 13ʳ/ 19/ 33 Claudian 8. 33 (*cumulos*), 18ʳ/ 28/ 48 Claudian (*Gothunni*), 18ʳ/ 28/ 48 SHA Vopiscus *Prob.* 18. 2 (*Gautunni*), 18ʳ/ 28/ 49 Tac. *Germ.* 43 (*Gothini*, but never *Gothunni*, as implied by 19ʳ/ 30/ 51-52), 7ʳ/ 11/ 18 and 26ᵛ/ 41/ 69 Amm. Marc. 27. 8. 5 (*Vecturiones*).

64. 3ᵛ/ 6/ 9 (Ausonius *epigr.* 109): *Britto, ferturque* (in the 1582 edition actually misprinted as *ferturqne*) as in the editions 1517; 1540; editions 1551; 1558; 1568; 1575 have *fertur ferturque* (in 1494 and 1515 there is a lacuna before *ferturque*); 4ʳ/ 6/ 9 (Ausonius *epigr.* 110): *desinet* as in the editions of 1558 (v.l.); 1568 (v.l.), following Mariangeli Accursii *Diatribae* (Rome, 1524), while editions 1494; 1515; 1517; 1537; 1540; 1551; 1558; 1568; 1575 have *desinat*; 4ʳ/ 6/ 9 (Ausonius *epigr.* 112): *et homo* (with editions 1494; 1515; 1517; 1537; 1540), while editions 1551; 1568; 1575 have *et bono* or *et Bono*; 4ᵛ/ 6-7/ 11 (Mela 2. 78): *Albionem ... Bergiona* (editions 1540; 1577), while that of 1526 has *Albiona ... Bergion*; 17ᵛ 28/ 47 (Mela 3. 9-10): *Gronij Praesamarci, Tamarici Nerij* (with editions 1540; 1577), while that of 1526 has *Groni Praesamarchi* and *Herri* with the third name missing. In other cases readings appear and disappear, see e.g., 4ʳ/ 6/ 10 (Caes. *B.G.* 8. 31. 4): *Oceanoque* (as in the edition e.g., 1540), while the editions e.g., 1520 and 1606 have *Oceano*; see further 4ᵛ/ 7/ 12 (Plin. *n.h.* 3. 125): *sitos* as in the editions 1513; 1524; 1525; 1530; 1535; 1536; 1540; 1553; 1554; 1561-1562, while *siti* is found e.g., in 1518 and 1526; and *prodentes* in 1518; 1524; 1525; 1543, but *prodente* in 1513; 1526; 1530; 1535; 1536; 1540; 1553; 1554; 1561-1562.

65. I. D. McFarlane, pp. 527-31.

66. A few examples from quotations 1ᵛ/ 2/ 3 from Prop. 4. 3. 37 *in tabula* instead of *e tabula*; or 3ᵛ/ 6/ 9 in adducing Martial 11. 21. 9 Buchanan has *bracchae Brittonis*, while the sixteenth-century editions have *brache, braccae* or *brachae* and invariably *Britonis*; but *Britto* is common in other authors (see note 64). More misprints are registered by Th. Ruddiman in his edition and by T. C. (= Thomas Crawford), *Notes and Observations on Mr. George Buchanan's History of Scotland* (Edinburgh, 1708); I have not checked the long excerpts from various authors in the third book.

67. 3ᵛ-4ʳ/ 6/ 9, cf. Ausonius *epigr.* 108-12 and 14ᵛ/ 22/ 38, cf. Lucan 1. 448.

68. 4ᵛ/ 7/ 12; for the variants in sixteenth-century editions see note 64. The conjecture *nomine* is explicitly rejected by Th. Ruddiman p. 412.

69. Arrian: 18ʳ/ 28/ 48; the word *Getini* for which Buchanan refers to Arrian has been preserved by Stephanus of Byzantium s. v. Γετία (p. 206 Meineke): 'Αρριανὸς δὲ Γετηνοὺς αὐτούς φησι, see also 19ʳ/ 30/ 51. Lucretius: 1ᵛ/ 2/ 3 (in the Edinburgh manuscript there are two additions in the margin here which may indicate that the text was rephrased: nam ante Caesarem natum Britanniae Lucretius meminit Aristoteles (*in mg.*: longe prius apud graecos) ... post (*in mg.*: Caesarem) Propertius ...

70. 6ʳ/ 10/ 16; 24ᵛ/ 39/ 67; 38ʳ⁻ᵛ/ 61/ 102, cf. Th. Ruddiman pp. 414; 418; 419 et saep.

71. 16ᵛ/ 26/ 44, cf. Caes. *B. G.* 6. 18. 1; for the passage on the *Attacottae* (*sic*) cf. 19ᵛ/ 31/ 53; the form *Attacottae* occurs neither in ancient authors (though the editions of Ammianus have a variety of readings at 26. 4. 5: *Ataciti, Atacitti* and *Attacotti* and at 27. 8. 5 also *Actacotti*) nor in contemporary writers; Lhuyd correctly says *Attacotti* (38ʳ), and so does Buchanan himself elsewhere.

72. 8ᵛ/ 13/ 22, cf. Markianos F (*Geographi Graeci Minores I*, p. 560 Müller = Steph. Byz. s. v. Αἰβοῦδαι p. 37 Meineke), cf. Ptol. 2. 2. 10; Solin. 22 (addition p. 219 Mommsen); see also Pomp. Mela 3. 54, the Edinburgh manuscript has several corrections here, especially after *Martianus Capella*.

73. 14ʳ/ 22/ 38 and 17ᵛ/ 27/ 47.

74. 4ʳ/ 6/ 9.

75. Th. Ruddiman, p. 410 points out that this passage is not in the Edinburgh manuscript and assumes that it was written in haste when the manuscript was already with the printer, and inserted later.

76. 18ʳ/ 28-29/ 49.

77. 19ᵛ-20ʳ/ 31-32/ 53-54.

78. Lhuyd 37ᵛ-38ᵛ.

79. 20ʳ/ 31/ 54 (in the Edinburgh manuscript: *sylvas*), cf. *Paneg.* 6. 7. 2 (the edition of 1520 reading *Pictonum sylvas*, of 1576 *Pictonum silvas*); Lhuyd (37ᵛ) has *Pictonum sylvas*, cf. above note 53.

80. 25ʳ/ 40-41/ 68-69; Lhuyd does not say *solos tum Brittones insulam incoluisse*, but *solos Britannos insulam habitasse*; in taking this to be from a panegyricus for Maximinian by Mamertinus Buchanan follows Lhuyd — or independently of him Rhenanus's hesitant attribution (see e.g., edition Basle 1520, p. 268).

81. Thus the editions of 1520 and 1576, except that both have *etiam tunc* and *signisque*, 1520 *Hybernis* and *Rhomanis* and 1576 *hybernis* and *pictis*; this is also Lhuyd's text (37ʳ). Scaliger seems to have suggested *Hibernis* for *Hybernis*.

82. 25ʳ/ 41/ 69, see also 18ᵛ/ 29/ 50, cf. Orosius 1. 2. 81 and Beda 1. 1 (pp. 16-18, Mynors with note 1, p. 16).

83. Even in the earlier passage to which Buchanan refers (18ᵛ/ 29/ 50), he cites Bede only for the fact that the colonists first went to Ireland, before going to Britain; here he introduces his interpretation carefully with the words "si ego eum recto intelligo" (25ʳ/ 41/ 68). 12ʳ/ 19/ 33 Buchanan rejects the view that the Picts were of Saxon origin and shows that Claudian 8. 31-33 does not mean this, and that Bede's evidence tells against it (1. 1, p. 16, Mynors).

84. 26ʳ/ 42/ 71-72; *scuta Brigantes* is the reading of the Edinburgh manuscript; the printed editions (at least 1582 and 1697, not 1715) have *Scutabrigantes* for the rejected reading, which Buchanan presupposes earlier (23ʳ/ 36/ 62); see appendix.

85. For Buchanan's friendship with Julius Caesar Scaliger see McFarlane, pp. 89-90; 275 et saep. J. J. Bernays, *Joseph Justus Scaliger* (Berlin, 1855), p. 31, maintains that when the younger Scaliger was sent to Bordeaux in 1551, Buchanan taught there; but this is not correct.

86. According to I. D. McFarlane, p. 173 it was in De Mesmes's circle that Buchanan got to know the younger Scaliger; for Buchanan's later stay in France see ibid., pp. 160-90.

87. The conjecture was published in: J. Scaligeri ... *Castigationes in Catullum, Tibullum, Propertium* (Paris, 1577), p. 159 (*ad* Tib. 4. 1. 149; repeated in the edition Utrecht, 1582, p. 151) and defended by Scaliger explicitly in the new edition of the *Castigationes* ... (Heidelberg, 1600), p. 181, after it had been rejected e.g., by W. Camden, *Britannia* (London, 1586), p. 40 and by M. A. Delrio, *Syntagma Tragodiae Latinae III* (Antwerp, 1594), p. 522; it was later also rejected by C. Barth (ed.), *Claudiani Opera* (Hamburg, 1650), p. 261. On Scaliger as textual critic see A. Grafton, *J. Scaliger* (Oxford, 1983).

88. 1577, p. 159: "Sed et Seneca in ἀποκολοκυνθώσει idem testatur in choricis anapaestis Et caeruleos Scotobrigantes pro quo ineptissime hodie editur scuta Brigantes. Quare et Scoti hanc gentis suae antiquitatem mihi debent qui primus illum locum emendavi: quem ipsi hactenus suae gentis testem Claudiano antiquiorem non haberent."

89. Buchanan, who occasionally contrasts those "qui ... ex professo scripserunt historiam" with poets who have the licence "ut familiarum, et nationum originem fabularum figmentis ornare conentur" (15ᵛ/ 24/ 42), often warns against the reconstruction of history on the basis of insufficient evidence (see e.g., 14ʳ–17ʳ/ 22–27/ 38–47, also especially with regard to the use of names, see e.g., 4ʳ⁻ᵛ/ 6–7/ 10–11; 21ᵛ/ 34/ 58; 26ᵛ/ 43/ 72–73, though he relies on names very extensively himself). At the same time he emphasizes the lack of reliable early indigenous sources (e.g., 14ʳ⁻ᵛ/ 22–23/ 37–39) and of early information about Britain from Greek and Roman authors (see e.g., 8ʳ⁻ᵛ/ 13/ 22; 16ᵛ–17ʳ/ 26–27/ 45–46; 25ʳ/ 40/ 68; 26ʳ/ 42/ 71, see also on its limited value e.g., 14ʳ/ 22/ 38). Stating occasionally that restat ut vestigia persequentes coniecturis, si fieri potest, ad veritatem perveniamus (19ʳ/ 30/ 51), he argues with the help of words, especially names (see e.g., 4ʳ/ 6/ 10; 4ᵛ/ 7/ 11; 20ʳ/ 32/ 54; 20ᵛ/ 33/ 56; 21ᵗ–24ᵛ/ 30–40/ 57–67; 25ᵛ–26ʳ/ 41– 42/ 70–71, showing great circumspection: 4ᵛ/ 7/ 11–12; 23ᵛ/ 38/ 64; 24ʳ/ 39/ 65) with the help of monuments (e.g., 6ʳ/ 9–10/ 15–16), of ancient authorities (throughout, see also note 92, stressing their importance: 1ᵛ–2ʳ/ 2–3/ 3–4; 6ʳ/ 9–10/ 15–16; see also note 91), of actual habits and practices or religious beliefs (18ᵛ–19ʳ/ 30/ 51; 20ʳ/ 32/ 54), of old indigenous sources (e.g., 6ᵛ/ 10/ 16; 7ʳ/ 11/ 18; 18ᵛ/ 29/ 50 (*nostri annales*); 19ᵛ/ 31/ 53), of oral tradition (11ᵛ/ 18/ 31; 12ʳ/ 19/ 32), of contemporary names (20ʳ/ 32/ 54), of contemporary witnesses (8ʳ⁻ᵛ/ 13/ 22), and of his own experience (7ᵛ/ 11/ 19; see also 13ᵛ/ 21/ 37). However, he is highly sceptical with regard to allegedly old local tradition (8ʳ/ 13/ 22), emphasizes what appears improbable (e.g., 4ᵛ/ 7/ 12; 68ʳ/ 100/ 178) or likely (73ᵛ/ 113/ 193), at least to him (82ʳ/ 127/ 216) or leaves the judgment in doubtful cases to the reader (64ʳ/ 99/ 167) or explains why he favours a particular version (51ᵛ/ 81/ 136).

90. 1ᵛ/ 1/ 2 and his remark on Strabo 8ᵛ/ 13/ 22: "Straboni ... fortasse venia danda sit quod ea parte orbis nondum satis explicata (Edinburgh manuscript: explorata) famam incertam secutus videri possit"; see also 14ʳ/ 22/ 38; similarly Lhuyd 17ʳ and with regard to Ptolemy 24ᵛ.

91. 1ᵛ/ 2/ 3–4; 4ʳ⁻ᵛ/ 6–7/ 9–11; 14ʳ/ 22/ 38/; 18ᵛ/ 28/ 48–49; 25ʳ/ 40/ 68; 26ʳ/ 42/ 71; 26ᵛ/ 42/ 72; 28ʳ/ 45/ 76.

92. E.g., 6ʳ/ 9/ 16; 16ᵛ/ 26/ 44; 25ʳ⁻ᵛ/ 40–41/ 68–70; 26ᵛ–27ʳ/ 43/ 73.

93. E.g., 25ʳ/ 40/ 68; 26ʳ/ 42/ 71.

94. I cannot here give an exhaustive account of Buchanan's attitude to the medieval tradition and the extent to which he draws on medieval sources. In the first four books he frequently relies on Bede, occasionally on Gildas (14ʳ/ 22/ 38; 25ᵛ/ 41/ 70; an excerpt: 32ᵛ/ 52/ 87), Gregory of Tours (3ᵛ/ 5/ 9), William of Malmesbury (3ᵛ/ 5/ 8; 26ʳ/ 42/ 71) and Geoffrey of Monmouth (3ᵛ/ 5/ 8; 26ʳ/ 42/ 71), whom he vigorously attacks 16ʳ⁻ᵛ/ 24–26/ 41–44 (see also 27ᵛ/ 44/ 75); he also refers to anonymous accounts.

95. John of Fordun, *Chronica* 45 (I, p. 12); on his construction and its antecedents see W. F. Skene in his introductions (see notes 13 and 29) I, pp. XXXV–XXXVII and II, pp. LXXIV–LXXVII. John Major assumes (II.1, f. XXIIᵛ) that there were fifteen kings

between Fergus I, son of Ferchard (cf. I.11, ff. XVIII^v-XIX^r), and Fergus II, son of Erth; but later he gives a genealogy with more than thirty generations between the two (IV.11, ff. LXV^v-LXVI^r). On the various lists of kings of the Scots and Picts see (after W. F. Skene (ed.), *Chronicles of the Picts, Chronicles of the Scots* ... (Edinburgh, 1867), and A. O. Anderson (ed.), *Early Sources of Scottish History A.D. 500 to 1286*, (Edinburgh, 1922), 2 vols., who present the material) M. O. Anderson, *Kings and Kingship in Early Scotland* (Edinburgh, 1973, ^{2}1980) (also on John of Fordun, see index).

96. *Scot. Hist.* I-VI, ff. 4^r-111^v 4-109; on Boece see *University of Aberdeen Quatercentenary of the Death of Hector Boece* (Aberdeen, 1937), especially J. B. Black, pp. 30-53 on the *Historia*, on John of Fordun as Boece's source, pp. 36-37, on his methods of inventing the early history, pp. 37-42, on his alleged sources, pp. 47-53; cf. also T. D. Kendrick (see note 30), pp. 65-69. For the view that Boece fell victim to a forgery see also Th. Innes (above note 6) I, pp. 130-69, esp. pp. 146-48, 166-68; also on John of Fordun pp. 123-30 and John Lesley pp. 169-71.

97. *De origine....* (see note 11) books II-IV, pp. 83-129: for Vergil's doubt as regards Fergus I see his *Historia* III, p. 52, for Lhuyd's criticism of Boece's early history, *Fragmentum*, 32^r-36^v.

98. Buchanan rejects the story of Diocletian, Labana and their daughters (15^{r-v}/ 24-25/ 40-42), as it was previously rejected by J. Major I.1, f. I^r, while ignored by Boece, Polydore Vergil and Lesley, the story of Brutus (15^r-16^v/ 25-26/ 41-43, previously rejected by J. Major I.1, f. I^{r-v} and Polydore Vergil, I, pp. 15-18 with reference to William of Newburgh, while generally accepted, even by Lhuyd 8^{r-v}; 16^v) and the story of Gathalus (16^v-17^r/ 27/ 45-46), as previously rejected by Vergil III, pp. 52-53, while accepted e.g., by Boece I, ff. 1^r-2^v and Lesley I, pp. 45-46. Early traces of the story of Brutus are found in Nennius's *Historia Brittonum* (pp. 127; 149-54 Mommsen: Bruto, Britto, Brito, Britus) and Geoffrey of Monmouth's *Historia Regum Britanniae* (pp. 224-59, Griscom), of Gathalus in John of Fordun's *Chronica* (Gaythelos I, pp. 8-17: 9-16 with remarks on earlier versions by Skene II, pp. 381-82), and of Diocletian in the *Chronicles of England*, printed by W. Caxton (1480). Geoffrey's story was not only used later by Latin chroniclers (see L. Keeler, *Geoffrey of Monmouth and the Late Latin Chroniclers 1300-1500*, Berkeley, 1946), but also translated and transformed into poems (e.g., by Wace) and expanded as the *Brut* chronicles ("the continuations of the vernacular versions," see A. Gransden (cf. note 29) pp. 202, 480) and printed as the *Chronicles of England* (ed. F. W. D. Brie I/II, Early English Text Society, 131 and 136 (London 1906-1908); see also F. W. D. Brie, *Geschichte und Quellen der mittelenglischen Prosachronik "The Brut of England ..."*, Habil.schrift, Marburg, 1905, and M. D. Legge, *Anglo-Norman Literature and its Background* (Oxford, 1963). Although William of Newburgh had already expressed doubts about the Arthurian legend (*Historia Rerum Anglicarum*, in R. Howlett (ed.), *Chronicles of the Reigns of Stephen, Henry II....* (London 1884-1889) 4 vols., Rolls Series 82, I, pp. 11-18), we find John Leland defending it still in 1544 especially against Polydore Vergil: *Assertio inclytissimi Arturij regis Britanniae* (London, 1544), and this defence is made available to an even wider public in a translation by R. Robinson 1582 (London, reprinted together with *The Famous Historie of Chinon of England* by W. E. Mead, Early English Text Society, 165, London, 1925), in the very year, when Buchanan published his *Historia*, an interesting coincidence.

99. 15^r-16^v/ 24-26/ 40-44.

100. 15^r/ 24/ 40; 16^v/ 26/ 44.

101. 15^v/ 24/ 42; see also 16^v/ 26/ 45 (Brutus) and note 93.

102. E.g., 1^v/ 2/ 3; 3^r/ 4/ 7; 3^v/ 4-5/ 8-9; 4^r/ 6/ 10; 22^r/ 35/ 60; 25^v-27^r/ 41-43/ 70-73.

103. See above note 27 et saep.

104. E.g., 2^v/ 3/ 5.

105. 26^v-27^r/ 43-44/ 73; cf. Iustin. 42. 3. 4; Liv. *perioch.* 77; see also the remark about

the *scuta angusta* (26ᵛ/ 42/ 72) mentioned only once by Livy (38. 21. 4).

106. He is, in fact, given a place by J. E. Sandys, in his *History of Classical Scholarship* (Cambridge, 1908), II, pp. 243–46, but only referred to as poet by R. Pfeiffer, *History of Classical Scholarship 1300–1850* (Oxford, 1976), p. 144; W. A. Lindsay denies that Buchanan was a scholar (in: D. A. Millar (ed.), *George Buchanan* ... (see note 7) p. 205), but on the grounds that he could not write verse correctly.

107. 4ʳ/ 6/ 10.

108. John Leland: 21ᵛ/ 34/ 58; D. Monroe: 8ᵛ–12ʳ/ 13–18/ 22–32; also Boece: 7ʳ/ 11/ 18 and more often later, but see also note 109.

109. mild irony: J. Annius: 15ᵛ/ 24/ 41–42; a number of people are criticized in a friendly manner (examples taken from the first two books only), e.g., Th. Elyot: 1ʳ/ 2/ 2 and 2ʳ/ 3/ 4; J. Goropius 4ʳ/ 6/ 10; Pomponius Laetus: 18ʳ/ 29/ 49; R. Caenalis: 18ʳ/ 29/ 49; P. Vergil: 21ᵛ/ 34/ 58; Boece: 5ʳ/ 7–8/ 12–13; 8ʳ/ 12/ 21; 26ᵛ/ 43/ 72; 27ᵛ/ 44–45/ 75–76 Buchanan rebukes Lhuyd for his criticism of Boece without accepting Boece's view which he himself often criticizes without naming Boece: e.g., 6ʳ⁻ᵛ/ 10/ 16; 9ʳ/ 14/ 23; 12ʳ/ 19/ 33.

110. Loc. cit. (see note 8) p. 21. On the emergence of humanist historiography in Italy and its influence on other countries see now E. Cochrane, *Historians and Historiography in the Italian Renaissance* (Chicago, 1981).

Appendix (addition to note 44)

Buchanan gives a curious mixture of various readings for a place in Moesia (23ᵛ/ 38/ 64): *Singindunum* (Ptol. 3. 9. 3) instead of *Singidunum* (ed. 1475, also Müller ed. 1883), while the editions of 1533 and 1546 and the translations of 1540 and 1562 have *Sigindunum* (alii alia). A little later (23ᵛ/ 38/ 64) he has *Carrodurum* together with other places ending in *-durum*, though the actual name is *Carrodunum* (Ptol. 2. 14. 4) and could well have been listed a little earlier. Where he mentions the *Nonantum promontorium* (5ᵛ/ 8/ 14) and again the *Nonantum Mula* he seems to have misunderstood Ptolemy's Νοουαντῶν χερσόνησος (2. 3. 1; 2, also misspelling it). Again, when Buchanan speaks (21ʳ/ 34/ 57) of *Ebora, quae felicitas Iulia Hispanis cognominatur*, he has misread his source (Plin. *n. h.* 4. 117), where *Felicitas Iulia* is mentioned as name of Olisippo, whereas *Ebora* is given its correct name *Liberalitas Iulia* in the following line; see Buchanan himself: 24ʳ/ 39/ 66, where he distinguishes between Pliny's *Ebora* and Ptolemy's *Ebura* (2. 5. 6). Similarly in giving several examples of *Noviomagus* from Ptolemy, Buchanan lists (24ʳ/ 38/ 65) besides *Nouiomagus Biturigum* (2. 7. 7) *Nouiomagus in Santonibus* who are referred to in Ptolemy in the previous line, but seem to have no place of that name, only *Novioregum*, not mentioned by Ptolemy, but in the *It. Ant. Aug.* (459. 2; ed. of 1512: 78ʳ). In several cases he gains additional examples by including mutually exclusive readings. He registers (22ᵛ/ 36/ 61) *Arabrica altera .. in Lusitania* (correctly, according to Ptolemy 2. 5. 6); but before that he also has *Arabrica Plin. conuent. Braca.* for which there is no evidence in Ptolemy, and confusion has to be ruled out, as he also lists *Abobrica* (cf. Plin. *n. h.* 4. 112) and *Axabrica* (Plin. *n. h.* 4. 119: *Axabricensis*, where some editions before 1526 have *Taxabricenses*, which modern editors change into *Arabricensis*). If Buchanan had anticipated this conjecture, he should have omitted *Axabrixa* later, and the additional information *conventus Bracarensis* on *Arabrica* is not correct, as Buchanan who spent so much time in Portugal must have known. Of the three places with the name *Augustobrica* (22ᵛ/ 36/ 61), only two exist, one *in Pelendonibus* (Ptol. 2. 6. 53), the other *in Vectonibus* (Ptol. 2. 5. 7) which is identical with *Augustobrica in Lusitania* (see also Plin. *n. h.* 4. 118). From the *Itinerarium Ant. Aug.* Buchanan lists (24^r/ 39/ 65) *Vacomagi* and adds *Vicomagi* as *pars Pictorum* from Ptolemy; in fact only *Vacomagi* are mentioned, and they by Ptolemy (2. 3. 8), where, however, the Ulm edition of 1482 reads *Vicomagi*.

Earlier Buchanan has *Novidunum in Tribocis* (23^r/ 37/ 63) from Ptolemy; but *in Tribocis* only other places are mentioned (Ptol. 2. 9. 9); it is not clear which city he is thinking of, most probably under the heading *in Gallia* of Νοιόδουνον (2. 8. 7; but see E. Lickenheld in Pauly Wissowa *R. E.*, 17 (1936), coll. 1189–90 s. v. *Noviodunum* 1 - 3), despite the difference in spelling (consistently found in the sixteenth-century editions of Ptolemy, whereas the earlier editions have various other forms). He is probably influenced by other places of the name *Noviodunum* of which he gives four: *in Scotia Nouiodunum vel Dunum novum in Coualia* (no source), *in Vindelicis, Rhaetia et Norico: Noviodunum* from Ptolemy, *in Sarmatia et Dacia: Nouiodunum ad ostium Dannubii* from Ptolemy and *item Nouiodunum alterum* from Ptolemy, though Ptolemy has but two: *Noviodunum in Pannonia superior* (2. 14. 4; see Müller *ad loc.*; in sixteenth-century editions *Novidunum*) and *Noviodunum in Moesia* on the Danube (3. 10. 2 and 5, in sixteenth-century editions *Nuiodunum*, again spelt in the most diverse manner in the earlier editions). To gain an additional example Buchanan says (23^v/ 38/ 64) *Octodurum vel Octodurus Caesaris*, though Caesar (3. 1. 4) writes *Octodurus*, and *Octodurum* is found in Ptolemy as a name of a place in Spain only (2. 6. 4), also mentioned by Buchanan under the heading *In Hispania*. Besides *Ganodurum in Gallia* (23^v/ 38/ 64) from Ptolemy (2. 9. 10) he has *Gannodurum* under the heading *In Rhetia, Vindelicis et Norico*; here he uses the spelling which prevails in the editions of Ptolemy at 2. 9. 10 (1475; 1482; 1513; Latin translations: 1540; 1562, while the editions of 1533 and 1546 have Γανόδουρον) to add a further example, though there is no record of a further place of that name there. That Buchanan is rather careless at times or even deliberately misleading his readers is indicated by the fact that although he accepts and defends Scaliger's conjecture *Scotobrigantes* (26^r/ 42/ 72) he claims elsewhere that Seneca speaks of the *Brigantes in Albio* (23^r/ 37/ 62), though this presupposes the reading *scuta Brigantes*. Finally, instead of *Breviodorum* he cites (23^v/ 38/ 64) *Breuiodurum* from *It. Ant. Aug.* (385. 2), as this form seems to fit better into his list.

Native Influences on George Buchanan

John Durkan

This paper is concerned to re-examine mainly the pre-Reformation period of Buchanan's life of which his *Vita* tells us something but scarcely enough. Such a scrutiny is hampered by among other things the absence of early correspondence apart from a few fairly uninformative preliminary epistles in his printed works. When the poet arrived in St Andrews in 1566 to take over as principal of St Leonard's college, the university now had three former members of the college of Guienne in Bordeaux, two of whom, John Rutherford and himself, had tutored in the family of Michel de Montaigne.[1] Buchanan could of course meet Scots and occasionally Englishmen at Paris where much of his time abroad was spent. How significant for his work were these contacts with his fellow Britons? This is surely a question worth broaching again, now that a new flood of light has been shed on his connections in mainland Europe.

Beginning not quite at the beginning, we start with his maternal uncle, James Heriot, who financed the young Buchanan's first Paris stay. Little is known of this uncle, except that he formed hopes of his nephew's talent by his performance in school in Scotland: and Buchanan confesses that during these two years he studied Latin versification largely because he wanted to. Unexpectedly the uncle died before 18 February 1522 and the experiment ended with the boy's abrupt return.[2] Who was Heriot? He must have been quite a young man, for he was a Paris graduate of 1504 who continued with studies in civil law at Orléans in 1507, when already beneficed in Glasgow diocese as vicar of Dumfries, though initially from St Andrews diocese.[3] He became official of Lothian, with his head-quarters from August 1516 in Edinburgh in the church of St Giles, and about the same time canon of Ross. One of his colleagues in the official's court was James Foulis, the earliest Scot to publish neo-Latin verse, not without mention of that very church.[4] Buchanan must surely have held Foulis's book in his hand and been appreciative of its relative metrical diversity and emotional range from the encomium of Patrick Panter, Greek and Latin scholar, to the Dunbar-like satire on the easy-going Edinburgh merchants at the mercy of their wives' infidelity and expensive tastes. Foulis's case paralleled Buchanan's remarkably, for he too had been a poor boy whose maternal uncle financed his studies, after his father, Henry, with his mother and others of his family had died in the plague.[5]

But, though this has hitherto been far from obvious, Foulis was not altogether unknown to the Buchanans themselves, and, despite no record in George's work, may have had some hand in the poet's early development. In 1518, along with George's uncle, Foulis, then prebendary of Bothwell (he married later), witnessed a deed by Buchanan's brother, as heir of their father, Thomas of "Laidloan," or Ledlewan, the site of the family estate of Moss, and this deed approved the resignation of lands in Petty, Kincardineshire. Again we find a sasine of land in north High Street, Edinburgh, in favour of Foulis in common with the executors of Buchanan's father who were John Heriot, vicar of Drymen and the poet's brother, Thomas: casualties were payable to Foulis as superior. Moreover in September 1528, Thomas Buchanan of Moss, the poet's brother, is again found in Edinburgh constituting procurators to claim these same lands in Kincardine with a mandate to George Heriot, goldsmith, to seal the procuration with his seal.[6] As this took place in Walter Chepman's writing office, the Chepman of printing fame, familiarity of the Buchanans with literary circles in the city seems certain. But a further question raises itself: when did Buchanan's father die? Before Flodden — for a deed of July 1513 assigning lands in Arnprior, attached to Inchmahome priory, designated Buchanan's mother as widow. After Flodden — if we credit another deed of November 1518 describing the father as having died "under our Sovereign Lord's banner at the field of Flodden, 9 September 1513." (This was a precept of *clare constat* whereby William, earl Marischal, infefted Robert as heir to his father, Thomas Buchanan, in the third of the Petty lands.) Somebody was not telling the truth and the reason is plain: the freedom from certain duties granted to the heirs of those dying on Flodden field.[7]

Foulis, it is worth remembering, was still at the court of James V when Buchanan revisited Scotland in 1534. Giovanni Ferrerio, himself at court in 1528–31, met Foulis whom in his *Auditum visu praestare* of 1539 he characterised as still a "poet to his fingertips."[8] A close associate of the reforming abbot of Cambuskenneth, Alexander Myln, Foulis in 1535 certified the accuracy of its monastic register to which he prefixed his arms with some verse. He also audited the monastic accounts in association with John Dingwall, Adam Otterburn and John Campbell of Lundy, of some of whom more anon.[9] Some of Foulis's epistolary prose is still extant, but the prose Latinity of these royal secretaries remains unexamined.[10]

Buchanan's teacher at St Andrews was John Mair, whom he willingly followed to Paris, finishing his arts course under a member of the school of Mair, Robert Wauchope. In his impoverished state he meantime acted as servitor to another member of the school, the former Paris rector, William Manderston, then at the college of Ste Barbe.[11] The theme of Mair's influence on Buchanan's political theory in the *De Jure Regni* has been well ventilated and, of course, Buchanan was to compose a stinging epigram on his old teacher. Yet it may have been in Mair's class that the poet first encountered the *Sphaera* of Joannes de Sacro Bosco. In his lectures on the Nicomachean ethics of Aristotle, Mair makes more classical references than usual, sometimes, as with Euripides and Theognis, merely echoing a reference in the text of Aristotle, though we have to remember the edition of Theognis and Phocylides of Girolamo Aleandro, whose Paris lectures the young Mair attended. Often Mair cited Hesiod in Leonardo Bruni's version or a line from some favourite Latin poet like Juvenal, quite as often taking time off to give his hearers some biographical details from Aulus Gellius. Once in the middle of his syllogisms he commended Pindar to them as an outstanding lyricist.[12] Despite this, Buchanan soon came to share the scorn of Thomas More and Juan Luis Vives for all late scholastic dialectical niceties.

Sir Thomas More's epigrams, with their Erasmian commendation, could scarcely have been without impact on the juvenile apprentice epigrammatist. His Paris contemporary and fellow Scot, Florence Wilson, quoted More's "Paraenesis ad virtutem veram," an epigram comparing life's vain pleasures to the withering of an early rose.[13] To Buchanan the anti-tyrannical epigrams may well have appealed, especially "Populus consentiens regnum dat et aufert."[14] Whether Buchanan's later claim in his defence to the Lisbon inquisitors that he based his play, "quantum materiae similitudo patiebatur," — for such analogues are necessarily defective in the *Baptistes* as elsewhere, — on More's treatment by King Henry VIII, is verifiable or not, there seems no reason for him not sharing the general appreciation of More. At the Scots court *c.* 1536, following a letter from Rome to James V on the death of John Fisher, the scribe of the royal letter-book entered some epigrams of "uncertain author" (actually by Joannes Secundus) regretting the fall of More, and the theme would find a welcome before a French student audience.[15]

It has to be remembered that, about the date of the play, Buchanan was commending the work of the quite orthodox François de Sagan.[16] It is not generally known just how many Englishmen were attracted to the German nation in Paris in the twenties and thirties. One of them, Nicholas Wilson, York diocese, incorporated with Buchanan, was a lifelong friend of both Fisher and More; Richard Pate, nephew of Longland, bishop of Lincoln, who, living into Elizabeth's reign, died at Catholic Louvain, was fresh from his studies at Bruges with Vives; Walter Abercromby, a Scot, was soon to join Linacre's new College of Physicians and John Redman, York diocese, would have as a pupil Buchanan's friend, Roger Ascham.[17] However, can such a putative regard for More be squared with Buchanan's epigrams in praise of Thomas Cromwell and Henry VIII? The date of these seems to be 1539 when the poet sought sanctuary in England and it is likely that the "bundles from the poor harvest of a barren mind" that he offered Cromwell then included his only printed work, the translation of Linacre, but also a manuscript book of poetical offerings of the kind: even so, the opening lines to Henry confessed that rumours concerning him were less flattering.[18] The Linacre it might have been politic to exclude from the gift, since as late as 1533, in a note to the reader, Buchanan had drawn attention with obvious approval to the fact that both the Linacre original and his Latin version were dedicated to the Princess Mary and that she was the daughter of the recipient of the Vives dedication, Catherine of Aragon.[19]

Florence Wilson, from Hector Boece's university of Aberdeen, was in Paris from about 1526 and friendly to Buchanan, gifting to him the Hebrew dictionary of Sebastian Munster.[20] Boece's visit to Paris in 1527 with his Scots history coming from the press that year must have been a thrilling occasion for Buchanan: here was a good companion, one who had known Erasmus and brought eloquence to his tale of Scotland's antiquities, a tale commended by among others the future bishop of Aberdeen, William Gordon. Then seems the best date for Buchanan's "epitaphium Alexandri Gordonii," second earl of Huntly; Gordon stayed with Ferrerio in Paris before proceeding to Angers, hence its appearance at the end of Ferrerio's manuscript history of the Gordons.[21] Wilson, who held a benefice in Fisher's diocese, himself offered Cromwell a treatise of history, but his main contribution lay in his brief commentaries on isolated psalms using the Hebrew text.[22] The idea of Latin paraphrases had not yet been taken up by Buchanan. The first Scot in the field was Roderick Maclean who at Rome in 1549, following verses on Columba of Iona, inserted in a blank space a paraphrase of Psalm 1, with a broad hint that he had more up his sleeve: "O pius, O foelix, O vir sine fine beatus, / Vitat iniquorum qui mala facta virum."[23] Wilson was for a time tutor to Wolsey's son as also was Thomas Lupset, he who had seen Linacre's version of Galen's *De sanitate tuenda* through the press. In October 1526 Winter, Wolsey's son, was "nowe with a Scottysshman, a kynd and very gentyll person and well lyerned, and doth all the pleasure he can for Mr Deane" (Winter was dean of Wells). Lupset moved to Paris by February 1528 when Buchanan had arrived, though Winter no longer lodged with the unidentified Scot.[24]

Manderston left Paris early in 1528, which must have exacerbated the poet's situation, though by 1532 he had taken on the tutorship of the young earl of Cassillis, Gilbert Kennedy. For Kennedy Buchanan translated Linacre's *Rudimenta* into Latin, as earlier the young More commended Linacre's *Progymnasmata*.[25] On returning to Scotland, Buchanan stayed with Cassillis, and it is likely that there he saw a manuscript of William Dunbar's "Dreme," a paraphrase of which Buchanan produced, as the Kennedy family had close poetic associations with Dunbar and this is not among that poet's works known to have been printed by Chepman and Myllar.[26] Ferrerio, who claimed to have lived on friendly terms with Buchanan and to have "loved him as a brother," was no longer at court when Buchanan went there, but acting as preceptor to the monks of the northern abbey of Kinloss.[27]

At James V's court where Buchanan was soon employed as tutor to the king's son by Elizabeth Sauchie, the poet met time-servers whom he lampooned, but others too like the chancellor, Gavin Dunbar, for whom he had an admiring epigram, a good man and learned as he was later to say, though lacking in civic wisdom, for indeed Dunbar was educated at Paris and Angers.[28] But a genuine friend of these years was Adam Otterburn, to the English always an acceptable envoy yet in custody and disgrace for some months before Buchanan was forced to flee Scotland. James Foulis had been his deputy as Lord Advocate. At one point when there was pressure from above to depose the popular Otterburn from his post as provost, Foulis was among the crowd that chanted, "Otterburn, Otterburn!" Otterburn too was a Latinist of some ability and a stimulus to Buchanan's poetic talents. It was he who had hired for Edinburgh the Aberdeen Latin poet, Adam Mure.[29] When Otterburn composed some Latin hexameters on a court sycophant, John Dingwall, Buchanan, who could scarcely have known Dingwall who died in 1532, offered an improved version. Dingwall was, it seems, a priest son of a priest to whom his father had left not one penny, a theme no doubt ensuring the epigram's post-Reformation survival. From being a humble notary in his native town of Dingwall, his days ended in luxury. He proudly exhibited many titles on the shield of arms above his grave as though the Dingwalls had been a noble family of long standing. Recent distinctions he had won at the Roman curia, till his final years as provost of the royal Trinity collegiate church.[30] In a further epigram Otterburn is made to complain that in these poetic contests he provided the cloth, ideas, that is, which Buchanan merely wrote up. If one remembers that Otterburn traded on the side in fine cloths and ironware (hence references to ancient dyes and to Vulcan and his assistants), the epigram begins to yield its secret.[31] No sooner had Buchanan agreed that Otterburn's "gems" needed something to set them off, than he crushingly called them insubstantial, "istos fumos," as though only Buchanan's divine creative gift gave Otterburn's offerings any substance.[32]

While at court Buchanan kept the company not only of the orthodox Otterburn, but of certain Lutherans, nine of whom abjured and five of whom were burnt in the king's presence in Edinburgh. One was a Dominican friar called Kelour who had put on a Passion play in Stirling in which contemporary prelates were lampooned under cover of attacking the Pharisee enemies of Christ. In evidence Ferrerio adduced against Buchanan there is a clear reference to certain others who were present at the wedding of a Cambuskenneth canon regular, Thomas Gibson or Cocklaw, vicar of Tullibody. One of those associates was Robert Logie, novice master. It is likely that both Gibson and Logie knew Buchanan from his Paris days, presumably as associates at the Augustinian study house of St Victor of Robert Richardson. At least when as religious refugees they reached England in 1540, soon after, in 1544, both were twice naturalised, once as Scotsmen and once as Frenchmen.[33] The above-mentioned Richardson, another Cambuskenneth canon, was certainly known to Buchanan as both studied together under Mair in St Andrews in 1525. Richardson was also the person who introduced Ferrerio to the abbot of Kinloss as he passed through Paris in 1528.[34] A further Cambuskenneth connection is that when David Panter succeeded Myln as abbot, Buchanan claimed to have had the offer of tutoring him in Greek.[35]

Excluded from the Scottish court in spite of James V's initial welcome, Buchanan had access to the French court before the death of Francis I in 1547, for a certain Pierre des Mireurs writing to Jean de Morel declared that the French king, seeing his mock defence of the procuress, not only expressed a wish to see him, but also "strenuously exhorted him to proceed in poetry as he had begun and always to publish something worthy of his genius, conceding the poet the fullest authority to do so."[36]

Returning to Paris on his release from the prisons of the Inquisition in Portugal, Buchanan brought with him the psalm paraphrases he had written there, the first of which Henri Estienne printed in 1556. He also had renderings of Simonides (both of Ceos and of Amorgos), which Guillaume Morel published along with other Latin renderings of Theognis, Phocylides, etc. in a twin volume with the Greek originals issued in 1553 by Adrien Turnèbe. One surmises that Buchanan probably knew the young ex-St Andrews student, John Hepburn, who in 1556 celebrated in preliminary verse in a Paris book, René Guillon's guide to Greek metric, the *Gnomon*.[37] Meantime Buchanan held a post in the college of Boncourt, from which he retired at the end of the session 1553–54. A letter in another Morel publication, *Jephthes*, explained why: he had taken up a new assignment as tutor to the son of the Marshal de Brissac. This becomes clear from a letter of Denys Lambin's to his successor at Boncourt at the start of the new 1554–55 session, "I am glad that you have succeeded Buchanan, both because it is an honour for you to be chosen in the place of a very learned man," and because his correspondent now had more leisure for letter writing.[38] The maturing of earlier influences rather than fresh native contacts looked the programme for the future.

It is hard to reconcile Buchanan's assurances that he was reading works of controversial theology just prior to his return home in view of his public poetic statements up to 1558, though he might well have shared in discussions with such as George Hay in Paris from 1552.[39] He himself pointed out in his history that in Scotland religious debate had died down ("jacuisse") in 1557–58,[40] and the recently discovered original text of the *Vita* (Rostock, 1595) confirms this. It reads not "tum domi conquiescere caeperant, Scotis a tyrannide Guisiana liberatis," but instead, giving quite a different sense, "tum domi conquiescere caeperant. Scotis a tyrannide Guisiana liberatis, eo reversus, nomen Ecclesiae Scotorum dedit." Thus only when Mary of Lorraine was dead did Buchanan return and join the new kirk party in Scotland: as late as 1558 the Guises were still his heroes. Nor was it at all precise what his religious allegiance was, for he certainly was friendly with Charles Utenhove whose religious allegiance was more to Erasmian Basle than to Geneva and Buchanan was soon friendly in Scotland with Alexander Cockburn, a Basle student of 1555, whose accomplishments in three languages he celebrated in 1564 after Cockburn's early death at Ormiston, where his tomb carries, with a few variants, Buchanan's verse epitaph.[41]

In Scotland it would be Buchanan who urged the young Patrick Adamson, whom he clearly favoured at first, to print his first verses attacking the "papists" of Aberdeen. He also found the company of William Ramsay at St Salvator's stimulating. One of the European propagandists for Buchanan, a Low Countries scholar at Orléans, Obert van Giffen, was anxious to obtain the poet's epigrams. Two letters elicited no reply. Encouraged, if not prompted, by some Scots students at Orléans, among whom he named John Gordon of Huntly, David Cunningham of Cunninghamhead and David Guthrie of Hilton, he despatched a third letter.[42] The epigrams were versions from the Greek, to be published, on his suggestion, by Plantin. He also asked Buchanan as an intimate of Ramsay whom he correctly described as a former professor at Wittenberg (where, indeed, he had been in 1544) to forward Ramsay's versions as well. In a letter to Plantin, van Giffen gave Ramsay's name as *Raverdus*, but the description of himself and Buchanan as "two outstanding Scotsmen" hardly allows identification with a foreign legist, Raewerd, and in the event van Giffen got the name right in the letter that reached Buchanan.[43] Ramsay had obviously left Wittenberg by 1548 when he was book-buying in Paris. From there he came to teach in the university of Bordeaux in 1550 on the recommendation of Jean de la Taste and and perhaps also of Patrick Buchanan, who had been asked to act as recruiting agent for new staff in the college of Guienne.[44] From Bordeaux Ramsay soon returned to Scotland in 1555, lecturing in Greek in Glasgow and Edinburgh before being appointed by Mary of Lorraine to a short-lived royal lectureship.[45] Along with Adamson he is honoured in 1590 in the Latinised version of Gui du Faur de Pibrac's French quatrains published in Poitiers by Thomas Bickerton (Bicartonus), a former St Andrews man.[46]

But before his appointment as principal of St Leonard's College in 1566, Buchanan had been active at the court of Mary, Queen of Scots. The sole printing press in the city for a time was that of Robert Lekprevik, an open propagandist for the new ecclesiastical regime. The poet himself had begun to appear in General Assemblies in 1563. In that year a reply to Quintin Kennedy's Catholic defence of the mass circulated in manuscript was called for. This reply, prepared by a leading minister, George Hay, was *The Confutation of the Abbote of Crossraguel's masse*. At the end were two hitherto unidentified lines attacking the mass, unsigned, but Buchanan's. Anonymity was safer for the present, if only because Buchanan's old patrons, the Kennedys, might be upset. It was Adamson who in his verses of 1564 carried on the attack on the abbot, presumably on Buchanan's behalf, by which time Buchanan had found a new patron in Mary's Protestant half-brother, the Lord James Stewart, prior of St Andrews. But the abbacy had become vacant by Kennedy's death and Buchanan, who had no hankering for spiritualities or for preaching, was concerned to retain his hold on the temporalities of Crossraguel from which the queen paid him a pension. It is possible that the poet feared a papal provision of an alternative candidate at the request of Cassillis. Hence the anti-papal and anti-monastic temper of his verse at this time, especially the revived and revised *Franciscanus* to which the Lord James was prepared to accept a dedication. The wedding of Mary to Lord Darnley in 1565 led to further complications. It was felt desirable to counter the Catholic and Italian influence at court represented by David Riccio, not by the anti-Italian phobia to which Knox was inclined, but by something more subtle, works by Italians themselves construable as anti-papal polemic. There lay to hand the Basle edition of Celio Secondo Curione's pasquils. These were reissued in Edinburgh as *Pasquillorum versus aliquot* (1565), with a few additions by George Buchanan, Scot. The discovery of these was made simultaneously by Professor William Beattie and myself working in tandem.[47] With the exception of the anti-mass lines previously printed in Hay's book, they were all, with additions, and some postliminary lines by Patrick Adamson, included in the first 1566 edition of the *Franciscanus* at Basle; but, strangely, the preface to the Lord James was left out, explicable it may be in terms of his temporary disgrace, or, because, at the time of going to press, Darnley might have been alienated. Likewise in 1565 Lekprevik issued a cento of anti-monastic verses by Lelio Capilupi, *De vita monachorum*, based on Basle and Venetian editions. Though these exotic productions of Lekprevik, surely pointing to Buchanan's influence, seem aimed at Riccio's sway in court, he and Buchanan were still on good terms in 1564 prior to Darnley's arrival.[48]

A final word ought perhaps to be said on the *Historia*. It is clear that he could have had easy access to archives in the care of successive secretaries and clerks register. Yet his only mention of one, Laurence Telfer, "a man honest and learned," a judgement parallelled in Ferrerio, was in connection with a far-fetched tale that Telfer had seen James IV cross the Tweed alive after Flodden.[49] Similarly his use of the courtier, Sir David Lindsay, was merely to note his story of a monitory apparition that James saw before the campaign that ended in the battle.[50] True rhetorician that he was he could seldom resist a good story, though he warned his readers that Macbeth made better theatre than history.[51] He resisted Humphrey Lluyd's attack on Boece partly because Lluyd seemed to be purveying new fables for old, older ones he preferred. The *Historia* has been described as two books in one; in fact it is three. One is the geographical and antiquarian section where Buchanan was supremely fitted to provide the necessary dressing of classical learning, drawing not only on Strabo and Tacitus, as did Mair and Boece, but on other sources more recondite. He had never been to the Western Isles or even to the Orkneys where Ferrerio had gone. But he had met the Isles chronicler, Donald Monro, at General assemblies and made full use of his manuscript.[52] He was clearly nervous that Catholicism might return via the Highlands or via Aberdeen, where his relative, Adam Heriot, was first minister. In the second section, where there is an episodic feel to much of the narrative, he was limited by his sources, Fordun and Boece, and that part is interesting less for new material than for the rephrasing and recombining of old materials into a fresh and colourful synthesis: indeed antiquarian skills were being used less to kill than to refashion old myths. We must ask ourselves how he got access to the *Liber Pasletensis*, the form Fordun took in the Black Book of Paisley. That could scarcely have been possible except through the Hamiltons with whom George and Patrick were both associated till at least 1560; for the Black Book was still at Paisley in 1617.[53] In the more modern third section, he had stories current in his family and at school plus personal experiences to draw on. The Kennedy clan, with soundest reason the bishop-founder of St Salvator's college, always had a good press from Buchanan who tended to two categories of men, the bad and the good. Mair's analytical approach is not Buchanan's, but the demands of eloquence were not always over-riding: there are many signs of critical weighing of evidence. But he could not aspire to the neutral style that the Catholic, John Leslie, at least in his first, the Scots, version, affected. Yet Sir James Melville wrote him off as a "stoick philosopher,"[54] and in his *De Iure Regni* there are Stoic echoes and he did cite lines out of Seneca's *Thyestes* on the ideal king as a space-filler maybe when his work was already at the press. But Seneca was in the air that contemporaries breathed. The play presented before Queen Elizabeth at the Christmas season 1564–65 is sometimes represented (for instance by J. van Dorsten) as Buchanan's *Alcestis*. The earl of Leicester was certainly present and Paul de Foix (*Foxius*), the French ambassador with his attendant Utenhove. Utenhove adverted to the moving performance in lines addressed to Elizabeth and highlights *Alcestis* as a play every bit as moving and this in the 1568 Basle edition of the poems of Buchanan. Yet there is no reason to deduce that Buchanan too was there. The play in fact was acted by the Children of the Chapel under their master, Richard Edwards, and was his *Damon and Pythias*, whose printing was held up till 1571 when Buchanan might have taken Utenhove's hint and read it. It included a few lines borrowed from Seneca's *Octavia*, lines not so remote in sentiment from Buchanan's selection from *Thyestes*.[55]

The foregoing implies that Buchanan's Scottish output could be greater than has survived. Otherwise we might conclude that the well of poetic inspiration dried up as soon as he set foot on his native soil, at least in his younger days. Latterly had he become convinced that poetry after all was not more perfect than history? Sir James Melville thought Buchanan "was easely abused and sa facill that he was led with any company that he hanted for the tym." There was a good side to this gregariousness: Beza could encourage him from afar with his competitive imitation of Buchanan's "Pictor et Pistor," but he needed and got encouragement nearer home.[56] The *Historia* itself was written at the prompting of friends, most of them Scots, who considered his verse trivial and believed there was more scope for immortality for him as an historian. How wrong they were the reprints of the psalm paraphrases alone will show. Yet his history was to prove immediately more durable than those of either Boece or Mair, and in some of its judgements, for instance of the "good Regent," the former Lord James, it has seldom been questioned even in modern times. If then, Buchanan's French connections are still seen to be basic and much more central for the bulk of Buchanan's production, part of the answer could be that he was more often out of Scotland than in it in his creative middle years.

University of Glasgow

Notes

1. For William Ramsay, J. Durkan, "The Royal Lectureships under Mary of Lorraine," *SHR*, lxii (1983), pp. 73–78; J. Durkan, "John Rutherford and Montaigne: An Early Influence?", *BHR*, xli (1979), pp. 115–22.

2. I. D. McFarlane, *Buchanan* (London, 1981), pp. 541–43, for text of *Vita*.

3. Paris, Sorbonne, Archives de l'université, Registre 91, fs 62, 70ᵛ, 72ᵛ; J. Kirkpatrick, "The Scottish Nation at the University of Orleans," *Miscellany of the Scottish History Society*, ii (1904), pp. 79–80; *Diocesan Registers of Glasgow* (Grampian Club, 1875), ii, p. 430.

4. D. E. R. Watt, *Fasti ecclesiae Scoticanae medii aevi* (Scottish Record Society, 1969), p. 326; *Extracts from the Records of the Burgh of Edinburgh* (Scottish Burgh Records Society, 1869), i, p. 185; J. IJsewijn and D. F. S. Thomson, "The Latin Poems of Jacobus Follisius or James Foullis of Edinburgh," *HL*, xxiv (1975), pp. 102–52.

5. ibid., p. 143; *The Dictionary of National Biography* is mistaken re father's name which was Henry, *Protocol Book of John Foular 1503–13* (Scot. Rec. Soc., 1941), nos. 8, 835 (his father was dead by Oct. 1503).

6. Edinburgh, West Register House, transcript held for National Register of Archives (Scotland) 0005, Ms inventory of writs of Viscount Arbuthnot, nos. 135, 222, 225; Scottish Record Office, Protocol Bk. Vincent Strathauchin, i, fo 180; SRO, Protocol Bk. Thomas Kene, f. 11ᵛ.

7. Re Arnprior, SRO, Cardross writs GD15/183/2; re Petty, Arbuthnot writs, no. 225; *Acts of the Parliaments of Scotland*, ii (1814), p. 278.

8. Cited in J. Stuart, *Records of the Monastery of Kinloss* (Edinburgh, 1872), xx.

9. *Registrum monasterii de Cambuskenneth* (Grampian Club, 1872), viii–x, p. 183.

10. D. Hay and R. K. Hannay, *The Letters of James V* (Edinburgh, 1954), xi, p. 233; letters assigned to Foulis are in the Tynninghame ms.

11. I. D. McFarlane, *Buchanan*, pp. 25, 27.

12. *Ethica Aristotelis Peripateticorum principis cum Jo. Maioris commentariis* (Paris, 1530), sample references, fs 4 (Aulus Gellius), 4ᵛ (Hesiod), 14 (chameleon), 16 (Juvenal), 31 (Euripides), 168 (Theognis); *Quaestiones logicales m. Joannis Maioris* (Paris, 1528) f. xʳ describes Pindar as "liricum illum insignem."

13. L. Bradner and C. Lynch, *The Latin Epigrams of Thomas More* (Chicago, 1953), pp. 35–36, 158; G. Marc'hadour, "La poésie latine de Thomas Morus," *RoczH*, xxvi (1980), pp. 35–43; for mention of lines critical of More, I. D. McFarlane, "George Buchanan's Latin Poems: From Script to Print," *The Library*, xxiv (1969), pp. 296, 319.

14. Bradner and Lynch, op. cit., pp. 52, 175

15. J. M. Aitken, *The Trial of George Buchanan before the Lisbon Inquisition* (Edinburgh–London, 1939), discusses some of the evidence on pp. 129–35. All four epitaphs on More, though for the Scots scribe of uncertain authorship, can be ascribed to Janus Secundus. They follow a long letter of Paul III to James V re the death of Fisher in SRO, Cunninghame of Caprington Muniments GD 149/264, fs 75–77, printed in *Letters of James V*, pp. 293, 309. They are "Quis jacet," "State viri," "Rex mes" and "Ad Styga." For their authorship, see H. de Vocht, *Acta Thomae Mori* (Louvain, 1947), pp. 199, 200, 203 and A. Blanchard and J. Chomaret, "Spicilegium Moreanum," *Moreana*, no. 74 (1982), pp. 77–92 (with references to earlier articles by Blanchard in nos. 36, 41).

16. I. D. McFarlane, *Buchanan*, p. 109.

17. Archives de l'univ., Reg. 15, f. 132 and Bibliothèque Nationale, Ms Lat 9952, f. 19ᵛ (Buchanan), 20ᵛ (Redman), 21 (Wilson) and later in 1529 incorporated, f. 78 (Pate); for Wilson, see *DNB*; for Pate and Redman, see A.B. Emden, *A Biographical Register of*

the University of Oxford, 1501 to 1540 (Oxford, 1974), pp. 435, 482; for Abercromby, J. Durkan, "Scottish 'Evangelicals' in the Patronage of Thomas Cromwell," *Records of the Scottish Church History Society*, xxi (1982), pp. 127–28.

18. P. J. Ford and W. S. Watt, *George Buchanan, Prince of Poets* (Aberdeen, 1982), pp. 154, 156 (i.e. *Misc.* xiii, xv).

19. Buchanan, ed. Ruddiman-Burman, *Opera Omnia* (Leiden, 1725), ii, pp. 646, 699. In 1533 there was still a possibility of marriage between James V and Princess Mary.

20. Durkan, "Early Humanism and King's College," *Aberdeen University Review*, clxiii (1980), pp. 268–70.

21. *House of Gordon* (Aberdeen, New Spalding Club, 1907), ii, p. 26; I. D. McFarlane, *Buchanan*, p. 510.

22. Durkan, "Scottish 'Evangelicals'," p. 129; Durkan, "Early Humanism and King's College," p. 268.

23. *Roderici Maclenii Hectorogenis Scoti Gathelici Ionitae de Intuitu Prophetico D. Columbae Ionidos Liber Primus* (Rome, 1549), sig. M^{vi}.

24. J. A. Gee, *The Life and Works of Thomas Lupset* (New Haven–London, 1928), p. 127.

25. Archives de l'univ., Reg. 91, f. 248^v shows him as "reformer" in the German nation at Paris in February, but f. 149 shows him replaced as "shortly before he had sought his native land."

26. W. Beattie, *The Chepman and Myllar Prints* (Edinburgh Bibliographical Society, 1950), pp. vii–viii, lists the Dunbar prints.

27. Aitken, *Trial*, xxxiii; on Ferrerio, see Durkan, "Giovanni Ferrerio, Humanist: His Influence in Sixteenth-Century Scotland," *Studies in Church History xvii: Religion and Humanism*, ed. K. Robbins (Oxford, 1981), pp. 181–94.

28. Epig. i, 43 in *Opera Omnia*, ii, 370; on Dunbar's studies, J. Durkan and J. Kirk, *The University of Glasgow 1451–1577* (Glasgow, 1977), p. 207.

29. Otterburn incepted in arts in 1500; for his graduation details, Archives de l'univ., Reg. 91, f. 31^v, 38, 44; *Extracts from Records of the Burgh of Edinburgh*, ii, 48; J. Durkan and W. S. Watt, "Adam Mure's *Laudes Gulielmi Elphinstoni*" *HL*, xxviii (1979), 199–233.

30. Epig. ii, 15, 16 in *Opera Omnia*, ii, 379–80; for Dingwall as protonotary, archdeacon of Caithness, subchanter of Moray, etc. see *Registrum magni sigilli regum Scotorum* (Edinburgh, 1883), iii, 181, 281, 1065; J. Knox, *History of the Reformation*, ed. W. C. Dickinson (Edinburgh, 1949), i, 18.

31. On Otterburn, see J. A. Inglis, *Sir Adam Otterburn of Redhall* (Glasgow, 1935).

32. ibid., p. 43 (satin, velvet), p. 66 (holland cloth, silk, iron).

33. D. Calderwood, *The History of the Kirk of Scotland* (Wodrow Society, 1842), i, pp. 123–24; *Aliens in England* (Huguenot Society, Publications no. 8), pp. 105, 155 (both had been in England since 1540 but only naturalised in 1544).

34. R. Richardinus, *Commentary on the Rule of St Augustine* (SHS, 1935), 62 (Mair his teacher), 127 (mention of Robert Logie); J. M. Anderson, *Early Records of the University of St Andrews* (SHS, 1926), 220, where Richardson is incorporated as a canon of St Andrews, the Scottish study house.

35. Aitken, *Trial*, pp. 26–27.

36. P. de Nolhac, "Documents nouveaux sur la Pléiade: Ronsard, Du Bellay," *RHLF*, vi (1899), p. 359.

37. Published by Wechel; Anderson, *Early Records*, p. 263.

38. H. Potez, "Deux années de la Renaissance," *RHLF*, xiii (1906), p. 683, and for evidence that Lambin's correspondent was at Boncourt, ibid., ix (1902), p. 401.

39. W. A. McNeill, "Scottish Entries in the *Acta Rectoria Universitatis Parisiensis* 1519 to *c.* 1633," *SHR*, xliii (1964), p. 76.

40. *Opera Omnia*, i, p. 562, lib. xvi, cap. xix.

41. H. G. Wackernagel, *Der Matrikel der Universität Basel* (Basle, 1956), ii, p. 95; *Opera Omnia*, ii, p. 384, *Epig. lib ii*, p. 26; *The Royal Commision on Ancient and Historical Monuments of Scotland; East Lothian* (Edinburgh, 1924), p. 80, with facing plate.

42. *Opera Omnia*, ii, pp. 724–26; Archives départementales de Loiret, Univ. d'Orléans, livre des procureurs D124, f. 455; other Scots enrolled then were Thomas Maitland of Lethington and Andrew Ayton.

43. The Van Giffen letter to Plantin is cited in I. D. McFarlane, *Buchanan*, p. 260.

44. "This buk cost in pareiss 1548 off Scottis mony xv s," on Aelianus (Graece), Rome, 1545; Ramsay's books are discussed in D. W. Doughty, "Renaissance Books, Bindings and Owners in St Andrews and Elsewhere: The Humanists," *The Bibliotheck*, vii (1975), 117–28; F. Cerda y Rico, *Clarorum Hispanorum opuscula selecta et rariora* (Madrid, 1781), i, pp. 121, 135, 137–43.

45. Durkan, "The Royal Lectureships," *SHR*, lxii, pp. 75–76.

46. *Vidi Pibracii 126 Tetrasticha*, transl. by Bicarton, Poitiers, 1590, with additional verses of his own, p. 46. On p. 42 he states that he was taught by Buchanan to refer to Dundee as "Taodunum" rather than "Deidonum."

47. *Buchanan*, 215–18; J. Durkan and W. Beattie, "An Early Publication of Latin Poems by George Buchanan" *The Bibliotheck*, xi (1983), pp. 77–80.

48. M. Lee, Jr, *James Stewart, Earl of Moray* (New York, 1953), pp. 162, 164 (about this time, Moray complained that the number of his friends "is grown marvelous scant").

49. *Opera omnia*, i, p. 463, lib. xiii, cap. xli. Telfer had been a fellow student of Buchanan's maternal uncle, Sorbonne, Reg. 91, f. 70^v, 72^v; later a scribe in Patrick Panter's office, he succeeded him as secretary in 1520, *Letters of James V*, pp. 67, 69–70.

50. *Opera omnia*, i, p. 458, lib. xiii, cap. xxxi.

51. ibid., i, p. 201, lib. vii, cap. xiii.

52. *Monro's Western Isles of Scotland and Genealogies of the Clans*, ed. R. W. Monro (Edinburgh, 1961), pp. 11, 26; *Opera omnia*, i, pp. 32, 43, lib. xxxii, cap. xliii.

53. D. Murray, *The Black Book of Paisley* (Paisley, 1885), pp. 48–51, where Murray denies its Hamilton connection, though on his own evidence Lord Claud Hamilton referred to it in 1573 (Murray postulates another "black book" here) and in the earl of Abercorn's presence (the Abercorns being Hamiltons) it was produced by the boy welcoming King James to Paisley. Another who had seen it was Sir William Sinclair of Roslin. For Buchanan's interest in northern parts, see now a generalised exhortation to support the magistrates and "the good," i.e., the king's party, in SRO, Caprington Muniments, GD 149/265, section 2, f. 18, "Buchanan's opinioun anent the ordering of the North 1569."

54. Cited in *Buchanan*, pp. 484–85; R. A. Mason, "*Rex Stoicus*: George Buchanan, James VI and the Scottish Polity," *New Perspectives on the Politics and Culture of Early Modern Scotland*, ed. J. Dwyer et al (Edinburgh, 1982), pp. 9–33.

55. Ad sereniss. iuxta ac eruditiss. Angliae Reginam Elizabetham in Alcestin Epigrammata"; J. A. van Dorsten, *The Radical Arts* (Leiden, 1970), p. 46; *Damon and Pythias* (Malone Society Reprints, 1957), introduction and lines 861 ff. Cf. J. S. Cunliffe, *Early English Classical Tragedies* (Oxford, 1912), p. lxxiii.

56. T. de Bèze, *Poematum editio secunda* ([Geneva], 1569), 160 "Pistoris et Pictoris certamen, ad Buchanani mutationem." Reference has already been made to the stimulus More may have afforded Buchanan: Aitken's case for More's example as an influence on the *Baptistes* might have been strengthened by reference to the "Baptistes" epigrams of More, Bradner and Lynch, op. cit., pp. 92–93, 213–14 (More's Epig. 211 cites Thyestes in this connection).

George Buchanan and the "Satyra in Carolum Lotharingum Cardinalem"

Philip Ford

Carmen quidem Buchanano non prorsus indignum, at vivido minus impetu, tardante iam vires ingenii senecta, effusum, cuique etiam, ut credibile est, ultima auctoris lima nunquam accessit.[1]

Such was Robert Freebairn's opinion of Buchanan's satirical poem against the Cardinal of Lorraine, written in the aftermath of the Massacre of Saint Bartholomew (1572). Because of the somewhat marginal position it holds in the corpus of Buchanan's poetry, partly as a result of doubts concerning its authenticity, this satirical swan song has received relatively little attention. The first time it appeared in print was in 1590 in a collection of poems of a largely Protestant nature published by Israel Taurinus (a pseudonym of the Geneva printer Jacobus Stoer): the *Selectorum carminum ex doctiss [imis] poetis collectorum, et nunc primum in lucem editorum libri quatuor*. It is clearly attributed to Buchanan, along with 30 other poems by the Scottish Humanist, and is to be found in the company of a number of other poems which deal with the French religious wars. Book II of the collection, *Guisiaca*, sub-titled *In tumultus gallicos,* contains several compositions on the theme of the Saint-Barthélemy, where it is interesting to note the currency of certain images associated with the events (for example, the battle of the giants, Hercules and the Hydra). The poem next appears in print in Robert Sibbald's *Commentarius in Vitam Georgii Buchanani*, published in Edinburgh in 1702. Sibbald had received his copy of the poem, which has a number of variants from the Taurinus version, from Dr. John Jamieson, "qui plane persuasus erat, eam fuisse Genuinum Buchanani faetum."[2] After this, it found its way in 1715 into Ruddiman's edition of the *Opera omnia* as a slightly self-apologetic appendage, sandwiched between the *Alcestis* and the *De metris Buchananaeis libellus*. In addition to the printed sources, a manuscript copy of the poem dating from the early seventeenth century is in the possession of the Bodleian Library. In what follows, I propose to consider the circumstances surrounding the composition of the "Satyra," examine its authenticity, and assess its poetical qualities.

Briefly, the events surrounding the Massacre of Saint Bartholomew were as follows. After the marriage of the Protestant Henri de Navarre to Marguerite de Valois, King Charles IX's sister, Paris was full of Huguenot nobles who were celebrating the event. Four days after the wedding on 22 August 1572, a shot was fired at the Huguenot leader, Gaspard de Coligny, and Henri, duc de Guise, was clearly implicated in the attempted murder. His father, François, had been assassinated in 1563 by the Huguenot Poltrot de Méré. The Huguenots demanded justice from Charles IX, but his mother, Catherine de Médicis, persuaded him that they were now plotting to overthrow him and gained his consent to massacre the Protestant leaders gathered in Paris. On the morning of 24 August, this task was duly begun, starting with the mortal wounding, defenestration, and mutilation of the Admiral de Coligny. Similar events followed in other French cities, notably Lyons.

Buchanan lost personal friends in the slaughter, including the Humanist Pierre de La Ramée. Since his return to Scotland around 1561 in the train of the young Mary Stuart, he had produced relatively little new poetry, but was devoting his time to more important issues on behalf of his country. However, the Massacre so shocked the Protestant world that, like Juvenal, Buchanan must have decided "difficile est saturam non scribere." The "Satyra" was one of several compositions that Buchanan felt impelled to write, and elsewhere in his writings it is not the Cardinal of Lorraine who bears the brunt of the attack. An unpublished poem, "De Casparo Colignio Fran[ciae] Admirallio" puts the blame for the Admiral's death quite squarely on Charles IX:

> Quisquis es, o hospes, mea te haec exempla monebunt
> Quantis, quam subitis obnoxia vita periclis,
> Quamque sit infido non tutum fidere regi.[3]

Catherine de Médicis does not escape blame either, and in *Miscellany* 22 as well as a number of unpublished epigrams, she is the subject of Buchanan's wrath as a result of her part in the affair. However, the "Satyra" clearly singles out the Cardinal of Lorraine as the principal culprit which, given that he was absent in Rome at the time of the massacre, may seem strange.

On internal evidence, it seems unlikely that the poem was completed immediately after the massacre, although we have a *terminus ad quem* in the death of the Cardinal of Lorraine on 20 December 1574: in Buchanan's poem he is still very much alive. However, a further clue may be provided in the allusions to the various fortunes of the Guises in the opening of the poem. In ll. 11–12, Buchanan writes:

> fugiendo dimicat ille,
> Et vicisse putat, si visum evaserit hostem.

This appears to be a clear allusion to Henri, duc de Guise, who was responsible for so much of the slaughter in Paris, and who narrowly escaped death at the siege of La Rochelle in February 1573. The "Satyra" would thus have been written some time after this event.

Whatever the exact date of composition of the poem, it has lost none of the outrage which Buchanan must have felt on hearing of the events. It is a visionary poem, fulminatory and hyperbolic in tone, eclectic in style.[4] The opening (1–12) reflects upon God's punishment of the Guise family as a whole, depicting them as a new breed of Giants fighting against heaven. Lines 13–21 concentrate on the fate of François, duc de Guise, who, as we have seen, had been assassinated in 1563 following his part in the Massacre of Wassy in the previous year, although the cardinal is forewarned of a yet worse fate (22–32). The after-life and all its punishments cannot equal the torments of his own guilty mind (32–43) which must constantly receive new fuel at the sight of the devastation which he has caused (43–47). More specifically (47–58) he is accused of hastening the deaths of his father and uncle (Claude, duc de Guise, whose death in 1550 was attributed by some to poison, and Jean, Cardinal de Lorraine, who died in the same year); and also, obliquely, of irregular sexual liaisons with Catherine de Médicis and his own sister-in-law Anne d'Este (wife of François de Guise). Both these accusations were current at the time.[5] Lines 59–70 dwell on the cardinal's inevitable fears of divine retribution, while lines 71–80 take on an Erasmian pathos in depicting the horrors of war in France. Anyone unmoved by the plight of his country must not be human, but rather, one of the Furies (81–104).[6] However, if Lorraine is not sated with the sight of so much carnage, Buchanan exhorts him (in a passage reminiscent of Ovid, *Metamorphoses* VIII.877sqq. on Erysichthon) to devour the very corpses, and even his own body, in order to provide himself with a fitting tomb. Only on his death can a new Golden Age of peace return to France.

The subject matter of the satire, then, is a blend of contemporary rumour, classical mythological allusions, and Erasmian eirinic propaganda. This last element is interesting in that it demonstrates a notable continuity in Buchanan's thought on essential issues from his early days in Paris right up until the last years of his life. The "Satyra," like *Miscellany* 23 on the capture of Vercelli in 1553 and *Silvae* 7 on the birth of James VI in 1566, clearly bears the marks of Erasmus's thinking on the subject of war, particularly in the long *Adage* 3001, "Dulce bellum inexpertis." One passage in particular on the horrors which come in the wake of war furnishes Buchanan with a number of details for his own composition.

> Ut interim non referam illa vulgaria prae his leviaque: protritas
> passim segetes, exustas villas, incensos pagos, abacta pecora,
> constupratas virgines, tractos in captivitatem senes, direpta
> fana, latrociniis, praedationibus, violentia plena confusaque
> 5   omnia. Utque taceam illa quae felicissimum etiam ac iustissimum
> bellum consequi solent: expilatam plebem, oneratos proceres, tot
> senes orbos, et simul in caede liberorum infelicius occisos quam

si hostis mali sensum una cum vita sustulisset, tot anus destitutas
et crudelius quam ferro peremptas, tot matronas viduas, tot
10   liberos orphanos, tot domus funestas, tot opulentos ad inopiam
redactos. Nam de morum pernicie quid attinet loqui, cum nemo
nesciat universam vitae pestem semel e bello proficisci? Hinc
pietatis contemptus, hinc legum neglectus, hinc ad quidvis audendum
sceleris promptus animus.[7]

For some examples of parallels between Buchanan's poem and Erasmus, apart
from the general tenor of the poem, compare:

                    pietatem expellere mundo
        Conata est, scelerique suas permittere habenas   (5-6)

and Erasmus ll. 12-14;

        Aspice tot viduas, puerosque parentibus orbos,
        Sedibus eiectae tot mendicabula plebis,
        Inter fumantes villas ...   (74-76)

and Erasmus ll. 9-10, 6, and 2;

        Sed tectum exuviis hominis crudelius ipsis
        Esse aliquid Furiis, imo Phlegethonte creatum   (98-99)

and Erasmus, ed. cit., p. 26, "tradidere bellum ab Inferis immitti, idque Furiarum
ministerio";

        Semianimes artus et adhuc spirantia membra
        Ore vora, crepitentque avidis sub dentibus ossa   (110-11)

and Erasmus, ed. cit., p. 34, "Non veriti sunt vesci ferarum exstinctarum ca-
daveribus, dentibus laniare carnem exanimem, haurire sanguinem, exsugere
saniem, et viscera, ut ait Ovidius, in viscera condere." This last passage appears
to have suggested some of the wording for the gruesome image of the cardinal's
self-ingestion, cf. 115-16, "in tua viscera conde / Viscera." There can be little
doubt, therefore, that Erasmus exercised a considerable influence both on the
substance and the wording of the poem.

So far, we have been begging the issue as to whether the "Satrya" can be ascribed
with certainty to Buchanan. On stylistic grounds, there seems to be no reason
for doubting its authenticity, although it is apparent that even when he was well
into his sixties, Buchanan was able to adapt his *elocutio* to new circumstances and
demands. One telling point is that the poem contains reminiscences from his earlier
compositions, a practice which he frequently followed in his later poetry. Compare, for example:

                    quamvis media sitientis in unda
        Aspiceres poenam Phrygii senis, et sua semper
        Excrescens in damna iecur, revolubile saxum   (36-38)

and *Miscellany* 24 on the death of Calvin:

> Inter aquas sitiens, referens revolubile saxum,
> Vulturibus iecur exesus; (56–57)

>   quam te nunc conscius horror
> Exagitat vesani animi (41–42)

and *Franciscanus* 203–05:

>   [nec] te saeva relinquet
> Tempestas vesani animi; te conscius horror
> Mentis aget vigilem;

> Aut flammis foedata aut deformata ruinis
> Oppida, disiectis tot rura inculta colonis (72–73)

and *Silvae* 7. 7–8:

>   repara flammis foedata, ruinis
> Convulsa, et pulso cole squalida tecta colono.

From the point of view of versification also, the "Satyra" conforms closely to Buchanan's usual practices. In accordance with metrical *decorum*, the number of elisions in the "Satyra" is relatively high (42.65 per 100 lines), reflecting the practice of Juvenal as is the case with Buchanan's other satirical poetry (e.g., the *Franciscanus*). However, in common with his previous poetry and classical Roman usage, he avoids the elision of long syllables before short ones (for one exception see line 42, "vesanī ănimi"), and there are no elided monosyllables. Line 33 contains the only monosyllabic line ending ("Omnibus ex aequo, nec poena, sed exitus hinc ad"), and l. 55 has a short final *o* in *libido*, which conforms with Buchanan's practice of treating final *o* as common. (This, however, was a normal Renaissance usage.) Thus, the poem gives rise to no apparent reasons for doubting its authenticity on stylistic or metrical grounds, and in fact contains many of the hall-marks of the Scotsman's verse. This, in addition to the clear attribution to Buchanan in the Taurinus edition, should allay most fears on the subject.

Although in some ways the style of the "Satyra" represents a change of direction, a move towards the hyperbolic style which d'Aubigné would later exploit in *Les Tragiques*, it contains few devices that cannot be found elsewhere in Buchanan's writing. The tone may be more serious than earlier, wittier satires, but then the horror of the subject called for nothing less than this.

This tone is created by a limited number of rhetorical devices. Apostrophe is central in this respect, as the bulk of the poem (lines 22 onwards) consists of a direct address to the Cardinal of Lorraine. Linked with this is the use of interrogation in this section (e.g., 45–47, 63–66) along with verbs in the imperative mood (43–44, 48, 50, 71, 74, 105, 111, 115). These devices serve to create a highly personal tone, underlining the poet's outrage in a manner reminiscent of Juvenal.

Enargeia, vividness of description, is exploited to the full in the poem, especially
in order to emphasize the horrors which the cardinal has produced in France,
while the hyperbolic tone is further enhanced by enumeration and repetition.
Alliteration and the careful control of rhythm also play their part, as elsewhere
in Buchanan's poetry, in reinforcing the message in the most effective possible
manner.

The full force of this style comes across in line 104–17:

> At tu si caede cruentum
> Non poteris satiare animum, tua lumina pascant
> Viventum sordes, lacrymae, suspiria, luctus,
> Passim exstinctorum laceri crudeliter artus.
> Aut si carnifices oculos lassare tuendo
> Non poteris, pars ulli tui ne sit scelerum expers,
> Semianimes artus et adhuc spirantia membra
> Ore vora, crepitentque avidis sub dentibus ossa;
> Atque epulis tandem satur immoriare petitis.
> Aut explere tibi si nulla cadavera possunt
> Sanguinis ingluviem insanam, tua dente cruento
> Ipse tibi lania membra, in tua viscera conde
> Viscera: sic digno vita potiere sepulchro,
> Exitio factis, dape conveniente palato.

Such a section is typical of what Imbrie Buffum would call, in relation to d'Aubigné,
the baroque style, although it would not be necessary to go too far in classical
literature — certain passages of Ovid's *Ibis* and *Metamorphoses* or of Seneca's
tragedies — to find similar descriptions.[8] It clearly indicates Buchanan's poetic
skills and his ability to continue adapting as circumstances demanded.

So far, I have avoided perhaps the most obvious question concerning the poem:
why should the Cardinal of Lorraine have been singled out for attack when others
were almost certainly more guilty? Although it now seems unlikely that the
Massacre was prepared far in advance, contemporary accounts from both Catholic
and Protestant writers were unanimous in seeing the events as having been long
planned and clearly worked out. Thus, the cardinal's absence in Rome at the time
is attributed both by the Protestant Hotman and the Catholic Capilupi to his desire
to be out of France when the slaughter took place, in order to avoid suspicion.[9]
Moreover, Capilupi lavishes considerable praise on the cunning of Charles IX
and his advisers in luring the Huguenots to Paris and butchering them so successfully. When the events were reported to the papal court, he writes, there was
general rejoicing, and after a service of thanksgiving on 8 September at the Church
of San Luigi dei Francesi, the Cardinal of Lorraine had a plaque placed on the
doors celebrating the event. Capilupi reports:

> Testatus etiam est idem Lotharingus, incredibile beneficium, non Galliam
> modo, sed Christianum orbem universum accepisse: seque incredibiliter

laetari, tam praeclari facinoris, suam potissimum familiam, eiusdem Dei singulari clementia, administram extitisse. Confirmatur veluti res certa, coniurationem hanc opera imprimis eiusdem Cardinalis inter Pontificem, Gallum & Hispanum ita factam esse.   (pp. 86–87)

Thus, whatever the cardinal's actual part in the affair, he seems to have been quite anxious to be associated with the planning and success of the venture after its completion.

The sincerity of Buchanan's outrage cannot be called into doubt. However, for a partial explanation of the attack on the Cardinal of Lorraine and the Guise family as a whole, we probably need to look closer to home than Paris. Mary Stuart was the niece of the cardinal. Since her enforced abdication in 1567, she had been living as a virtual captive in England, and the Scottish lords had been doing their utmost, aided by Buchanan, to have her tried for treason. The abortive Ridolfi plot, in which Mary was implicated and which had planned a Catholic uprising in England to place the Scottish Queen on the throne, had been discovered in 1571, providing further evidence of her treachery. Thus, the opening twelve lines of the "Satyra" can be seen to apply as much to Mary as to any other member of the Guise family, and any association with the events of the Saint-Barthélemy, however remote, might be seen as representing another nail in the Scottish Queen's coffin.

Whatever the full motivation for the "Satyra," its importance and interest in the corpus of Buchanan's writing are undeniable. Certainly, as Freebairn indicated, there are some passages which would have benefited from a *dernier coup de lime* to clarify their meaning (e.g., 49–50 and 56–57, where the confusion is underlined by hesitation over punctuation in different editions). Nevertheless, even as it stands, the poem is an impressive composition whose impact on a modern audience can hardly be less forceful than it was on contemporary readers. How many people would have seen it around the time of composition is difficult to estimate. However, the different versions of the poem (Taurinus, Sibbald, and Bodleian MS) indicate several original sources, which may have been at least partly revised by Buchanan—the hesitation between the indicative and the subjunctive in different *états* of the poem is typical of him. Of course, it is impossible to determine what influence the composition may have had on other writers, although d'Aubigné for one was certainly acquainted with the Scotsman's other long satirical work, the *Franciscanus*.[10] However, what is clear is that right up until the end of his poetic career, Buchanan continued to be in the forefront of literary developments, showing that, if his outlook on life had remained remarkably stable, his literary creativity could certainly not be accused of any such conservatism.

Clare College, Cambridge

Notes

1. Cited in George Buchanan, *Opera omnia*, ed. Thomas Ruddiman and Peter Burman, 2 vols. (Leiden, 1725), I.b4ᵛ. References to Buchanan will be based on this edition.

2. *Commentarius in Vitam Georgii Buchanani, ab ipsomet scriptam* (Edinburgh, Georgius Mosman, 1702), p. 67.

3. See Bibliothèque Nationale MS français 22561, f. 80ʳ.

4. Buchanan includes reminiscences of quite a wide range of poets in the "Satyra," compare, for example: "poena didicere magistra" (3) and "vita didicere magistra" (Juvenal 13. 22); "permittere habenas" (6) and Tibullus 4. 1. 92 where the expression occurs in the same metrical position; "plaudere somno / Ipse sibi assuetus" (14–15) and "mihi plaudo / ipse domi" (Horace, *Satires* 1. 1. 66–67); "Romanique decus columenque senatus" (24) and "grande decus columenque rerum" (Horace, *Odes* 2. 17. 4); "populo plaudente" (30) and Ovid, *Ibis* 165 for the expression in the same metrical position; "micat ignibus aether" (63) in same metrical position in Vergil, *Aeneid* i.90; "taboque natantes / Sanguinis innocui campos, inhumataque passim / Ossa virûm, laceros artus" (76–78) and Vergil, *Aeneid* iii.625–27 "sanieque exspersa natarent / limina; vidi atro cum membra fluentia tabo / manderet...", etc.

5. cf. Agrippa d'Aubigné, *Les Tragiques* I.1001–04:

> Et puis le cramoisi encores nous avise
> Qu'il a dedans son sang trempé sa paillardise,
> Quand en mesme suject se fit le monstrueux
> Adultere, paillard, bougre et incestueux.

6. Buchanan echoes these sentiments in an epigram concerning the cardinal, *Epigrams* II, "Icones" 22:

> Iam furor humanus Furias lassarat, inermes
>   Torpuerant angues, torpuerantque faces;
> Cum te vis inimica bonis, Carle, edidit, unus
>   Pro Furiis possis qui satis esse tribus.

7. The text is based on the edition of the Adage by Yvonne Rémy and René Dunil-Marquebreucq, Collection Latomus, 8 (Brussels, 1953), p. 24.

8. Imbrie Buffum, *Agrippa d'Aubigné's 'Les Tragiques': A Study of the Baroque Style in Poetry* (New Haven and Paris, 1951).

9. See Ernestus Varamundus Frisius (= François Hotman), *De furoribus gallicis, horrenda et indigna Amiralii Castillionei, nobilium atque illustrium virorum caede ...* (London, Henricus Bynneman, 1573), p. xxv, and Camillo Capilupi, *Lo stratagema de Carlo IX re di Francia contro gli Ugonotti rebelli di Dio e suoi* (n.p., 1574), p. 13.

10. I. D. McFarlane points to a textual reminiscence of the *Franciscanus* in Agrippa d'Aubigné, *Les Tragiques* (London, Athlone Press, 1970), p. 69.

George Buchanan's Psalm Paraphrases: Matters of Metre

Roger Green

The remarkable popularity of George Buchanan's metrical Psalm Paraphrases is largely due to his possession in abundance of two qualities demanded by this common form of literary and spiritual exercise: an imaginative understanding of the sacred text and a manifold sensitivity to classical Latin poetry. One aspect of the latter quality will be dealt with in this paper, which will briefly discuss the variety of his metres and ask, which metres did he choose, and why? how did he compose? did he make metrical mistakes, and, if so, were they corrected? Work on this theme began as early as 1566, within a year of the first publication of the complete Paraphrases, when Plantin appended to his edition an analysis of the *Carminum Genera* which has been frequently reprinted in later editions. Metrical matters were subsequently pursued by Ruddiman who, although no Bentley, was for his times an impressively knowledgeable and careful editor;[1] and although the volumes issued to commemorate Buchanan's birth in 1906 are not noteworthy in this regard, the quatercentenary of his death has seen renewed interest, especially in Professor McFarlane's magisterial biography[2] and Dr Philip Ford's book on the poetry of Buchanan[3] — which arrived on my desk twelve days before this paper was due to be read.[4]

Buchanan's variety is his most obvious characteristic, and emerges clearly from the following table, which is, essentially, Plantin updated. Frequency of Buchanan's metres, with models:

iambic trimeter + dimeter	28	Hor., Prud., Boeth., Paul.
hexameter + iambic trimeter	16	Hor., Prud., Boeth.
Alcaic stanza	16	Hor., and others
iambic dimeter	14	Prud., Sed.
Sapphic stanza	10	Hor., and others
hexameter	10	everybody
Alcaic hendecasyllable	8	Prud. (Claud.)

second asclepiad[5]	6	Hor.
third asclepiad	4	Hor.
sapphic + glyconic	4	Boeth.
trochaic tetrameter	4	Prud.
elegiac couplet	3	everybody
iambic trimeter	3	Hor., Prud.
3 glyconics + pherecratean	3	Cat.
fourth asclepiad	3	Hor.
first asclepiad	3	Hor.
first archilochian	2	Hor.
iambic trimeter + pentameter	2	Boeth.
sapphic hendecasyllable + iambic dimeter	1	—
second archilochian	1	Hor.
glyconic, asclepiad, greater asclepiad	1	Prud.
two trochaic dimeters + trochaic dimeter catalectic	1	—
trochaic dimeter + iambic dimeter	1	—
hexameter + anapaestic dimeter catalectic	1	—
hexameter + iambic dimeter	1	Hor., Aus.
anapaestic dimeter	1	Sen., Boeth.
iambic dimeter catalectic	1	Prud.
hexameter + iambic dimeter + hemiepes	1	Hor.
hexameter + hemiepes + iambic dimeter	1	—

With his 29 metres (or 30; the reason for this hesitation will emerge later), he is well ahead of both classical and neo-Latin poets. His closest rivals in the ancient world are Boethius (26), Horace and Ausonius (20), Prudentius (18), followed by Seneca (whose manuscripts do not allow an exact computation) and Catullus with 10; and among his contemporaries — at least those whose complete works are readily available for consultation — he easily outstrips Erasmus (18), Marullus (16), Secundus (15), Flaminius and Crinitus (11), and Politian (10). There were indeed poets who used more metres in paraphrases: Gagnay used at least 40, and one writer later in the century is reported to have used 100,[6] but these freakish compositions rapidly found the oblivion which their unreadability deserved. As the table shows, all but 5 of Buchanan's metres are classical; 2 of these are common in mediaeval verse, and the 3 combinations which are novel are in fact close in structure and composition to classical models. Three groups may be distinguished: a group of the 7 commonest metres, which account for 102 poems, or slightly more than two-thirds of the total; then a group of 11 metres, used between two and six times each; and another group of 11 metres which are used once each — these form quite a long tail, but this is also characteristic of the classical poets, who enjoyed experimenting within the guidelines of familiar metrical units.

How did Buchanan choose a metre for a particular poem? Some of his contemporaries, notably Macrinus, essayed versions of a particular psalm in more than one metre, but Buchanan's goal, perhaps from the beginning, was to paraphrase the whole Psalter, and although a later writer is said to have written two complete versions in hexameters and distichs,[7] the idea of trying to render every psalm, or even a large number of the 150, in different metres would be out of the question even for such a painstaking writer as he was. It is much more probable that he decided upon an appropriate metre and then stuck to his decision. Whether he ever made any changes in this regard is uncertain: in a letter of 1579[8] he says he had been thinking of changing whole Psalms, and therefore he might have changed their metres also; but the clear implication of the document is that advancing years in fact prevented him. The evidence for early drafts of the paraphrases is scanty,[9] but a review of manuscript and printed evidence shows only two apparent changes of mind in regard to metre, and they are not genuine exceptions to the rule. Psalms 105 and 129 both appear in a different metre in later versions, but what Buchanan has done is simply to conflate into one single line what were originally two short ones, so creating a trochaic tetrameter catalectic out of two trochaic dimeters, one catalectic, one not. To put it less technically, he has added a line such as "facta gentibus per orbem" to "praedicate illustria" to make "facta gentibus per orbem praedicate illustria"; in some places verbal alteration was necessary in order to avoid hiatus in the middle of the new lines (and Buchanan took the chance to make other variations, affecting style and sense).[10] Inspection of some early editions of Prudentius, which vary between these two formats in their presentation of *Cath.* 9 and *Perist.* 1, has confirmed the explanation which I suggested at the conference. The later format of the Psalms is that found in editions of 1562 and 1564, but also that of the editions of fifty years earlier printed with the commentary of Antonius Nebrissensis; the earlier, two-line format, could have been seen by Buchanan in the *editio princeps*, or in editions of 1501 and 1503, or (more probably) in those of 1527 (Paris) or 1553 (Lyon). Which of these he consulted, it seems unfortunately impossible to determine.

The original choice of metre for a psalm was obviously important: how did Buchanan decide? Perhaps on the basis of the tone of a psalm; but although interesting suggestions have been made in the case of certain individual psalms, especially the elegiacs (which I discuss later), I doubt if the suggested criteria can be applied to all the poems in a particular metre. Too many awkward questions can be raised. Why, for example, the Sapphic stanza and not, say, the Alcaic for Psalm 23? Why is the parallelism of Hebrew poetry subjected to various metres, some of which are stanzas, some couplets, some single lines? Doubtless the choice was sometimes determined by particular words that could hardly be avoided, such as *decempeda* in Psalm 60, or the common *sollicitudo*; but aesthetic considerations as well as such practical ones are important to Buchanan, who like Horace has an ear for the melodiousness of long words, as in "sepulchrique irremeabilis / tenebricosis sub latebris iacent" (49. 35–36).[11] Then there were the demands of variety; hardly ever does one find two successive Psalms rendered in the same metre.

His initial choice would have been eased by two characteristics of Latin metre. Firstly, it is possible to combine metrical units, so that if he began in one metre and then found a verse which seemed to demand another, he might combine the two, with a result as in Psalm 8, where a Sapphic line is followed by an iambic one. This is admittedly a unique pairing, but many other examples of such combinations were offered in Horace's *Epodes* and elsewhere. Secondly, there is the considerable similarity of some Latin metrical units: a word such as *decempeda* which has just been mentioned seems to cry out for the iambic metre, but also fits perfectly into the Asclepiadic, and is so used in Horace, *Odes* 2. 15. 14. On two occasions the famous Ambrosian *incipit* "aeterne rerum conditor" becomes the first line of an Alcaic stanza by the addition of three syllables.

It is not entirely clear whether in choosing a metre Buchanan felt a need to avoid the metres of his predecessors. The earliest sets of paraphrases seem to have been written independently — critics complain that the genre is hackneyed, but not of plagiarism, which seems to enter later; Arthur Johnstone, for example, in his first psalm shows such a debt to Buchanan, a compliment to a classic. But Buchanan may well have known some earlier versions, and a comparison is instructive. His choice of metre coincides with Gagnay's in only one place out of a possible seventy-five;[12] in only one case (Psalm 65 [64]) does he choose the same metre as Macrinus, who produced at least thirty paraphrases between 1530 and 1540; one of the ten paraphrases by Musius which I have seen uses the hexameter which in Buchanan's version of the same Psalm (11/12) forms one of the two lines of a couplet. This negative correlation seems to be significant, and a deliberate preference seems clear in the case of one particular metre, the elegiac couplet. This metre had been used for complete versions by the Frenchman Bonade (1531) and the Germans Hessus (1537) and Spangeburg (1544), who are presumably the predecessors mentioned by Gagnay in his preface, and in versions of various psalms by Obsopaeus (1531), Melanchthon, Micyllus and others in a volume of 1532, by Bourbon (1533: evidently one only, at least in the *Nugae*), and by the Spaniard Gomez (1537). In following the principle of variety Buchanan, along with Gagnay, Bèze and Rapicius, stands in the tradition of Macrinus and his close followers Cornelius Musius and Scaevola Sammarthanus.

Buchanan's avoidance of the elegiac metre is not in fact total; he uses it three times, a fact which invites investigation. As Dr. Wall has pointed out,[13] Psalm 137 recalls the poetry of Ovid in exile; in fact the third line "illa animum subiit species miseranda Sionis" is a close reworking of *Tristia* 1. 3 "cum subit illius tristissima noctis imago." This classical model is for obvious reasons not reflected throughout the paraphrase, but it may have moved Buchanan to relax his initial embargo on the metre. (This speculation gains some probability from the fact that Psalm 137 was among the first of Buchanan's paraphrases to appear,[14] but it need not necessarily have been written before the other two in the same metre.) Of these two, Psalm 114 also begins with the theme of exile, but is less obviously Ovidian, especially when the mood changes to one of exultation; Israel came out of Egypt, but Ovid remained in Bulgaria. The other one (88) is extremely gloomy (though very powerfully written), and the tone may account for the metre; but one must remember that the elegiac is the metre both of epitaph and epigram (and indeed, as Gagnay pointed out, of erotic verse). There may be a better explanation, but it does not seem to involve any classical model.

The hexameter, like the elegiac couplet, is ubiquitous in Latin of all periods; one might have expected it to be used either more often, or not at all in a collection of mainly lyric metres. A rough analogy is provided by the metrical interludes, in lyric metres, of Boethius's *Consolatio Philosophiae*, which include, at the exact centre of the work, a most impressive poem in hexameters (which Buchanan certainly knew).[15] Although Buchanan is generally unconcerned with such structural markers, it should be noted that he uses the hexameter for the first Psalm, and for the last Psalm of Book 3, and the first one of Book 5. His hexameter paraphrases are longer than average, and there is also a preference for the *metrum heroicum* in certain contexts: in some poems it is used to express divine majesty (18, 45, 89, 104), in others to describe the history of the people of Israel (78, 107, 132, 135); in 85 Buchanan recalls the famous fourth eclogue of Vergil. The hexameter is not used, as might be expected on these criteria, in 105 and 106; this is because the writer takes care to vary the metres of consecutive poems. Psalm 119 is very long, but consists of short sections for which the hexameter would be unsuitable because of the ethical content and jerky style.

Two other common metres in Buchanan are the Sapphic and Alcaic; their presence is not surprising, and they require no comment, except perhaps the observation that Buchanan seems to be unaware (unlike Macrinus) of the conventions observed by Horace in order to make the third line of the stanza a fluent transition from the melodious *da capo* of the first two lines to the tripping final line.[16] Of the other metres in his commonest group, the most frequent is the iambic couplet or epode, used in the majority of Horace's *Epodes*, and by Prudentius, Paulinus of Nola and Boethius; next in frequency is the combination of hexameter and iambic trimeter, used by Horace in his sixteenth *Epode*, famous for its description of the Isles of the Blest, by Erasmus in the long poem at the head of his *Adagiorum Collectanea* of 1500, and doubtless elsewhere. There is also the iambic dimeter, used continuously, for which the models are Ambrose, Prudentius and Sedulius.[17] Between them these three metres account for over one-third of the paraphrases, and this preference calls for explanation. It does not seem to be due to a perceived unity in tone among the poems concerned; it might be the result of the fluency developed by Buchanan in writing his dramas, where they preponderate; or he may have been influenced by the thirty paraphrases in various iambic metres produced by Flaminius in 1546, which have not as yet, however, produced any certain similarities that are not to be explained by the original text. Alternatively, the explanation may lie in the poems of Prudentius, who used iambic metres of some kind in nine separate poems, including five of his twelve hymns. It is highly likely that Prudentius is also the source of the seventh metre of the first group, the continuous Alcaic hendecasyllables, for which Plantin, followed by Ruddiman, also suggested Statius and Claudian. Statius never used the metre; Claudian cannot be set aside so easily, since there is a certain echo of the poem in question in Buchanan's "de Amore Cossaei et Aretes,"[18] but it may be that Claudian's *epithalamium* was consulted only when writing a poem in that genre and that the sacred poet was followed for the Paraphrases.

The important role played by Prudentius in the Paraphrases is conspicuous elsewhere; three of Buchanan's other metres are found in no other ancient poet, and there are several that are common to both Horace and Prudentius. His preference recalls Erasmus (see *Ep.* 492, for example), and it is noteworthy that Prudentius is preferred to Catullus, of whom there is not much sign in the Paraphrases, though his poem 76 contributes importantly to Psalm 78 (note the recurring phrase *benefacta priora*). Unlike Macrin and Gagnay, Buchanan avoids both the hendecasyllable and scazon, which are characteristic metres of Catullus. But Buchanan's interest in Prudentius is shared with Macrinus, who often writes in a similar vein to Prudentius, and cites him in his *Paeanes* of 1538.[19] It is not possible to say whether Macrinus drew Buchanan's attention to Prudentius, or *vice versa*; the lack of evidence about their acquaintance should not, as McFarlane has pointed out, be taken as conclusive.[20] But in view of Prudentius's wide popularity, it is perhaps more likely that they acquired their knowledge of Prudentius independently.

Once Buchanan had chosen a metre, how did he then set about versifying the material? For the metres of Horace there existed various aids, ancient and modern, as Dr Ford has demonstrated;[21] for Boethius there was, as in the case of Horace, a review of his various metres by Perrottus, often published with the text and easily available, as well as textbooks by Agricola and Murmelius. For Prudentius, however, it seems that no such work, at once simple and systematic, existed. Although contemporary editions contain basic descriptions of his metres, other material is partial; two metres are dealt with by Bede, the mediaeval grammarian, and certain hymns by commentators on the Breviary,[22] but some commentators avoid matters of metre altogether. This impression, if correct, suggests that Buchanan actually composed as I believe Latin poets had done for the last 1000 years — by direct examination of their models and inference from them. This method of composition is confirmed by the presence in the Paraphrases of many borrowings from both Prudentius and Horace, and a few from Boethius; for example, Prudentius's phrase *lingua retexere* (*Cath.* 5. 81) is used in Psalm 40. 24, and also provides the basis for *fata retexere* in 49. 23; such similarities are all the more significant because of the great gulf in style between the flamboyant Spaniard and the sober son of Strablane. Similarly, Horatian phrases are taken over, such as *oculo irretorto*[23] of *Odes* 2. 2. 23 in 33. 59, or generate similar phrases, as *multa petentibus* (*Odes* 3. 16. 42) generates *busta petentibus* (28. 4) or *oracla petentibus* (99. 24).

Buchanan's earliest knowledge of metre, including the fundamental matter of prosody, was no doubt derived from a textbook such as that of Alexander Villa Dei or the more modern Despauterius,[24] but material of this kind will not have taken him very far towards his ambitious programme of paraphrasing the whole Psalter in different metres. Nor will he have benefited in this regard from studying the ancient grammarians. The majority of those now collected in Keil's edition were available in his youth (though some of the most lucid were first edited much later), but as guides to verse composition they had grave limitations. The manuscripts have numerous lacunae, and the works often defy comprehension in modern texts; they tend to concentrate on the origins and interrelationships of metres, and deal only with the metres of Horace; one of them, the treatise ascribed to Caesius Bassus, breaks off after five metres only. In one case, that of Terentianus Maurus, whose versified treatise, bound together with that of Caesius Bassus, was in Buchanan's possession before passing to St Leonard's College and then the Library of St Andrews University,[25] it can be demonstrated that Buchanan took little note of their instruction. In ll. 1048ff. Terentianus explains at length that one should not place a short vowel before a combination of 's' and another consonant, as would happen in the word groups *quisque scire, quisque scribere, ante scire*; this is something that Buchanan does very often in the paraphrases and elsewhere.[26] If Buchanan had known his Terentianus better he would surely have observed this rule faithfully; but if he was making inferences from ancient texts, it can easily be understood how a negative rule of this kind could have escaped him. It is also possible that he was relying on the authority of one of the few poets to whom this practice does not apply, such as Propertius, or on the analogy of Vergil and others who relax the ban before a Greek proper name that could otherwise not be admitted; on this point no clear guidance would be given by Prudentius, who is anomalous and inconsistent.

This small but significant detail of prosody leads me to my last question, that of Buchanan's accuracy. At the quatercentenary celebrations of Buchanan's birth in 1906, a paper was given by Professor Lindsay, whose knowledge of the Latin language and Latin metre was perhaps unequalled in his day, in which he castigated Buchanan for metrical failings.[27] Ripples caused by the stone which he threw into the pool of Buchanan scholarship — though he was not the first to do so — are still observable; the reactions of those who spring to Buchanan's defence are instructive, and indeed raise questions not without importance to neo-Latin

studies as a whole. Lindsay cited only one example, which is not from the Paraphrases, but the *Miscellaneorum Liber*; this version may well not be authentic.[28]
How stands it with the paraphrases? A number of *prima facie* cases must, as Lindsay realised, be struck off the charge-sheet. Classical scholars before Ritschl were
dimly, if at all, aware of certain refinements of classical iambic verse; and the
indifferent treatment of *-ii* and *-i* was typical of the sixteenth century. In dealing
freely with Hebrew names Buchanan was following the example of the early Christian poets (and indeed classical ones); though in 136. 25 one may conclude from
variant versions that he was sensitive enough to change what he first wrote. Besides the relative immaturity of classical scholarship, there is the inefficiency of
printers to be considered. Two types of printer's error mentioned by Stephanus[29]
are common: the transposition of words (e.g., at 53. 41, 63. 9, 87. 21, 92. 13),
and the use of a wrong letter, which is not always obvious: in 10. 37 *multimodis*,
though unsound metrically, for a long time replaced *multinodis*, a rare word (found
in only two ancient poets, one of them Prudentius), and undoubtedly correct.
Sometimes a contracted form is used in place of the uncontracted form, or vice
versa (*lamna/lamina*; *saecla/saecula*; *puertiae/pueritiae*). The faulty *servat et in morem* of
103. 15 in many versions may be due to the use of the ampersand to express *ac*,
which Buchanan doubtless wrote, believing, like scholars until the present century, that it was long by nature; the mistake *et terrificas minas* for *et tetricas minas*
in 91. 6 may be due to poor handwriting.

If such factors are taken into account, certain errors are not easy to find. Two
of the most probable examples must here suffice: 31. 38 *per luctus et suspiria*, and
44. 55 *recta pes; etsi penitus abiecti interim*. In both cases the third syllable is long,
but ought to be short; in the second case the poet may have forgotten that *pes*
is a syllable long by nature (did the writing of the *de Prosodia* jog his memory?).
It is possible that he would have appealed to the practice of Ausonius in certain
poems (some of which were currently being edited for the first time by his friend
Elie Vinet), but it is not likely that he would use this authority in only two places
out of several hundred, especially since there is no mention of Ausonius in the
de Prosodia. (An analogous reservation arises over Ruddiman's appeal to Seneca
to justify *mox humi comis iacet arefactis* in 90. 27).

It is no easier to be certain whether these examples were ever corrected by the
author. Ruddiman is content to print any version which he considers metrically
correct, choosing a version without worrying about the reading's authenticity, just
like any classical editor before Lachmann and many after him; but at least in
these cases there are grounds for suspicion. Vautrollier's *luctus per et suspiria* has
per in a position that is anomalous; the reading *moerore fracta luctibus* in Le Preux,
1581 should be rejected because it lacks a copula, and is probably a mistake for
moerore fracta et luctibus, which is printed by Plantin, 1582, and which may be
authorial, although the combination of singular and plural is a little suspicious.
The second of the passages cited above is corrected by Vautrollier alone; this is
rather surprising, since most of the *prima facie* revisions of style and sense and

most of the corrections of typographical errors are offered by more than one of
the later versions.

It is clear, at least, that questions of this kind, of which there is a fair number,
require careful consideration and more detailed treatment than can be given here.
Such a complex treatment of small matters may appear reminiscent of the approach of a music critic who delights in finding wrong notes in a musical
performance — or rather a musical score — but it is surely more appropriate to an
editor than the hagiographical approach that is sometimes to be detected even
in Ruddiman, or the hasty hypercritical approach (in this case) of Lindsay. There
are meatier matters than metre, but matters of metre do matter; they matter
because they enable us to see a leading classical scholar at work, because they
shed light on the creation of a popular text-book, and because they contribute
to an understanding of the quality of the poet to whom contemporaries happily
gave the title *poetarum nostri saeculi facile princeps*.

University of St Andrews

Notes

1. *Georgii Buchanani ... Opera Omnia* (Leyden, 1725), II, 1ff. and II, 607ff.

2. I. D. McFarlane, *Buchanan* (London 1981). Henceforth cited as 'McFarlane.'

3. P. Ford, *George Buchanan, Prince of Poets* (Aberdeen 1982). Henceforth 'Ford,' or
'Ford-Watt' if the reference is to their accompanying commentary on the *Miscellaneorum
Liber*.

4. The opportunity has been taken to slim down the original and add a small amount
of new or better digested material.

5. The terminology follows that of R. G. M. Nisbet and Margaret Hubbard, *A Commentary on Horace Odes Book 1*, xxxviii and n. 4.

6. J. A. Gaertner, "Latin Verse Translations of the Psalms, 1500–1620," *HTR*, 49
(1956), 273.

7. J. A. Gaertner, ibid., p. 273.

8. McFarlane, p. 263.

9. McFarlane, pp. 249ff.

10. These matters will be discussed elsewhere in the necessary detail.

11. My mode of reference perhaps requires justification. The psalm is referred to by
an Arabic numeral in accordance with the current trend among classicists; the second figure
refers to the line of the Paraphrase, not the verse of the psalm. The latter practice is followed by Ruddiman and some other editors, but creates great difficulty for the reader who
uses an unnumbered text; whereas numbering by line, pioneered by Vautrollier but not
common, gives such a reader a better chance.

12. Gagnay's work, published in 1547 apparently against the advice of his mentor, is
prolix, prosaic, gangling and unmusical; to a classicist of Buchanan's calibre perhaps
unreadable. He wrote better verse in his *editio princeps* of Claudius Victor (or Victorius)

of 1536, where he rewrote the poem freely in places where he could not read the manuscript (see *Poetae Christiani Minores*, ed. C. Schenkl [*Corpus Scriptorum Ecclesiasticorum 16, pt. 1*] [Vienna 1888], 437ff.).

13. J. Wall, "The Latin Elegiacs of George Buchanan (1506–1582)," in *Bards and Makars*, edd. A. J. Aitken, M. P. McDiarmid, D. S. Thomson (Glasgow, 1977), pp. 184–93.

14. In H. Stephanus's anthology of 1556, along with eighteen others; see McFarlane, p. 250f. But the 'Ovidian' couplet is absent from the early versions.

15. Cf. Psalm 68. 1 "O qui perpetuis orbem moderaris habenis" and Boeth. *Cons. Phil.* 3., metr. 9. 1 "O qui perpetua mundum ratione gubernas."

16. Nisbet and Hubbard, pp. xlff.

17. In Buchanan's *de Prosodia* (*Opera omnia*, II, 709ff.) Sedulius is offered as a model for the dimeter, and Prudentius for the trimeter, but all three were well known.

18. Ford-Watt, p. 183.

19. As noted by I. D. McFarlane, "Jean Salmon Macrin," *BHR*, 21 (1959), 325ff.

20. McFarlane, p. 98.

21. Ford, pp. 12ff.

22. See the paper of Dr Ann Moss (p. 371).

23. Perhaps in a different sense: see *Opera omnia*, II, 35 and Ford-Watt, p. 184.

24. Ford, pp. 16ff.

25. *Terentiani Mauri venustissimus de litteris, de syllabis et metris Horati liber* (Paris, 1510): Typ FP.B10PT.

26. Ford, p. 33.

27. W. M. Lindsay, "Buchanan as a Latin Scholar," in *George Buchanan: a Memorial 1506–1906*, ed. D. A. Millar (St Andrews, 1907), pp. 208ff.

28. McFarlane, p. 114. In Par. Lat. 8140 and 8141 the reading is *ludisque sacratae iocisque* in "Calendae Maiae," l. 3 (Ford-Watt, p. 152), after the initial line *salvete sacris deliciis sacrae*. This creates a play on words entirely typical of Buchanan; cf. Psalm 91. 47/48, "fato eximam; exemptoque honorum / eximium decus arrogabo."

29. In his address to the reader (pp. 94f.) that follows his selection of Psalm Paraphrases printed in 1556. A collection of the writings of printers about their art would be illuminating.

Buchanan's Poetry on Rome

Bernhard Kytzler

Usually, it is a fascinating phenomenon when there is an author of great genius treating a traditional theme of great importance. Buchanan as a Latin poet is no exception to this rule. The following paper aims at showing in which way he handles a theme of age-old tradition, handed down to him through many centuries: the City of Rome and her empire, her fame and her failures, her glory and greatness as well as her vices and her fall.

Indeed we observe in the poetic production devoted to Rome, from the ancient classics to the medieval authors and on to the Renaissance writers, a two-fold antagonistic intention: praises versus pamphlets, hymns versus satires, *laudatio* versus *vituperatio*. This Janus-head, showing on one side admiration, on the other condemnation and contempt, reappears quite clearly in the writings of Buchanan. However, there is no balance between these contradictory points of view: the conventional formulae for the praise of Rome are to be found just once; whereas on the other side there is quite a number of bitter and sarcastic epigrams strongly attacking Rome — a disproportion which, by the way, is indeed to the advantage of the modern reader who is much more entertained by these pasquils and pamphlets than amused by the countless celebrations of Rome's greatness and glory.

Although there is only one piece of poetry in Buchanan's books praising Rome, none the less this single epigram deserves attention. It is, in fact, not an original poem, but a translation "e Graeco."[1] Interestingly enough, Buchanan is not the only Humanist who gave us a Latin version of these three Greek disticha: the original (AG IX.291) is composed by Krinagoras of Mytilene, a contemporary of Augustus and protégé of Octavia;[2] besides Buchanan, a scholar as great as Henricus Stephanus (1528–98) has translated this poem; and so did Franciscus Bellicarius (1514–91).[3] Since this is not the place to discuss the questions of the Greek text, let us look here only at Buchanan's version of ll. 3–4.

These lines seem to explain that Rome's power shall never be weakened as long as she keeps in mind that Caesar is always giving the right commands:

'Ρώμης οὐδ' ὅσσον βλάφει σθένος, ἄχσι κε μίμνη
δεξιὰ σημαίνειν χαίσαρι θαζσαλέη.

Bellicarius renders this as

modo fida supersit
promptaque ad imperium dextera Caesaribus,

whereas Stephanus has in l. 4

Caesaris invicta sceptra tenente manu

and Buchanan understands it as

Non tamen aeternae divina potentia Romae
incolumi nobis Caesare fracta cadet.

So we have Buchanan saying "As long as Caesar is safe," whereas Stephanus says "as long as the invincible hand of Caesar holds the sceptre" and Bellicarius gives us "if only the faithful hand of the Caesars remains and is ready to reign." Without discussing the problems of the Greek original, we shall refer here only to the form of Buchanan's translation.[4]

It is interesting to see how he introduces into the Latin version conventional formulae which are to be found not in the Greek text but which stem from the Latin tradition. Most striking is the addition of two adjectives in line 3: instead of the simple 'Ρώμης ... σθένος = "power of Rome" we read the resounding phrase "aeternae divina potentia Romae" = "Eternal Rome's divine power." That brings in the phrase about the "Eternal City," coined, as it seems, by Tibullus (2, 5, 23). Buchanan's rendering of this part of the poem is quite opposed to the less rhetorical, more precise translation of Bellicarius's "Latias ... vires" or to the version of Stephanus who combines exactness with the dramatic impact of prosphonesis in the allocution "Tua, Roma, potentia."

Now from the translator to the poet. When we devote the main part of this essay to Buchanan's original writing on Rome — perhaps better: against Rome —, then we soon find an epigram which also might be called "e Graeco," if not for its full length, then at least for a considerable part. And again there is another Latin version of this poem. The original is composed by Alpheios of Mitylene (AG IX.526).[5] It seems that Faustus Sabaeus (1488–1558), Custos and Curator of the Vatican Library, in the same way as Buchanan, felt the need to add a final point to the text: therefore he calls the way to Heaven, the only place left after Rome has taken over all earth, *inaccessus*, unapproachable. Against this "Roman," i.e., "Catholic," version, Buchanan sets his "protestant" sarcasm (*Fratres* XVI). He explains that Heaven has been reached by the pious people of early Christian Rome, so that now, for the Papal Rome of his time, there is only one more way to go: to Hell.[6] Here an idea, handed down through many generations, ennobled in the lines of Vergil's *Aeneid* (VI. 781–82)

                              illa inclyta Roma
             imperium terris, animos aequabit Olympo,

here in the hands of Buchanan the idea is led to an unexpected climax: praise
has become part of a pamphlet, Great Rome takes now no longer the way to
Heaven but to Hell. We might say that this epigram shows best Buchanan's attitude toward Eternal Rome and her literary tradition: he remembers the glorious
past but detests the ignoble present[7] — the Janus-head of admiration and hate,
referred to at the beginning, is clearly a reflection of the scholar's vast learning
on the one side and of the citizen's vivid engagement in the political and religious
struggle of his time on the other.

    There is another epigram in which Buchanan uses the same thought-pattern
for a personal pamphlet against Pope Pius (*Fratres* X):

             Vendidit aere polum, terras in morte relinquit,
                Styx superest Papae, quam colat, una Pio.

        He sold Heaven for money, in death he left behind the earth —
           only Hell is left for Pope Pius to live in.[8]

Again the pattern Earth plus Heaven is given a poignant point against the pope
by introducing Hell as his last resort. Here we observe something that reappears
time and again in Buchanan's poetry: like a painter who produces sketches and
pictures of the same model or motif more than once, so Buchanan uses the same
literary motif several times with different shades and various connotations. In fact
we find the contrast of Earth and Hell a third time, incorporated in a poem directed
against another pope:

        Stare diu haud poterant mundusque & Julius una,
            omnia perdendi tam ferus ardor erat.
        Ergo ne ante diem mundi structura periret,
            ad Styga discessit Julius ante diem.   (*Fratres* XI)

    They could not exist together for a longer time, the world and Julius,
        so strong was his desire to destroy all things.
    Therefore in order that the structure of the world may not collapse
                                        before its day,
        to Hell went Julius before his day.

    The popes are often the target of Buchanan's sarcasm.[9] There are two more
epigrams belonging to this group: one against Pope Paul, playing on the assonance
of *domus* and *dominus* (*Fratres* XII), and another one that attacks no less than three
popes at once (*Fratres* XIII):

             Paedicat Paulus, contemnit foedera Clemens,
                sacrilega tractat Julius arma manu.
             Et quisquam sceleris nomen formidat inane,

auctores scelerum qui videt esse Deos?

Paulus abuses young boys, Clemens breaks treatises,
   Julius uses unholy arms,
  so who is going to fear the empty name of crime,
   if he sees men committing crimes being like Gods?

Without discussing the allegations, we should note the masterly use of alliteration put to work in order to underline the main words, connecting *paedicat Paulus,
contemnit ... Clemens.*

   Another group of poems is bound together by the notorious figure of that famous
Roman institution called *Pasquinus.*[10] A longer piece (*Fratres* XVII) gives in sixteen lines a picture of this statue and at the end launches an attack against certain
"purpureos ... cinaedos." The Pasquillus-epigram n° IV plays with the word *paulus,*
which is the name of the pope as well as an adjective meaning "small." Pasquillus,
asked what he thinks about this pope, answers "There is nothing that became just
a little bit better under Pope Paul — and there is nothing worse than Paul."

Praesule de Paulo, praesul doctissime vatum,
   Pasquille, dic quid sentias?
Nec melius paullo quidquam est antistite Paulo,
   et pejus est Paulo nihil.

The word *praesul,* equally given to the position of the pope and to the function
of Pasquillus, adds an intricate slander to the open attack of this epigram.

   So far we have looked at short poems only, epigrams making a point against
a person or a vice, using amusing puns and playful alliterations. There is, however,
a longer poem of thirty-five lines, showing the master's hand probing to reach
the extreme (*Fratres* XIV). Again we find a companion piece, a prelude, so to
speak, to the fully orchestrated concerto (*Fratres* XV); it numbers six lines only,
and it introduces the idea of the shepherd: in a form of typological approach sarcastically used, the shepherd, who once founded the City, Romulus, and the
shepherd, who is now the ruler of Rome and the Church, are set against each
other. This time-spanning allusion is combined with a play on the word *lupus.*

Non ego Romulea miror quod pastor in urbe
   sceptra gerat, pastor conditor urbis erat.
Cumque LUPAE gentis nutritus lacte sit auctor,
   non ego Romulea miror in urbe LUPOS.
Illa meum superat tantum admiratio captum,
   quomodo securum servet ovile LUPUS.

I am not astonished that in the City of Romulus a shepherd
   holds the sceptre: a shepherd was the founder of the city.
And since the founder of this nation was nourished with wolf's milk,
   I am not astonished to see wolves in the City of Romulus.

But one thing fills me with astonishment beyond reason,
  how is it that the wolf serves the careless sheep?

Certainly, Buchanan was not the only poet to play with the pun on *lupus*: Georgius
Tilenus (1557–90) for instance has an epigram on that theme;[11] there are probably more of them. But most certainly it could not escape Buchanan's brilliant
mind that the word *lupus* is capable of bringing in many more connotations. It
seems he could not resist the temptation to burn up in one fantastic firework all
the ammunition waiting to be used by someone prepared to bring out all the hidden power of this particular field of words. The result is a poem playing not only
with the word *lupus* like the one before, but a poem that introduces *lupus* and *lupa*,
lupercus, *lupinus*, *lupercal* and *lupanar*. In fact these words reoccur twenty-three times
in the thirty-five lines of *Fratres* XIV. The end assembles them all: if you look
at Rome,

> nihil comperies nisi LUPERCOS,
> LUPERCALE, LUPOS, LUPAS, LUPANAR.

Now this tour de force is in itself astonishing enough. But I would like to suggest
that it is meant moreover to ridicule a very famous sonnet on Rome and her ruins:
Castiglione's "Superbi colli," composed by the author of the "Cortegiano" in Italian,
later translated into Latin at least three times, that is by the Belgian Flamingus
and the Italians Niccolo d'Arco and Lazzaro Buonamici.[12] Certainly Buchanan's
introductory line

> Hi colles ubi nunc vides ruinas

is a close echo of Castiglione's beginning

> Superbi colli e voi sacre ruine,

and it is quite similar to the versions of Flamingus

> En dominae colles urbis sacraeque ruinae

and also that of d'Arco

> Excelsi colles urbi sacraeque ruinae.

Line 2 also is an echo of the Italian sonnet or of one of its Latin versions;[13]
moreover both poems go on to reflect on the past of the Eternal City: Castiglione
enumerates her "opere divine" such as *teatri, archi, colossi* and so on, Buchanan
on the contrary dwells on the theme of the wolves once hunting in the very same
places. But not only in the beginning and also in the progress of the main thought
there is a parallel—there is also one at the end. Castiglione finishes his sonnet
with a play on the words *fine* and *tempo*, repeating *fine* three times and *tempo* four
times. Similarly Buchanan repeats at the end of his poem all the key-words of
his song of hate, as quoted above. I would like to suggest that Buchanan disliked

the soft sentimental song of the sonnet, and that his clear mind intended to replace it — or at least, to balance it — by another poem, that at once amused the reader and seduced him to think of Rome's vices only. Buchanan himself in fact expressed a much more balanced view in his dialogue *De iure regni apud Scotos*, where he counterbalances the examples of Roman vices with examples of Roman virtue, where he brings in immediately after the dark figure of Romulus the pious King Pompilius Numa.[14] But here in the pamphlet, playing on all the puns that possibly could be made by using the root *lupus*, here Buchanan leaves aside the role of the philosopher and lets his temper go in order to fight for what he feels is right and to attack what he feels is wrong.

At the end of this short survey two questions may be raised: 1) What is the place of Buchanan in the tradition of Latin poetry about Rome? 2) What is the position of the poems about Rome within the work of Buchanan?[15] To look at the second question first: Buchanan's poetry on Rome as we have seen is relatively small. In fact we have taken into consideration no more than ten poems with a total of less than one hundred lines only. However, we find in them all the elements that mark the appearance of a powerful poet and of a Humanist of highest rank. As for the first question, we might give two answers: 1) Buchanan apparently knows very well the traditional topoi and formulae of the *Laudes Romae* — as well as he knows contemporary *cantica*, e.g., Castiglione's, on the old theme. Here we observe him fully integrated into the stream of European thinking about a widely spread topic. 2) What makes him stand out of this stream as a particular figure of special interest, is his way of using material handed down to him: he is not merely repeating well-known thought-patterns, but he gives them an unexpected twist, he likes to lead them to an end even contradictory to what they once were meant to say. Here we observe Buchanan as an original thinker, as a poet and pamphleteer, who uses whatever he finds in his own personal way. A great scholar, the centenary of whose death was commemorated last Year,[16] describes Buchanan's qualities with these words: "Als Humanist vereinigt er caledonische Gediegenheit mit der Grazie der Franzosen, unter denen er seine Bildungsjahre verlebte. Seine lateinischen Dichtungen wurden von dem einstimmigen Urtheil des Zeitalters hoch über alle italienischen Leistungen auf diesem Felde gestellt, denen sie an Formgewandtheit gleich und an poetischem Mark überlegen sind. In der That lesen sich die oft sehr ausgelassenen Elegien und Jamben wie wenn ihr Verfasser das Latein als Muttersprache gelernt hätte, und diese Stücke bewähren seinen Dichterberuf für alle Zeiten."[17]

Notes

1. "Liber Primus Epigrammatum," no. X. All quotations from Ruddiman's edition.
2. On this epigram cf. Eduard Norden, "Das Germanenepigramm des Krinagoras," in *Kleine Schriften*, ed. Bernhard Kytzler (Berlin, 1966), pp. 179–90.
3. These texts may be found in: *Roma Aeterna*, ed. Bernhard Kytzler (Zürich, 1972), p. 587.
4. On Buchanan's translations from the Greek, cf. I. D. McFarlane, *Buchanan* (London, 1981), pp. 185 sqq.
5.   Κλεῖε, θεός, μεγάλοιο πύλας ἀκμῆτας Ὀλύμπου·
       φρούρει, Ζεῦ, ζαθέαν αἰθέρος ἀκρόπολιν.
       ἤδη γὰρ καὶ πόντος ὑπέζευκται δορὶ Ῥώμης
       καὶ χθών· οὐρανίη δ' οἶμος ἔτ' ἔστ' ἄβατος.
Shut, o god, the tireless gates of great Olympus, keep, o Zeus, the holy castle of heaven. Already sea and earth are subdued by the Roman arms, but the path to heaven is still untrodden. (Translation by W. R. Paton, *The Greek Anthology*, Loeb, London, 1917.) The version of Sabaeus in *Roma Aeterna* (cf. n. 3), p. 588.
6. About the parallels with Du Bellay's *Antiquitez* cf. McFarlane (cf. n. 4), p. 166.
7. About the conduct of the popes cf. McFarlane (cf. n. 4) p. 3.
8. Translation of Fred J. Nichols, *An Anthology of Neo-Latin Poetry* (New Haven & London, 1979), p. 469.
9. cf. n. 7.
10. cf. McFarlane (cf. n. 4), p. 3.
11. Reprinted in *Roma Aeterna* (cf. n. 3), p. 518.
12. Reprinted in *Roma Aeterna* (cf. n. 3), p. 636; pp. 478–80.
13. Castiglione: "Che il nome sol di Roma ancor tenete"; Flemingus: "quae veteris Romae non nisi nomen habent"; d'Arco: "queis Romae nomen vix tenuisse datum est"; Buonamici: "quis modo nunc Romae nomen inane manet"; Buchanan: "et tantum veteris cadaver urbis."
14. Edition of 1579, p. 45.
15. About the possibility that Buchanan managed to visit Rome during his sojourn in Italy cf. McFarlane, p. 176.
16. Cf. *Acta* of the Jacob Bernays Conference, ed. Jean Bollack & A. Laks (Lille, 1985).
17. Jacob Bernays, *Joseph Justus Scaliger* (Berlin, 1855), p. 19.

An Acrostic Tribute to Thomas Ruddiman and his Edition of Buchanan's Works

J. G. Macqueen

Ⓐll of us who are gathered here today to commemorate the quatercentenary of the death of George Buchanan will be well acquainted with the fundamental contribution made to Buchanan studies by the edition of the *Opera Omnia* produced in the early eighteenth century by Thomas Ruddiman. Many of us too will know something of the story of Ruddiman's life:[1] how he was born in 1674, the son of a crofter at Raggel, in the parish of Boyndie, in the county of Banff, and how at the age of sixteen he made his way on foot to King's College, Aberdeen, where he graduated M.A. in 1694. For the next five years he worked first as a tutor, and then as schoolmaster of Laurencekirk, in the Mearns. There, in 1699, he was introduced to Dr Archibald Pitcairne, the celebrated Edinburgh doctor, controversialist and Latin poet, who invited him to come to the capital. Soon afterwards he found employment in the library of the Faculty of Advocates, and was able to start on his long career as librarian, printer and scholar. By the early 1720s he was a prominent figure in Edinburgh life, and his edition of Buchanan's *Works*, though it caused much historical and political controversy, had, together with his *Rudiments of the Latin Tongue*, given him a widespread and enduring reputation as a Latinist.

All this is well known and I summarise it here only to provide a background for the life and work of another Scot, almost totally unknown, whose life and career, at least in their earlier part, offer an almost exact parallel to those of Ruddiman, and whose surviving work, undistinguished as it is, shows how their paths may have crossed, and, more important, how the tradition of Latin verse composition, still at that time strong in the north-east of Scotland, could provide a man both with an income at a time of necessity and with a life-long means of self-expression and personal satisfaction.

James Gatt[2] was, like Ruddiman, born in Banffshire, in the parish of Cullen, on January 10th, 1700, and began his education at the local parish school. Like Ruddiman too, he went on to King's College, Aberdeen, and Mr Jacobus Gatt, Cullenensis, duly appears on the list of graduates for April 9th, 1719.[3] The next few years were spent, like Ruddiman's, as tutor at various private houses, and in 1722 he too moved to Edinburgh, though in his case it was not to take up employment but to enroll as a student of theology at the College. It was here that his talent as a Latin poet could be put to practical use. Like many students, past and present, he found his resources inadequate, and so was forced to look about him for patronage and financial support. Such use — or misuse — of the Muse was at that time by no means unknown in Edinburgh. "A considerable number of needy and thirsty men," to quote a scholar of an earlier generation,[4] "formed an Edinburgh Grub Street — broken schoolmasters, law-clerks, and students who had failed of a profession. They hung on the skirts of fortune, poor starvelings, not too reputable or sober, who were ready with pen to indite funeral elegies in English, Scots, or Latin verses, on the 'universally lamented' or 'deplorable' death or some 'incomparable' lord or citizen; or an epithalamium on the wedding of some person of quality." If a composition met with approval, the poet would receive a few shillings as payment for his efforts. Gatt of course was by no means a broken man, but an eager student and aspirant to the ministry, and he had the warm approval of William Hamilton, the eminent professor of theology at the time. So he could direct his talents at higher targets than mourning merchants and petty gentry. Soon we find him appealing in Latin verse to no less than the Barons of the Exchequer, who were so impressed by his talents that they granted him a bursary for his pains, and in return received a further poem each year when payment was made. Other poems were addressed to eminent citizens such as Adam Cockburn, the Lord Justice Clerk who is best known for having a quarter of a century previously been a member of the board of enquiry into the massacre of Glencoe, and one, to which I would like to draw your attention today, is dedicated to his Banffshire compatriot, now a man of some substance and a scholar of renown — Thomas Ruddiman.

The poem to Ruddiman, as copied out by Gatt nearly twenty years later, is in two parts. The first in an encomium on Ruddiman, and the second a personal address, suitably laced with self-denigration, which serves to explain the author's purpose in sending it. Unfortunately for us, that purpose remains rather obscure. "Admit me to the roll of young men on whom you bestow your favour," says Gatt in the final lines; but the "devouring cares" a few lines earlier suggest that he was looking for something more practical than the favour of friendship. George Chalmers, Ruddiman's late eighteenth-century biographer, mentions that the great man gave active assistance to literary friends;[5] but this assistance was not necessarily financial. Perhaps what Gatt wanted was admittance to one of the numerous literary clubs of the capital.[6] In several of these Classical lore and Latin verse were encouraged, and it may be that Gatt saw in one of them an opportunity to meet leading members of Edinburgh society, and exercise his literary and poetic talents. We simply cannot tell. Ruddiman was certainly a leading light in one of these clubs, and it was its policy to have a bias towards Classical studies, and to bring in young Presbyterian clergymen and students of divinity so that they could listen to the disputations.[7] But if Gatt ever succeeded in gaining admission, he might not have enjoyed the strong support for the Stuart cause which was to be found there, or the baiting of young theologians which, we know from the Boswell papers, gave delight to such young legal wits as Henry Home, later Lord Kames.

The first part of the poem is of greater interest. It is, as you can easily see from the way in which Gatt has laid it out, an acrostic in form, the initial letters of the lines forming the words MAGISTER THOMAS RUDIMANNUS. It begins with a rather amusing appeal to his Muse to calm down, and not allow herself to be over-excited by the prospect of extolling Ruddiman, the "gloria ... gentis praeclara Boinae" of line 3 (it is to be remembered that he was born in the parish of Boyndie). So much in control of his acrostic form is the poet in these early lines that he can afford to indulge in word-play on Ruddiman's name, first in lines 5 and 6, where the "nitidissima fama minime rudis Rudimanni" (the brightly gleaming fame of Ruddiman — no "rude man" he!) has spread throughout the world, and again (and much less attractively) in the vocative "Ruphandre" in line 8, a barbarous compound, as we can see from the gloss in the top right-hand corner of the page, of the Latin *rufus* and Greek ἀνήρ, ἀνδρός to translate "Ruddy Man." One can almost feel the scholarly Ruddiman squirm as he read it, and perhaps Gatt was right to apologise so profusely for his poem's defects, and to suggest (l. 37) that he should stop, "nausea ne obrepat tibi"!

Then follows a reference to Ruddiman's scholarly work in Latin (ll. 9ff.). Like a second Buchanan, he banishes every solecism from the Latin language, and recalls honeyed Philology (Phīlologīam!), long imprisoned in filthy squalor. The reference is presumably to Ruddiman's *Rudiments of the Latin Tongue*, which had appeared in 1714, for in 1724, the date of our poem, the larger *Grammaticae Latinae Institutiones* had not yet appeared.

Lines 13–14 are of considerable interest. Without doubt, says Gatt, later generations will say that it is due to you that the Augustan age of Buchanan is being born anew for the Scots.[8] We are now quite used to employing such phrases as "Augustan poetry," the "Augustan period" and the "Scottish Augustans"; but in 1724 this was by no means the cliché which it is today. The earliest reference given by the OED for this use of the word in English is for the year 1712, when the adjective "Augustan" is used of the reign of Charles II, and it was not, as far as I can see, until 1756 that it came into use with reference to the early eighteenth century. Gatt not only — uniquely, as far as I know — refers to the age of Buchanan as "Augustan." He also, by implication, calls the early eighteenth century in Scotland an Augustan period; and he must have been one of the first, if not *the* first, to do so. All this is particularly apposite in a poem which has just referred to Ruddiman as "magnae spes altera Romae," "the second hope of great Rome."

Then (l. 15) comes a passage which pays tribute to Ruddiman's monumental edition of Buchanan. The date on the title page of this work is of course 1715, and it may seem at first sight that Gatt's praises of it, though fulsome, are, like those of the *Rudiments*, a little out of date. But it must be remembered that although the book was ready for publication by September, 1715, the sudden departure of its publisher, Robert Freebairn, to join the forces of the Old Pretender caused the postponement of its sale in Scotland until 1722.[9] Thus the appearance of the weighty two-volume folio edition was for Gatt an exciting event of the fairly recent past. Impressive these volumes certainly are, both as works of scholarship and as products of the printer's art. Yet it is, I think, taking things rather too far to suggest, as Gatt does (ll. 17–18) that they force the products of the *Officina Plantiniana*[10] in Antwerp into second place in the contemporary book-production league. And certainly Ruddiman's *prooemia* and other editorial contributions did not, as Gatt claims in line 19, strike all men senseless and speechless with amazement. On the contrary, they provoked the most bitter disagreement and long-lasting controversy, which was to go on until Ruddiman's death in 1757. But despite all this there is, I think, some justification in Gatt's claim (l. 20) that the light of Ruddiman's scholarship had revealed Rome to the contemporary world. His works did indeed uncover all the secrets of the ancient tongues — or at least the secrets of the Latin tongue. For although "linguae utriusque" (ll. 22–23) would normally mean "of both Latin and Greek" there is little trace in Ruddiman's scholarly work before 1724 that he had any particular interest in Greek. This makes me wonder whether Gatt used the phrase to refer, not to Latin and Greek, but to Latin and Scots, with particular reference to Ruddiman's work on the poems of Gavin Douglas, published by Freebairn in 1710. Whatever the truth of this suggestion, there is a great deal to justify Gatt's congratulations, with their Vergilian echo, in the final lines,[11] and his claim that, thanks to Ruddiman, sublime learning would be immortalised for a grateful age to come. Indeed it is not until the present day that his edition of Buchanan is being superseded.

I can find no evidence to show if Gatt's plea was successful, and if he was in fact admitted to the circle of Ruddiman's friends. If he was, it could have been a very uneasy friendship, for Ruddiman was a strong Jacobite with quietist leanings, while Gatt, was, at least in later years, a conventional Presbyterian and convinced Hanoverian. But if they did meet, their mutual interest in Latin language and literature may have offered ample scope for discussion of topics which avoided both politics and religion.

Gatt's connection with Edinburgh and its literary society was not to last for long. In 1727 he was licensed "with distinguished approbation" by the Presbytery of Linlithgow to preach the Gospel,[12] and two years later he was appointed assistant to the minister of the parish of Gretna, in Dumfriesshire. On the death of the minister in the following spring, he became his successor, and remained in Gretna for fifty-seven years until his death in 1787, despite an invitation to move back to Edinburgh, "preferring" as the records of the Church of Scotland tell us "his rural and pleasant retirement to all the fascinating society Edinburgh contained." But throughout his long and often hard life in Gretna he retained his fluency in Latin, and made constant use of the language. In 1724 he had begun a Latin diary, making short weekly entries, mostly devotional in character, but not infrequently referring to incidents of his everyday life. This he continued to do until 1779, and as time went on the entries were increasingly in verse, making use of a wide variety of metres. He also followed the old-established tradition of translating Scripture into Latin verse by composing a version of the Book of Proverbs. In 1741 he decided to make a collection of some of his original Latin poems, and so began *Jacobi Gathei Miscellanea Metrica*. The early poems of the collection go back to the 1720s, and among them is the poem to Thomas Ruddiman which has been my main consideration today. But the urge to compose was too strong to allow Gatt to be content with works from the past. Soon the notebooks began to contain new work — "Deliciae Gratinienses"; "Deliciae Collinienses"; "In Parentes et Amicos"; "De Natalibus"; "De Educatione"; "De Providentiae Benignitate"; "De Conversione"; "De Coniugio"; and many other poems on contemporary or near contemporary events also occur, some of only local interest, others on matters of national or even international importance. We have for instance, "De Tempestate quae incepit quarto et vicesimo die Januarii et duravit ad sextum diem Martii, A.D. 1745"; or "De Schismate in Ecclesia Scoticana"; or "De Cometa" (dated January 31st, 1744, for those with astronomical interests); or "De Porto Bello Subacto"; or "De Proelio Dettingensi"; or "De Naumachia Thoulonensi." Increasingly in fact the man of God found that his talents were best suited to poems of battle: — and in the mid-eighteenth century there were plenty of these about which he could write! But while he could compose with considerable vigour on wars in Europe or the Americas, his attitude proved rather different when, late in 1745, he was faced by the reality of Bonny Prince Charlie's Highlanders passing through Gretna on their way south into England. Abandoning his Manse, and leaving his wife to face the rebels, he fled across the Solway and hid in Cumberland until the danger was past. Only in February 1746, when the Prince's forces were again north of the border and well clear of Gretna, could the minister sit down to write a poem "De Proelio Commisso ... prope Prestonpans" (in the interests of brevity I shorten some of his titles considerably), and follow it with "De Obsidione Castelli Edinburgensis"; "De Progressu Montanorum ex Lothiana in Angliam"; "De Regressu Montanorum ex Anglia" and so on through hundreds of elegiac couplets to a triumphant "De Praelio ... facto in Culloden Muir," and "De Ruina Montanorum et reditu Gulielmi Augusti Principis Cumbriaci et Brunswick-Lunenbergensis, Summi Regiarum Copiarum Praefecti in Britannia, ad Angliam."

The Forty-Five seems to have been the only large-scale incident to disturb the life of the minister of Gretna. After that he has little to write about except the innumerable battles of mid-eighteenth-century Europe. Occasionally there is a variation: — exciting events such as earthquakes in Lima in 1746, or in Lisbon in 1755; or a *genethliacon* on the birth of the Prince of Wales, or an *epithalamium* on the marriage of George III. There are still some poems of more personal interest: — "De Ponte super Fluvium Cirtelum (Kirtle Water) ... in Parochia Gratiniensi"; or "De Odontalgia aut Dolore Dentium qui me male habebat anno 1747"; or (the most marvellous title of all) "De Mola Serica Derbyensi; in qua sunt 26,586 rotae, 77,746 motus, 4 ampla et alta cubicula super se invicem posita; una rota magna totam agitat machinam tribus vicibus intra horae minutam; unoquoque rotationis tempore, 73,728 ulnae anglicanae serici plicantur; et spatio unius diei et noctis 318,504,960 ulnae conficiuntur. — ac quod mirari subit, tertia vel quinta pars motuum, aut dimidium earum, sisti potest, reliquis minime impeditis vel obstructis." After a title like that, one would have thought that there was nothing left to say in the verses to follow; but in fact Gatt, as a good Christian, avoids mere repetition by making the poem deal not with silk-weaving but with the superiority of the works of God to those of man.

So, over fifty years and more, the minister of Gretna made entries in his diary, and composed and wrote out in his note-books more than 200 Latin poems which cannot ever have been seen by anyone other than a few local doctors and schoolmasters and the ministers of neighbouring parishes. His manuscripts remain in the possession of the minister and Kirk Session of Gretna, and to them I owe a great debt of gratitude for allowing me to examine them. What would have happened if Gatt had accepted the invitation to return to Edinburgh we cannot say. Perhaps his connection with Ruddiman would have prospered; and perhaps his scholarly and poetic skills, stimulated by the intellectual activity of the metropolis, would have enabled him to emerge, as Ruddiman did, "Buchananus ut alter" (to quote his own poem), as a not inconsiderable figure in the history of Scottish neo-Latinity.

University of Bristol

Text and Translation

Acrostichis ad Magistrum Thomas Ruddimanum

Anno Domini 1724

M	usa quiesce, precor, dudum torpore sepulta;
A	urea serta voras spe frustra aut laurea; sensi:
G	loria at exulto gentis praeclara Boinae;
I	n quantum emicuit! Doctas quot flammifer oras
S	ol gemma rutilante beat, nitidissima fama
T	ot minime rudis est Rudimanni didita terris.
E	ximias opulenta stupet vicinia dotes
R	espiciens Ruphandre tuas; teque invidet omnis
T	erra Caledoniis, merito; Buchananus ut alter
H	orridula veterum pulsa stribligine prorsus,
O	bseptam squalore tetro tu Philologiam
M	ellifluam revocas, magnae spes altera Romae:
A	cceptum indubie referent tibi sera nepotum
S	ecula quod Scotis Augusta en nascitur aetas;
R	ursus ab integro, Buchanani, cuius opimos
U	beris ingenii fetus tu iam redivivos
D	as pulchris ornando typis, queis Plantiniani
I	udice me cedent; tua tersa prooemia cunctos
M	iraclo stupidos defigunt, ut nihil ultra.
A	uricomam tendente facem te, Roma patescit.
N	ulli non opera et tua nunc dignissima Cedro
N	ota prius paucis pandunt mysteria linguae
U	triusque; novis macte o virtutibus esto:
S	ublimis memori Doctrina sacrabitur aevo.

Line numbers: 5 (at "ol gemma"), 10 (at "orridula"), 15 (at "ursus ab"), 20 (at "ulli non").

Ecce ego qui curis conflictor edacibus, hasce 25
   Nugas mitto tibi Compatriota tuus:
Imis te exposco precibus ne munera temnas;
   Conatum laudes, prorsus acumen abest.
Quot sunt errores, totidem mihi crede dolores.
   Obstrepuit dolor; at carmina cudit amor. 30
Iacobus memini Gilbertus doctus amicus
   (qui mihi dum vivo certo colendus erit)
Me comite invisurum temet,[13] si forte vacaret,
   Pollicitus semel est anteriore hyeme,
Mira canens de te, cuius praeclara per orbem 35
   Fama volat nullo demoritura die.
Nausea ne obrepat tibi, desino; parcito mendis:

Versus cum calamo provolitante fluunt.
Haec raptim male nata licet, ne sperne; referto ast
　　Me iuvenum in censum, queis Rudimanne faves.　　40

My Muse, long buried in lethargy, be silent, I pray you. You are eager
for garlands of gold or of laurel, I know, though your hopes are vain. Yet
I rejoice in the outstanding glory of the people of Boyndie. How far its beam
has spread! The brightly gleaming fame of Ruddiman — no 'rude' man he! —
has spread to every land where the fiery sun, with his red-glowing eye, blesses
shores where learning flourishes. The rich area where you live, Ruddiman,
is astounded as it gazes on your outstanding gifts. Every other country feels
envious that you belong to Scotland, and rightly so. Like a second Buchanan,
you eliminate every rude barbarism from the texts of the ancients, and bring
back the honeyed sweetness of linguistic study, long imprisoned in filthy
squalor. You are the second hope of great Rome. Without doubt in times
to come future generations will say that it is due to you that the Augustan
age of Buchanan is being reborn anew for the Scots — Buchanan, the splendid offspring of whose fertile genius you are now reviving and offering again
in a new edition, beautifully printed, volumes to which, in my opinion, the
products of the Plantin press will yield place. Your elegant prefaces astound
all men, as nothing else can, and strike them dumb with amazement. When
you hold the golden-haired torch aloft, Rome is revealed in its light. Now
too your works, worthy of immortality,[14] reveal to all the secrets of both
tongues, known previously to few. Heartiest congratulations! Sublime Learning will be immortalised for a grateful age to come.[15]

　Herewith I, your fellow-countryman, who am tormented by devouring
troubles, send these poor verses to you. I beg you from the bottom of my
heart not to scorn the gift. Commend the attempt, though talent is utterly
lacking. Every error in them, believe me, causes me pain. Anguish has
hindered my verse; but love forges the lines. Our learned friend James
Gilbert, I remember (and I must certainly honour him as long as I live),
promised once last winter that he would visit you, if time were available,
and take me with him, and he sang your praises, for your fame and glory
spread throughout the world and will never die. I say no more, to avoid
sickening you. Pardon my errors. The lines flow with the pen rushing ahead.
Hurried and ill-begotten though these verses be, do not reject them, but
admit me, Ruddiman, to the roll of young men on whom you bestow your
favour.[16]

Notes

1. For full details see Douglas Duncan, *Thomas Ruddiman: a Study in Scottish Scholarship of the Early Eighteenth Century* (Edinburgh, 1965).

2. For biographical details of Gatt I am indebted to his own writings, and to the manuscript biography written almost forty years after his death by the Rev. David Smith, minister of the neighbouring parish of Morton, and preserved with Gatt's papers in Gretna Church.

3. P. J. Anderson (ed.), *Officers and Graduates of the University and King's College Aberdeen, MVD-MDCCCLX* (Aberdeen, 1893), p. 224.

4. Henry Graham, *Scottish Men of Letters in the Eighteenth Century* (London, 1901), p. 5.

5. George Chalmers, *The Life of Thomas Ruddiman A.M.* (London, 1794), p. 98.

6. D. D. McElroy, *Scotland's Age of Improvement: a Survey of Eighteenth Century Literary Clubs and Societies* (Washington, 1969).

7. G. Scott and F. A. Pottle (eds.), *The Private Papers of James Boswell* (privately printed, 1928-34), XV, 314.

8. There is a problem here. Gatt puts a semi-colon after *aetas* at the end of l. 14, and another after *cedent* in l. 18. The text, thus punctuated, offers no explanation for the genitive *Buchanani* in l. 15, and one or other of the semi-colons must, I think, be disregarded. If the second were taken as a comma, *Buchanani* would depend on *tua ersa prooemia* in l. 18 ("Your elegant prefaces to Buchanan ..."), and *rursus ab integro*, which comes immediately before *Buchanani*, would have to be taken as part of the relative clause *cuius ... typis*, which already contains *iam*. All this is possible, but extremely unlikely. Much more probably the first semi-colon is to be totally disregarded, and *Buchanani* is to be taken with *aetas*, and *rursus ab integro* with *nascitur* ("The Augustan age of Buchanan is born anew"). Probability becomes certainty when one compares Vergil, *Eclogue* iv.4-5:

> ultima Cumaei venit iam carminis aetas;
> magnus ab integro saeclorum nascitur ordo.

Clearly what Gatt has written is a blending of the two Vergilian lines. His punctuation, like that of other eighteenth-century authors, in many places does not conform to the accepted rules of twentieth-century orthography.

9. Duncan: op. cit. n. 1, p. 63 and note 75.

10. Founded in Antwerp by Christophe Plantin in 1555.

11. Vergil, *Aeneid*, ix, 641:

> macte nova virtute, puer; sic itur ad astra!

Apollo is addressing the young Ascanius who has just killed Remulus.

12. Hew Scott (ed.): *Fasti Ecclesiae Scoticanae* (London, 1866), Part I, pp. 618-19.

13. Gatt's scansion is questionable in several places (e.g., at the end of l. 3); here it must be wrong. Perhaps he intended to write *te* rather than *temet*?

14. The phrase *dignissima cedro* (literally "worthy of cedar-oil," which was used to preserve books from decay) is derived from Horace, *Ars Poetica*, ll. 331-32 ("carmina ... linenda cedro") and Persius I, 42 ("cedro digna locutus").

15. The translation offered is based on the use of *sacrare* in Horace, *Odes* I, 26, 11:

> hunc Lesbio sacrare plectro
> teque tuasque decet sorores.

Gatt may however have used the verb in its more common meaning of "render sacred" or "hold sacred." In that case the translation would be "Your sublime learning will be held sacred by a grateful posterity."

16. I am extremely grateful to Niall Rudd for his valuable comments on this paper. He is of course in no way responsible for its remaining defects.

New Poems by Buchanan, from Portugal

John R. C. Martyn

After George Buchanan had "escaped" from Portugal in 1552, despite some efforts by King John III to retain his services, it seems that the Humanist "washed his hands" of the country which had caused him so much aggravation, ridiculing it with stinging attacks, in poems on Portugal, Brazil, Rome, the popes and even King John III.[1] He may have continued for a while working on profane poems he had started, or based on experiences he had had, in Portugal,[2] but he was soon completely immersed in literary and educational circles and activities, first in France (1552–61), and then in Scotland, and by 1568 he had become a Protestant, active in attacking Mary Queen of Scots, and in furthering the Scottish Reformation, even being friendly with the English.[3] Portugal was no doubt by then a distant and unpleasant memory, and there is no sign of his having communicated with Portuguese scholars, or noblemen, not even with his old friends Diogo de Teive and Jean de Costa.[4] Meanwhile, one would imagine that his condemnation by the Portuguese Inquistition, and the total banning of his works by the Portuguese *Index* of 1581, backed up by those of Sixtus V in 1590, and Clement VIII in 1596, would have meant an end to his poems (satires and epigrams especially) being freely read in Portugal. But the reverse seems to be true. His poems continued to circulate there, including some that never appeared, it seems, in later collections of his works.

The first such poem is an epigram (a couplet) located in a manuscript in the Torre do Tombo, Lisbon, number 2209, entitled *Miscela*, amongst the *Manuscritos da Livraria*. The date of this collection of Latin and Portuguese poetry (plus a few prose texts in Latin) is about 1580, to judge from dated works within the collection.[5] The poem appears on an unnumbered folio near the start of the *Miscela*, and it contains thematic material, and irony and wit, that are typical of Buchanan's work during his Portuguese visit. The Latin is as follows:

> Ex Epigrammate Comparandum est Praemium a Buchanano
> Lusce puer, fac⟨i⟩em luscae concede parenti;

ut tu verus amor, sic erit illa Venus.
faciem: *legitur fort*. fucem   *post* ut *legitur* sis, *sed del.*

One-eyed boy, grant light (splendor) to your one-eyed mother:
    Just as you will be a true Cupid, so she will be a true Venus.

Just below this epigram, but in the same hand (although less legible) is another
epigram that seems to be connected with Buchanan. There is no heading or name
above or below it, although there are letters (of a sort) directly above it (Q CO).
Their meaning eludes me. Beneath is a new dedication (to Ludovicus de Sylva),
which suggests that the top two epigrams are a pair. The second runs as follows:

Divinam spherae spheram cum Principe Romae
    postulat a nobis qui regit astra poli.

He who rules the stars of Heaven, demands from me, and (*cum*) from
the Prince of Rome's 'sphere' (world), a 'sphere' (poem) that is divine.

The play on the word *sphera*, and the ironical treatment of Rome and the Pope,
certainly suit Buchanan's style, although the Latin is awkward (it might be "God
and the Pope demand from me …", but *postulant* would be expected). It seems
that Buchanan first started work on his *magnum opus*, the *De Sphaera*, while still
in Portugal, and was working hard on it in France in the 1550s;[6] like the Pope,
he failed to complete its 'divine' message (sadly, pre-Copernican) by the time of
his death in 1582. There do not seem to have been any other *sphaera* poems in
Portugal at that time.

A third poem connected with Buchanan in this *Cancioneiro* (or *Carminum Liber*),
is the eulogy of twenty-two lines attached to the preface (p. 5) of Diogo de Teive's
Commentarius de rebus in India apud Dium gestis anno salutis nostrae MDXLVI, dedicated to King John III, and published in Coimbra in 1548, the year their leader
and close friend, André de Gouveia, died most unexpectedly, and two years before their incarceration by the Inquisition, together with Jean de Costa, who had
also donated a liminary Latin poem to Teive's history (26 ll.): the work seems
to have been an ill omen for the three professors. In his poem, Buchanan praises
the King's world-wide empire, and Teive's literary genius. The *cancioneiro* version
is as follows, with my translation beside it:

Georgi Buchanani Ad Emmanuellem Regem. (sic!)

(Ad eundem invictissimum Regem — Ioannem III — de hoc commentario G.B.
in 1548 ed. [*C*])

Cum tua sceptra Asiae gens, Europaeque timeret et tremeret fasces terra Libyssa tuos:	When the people of Asia and Europe feared your sceptre, and the Libyan land trembled at your rule;
Iamque iugi patiens Indus: nec turpe putaret	And the Indus already endured your yoke, nor did the Ganges

a domino Ganges poscere iura Tago:

Inque tuis Phoebus regnis Oriensque
                                                    Cadensque
vix longum fesso conderet axe diem:

Et quaecumque vago se circumvolvit
                                                    Olympo
luceret ratibus flamma ministra tuis:

Gaudebat tibi devictus, sibi redditus
                                                    Orbis
nosse suos fines, iustiamque tuam
                                                    (-titi-C)
Una aberatque oberatque tuis Mors
saeva
                                                    triumphis
carpere victricem scilicet ausa manum.

Et comes huic tenebris nisa est oblivio
                                                    caecis
fortia magnanimum condere facta
                                                    ducum.
Donec Apollineis se Tevius induit armis

et spolia e victa Morte superba tulit.

Victurisque iubet chartis iuvenescere,
                                                    vitae
prodiga pro patria pectora laude suae,
                                                    (-riae C)
Proque aevi paucis quod Mors praesci-
                    derat annis (praeciderat C)
reddit ab aeterna posteritate Decus.

Iure ergo invictus Rex es? quando omnia
                                                    vicens (es; C)
accessit titulis Mors quoque victa tuis.

think it disgraceful to demand laws
                                        from Tagus, its lord;
And Phoebus, rising and setting, still in
                                        your kingdom
scarcely ended the long day with
                                        tired axle;
And whatever flame (star) rotates in the
                                        open sky,
shone to serve your ships;

The World overcome by you, restored
                                        to itself, rejoiced
to know its own boundaries, and
                                        your justice;

Savage Death alone was absent from
    your triumphs, and hindered them,
in fact, Death dared to revile your
                                        conquering hand.
And its companion, Oblivion, strove
                                        with dark shadows
to conceal the brave deeds of
                                        great-hearted leaders.
Until Teive girt himself with Apollo's
                                        arms,
and took proud spoils from
                                        conquered Death.
He orders, with pages that will live on,
                                        breasts,
prodigal with life, for the glory of
    their country, to grow young again,
And in return for the few years of life
                                        which
Death has cut out (before time), he
    gives Glory from eternal posterity.
And so you are justly the unconquered
                                        King, since
Death that conquers all has been
    conquered and added to your titles.

After the poem, the scribe added its source: "Hoc epigrama translatum fuit ex
quodam commentario quem de rebus apud Dium gestis Tevius inscripsit, super
quae Georgius Buchananus hoc mirabile epygrama composuit." His literary judgement is an improvement on his historical knowledge!

A different *Cancioneiro*, that contains a nobleman's collection of Latin and Portuguese poems, made in about 1600, the *Cancioneiro de Corte e de Magnete*, recently
edited by A.L.-F. Askins,[7] also provides us with a short poem by Buchanan,
similar to one in later editions of his works. It is one of the anti-Rome poems
which he wrote in Portugal, revising it afterwards, *Fratres* I,17, *In eandem*. In the
Cancioneiro, its title is simply "*Versos de Bucanano*." The second couplet is almost

totally different, and preferable in my view, l. 4 especially; there are sixteen variants in all:[8]

(a) Roma armis olim ratibusque subegerat
                                        orbem
   atque eaedem vires orbis et urbis erant.

(b) Roma armis terras, ratibisque
                        subegerat undas,
   atque iidem fines urbis et orbis erant.

Sidera restabant; penetravit sidera
                                  quondam
   Pontificum veterum relligiosa fides.

Vincere restabat caelum; perfregit
                              Olympum
   priscorum pietas aurea Pontificum.

At bona posteritas, caeptis ne cedat avitis,

   Tartara praecipiti tendit ad ima gradu.

At bona posteritas, ausis ne cedat
                                  avitis,
   Tartara praecipiti tendit ad ima
                                  gradu.

(l. 2, *caedem* legitur)   My version of (a) follows:

> Rome once conquered the World with arms and ships,
>   and the power of the World and of Rome were the same.
> Heaven remained; the early Bishops' pious faith
>   penetrated Heaven at some time past.
> But fine posterity, so as not to yield to their ancestors' beginnings,
>   marches with headlong step down to the very bottom of Hell.

The punch-line, unchanged in later editions, would hardly have pleased the Portuguese Church around 1600; the collection must have been very much a *private* one.[8]

These four poems, three certainly by Buchanan, give us a most interesting and hitherto unexpected picture of his continued popularity with some Portuguese readers, nearly thirty years after his departure from Portugal, and twenty years after his poems had been damned on the local *Index*. A different tradition was established, it seems, and continued at least until the end of the century. Other new poems, or known poems with variants, may well appear when the large collection of *Miscela* at the Torre do Tombo is catalogued, unfortunately not likely to happen in the near future.

University of Melbourne

Notes

1. *Fratres*, I, 28, "Adventus in Galliam" begins "Jejuna miserae tesqua Lusitaniae / Glebae-que tantum fertiles penuriae," repeated at the end; *Fratres* 1, 29, 30 revile Brazil's settlers (*vel Sodomitas*); *Fratres*, I, 15–17 ridicule Rome, where "Nihil comperies nisi Lupercos, Luper-cale, Lupos, Lupas, Lupanas"; *Fratres* I, 10–14 attack the venality of *Pius*, *Julius*, *Paulus* and *Clemens*; and *Misc.*, 5 attacks King John III for profiteering; if his "pepper-stall" is closed, he will starve!

2. I. D. McFarlane, *Buchanan* (London, 1981), p. 152, argues that Buchanan waited until he had left Portugal before writing down some poems inspired by his experiences there, such as the eight against Beleago (p. 153) and some of the Leonora poems (p. 155); but with his brother there to remove libellous poems, there's no real reason why Buchanan should not have circulated all these diatribes in Coimbra; and some certainly stayed around for many years.

3. See McFarlane, op. cit., pp. 159–90 (France) and 206–46, 320–28 (Scotland, England).

4. No letters between them appear in McFarlane's appendix B.

5. As established by Arthur L.-F. Askins on p. 131 in his article "Diogo Bernardes and Ms. 2209 of the Torre do Tombo," in *Arquiv. do Centro Cult. Portug.*, xiii (1978), 127–65. I am grateful to him for showing me the third and fourth poems in this article.

6. Working in Coimbra with Nicolas de Grouchy, who was editing Aristotle, and then in France with Vinet, Finé, Jean-Pierre de Mesmes and others, as described by McFar-lane, op. cit., pp. 356–58.

7. A.L.-F. Askins, *Cancioneiro de Corte e de Magnete* (Univ. Calif. Press, 1968), p. 143.

8. While writing this article, I heard from Professor McFarlane that these variants over-lap with others to be found in French documents and printed sources before 1615, which suggests that they are genuine. In the second stanza, however, the chiastic anaphora of *sidera*, and neat climax in *fides*, seem to be unique, and very effective, readings. Unlike with his liminary poem to Martin Azpilcueta's *Enchiridion* (cf. McFarlane, op. cit., pp. 152–53), in the titles of all these poems (except the *sphera* epigram), Buchanan's name is in no way concealed, which is surprising.

The Tragedies of Buchanan, Teive and Ferreira

John R. C. Martyn

I shall concentrate mainly on a single element common to the tragedies of Buchanan, Teive and Ferreira; however, it is one that plays a key rôle in their structures and dramatic power, namely the Prophetic Dream. In so doing, I hope to show the special significance of Buchanan's dramas, in particular his *Jephthes*, a source ignored by Soares in his 1977 edition of Teive's *Ioannes Princeps*,[1] and by Adrien Roig in his recent edition of the *Castro*, and biography of its author, Ferreira.[2]

In Book II of Vergil's *Aeneid*, ll. 270–97, Hector's ghost appears to the sleeping Aeneas, looking as ghastly as he did when Achilles had finished dragging his dying body around Troy behind his chariot, a symbol of Troy's savage destruction by the Greeks. The apparition warns Aeneas of his imperial destiny, while stressing the hopelessness of saving Troy. For the rest of the dramatic account of Troy's fall, Aeneas alternates between his immediate duties as an epic warrior and leader, and his long-term obligations as preserver of his family and of the Trojans who survived. For the moment, he ignores Hector's warning, even when reinforced by the priest Panthus, and instead leads a band of young Trojans against the invaders, described in lines 355–59 with a powerful simile:

> inde lupi ceu
> raptores atra in nebula, quos improba ventris
> exegit caecos rabies, catulique relicti
> faucibus exspectant siccis, per tela, per hostes
> vadimus haud dubiam in mortem ...

The *atra nebula*, *caecos* and *rabies* give a nightmare quality to the imagery. The *catuli* remind us of young Ascanius and the *Penates* waiting at Aeneas's home.

The same image appears in Buchanan's *Jephthes*, in the very dramatic opening scene that follows the Angel's ill-omened prologue, Act I, ll. 95–102.

Vidi luporum concito cursu gregem
Rictu cruento, spumeo, rabido, unguibus   95
Saevum recurvis praecipite ferri impetu
Imbellia in pecora, vidua pastoribus.
Tum pavidi ovilis fida custodia canis
Lupos abegit; atque ad infirmum pecus
Trepidi timoris exanime adhuc memoria,   100
Denuo reversus, e sinu timidam meo
Agnam revulsam dente laniavit truci.

The Queen, Storge (the Greek for maternal love), explains her grief to her daughter, Iphis: "Night visions so terrify me, in my misery, and grim dreams disturb
me, as I toss and turn." (76–77 nocturna sic me visa miseram territant / et dira
turbant inquietam insomnia.) In ll. 94–102, she describes the nightmare: a pack
of ravenous wolves (note *rabido*) attack a flock of sheep, until driven off by the
faithful, guardian sheep-dog (*ovilis fida custodia canis*); but the devoted dog, to
Storge's horror, proceeds to tear the lamb from her embrace (101–02), ripping
it apart with its *dente truci*. The jaw seems right for a death-hold by any single
dog, or wolf. In Euripides's *Hecuba*, the Queen dreams of her daughter, Polyxena,
being sacrificed to the shade of Achilles, a similar, although self-explanatory
nightmare: ll. 90–94:

εἶδον γάρ βαλιὰν ἔλαφον λύκον αἵμονι χαλᾷ
σφαζομέναν, ἀπ' ἐμῶν γονάτων σπασθεῖσαν ἀνοίκτως·
καὶ τόδε δεῖμά μοι· ἦλθ'ὑπὲρ ἄκρας
τύμβον κορυφᾶς
φάντασμ' Ἀχιλέως·

Compare this with Erasmus's version, used by Buchanan in composing his *Jephthes*:

Vidi siquidem cervam variam
(visu miserum)
nostro e gremio vi direptam,
quam laniat lupus ore cruento.   ore: ungue *codd. aliquot*
Terrebar et hinc: summum in tumulum
umbra ferocis venit Achillis.

The manuscripts are divided between *ore* and *ungue*; the latter translates Euripides,
but *ore* was Erasmus's final choice, and seems preferable to me, although J. H.
Waszink chose the "claw" in his recent edition of the play;[3] but it is more appropriate for a member of the cat family than for the dog's. Shortly after, Storge's
description of her daughter as her *sola spes* is a somewhat inappropriate reworking of Hecuba's reliance on her only surviving son, in Erasmus's version (ll. 88–89):
qui iam solus / generis superest ancora nostri.

Quae sola spes et familiae solacium
superest, senectae columen unicum meae.

Buchanan also copied in part the setting for the nightmare, as translated by Erasmus:

Euripides, *Hecuba*, 70-71

ὦ πότνια χθών,
μελανοπτερύγων μῆτερ ὀνείρων

Erasmus, *Hecuba*, 78-79

tellus,
gignens atris somnia pennis...

Buchanan, *Jephthes*

nox mihi conscia curae,
nigris referens somnia pennis...

Just as Clytaemnestra is increasingly suspicious of danger to her young daughter, Iphigeneia, in Euripides's *Iphigeneia at Aulis* (the other Greek play translated by Erasmus), even so Queen Storge senses that the nightmare means mortal peril to her only surviving child, Iphis. But Iphis dismisses her mother's forebodings, and her horror of war: caedes, cruores, vastitatem, incendia / Profana, sacra, mixta (128), "butchery, bloodshed, devastation, infernos, confusion of sacred and profane," and its effects:

dolor dolori, luctui est luctus comes:
fratrem patremque perculit belli furor.   (134-35)

"Misery joined to misery, mourning to mourning; the madness of war has laid low my brother and my father alike." Instead, Iphis foresees her father's safe and truly glorious return (*incolumnis, laude cumulatum*), as victor in a just war, sanctioned by the Lord God (*bella qui suasit, Deus.* 143-45).

The Iphigeneia parallel increases the dramatic irony. As the Angel had pointed out, Jephtha had made a rash vow to God, that if he had God's help in defeating the Ammonites, he would sacrifice to him the very first *thing* that met him as he returned to his palace. Presumably some unlucky animal, or slave-attendant. Any young princess would be expected to wait demurely beside her mother. But the first word of l. 495, *Prodeo* ("I am coming out") neatly depicts the girl's impetuosity, her inability to wait in the Palace. Like the rash sister of Horatius, who ran forward to greet her triumphant brother, but burst into tears at the sight of her fiancé's spoils draped over her brother's shoulder. Livy suggests she got what she deserved, her brother's sword right through her heart. For Iphis, the sword is delayed.

But before we look at Jephtha's reaction, let us trace the sacrificial vow, the *victima* theme, throughout the play:

1. 58–59   *Angelus*
                  Quodcumque primum se obviam ferret sibi,
                  promisit *aris* se daturum *victimam.*

2. 417–18   *Chorus*
                  Festas *victima dux gregis*
                  aras imbuat:

3. 484–87   *Jephthes*
                  Quod primum ad aedes sospiti occurret meas,
                  tuas ad *aras imbuet* grata hostia
                  suo cruore; tuis beneficiis licet
                  par nulla possit comparari *victima*

4. 726–29   *Symmachus*   Oblata poterit perdere omnes *victima?*
                  Jephthes   Quae sola generis supererat spes *filia.*
                  S.   Hanc immolabis? Quae iubet necessitas?
                  J.   *Quod prima* nobis obvia redeuntibus.

5. 803–06   *Chorus*
                        patrio sed mactatu
                  victima diras *imbuet aras,*
                  et vice *brutae pecudis:* jugulo
                  calidam sanguinis evomet undam

6. 1144, 48   *Storge*
                  arae cruentae *victimis* nefariis. (cf. nefanda cruentus
                                          victima 734)
                  et me trucida *victimam* cum *filia.*

7. 1320   *Iphis*
                  Devota morti et consecrata *victima.*

8. 1372–73   *Nuntius*
                  Cum staret *aras* ante tristes *victima*
                  iam destinata *virgo*

Note also 1016–17 (Sacerdos) sacris *victimas* non quaslibet / mactare.

Both the Angel and Jephthes use the neuter, the first *indefinite*. Note the Chorus's expectation of a welcome-home sacrifice, but with *festas aras*; so *grata hostia* in l. 487. By l. 803, the Chorus suspects the worst, but it cannot complete the equation; the dumb animal is now only a parallel, *vice* ("in the manner of"). By l. 1144, Storge completes the picture, offering *herself* as a victim, together with her daughter — who stands before the "sad altars" as a virgin in the final messenger-speech. A key theme, skilfully developed throughout the play.

    Jephtha's first words in l. 499, *me miserum*, set the scene's irony and grim ambiguity at once. The highly dramatic dialogue that follows is worthy of Euripides at his best, like the poignant one between Agamemnon and his over-loving, over-trusting daughter, Iphigeneia. Like the Greek, Buchanan's dialogue uses stychomythia, on the surface an unexpected medium for such an emotional scene. The daughter, Iphis, is bubbling over with joy, and grows increasingly perplexed, while her father is shuddering with misery, and increasingly evasive. Finally he has to escape, leaving the tidying-up to his friend, Symmachus.

In the final scenes, Iphis, like Iphigeneia, shows more courage than her parents, and accepts her fate, for the good of her people, and for the sake of her father. Her patriotism perhaps simply reflects the Euripidean model, but it could either be a case of artistic self-delusion, or be implicit in God's threat of punishment if the vow is not fulfilled. Storge again criticizes the madness of war, and the primitive barbarity of such a rash covenant with God, but to no avail. Her final words contain a grim, uncompromising surprise:

> Quo fortiore nata tulit animo necem,
> Hoc angit animum tristior meum dolor.

"The braver my daughter was in bearing her death, the more bitter the pain that torments my mind." Iphis's great courage is not only no consolation, but provides the ultimate insult to her mother.

As I argued recently in *Humanistica Lovaniensia*,[4] it is likely that George Buchanan staged his four Latin tragedies between the years 1541 and 1544,[5] on the annual feast of St John the Baptist, it seems, the plays being performed before[6] the people of Bordeaux and the staff and students of the College of Guyenne, acted by its most talented Latinists, including the young Michel de Montaigne. I suggest that the leading rôles of young females were played by the precocious son of the Lord Mayor of Bordeaux, even though he does not say so explicitly in his *Essays* I,25.[7] The Latin plays written by Buchanan, Guérente and Muret were an integral part of the educational theories of the College's Principal, the brilliant administrator and Humanist, André de Gouveia, theories fully endorsed by Buchanan, and much admired by Montaigne. However, the possibly heretical message of his *Baptistes* and to a lesser degree of his *Jephthes*, both of which later on became favourites with the Lutherans, as well as his outspoken anti-franciscan poems, may have made Buchanan feel uneasy, especially at a time when the first heretics were being burnt in the Bordeaux area. After teaching in other schools in Paris and Toulouse, he finally left his adopted country, France, fortunately following an invitation from his old friend, André de Gouveia, to join him as professor at the new *Collegium Regale* in Coimbra, recently founded and richly endowed by the humanistic King of Portugal, John III. Several famous teachers, and scholars, from Bordeaux also joined André, including Diogo de Teive, João de Costa, Nicholas de Grouchy, Patrick Buchanan (the Humanist's brother), Elias Vinet, Arnaldo Fabricio and Guillaume Guérente.

Unfortunately André got sick with a stomach disorder, or more probably with arsenic-induced colic,[8] less than a year after the highly auspicious opening of the Royal College, when fit and well, and in the best of spirits, it would appear. He died most unexpectedly, with no friend present, and without time to confess, on 9 June 1548. At once trouble broke out between André's colleagues from Bordeaux, and a Paris-based faction, led by Diogo de Gouveia the Younger, but dominated and controlled through his agents by that rabid old critic of Erasmus and hunter-out of heresies, Diogo de Gouveia the Elder, one-time confidant of the Kings of Portugal and renowned Principal of the College of Ste Barbe in Paris. His college's recent closure was due to financial pressures (not paying the rent), arising in part from the young King's preference for Coimbra and André's college for the future training of administrators, priests and teachers for the great Portuguese empire. With his nephew, André, out of the way, old Diogo could turn the Inquisition on to André's friends, Da Costa, Teive, and Buchanan. They were formally denounced as heretics by his other nephew, and new Principal of the Royal College, Diogo de Gouveia the Younger. The trio were sufficiently astute, and innocent of real heresy, to avoid excommunication, or worse. However, incarceration in prison and then in primitive monasteries was deleterious both for their health and for their morale, although it did give Buchanan a chance to work on his superb Latin version of the *Psalms*. Thanks to the influence of King John, such as it was when up against the Spanish Inquisition, recently introduced into Portugal (by him, admittedly), the Humanists were released after less than two years of confinement, and Buchanan escaped to France, and from there eight years later to the Scottish Reformation.

Diogo de Teive was in fact allowed to return to the now emasculated College of the Arts, as its Principal, but only for two years (1552–54); soon afterwards, the Jesuits took over *in toto* (September 1555), despite opposition from the King. To prove his faith, Teive had entered the Church, and turned to writing for the Court. Among his many Latin eulogies of the King, perhaps the most elegant is his one surviving tragedy, *Ioannes Princeps*, which describes the poignant death of the young prince, John, recently married to Joanna, daughter of Charles V, and the King's last hope of a direct, legitimate successor to his throne.

It seems certain that there were regular dramatic performances at the *Collegium Regale* while André was in charge, that continued long after his death.[9] Besides the four Latin plays by Buchanan, two other plays were written by Teive, based on the stories of David and of Judith, but neither survives. However, Teive was not the only budding dramatist to see Buchanan's plays performed on the College stage. Between 1543 and 1551, young António Ferreira was studying for an Arts, and then a Law degree, enrolled for most of the time at the Royal College. According to the excellent study of his life by Adrien Roig,[9] this was the best period in António's career, with stimulating teachers (like Teive and Buchanan), passionate love-affairs, close friendships and exciting literary experimentations, in Portuguese especially. While at the College, he established himself as an exciting and key figure in the development of Portuguese poetry, the future "Horace of Portugal," composing both lyric poetry and lively comedies, and working on the first draft of his famous tragedy on *Inez de Castro*,[10] although it was not published until 1587, about thitry-three years after the appearance of Teive's *Ioannes Princeps*. Soares, in his edition of Teive's play, provides several examples of Ferreira's debt to Teive,[11] but he should have reversed the process. Certainly Ferreira greatly admired his old teacher and friend, and it is very likely that they exchanged notes in composing their plays, but I am far from convinced that Ferreira owed anything of importance to Teive: it was a very different matter with Buchanan.

Buchanan's plays were written for public performances, and were revised in the light of early productions. Teive's tragedy, however, although based on an actual historical event, and forecasting Portugal's imminent surrender to Spain, was written in a dramatic vacuum, as a purely academic eulogy and *consolatio* for the grieving King. As a *persona vix grata* with the Inquisition, Teive was by then but a shadow of the relatively free-thinking and outspoken Humanist of André's day. His Latin play is beautifully composed, but it lacks any real dramatic power, with stereotype and lifeless characters, long set-speeches, very little movement, minimal pathos, repetitive sycophancy and often banal philosophising.

This can be seen to some extent in his prophetic dream, Act I, ll. 27-96:

REGINA: Praesaga mens aliquid sinistrum enuntiat,
            nam multa uigilans, multa maesta somnians
            mecum ipsa meditor, cumque prorsus pellere
            et submouere hanc aegritudinem uolo,   30
            cum liberare conor his angoribus
            mentem inquietam, grauius atque acerbius
            agitatur illa, nec quidem ullo me otio,
            ulla quiete perfrui maestam sinit.
            Cum superiore nocte in his euoluerer   35
            defessa prorsus cogitationibus,
            ignara ferme somni et inscia lumina
            tandem occupauit durus et grauis sopor.
            Verum inter illa mihi uidebar somnia
            tam maesta uigilans esse; sed cum denuo   40
            animo reuoluo, denuo rem cogito,
            et torpor artus et animum angor occupat.

REX: Quid uana nobis praedicas insomnia?

REGINA: Vtinam illa uana et falsa caderent! Nec
            quidem
            quod uera ducam refero, sed quod maximum   45
            nobis timorem nocte tota incusserint
            et triste curis pectus infestauerint.
              Bis quina nobis lumina a Deo data
            credula putabam, quibus ut aureum iubar
            nostrum micabat corpus utque his omnia   50
            oculis uidebam, sic uidebar omnibus
            latisque terris fulgor eluxit meus.

Sed dira nostrum femina premebat latus.
Quid feminam dixi? Horribile portentum erat,
squalore, macie foeditateque efferum,   55
prae se furorem immanitatemque indicans;
excelso ab umero pharetra pendebat grauis,
immane robur foeda gestabat manus
arcus superbi, quem furore percita
(talis erat oris forma prodigio truci)   60
in nostra dirigebat atrox lumina
et singulis singula adimebat ictibus;
quotiesque lumen aliquod auferebat, heu!
toties putabam ui mihi cor erui.

Sed fessa uulnere repetito saepius,   65
tandem quieuit; unicoque lumine
mihi relicto ceterorum incommoda
solabar. Ingens sed timor nostram undique
mentem occupabat et pauore maximo
oppressa, ut illo mihi relicto lumine   70
frui daretur, supplici orabam prece.
Sed illa nullis precibus, ut tigris fera,
pietate nulla commouetur: unicum,
quod reliquum habebam lumen, abstulit mihi.

Tum quantus animum exulcerauerit dolor   75
quantusque maeror impetu saeuo egerit
suoque prorsus de statu deiecerit,
nequeo explicare. Taetra uisa protinus
caligo caecis nubibus cuncta occupans
obruere terras, cuncta diris questibus   80
late sonabant, cuncta lamentationibus
oppleta, quippe mundi euersi imaginem
prae se ferebant. Sic diu maestissimis
iacui tenebris consepulta, paruula
scintilla donec lumine exit ultimo,   85
quod lucis expers tum iacebat pristinae.

Haec me refecit et tenebrarum chaos
densissimum illud orbe toto depulit,
sed alia facies luminis primi fuit
aliusque lucis fulgor. His insomniis   90
nimium molestis praeterii noctem integram;
et adhuc (fatebor uera) pectus territant
stupidamque mentem tristibus curis premunt.

REX: Narrare tandem desine mihi somnia,

quae uera quamuis, exitu incerto accidant.   95
Habenda nulla Christiano bis est fides.

Soares argues that this has debts to the two similar appearances in Seneca's plays, first, that of Hector to Andromache in the *Troades*, ll. 438-460:

Partes fere nox alma transierat duas
clarumque septem verterant stellae iugum;
ignota tandem venit afflictae quies   440
brevisque fessis somnus obrepsit genis,
si somnus ille est mentis attonitae stupor;
cum subito nostros Hector ante oculos stetit,
non qualis ultro bella in Argivos ferens
Graias petebat facibus Idaeis rates,
nec caede multa qualis in Danaos furens
vera ex Achille spolia simulato tulit,
non ille vultus flammeum intendens iubar,
sed fessus ac deiectus et fletu gravis
similisque nostro, squalida obtectus coma.   450
iuvat tamen vidisse. tum quassans caput:
"dispelle somnos" inquit "et natum eripe,
o fida coniunx; latcat, haec una est salus.
omitte fletus! Troia quod cecidit gemis?
utinam iaceret tota. festina, amove
quocumque nostrae parvulam stirpem domus."
mihi gelidus horror ac tremor somnum expulit,
oculosque nunc huc pavida, nunc illuc ferens
oblita nati misera quaesivi Hectorem;
fallax per ipsos umbra complexus abit.   460

Secondly, that of Crispinus to Poppaea in the *Octavia*, ll. 712-39:

Confusa tristi proximae noctis metu
visuque, nutrix, mente turbata feror,
defecta sensu. laeta nam postquam dies
sideribus atris cessit et nocti polus,
inter Neronis iuncta complexus mei
somno resolvor; nec diu placida frui
quiete licuit. visa nam thalamos meos
celebrare turba est maesta; resolutis comis
matres Latinae flebiles planctus dabant;   720
inter tubarum saepe terribilem sonum
sparsam cruore coniugis genetrix mei
vultu minaci saeva quatiebat facem.
quam dum sequor coacta praesenti metu,

diducta subito patuit ingenti mihi
tellus hiatu; lata quo praeceps toros
cerno iugales pariter et miror meos,
in quis residi fessa.   venientem intuor
comitante turba coniugem quondam meum
natumque; properat petere complexus meos   730
Crispinus, intermissa libare oscula;
irrupit intra tecta cum trepidus mea
ensemque iugulo condidit saevum Nero.
tandem quietem magnus excussit timor;
quatit ossa et artus horridus nostros tremor
pulsatque pectus; continet vocem timor,
quam nunc fides pietasque produxit tua.
heu quid minantur inferum manes mihi
aut quem cruorem coniugis vidi mei?

NUTRIX

Octaviae discidia planxerunt sacros
inter penates fratris et patrium larem.
fax illa, quam secuta es, Augustae manu
praelata clarum nomen invidia tibi
partum ominatur. inferum sedes toros   750
stabiles futuros spondet aeternae domus

The first of these passages is very close to Vergil's in *Aeneid* II, except for the ending, where Hector asks his wife to save their son, victim finally of Ulysses's guile, as he leaps to his death from Priam's tower. The dream adds little to the plot, except to remind us of Hector, and of his son's unfulfilled rôle in rebuilding Troy. Poppaea's nightmare is more original and colourful. Its macabre nature is typical of Seneca, although the *Octavia* was almost certainly not written by him. The Nurse's reaction and misleading interpretation of Nero's future and of Poppaea's marriage prospects do provide some dramatic irony, but the scene has little real bearing on the plot. Soares suggests that Teive used several words from Seneca, but they are all commonplace material, to be found in any nightmare situation, words like night, peace, fear, terror etc. Far more significant are Teive's debts to Buchanan, his *Jephthes* in particular. Like the forceful *truci* that emphatically ends Storge's dream (l. 101), and describes the *prodigio* in Teive's (l. 60); and *eheu* opens Storge's lament, and marks the eye's loss in Teive's (l. 63). The King dismisses the Queen's dream as uncertain and unchristian (ll. 94–96), just as Iphis reinterprets her mother's fears. Like Storge, the Queen loses what she loves most, her last eye (*unicum lumen*, ll. 73–74), equal to Storge's *timidam agnam*. In both cases their future loss is expressed symbolically, unlike the explicit references to the son of Andromache, and to Nero's fate, and likewise to Achilles in the *Hecuba*.

Admittedly the atmosphere of misery and grief is hinted at with the mourners, led by Agrippina, who drive Poppaea into a chasm (ll. 722–26), but the *diris questibus, lamentationibus* and *maestissimis tenebris* of Teive's Queen (ll. 80–83), are much closer to Storge's *dolor* and *luctus* on ll. 114 and 134. But whereas Buchanan lets the sacrificial victim herself ridicule her mother's gloom, with heightened irony and dramatic power, Teive leaves it to the Queen's husband to dismiss her fears, almost casually. The *dira femina* (l. 53) is a compound of Seneca's *Hector* and Poppaea's Agrippina, with touches of a vengeful Diana. The total effect is somewhat ludicrous, with the monstrous fury, the prolonged assault on the Queen's many eyes, and her very slow recovery of sight. However, Teive's Latin is almost always exemplary, as in the contrast in ll. 83–85 between the *maestissimis tenebris consepulta*, with its grim, sibilant burial imagery, and the *parvula scintilla*, two *diminutives de tendresse*, for the first flicker of returning light.

Ferreira dedicated some poems to Teive, and like him, mourned the premature death of the newly-wed prince John. Both of their tragedies have themes taken from Portuguese history, a novel feature in European drama, and their plots and scenes, and many of their sentiments and images are very much alike, whoever imitated whom. However, I suggest that it was Buchanan's plays, especially his *Jephthes*, that in fact gave the original impetus and inspiration to both of them. In Ferreira's drama, its superbly controlled pathos, its realistic characterisations and its important political and moral themes are greatly indebted, in my view, to the brilliant Scottish playwright and teacher, George Buchanan.[12]

Again, this can be seen if we look at Inez' nightmare, Act III, Scene 2:

> Adormeci tam triste, que a tristeza
> Me fez tomar o sono mais pesado   45
> Do que nunca me lembra que tiuesse.
> Então sonhei que estando eu so num bosque
> Escuro, & triste, de huma sombra negra
> Cuberto todo, ouuia ao longe huns brados
> De feras espantosas, cujo medo   50
> M'arrepiaua toda & me impidia
> A lingua, & os pes, eu co'alma quasi morta
> Sem me mouer, meus filhos abraçaua.
> Nisto hum brauo Lião a mim se vinha
> Co a catadura fera, & logo manso   55
> Para tras se tornaua. Mas em s'indo,
> Não sey donde sahiam huns brauos Lobos,
> Que remetendo a mim com suas vnhas
> Os peitos me rasgauam. Então alçaua
> Vozes aos Ceos, chamaua meu Senhor;   60
> Ouuiame, & tardaua. E eu morria
> Com tanta saudade, que ind'agora

Parece que a cã tenho. E est'alma triste
Se m'arrancaua tam forçadamente,
Como quem ante tempo assi deixaua   65
Seu lugar, & deixaua pera sempre
(Que este na minha morte era o mòr mal)
A doce vista de quem me ama tanto.

AMA

Ay, & como estaria essa tu'alma
Tam morta! Deos te guarde! Mas as vezes   70

I went to sleep, so sad, that the sadness
Made me fall into the heaviest slumber   45
That I ever remember experiencing.
I dreamt, then, that I was alone in a wood,
Gloomy and sad, completely wrapped
In darkest shadow, when I heard far off
The roar of frightful beasts. The terror inspired by them   50
Made my body tremble and paralyzed
My tongue and my feet; my spirit nearly lifeless,
Without moving, I embraced my children.
At this point, a ferocious lion came towards me,
With a wild appearance; then, immediately tamed,   55
It retraced its steps. But as it left,
Some ferocious wolves came out from somewhere,
Which, leaping upon me, with their claws
Were tearing at my breast. So I implored
The Gods with loud cries, I called on my Lord;   60
He heard me, and was too late. I was dying
Of such intense, sad longing that it seems I am still
Oppressed by it. My sad soul
Broke away from my breast so reluctantly
As if it was leaving its dwelling-place   65
Prematurely, and was being separated for ever
(And in my death this was my greatest evil)
From the sweet sight of him who loves me so dearly.

NURSE

Alas! How your soul must have been
Crushed! May God protect you! But sometimes   70

The nightmare is very close to Storge's. Inez sees a ferocious lion approach her
and her children (ll. 54 f.), but suddenly withdraw, only to be replaced by a pack
of ferocious wolves, that rush upon her, and tear at her breast with their claws.

In Storge's dream, wolves attacked her and her lamb, but were driven off by the sheepdog, which then turned on her and tore the lamb from her lap with its cruel fangs. Storge's interpretation of it as death for her daughter is dismissed by an optimistic Iphis, just as Inez' vision of her own death is dismissed by an optimistic and reassuring nurse, or foster-mother (I.13: no amor mãy). The symbolism of the animal attacks in both cases involves all-conquering, recently returned Kings, Jephtha and Alfonso respectively, and death for their unfortunate daughter, Iphis, and daughter-in-law, Inez.

Both girls become victims of what purports to be "for the good of the State." In both plays, the King seems horrified, initially, at the sacrifice of innocence, whereas each girl meets her death with some peace of mind, thanks to a clear conscience. As Watson Irvine well argued in an otherwise disappointing article on this topic,[13] these two themes, the Machiavellian justification of what is necessary for the State, however immoral and unjust it may be, and the victim's final peace of mind and guiltlessness, are in neither case to be found in the Senecan, or in the Euripidean tradition. But both are pronounced themes of the *Baptistes*, and thence of the *Castro*. I agree with this view, but suggest that the *Jephthes* had a far greater influence than the *Baptistes*, as in the dramatic irony and animal imagery of both nightmares, in the pathos of the girls' innocence and trustfulness, and in their deaths, due to excessive and impulsive love, for Jephtha and for Pedro, respectively. In both plays, the girl's death is vividly and fully reported by a messenger, as in Greek tragedy, leading to unforgiving reactions from Storge and Pedro alike, whereas Teive's medical bulletins have little or no dramatic power, and the messenger in the *Baptistes* uses just one line to confirm the Chorus's fears. In both cases, the prophetic dream prepares the stage most effectively for the final showdown, between Iphis and her father, and between Inez and Alfonso, thereby creating two of the best scenes in early Renaissance drama, certainly very different from the catalogue of misery in Teive's lifeless eulogy of prince and King; in fact they are comparable with the best scenes in Classical drama.

University of Melbourne

Notes

1. Nair de Nazaré Castro Soares, *Diogo de Teive: Tragédia do príncipe João* (Coimbra, 1977). Cf. my review in *AUMLA*, 53 (1980), 104–05.

2. Adrien Roig (a) *La Tragédie "Castro" d'António Ferreira* (Paris, 1971) and (b) *António Ferreira: études sur sa vie et son œuvre (1528–1569)* (Paris, 1970).

3. J. H. Waszink *Opera Omnia Desiderii Erasmi Roterodami* I, 1 (Amsterdam, 1969), p. 227.

4. "Montaigne and George Buchanan," *HL* XXVI (1977), 132–42.

5. In fact he had translated Euripides's *Medea* a few years before in Paris, while improv-

ing his Greek. See P. J. Ford *George Buchanan: Prince of Poets* (Aberdeen U.P., 1982), pp. 70-71.

6. Not "by," as in I. D. McFarlane's translation of *apud* in his *Buchanan* (London, 1981), p. 117, one of the few blemishes in an excellent biography of the Scotsman.

7. Essays, I, 25: "avant l'aage 'Alter ab undecimo tum me vix ceperat annus' j'ay sou-stenu les premiers personnages és tragedies latines de Bucanan, de Guérente et de Muret, qui se représentèrent en notre collège de Guyenne avec dignité." It would be natural for a young boy fluent in Latin to play a girl; embarrassing in later years?

8. I hope to provide medical and other evidence to support this claim in a forthcoming monograph.

9. Op. cit (b), p. 73.

10. Cf. Roig op. cit. (b), pp. 102-03, ending "tout le théâtre d'António Ferreira serait ainsi lié à sa vie d'étudiant à Coimbra."

11. Op. cit, pp. 97-132; cf. also R. Lebègue, *La Tragédie religieuse en France (1514-1573)* (Paris, 1929), p. 253: "*Jephthes* doit certainement plus à Euripide qu'à Sénèque."

12. Cf. J. P. Wickersham Crawford *Spanish Drama before Lope de Vega* (Oxford UP, 1937), p. 162: "It is to these college performances that we owe Ferreira's *Castro*, the first Portu-guese tragedy written according to Classical models."

13. Anthony Watson, "George Buchanan and António Ferreira's *Castro*," *BHS* 31 (1954), 65-77.

Buchanan and Classical Drama[1]

P. G. Walsh

The main focus of this paper is *Jephthes*, undoubtedly Buchanan's greatest achievement in the field of drama; but it will be useful to devote preliminary if brief attention to his translations of *Medea* and *Alcestis*, and to his other original play *Baptistes*, in order to trace our playwright's developing dramatic talent and maturing Classical sensibility.

Though Buchanan learnt some Latin before leaving Killearn for France in 1520, it was in Paris that he laid the foundations of his career as dramatist. There he developed his remarkable facility at Latin versification, to earn the accolade of the younger Scaliger: "unus est in tota Europa, omnes post se relinquens in latina poesi."[2] In Paris too he took up the serious study of Greek so successfully that by 1530 at the age of twenty-four he was thoroughly versed in both languages.[3] A letter written many years later to Daniel Rogers[4] reveals that he translated Euripides's *Medea* to develop his knowledge of Greek, and this must have been in these formative years in Paris. The evidence of the Latin autobiography, which states that the composition of *Medea* followed after *Baptistes*[5] as the second of the four tragedies mounted at the Collège de Guyenne at Bordeaux, is only apparently contradictory; we can easily reconcile the conflicting evidence by assuming that earlier in Paris he had already roughed out a translation of *Medea* into Latin prose and had then, following the pioneering example of Erasmus, shaped the prose-version into verses; later at Bordeaux during his initial period of hectic pedagogy in 1542–43, he will have put the *manus extrema* to his translation after having earlier completed *Baptistes*.

Thus the translation of *Medea* at Paris formed his early apprenticeship to dramatic composition, and the work as published in 1544 bears some of the marks of the novice. McFarlane disagrees,[6] believing that the work as published was distinctly different from any earlier version. He suggests that Buchanan has translated *Medea* from the text of the 1537 edition of Hervagius, which of course could not have been available to him in his earlier years in Paris.[7] In fact, however, the Hervagius edition is slavishly identical with the Aldine, except for one or two marks of punctuation which may be misprints. The likelihood is that Buchanan translated the 1503 Aldine edition of Euripides at Paris, and that the revision at Bordeaux was rudimentary.

There are two internal reasons which encourage the speculation that the 1544 translation of *Medea* is substantially the work of the less mature Buchanan. First there are errors in translation; our forthcoming edition lists over thirty of these. The achievement is nonetheless impressive. *Medea* is notoriously corrupt textually in its choral odes, and the Aldine text is seriously deficient; and since the great Greek Thesaurus of Henri Estienne (Stephanus), the basis of every Greek lexicon down to Liddell-Scott-Jones, did not appear until 1572, Buchanan was dependent on such less comprehensive aids as Guarino, Toussain, and Budé's *Commentarii linguae graecae*. Given the difficulties, the translation is meritorious, but it does not match the accuracy of Buchanan's later rendering of *Alcestis*. Secondly, there are metrical criteria for dating the translation of *Medea* early. Fries and McFarlane draw attention to a technical deficiency in Buchanan's deployment of the anapaestic dimeter; in no fewer than a hundred lines of *Medea* there is no diaeresis between the two halves of the line. Both Euripides and Seneca regularly observe the diaeresis, but interestingly Erasmus in his translations of Euripides's *Hecuba* and *Iphigenia at Aulis* does not. In his three other dramatic compositions Buchanan avoids this solecism, so that the pattern is clear: *Medea* was composed first after close study of Erasmus, and by the time Buchanan turned to *Baptistes*, closer study of Euripides and Seneca had taught him to observe the diaeresis in the anapaestic dimeter.[8]

This mention of Erasmus as model—Buchanan speaks admiringly of his achievement as translator in the prefatory letter to *Medea*[9]—prompts the suggestion that the comparative merits of the two translators would repay detailed study. Erasmus is the pioneer, and a man who works at breakneck speed because his projects are so many. These limitations enable Buchanan to win the palm. He is certainly more succinct and disciplined than Erasmus; his handling of the iambic trimeter is more mellifluous; and some of his choral odes, notably in *Alcestis*, stand comparison with the originals in Euripides.

Buchanan's entry into drama by way of Euripides has significant results; Euripides is much more important as a formative influence than is Seneca. Buchanan clearly read Seneca's plays as part of his apprenticeship; in our edition we draw attention to close reminiscences of *Hercules Furens*, *Phaedra*, and *Troades*. But the influence of Seneca is superficial rather than deep. First, structure; in his two original plays Buchanan ignores the "law" of five acts laid down by Horace in his *Ars Poetica*[10] and meticulously observed by Seneca; both the biblical plays have seven acts, which accords with the more flexible Greek convention of five, six or seven parts. Secondly, characterisation; Buchanan does not exploit obvious opportunities of incorporating Senecan strands into his characters. In *Baptistes* Herod bears no close resemblance to any of Seneca's tyrannical kings; nor does John the Baptist reflect any of the traits of Hercules, the Stoic exemplar of virtue who likewise made his way to heaven. In *Jephthes*, Storge is not invested with elements of the persona of Clytemnestra in Seneca's *Agamemnon* as she mourns the death of Iphigenia, and Jephthes himself is not enriched by reminiscences of Seneca's Oedipus, though both curse themselves for past misdeeds. The only clear evidence of thematic influence from Seneca comes in the final act of *Jephthes*, where motifs of Seneca's *Troades* are visible,[11] as we shall later see. In all these fundamental respects Euripides is much the more important as a formative influence. Seneca comes into his own in the more superficial realms of sentiment and style. Certain rhetorical commonplaces (the nature of kingship in *Baptistes*, the contrast between king and peasant in *Jephthes*, and above all the uncertainty of fortune in both) and certain tricks of style and metre betray the influence of Seneca, but it does not impinge at the deeper levels of plot, character or fundamental theme.

When Buchanan began to teach at Bordeaux, he was required to compose annually a Latin play for performance by his pupils. *Baptistes* was the first to be performed there in 1543, but Buchanan did not publish his text until over thirty years later in 1577, and only then in response to vigorous promptings. The reason for this hesitancy is manifest in the prefatory letter to James VI of Scotland; in this letter he calls the play a *foetus abortivus*, a premature offspring. What exactly does he mean? Critics have been distracted from a proper consideration of the deficiencies because their attention has been directed predominantly to unravelling the play as a *pièce à clé*, visualised in terms of the personalities at the French or Scottish or English court.[12]

The extraordinary prologue to the play may not be as helpful in illuminating these deficiencies as at first appears. Buchanan here speaks *propria persona* to complain of carping critics and to categorise the play and its message. But if we remember that this was Buchanan's first play to be performed, and that it was mounted before schoolboys, we have to ask ourselves why the author waxes so bitter about captious criticism. It is noteworthy that such a personal introduction is quite inappropriate to the performance of a tragedy, as distinct from a Terentian comedy. Moreover, the play stands quite well without it, since the long speech of the rabbi Malchus which follows itself bears all the marks of a prologue. It is tempting to conclude that the prologue was not a part of the original production, but was appended shortly before publication in 1577, after Buchanan had incurred criticism of his other dramatic works. And if this suspicion is justified, the emphasis laid in the Prologue (and in the sub-title) upon calumny as the unifying theme may be retrospective, a valiant attempt to lend unity and coherence to a disjointed plot.

The fundamental flaw in the play is that it carries two separate and unconnected themes. The first is the conflict between the religious establishment, represented by the rabbi Malchus, and the reforming prophet John himself. The second is the theme of corrupt kingship as personified in Herod and challenged by John's *nuda virtus*. The fact that both topics, the need for religious reformation and the arbitrary nature of royal power, were burning sixteenth-century issues made the prospect of John as a tragic hero attractive, and McFarlane is able to cite half-a-dozen other dramatic productions devoted to him in the 1530s and 1540s.[13]

Buchanan's retrospective self-criticism of his play as a *foetus abortivus* must be directed at this weakness in plot and structure, and more generally at his own failure to observe the Aristotelian canons for tragedy. There is an enormous gulf between *Baptistes* and *Jephthes* in this respect. *Baptistes* is a biblical play which is essentially faithful to the narrative-account of the New Testament, and as such is the heir to the medieval tradition of sacred drama; though *Jephthes* likewise has a biblical theme, it is more freely handled according to Aristotelian precept and Euripidean practice.

If we analyse *Baptistes* according to the Aristotelian "rules," a major problem is the nature of the hero. John the Baptist is on every count the antithesis of the Aristotelian hero, who must be a man between moral extremes, a man not out-standingly good or just. He must also be highly renowned and prosperous; from this point of view a Job amongst biblical characters would be more appropriate than a John.[14] But Aristotle would have regarded the defects in the plot as even more serious. John's death is not the result of his own error or flaw (*harmartia*), but is induced externally by the request of Salome and her mother Herodias. There is no reversal (*peripateia*) and no recognition (*anagnorisis*). Finally, the play is episodic. "I call a plot episodic" says Aristotle "when the episodes or acts succeed each other without probable or necessary sequence."[15] The episodic nature of *Baptistes* results from its presentation of the two unrelated themes. Buchanan could have interconnected the two conflicts of prophet *versus* religious establishment and naked virtue *versus* tyranny; he could have created the rabbi Malchus as a clerical Iago responsible for poisoning the minds of queen Herodias and of Herod, so that in consequence of Malchus's calumny they were induced to encompass John's destruction. If that had been the sequence of events in the play, calumny would indeed have been its appropriate subtitle.

The reason why Buchanan did not stage a tragedy on these lines was that he wished to remain faithful to the gospel-account, and there is no hint in scripture that John's criticisms of the Jewish religious establishment caused his death. So, as McFarlane rightly remarks, "When one has finished reading the play, one does not feel that calumny is the major theme."[16] What Buchanan has done is to augment the basic outline of the gospel-narrative with imaginative dialogues exploring the theme of *ecclesia semper reformanda*; and the result is a series of sepa-rate and disconnected episodes, so that the play contains little action. As Lebègue remarks of Buchanan with regard to this play, "il s'est peu soucié de l'action dra-matique."[17]

We must not of course insist on the Aristotelian "rules" as the sole criteria of a good play; the *Baptistes* contains memorable characterisation in the persons of Malchus and John, and a Christian reader may well find inspiration in John's attitudes towards the claims of God as against earthly powers, and towards the prospect of spiritual life succeeding physical death. But the point which must be stressed is that the advance from *Baptistes* to *Jephthes* represents an advance from a biblical, historical, non-Aristotelian conception of tragedy towards one which, in the words of Buchanan's contemporary Roger Ascham, "is able to abide the true touch of Aristotle's precepts and Euripides's examples."[18]

Between the composition of *Baptistes* and that of *Jephthes* Buchanan must have studied Aristotle's *Poetics* with care. In his recent study of Buchanan's theory and practice as a poet, Philip Ford rejects this thesis of Aristotelian influence on the *Jephthes* because "it was not until later in the century that the Greek philosopher's views began to exercise any influence in this field in France."[19] But Ford is thinking of the diffusion of the *Poetics* in the vernaculars, and it is certainly true that the first translation, that by Segni into Italian, did not appear until 1549. But Buchanan was by now capable of mastering Aristotle not only in his Latin dress but also in the Greek original, and three different editions of the *Poetics* had been published by 1536, the year which also saw the publication of the revised Latin translation by Pazzi.[20] McFarlane's account of Buchanan's sojourn in Bordeaux offers food for speculation here, with the information that Aristotle was one of the authors read at the Collège de Guyenne,[21] and more important that Buchanan was on friendly terms with Julius Caesar Scaliger, the greatest sixteenth-century authority on the *Poetics*.[22] The arguments for a knowledge of the *Poetics* developed by Buchanan at Bordeaux seem to me to be overwhelming. He has certainly created in Jephthes a hero renowned and prosperous, as Aristotle demands. There is a *hamartia*, the taking of the vow; a *peripateia*, when the vow impinges on his only daughter; and an *anagnorisis* which is powerful in the development of the action. Above all, the play is not episodic, but is built up cumulatively to create highly effective Aristotelian drama, in which the unities are observed. The *Book of Judges*[23] tells us that there was an interval of two months between Jephthes's return and the sacrifice of his daughter; by enclosing both in "a single revolution of the sun," as Aristotle demands, Buchanan tacitly abandons his fidelity to the Old Testament chronology, and observes the Aristotelian unity of time.[24]

So much for the Aristotelian theory. I should now like to examine *Jephthes* act by act to establish how Buchanan has achieved his aim by close structural imitation of the two plays of Euripides which had been translated by Erasmus, namely *Hecuba* and *Iphigenia at Aulis*.[25] In reading *Jephthes* side by side with the two models by Euripides, one is powerfully reminded of the Greek motto of the University of Edinburgh, *diploun horōsin hoi mathontes grammata* ("Those who have learned letters have a double vision"). Men of learning see the world both directly through their own eyes, and vicariously through the eyes of earlier creative writers. So they exploit the vision of poetic predecessors to unite it with their own, and they thereby achieve that complex presentation of situations and characters which we dignify with the name of creative imitation. In the case of *Jephthes* we are speaking not merely of verbal evocation, of the reminiscence of an apposite phrase of

Horace, Ovid or Vergil, but of thematic imitation, in which the structure of a whole act is derived repeatedly from the Euripidean models.

The biblical account of the history of Jephthes in *Judges*, chapter 11 is short and lacking in circumstantial detail. This allowed Buchanan considerable scope to indulge his creative imagination in plot, character, and situation. He visualised the sacrifice of Jephthes's daughter through the eyes of Euripides, whose *Iphigenia at Aulis* enacts Agamemnon's sacrifice of his daughter Iphigenia to appease the goddess Artemis as the prelude to the Trojan War, and whose *Hecuba* incorporates the sacrifice of Polyxena, virgin daughter of Priam and Hecuba, to appease the shade of Achilles in the aftermath to the same war. Buchanan had studied Erasmus's Latin versions of these plays during his apprenticeship as translator, and now he exploits that knowledge by his choice and treatment of the Jephthes theme.

Before we turn to analysis of the play we must briefly consider the significance of the names of the characters. The only name taken from *Judges* is that of Jephthes himself; the others are invented by Buchanan who follows the convention of ancient comedy and satire. The wife of Jephthes is called Storge, which in Greek denotes dutiful love rather than sexual passion. The name initially establishes her firmly as a mother rather than as a wife; and the choice of a Greek rather than a Hebrew name directs us towards Clytemnestra and Hecuba, the ravaged mothers in the plays of Euripides. The name Iphis, invented by Buchanan, for Jephthes's daughter may have three points of reference. First, it sounds cognate with Jephthes. Second, it recalls the Iphis of Ovid's *Metamorphoses*;[26] in Ovid's story Iphis is born a girl but reared as a boy, because her father Ligdus had commanded that if a girl were born to him she should be put to death. The connecting theme in Ovid and in Buchanan of the girl whose father wills her destruction is surely not coincidental. But thirdly and most important, Iphis is an alternative form, found in the Greek of the Alexandrians,[27] for Iphigenia; Jephthes's daughter is thus depicted as a second Iphigenia. The only other named character in the play is Symmachus, his Greek name indicating his role as trusty war-comrade.

The play opens with the prologue delivered by an angel. He first recounts the troubled history of Israel, then outlines the victory of Jephthes over Ammon, and finally acquaints the audience with the disastrous vow by which Jephthes has promised to sacrifice, upon his return home, the first of his possessions on which his eye falls. The angel is the appropriate Hebraic equivalent for the all-seeing deity or ghost which performs a similar function in individual plays of Euripides and Seneca. Sypherd, in his excellent book on the history of the Jephthes theme,[28] suggests that Mercury in the *Amphitruo* of Plautus is the inspiration here, but that connexion is more apparent than real. The entire first act, including the prologue, is modelled on the first episode in Euripides's *Hecuba*, in which the ghost of Polydorus, son of Priam, delivers a prologue of similar length which likewise outlines the troubled history of his afflicted land, together with the circumstances presaging the sacrifice of his sister Polyxena. That *Hecuba* is Buchanan's model here is demonstrated by the fact that Polydorus's prologue is followed by a grief-stricken dialogue between mother and daughter, Hecuba and Polyxena; so too in *Jephthes* a dialogue now ensues, after the angel's prologue, between the mother Storge and her daughter Iphis.

If we needed further proof that Buchanan is consciously shaping his preliminary act after *Hecuba*, it is provided when both mothers recount to their daughters parallel dreams. Hecuba relates how in sleep she seemed to hold in her lap a dappled fawn, but a wolf wrenched it away and rent it with bloody claws; the dream presages the sacrifice of Polyxena, torn from Hecuba's embrace, on the altar of the Greeks. Buchanan's adaptation is masterly. Storge recounts how in *her* dream a wolf attacked the sheepfold, and the trusty sheepdog drove off the wolf. But on its return the dog itself snatched the lamb from Storge's arms and tore it with cruel teeth.[29] This prophetic image of the death of Iphis at the hands of her own father Jephthes is creative imitation at its finest. Throughout this scene in *Jephthes* it is notable how Iphis's attempts to reassure her mother Storge parallel the initial gaiety of Polyxena in *Hecuba* until Polyxena is told of the grim news of her future.

The first Choral Ode follows, recited by the band of Jewish women in two of the favourite metres of Seneca, the Lesser Asclepiad and the Sapphic. The theme of God's displeasure that has brought suffering to Israel is introduced by an invocation to the river Jordan. Buchanan here exploits a choral ode in *Iphigenia at Aulis*[30] where the description of the situation at Troy likewise begins with the citation of the river Simoeis, and there is a clear echo of that passage in *Jephthes*. But as we have noted, *Hecuba* is the main Euripidean quarry in this first part of the play; and we observe how when the Chorus announces the arrival of the messenger from the battlefield, the line has been adapted from the end of the first episode of *Hecuba*, which similarly announces the arrival of Odysseus bearing news.[31]

Act II of *Jephthes* consists of a dialogue between the messenger and the Chorus, during which the messenger details Jephthes's military victory. It was necessary for Buchanan to incorporate this historical content into his play so that the drama could unfold on Aristotelian lines, and represent the change of Jephthes's fortunes from good to bad. But there was no scene of this kind in either of the plays of Euripides translated by Erasmus. Buchanan must accordingly roam further afield in search of a model for creative imitation. As Lebègue notes, there are striking evocations in this act of Plautus's *Amphitruo*.[32] As any student of Buchanan's poetry knows, Buchanan is constantly employing the language of Roman comedy, but here we speak of the creative imitation which invests a whole scene with Plautine subject-matter. The flavour, however, is wholly different in *Jephthes*. In Plautus the rascally slave Sosia rehearses how he will tell Alcmena of her husband Amphitruo's victory: first how Amphitruo offered peace with justice rather than battle, but when this met with a haughty reply from the Teleboians, how he routed the enemy from the field. Buchanan uses the same sequence of topics for the messenger's speech, but the tone is more solemn and triumphant, as is appropriate.[33] Then, at the climax of the messenger's account, when his speech declaims how the sky was rent with lightning and thunder as a portent of divine favour, Buchanan merges with the Plautine sequence a reminiscence of the eighth book of Vergil's *Aeneid*, where a similar portent from the sky presages the arrival of Venus with the arms of Aeneas manufactured by Vulcan.[34]

The tidings of victory are followed by the second Choral Ode, in which the victory is attributed to the God of Israel, and festive rejoicing proclaimed. The ode begins in iambic dimeters and ends with glyconics. We should be sensitive to the implications of such metrical variations. Though the iambic dimeter is very occasionally found in Classical poetry, it is preeminently the medium of the great fourth-century innovation in Christian poetry, the Ambrosian hymn. In this celebration of divinely-guided victory, we hear repeated echoes of the hymns of Ambrose and Prudentius,[35] and in combination with these echoes the metre imparts a sacred flavour to the ode, suggesting to the reader the baptism of the Classical form. Then in the ensuing glyconics are clear reminiscences of Lucretius, Horace and Ovid,[36] so that in sum we find that synthesis of Christian and Classical *auctores* which is characteristic of much Renaissance poetry.

Now follows in Act III an extended dialogue between the warrior-leader and his daughter. Jephthes arrives home from battle to be greeted by an exultant Iphis, but recollection of his vow turns his joy to silent consternation. Clearly Buchanan found the model for this whole act in Euripides's *Iphigenia at Aulis*; the verbal echoes[37] of Erasmus's translation to which Sharratt has drawn attention are an indication of a deeper and more fundamental debt to Euripides. At this stage of the play, Jephthes cannot bring himself to reveal to his daughter the true reason for his displeasure, and there is a recurrent dramatic irony as the audience shares with Jephthes the knowledge as yet concealed from his daughter. This ironical sequence is adapted from the parallel dialogue in *Iphigenia* between Agamemnon and his daughter; the king knows, and the audience knows, that Iphigenia is to be sacrificed, but the girl in her ignorance is baffled by the frowns and tears of her father. The debt to Euripides in this act extends even to the manipulation of characters on stage. In Euripides, Iphigenia leaves the stage as Clytemnestra enters to be told the fiction that her daughter is to marry Achilles; in *Jephthes* the girl is ordered off-stage by her father to permit the entrance of Symmachus the comrade-warrior, whose dialogue with Jephthes is to provide the stuff of Act IV.

The third Choral Ode in the Pherecratean metre is a condemnation of the malice and back-biting which the Chorus, sharing the ignorance of Iphis, believes is responsible for Jephthes's apparent displeasure with his daughter. But the ode is perfunctory; Buchanan is anxious to resume the action.

The three acts which now follow bring cumulative pressure to bear on Jephthes to renounce the terms of his vow. First Symmachus elicits the facts, and seeks to dissuade his commander with the arguments of common-sense. Next the rabbi uses his priestly authority to persuade Jephthes that his proposed course of action is both unnatural and displeasing to God. Finally, as climax comes the pressure from kin — from Jephthes's wife Storge and from the innocent Iphis herself.

Though there is in neither of the plays of Euripides translated by Erasmus a closely similar parallel to inspire the dialogue of Act IV between the general and his trusty lieutenant Symmachus, Buchanan here ingeniously exploits the structure and argumentation of the initial scene of *Iphigenia at Aulis*. In that play Agamemnon reveals his distress and the reasons for it to his old and trusty slave, and thus obliquely to the audience; the priest Chalcas has ordered the sacrifice of the king's daughter Iphigenia to propitiate Artemis. Once again there are verbal echoes in *Jephthes* of Erasmus's translation which direct the vigilant reader to this parallel scene in Euripides; so we are enabled to observe the similarity when Jephthes reminds Symmachus of the occasion and nature of the vow which is to make Iphis a victim like Iphigenia. Then Jephthes proclaims the happiness of the low-born in contrast to the misery of those in high estate, just as Agamemnon in Euripides utters similar sentiments, though Erasmus allots the speech mistakenly to the old slave.[38] It is interesting to note that when Symmachus challenges these sentiments of Jephthes—that it is better to be an untroubled nonentity than a harassed statesman—the rebuttal echoes the words of Sallust's exordium to the *Catiline*, that to live inert and inglorious is a species of non-existence.[39]

The Choral Ode which follows laments the mutability of fortune in anapaestic dimeters. Though the message is appropriate to the dramatic change in Jephthes's situation, Buchanan seems all too aware that it is the most threadbare of Senecan themes, and he seeks to relieve the monotony by sucessive evocation of Lucretius, Ovid, Horace and Statius.[40] Even so it is the kind of ode which a Buchanan (or a Seneca) could have composed in bed or between dinner-courses, and this impression of facile versification is reinforced when we read that sadness follows joy as darkness follows sunlight, and harsh winter follows spring.[41] Alas, harsh winter does not follow spring, but the critical faculties of the hearer are as numbed by the clichés as those of the composer. Buchanan is writing mechanically on an undemanding theme.

Act V represents the intellectual kernel of the drama, the point at which the theological implications of vows are probed, and the contemporary controversies are aired. Two main issues are being resolved here; first, the extent to which an individual's vow is binding if it impinges on the welfare of a second party, here Iphis; and second, the issue of ritual sacrifice. Buchanan cannot look to Euripides for guidance on these themes, and this act is wholly non-Classical in its inspiration. The condemnation by the rabbi of Jephthes's unflinching adherence to his vow closely approximates to the view of St Thomas Aquinas, whose *Summa*[42] approvingly quotes the judgment of St Jerome[43] that Jephthes was foolish in making the vow and impious in adhering to it. Buchanan's *auctores* in this theological dialectic are not the Classical dramatists but the writers of the Old Testament. The theme that God finds bloody sacrifices unacceptable is pervasive in *Isaiah* and in *Psalms*, and it is taken up repeatedly by the fourth-century Christian poets whom Buchanan knows well, Prudentius and Paulinus of Nola.[44] Characteristically, however, Buchanan combines with these Hebraic and Christian evocations a reminiscence of Ovid's *Metamorphoses*, a passage in which Ovid likewise protests against the ascription to the gods of the cruelty with which men ritually slaughter innocent animals.[45]

The ensuing Choral Ode again finds Buchanan hard-pressed to achieve a theme which is both relevant and original; again he has recourse to sentiments about life's uncertainties, and finds creative satisfaction in the facility with which he incorporates evocations of a wide range of classical authors; his hope is that his readers will capture and savour the reminiscences. But such evocation surely gets out of hand when in addition to the recognisable borrowings from Vergil, Horace and Ovid, Buchanan builds into this ode a sustained echo of the comic novel of Petronius;[46] the relevance of the theme of the unscrupulous legacy-hunters of Croton to the tragic situation of Jephthes seems remote. Perhaps the most apposite of these literary echoes here is a reminiscence of a dramatic fragment of Ennius. In the prefatory letter (addressed to Jean de Luxembourg) to his translation of *Medea*, Buchanan cites this early Latin poet as a formidable predecessor in the art of translating Greek drama into Latin verses;[47] Ennius, like Erasmus, wrote an *Iphigenia* which was a close imitation of *Iphigenia at Aulis*. Buchanan here imitates one of the dozen surviving fragments of Ennius's play, as is shown by his parade of the rare word *praeterpropter*, "here or thereabouts."

The penultimate act brings mother and daughter on stage to confront Jephthes in the emotional climax — the final desperate appeal for the renunciation of the vow. Buchanan here adopts the structure and motifs of Euripides's *Iphigenia at Aulis* at the point where Agamemnon is similarly confronted by Clytemnestra and Iphigenia. In *Jephthes*, Storge begins the action of the scene by lamenting that her daughter has been robbed of impending marriage, and of the hope of husband and children. There is a hint of this theme in the Book of Judges, since Jephthes's daughter retires to the mountains for two months to lament her wasted virginity; but it is much more explicit in the developed legend of Iphigenia in the Classical authors. In Euripides, Agamemnon pretends that Iphigenia is to marry Achilles, and more strikingly the theme of deprivation of marriage is taken over by Lucretius in his celebrated depiction of Iphigenia as a victim of *superstitio*.[48] Storge now urges Iphis to make a personal appeal to her father; the girl's moving speech closely parallels Iphigenia's in the Greek play. When Jephthes appropriates to himself the entire blame, and Iphis proclaims that harsh necessity is his master, she is echoing the sentiments of Iphigenia; likewise when she pleads with her mother not to be angry with Jephthes.[49]

Some critics here suggest that Buchanan's Iphis is a more mature and majestic character in the acceptance of her fate than is Iphigenia. Michael Mueller in his *Children of Oedipus* draws attention to the observation of St Ambrose, that the willing acceptance by Jephthes's daughter of her fate transforms the rash vow into a species of noble martyrdom.[50] This is the direction in which Buchanan has guided the basic elements of Iphis's characterisation away from the similarities to the heroine of Euripides's *Iphigenia at Aulis*. These similarities include not only the marriage-motif already mentioned, but also an extraordinary emphasis on the patriotism of Iphis; "I offer my life" she says "to my father and to my country." The ritual sacrifice of Iphis in itself hardly demands the repeated emphasis on patriotism which it receives, although it can be claimed that her free acceptance of the term of the vow ensures for Israel the fruits of her military victory. But Buchanan is surely visualising Iphis here as a second Iphigenia; in the frame of the Trojan war the sacrifice of the daughter permits the Greek ships to sail on their errand of public vengeance.

So too in the Choral Ode which follows Buchanan's emphasis on the fame of Iphis as a patriot, and his condemnation of those who lack such patriotic altruism, seem excessive if the heroism is visualised within her national boundaries; Iphis has now assumed the role of international martyr in which the persona of Iphigenia is subsumed. It is notable that Buchanan here borrows from Erasmus's rendering of Euripides the image of the warrior-girl, the girl with a man's spirit (*animi virilis*).[51] It is surely not fanciful to suggest that Buchanan thinks here of another virgin patriot, of the Joan of Arc who resumed her male attire before being burned at the stake as a martyr for France.

Buchanan's final act is likewise structured after *Iphigenia at Aulis*. In both plays a messenger reports the details of the sacrifice to the stricken mother. But there is a vital difference in the denouement of the two plays. In Euripides's drama Iphigenia is miraculously removed, and a hind found in her place; but there is no such deliverance for Iphis in *Jephthes*. So Buchanan can adapt only the preliminaries to the sacrifice from *Iphigenia at Aulis*; for example, there is a crowd of onlookers at the ritual much more appropriate to the Greek context than to the Hebraic one, and again, Jephthes cloaks his eyes at the fatal blow just as Agamemnon does.[52] But Buchanan now looks elsewhere for inspiration, and *Hecuba*, the other play of Euripides translated by Erasmus, was a useful quarry. Just as Iphis in *Jephthes* has to encourage the priest to strike—"at tu, sacerdos, quid metuis?"—so does Polyxena in *Hecuba*.[53] And it is here in the final act that Seneca comes into prominence; the passage of the *Troades* in which Astyanax, the young son of Hector and Andromache, is ritually murdered, is repeatedly evoked here, especially in the messenger's description of the morbid fascination of the crowd, and in the portrayal of the victim who alone is dry-eyed amidst the throng of weeping bystanders.[54]

This paper has attempted to demonstrate the truth of the perceptive observation of Roger Ascham, that *Jephthes* "is able to abide the true touch of Aristotle's precepts and Euripides's examples." In its essence the structural scheme is simple; five of the seven acts are based on similar scenes in Euripides's *Hecuba* or *Iphigenia at Aulis* or both. Into them is sewn another act inspired by the *Amphitruo* of Plautus, and another for which the Bible and Christian poets furnished sustained reminiscences. In the terms familiar to us from Roman rhetoric, this process of imaginative recreation and structuring represents *inventio* and *dispositio*. Each act is then invested with the appropriate *elocutio*, which involved the artistic evocation of a wide range of Latin poets and prose-writers, both Classical and Christian. By his close observation of Aristotelian theory and Euripidean practice, Buchanan has transported us a whole world away from his lesser achievement in *Baptistes*. For this reason, I believe, the celebrated tribute of Sir Philip Sidney in his *Apology for Poetry*, that "The Tragedies of Buchanan doe justly bring forth a divine admiration," should be applied more enthusiastically to *Jephthes* than to *Baptistes*.

University of Glasgow

Notes

1. This paper was composed shortly after the completion of the edition of *The Tragedies of George Buchanan* (Scottish Academic Press, 1983). I should like to express my debt to my collaborator in that edition, Dr Peter Sharratt; he has already made a perceptive study of the Classical sources of *Jephthes* in the *Acts of the Fourth Neo-Latin Conference*. The second crutch supporting me in the production of this paper has been Ian McFarlane's monumental *Buchanan* (London, 1981). A most useful analysis of *Jephthes* visualised in the tradition of Greek drama can be found in Martin Mueller's *Children of Oedipus* (Toronto, 1980).

2. Quoted in Sandys, *A History of Classical Scholarship* (Cambridge, 1908), I, 245.

3. See McFarlane, *Buchanan*, p. 31.

4. The letter was written from Edinburgh in November 1579; *Opera omnia* (1725), II, 755.

5. "quae prima omnium fuerat conscripta (cui nomen est Baptista) ultima fuit edita; ac deinde Medea Euripidis." Text conveniently in McFarlane, *Buchanan*, App. G.

6. *Buchanan*, p. 120.

7. C. Fries, "Quellenstudien zu G. Buchanan," *Neue Jahrbücher für die klassische Altertum*, II, 4 (1900), 177ff., II, 5 (1900), 241ff., is cited in support of this suggestion, but Fries was aware of the status of the Hervagiana (p. 185, "nur ein genauer Nachdruck der Aldina").

8. Other metrical peculiarities allow us to observe a progression in metrical orthodoxy from *Medea/Baptistes* to *Jephthes* (for example, Buchanan has eliminated use of the anapaest in the fourth foot of the iambic dimeter in *Jephthes*, but it appears three times in *Medea* and five times in *Baptistes*), but there is no other notable difference between *Medea* and *Baptistes* with the exception of the repeated solecism utǐ in *Medea* 361, 473, 631.

9. "... praesertim cum non ignorarem hanc a plerisque rem prius tentatam uni Erasmo ita successisse ut iuxta ab incepto me deterrere debuerit illorum casus atque huius felicitas."

10. *A. P.*, 189f.

11. Both Sharratt and Mueller draw attention to the influence of the *Troades* (see n. 1 above).

12. For a summary account of the various theories, McFarlane, *Buchanan*, pp. 382ff.

13. *Buchanan*, pp. 381ff.

14. Aristotle, *Poetics*, 1453a.

15. *Poetics*, 1451b.

16. *Buchanan*, p. 389.

17. R. Lebègue, *La tragédie religieuse en France 1514–1573* (Paris, 1929), p. 216.

18. *The Scholemaster* (ed. Mayor), p. 169.

19. Philip J. Ford, *George Buchanan, Prince of Poets* (Aberdeen, 1982), p. 72.

20. Of course there were also thirteenth-century codices of the Latin *Poetics*, on which see Lobel's British Academy lecture (1931).

21. *Buchanan*, p. 82. The philosophical works would be the main subject of study, but Buchanan could have been stimulated to pass on to the *Poetics*.

22. Though Scaliger's *Poetices libri septem* did not appear until 1561, the subject was preoccupying him for most of his thirty years in France (1525–55).

23. *Judges*, 11. 37–9.

24. *Poetics*, 1449b.

25. See now the edition by J. H. Waszink (Amsterdam, 1969).

26. Ovid, *Met.* 9.666ff.

27. See Liddell-Scott-Jones, s.v. ἰφιγένεια.

28. W. O. Sypherd, *Jephthah and his Daughter* (Newark, Delaware, 1948).

29. Erasmus, *Hec.*, ll. 99ff.; Buchanan, *Jephthes*, ll. 94ff.

30. Erasmus, *I. A.*, ll. 1015f.: "ilicet sacrum Simoentis amnem / vitreo qui gurgite vorticosus ..."; *Jephthes*, ll. 147ff.: "Iordanis vitreo gurgite qui rigas / convalles virides...."

31. Erasmus, *Hec.* l. 238: "sed ecce Ulysses huc citus movet gradum ..."; *Jephthes*, l. 220: "sed ecce celeri nuntius properat gradu...."

32. Lebègue (n. 17), p. 236.

33. Plautus, *Amphitruo*, ll. 206ff.; *Jephthes*, ll. 254ff.

34. Vergil, *Aen.* VIII, ll. 524ff.; *Jephthes*, ll. 306ff.

35. Compare ll. 341f., "o aurei dux luminis / sol ..." with Prudentius, *Cath.*, 2.25, "lux ecce surgit aurea ..."; ll. 342f., "qui ... vices diurnas temperas" with Ambrose's "Rector potens, verax deus / qui temperat rerum vices ..."; 347f., "iubar beatum in liberos/fundis nepotes Isaci" with Ambrose's *Splendor paternae gloriae*, ll. 7f.: "iubarque sancti spiritus / infunde nostris sensibus."

36. Compare l. 370, "arces ... igneas," with Horace, *C.* 3.3.10; l. 384 with Horace, *Ep.*, l. 5.29; l. 385 with Ovid *Fasti* 6.38; and note the Lucretian vocabulary at l. 389, etc.

37. Note esp. ll. 495f., "ut laeta ac lubens/ conspicio vultus" and Erasmus, *I. A.*, l. 851, "laeta lubensque conspicor"; l. 521, "nobis pariet absentiam haec absentia" and *I. A.*, ll. 872f., "etenim hic dies praesens absentiam mihi/ tibique pariet, gnata, quam longissimam."

38. *Jephthes*, ll. 628ff.: "felice natum sidere illum existimo/ procul tumultu qui remotus exigit/ ignotus aevum tuta per silentia," and Erasmus *I. A.*, ll. 20ff.: "nam felicem censeo sane/ ego mortalem, quisquis tutum/ ignotus et inglorius aevum/ transmisit."

39. Compare ll. 632–41 with Sallust, *Cat.*, l. 1–3, 2.7.

40. See l. 793 and Horace, *C.* 4. 11. 22ff.; 802 and Ovid, *Met.* 15.626; l. 803 and Lucr. l. 99; l. 806 and Statius, *Theb.* 9.747.

41. l. 821: "ut veri aspera bruma tepenti ..."

42. Aquinas, *S. T.*, 2a2ae 88.2.

43. Jerome, *Adv. Jov.* (P.L. 23, 252).

44. See Paulinus, *Ep.* 11.7, *Poem.* 32.24; Prudentius, *Perist.* 10.1007.

45. ll. 933f. and Ovid, *Met.* 15.127ff.

46. ll. 1094ff. and Petronius, *Sat.*, 116f.

47. "haec ipsa quondam fabula ab Ennio prius versa fuerat."

48. l. 1126 and Lucr. l.96ff.

49. Harsh necessity, *Jephthes*, ll. 1261, 1271 and Erasmus, *I. A.*, l. 2087; plea to the mother, l. 1271 and *I. A.*, l. 2082.

50. Ambrose, *De off. min.*, 3.12.

51. l. 1333: "animi nimium virgo virilis, licet iniuria tibi fatorum ...," and *I. A.*, l. 2000, "beata es tam virili pectore, / at ex parte sortis ac deae felix parum."

52. *Jephthes*, l. 1430 and *I. A.*, l. 2232.

53. *Jephthes*, l. 1424 and *Hec.*, l. 609.

54. Morbid fascination of crowd, l. 1404 and Seneca, *Troades*, ll. 1128f.; dry-eyed victim, l. 1380 and *Troades*, ll. 1099f. (Astyanax).

ITALY

Portrait of a Venetian as a Young Poet

Joseph R. Berrigan

For the past decade I have been studying the literary output of a precocious Venetian patrician, Gregorio Correr.[1] I have published editions of his fables, satires and tragedy and written on these works as well as on his educational treatise and his Vergilian pastoral, the *Licidas*.[2] My principal and indispensable text has been his holograph in the Marciana of Venice.[3] This manuscript, in his own hand, preserves those works of his that he wished to survive, in the way he wished them to survive. I shall confine my remarks to the young Correr or Correr the young poet, for almost all of his extant youthful works are poetic; the only exception is his collection of fables, which he composed while he was at work on his tragedy, the *Progne*. The second part of the Marciana codex consists of the fables and four longish prose works — the *Soliloquy*, an oration at the Council of Basel, and two letters, one to Cecilia Gonzaga, the other to a Carthusian novice.[4]

Pride of place in the Marciana text is granted to the *Progne*, as the work he was the proudest of having written. My own introduction to him, however, is a short poem of four distichs dedicated to Gregory XII. Correr's own title for the poem is "Epygramma cum viseret tumulum Gregorii papae xii."[5]

> Optime pontificum, caelo dignate, nepotem
> Aspicis ad tumulum relliquiasque tuas.
> Non licuit puero quondam dum vita manebat
> Ora neque aspectus usque videre tuos.
> Me tamen esse tui memorem voluere parentes
> Deque tuo dictus nomine Gregorius.
> Salve, sancte pater, tuque, o fidissima quondam
> Curarum requies, hospita terra, vale.

Here we have a most important clue to Gregorio Correr's personality. He was conscious of being a Venetian aristocrat, as Poggio Bracciolini would discover when he made disparaging comments on the patricians of Venice, but he was especially proud of his relationship to Pope Gregory XII, after whom he had been named. Unable to see his distinguished namesake while he still lived, Gregorio Correr visited his tomb and composed this brief poem to honor his memory, to express his gratitude, and to abide by his parent's injunction:

> Me tamen esse tui memorem voluere parentes.

His very name would be an unfailing reminder of this papal connection.

While he was at Mantua as a student of Vittorino, he composed an ode for the successor of Gregory XII, the last pope elected, not by the College of Cardinals, but by a church council, that of Constance. Martin V was honored by Correr with an ode modelled upon the *Carmen saeculare* of Horace. Thus the doughty old Roman aristocrat, scion of the Colonna clan, is cast in the role of Horace's hero, Augustus Caesar. Martin, like Augustus, had brought unity, peace and the blessings of plenty. Like Augustus he deserved a long life:

> Augeas serus numeros beatorum.
> Hic pedes sacros veneretur orbis,
> Te diu terrae videant beatum
>   Et tua Roma.
> Te Palatinae venerentur arces,
> Te diu reges positisque telis
> Exterae gentes valeant nihil te
>   Visere maius.[6]

It was in Mantua that Correr composed most of these poems, under the guidance of Vittorino da Feltre. An early instance of this Mantuan prosody is his *Licidas*, a pastoral shaped after the second eclogue of Vergil. Vittorino liked to have his students compete with one another and Correr found that one of his contemporaries was much more facile than he in the crafting of hexameters. He would not return to that verse until he had left for Rome, where he would write the Satires and his educational treatise. The *Licidas*, whatever competition it may have encountered, is a lovely poem and can be appreciated for its own pastoral charm. Like its Vergilian pattern it celebrates the love of one shepherd for another and his feeling of desperation at being rejected. One can only wonder at the significance of such a topic for a teenager in the 1420s. What can be definitely seen and felt is the greater intensity with which Correr pictures his abandoned shepherd. He intends to leave his beloved country and go into exile:

> Scythicas durare pruinas
> Certum est aut contra nascentem visere solem
> Auroramque sequi, vastis regionibus exul.[7]

There then appears in the graceful lines of the pastoral the kind of violence that we shall have to note again and again:

> Ante tamen stabulis ignes inducere nostris
> Spesque meas olim teneros cum matribus agnos
> Urere.[8]

This kind of imaginary arson, with the intentional destruction of his beloved flock, has no precedent in Vergil but it smacks of the violence and bloodshed that had already appeared in his ode to Martin V. There we read in the second stanza that Christ returned to heaven in joy,

> scelestas
> Deserens terras et adhuc recenti
> Sanguine tinctas.

But those are only hints when they are compared with the tragedy that Correr undertook after forsaking the hexameter. He always felt that the *Progne* was his greatest achievement; he refers to it in many of his other works and records the satisfaction he felt in witnessing the impact it had upon its readers. It should have indeed, for this time he took as his model the *Thyestes* of Seneca and enacts the grim, gory tale of Tereus, Philomela, and Progne. Correr fills his drama with savage actions and even more savage words from the appearance of Diomedes, the Thracian horse-lord, through the rape of Philomela and the murder of her entourage, to the final horrific slaying of Itys and Tereus's banquet. On occasion Correr seems self-indulgent in his wallowing in rhetorical and actual violence. Some of it indeed may be due to Seneca but Correr had, after all, chosen to imitate him.

Another element of Correr's personality surfaces in the dialogue between Progne and her nurse: the author's profound distrust, even hatred of women. There has been a glimpse of this misogyny in the ode. In the fourth stanza the "pueri et virgines" had prayed,

> Occidat serpens, lateat novercis
> Herba veneni.

In the play, the nurse had unwittingly suggested the slaughter of Itys to her mistress and begged her not to do the deed:

> Factura deinceps omne femineum genus
> Nocens?[9]

Progne proceeds to her dire, quite unmotherly action and receives this accolade from her husband, once he has eaten his meal:

> O novercales manus!
> Quae Cholchis unquam tanta commisit scelera?[10]

While he was engaged in composing this tragedy, Correr undertook a lighter task to refresh his spirit. He wrote a set of Aesopic fables to match a set that another of his fellow-students, Ognibene de Lonigo, had translated from the Greek.[11] Correr wrote sixty apologues to go with Ognibene's forty. Inspired as they are by the relatively gentle Greek fabulist, Correr's fables are in general much lighter than the *Progne*. Occasionally, however, his misogyny and fascination with violence reappear. The grim little story of the two adulterers and each other's wife ends with the moral that those who get married often find themselves in the same plight.[12] He underscores the dangers of beauty and its possession with the story of the Monkey and the Fox, in which the latter uses the sad state of a plucked vulture to drive home the peril of being too fine.[13] Another monkey learns the same lesson in his own person, when he is chained and beaten by an actor who had tricked him with a display of finery.[14]

After leaving Mantua for Rome and the household of his uncle Antonio, the Cardinal of Bologna, he continued for a short time to compose poetry.[15] The principal fruits of this effort are the educational treatise on Vittorino's school and his book of six satires. He may have changed his residence and altered his mode of composition, but some of the same traits reappear in these later works. Violence and misogyny are fused in these lines from the *Quomodo*:

> Coram patre puer nunc peierat et bibit, audet
> Omne nefas, ludit, lenonum dedecore emptas
> Servat amicitias....[16]
> Mox tibi decrepito, si quid de moribus huius
> Poeniteat demum, tenue et miserabile guttur
> Elidet; ficto gemitu lugubre feretrum
> Componet sed tu porrectis calcibus ibis.[17]

Two other subjects concern Correr later in the poem: the nature of Venetian civilization and the difficulty of becoming a poet. The rest of his life he would spend in such cities as Rome, Florence and Verona, but he would return to Venice only in death. Surely part of the reason can be seen in his description of contemporary Venice and its low estimation of liberal learning.

Other than mirroring once again Correr's poor opinion of most of his contemporaries and his extraordinary regard for Vittorino, the Satires deal with that other theme of the *Quomodo*, the near impossibility of becoming a poet in his age.[18] He had tried his hand at a pastoral, a tragedy, a Horatian ode, distichs and now he experimented with satires. They were to be his last major poetic work. Falling under the influence of his cardinal-uncle, he gave up the self-proclaimed difficulties of being a Quattrocento poet and dedicated himself to the clerical life and the studies appropriate to it. He details this transition in his *Soliloquy*, written after the death of Cardinal Antonio, some fifteen years after his departure from Mantua.[19]

I began this paper with a short poem of eight lines that Correr wrote for his papal grand-uncle. I would like to conclude it with another eight-line poem, entitled "Responsio ad Amicum:"[20]

Pauca quidem meritis tribuit fortuna maligna
   Parca manu rerum quas valet ipsa dare.
At tibi secretos pandit natura recessus
   Ingeniumque simul nobile larga dedit
Et doctas artis et fidum pectus amicis
   Iusque in divitiis non habet illa tuis.
Perge modo. Invitam coges vincesque merendo,
   Ipsa sibi quamquam mens bona sit pretium.

I would like to believe that this Boethian balance represents Correr as he takes leave of his poetic efforts and that he applies the salutary message of these lines to his own life. Among those things that Fortune controls are not only wealth and power but also poetic fame; he advises his correspondent to forego all of that, to be satisfied with the gifts that Nature had provided him and most of all to remember that "a good mind is its own reward."

Notes

1. The most recent biographical treatment of Gregorio Correr is by Laura Casarsa: "Contributi per la biografia di Gregorio Correr," *Miscellanea della facoltà di lettere* (Trieste, 1979), 29–88.

2. *Fabulae Aesopicae Hermolai Barbari et Gregorii Corrarii* (Lawrence, 1977); "Liber Satyrarum," *HL*, 22 (1973), 10–38; "Gregorii Corrarii Veneti Tragoedia, Cui Titulus Progne," *HL*, 29 (1980), 13–99; "Early Neo-Latin Tragedy in Italy," *ACNL Lovaniensis* (Munich, 1973), 85–93; "The *Libellus Fabellarum* of Gregorii Correr," *Man*, 19 (1975), 131–38; "The 'Quomodo educari et erudiri debeant pueri' of Gregorio Correr," *Classical Bulletin*, 56 (1979), 23–26; "The Latin Aesop of the Early Quattrocento," *Man*, 26 (1982), 15–23; I read papers on the *Licidas* and the other minor poems of Correr at the Manuscripts Conference in Saint Louis in 1981 and 1982.

3. Venice, Bibl. Naz. Marciana, lat. xii 155 (3953).

4. Bibliography for these works may be found in Casarsa, 43, 44, 48, 50.

5. This poem is on f. 19^v of the Marciana manuscript.

6. The ode's publication is discussed in Casarsa, 39n; it is found on ff. 18^v–19^v of the Marciana manuscript.

7. This pastoral runs from f. 21^r through f. 22^v of the Marciana manuscript; these are ll. 85–87.

8. ibid., ll. 88–90.

9. *Progne*, ll. 723–24, p. 74 of my edition.

10. ibid., ll. 1042–43, p. 96.

11. See my article, "The Aesopic Fables of Ognibene da Lonigo," *Classical Bulletin*, 56 (1980), 85–87.

12. This is Correr's forty-sixth fable, p. 178 of my edition.

13. Thirty-fifth fable, p. 158.

14. Thirty-third fable, p. 154.

15. See Casarsa, 42.
16. Ll. 62–65. For bibliography see Casarsa, 37.
17. Ll. 69–72.
18. See my edition, especially p. 11.
19. See Casarsa, 50–51.
20. This is found on f. 20^v of the Marciana manuscript.

Methoden und Motive der
Platoninterpretation bei Marsilio Ficino

Paul Richard Blum

Daß Marsilio Ficino Platon gelesen habe, ist nicht gerade eine originelle Feststellung, ist doch der Florentiner Platoniker vor allem durch seine Platonübersetzungen bekannt und bedeutend.[1] Dennoch ist diese Behauptung nicht gänzlich überflüssig, denn man hat auch Platoniker sein können, ohne Platons Schriften direkt gelesen zu haben, auch Ficino war es in einer frühen Phase, und nicht aus eigenem Antrieb unterzog er sich der Mühe des Studiums der primären Quellen.[2] Daß nun seine Lektüre sein Bild von Platon, seinen Platonismus entscheidend modifiziert habe, sei einmal angenommen — es gehört zu den schwer hintergehbaren Hoffnungen eines jeden Verteidigers der klassischen Studien —, halten wir aber fest, daß Ficinos Platonismus und sein Platonlektüre genuin zweierlei sind. Hinzukommt, daß bekanntlich viele Strömungen in Ficinos Denken einfließen: Augustinismus, Neu- und Pseudoplatonismus, Scholastik, um nur einige zu nennen. Alle diese Facetten wird man einerseits tunlich auseinanderzuhalten versuchen, wenn man eine Embryologie seines Denkens betreibt, sie werden andererseits ebenso sinnvoller Weise ineinander verschwimmen, wenn man die Philosophie Ficinos als etwas Eigenständiges (früher hätte man "System" gesagt) darstellen will.[3] Keiner der beiden Versuche soll hier angestellt werden, es wäre auch nicht der richtige Ort, vielmehr möchte ich damit experimentieren, Ficinos Stellung zu Platon in einer Skizze seiner Übersetzungs- und Kommentierungstätigkeit herauszupräparieren. Und dies einmal, um die Fallstricke der vielen anfallenden "ismen" zu vermeiden, zum anderen aber, um etwas über die Art und Weise der Lektüre einer unbezweifelt autoritativen Quelle zu erfahren.

Über seine Platonübersetzungen selbst ist hier nicht viel zu sagen, es ist die erste vollständige lateinische Ausgabe gewesen, ihre Verbreitung war beachtlich, über ihren sprachlichen Wert bin ich nicht kompetent zu urteilen, doch wird er — wenn auch nicht einhellig — zumeist hoch geschätzt, zumal in der neueren Zeit.[4] Aus der Entstehungsgeschichte dieser Übersetzung sei aber darauf hingewiesen, daß die ersten zehn Dialoge, beginnend mit Hippias maior bis zu Parmenides

und Philebos, auf Wunsch Cosimos ausgewählt wurden.[5] Dieser hatte die Übersetzung zusammen mit den Hermetischen Schriften erbeten, nachdem er zuvor
Aristoteles in der Version von Argyropulos studiert hatte.[6] Cosimos Intention,
und wie Ficino sie referiert, ist notierenswert:

> quibus omnia vitae praecepta, omnia naturae principia, omnia divinarum
> rerum mysteria sancta panduntur.[7]

Ergiebiger und der Interpretation zugänglicher sind seine Beigaben verschie-
dener Art. Deren Formen sind vielgestaltig, sie reichen von Dedikationsschreiben
und Vorworten über Kapitelüberschriften, vorgeschaltete Kommentare zu einzelnen Kapiteln, die sich zu Traktaten ausweiten, Vorlesungen zum Text bis hin
zur Travestie, wie ich seinen Symposionkommentar nennen möchte.

Die allgemeinste Form ist das Argumentum, auch Epitomae genannt,[8] welches
jeder Schrift,[9] beim "Staat" und den Nomoi auch den einzelnen Büchern, voran-
gestellt ist. Die Argumenta lehnen sich nicht eng an den Text an, sondern klären
Vorfragen, bieten Sacherläuterungen zu den anstehenden Themen und stellen
Bezüge zu den übrigen Schriften Platons her. Hier zitiert Ficino frei aus allen
ihm sonst wichtigen Autoritäten, er hebt die ihm vordringlichen Themen der
Schriften hervor, auch finden Überlegungen zu Platons Stil hier ihren Platz. Die
Eigenständigkeit der Argumenta erkennt man auch daran, daß sich ihnen in
einigen Fällen (Parmenides, Philebos, Sophistes, Phaidros, Timaios) noch Kapitelsummen anschließen, die präziser über die platonischen Inhalte Auskunft
geben. Erweitert werden die Argumenta gelegentlich (Parmenides, Philebos,[10]
Phaidros, Politeia VIII, Timaios) zu umfangreichen Kommentaren, in denen der
Platoniker seine gesamte Gelehrsamkeit ausbreitet, und die seine anderen Werke,
besonders die Theologia Platonica ergänzen. Die größten Teile des Parmenides-
kommentars sind eine Darstellung der neuplatonischen Metaphysik des Einen
(es wird hervorgehoben, daß die Dialektik keineswegs, sondern Theologie Ge-
genstand des Dialogs ist),[11] dagegen offenbart der Kommentar zur Hochzeits-
zahl (Politeia VIII) seine Interessen für mathematische Spekulation, während der
Timaioskommentar zu einem kosmologischen Traktat gerät.

Aus diesen Beobachtungen können wir festhalten, daß Ficino ein differenziertes
Verhältnis zu Platons Schriften hat: Er ist — außer der Übersetzung — zu strenger
sachlicher Nähe ebenso in der Lage wie zu weiter fortschreitender Distanz und
Selbständigkeit gegenüber der Autorität. Eine besondere Rolle kommt in diesem
Sinne seiner Bearbeitung des Symposions zu. Dieser Kommentar, fast doppelt
so umfangreich wie das Symposion, verzichtet auf besondere Kapitelsummen ebenso wie auf das sonst übliche Argumentum und er hat — zusammen mit dem
Timaioskommentar — die Auszeichnung bekommen, in den Platonausgaben abgedruckt zu werden. Tatsächlich finden sich in Ficinos Convito verschiedene
Stufen der Nähe und Distanz zum Text und zur Sache, weshalb eine ausführ-
liche Besprechung hier vielleicht angebracht ist.

Eine Travestie kann man den Convito deshalb nennen, weil er den platonischen

Text selbst in der literarischen Form eines Gastmahls, bestehend aus analog
gebildeten Reden, kommentiert. Der Ort ist Florenz, die Sprecher sind Freunde
Ficinos, auch die Zeit, eine Gedenkfeier zu Platons Geburts- und Todestag, ist
angegeben.[12] Auch hier nehmen die Redner auf einander Bezug, jedoch ist das
Gastmahl szenisch kaum ausgeführt. Die einzelnen orationes haben statuarischen
und bisweilen traktathaften Charakter. In ihrer Abfolge fehlt ihnen ein wesent-
liches kompositorisches Element: Der graduelle Aufstieg, die von Rede zu Rede
sich präzisierende Erarbeitung des Eros-Themas, die bei Platon in der Diotima-
Rede kulminiert und dann einen komödienartigen Ausklang bietet, das alles ist
bei Ficino verschwunden, für ihn trägt jede Rede mit gleicher Ernsthaftigkeit unmittelbar zum Hauptthema bei. Die charakteristisch Platonsche Dialektik der
einander überbeitenden, ablösenden, relativierenden oder ersetzenden Zugangs-
weisen zu einer Fragestellung, zumeist durch die Sokratische Kunst geleistet, hier
durch die Abfolge der Redebeiträge, die immer schon von Ungenügen und Vor-
läufigkeit gekennzeichnet sind, diese literarisch-philosophische Methode gibt Ficino auf zugunsten einer zwar vielseitigen, aber immer um gleiche Reflexions-
höhe bemühten Ausarbeitung eines komplexen, aber auch durchgängig kohären-
ten Gegenstandes, nämlich seiner Lehre vom Amor. Typisch ist hierfür die Rede
des Eryximachos, der sie übrigens selbst für unvollständig erklärt.[13] Der Beitrag
der medizinischen Kunst zum Thema Eros wird bei Platon von Aristophanes'
Schlucken, Gurgeln und Niesen begleitet und von ihm selbst durch den phan-
tastischen Mythos von der Entstehung des Menschen abgelöst. In Florenz nimmt
der Mediziner Ficino die Sache befremdlich ernst. Er läßt an einer Kosmologie
arbeiten:

> Tria nobis deinceps ex nostri Eryximaci mente tractanda videntur. Primum,
> quod amor omnibus insitus per cuncta porrigitur. Alterum, quod omnium
> que secundum naturam sunt operum effector atque servator. Tertium, quod
> artium singularium est magister et dominus.[14]

Hatte Ficino keinen Humor? Übernahm er die literarische Form, ohne die
Methode verstanden zu haben? Durchaus nicht, im Gegenteil. Humanistisch aus-
gebildet, hatte er einen Sinn für stilistische, rhetorische, literarische Feinheiten.
Er weiß mythische Formen auszulegen — und als solche behandelt er die Aristo-
phanes-Rede —, er weiß auch, wann sie sich der Auslegung entziehen.[15] An den
Sophistendialogen lobt er die taktische Zurückhaltung, mit der Platon sich für
seine Gegner unangreifbar macht,

> ne (...) venenosa in eum impudentissimae linguae tela retorqueant. Ergo
> partim ironia, partim risu, saepe ioco, et ludo, saepius honesta quadam
> redargutione immeritam sophistis auctoritatem conatur adimere. Id qui-
> dem in sophista acutissime perficit. Idem in Gorgia elegantissime. Facete
> admodum, et urbane in Hippia. Scite et argute in Euthydemo, Artificiose
> etiam in Protagora, saepeque similiter.[16]

Auf Albinos (Alcinous) sich stützend unterscheidet er bei Platon drei Typen von Dialogen:

> Aut enim solum inquirit, falsave confutat dialogus, aut solum vera exponit ac docet, aut in utroque versatur. Primus inquisitivus et contentiosus. Expositivus alter. Postremus mixtus est dictus.[17]

Ähnliches vermerkt er im Schriftenverzeichnis Platons:

> Aut enim sophistas confutat, aut adolescentes adhortatur, aut docet adultos,

mit der bedeutsamen Konsequenz:

> Quae in epistolis, vel in libris de legibus, et Epinomi Plato ipse suo disserit ore, certissima vult haberi. Quae vero in caeteris libris Socratis, Timaei, Parmenidis, Zenonis ore disputat, verisimilia.[18]

Das bedeutet, Ficino erkennt nicht nur die taktische und didaktische Funktion vieler Partien bei Platon, er ist sich auch der zetetischen und hermeneutischen Methode bewußt und hält — in summa — die Werke Platons in höchstem Maße für auslegungsfähig und -bedürftig.[19] Wie in jeder Hermeneutik — das braucht hier nicht betont zu werden — bedarf es auch für Ficino zur Interpretation eines Vorbegriffs von dem, was eruiert werden soll. Ficino nennt den "stylus" Platons

> non tam humano eloquio, quam divino oraculo similem (…) semper (…) arcana coelestia complectentem. (…) ita Platonicus stylus continens universum, tribus potissimum abundat muneribus, philosophica sententiarum utilitate, oratorio dispositionis elocutionisque ordine, florum ornamento poeticorum, et ubique divinis utitur testibus, tum etiam certissimum de architecto mundi deo perhibet testimonium.[20]

Mit anderen Worten: Die gewisse Hoffnung, in Platon die Prinzipien des Seins und das Summum bonum zu finden, leitete nicht nur seinen Mäzen Cosimo — wie schon zitiert —, sondern auch den Übersetzer Ficino selbst. (Wäre er nur an Methodischem interessiert gewesen, hätte er den Parmenides für eine logische Übung halten können.) Unter diesem Vorverständnis, das er zweifellos aus neuplatonischer und christlicher Quelle bezog, las und interpretierte er Platon. Auch das ist nichts Überraschendes, aber es hilft, seine Kommentierungsformen zu interpretieren. Alles, was bei Platon nicht nur ausdrücklich mythisch oder allegorisch, sondern auch was "facete" klingt, muß Ficino für Dissimulation (der lateinische Begriff für εἰρωνεία) halten, denn:

> Pythagorae, Socratisque et Platonis mos erat, ubique divina mysteria figuris, involucrisque obtegere, sapientiam suam contra Sophistarum iactantiam modoste (sic!) dissimulare, iocari serio, et studiosissime ludere …[21]

Diese spezifische Interpretation der platonischen Ironie hat einerseits eine Stütze in dem immer wiederkehrenden Bild vom Weisen, der seine Lehre vor der profanen Masse verbirgt, sie findet sich aber besonders leicht dann, wenn Platon christlich umgedeutet werden soll, so bei Augustin, Proklos und — in sehr ähnlicher Formulierung — bei Abaelard.[22] Ficino scheint aber sein Verfahren als erster mit hermeneutischer Konsequenz durchzuführen. Wenn er Platon interpretiert, muß er durch die "involucra" hindurch die Wahrheit direkt ansteuern. Schon deshalb benötigen die platonischen Schriften Argumenta, um wenigstens im Ansatz die Leitideen und stilistischen (in Ficinos Sinn) Probleme aufzudecken.

Aus dieser Notwendigkeit erklärt sich auch, warum im Convito die Reden zunächst meistens gar keinen Bezug auf den platonischen Text nehmen. Vielmehr beginnen sie durchwegs mit Präliminarien, so der ganze Kommentar mit einer dem Symposion durchaus fremden Kosmogonie, und wenn hierbei die Vorlage zitiert wird, dann um die dort nur angedeuteten Quellen wie die Orphica oder um Parallelen aus anderen Dialogen ausführlich aufzuarbeiten. Erst danach folgt eine textnähere Auslegung, die sich passagenweise zu punktuellen Wortauslegungen verengt.[23] In das Gewand eines platonisierenden Gastmahls gekleidet, finden wir also nebeneinander drei typische Formen mittelalterlicher Kommentarliteratur, die Wortauslegung, den quaestionenartigen Sachkommentar, der das Thema besonders hinsichtlich anderer Autoritäten ausweitet und den sich verselbständigenden Traktat. (Auch die Sensus-Lehre kommt ins Spiel.) Ähnlich wie dort ist auch bei Ficino die definitive Stellungnahme unter einer Fülle von Nebenerörterungen und Zitaten schwer auszumachen.[24] Jenseits des Mittelalters aber liegt Ficinos Sinn für die Präsentationsform von philosophischer Lehre, die sich nicht zuletzt in der Übernahme der oratorischen Form äußert. Dafür spricht die gattungsstiftende Wirkung des Convito.[25]

Fragt man sich also, warum er das Symposion nachahmt — und dies, wie gesagt, in letzter Konsequenz unsachgemäß — so genügt nicht etwa ein Hinweis darauf, daß er die Akademie habe wiedererstehen lassen wollen, denn auch dafür hat es Gründe geben müssen.[26] Einer lag offenbar in der Einsicht gerade in die historische Distanz Athens von Florenz — immerhin werden die Reden im Convito mit der Feststellung eröffnet, für 1200 Jahre seien die jährlichen Platonfeiern unterlassen worden, bis endlich in unserer Zeit ...[27] —, denn nur etwas, das unmißverständlich vergangen ist, kann man wiederbeleben wollen, sonst setzt man einfach fort. Andererseits besteht bekanntlich bei Ficino wie bei anderen Renaissancephilosophen die Tendenz, Platon mit vielen anderen Autoritäten zu amalgamieren. Deshalb müßte hier eine Erörterung seiner Stellung zu Plotin, Augustinus, dem Hermetismus usw., so wie seiner unglaublichen Anstrengungen, Platon zu christianisieren, folgen, nicht zuletzt auch seine Zugehörigkeit zur Tradition von der ungeschriebenen Lehre Platons.[28] Doch stehen diese Versuche nicht im Gegensatz zur historischen Perspektive auf die Antike, sondern dienen der unverzichtbaren Vermittlung der fernen mit der eigenen Kultur:

Amo equidem Platonem in Iamblico, admiror in Plotino, in Dionysio veneror,[29] sagt Ficino. Was immer ihn sonst zu den anderen Autoren hinziehen mag, sie sind ihm zugleich Brücken zu seinem Verständnis von Platon. Entscheidend aber ist, daß Ficino keinem Eklektizismus im schlechten Sinne huldigt, indem er der Sache und der Genese nach unvereinbare Lesefrüchte kontaminiert.[30] Denn jedenfalls hinsichtlich Platons kann man ihm keinen Mangel an Lektüre und Untersuchung unterstellen. Vielmehr ist er—beginnend mit Studien der lateinischen platonischen Literatur, vor allem Augustinus—darauf ausgegangen zu erfahren, was Platon selbst und wirklich gedacht hat: "ut (...) Platonicam aperiamus sententiam."[31] Seine beachtliche Kommentartätigkeit zeigt, daß er glaubte, eine zutreffende Interpretation gefunden zu haben, ob er dabei vielleicht irrte oder doch den richtigen Schlüssel gefunden hat, ist eine andere Frage aus einer anderen Zeit.[32]

Anmerkungen

1. Abgekürzt wird im folgenden zitiert: Marsilio Ficino, *Opera* (Basileae, Henricpetri, 1576); (Reprint Torino, 1962): *Op.* (ab p. 1013 = Bd. II).—*Supplementum Ficinianum*, ed. Paul Oskar Kristeller (Florentiae, 1937; Reprint 1973): *Supp. I/II.*—Platon, *Opera tralatione Marsilii Ficini* (Basileae, Froben, 1539): *Plat.* (mir vorliegende Ausg., offenbar weitgehend seitenidentisch mit der 1. Ausg. Florenz [1484], cf. *Supp. I*, p. LX sq.).

2. *Op.* 929: Cristoforo Landino und Cosimo il Vecchio haben ihm geraten, Griechisch zu lernen und Platon im Original zu lesen. Cf. Raymond Marcel, *Marsile Ficin (1433–1499)*, Les Classiques de l'humanisme, Études 6 (Paris, 1958), p. 197 sq.

3. Paul Oskar Kristeller, *Die Philosophie des Marsilio Ficino*, Das Abendland, NF 1 (Frankfurt, 1972), pp. 4–7.

4. Z.B.: Jean Festugière, *La philosophie d'amour de Marsile Ficin et son influence sur la littérature française au XVIᵉ siècle*, Études de philosophie médiévale 31 (Paris, 1941), pp. 145–52; Marcel, *Ficin*, p. 252, Anm. 2; Charles Huit, *La vie et l'œuvre de Platon* (Paris, 1893; Reprint Hildesheim/New York 1973), Bd. II, pp. 441–43; Heinrich von Stein, *Sieben Bücher zur Geschichte des Platonismus* (Göttingen, 1862–1875; Reprint Frankfurt, 1965), Theil II, pp. 129–60, bes. 147 (mit älterer Literatur); Daniel Georg Morhof, *Polyhistor literarius, philosophicus et practicus*, ed. 4a. (Lubecae, 1747; Reprint Aalen, 1970), II.1.7.15, Bd. II p. 39: "Quia enim potius Dogmaticus fuit et Philosophus, quam Philologus et Criticus, mirum non est, si in Platonis textu interpretando non usque adeo scopum tetigerit." Cf. unten Anm. 32.

5. *Supp. I*, p. CLI sq.

6. *Xenocratis de morte*, Praefatio, *Op.* 1965.

7. ibid.

8. "Argumentum" in: *Plat.* passim; "Epitomae" in: *Op.* passim.

9. Ausnahmen bilden *Clitopho*, *Plat.* 301, den schon Ficino für unecht hielt (*Supp. I*, p. CL), und *Convivium*, dazu unten.

10. Über Besonderheiten des Phileboskommentars s. Michael J. B. Allen, "Introduction," in: Marsilio Ficino, *The Philebus Commentary*, Publications of the Center for Medieval and Renaissance Studies, UCLA, 9 (Berkeley, etc. 1975).

11. Dazu besonders Raymond Klibansky, "Plato's Parmenides in the Middle Ages and the Renaissance," *MRS*, 1 (1943), 281–330, ergänzter Nachdruck in: Ders., *The Continuity of the Platonic Tradition during the Middle Ages (...) together with Plato's Parmenides (...)* (München, 1981), hier 312–25 (32–45).

12. Die Frage nach der historischen Wirklichkeit eines solchen Gastmahls (ausführlich: Raymond Marcel, "Introduction," in: Marsile Ficin, *Commentaire sur le Banquet de Platon*, Les Classiques de l'humanisme, Textes 2 [Paris, 1956], pp. 28–36) ist hier irrelevant: der veröffentlichte Text stammt von Ficino. Inzwischen erschien: Marsilio Ficino, *Über die Liebe oder Platons Gastmahl, Lateinisch-Deutsch*, ed. Paul Richard Blum, Philosophische Bibliothek, 368 (Hamburg, 1984).

13. *Plat.* 424 (188 e): "Forte et ipse multa quae ad laudandum Amorem pertinent, praetermitto, neque sponte tamen."

14. *Comm. in Conv.* III, 1, ed. Marcel, p. 160.

15. ibid., I, 4 [3], ed. Marcel, pp. 143–44, zu Alcestis und Orpheus.

16. *Argum. in Prot.*, *Plat.* 224, *Op.* 1296.

17. *Argum. in Men.*, *Plat.* 13, *Op.* 1132; *Alcinoi de doctrina Platonis* 6, *Op.* 1948.

18. *Platonis vita*, *Plat.* fol. α 4^r, *Op.* 766.

19. Stein, *Sieben Bücher* (s. Anm. 4), III, 147 zu der eben zitierten Stelle: "und es ist leicht abzusehen, welche verwirrende Wirkung dies Nichtverstehen der dialogischen Absichten Platons sowol überhaupt als auch namentlich durch Ueberschätzung des in jenen ausgezeichneten Quellen Enthaltenen mit sich führen musste."

20. *Plat.* fol. α 2^r (prooemium), *Op.* 1129.

21. *Comm. in Parm.*, *Op.* 1137; cf. *Argum. in Euth.*, *Plat.* 253, *Op.* 1303.

22. Augustinus, *Civ. dei* VIII, 4; Proklos, *Theol. Plat.* I, 5; Abaelard, *Intr. ad theol.* I, 19, *PL*, 178, 1022: "semper philosophia arcana sua nudis publicare verbis dedignata sit, et maxime de anima, de Diis per fabulosa quaedam involucra loqui consueverat"; zit. bei: Tullio Gregory, "L'anima mundi nella filosofia del XII secolo," *Giornale critico della filosofia italiana*, anno 30, 3a serie, vol. 5 (1951), 494–508, hier: 497.

23. Etwa so: *Comm. in Conv.* IV, 2, ed. Marcel, p. 169: "Summa vero nostre interpretationis erit huiusmodi. Homines, id est hominum anime. Quondam, id est, quando a deo creantur (...)"; oder V, 2, p. 179: "Post hec diffusius enumerat Agathon, quot ad huius dei formosam spetiem requiruntur. Iuvenis inquit est, tener, agilis, concinnus et nitidus. Nobis autem primum querendum quid hec ad pulchritudinem conferant (...). — Cf. auch Michael J. B. Allen, "Cosmogony and Love: the Role of Phaedrus in Ficino's Symposium Commentary," *JMRS*, 10 (1980), 131–53.

24. Kristeller, *Ficino*, p. 6, ders., "The Scholastic Background of Marsilio Ficino," in: Ders., *Studies in Renaissance Thought and Letters*, Storia e letteratura, 54 (Roma, 1956), pp. 35–97; Ders., "Florentine Platonism and its Relations with Humanism and Scholasticism," *Church History*, 8 (1939), 201–11; cf. ders., "Lay Religious Traditions and Florentine Platonism," in: Ders., *Studies*, pp. 99–122 (über Werkgattungen bei F.).

25. John Charles Nelson, *Renaissance Theory of Love* (New York, 1958), p. 69. Ein Vorgänger war evtl. Lorenzo prete pisano, mit den Dialogen *De amore* (nach 1435): Paola Zambelli, "Platone, Ficino e la magia," in: *Studia humanitatis: Ernesto Grassi zum 70. Geburtstag*, Humantistische Bibliothek I, 16 (München, 1973), 121–42, hier: 127 sq.

26. Kristeller, *Ficino*, p. 14.

27. Ed. Marcel, p. 136.

28. Für diesen ganzen Komplex ist aufschlußreich: *Theologia Platonica* XVII, *Op.* 386–96,

Marsile Ficin, *Théologie platonicienne de l'immortalité des âmes*, Les Classiques de l'humanisme, Textes 3–5 (Paris, 1964–1970), Bd. III, 148–74. Auch der Brief an Martin Uranius, *Op.* 899, ediert und erläutert in Raymond Klibansky, *The Continuity of the Platonic Tradition during the Middle Ages* (London, 1939; Reprint München, 1981) (cf. Anm. 11), pp. 42–47; E. N. Tigersted, *The Decline and Fall of the Neoplatonic Interpretation of Plato*, Commentationes Humanarum Litterarum, 52 (Helsinki/Helsingfors 1974), Ficino bes. pp. 18–20 u. 24 sq.

29. *Epist.* XI, *Op.* 925.

30. Z.B. Tigersted, *Decline*, p. 20; Rudolf Pfeiffer, *Die klassische Philologie von Petrarca bis Mommsen* (München, 1982), pp. 80 u. 96, spricht von "mystischem Symbolismus."

31. *Epist.* VII, *Op.* 855: "Ego igitur divi Augustini primum authoritate adductus, deinde multorum apud Christianos sanctorum hominum testimonio confirmatus operae pretium fore censui quandoquidem mihi philosophandum esset, ut in academia praecipue philospharer, verum ut doctrina Platonica (...) latius refulgeret, libros Platonis omnes e Graeca lingua transtuli in Latinam." Danach habe er die *Theologia Platonica* verfaßt, "ut mentem eius potius quam verba sequamur, sublatisque Poeticis velaminibus Platonicam aperiamus sententiam divinae legi undique consonam."—Cf. Alessandra Tarabochia Canavero, "S. Agostino nella teologia platonica di Marsili Ficino," *Rivista di filosofia neoscolastica*, 70 (1978), 626–46.

32. [Johann Jacob Brucker], *Historia philosophica de ideis tum veterum imprimis Graecorum tum recentiorum philosophorum placita enarrantur* (Augustae Vindelicorum, 1723), p. 33 zu Ficino: "Saepe tamen, ubi litera sententiae suae non favet, nescio quae mysteria allegoriarum subsidio quaerit, totusque Platonis amore captus est."

The Making of the *De partu virginis*

Charles Fantazzi

One of the most gratifying rewards of the arduous task of textual criticism is the opportunity to catch a glimpse of the poet at work in the various phases of the creative process. There is presently an awakened interest in the work of art *in fieri*, whether it be the study of the sinopias of frescoes, the notebooks of composers, or the *sudate carte* of poets and novelists. Some aesthetic critics,[1] indeed, esteem that a work is not perfectible at all, but goes through successive stages of organic development, of which the published version may be regarded as merely an accidental final stage.

The Neapolitan *Cinquecento* offers a perfect exemplification of the meticulous, uncontented poet in the figure of Jacopo Sannazaro. His contemporaries did not fail to notice this quality in him. Giraldi called him a *poeta statarius*,[2] while Pontano jokingly applied to him the anecdote of Apelles concerning his fellow painter Protogenes, that he did not know when to lift his hand from the canvas.[3] While this ceaseless *labor limae* is evident in the various revisions and variants of his vernacular poetry, it is even more accentuated in the Latin poems, and most notably in the *De partu virginis*. In Pontano's dialogue, *Actius*, the chief speaker, who is, of course, none other than Sannazaro himself under his academic name, defines the poet's function as "dicere apposite ad admirationem,"[4] and adds that this quality of "meraviglia," as it was termed in *Cinquecento* poetics, could be achieved only through technical perfection of metre and diction.

The editing and revising of the *De partu virginis* through its long years of gestation can be followed at close hand. We are in possession of a clandestine edition of an early version of the first book, which appeared in Venice probably around 1520,[5] several manuscripts with authorial variants written in as they were transmitted by the poet,[6] two autographs in the Laurentian library with numerous erasures and interlineations,[7] a group of letters to Antonio Seripando,[8] older brother of Cardinal Girolamo Seripando, explaining some of the revisions, and the final edition of 1526 authorized by the poet.[9] The letters to Seripando are extremely candid and at times even petulant. The poet inveighs against those purists who required a Vergilian exemplar for every word that appeared in the poem. He calls them "ignoranti bestie,"[10] very strong language for the mild-mannered Sannazaro, and argues that even in Vergil there are words that are not deserving of emulation. Most objections, however, came from those who took exception to what they perceived as too great a freedom used in the treatment of religious matters. Here the poet was vindicated by the authority of learned prelates, especially Sadoleto and Giles of Viterbo, who defended his modest poetic liberties. He later inevitably incurred the astringent criticism of Erasmus in the *Ciceronianus*, where he is credited with writing on a religious subject with grace and liveliness, but censured for not having treated sacred material in a more sacred manner.[11]

The matter of religious decorum and the harmonization of the Gospel story with classical motifs and language were of great concern to the poet. Sannazaro was attempting something very different from all his predecessors in this genre. He was, of course, familiar with the early Christian poets, whose writings had received some impetus from the set of three volumes, *Veteres poetae Christiani*, published by Manutius in 1501. But Juvencus's rather crude paraphrase was more of an apologetic work than a poem in its own right, and Sedulius's *Carmen paschale*, though artistically superior, was too didactic in its intent. Soon after the publication of the Manutius collection, the *Parthenice* of the Carmelite poet, Giambattista Spagnuoli, usually known as Mantuan in English, also appeared. It is about twice the length of Sannazaro's poem, quite prolix and often uninspired, but not without some influence on the later poem. While the two poems are widely separated in their perfection of form, they are even more distinct in their approach. Mantuan dresses up the Christian mysteries in classical garb, embroidering his tale with numerous mythological allusions. In Sannazaro's poem, on the contrary, as Edgar Wind aptly remarks, "the Vergilian tone has acquired a twist of mystical ardour, which is unmistakably Christian."[12] With his religious mentor, Giles of Viterbo, Sannazaro was persuaded that the rays of divine truth were covered with poetic veils. He says plainly in writing to Seripando that he follows St Augustine in the belief that Vergil could have prophesied the coming of Christ. In demonstration of this he incorporates into the Third Book a close paraphrase of the *Fourth Eclogue*, a poem often quoted by Giles. For this reason, too, he has Proteus deliver a prophecy although he discreetly has the river Jordan serve as the elusive sea-god's mouthpiece. The classical figures of the poem are not mere ornaments, but almost instruments of divine revelation. Vergil occupied a special place in all of this. If Vergil was often regarded as an *anima naturaliter Christiana*, then we must truly consider Sannazaro a new Vergil in Christian guise, born on those same Parthenopean shores so dear to the Roman poet.

I should like to examine some of the more important revisions in the first book from the early *Christeid* (which was the title of the Venetian printing) through the corrections of later manuscripts to the autographs of the Laurentian library with their erasures and additions. Some of these changes are commented upon by Sannazaro himself while others I have ventured to explain. Most of the corrections are an improvement, but not all, in my opinion. Some are of Sannazaro's own devising, others were suggested to him by his circle of friends, Seripando, Sadoleto and especially the poet Antonio Tebaldeo. Interesting insights into the creative process and the role of poet as editor of his own work should emerge from such an investigation.

The opening invocation reveals Sannazaro's firm belief in the gift of poetic inspiration and his unabashed devotion to the Muses of pagan antiquity. His entreaty is genuine, not merely conventional, for in his view piety could not be separated from eloquence. In Pontano's dialogue, *Aegidius*, the Muses are credited with omniscience of natural events.[13] They are constantly invoked in Sannazaro's poetry, but here with even more relevance since, as he says, they too draw their origin from heaven and, virgins themselves, are gratified by the reverence owed to virginity. In the *Christeid* there was more specific mention of hallowed places of the Muses, which may have offended some critics, and in the Ashburnham autograph there were three additional lines, subsequently deleted, but still clearly visible, in which the poet pays personal homage to the Muses, who, he declares, had brought him up in the love of the liberal arts

> ut sine Pierio nil sit mihi dulce paratu.[14]   (f. 12 ter)

The last word was originally *lepore*, "alla lucreziana," as he explains to Seripando, but even this term seems to have been considered improper by his critics. Sannazaro argues in opposition that any poetic ornament or fiction that was not detrimental to religion was worthy of inclusion in his poem.

Only after this lengthy invocation of the Muses does the poet turn to the Blessed Virgin herself to seek her benediction. In addressing her he uses the appellation frequently used by Vergil of goddesses, *alma parens*, as well as *diva*, used also by Mantuan. Sannazaro could not bring himself, however, to refer to Christ as Apollo or to the Virgin as a nymph, as he tells Seripando, an overt refutation of Mantuan's use of that term in the very opening line of his epic announcing the theme of the Palestinian nymph. While Mantuan is lavish in his epithets of Mary, star of the sea, Sannazaro is content to refer to his humble devotion in the rites and ceremonies of the shrine cut into the rock overlooking his beloved Mergilline. In the *Christeid* the tone was more paganizing in the use of phrases redolent of ancient worship, but in the definitive version this passage undergoes a subtle Christianization.

The opening scene of the poem represents Almighty God looking down from his heavenly heights at the triumph of the infernal forces as they drag man into the depths of hell. As in Vergil's underworld, Tisiphone, one of the Furies, leads the phalanx of her savage sisters in their bloody revenge. Here a few simple changes in one line reveal Sannazaro's deft art of revision. Without having to make any rhythmic or contextual alterations, he converts "immites stimulantem ad furta sorores" into the much more forceful "immanes stimulantem ad dira sorores"

(l. 36). Offended at this victory of the forces of evil, God determines to rescue man by creating a new Eve. To signify Mary's role in the drama of redemption the poet struggled to find adequate and terse expression. He swears on his faith to Seripando that he was never satisfied with these lines and asks for some suggestion for emendation. The manuscripts fully testify to the poet's quandary at this point with various re-wordings and rearrangements of words. Perhaps Sannazaro had in mind a distich from Sedulius:

> Sola fuit mulier patuit quae ianua leto
> et qua vita redit sola fuit mulier.[15]

Although the poet did not like his original phrasing it seems to me that in this case the final compromise is inferior. The *Christeid* reads:

> Nec mora, cum fuerit tantorum sola malorum
> foemina principium, reparet quoque foemina damnum. (ll. 45–46)

This is expanded to four lines, (in the Laurentian autograph the two additional lines are added in the margin):

> Cumque caput fuerit tantorumque una malorum
> foemina principium lacrimasque et funera terris
> intulerit, nunc auxilium ferat ipsa modumque
> qua licet afflictis imponat foemina rebus. (ll. 51–54)

I think it is quite clear that the *amplificatio* is less effective than the epigrammatic terseness of the first version. Perhaps once again Sannazaro was tempted to expand the theological content to the detriment of the poetry.

   The mission of the angel Gabriel to Earth is a delightful interlude, which shows off Sannazaro's great skill in interweaving and re-composing snatches of Vergil. The simile of the swan hastening its flight to the Caystrian marshes sighted from the air is a lovely amalgam of Vergilian reminiscences. In God's instructions to his messenger there are some interesting revisions. Twice in this short speech Sannazaro had used the word *Tonans* to signify the Almighty, a word sanctioned by the usage of Juvencus, but emended here, I think, because he felt it was awkward for God to refer to himself by this title. Thus "domoque habitare Tonantis" (*Christeid*, l. 59) becomes "nostros aeternum habitare penates" (l. 72) and "ut foret aeterni sobolem quae sola Tonantis / conciperet" (*Christeid*, ll. 62–63) is changed to the dogmatically more precise: "ut foret intacta sanctum quae numen in alvo / conciperet" (ll. 75–76).

   As so often in Renaissance paintings the Virgin is depicted as immersed in the reading of the Scripture when the angel approaches. Here again, under the influence of the cabalistic merging of Christian and pagan themes, Sannazaro presents her as wrapt in admiration of the future mother of God as foretold by prophets and Sibyls. In one line the doctrinal once again seems to have won out over the more poetic, at least to my perception, "felicemque illam felici et sidere na-

tam" of the *Christeid* (l. 90) which remains without erasure in the Laurentian autograph, gives way in the printed text to the metrically more awkward "felicemque
illam humana nec lege creatam" (l. 103).

The simple salutation of the angel seems to have resisted easy translation into
classical verse. The letter to Seripando has several variants, which do not occur
in any of the manuscripts. Here again the version of the *Christeid* seems to be more
fluent and unencumbered. "Salve, o nostris lux addita rebus" (*Christeid*, l. 96) is
changed to "Oculis salve lux debita nostris" (l. 109). *Debita* for *addita* is probably
a theological nicety, emphasizing the providential role of Mary in the divine plan
of redemption. The Virgin's perturbation at the angel's words, as the Gospel tells
us, "turbata est in sermone eius," was quite literally translated at first; "stupuit
dictis conterrita virgo" (*Christeid*, l. 102). Later, seemingly in response to criticism,
Sannazaro changed *dictis* to *visu*, explaining that the emotion would then be more
consonant with the following simile of a young maiden awaiting the arrival of
her future spouse on the shore of Mycone. In the end he rejected both words and
settled for an innocuous *confestim*. The simile also was probably too explicit and
too secular in its reference to the ship bearing the maiden's father and the promised spouse — "patrem et sperata viri connubia portans" (*Christeid*, l. 111), for this
human cargo is changed to the exotic wares of Arabia and Canopus in the final
version.

The delicate matter of Mary's vowed virginity, which prompts her to demur
at the angel's annunciation, is handled with great circumspection. The Gospel
words quoted in the margin are simply "quomodo fiet istud, quoniam virum non
cognosco." In the *Christeid* Sannazaro used the rather forceful expression "tactus
exosa virum taedasque jugales" (*Christeid*, l. 136), echoing Daphne's sentiments
before Apollo's advances in the first book of the *Metamorphoses* (I.483). This is considerably mitigated in the final version to "mene attactus perferre viriles / posse
putas?" (ll. 158–59) influenced perhaps by Mantuan's "tactus non passa viriles."

The angel's reassurance to Mary that the power of the Holy Spirit would come
upon her is very skillfully adapted to epic language and suffered hardly any revision. The last line of the angel's words, "quia non erit impossibile apud Deum
omne verbum," proved somewhat refractory to the exigencies of the meter. Seripando seems to have objected to the adjective *exsuperabile*, a good Vergilian min-
tage, which was then changed to the less poetic *superabile*. At this point in the letter Sannazaro gives vent to a petulant explosion of artistic frustration, cursing
the day he ever attempted this unending task. He exclaims that he should have
left these fatigues to the popes or those who devour the revenues of Christ. Paradise could have been attained without such sacrifice, he remonstrates, but then
resigns himself in the prayer, "Ma lodato sia Dio di ogni cosa."[16]

Mary's *fiat* receives some subtle modifications in the final revision, which ac-
centuate her complete acquiescence to God's will. *En adsum*, a lovely phrase, worthy of evangelical piety, remains the same in both versions, but the remaining
part of her response, "accipio venerans tua iussa tuumque / dulce sacrum, pater

omnipotens" (ll. 181–82), is an improvement on the impersonal "accipio libens mandata Tonantis," which may owe something to Mantuan. In the *Christeid* Sannazaro in a rather naturalistic sequence had the angel depart at this point, and had Mary entrust a message to him for the dwellers in heaven. This is followed by the mysterious infusion of the Holy Spirit into the womb of the virgin, described in appropriately mystical language. Mantuan's image of the inflation of a bellows is decidedly gauche, by comparison. In the final revision this episode is placed before the farewell to the angel, making her prayer to him to bear witness to her virginity in heaven more understandable.

The next scene transports us to limbo, with numerous reminiscences of Vergil's underground, where Fame has already brought the news of the world's future redemption. With very effective dramatic invention, Sannazaro has the prophet David foretell in a vivid *repraesentatio* salient events in the life of Christ and his mother. There is evidence of extensive revision in this section with relevant discussion in the letter to Seripando. In an earlier letter there had obviously been some dispute about the propriety of this device, which the poet defended, explaining that things seen only vaguely in the past are now set vividly before the prophet's eyes. In his prophetic ecstasy David foresees the passion of Christ, which Sannazaro presents in graphic terms. There are not too many revisions in this section and those that do find acceptance are all in the cause of greater simplicity. To give but one example, the rather stilted "alti regnator Olympi / horrendum attonito spectaclum praebeat orbi" cedes to the more poignant "hominum lux illa decorque / pendeat" (ll. 327–38).

From the lifting of Christ upon the cross Sannazaro passed immediately in the *Christeid* to the convulsions of nature that bore testimony to his death. He later added a marvelous *pezzo forte*, the lamentation of Mary beneath the cross, worthy of the best traditions of the vernacular *pianti della vergine*. It is a passage of 35 emotional lines (333–68) compared to the more than 100 repetitious hexameters of Mantuan. Variants are plentiful here and for the most part tend to reduce the high pitch of emotion. In one line *discissa* and *laniata* are changed to the less violent *demissa* and *effusa*. A slight change in the order of words brings out a forceful epanalepsis in "quis me miseram, quis culmine tanto." To describe the virgin's despair, Sannazaro usurps a line from Vergil's *Fifth Eclogue* depicting the sorrow of the mother of Daphnis, who lifts her cries to the stars. "Crudelia dicit sidera" (ll. 339–40) is a rather daring utterance, which caused some theological hesitation in the poet but, having passed muster with sterner theologians, it was allowed to remain. He also uses to very good effect single words and sentiments taken from the lament of the mother of Euryalus over the lifeless body of her son. In one place, however, pedantic criticism of the word *aerumnas*, not found in Vergil and therefore considered inadmissible, resulted in the worsening of one line (l. 351).

The account of the mourning of nature at the death of Christ borrows a few particulars from Vergil's account of the cataclysms that followed upon the death of Caesar. One felicitious change of diction is owed to the Vergilian passage. Of the darkening of the sun's rays the homely word *fuligine* is replaced by *ferrugine*, of more poetic currency. From these celestial manifestations David's prophecy returns to his own surroundings as he relates the future deliverance of souls from the prison of limbo after Christ's redeeming death. This gives the poet the opportunity to paint in epic language the regions of the underworld, which he does with great virtuosity, rearranging lines from Vergil's description of infernal monsters in the Sixth Book. The only significant addition to the *Christeid* is a group of three lines (ll. 404–06) in which the inhabitants of limbo exalt the arrival of the victorious Christ in their midst with shouts of acclamation. These lines serve as a good preparation for the following rather remarkable tableau of Christ as charioteer driving a chariot drawn by the four living creatures from the vision of Ezechiel and the *Apocalypse* representing the four evangelists, a passage which may also owe something to the twenty-ninth canto of the *Purgatorio* (xxix.106–54).

These have been but a meagre sampling of some of the more significant changes performed in the text of the first book in Sannazaro's subtle and even exasperated elaboration. Unlike Petrarch, however, whose hopes for the *Africa* were misplaced, Sannazaro's efforts were rewarded. The poem was immensely popular from the first, and constituted, as Professor Dionisotti has said,[17] the trump card of his whole literary career.

University of Windsor

Notes

1. Cf. Paul Valéry, *The Art of Poetry*, transl. Denise Folliot (New York, 1958), p. 177.
2. Lilio Gregorio Giraldi, *De poetis nostrorum temporum*, ed. Karl Wotke (Berlin, 1894), p. 16.
3. ibid., p. 16.
4. Giovanni Pontano, *I dialoghi*, ed. Carmelo Previtera (Florence, 1943), p. 147.
5. Marciana 2559.
6. Vatican lat. 3360 and codices 3259 and 3357 of the Biblioteca Nazionale di Napoli.
7. Codex XXIV, 44 and Ashburnham, 411.
8. Jacopo Sannazaro, *Opere volgari*, ed. Alfredo Mauro (Bari, 1961), pp. 368–88.
9. Antonio Frezza, Naples, May 1526, and Minizio Calvo, Rome, December 1526.
10. Mauro, op. cit., p. 381.
11. "praeferendus est Pontano, quod rem sacram tractare non piguit, quod nec dormitanter eam nec inamoene tractavit. Sed meo quidem suffragio plus laudis erit laturus, si materiam sacram tractasset aliquanto sacratius." Desiderio Erasmo da Rotterdam, *Il Ciceroniano*, ed. Angiolo Gambara (Brescia, 1965), p. 278.
12. Edgar Wind, *Pagan Mysteries in the Renaissance* (Oxford, 1980), p. 20.
13. Previtera, op. cit., p. 248.
14. Lines from the poem are given according to a critical edition that Professor Alessandro Perosa and I are preparing.

15. Sedulius Scotus, Hymnus I, ll. 7-8, *Opera omnia*, ed. Johannes Huemer (Vienna, 1885), p. 154.

16. Mauro, op. cit., p. 378.

17. "Il *De partu virginis* fu per il Sannazaro la carta decisiva di tutta la sua vita di scrittore." Carlo Dionisotti, "Appunti sulle *Rime* del Sannazaro," *GSLI*, 95 (1963), 193.

Roman Law and Constitutional Thought in Machiavelli

John H. Geerken

In the year 1520, or thereabouts, Machiavelli composed a short treatise entitled, "A Discourse on Remodelling the Government of Florence" — a piece hitherto largely ignored because overshadowed by Machiavelli's better-known works.[1] This neglect is unfortunate for the essay could be taken to function in the corpus of Machiavelli's writings as a kind of distillation of his reflections on historic and contemporary constitutions, especially those of Rome and Florence. Not only does it have distinct linkages to *The Prince* and the *Discourses*, but as one of his last works, it is a product of Machiavelli's greatest intellectual maturity, showing him, in some respects, to be beyond ideology and partisanship. In any case, it is a work that most clearly reveals Machiavelli the law-giver; in one place he explicitly refers to "this republic of mine," while in another he alludes to his trying "to design a republic."[2]

For all that, it must be acknowledged that what Machiavelli meant by that which goes under the rubric *re publica* must be approached with some caution. Although the term *re publica* is a familiar one in the traditions of legal and political discourse which he inherited, it is not customary to think of Machiavelli as standing within those traditions. Repeatedly he comments in his works that he is making a new way.[3] Furthermore, the conventions of Machiavelli scholarship have been such as to locate the Florentine neither among the founders or reformers of republics, nor among those who make up the tradition of Roman Law. As J. G. A. Pocock has put it, "*virtus* ... and *ius* inhabit different conceptual universes."[4]

However, a careful examination of "The Discourse on Remodelling the Government of Florence" — not in isolation, but against the background of *The Prince* and the *Discourses* on Livy, as well as the legal and political ambience of Florence itself — suggests that, in fact, a case can be made for precisely such conceptual coexistence. In his writing of what I shall be calling the "Remodelling Discourse," Machiavelli was in no way repudiating his earlier works, but sharpening and underscoring the views he had there set forth. What linked these works — and all his major works together — was Machiavelli's abiding concern with constitutions —

i.e., with the problem of founding a lasting republic — and what forged a major part of these links was, among other things, his understanding of the elements of Roman legal thought. This is not to say that Machiavelli was a lawyer, or that he was especially or unusually interested in the law, or that he was educated in the law (although there is some circumstantial evidence that his father — himself a lawyer — might have had such an education in mind for his son).[5] What is claimed is that the conceptual patterns which are revealed in the Machiavellian corpus have an identifiable legal component, and that that legal component must be seen as mediated by an ambience of legal and political discourse in Florence that was saturated with Roman Law.[6]

Now, what does Machiavelli say in the "Remodelling Discourse" that enables it to function in the wider sense thus noted? The treatise may be divided into four parts: an introductory critique of Florentine institutions and procedures from 1393 to 1520; an analysis of proposed measures of reform; then, the body of the essay in which Machiavelli sets forth his specific recommendations regarding the distribution of offices; and a concluding exhortation to the pope, Leo X, to whom the work is addressed.

The diagnostic introduction is a model of compact constitutional criticism. In the three printed pages or so that make it up, Machiavelli surveys 127 years of Florentine history and concludes that the city has had, in effect, no constitution. Seven times he invokes the criterion of endurance: good constitutions are fitted to last, bad ones are not; eight times he cites the theme of Florentine constitutional failure. And the reasons to him are clear: Florence has been unstable because her methods of governing are always varying; her public officials enjoy no prestige, while some of her private citizens enjoy too much; the *Signoria* has too much arbitrary power over life and property — there being no machinery for appeal; and the people are denied their share of power.[7] Accordingly, the constitution of Florence is no true mixed constitution, but a specious hybrid, sometimes of an aristocracy and a republic, as under Cosimo; sometimes of a princedom and a republic, as under Lorenzo. In neither case, however, does the government conduce to the common good. "The reason why all these governments have been defective," he concludes in this first section, "is that the alterations in them have been made not for the fulfillment of the common good, but for the strengthening and security of the party [in power]."[8]

Proceeding to his criticism of contemporary proposals for reform, Machiavelli declares that constitutional stability does not lie in the direction of turning the clock back to the time of Cosimo's aristocratic republic. For the times and the people have changed: the people no longer approve of the government as they did Cosimo's; they have become accustomed to equality. For its part the Medici family, having grown great, is no longer intimate and friendly with the people. The military and diplomatic situations in Italy have changed; the people have fallen out of the habit of paying taxes. In sum: it is no longer possible to put the same Medicean stamp on different Florentine material. In consequence, any change in the constitutional order must begin with existing realities, not a priori formulas.[9]

This understood, the central question then becomes one of inclusiveness: should the new government include more people or fewer? Oligarchies for Machiavelli fail from the outset because their lack of firmness makes them either rise to princedoms or sink to republics. In either case they are incapable of security or glory. Princedoms he will not discuss because they do not befit a *populus* accustomed to equality, and they are too difficult to establish without the requisite conditions and facilities. (He does not add, as he might have, that he has discussed princedoms elsewhere.) So that leaves only the form of the republic — which brings Machiavelli to the main part of his discourse.[10]

"Those who organize a republic," he affirms, "ought to provide for the three different sorts of men who exist in all cities, namely, the most important, those in the middle, and the lowest."[11] The most important people should get the most important offices inasmuch as their ambition for those offices must be appeased. This leads Machiavelli to recommend the abolition of the old *Signoria* and the creation of a new one of sixty-four members, half of whom would assume for a year the magistracy (together with the Gonfalonier of Justice), while the other half would assume for that same year an advisory and consultative role. At the end of the year these functions would be exchanged between the two groups. And as membership in these groups is for life, and as those of lesser rank would never be admitted, the perennial problems growing out of mismatched rank, status, and ambition between public office and private individuals would be solved.[12]

By the same token, "since there are three sorts of men,... there [should] also be three ranks in a republic, and not more."[13] For those of middling importance there is established a Council of Two Hundred, membership in which is denied to those in the first and third ranks, but which is for life to those in the second. It would assume the functions now performed by "the jumble of councils" (the phrase is Machiavelli's) that has long plagued Florence.[14]

The third and final class of men — "which is the whole general body of citizens"[15] — is awarded a Grand Council of One Thousand, or at least Six Hundred. And this council would allot all other offices and magistracies except those pertaining to the aforementioned classes of men and their respective councils. The balance of Machiavelli's discussion is then devoted to recommendations for secret voting procedures (pouching), for levying an infantry, for the establishment of a court of appeal with the power of secret judgment, and for other details of implementation.[16]

But two other features of this constitution must be noted. Machiavelli has described a pyramidal sandwich of power: the best and fewest at the top; the more and better in the middle; the most and least important at the bottom. But by instituting the office of Provost, and by staffing it with four Provosts drawn only from the lowest level, Machiavelli has moved in the direction of constitutional checks and balances: for the Provosts are charged with observing and vetoing the decisions of the two higher levels, and their powers are reinforced by machinery for appeal.[17]

The second notable feature is that appointment to the life-time offices of the *Signoria* (level one) and to the Council of the Selected (level two) is to be made by Leo X, "since you have the military and criminal justice in your hand, the laws in your bosom, and all the heads of government as your supporters."[18] At least seven times in the six pages of this section Machiavelli refers explicitly to the pope's authority — most emphatically when he declares that "in order to make these changes and to support and regulate the above-mentioned groups,... Your Holiness ... must have ... as much authority ... as is held by the entire people of Florence."[19] Between the lines of this remark is the unspoken assumption that the *imperium*, or highest public power of Florence (at least theoretically) resides in the *populus liber*. Yet Machiavelli is also realistic enough to acknowledge the very real fact of Leo's power. He holds the *imperium* since he has the military and criminal justice in his hand and the laws in his bosom. But what is remarkable about Machiavelli's treatment of Leo's authority is that the latter should hold it only during his lifetime and then have it remanded through the constitutional reforms Machiavelli is advocating to the Florentine people. Seven times within four pages Machiavelli makes use of such phrases as "during your lifetime," or "after the lifetime of Your Holiness" to betoken the fact that the distribution of public power just described is in fact a monarchical order; but also that that order must be transformed on Leo's death if it is to survive.[20] This transformation can be accomplished, Machiavelli suggests, by filling vacancies occasionally by nomination not of the pope, but of one of the councils. Were this to happen government would be so ordered that "it will administer itself and.... Your Holiness will need only to keep half an eye turned on it."[21] In sum, a true and lasting republic can be allowed to evolve from a *de facto* monarchy. So confident, in fact, is Machiavelli in this possibility that he proceeds to deny any alternative: "There is no other way for escaping these ills," he concludes, "than to give the city institutions that can by themselves stand firm. And they will always stand firm when everybody has a hand in them, and when everybody knows what he needs to do and in whom he can trust, and no class of citizen, either through fear for itself or through ambition, will need to desire revolution."[22]

Such, then, is Machiavelli's prescription for a perfect republic (that phrase, too, is his). It is his constitutional thought in microcosm. And though the bulk of it has to do with specifying the component parts, their arrangement, interrelationship, and functioning, it is possible to examine the work for its first principles — especially those first legal principles that seem to bear the strongest imprint of the Roman Law tradition.

Parenthetically, it should be stated how the term "principle" functions in this context. I use it in the sense of beginnings, the basic views of law and justice that produce specific rules. Preoccupation with specific rules does not preclude the existence of such principles, even if the rule-maker does not explicitly formulate them, or is aware of these principles. Neither Roman lawyers as a group, as Schultz has shown,[23] nor Florentine lawyers as a group, as Martines has shown,[24] were given to self-analysis and research into or formulation of underlying first principles. Nevertheless, it is possible by a process of deduction to derive what the governing principles of Roman and Florentine jurisprudence were. In Machiavelli's case, we know from his recommendations at the opening of the Livy *Discourses*, Book III, that a polity return periodically to its first principles. But what his own were in the areas of law-making and constitutions he chose not to make explicit.

With regard to the "Remodelling Discourse" it is clear that the most important such first principle is the primacy of the *universitas*, the whole. In the case of ancient Rome, her striving for a unitary state, her consciousness of her particular destiny, her sense of historical mission to organize and direct the world by means of her arms and laws — in which areas she admitted no superior — contributed to the rise of the notion of *Roma communis patria*,[25] a sense of blood-brotherhood[26] that expressed itself legally in distinctions between Romans and non-Romans, in provisions virtually equating citizenship and nation, and in the formulaic usage of the phrase "arms and laws," often found in legal writings, even as late as Justinian.[27]

In parallel fashion, the *universitas* came first for the Florentine jurists — whether that *universitas* be one of guild, nation, or especially city.[28] Since the mid-fourteenth century Florentine lawyers had refined the Bartolist doctrine that the *princeps* of Roman law was the *civitas* of Florentine law.[29] The doctrine that the city was prince unto itself (*civitas sibi princeps*) included the notion that the city as an *universitas superiores non recognoscens*, it recognized no superiors.[30] Accordingly, it exercised the *plenitudo imperialis potestatis*, and like the emperor of Roman Law could be above the law, *princeps legibus solutus*.[31] Consider, for example, Francesco Guicciardini's understanding of the primacy of the city in his account of the conduct of a Florentine magistracy (The Eight of War) during the Pazzi conspiracy of 1478:

> That magistracy ... had been established with immense authority in criminal matters.... Given a free and absolute power over crimes concerning the state, it was restrained by no laws in this sphere of things. The men who held the regime in their hands devised the office of the Eight so as to have a club for smashing the head of anyone who might wish to vilify or change the government. And though it was born in violence and tyranny, yet the outcome was very salutary. For as anyone in this land knows who has experience of things, if the fear of this magistracy — a fear caused by its swiftness in discovering and judging crimes — did not hold back the wicked, one could not live in Florence.[32]

Guicciardini was four years out of law school when he wrote these lines around 1509. Machiavelli had three years yet remaining in his secretarial post at the chancery. But he, too, would eventually come to write in the *Discourses* III.41:

"For where the very safety of the country depends upon the resolution to be taken, no considerations of justice or injustice, humanity or cruelty, nor of glory or of shame, should be allowed to prevail. But putting aside all other considerations, the only question should be: what course will save the life and liberty of the country?"

(From this kind of thinking—that the *princeps*, whether city or prince, is occasionally above the law, especially in emergencies—it is but a short step to the position that, again in necessity, the *princeps* is above morality.)

That Machiavelli still subscribes to the principle of the primacy of the *universitas* in the "Remodelling Discourse" is evident from his emphasis on the common good—indeed, his use of the concept as a criterion for distinguishing good constitutions from bad. I have already quoted a passage in which he faults Florentine governments for instituting changes that benefit party or faction, but do not fulfill the common good. That came in the first, diagnostic part of Machiavelli's treatise. But then at the end of the part in which he sets forth his recommendations, he affirms that a benefit of his scheme in its provision for the observation of office holders in office is that if some individual or group

> does things opposed to the common good through wickedness, somebody may be at hand to take from them that power and appeal their decision to another body, because it is not good that one kind of magistrate or council should be able to retard public business without someone's being there who can arrange for action. It is also not good that office-holders should not have somebody to observe them and make them abstain from actions that are not good.[33]

There is no departure from this principle in Machiavelli's other works, even in *The Prince* where his discussions of Cesare Borgia in chapter 7, of Agathocles the Sicilian in chapter 8, and of Lorenzo de' Medici in chapter 26 evaluate their respective doings against the criterion of usefulness to their subjects or to the good of the mass of the people, *bene all università delli uomini*.[34]

Implicit in the idea of the primacy of the *universitas* is a second Roman legal principle, the distinction between the public and private spheres. For the common good implies a private good, and invocations of common good usually imply some sort of contest between the good of some individual or group on one hand and the good of the state on the other. On this point Roman Law was quite clear. Justinian's *Digest* defines public law as that which looks to the things of the Roman state, and private law as that which looks to the utility of individuals.[35]

A parallel insistence on the separation of public and private spheres is evident in Machiavelli. The "Remodelling Discourse" locates a cause of Florence's constitutional problems in the fact, noted above, that public officials have too little dignity or prestige whereas some private citizens have too much. The private sphere threatens to usurp the public—a concern that preoccupied Machiavelli in his other works as well. Thus, in *The Prince* he will lay down two rules: first, that for an individual to become prince (i.e., change from private to public status) presupposes either great ability (*virtù*) or good fortune;[36] and second that only a man of great genius is likely to know how to hold public command if he has always lived in a private position.[37] Though it takes exceptional ability (or luck) to cross over from the private realm to the public, there are those, to be sure, who have done so. Agathocles the Sicilian, Paolo Vitelli, and Francesco Sforza are all examples. But the most praiseworthy of such men in Machiavelli's eyes is Julius II, discussed in chapter 11 as one who "merits great praise as he did everything to increase the power of the church [i.e., a public institution] and not of any private person."

It is in the Livy *Discourses*, however, that Machiavelli fully develops his thinking about the two spheres. At least seven chapter titles throughout the three books announce a specific concern with the topic,[38] although the work abounds in other references, examples, and discussion. The pattern nevertheless is clear: private citizens can, by virtue of their wealth, merit, or personality rise to a position whereby they can threaten the public good. Failure to watch prominent citizens, repress their insolence, or punish their crimes invites injury to the *re publica*. As Machiavelli puts it in *Discourses* III.28:

> ... it is often the great influence of such distinguished citizens that is the cause of states being reduced to servitude. And to prevent this the institutions of the state should be so regulated that the influence of citizens shall be founded only upon such acts as are of benefit to the state, and not upon such as are injurious to the public interests or liberty.

This is clearly consonant with what Machiavelli says in the "Remodelling Discourse" regarding the prestige of public officials and private individuals. Too much of the latter and not enough of the former creates a condition threatening the roles and functions of the two spheres. For there are for Machiavelli two spheres, one public and one private, and they coexist in a kind of tension. Aggressive (and unavoidable) individual ambition he locates in the private sphere; the laws to restrain that ambition in the public sphere. However, those laws are only as effective as those who enforce them, and if the latter are lax in this responsibility by virtue of indifference, complacency, ineptness, false sentimentality, or corruption, they have the effect of relaxing the tension of legal restraint and thereby create conditions in which private ambition can more freely exercise itself. If this process is unchecked the public order will be subverted, and the interests of private individuals will dictate the agenda of the *re publica*. This is, in fact, how Cosimo de' Medici came to power.[39]

Private individuals, of course, do not act alone: they lead partisans, head factions, and represent family and class interests as well, with their respective forms of collective ambition and hopes for aggrandizement. That these, too, threaten the state then leads Machiavelli from the public-private dichotomy to a third (and for us, final) legal conception derived from Rome: the notion of constitutional checks and balances.

Machiavelli's analysis of a perfect constitution dominates the first book of the Livy *Discourses* and receives particular attention in chapter 2. There Machiavelli, borrowing extensively from the sixth book of Polybius's *History*, notes the origin of society, the establishment of monarchy, its degeneration into tyranny leading to revolution, the succession of aristocracy and oligarchy, and then, finally, democracy and mob rule—the latter returning the polity to the point where monarchy is reintroduced. The three good forms of government ineluctably degenerate into their corresponding evil forms because merit gives way to the principle of heredity and the children and grandchildren bring different attitudes to office—especially the willingness to inflict "injury upon public as well as private interests, each individual only consulting his own passions."[40] For Machiavelli the only way to stop the cycle—again following Polybius—is to take from each of the three good governments and form a single mixed polity:

> Hence, since those who have been prudent in establishing laws have recognized this defect, they have avoided each one of these kinds by itself alone and chosen one that partakes of them all, judging it more solid and stable, because one keeps watch over the other, if in the same city there are princedom, aristocracy, and popular government.[41]

The key word, though he does not tell us, is *watch*. But Machiavelli becomes so preoccupied in subsequent chapters with his account of Rome's defiance of the cycle, with her development of a mixed constitution in chronological stages, that he does not explain how the machinery of watching should take place in a perfect polity.

That deficiency, however, he repairs in the "Remodelling Discourse." The Provosts representing the companies of the people (the lowest level) are to take turns residing in the palace with the *Signoria*. It will be recalled that the *Signoria* is made up of sixty-four citizens, divided into two groups, one of which functions in a directive, the other in a consultative mode. Each group of thirty-two citizens is further divided into four groups of eight, with each of these smaller groups residing in the palace for a period of three months, therein assuming the magisterial and ceremonial functions of government. With each resident group of eight (to which is added the Gonfalonier for Life) is a resident provost from the ranks of the people, also serving on a rotational basis. Machiavelli further stipulates that for the Nine to do any business whatsoever one Provost must be present with the power of appeal to the thirty-two. For the thirty-two to do any business two Provosts must be present with power of appeal to the Council of Two Hundred; for the Two Hundred to function six Gonfaloniers of the people and two Provosts are necessary with power of appeal to the Grand Council, and that body, in turn, likewise requires twelve Gonfaloniers and three Provosts in order to proceed.[42] In sum, when Machiavelli writes about the three powers or classes keeping each other reciprocally in check, he has in mind a double process of observation and veto-appeal which will expose the workings of government and give substance to what we might call the principle of accountability. Whatever secret agreements, understanding, and policies might occupy the penumbra of politics at the higher levels, they must first be processed through a machinery of exposure, veto, and appeal before arriving at the point where they can be implemented.

Of course, Machiavelli's constitution was itself never implemented, just as much of his advice in *The Prince* and *Discourses* went unheeded in his own time and by his own countrymen. Nevertheless, his constitutional thinking, in its forms and sources does deserve consideration — if for no other reason than that it discloses how Machiavelli was groping for a way to express what we might call the idea of a loyal opposition. Though his constitution did not specifically envision anything like an opposition party, perhaps because his classical models where likewise omissive, he did recognize that there are opposing interests in government. For him the lessons of history made clear that since opposition in some form was always present and could not be avoided, it had to be accommodated. The result was a constitution of tri-partite forces and counterforces in equilibrium, much like a well-trimmed boat (to use Polybius's image). That Machiavelli's vessel never sailed does not deny the fact that in a period of renaissance he nevertheless sought to restore the *publica* to the *re publica*.

Scripps College

Notes

1. The work, hereinafter referred to as *RD*, is the *Discursus flodentinarum rerum post mortem iunioris Laurentii Medices*. I have used the version found in Niccolò Machiavelli, *Tutte le Opere*, ed. Mario Martelli (Florence, Sansoni, 1971), pp. 24–31. The quotations in English are taken from *Machiavelli: The Chief Works and Others*, transl. by Allan Gilbert (Durham, N.C., Duke University Press, 1965), 3 vols. *RD* is found in vol. I, 101–15. I have followed Gilbert's dating of the work. There seems to be little controversy over the date.

2. ... in questa mia repubblica..., Martelli, 27; Gilbert, I, 107, 109.

3. *The Prince*, ch. 15, *Discourses on the First Ten Books of Titus Livius*, Book I, Introduction.

4. Private correspondence with this author, June 16, 1980. For a survey of Machiavelli literature, see J. H. Geerken, "Machiavelli Studies Since 1969," *JHI*, 37 (1976), 351–68, and Quentin Skinner, *Machiavelli* (New York, Hill and Wang, 1981).

5. See my forthcoming article, "Did Machiavelli Study Law?"

6. On the Florentine legal ambience, see Lauro Martines, *Lawyers and Statecraft in Renaissance Florence* (Princeton, Princeton University Press, 1968).

7. *RD*, Gilbert, I, 101–04.

8. ibid., p. 103.

9. ibid., p. 105.

10. ibid., pp. 106–07.

11. ibid., p. 107.

12. ibid., pp. 108–09.

13. ibid., p. 109.

14. ibid.

15. ibid., p. 110.

16. ibid., pp. 110–13.

17. ibid., pp. 111–12.

18. ibid., p. 113.

19. ibid., pp. 109–10.

20. ibid., pp. 110–13.

21. ibid., p. 115.

22. ibid.

23. Fritz Schulz, *Principles of Roman Law* (Oxford, Clarendon Press, 1956).

24. Martines, 413.

25. Pliny, *Hist. nat.* III.5.39 in Schulz, 112.

26. Cicero, *in Verr.* II.v.67, 172 in Schulz, 111.

27. Cf. Vergil, *Aeneid* VI, 847ff.; Pliny, *loc. cit.*; for Justinian's constitutions, see Schulz, 118.

28. Martines, 25.

29. ibid., 121f., 422ff.

30. ibid., 438.

31. ibid., 426ff.

32. *Storie fiorentine dal 1378 al 1509*, ed. R. Palmarocchi (Bari, 1931), pp. 41–42, quoted in Martines, 410.

33. *RD*, Gilbert, I, 112.

34. The phrase is Machiavelli's, *The Prince*, ch. 26; Martelli, 297. It must be stressed that not all appeals to the common good—whether by Machiavelli or by other writers or lawyers—were of the highest-minded quality. Like more contemporary appeals to "national security" or "national honor," it was capable of politically-inspired abuse. For an example of such abuse in fourteenth-century Florence, see Martines, 406–07. Even in abuse, however, the notion of the common good underscores the primacy of the *universitas*.

35. *Digest*, I, 2.

36. *The Prince*, ch. 6.

37. ibid., ch. 7.

38. Cf. *Discourses*, I, 52; II, 13, 28; III, 28, 30, 34, 35.

39. ibid., I, 33, 52. Cf. *History of Florence*, IV, 28; VII, 2.

40. *Discourses*, I, 2. This passage is in the translation by Christian E. Detmold in *The Prince and the Discourses*, intro. by Max Lerner (New York, Modern Library, 1950), p. 114.

41. ibid., Gilbert, I, 199.

42. *RD*, Gilbert, I, 111–12.

1453 and all that: The End of the Byzantine Empire in the Poetry of Michael Marullus

M. J. McGann

I have time to speak today about only two of the many references which Michael Marullus makes to the end of the Byzantine Empire: the chronological connection which he draws between his own birth and the defeat of his *patria* (*Epigrams* 2. 32. 65-66) and his condemnation of an unnamed person whom he holds responsible for the loss of Constantinople (*Epigrams* 3. 37. 41-46).

Birth in Defeat

Vix bene adhuc fueram matris rude semen in alvo,
    Cum grave servitium patria victa subit.
Ipse pater, Dymae regnis eiectus avitis,
    Cogitur Iliadae quaerere tecta Remi:
Hic, ubi Pierio quamvis nutritus in antro,
    Mille tuli raram damna habitura fidem.

(*Epigrams* 2. 32. 65-70)

This is part of a long poem addressed to an Italian girl called Neaera, whose hand he seeks in marriage. Her cruelty has made him wretched, but this is nothing new. Even in the womb he was harried by Fortune: he had scarcely been conceived when his *patria* was defeated and enslaved (65-66). The inference seems clear: as Marullus was a Byzantine Greek and Constantinople fell on 29 May 1453, his conception occurred shortly before that date, say around the middle of May. This would give a probable date of birth in February, 1454. A somewhat earlier date of conception, which would assign his birth to late 1453, could not be ruled out. This is the reasoning which has produced the generally accepted view that Marullus was born in 1453 or 1454. It should be taken as pointing only to the *date* of birth, for it would be a mistake merely on the basis that *patria* is held to refer to Constantinople to infer that conception and/or birth necessarily took place in the city itself. A Byzantine Greek could speak of the fall of Constantinople as the defeat of his *patria* on grounds less substantial than having actually been born in the city. But the accepted date of birth depends on the identification of *patria* with Constantinople. In this part of my paper I hope to show that there are good reasons for rejecting this and proposing a new date of birth.

After speaking of the wretchedness of the period when his mother carried him in her womb (65–66), Marullus turns to his father, who was driven out of his "ancestral kingdom"[2] of Dyme and forced to take refuge in Italy (67–68), where he himself in spite of his poetic gifts "suffered a thousand unbelievable hurts" (69–70). Making allowance for the fact that he is trying to impress Neaera, we can say on the basis of the rather impressive "ancestral kingdom" that his father's family at least had roots and some standing in the place he calls Dyme. This has always been identified as Dyme in Achaea.[3] I have found no documentary evidence for the occurrence in Achaea in late Byzantine times of any of the Greek forms which could lie behind the name "Marullus,"[4] but it does appear during the fourteenth century elsewhere in the Morea, in Elis and Messenia, borne by persons of no very great distinction.[5] It should not however be forgotten that there was another Dyme, near the mouth of the river Maritza (Hebrus) in Thrace, about 200 miles west of Constantinople.[6] I have not located bearers of the name precisely in this area either, but it is attested, once more in not very elevated circumstances, further west in the neighbourhood of Thessalonike.[7] Whichever Dyme is meant, lines 67–68 suggest that the poet's father went directly from there to Italy. That this was not in fact so is clear from an account of his family history included by Giovanni Tarcagnota in his *Delle istorie del mondo*.[8] Giovanni's father, Paul Tarchaniotes, was a first cousin of Michael Marullus (the poet's mother, Euphrosyne Tarchaniotissa, was a sister of Paul's father, Demetrios Tarchaniotes).[9] Giovanni tells how his father Paul and two paternal uncles were orphaned in childhood. Paul was sent to live in Ragusa with his aunt's husband (the poet's father), who appears in the narrative as Manoli Marulo. His aunt (the poet's mother) was living in Calabria at the time. Later she was joined by young Paul and her husband Manoli, who had not received him with much kindness. Whether this crossing to Italy marks the final migration there of the poet's family is not clear. Further light has been thrown on the Ragusan episode by the discovery in the city records of evidence that "Emanuel Marulla, Grecus," a physician, who should be identified with the poet's father, resided in Ragusa during the years 1465–70.[10]

Marullus's own connection with the city is attested by *Epigrams* 4. 17, which is entitled *de laudibus Rhacusae*. In this poem he tells how in childhood he first gave utterance there to his grief as an exile (9–12):

> Amica quondam dulcis, ubi puer
> Primas querelas et miseri exili
>   Lamenta de tristi profudi
>   Pectore non inimicus hospes.

He was not however born in Ragusa, but was a *hospes* (12), a passing guest, who seemingly arrived at a very early age, before he had yet mastered articulate speech.

He is unlikely therefore to have been much more than four years old when he came to Ragusa.

The narrative of Giovanni Tarcagnota harmonizes well with the evidence of the city records concerning Emanuel Marulla. Giovanni offers no dates, but the point of departure for his account of family history is the death in action against the Turk in defence of the Morea of his paternal great-grandfather (the poet's maternal grandfather), Michael Tarchaniotes. The likeliest date for this would be 1460. Subsequently Michael's son Demetrios with his wife and children fled from Mistra to Corfu. Both parents died. An aunt then arrived from Coron and made arrangements for the care of the orphaned children. It was only then that Paul was sent to join his aunt's husband in Ragusa. This could very well have been in 1465 or even later. Certainly there is no conflict in chronology between the city records and Giovanni Tarcagnota's narrative.

Evidence is thus lacking that Michael's father was in Ragusa much before 1465. On the other hand a combination of the traditional date of birth with the indication offered by *Epigrams* 4. 17 would suggest that Michael himself had been taken there no later than 1458. This is inherently unlikely: Byzantine Morea remained, in spite of many disturbances, unsubdued by the Turks until 1460, and during the late 1450s young Michael would be likely to have enjoyed there the protection of his Tarchaniot grandfather and uncles[11] and very possibly of his father as well.[12]

The evidence concerning the Ragusan episode simply does not sit happily with the traditional date of Michael's birth. A more coherent picture emerges if we date Michael's arrival in Ragusa, as well as his father's, to c. 1465. On the basis of his learning to speak articulately there, his birth would be dated to c. 1461. The reference in *patria victa* would then be not to the fall of Constantinople in 1453, but rather to the conquest of the Despotate of Morea in 1460. By *patria* he means the Morea; to his friend Sannazaro he was after all *Spartanus* (*Elegies* 2. 2. 25).

That however was exceptional. Most contemporary references speak of him as *Constantinopolitanus*, and it may be surmised that this is how he wished to be described.[13] But a man can have two sets of roots. His elder contemporary Demetrios Raoul Kabakes, father of his friend Manilius Ralles, called himself "Spartan and Byzantine" and "both Hellene and Thracian,"[14] meaning in both cases probably that he was a Spartan of Constantinopolitan origin. Michael's situation may have been little different. His father was *patria Constantinopolitanus*.[15] Perhaps the basis for that description was the ownership of ancestral property at Dyme by the Maritza, from which his father might have fled to the Morea in the 1450s. In any case Michael was born there c. 1461. Doubtless as an exile in Italy he generally preferred the description *Constantinopolitanus*,[16] but when he came to date his birth, he did so by reference to the conquest of the land where he was born, the Morea.

A Question of Guilt

Quis furor est patriam vallatam hostilibus armis
   Tutantem externis credere velle viris
Ignotaque manu confundere civica signa
   Et sua non Graecis tela putare satis?   40
Ille, ille hostis erat, ille expugnabat Achivos
   Miles et eversas diripiebat opes,
Ille deos et fana malis dabat ignibus, ille
   Romanum in Turcas transtulit imperium:
Nec nobis tam fata deum, quam culpa luenda est   45
   Mensque parum prudens consiliumque ducis.
Hanc igitur miseri luimus longumque luemus,
   Dum nos Euxinus et lacrimae minuant.

[*BR* = ß]
39 Civilesque manus Ligurum confundere signis ß.
41–42 expugnabat opimum / Bosphorum et captas (captat *B*
  captae *R*) ß.
43 fana miles igni dabat ß.

(*Epigrams* 3. 37. 37–48)

In *Epigrams* 3. 37 (*De exilio suo*), a poem purporting to have been written while Michael was unhappily serving as a mercenary in the Balkans, he looks back in sorrow and anger to the fall of Constantinople itself. It would have been better to endure slavery at home than the indignities of exile, but better still to have died fighting for one's country against dreadful odds, inspired by the thought of home and family. Then (37) he reflects on the madness of entrusting the defence of one's besieged *patria* to foreigners, "confusing with an unknown band the standards of the state and believing that for Greeks their own weapons were not sufficient. That soldier was the enemy; he it was who took the Achaeans by storm and overthrew their wealth, who set fire to their gods and shrines and handed over to the Turks the Roman Empire. We must expiate not so much acts destined by the gods as the guilty imprudence of our leader's plans." The text, which is that of the printed edition of 1497, is curiously unspecific. Only line 44 ("handed over to the Turks the Roman Empire") points to the fall of Constantinople. The *externi viri* and the *ignota manus* are presumably foreign allies, but is the criticism directed at the allies of the Byzantines in general or at a specific contingent? *Ille miles* clearly refers to an individual, but he is blamed in such sweeping terms that one would hesitate to identify him. He must be distinguished from the imprudent *dux*, who can only be Constantine XII. There is however another, and earlier, version of these lines which is more specific.[17] Contained in MSS Riccardiani 915 (B) and 971 (R), it offers the unmetrical *miles* instead of *malis* (43) and a clear reference to Constantinople in *opimum/Bosphorum* instead of *Achivos/miles* (41–42), but most importantly at line 39 it identifies the allies whom the poet is attacking: *civilesque manus Ligurum confundere signis* ("confusing with Ligurian standards the forces of our citizens"). Once our thoughts have been directed to the role of the Genoese in the defence of the city, the reference in *ille, ille hostis erat* becomes clear. It is to Giovanni Giustiniani Longo, the Genoese commander of a contingent of mercenaries sent by the Genoese government from Chios. On his arrival in January 1453 he was put in command as *protostrator* of all the forces defending Constantinople and entrusted with the hopes of emperor and city.[18] His conduct was energetic and brave — until the last day of the siege. He was wounded, but his men succeeded in getting him away from the city. Accounts of the severity of the wound vary. That it was serious is suggested by the fact that he died within a few days, but there was a suggestion also that his "inglorious end" was the consequence rather of *tristitia*. In any case he did not die at his post, and his disappearance had at a critical moment inflicted a severe blow on the morale of the besieged. It was natural for some to hold him responsible for the defeat. The Genoese role subsequently came under scrutiny, and accusations of treason were made, particularly by Venice. Genoa felt obliged to defend its own and Giustiniani's conduct, and letters stating its case were dispatched to several parts of western Europe.[19]

Only with the help of *Ligurum* at line 39 in the earlier version are we able confidently to identify *ille miles*. The question should at least be raised why this clue does not appear in the edition of 1497 even though its absence leads to some degree of obscurity. It is not known when the poem was composed. It purports to have been written during Michael's period as a mercenary in the Balkans, which began when he was seventeen years old[20] and which on the basis of the first part of this paper and the evidence of *Epigrams* 1. 48. 1-14 may be assigned to the years 1478-80.[21] It is perhaps unlikely that this powerful piece is the work of a youth in his teens, and the fact that it forms part of Book III of the *Elegies*, which in general reflects his life in Florence, should perhaps incline us to date it to his Florentine period, which began in 1489.[22] All that can be said about the date of the changes which he introduced is that they were made at latest in 1497 and perhaps specifically for the printed edition of that year. The effect of the major change, at line 39, is to remove a dismissive reference to Genoa and to make it extremely difficult, if not impossible, to identify "the guilty man" as Genoese. A desire not to give offence to Genoa could be connected with its role in Charles VIII's strategy for his invasion of the Kingdom of Naples. In 1494 it provided a base for the invasion fleet. Even after Charles returned to France in 1495 with his Italian conquests in ruins, he still dreamt of an Italian kingdom, and Genoa would have remained central to his plans. Committed to the French cause by reason both of his links with the Prince of Salerno and the sons of Pierfrancesco de' Medici and of his hope that Charles would lead a crusade against the Turk, Michael could have felt it to be diplomatic to remove from his poem a reminder of the inglorious part Genoa had played in the fall of Constantinople. The now unspecific reference to the *miles* was allowed to remain, to puzzle many a reader with the vagueness of its denunciation.

The Queen's University, Belfast

Notes

1. All references to Marullus are to the text edited by A. Perosa, *Michaelis Marulli Carmina* (Zurich, 1951). Other poems referring to the end of the empire or to his exile include *Epigrams* 1. 6 (presumably); 22; 27; 48; 52; 63; 2. 17; 30(?); 36; 49; 3. 47; 4. 6; 17; 29; 32; *Hymns* 2. 6; 8; 3. 1; 2; 4. 1; *Neniae* 1; 2; 4.

2. The expression derives from Vergil, *Georgics* 3. 228, the context of which is the withdrawal of the defeated bull. It would be a mistake to suppose that this undercuts Marullus's use of the phrase though something of Vergil's pathos is perhaps conveyed.

3. In the *Index Nominum* of his edition (p. 242), Perosa offers Kaminitsa as the site of Dyme. See however *RE* 17. 2435ff., s.v. Olenos 4; A. Philippson, *Griechische Landschaften* 3. 1 (Frankfurt a.M., 1959), p. 196. Dyme is identified as Chiarenza by Girolamo Albrizzi, *Esatta notitia del Peloponneso volgarmente Penisola della Morea* (Venice, 1687), pp. 28–29.

4. For these see my discussion at *BHR*, 42 (1980), 403, n. 21.

5. See J. Longnon and P. Topping, *Documents sur la régime des terres dans la principauté de Morée au XIVᵉ siècle* (Paris, 1969), *Index Nominum*, s.v. Marulli, p. 297. In general of course full discussion of Michael's family background will be possible only after the appearance of the fascicles of the *Prosopographisches Lexikon der Palaiologenzeit* (Vienna, 1976–) containing the names "Maroules etc." and "Tarchaniotes."

6. *RE* 5. 1878, s.v. Dyme 2.

7. V. Laurent, *Échos d'Orient*, 30 (1931), 483–84; A. E. Laiou, *Peasant Society in the late Byzantine Empire* (Princeton, 1977), p. 329, s.v. Maroules Nikolaos.

8. G. Tarcagnota, *Delle historie del mondo* (Venice, 1562), part 2, book 20, f. 484ʳ.

9. See the family-tree at *BHR*, 42 (1980), 404.

10. B. Krekič, *Dubrovnik (Raguse) et le levant au moyen âge* (Paris, 1961), pp. 134–35. The identification of Emanuel with the poet's father was proposed by A. E. Vacalopoulos, *Origins of the Greek Nation. The Byzantine Period, 1204–1461* (New Brunswick, N.J., 1970), p. 245.

11. His grandfather's death in defence of the Morea is mentioned by G. Tarcagnota, loc. cit. That three uncles also died at this time is attested by Michael himself at *Epigrams* 1. 27. 10.

12. If Michael refers to the Achaean Dyme at *Epigrams* 2. 32. 67, it is likely that his father's expulsion from there occurred c. 1460. If he was forced out of the other Dyme, this might have happened at an earlier, perhaps a considerably earlier, date, and it is entirely possible that he then moved to the Morea, leaving it only under Turkish pressure c. 1460. For this possibility see below, p. 2–3.

13. It may be supposed that the occurrence of *Constantinopolitanus* in the title pages of *Epigrammata* (probably Rome, 1489) and *Hymni et Epigrammata* (Florence, 1497) reflects his own wishes. Marullus is so described also in the titles of most of the fifteenth-century MSS listed by Perosa in the Prolegomena to his edition, pp. VII–XXII, and in a reference

to his work as translator of four letters allegedly sent by Bayezid II to Alexander VI in 1494, Johannes Burckardus, *Liber Notarum, Rerum Italicarum Scriptores*, 32. 1, p. 553. He is called *Bizantius* by Paulus Cortesius, *De cardinalatu* (Castel Cortesiano, 1510), ff. 2^r, 81^r, and by Petrus Crinitus, *De honesta disciplina* (Basel, 1532) p. 179. In a letter of Lorenzo di Pierfranceso de' Medici to G. Lanfredini written in May, 1489, Michael's brother is called *nobile Constantinopolitano, Arch. di State di Firenze, Mediceo av. il Princ.* 51. 625, cited by G. B. Picotti, "Marullo o Mabilio? Nota polizianesca" in *Raccolta di studi di storia e critica letteraria dedicata a Francesco Flamini* (Pisa, 1918), p. 249, n. 7 (the relevant portion is on p. 250).

14. S. Fassoulakis, *The Byzantine Family of Raoul-Ral(l)es* (Athens, 1973), p. 83.

15. See *BHR*, 42 (1980), 401.

16. According to Petrarch, the Calabrian Leontius Pilata evinced a rather different attitude: in Italy he wished to be regarded as from Thessalonike, in Greece as an Italian, *Senilium rerum libri* 3. 6.

17. For the relative chronology see Perosa, pp. X–XIII.

18. For the date of his arrival and the confidence which he inspired see A. Pertusi, *La caduta di Costantinopoli*, 1 (1976), pp. LXVIII, 148 (Leonard of Chios, 43). For a general discussion see Pertusi, pp. 362–63.

19. C. Desimoni, *Atti della Società Ligure di Storia Patria*, 10 (1874), 296–97, cited by Pertusi, p. 363.

20. *Epigrams* 2. 32. 71–78.

21. It appears from *Epigrams* 1. 48 that Michael was in Italy and indeed formed part of a military force concerned with resisting the Turkish invaders at Otranto when Giulio Antonio Acquaviva was slain there on Feb. 7, 1481. It may be inferred that he had returned from the Balkans in time to join the forces opposing the Turks.

22. Picotti, op. cit. (above, n. 13), p. 250, n. 1.

Ockham and Valla on Enjoyment and Pleasure

Arthur Stephen McGrade

I know little about rhetoric, but I believe it is an approved tactic of that art to seek the good will of one's audience by starting with a display of candor and modesty. Let me begin accordingly by making clear that this paper is only a first report of what someone who has spent some time reading Ockham finds interesting in Lorenzo Valla's dazzling dialogue, *De voluptate*, "On Pleasure," or "On the True and False Good." I use only the second, 1433 version of the dialogue,[1] and I take it at face value. That is, I pay no heed to the tradition of interpretation in which Valla is a *non*-Christian hedonist, nor do I take up, except very briefly at the end, the extremely interesting issues raised by Dr Gerl's interpretation of the dialogue as a radical transformation of philosophy itself from sterile rationalism into living rhetoric.[2] Such results as emerge from this comparison must be accepted with these limitations clearly in mind.

To set the stage for what I have to say about Valla on pleasure, I must first indicate some salient aspects of Ockham's treatment of the topic.[3] Four points especially deserve notice. (1) Ockham is interested in the psychology of the topic and not only in its abstract morality. He investigates the genesis of various kinds of pleasure and the role of pleasure in the motivation of human behavior, and he discusses the psychology of our willing of ends and means with great thoroughness. I think Ockham's interest in psychological processes generally is an important, neglected part of his thought. In the case of pleasure, certainly, the psychological interest is prominent. (2) Perhaps the central psychological thesis in Ockham's treatment of pleasure is that there are two kinds of it, each with its own causal story. On the one hand is what we might call physical pleasure, or pleasure in the 'sensitive' soul. On the other hand is what we might call psychic pleasure, what Ockham calls pleasure in the 'intellectual' soul. The interesting thing about these pleasures, to my mind, is not so much their different ontological levels or locations as their different patterns of causation. Physical pleasure is caused directly by our perception of an appropriate physical object. There is a pleasure in a warm bath (my example) caused directly by the sensations of warmth and wetness. Psychic pleasure, Ockham argues, is not caused directly by the apprehension of an object. A crucial mediating role is played here by volition. Psychic pleasure is an effect of the will's acceptance of an object, psychic distress or sadness an effect of the will's rejection. As an example (my own again), consider the joys and sorrows of a sports fan who has chosen to root for a particular team. When his team wins he is happy, but this is because he wanted it to win. His attachment to the team is crucial. Without it the mere spectacle of the team's winning would bring no pleasure. (3) The next point concerns the causes of volitional acceptance or rejection. Ockham holds that we will some things because we will others. For example, a man willingly accepts a bitter, physically unpleasant medicine because he desires to be healthy. What about his desire for health? Let us assume that our man does not will to be healthy because he wills some further object. Now Ockham holds the interesting view that this independent, 'non-referring' voliton of an object can take two forms. The object willed for itself in a given case may simply be willed for itself, or it may be willed as the highest or best object which possibly could be willed. The man who wants to be healthy in the first way just wants to be healthy. He neither affirms nor denies that something else might be more desirable than health. The man who wills health in the second way does, as it were, affirm that health is the greatest possible human good. Would he be right? This brings me to the last aspect of Ockham's position I want to place before you. (4) According to Ockham, as I read him, a person merely following natural reason, without the aid of revelation, would be able to determine that Aristotelian εὐδαιμονία was objectively preferable to the alternative candidates for the *summum bonum* with which Aristotle compares it, but he would be unable either to assert or rule out the possibility of a higher good than εὐδαιμονία. Hence, his simply desiring such happiness in preference to other goods he was aware of would be neither sinful nor immoral. But to set this sort of happiness up as an absolutely ultimate value — as the greatest possible good — would be inordinate and culpable, it would be a sort of idolatry. For according to Ockham, there in fact is a higher, more desirable good, God. To love God above all else and for his own sake is the supreme ordinate act of non-referential willing. This cherishing of God is what he identifies as enjoyment (*fruitio*), and the psychic pleasure which is the natural effect of such loving completes his account of the essence of blessedness.

Anyone familiar with Valla can anticipate some of the points in the *De voluptate* which strike me as particularly interesting. In the first place, although Valla is concerned throughout to affect the way we live, this practical concern leads him to discuss the actual motives of behavior in ways that are at least roughly comparable with what we find in Ockham. Thus, Veggio the Epicurean's comprehensive and ingenious analysis of various human pursuits in Books 1 and 2 of Valla's dialogue not only establishes the irrationality of acting for the sake of abstract virtue; it also shows in some detail how the motivation of certain actions of which Veggio approves, but which are traditionally thought to be motivated by Stoic

or Aristotelian principles of virtue, can be explained and justified in a psychologically plausible way on hedonistic principles. I refer here to acts of justice and
mercy and to the goods of contemplation and tranquility. Ockham would not agree
with the particular results of Veggio's analysis. He would agree, rather, with Aristotle, in a passage criticized later in the *De voluptate*, that the virtues and their
objects are desirable apart from pleasure. Nevertheless, Veggio's analysis is the
kind of thing one finds in his own work. Another example of Valla as psycholo-
gist is the fine-grained analysis of the moral virtues in his third book. His digging
beneath the surface of such abstractions as 'courage' and 'temperance' in order
to discover the more specific qualities of temperament operative in particular actions seems to me to be thoroughly in Ockham's spirit.

A further point of interest in the dialogue is Valla's presentation, through Veggio and Catone, the overwhelmed Stoic, of a rather complete secular account of
human life. This is complicated to assess. From the Christian standpoint ultimately
dominating the *De voluptate*, it would be better if we could take the strong medicine
of Lactantius and Augustine, neither of whom has much interest in putting on
a non-Christian *persona* even temporarily. Valla's spokesmen for stoic virtue and
non-Christian pleasure are presumably intended to strike us as somewhat absurd
even before the Franciscan Antonio da Rho puts them both in their place by showing how virtue and pleasure ought truly to be understood. Still, one does not lavish
as much care on constructing a position as Valla does on Veggio's hedonism if
one thinks it entirely absurd. On Valla's account of the matter (through Antonio
da Rho), Epicureanism would not be absurd if it were not for religious considerations pretty well lost to the human race apart from Christianity. This is to say
that Valla, like Ockham, has a serious interest in thinking out what life would
be like for the natural man. He treats Christianity as coming (with revolutionary
impact, to be sure) into a human world which has been functioning without it,
rather than as permeating a cosmos unthinkable apart from it.

The last and greatest point of interest for an Ockhamist in the *De voluptate* is
Valla's treatment of the pleasure involved in enjoying God (Book 3, chapters
13–14). A detailed analysis of Valla's discussion of the *fruitio Dei* is beyond the
scope of this paper, but I believe that such an analysis against the background
of scholastic treatments of the subject would be rewarding. For all of his anti-
scholasticism on other occasions, Valla is here thoroughly scholastic in terminology,
debating whether God is the efficient or final cause of our delight in him,
distinguishing between *esse* and *bene esse*, substance and quality, receiver and received, and so on. In the course of this discussion, he explicitly rejects the scholastic
view that being as such is good (discreetly refraining from naming Augustine as
a principal source for this view), and he engages directly with the scholastic problem of determining exactly what it is in the love of God which is supremely good.
Valla's discussion of the love of God is the lynch-pin of his final account of the
true good. Just as loving God is for Ockham the only love which counts as an
unqualified fruition for the human spirit, so for Valla a presentation of the goal

of Christianity which evokes the enjoyableness of that goal is the only adequate response to the new spring of paganism in his time. Ockham's formidably technical style of argument does not invite us to think of him as a spiritually ardent man, yet I think he would be in sympathy with Antonio da Rho's bold assertions that nothing is done rightly without pleasure and that there is no merit in serving in God's army only with suffering endurance and not with a good will.

Whatever his sympathy with such statements, I think Ockham would disagree with Valla on other points. In the last part of this sketchy comparison of their views, I want to look at one or two of these. First, then, I think Ockham would regret the apparent loss in Valla of his distinction between the causal structures of physical and psychic pleasure. I take it he would accept Veggio's hedonism or something like it as an account of certain sub-rational psychological processes. He would think, however, that the causal relationship between desire and pleasure is just backwards in Veggio's attempts to explain our most distinctively human behavior. Here, he would insist, commitment to an object precedes and causes the pleasure involved in the enjoyment of that object. Commitment to, or volitional acceptance of, one's health; one's self; one's family, friends, community, or civilization; the principles of rational morality; or fate, or destiny, or God (all of these would count as possible objects of non-referring volition for Ockham) — one's willing of any or all of these need not be caused by the experience of pleasure already derived from them or from the expectation of pleasure to be derived from them in the future. And when the experience or expectation of pleasure is the basis of our willing of other things, this can only be because we make it our basis — that is, we are then using the other things and willing only the pleasure non-referentially.

The point is important enough to deserve further discussion; let us note here how the two views bear on the all-important matter of the love of God. Ockham insists, against the Dominican Durandus of St Pourçain, that in the state of blessedness it is God himself who is loved above all things and for his own sake, as he deserves to be loved. The intense pleasure involved in beatitude is a natural causal consequence of this prior act of cherishing God. On Valla's account, on the other hand, as he himself clearly sees, we do not seek God for his own sake but as the source of our own pleasure. At the beginning of the passage I have been discussing, Antonio da Rho remarks that we ought to love God more than ourselves, but as he proceeds it becomes clear that he does not mean we should love God for his own sake. This view is explicitly rejected. The Bible tells us to love God, it does not tell us to love him for his own sake. God himself, then, is not our true good. He is, rather, the source of our true good, which is the pleasure he produces in us.

From Ockham's standpoint, someone who loved God only because he gave him pleasure would be an inordinate egoist, certainly not a *beatus*. From Valla's standpoint, on the other hand, Ockham's conception of enjoyment looks psychologically inexplicable.

What are we to say about these positions? I offer the following observations as an aid to carrying the comparison further.

First, so far as the content rather than the expression of their views is concerned, Ockham would seem to be in a way more of a Renaissance thinker than Valla. I have in mind here the traditional picture of the Renaissance as a period emphasizing human dignity or the grandeur of human nature. Ockham's conception of human behavior as based on free commitment to intrinsically good or bad ultimate ends seems to me to have all the grandeur one could possibly ask for—indeed, perhaps too much. Valla's hedonism, on the other hand, supercharged as it is with appeals to the delights of the life to come, seems at least on the surface to fit more closely the traditional picture of the Middle Ages as a period in which this-worldly behavior was severely and arbitrarily constrained by prudential considerations of other-worldy reward and punishment. Of course, the situation is more complicated than my comparison in terms of traditional pictures suggests. Ockham's position is related to that of Bernard of Clairvaux, while Ockham's contemporary, Peter Aureoli (also a Franciscan), took a position on enjoyment rather like Valla's. And all discussions of enjoyment in the Middle Ages go back in one way or another to Valla's hero, St Augustine. Still, it does not look as if Ockham is any *more* medieval than Valla, except in form of expression.

What about form of expression? This is always important, especially if we include here a writer's evocative expression of a whole world of personal relationships, such as we find in Valla but not in Ockham. The difference is enormous. It can be argued, however, that Valla's creative eloquence is guided by a principle defended in the abstract by writers like Ockham. If we had to judge Valla on the basis of the abstract doctrine propounded in the *De voluptate*, we would, as we have seen, judge him for good or ill as a theistic ethical egoist. But such a judgment needs qualification. We can make better sense of his work if we read it in light of another principle, a principle clearly propounded in the abstract by the scholastics but far from apparent in the disputatious texture of their discourse. The principle I refer to is friendship, more precisely the love of friendship, *amor amicitiae*, the love we have for someone or something we value for her, his, or its own sake. I have found no discussion of this important Augustinian principle in the *De voluptate*, and yet, of course, the world Valla creates in his dialogue abounds precisely in friendship. This is most obvious in the elaborate courtesies and expressions of mutual regard of all the characters, but deeper forms of friendship are involved in Antonio da Rho's striking assertion (p. 255) that no one has ever existed who has desired, or been happy to see, evil for others, and in the ebullient account of God's generosity in creating the world for human beings and offering them divine blessedness. And the themes of human and divine friendship are combined in the picture of Christ advancing from his throne in heaven to take each redeemed person by the hand, extending the greeting of friend to friend.

Both an Ockhamist and a suitably jaundiced inhabitant of the modern world might question Valla's assumption that this is the only picture of human destiny an accomplished orator might be moved to accept and project. Faith is required to accept this picture, surely, and such faith involves a judgment about the intrinsic goodness of what is pictured. This is to say that Valla's project in the *De voluptate*, his rhetorically powerful projection of a Christian vision of human destiny, involves an unacknowledged, pre-rhetorical judgment about what deserves to be projected. But Valla's pre-rhetorical judgment, although unacknowledged, would be from Ockham's standpoint the right one.

How, then, are Ockham and Valla related on enjoyment and pleasure? What is the result of looking at a Renaissance Humanist like Valla from the vantage point of the scholasticism he so cordially detested? In dealing with these two writers — if I may refer to Ockham as a writer — I have found it helpful to distinguish, without separating, form and content. Valla's reversion to Lactantius and Augustine owes nothing positive to the scholastics, as far as I can see, in point of form. In deciding to write oratorically rather than dialectically and to heap abuse on philosophy, he properly regarded the scholastics as the enemy. But what Valla found in the church fathers and the doctrinal presuppositions of his own rhetorical objectives may well have been shaped by the scholasticism he rejected. I know nothing about Niccolò Niccoli, the spokesman for Christianity in the first version of the dialogue, but I was delighted to find that his replacement, Antonio da Rho, was not only a distinguished Humanist but also a Franciscan. When one compares his discourse on pleasure and the enjoyment of God with what earlier friars like Bonaventure, Aureoli, and Ockham wrote on these topics, one's immediate impression is that they are speaking different languages — that, indeed, they have different conceptions of what language itself is and what it is to speak as a human being, yet what they communicate seems mutually relevant and in some cases mutually supportive. In this present group of humanists, to whom nothing Latin is alien, it may be intelligible to suggest that medieval and Renaissance discussions of human nature and destiny both shed light on these important topics.

Notes

1. Lorenzo Valla, *On Pleasure: De voluptate*, transl. A. Kent Hieatt and Maristella Lorch (New York, Abaris Books, 1977).
2. Hanna-Barbara Gerl, *Rhetorik als Philosophie: Lorenzo Valla* (Munich, Wilhelm Fink Verlag, 1974).
3. For a fuller presentation, see my "Ockham on Enjoyment: Towards an Understanding of Fourteenth-Century Philosophy and Psychology," *Review of Metaphysics*, 34, 706–28.

Les théories de la beauté littéraire
de Marsile Ficin à Torquato Tasso

Alain Michel

La théorie de la beauté constitue assurément l'un des éléments principaux de la critique et de la création littéraires. Nous avons eu l'occasion de le souligner dans un ouvrage récent sur *La parole et la beauté*,[1] dont nous voudrions indiquer ici quelques intentions majeures, en les mettant en rapport avec la littérature néo-latine. Nous tiendrons compte d'autres travaux dont nous n'avions pu avoir connaissance au moment où nous rédigions notre livre, et notamment des recherches de M. Montgomery.[2] Celui-ci a essentiellement étudié l'image et l'imagination de Dante au Tasse. Nous nous bornerons à une période plus restreinte, puisque nous partirons de Ficin. Mais surtout, nous adopterons un point de vue un peu différent, non pas opposé mais complémentaire, qui nous est dicté par l'orientation de notre propre recherche. Nous essayerons de montrer comment certains théoriciens marquants du quinzième et du seizième siècles utilisent la terminologie antique pour fonder leur propre pensée. Une telle démarche est naturelle puisqu'ils parlent eux-mêmes le latin. Lorsqu'il leur arrive (comme au Tasse) de s'exprimer en langue vernaculaire, ils se servent encore des mêmes concepts.

Il ne s'agit pas seulement pour nous d'établir des relais historiques. Nous mettrons en cause toute une théorie du beau dans ses rapports avec la parole littéraire. Le vocabulaire de langue latine que nous allons étudier provient essentiellement de Cicéron et de ses traités de rhétorique. Nous croyons que l'orateur romain a été l'un des premiers à établir un ensemble de vocables qui, au delà des préceptes et de leur utilité immédiate, constituent une esthétique de caractère universel et valable pour tous les arts. Bien entendu, Cicéron n'a pas créé tous les termes dont il se sert. Il en doit une bonne part aux grecs: Platon, Aristote, les Stoïciens aussi et Épicure. Nous voudrions rappeler d'abord l'essentiel des notions qui se trouvent ainsi définies. Elles constituent un système ouvert, dont nous pourrons ensuite suivre les transformations (en même temps que l'influence) au temps de la Renaissance.

Une première remarque s'impose au sujet des anciens. Elle est relative au rôle considérable que la rhétorique joue chez eux. C'est elle, d'abord, qui définit les concepts littéraires. Son influence sur les *Poétiques* est évidents. Notons que ces dernières sont beaucoup moins nombreuses que les traités relatifs à l'éloquence. Aristote et Horace doivent aux techniques des orateurs une grande partie de leurs concepts: ornements, vraisemblance, usage des lieux, réflexion sur les tropes et les figures. Toutefois, il convient de nuancer ce que nous venons d'écrire. Il serait plus exact de dire que la rhétorique et la poétique puisent l'une et l'autre dans le trésor de la philosophie. Pensons par exemple aux idées d'imitation, de nature, sans parler de la vraisemblance et du vrai, que nous citions à l'instant. Précisement, Cicéron est entre tous celui qui a le plus insisté sur le rôle de la philosophie dans une création authentiquement littéraire. La pensée antique affirme donc le lien étroit qui existe entre rhétorique et poétique grâce à la philosophie.

Pouvons-nous, de façon brève et sommaire, retenir quelques notions qui sont appelées à fonder par la suite les problèmes qui domineront l'histoire littéraire? L'une d'entre elles concerne la fonction de la parole. Celle-ci peut informer ou persuader. Dans le premier cas, elle vise à la contemplation, dans le second à l'action. A l'intérieur de la contemplation, deux orientations sont possibles, qui ont aussi retenu l'attention des modernes: elle peut, comme disait à peu près Platon,[3] viser à la *mimésis* ou à la *diégésis*. Le philosophe d'Athènes avait tendance à condamner la première, qui lui paraissait trop éloignée de la vérité puisqu'elle était apparence d'apparence. Il ne condamnait pas en revanche le récit historique ou mythique, qui, s'appuyant sur la dialectique, tendait à reconstruire le réel et dont le discours pouvait s'épanouir en dialogue. Vint Aristote qui, dans sa *Poétique*, tenta la synthèse des opposés: le *mythos* des poètes faisait de l'imitation son principal moyen.

La question de la vérité prend ici toute son importance. Pour Platon, le beau est la splendeur du vrai. Aristote n'est pas du tout opposé à cette conception. Mais il veut scruter la nature d'une telle splendeur. Alors interviennent deux problèmes principaux, dont l'un concerne le langage et l'autre les réalités mises en causes — le référent.

Commençons par là. Nous parlions de vérité, de dialectique. Mais qu'en est-il de la morale? Doit-on distinguer l'esthétique et l'éthique? Et sinon, à quelle éthique doit-on se référer? Celle de l'âme, comme le pensent les Stoïciens (et ils rejoignent ainsi les Platoniciens), celle du corps, comme le croient les Épicuriens (on est tenté, avec Lucrèce, de rapprocher délectation poétique et *uoluptas* sensible), celle du corps et de l'âme, comme le pensent les Péripatéticiens, qui considèrent le composé humain dans sa complexité? Notons qu'une telle manière de poser les problèmes se rattache à la doxographie du bien suprême telle que Cicéron l'exposait dans le *De finibus*: nous rejoignons ici l'Arpinate.

Nous le rejoindrons aussi à propos du langage. Dans le livre III du *De oratore* et dans la plus grande partie de l'*Orator*, il formule une théorie des vertus de l'expression (*uirtutes dicendi*), dont on admet communément qu'elle provient de Théophraste:[4] un style parfait implique la clarté, la pureté (essentiellement grammaticale), l'*ornatus* et la grâce. Il n'est pas nécessaire de souligner la valeur et la fécondité d'une telle analyse: ces quatre rubriques (avec quelques transpositions) peuvent être appliqués à toute critique esthétique. Notons seulement que, s'il est vraisemblable que Théophraste les a mises en œuvre, on doit ajouter qu'Aristote les a esquissées au début du III de la *Rhétorique* (1404[b]). Il partait, quant à lui, du désir de concilier dans la beauté du langage deux vertus apparemment contradictoires: d'une part la clarté, la transparence (que peut se faire aussi pureté): elle constitue le meilleur moyen d'assurer le primat des choses sur les mots, du sens sur l'expression. Mais, d'un autre côté, il connaissait les dangers de la banalité. Il savait que le rôle de la parole belle est d'inspirer l'admiration, c'est-à-dire l'étonnement devant ce qui dépasse les idées toutes faites: il défendait donc, à côté de la simplicité, le merveilleux (Θαυμαστόν) qui paraît souvent s'opposer à elle. En revanche, il ne s'étendait pas beaucoup sur la dernière des vertus du style, dont Platon (sans la rattacher directement à une telle théorie) avait beaucoup parlé: la Χάρις, la grâce de convenance. Cicéron, au contraire, insiste sur la distinction entre le *pulchrum* qui naît, dans l'*ornatus*, de l'équilibre, de la plénitude, de la proportion) et le *decorum* (la "grâce" indicible et, comme on dira plus tard, comme Catulle le suggère déjà, "plus belle encor que la beauté").

On voit que la rhétorique antique propose dans toute leur complexité les questions relatives au beau: est-il lié à l'action ou à la contemplation, à l'imitation ou la narration, au corps ou à l'âme, à la simplicité ou au merveilleux, à la grâce ou à la beauté? Il faudrait ajouter le problème du sublime et celui du réalisme: faut-il idéaliser? Y-t-il une beauté de l'horrible? De telles questions nourrissent encore les poétiques de notre temps. Nous allons voir qu'elles ont d'abord été remises en honneur par la Renaissance.

Nous commencerons dans la Florence de Laurent le magnifique, auprès de Marsile Ficin.

Nul n'a si profondément médité sur la beauté. Il parle latin. Mais il traduit Platon et Plotin. Il exprime ainsi de manière parfaite ce qui constitue l'originalité du Quattrocento florentin. A travers la terminologie latine et la tradition cicéronienne, nous revenons à l'esprit même du Platonisme. Pour Platon, le beau était *splendor ueri* (si précisément nous parlons la langue de Cicéron). Ficin consacre toute sa méditation à l'idée de *splendor*. Elle implique d'abord une théorie de la lumière qui est médiatrice entre la matière et l'esprit, participe de l'une et de l'autre. Ensuite, elle permet, à la manière de Plotin et dans la tradition des *Ennéades*, de concilier Platon et Aristote. La lumière est à la fois forme et acte: elle délivre et détermine ce qui est en puissance dans la matière.

"Dès que la puissance de Dieu, qui surpasse tout, engendre les anges et les âmes, elle répand en eux, comme en ses fils, son propre rayon qui porte en lui une vertu féconde pour créer toutes choses. Ce rayon imprime en ceux qui sont plus proches de lui l'ordonnance et l'ordre du monde beaucoup plus expressément que dans la matière de ce monde. Voilà pourquoi cette peinture du monde, que nous voyons, brille tout entière d'un éclat particulier dans les anges et dans les âmes ..." (trad. R. Marcel)

"Diuina potestas omnia supereminens statim a se natis angelis atque animis suum illum radium in quo fecunda uis inest omnium creandorum, tamquam filiis clementer infundit. Hic in eis utpote si propinquioribus totius mundi dispositionem et ordinem multo pingit exactius quam in mundi materia. Quamobrem haec mundi pictura, quam cernimus, uniuersa in angelis et animis lucet expressior ..."(*De amore* V.4)

Il s'agit à la fois de l'amour et de la lumière. L'une exprime l'autre, dans l'esprit et dans la matière. La beauté est à la fois "la forme du bien," son "acte" et le "rayon" de la lumière divine qui produit la vérité. Une telle lumière, pour manifester sa splendeur, pour créer son espace, a besoin de miroirs. Les plus purs sont les meilleurs. Ce sont aussi les plus spirituels: l'ange, l'âme. La matière fournit elle aussi un reflet mais il est moins pur. Ainsi la beauté véritable réside dans la lumière de l'esprit qui s'exprime ou se reflète, selon la hiérarchie de ses perfections, dans les anges, les âmes et même les corps.

La doctrine ainsi exprimée provient à la fois de Plotin, du Ps-Denys l'Aréopagite et de Robert Grosseteste. Elle justifie une conception de l'imaginaire qui domine la *Divine Comédie*, où tant d'images dépeignent la rencontre de l'ombre et de la lumière.[5] Elle va survivre à travers la Renaissance jusqu'à la *Panaugia* de Patrizzi et jusqu'à Blaise de Vigenère.

Soulignons seulement un dernier terme. Il s'agit de la grâce (et nous rejoignons ici, d'une manière originale, la terminologie de l'esthétique antique). Ficin reconnaît qu'une beauté conçue selon de telles exigences ne peut être perçue que par la voie négative: "On ne peut définir absolument ce qu'est la lumière: mais on peut toujours dire ce qu'elle n'est pas." La formule est commentée de la manière suivante par son disciple F. Cattani da Diacceto: "Est itaque pulchritudo non per se ens, non per se uita, non per se numerus, non per se ordo, non per se proportio, sed gratia quaedam, splendorque ac flos boni ..." (*De pulchro* I.9). "La beauté n'est ni l'être en soi ni le nombre en soi, ni l'ordre en soi, ni la proportion en soi, mais une certaine grâce, splendeur et fleur du bien." Retenons ces formules. Nous en retrouverons l'application dans la suite de notre exposé. Pour l'instant, nous insisterons seulement sur deux mots: *flos, gratia*. Ficin et ses disciples cherchent la "fine fleur" du bien. Ils découvrent ainsi la grâce, *gratia*, qui est la fleur de la beauté. La liaison avec la "convenance" cicéronienne est évidente. Dans les deux cas, on revient à la Χάρις platonicienne. Mais Cicéron n'employait point Gratia en ce sens. *Gratus* a commencé à le prendre chez Horace, puis *gratia* chez Quintilien. De toute manière, le terme a un sens plus fort que *decorum*. Il signifie la puissance du plaisir esthétique, source de l'amour. Ficin lui-même, dans le passage que nous citions, exprime de manière très forte, le rapport qui existe à ses yeux entre *gratia* et *pulchritudo*: "Ubi Dei uultum illum sinu

suo insculptum introspicit (sancta mens angeli), inspectum ilico admiratur. Aui-
dissime illi semper inhaeret. Vultus illius diuini gratiam pulchritudinem dicimus.
Auiditatem angeli Dei uultui penitus inhaerentem uocamus amorem." (*De amore*
V.5). "Quand le pur esprit de l'ange voit intérieurement ce beau visage de Dieu
sculpté dans son sein, il admire assitôt ce qu'il a vu. Il s'attache à lui sans cesse
avec la plus grande avidité. Nous appelons beauté la grâce de ce visage divin.
L'avidité de l'ange, s'attachant profondément au visage de Dieu, nous l'appelons
amour ..."

La beauté n'est autre chose que la contemplation de la Face divine, gravée
dans notre âme et dans l'univers par le rayonnement divin, connue de manière
éminente dans les anges. Sans nous arrêter aux sources augustiniennes, diony-
siennes, thomistes, antiques et médiévales, nous devons souligner ici ce qu'on
pourrait appeler la métamorphose de la grâce.

Nous aurons à y revenir. Pour l'instant il faut d'abord montrer comment cette
réflexion religieuse et métaphysique trouve son application dans une esthétique
littéraire. Un nom s'impose: celui de Christophoro Landino[6] qui est disciple de
Ficin et qui le fait parler dans ses *Disputationes Camaldulenses*, en 1472, peu après
le temps du *De amore*. Il s'agit, comme on sait, d'un commentaire allégorique de
Virgile. Nous y trouvons (placée aussi sous le patronage d'Alberti) la mise en
œuvre de l'esthétique ficinienne. Nous retiendrons deux idées essentielles: 1° La
poésie de Virgile, dans L'*Énéide*, est essentiellement une démarche purificatrice
qui, au delà de l'action et sans la mépriser, nous conduit vers la contemplation.
Énée symbolise ce voyage spirituel vers l'absolu; 2° Dès lors, en suivant l'exemple de Virgile, il est permis de méditer sur la fonction de la poésie. Elle tend à
découvrir dans l'apparence un sens plus profond qui est celui de l'idée platonicienne. Elle permet au lecteur de saisir un tel sens grâce à plusieurs démarches.
D'abord, elle use de fiction (*figmenta*), pour favoriser, en révélant ce qu'elles ont
de feint, le dévoilement du vrai; ensuite, elle aide une telle démarche par les jeux
de l'ornement, du nombre et de l'amplification. Reconnaissons ici l'application
des enseignements venus de Platon. Certes, le philosophe chassait les poètes de
la cité. Mais la beauté constituait pour lui la splendeur du bien idéal dans l'apparence même et sa théorie du mythe, entendu comme belle fiction, était exactement celle que Landino utilise pour définir la poésie.

De Ficin aux *Disputationes camaldulenses*, nous avons ainsi mis en lumière une
théorie du beau qui coïncide avec le plus pur épanouissement du génie florentin.
Nous avons constaté qu'elle implique à la fois une affirmation de la valeur con-
templative du mythe et une métamorphose de la grâce. Tout cela développe la
problématique que nous avions trouvée chez les anciens. Mais, naturellement,
d'autres interprétations sont possibles. Nous allons les découvrir en poussant en
peu plus loin.

Nous devons en effet nous tourner vers l'école napolitaine. Son principal théoricien est Giovanni Pontano, qui rédige lui-même une œuvre poétique d'une grande
qualité et qui s'inspire de surcroît d'un admirable poète, son ami Sannazar. Celui-

ci donne son nom au principal dialogue théorique de Pontano: *Actius*.

L'auteur reste sans doute assez proche des Platoniciens que nous avons étudiés. En particulier, il insiste comme eux sur le rôle de l'inspiration. Le poète pratique un type de connaissance qu'on retrouve aussi dans les songes. Il est en "sympathie" directe avec la part spirituelle de l'univers. Notons que les termes employés ont un caractère original. L'auteur nous dit, s'exprimant comme un médecin, qu'une telle sympathie ressemble à une "contagion." De même, parlant du *furor* qui saisit le poète, il explique qu'un tel transport domine surtout les tempéraments où se manifeste un excès de bile noire (éd. Previtera, p. 145). Autrement dit, le génie poétique se trouve lié à la mélancolie.

La même idée existait chez Ficin. Elle s'inspire, pour l'essentiel, d'une tradition qui vient à la fois des médecins antiques et du *Problème XXX*, attribué à Aristote. Nous pouvons donc supposer que l'influence de ce philosophe existe chez Pontano. D'autres traits nous permettront d'indiquer la différence d'esprit qui existe entre lui et les Florentins.

D'abord, il met l'accent sur les problèmes de langage qui sont liés à la *compositio uerborum*, au choix et à la disposition des mots. Il étudie de manière détaillée, dans l'œuvre de Virgile, la séparation de leurs accents, le nombre de leurs syllabes, l'euphonie plus ou moins grande des rencontres entre les sons. Il explique que le charme, la dignité, la gravité naissent à cet égard de la variété des effets, laquelle assure la constante modulation du chant. Nous reconnaissons une réflexion sur la *compositio uerborum* qui, dans l'antiquité, avait été illustrée par Denys d'Halicarnasse. L'auteur l'applique de manière très originale à la versification virgilienne.

Il insiste sur un troisième aspect, lorsqu'il se demande quel est le devoir du poète. Voici sa réponse (p. 233): "Utriusque etiam, oratoris atque poetae officium est mouere et flectere auditorem: uerum quonam, quo, inquam, haec et commotio et flexio et maximum utriusque in hoc ipso studium? Oratoris scilicet ut persuadeat iudici, poetae ut admirationem sibi ex audiente ac legente comparet ..." Texte d'une richesse remarquable. Il situe, en effet, dans le champ de la culture la place de la poétique. Il montre à la fois ses ressemblances et sa différence avec la rhétorique. Et il arrive ainsi à une idée essentielle: la poésie vise à provoquer l'admiration. Nous sommes tout près du Θαυμαστόν aristotélicien. N'oublions pas que la notion jouait un rôle important dans la *Rhétorique*, qui était connue au quinzième siècle. Mais on peut constater, en scrutant les choses de plus près, que Pontano s'inspire de sources plus récentes qu'Aristote. D'abord, il déclare que l'essentiel de la poésie comme de l'éloquence, réside dans le *mouere*. Il rejoint ici la pensée de Cicéron qui disait dans l'*Orator* que le pathétique permet seul à la parole d'atteindre sa perfection. Il ajoutait qu'alors seulement on peut parler d'*oratio grandis* et atteindre une plénitude qui rejoint l'idéal et ne réside pas seulement dans le juste-milieu. Or voici ce qu'écrit Pontano (p. 237): "Assentior, ut semper existimauerim in quacumque ad dicendum suscepta materia atque in dicendi quoque genere magnitudinem sublimitatemque ipsam poetae esse propriam, nunquam mediocritate contentam." Le propre de la poésie est le sublime.

Pontano donne aussitôt comme preuve les *Géorgiques*, où Virgile a introduit le céleste dans le terrestre. Nous rejoignons ici certaines observations qui apparaissent aussi dans le *Commentaire* de Landino (mais nous sommes assez loin des *Disputationes camaldulenses*). Suivant à la fois la ligne de Cicéron et celle de Virgile (et montrant ce qu'elles ont de commun), Pontano dépasse Aristote et Horace. Il ne se contente pas de l'*aurea mediocritas*, il veut le sublime et il le trouve dans l'exaltation du pathétique, laquelle ne peut provenir que de l'admiration. La suite du texte, après avoir cité Cicéron, marque avec force qu'une telle pratique trouve sa pleine application dans l'histoire: "Nam historia, ubi magnifica esse uult, ubi heroica uideri ac grandis, et figuras et uerba de poetis mutuatur." Voici en somme le sommet de la poésie: il réside dans l'imitation des héros.

Nous pouvons mettre ici un terme à nos remarques sur Pontano. Nous avons vu qu'il part d'une philosophie assez proche de celle que développe Landino. Lui aussi s'inspire à la fois de Platon et d'Aristote. Mais il ne s'intéresse pas chez eux à la méditation transcendante, à la métaphysique de la lumière et du beau qui avait retenu Ficin. Il se tourne au contraire vers le langage et ses figures, vers l'esthétique du sublime, vers l'histoire et la psychologie. Il annonce la pensée baroque et classique qui conduira, en France, vers Corneille et en Italie vers Vico et son *Oratio de mente heroica*. Le médiateur qui lui permet de conserver la pensée platonicienne tout en l'infléchissant vers les problèmes littéraires et psychologiques, est Cicéron.

Il faudrait indiquer à la fois les tenants et les aboutissants, rappeler l'influence de Valla (si attentif au simple plaisir du langage) et de Sannazar, citer en aval les grands commentaires d'Aristote, qui reviennent au texte de la *Poétique*, mais qui s'appuient sur la même tradition cicéronienne, ou rappeler les premières éditions du *Traité du Sublime*. Nous nous bornerons ici à un exemple. Nous le tirons du *Naugerius* (ou *Navagero*) de Fracastor (1540). Là encore, l'auteur s'interroge sur la définition du poète. Il le fait dans l'esprit même du platonisme, en cherchant les caractères distinctifs. Il arrive à la formulation suivante: "alii siquidem singulare ipsum considerant, poeta uero uniuersale, quasi alii similes sint illi pictori, qui et uultus et reliqua membra imitatur, qualia prorsus in re sunt, poeta uero illi assimiletur, qui non hunc, non illum uult imitari, non uti forte sunt, et defectus multos sustinent, sed uniuersalem et pulcherrimam ideam artificis sui contemplatus res facit, quales esse deceret." "Car les autres considèrent la singularité même, mais le poète l'universel. Tout se passe comme si les autres étaient semblables à ce peintre qui imite le visage et les membres, tels qu'ils sont en réalité, et comme si le poète était pareil à celui qui ne veut pas imiter tel ou tel modèle, comme le hasard les fait, avec leurs nombreux défauts, mais, ayant contemplé l'idée universelle et belle entre toutes qu'il se fait de l'artiste, les représente telles qu'elles devraient être" (158b).

Nous sommes, on doit le souligner, au cœur de la pensée cicéronienne, transposée de la rhétorique dans la poétique. Dans l'*Orator* 7 sqq., l'Arpinate avait indiqué qu'on ne peut concevoir l'éloquence véritable qu'en dépassant les exemples

historiques et en se forgeant un modèle idéal. Panofsky a montré l'importance
de ce texte pour l'histoire de l'art. Nous en voyons ici le rôle dans la tradition
des poétiques. Il faudrait aussi analyser la structure et la progression du dialogue
proposé par Fracastor. Il se demande quels peuvent être les rôles de la poétique:
enseigner, plaire, émouvoir, Il marque l'intérêt des trois fonctions, en particulier
du *mouere*, mais il s'avise qu'elles appartiennent aussi à la rhétorique. Il arrive
donc à la distinction que nous avons indiquée. Il faut imiter l'idée. Elle possède
deux caractères: elle est universelle (et l'interprétation du platonisme prend ici
un caractère aristotélicien); elle est belle, liée essentiellement à la convenance.
Or, la premier caractère appartient aussi à l'éloquence, qui est capable, comme
Cicéron l'a montré, de s'élever aux types généraux. Reste donc la seule beauté.
Voici que, pour la première fois, se trouve affirmé le primat absolu de la beauté
en poésie. Elle réside pour l'essentiel dans la convenance; en fin de compte, on
peut définir ainsi l'*officium* du poète: il cherche par l'imitation ce qui est le plus
beau (*pulcherrimum*) en chaque genre; il doit "apposite et simpliciter dicere ex con-
uenientibus in unoquoque."

Nous sommes maintenant au seizième siècle. Nous constatons que les hommes
de la Renaissance, s'inspirant de la pensée antique, sont arrivés à distinguer plusieurs points de vue, tout en s'inspirant constamment d'une tradition platonicienne et aristotélicienne. Dans la lumière de Dante et de Platon, ils ont d'abord
insisté sur la contemplation purifiante. Puis, se rapprochant d'Aristote, ils sont
revenus à l'imitation en essayant de l'ennoblir par les figures du langage, par le
sublime psychologique et par les sources de la grâce. Ils ont en somme tendu à
dégager des symbolismes moraux et métaphysiques une esthétique toute pure.
Il s'inspiraient en cela de Cicéron, mais détournaient complètement les résultats
de sa pensée.

Le problème de la beauté, dans ce qu'elle a de spécifique, reste donc posé. Il
est possible de la mettre en œuvre dans les textes littéraires et poétiques. Mais
les questions métaphysiques demeurent. Il faut sans doute préciser à leur propos
quels sont les rapports de Platon et d'Aristote. La question est formulée d'une
façon particulièrement claire, dans la première moitié du seizième siècle, par
Nifo, humaniste padouan, ami de Jeanne d'Aragon, qui fut plus tard, en France,
l'un des maîtres à penser des libertins érudits, lorsque Naudé l'eut édité, en 1645.
Son *De pulchro et amore* (1531) (qui attend toujours une deuxième édition) résume
avec une ampleur remarquable les problèmes d'esthétique qui se posent après
Ficin. Il le fait en multipliant les références précises à l'antiquité, si bien que cet
essai peut apparaître aujourd'hui encore comme une des meilleures synthèses sur
l'esthétique humaniste à tous les sens du terme. Il mérite donc que nous essayons
de l'analyser. Nous verrons ensuite son influence sur l'un des plus grands maîtres
de la littérature universelle: Torquato Tasso.

La démarche de Nifo est assez sinueuse et dialectique. Il s'efforce de présenter
successivement tous les points de vue possibles sur le beau. Puis sa pensée va se
resserrer, atteindre l'essentiel.

Notons toutefois qu'il part de l'*Hippias majeur*. Platon y combattait le relativisme des sophistes, qui voyaient dans la beauté une pure convention, fondant l'idée de convenance ou de grâce. Nifo attaque dans un tel esprit l'enseignement de Protagoras (chap. 1). Au chap. 2, il lui oppose la doctrine stoïcienne, qui confond beauté et sagesse. Le chap. 3 évoque un des plus suggestifs parmi les textes de l'antiquité: les *Imagines* où Lucien décrit la belle Pantheia. L'auteur grec montrait qu'elle possédait toutes les qualités possibles; il évoquait la célèbre anecdote selon laquelle le peintre Zeuxis, pour peindre Hélène, avait combiné les beautés des plus jolies filles de Crotone. Une telle manière de voir semblait unir en les dépassant le point de vue des sophistes et celui des Stoïciens. Mais une question arrêtait alors le philosophe: le portrait de Lucien (comme celui de Zeuxis) a un caractère imaginaire. Une telle beauté, la beauté même existe-t-elle dans la nature? Nifo répond par deux arguments. Le premier relève de la théorie: l'idée existe par soi; Nifo suit ici Platon et Aristote vient à la rescousse, dans le *De caelo*: l'existence d'une réalité implique celle de son contraire. Or, la laideur existe ... Mais à la théorie s'ajoute un second argument, qui repose sur le fait et, si l'on ose dire, sur la pratique. Nifo était l'ami de Jeanne d'Aragon. Au chap. 5, il proclame que le beau existe dans la nature, puisque Jeanne existe. Et il fait son portrait détaillé: au moral, c'est une héroïne. Mais ses qualités physiques aussi méritent l'admiration et l'auteur les décrit avec minutie: yeux pers, cheveux châtains, corps parfaitement proportionné. Les beautés du tableau du Louvre se trouvent copieusement confirmées.

On pourrait s'arrêter ici. Mais l'auteur s'avise qu'il se rapproche dangereusement des théories soutenues par les sophistes. Dans l'*Hippias majeur* et aussi dans le *Gorgias*, Platon leur reprochait de confondre la beauté avec une belle jeune fille. Socrate, avec son impertinence coutumière, demandait s'il faut la confondre aussi avec une belle marmite. Autrement dit, la question posée est celle du nominalisme: la beauté existe-t-elle de manière universelle, indépendamment de ses applications ou de ses apparitions particulières?

C'est sans doute dans un tel esprit qu'il faut interpréter les chapitres 6 à 13. Nifo y critique une série de confusions qui se trouvent en rapport avec les diverses nuances de vocabulaire que nous avons observées dans l'antiquité. Le beau ne se confond pas avec le bien, ni avec les différentes valeurs qui le monnayent. Il ne se réduit ni aux biens extérieurs, comme l'or (chap. 7), ni aux biens du corps (chap. 8) comme la santé, ni au *decorum* (chap. 9), qui est lié à l'apparence, qui peut nous tromper et qui néglige l'invisible, ni encore à l'utile. De manière générale, il faut éviter de confondre le beau avec ce qui conduit vers lui. De même, tout en le distinguant du bien, il faut éviter de l'en séparer.

Au chap. 12 et au suivant, nous aboutissons ainsi à la doctrine des Néo-platoniciens. Le cheminement à travers les doctrines antiques est achevé: la beauté est le bien en acte, le rayon de lumière divine qui se reflète dans les anges et dans les âmes. Aux chapitres suivants (à partir de 14), Nifo développe la notion de *gratia*, dont il marque, en citant le *consensus* des philosophes (Socrate, Platon, Théophraste, Carnéade) la toute puissance: elle agit sur les hommes avec une sorte de violence et ravit leurs âmes.

Notons qu'au point où nous sommes arrivés, Nifo a reconstruit dans sa totalité, en marquant toutes les sources, la doctrine de Ficin. En particulier, il a distingué comme le maître florentin le *decorum* et la *gratia*. Mais maintenant, il va s'opposer, au nom d'Aristote, à cette tradition platonicienne. Il exprimera ainsi certaines nuances de l'esprit baroque. Car il ne croit pas (contrairement aux Platoniciens) qu'on puisse parler de beauté au sens propre si on traite de réalités simples, éternelles, spirituelles. La véritable beauté naît de l'agencement des parties; elle veut le mouvement et la vie et s'exprime dans les corps en même temps que dans les âmes, mettant ainsi en évidence le lien qui existe entre les uns et les autres. Aristote, précisement, insistait sur ces trois idées: le rôle du "faire" humain, de l'élaboration poïétique et technique; l'importance de la vie; l'union de l'âme et du corps dans toute expérience des valeurs, qu'il s'agisse de la vertu ou du plaisir. La beauté se trouve ainsi mise en relation avec un amour total, qui exalte tout le composé humain.

Nous sommes ici au point exact d'où partiront les "libertins érudits" pour dépasser le Platonisme de la Renaissance. On ira jusqu'à la pensée moderne, tout en ressaisissant certaines tendances fondamentales de l'Aristotélisme médiéval. Nifo est l'ami des médecins padouans. Il prépare à la fois l'esprit de la science moderne et, comme l'a montré M. de Gandillac,[7] la conception globale de l'amour que retrouveront les surréalistes.

Mais il ne nous est pas permis de nous arrêter ici. Nous devons aller jusqu'à la fin du seizième siècle. Parmi les théoriciens de la beauté poétique, nous ne retiendrons que le nom du plus grand poète. Il s'agit de Torquato Tasso. Nous allons constater qu'il connaît Nifo et qu'il se sert de lui pour exposer, à la fin de sa vie, les grands problèmes esthétiques qu'il a rencontrés. Il le fait notamment, vers 1594, dans un dialogue qu'il intitule le *Minturno* ou *Della bellezza*.

Avant d'y arriver, nous devons rappeler que l'auteur de la *Jérusalem délivrée* et de l'*Aminte*, le compagnon inspiré des grands madrigalistes a été, plus et mieux que Nifo, un théoricien de l'esthétique littéraire. Il ne s'est pas limité à la métaphysique du beau mais il en a connu, de manière précise, la poétique. Il l'a dégagée, dès 1564, dans ses *Discours sur l'Art poétique* (qui ne devaient être imprimées qu'en 1587). Il s'est alors montré disciple d'Aristote, encourant même à ce propos les reproches du platonicien Patrizzi. Il a soutenu que le poème épique est imitation à la fois vraisemblable et merveilleuse des vertus héroïques et qu'il exprime aussi la *vaghezza* des passions par des moyens qui appartiennent au *decoro*. Nous venons de citer deux mots italiens. Le second est une transposition fidèle d'une notion latine; le premier appartient en propre à sa langue. Nous rencontrons ici un type de problèmes qui intéresse au premier chef le spécialiste des études néolatines. Il s'agit de la traduction des termes employés par le latin technique. Nous constatons leur fréquence. Les notions qui interviennent alors ne peuvent s'expliquer qu'à partir du latin. Mais, naturellement, elles se trouvent gauchies; nous devons rendre compte de ces inflexions originales.

Il est clair, dans les *Discorsi*, que le Tasse ne se satisfait pas, au sujet d'Aristote, de l'interprétation qu'on trouvera plus tard chez nos classiques. Il insiste beaucoup plus sur l'émotion, sur la *uariatio* des ornements et sur le merveilleux. En cela, il suit la double tradition de Pétrarque et de Sannazar. Il s'enchante à la fois de la *vaghezza* et de la douceur ornée que les musiciens de son temps confèrent à chaque madrigal.

Le dialogue *De la beauté*, dont nous allons parler pour finir, tire, si l'on peut ainsi s'exprimer, les conséquences platoniciennes d'un tel état d'esprit. Torquato Tasso, sans renoncer aux leçons de Nifo, qu'il cite avec précision, va laisser le dernier mot à Ficin.

Il imagine un dialogue, à Naples, entre Antonio Minturno (qui fut lui-même un grand théoricien de la poétique) et Geronimo Ruscelli. Il s'agit effectivement de s'interroger sur la beauté poétique. On le fait à propos des œuvres de l'Arioste, et l'on y découvre, précisément, comme dans les *Imagines* de Lucien, l'image accomplie de la beauté: il s'agit même de la beauté toute nue, puisque c'est le portrait d'Olimpia. Mais l'auteur (par la bouche de Minturno) ajoute aussitôt deux remarques, qui vont précisément contre l'Aristotélisme de Nifo (Raimondi, t. II.311): 1° Olimpia n'est pas vraiment nue puisqu'elle a gardé, comme dit Pétrarque, un "voile" qui est son corps; 2° Les admirateurs de l'Arioste le glorifient d'avoir ajouté la vie au marbre antique. Il est vrai que telle est parfois la fonction des poètes. Mais il leur arrive aussi de rendre le vivant à l'immobilité de la pierre, par exemple lorsqu'ils peignent Niobé. Baudelaire aurait aimé une telle affirmation, qui rend ses droits au Platonisme.

Dans sa quête du beau, le Tasse va reprendre un à un les arguments de Nifo. Il les justifiera d'une certaine manière, mais en même temps il les retournera dans le sens de Ficin. Par exemple, il est vrai que le *decorum* n'est pas le beau (p. 314). Mais pour quelle raison? Voici la réponse: la plus belle des femmes n'a pas besoin que, par convenance, on lui donne des habits de reine: sur elle, tous les habits sont des habits de reine; elle illumine tout de sa beauté. L'idée de convenance n'a donc plus de raison d'être. De même, la beauté ne réside pas dans les biens du corps. Nous avons dit pourquoi: c'est qu'elle est dans l'âme et dans les anges. Et le Tasse, non sans avouer qu'il craint un peu de passer pour Pélagien (p. 315), affirme que Dieu ne cesse de créer des anges. Ce sont les belles âmes dans les beaux corps, ou, aussi, dans les beaux paysages: il observe en passant que la courbe du golfe de Naples est fort propre à favoriser la création des anges (p. 309 sq.).

Nous avons dit que le Tasse partait d'une méditation sur Arioste. Il notait que, chez ce poète, la beauté naît souvent de la description du terrible. Faut-il croire qu'elle est liée à la guerre? Cela nous renvoie aux Péripatéticiens comme Plutarque, qui disaient qu'elle est victoire de la forme sur la matière. Mais le

Tasse veut que la beauté soit paisible: elle exprime seulement la sérénité, la pureté de l'esprit (p. 324–27). De même, elle n'est pas apparence mais lumière et il faut croire à la lumière. Nous rejoignons Ficin dans ce qu'il a de plus profond (pp. 316–27: non "paraître" mais "apparaître").

Mais alors, qu'est-ce que la beauté? On ne peut guère répondre. Nous constatons qu'ici encore, le Tasse rejoint Ficin. Celui-ci nous disait bien que la beauté n'était pas l'être ou l'esprit en soi mais la grâce qui en fait la fleur. Il répondait ainsi d'avance aux objections de Nifo. Que dire de la beauté? Voici la réponse de Torquato Tasso: on ne peut rien en dire; elle est au-delà des déterminations. Elle est un je ne sais quoi qui purifie notre âme (p. 327 sq.). On sait l'importance que gardera dans le classicisme français ou dans le mysticisme espagnol la notion de "je ne sais quoi." Ajoutons que Ruscelli, l'interlocuteur de Minturno dans le dialogue, ne s'en satisfait pas. Quant à lui, il veut se contenter des beautés de la femme réelle: il s'en tient à Jeanne d'Aragon (p. 330). Le débat entre Ficin et Nifo, entre Platon et Aristote, reste donc en suspens. Rien de plus vrai qu'un beau visage: mais il apparaît peut-être comme le voile d'un mystère infini.

Nous pouvons conclure. Notons d'abord que l'histoire de la Renaissance nous a révélé l'existence et la portée des notions dégagées par l'esthétique antique. Nous avons pu aussi apprécier leurs métamorphoses, qui mettent en lumière les aspects créateurs de la poétique dans la période qui nous intéresse.

Nous avons décrit le débat entre Platonisme et Aristotélisme; nous avons noté le rôle de Ficin et de sa théorie de la lumière: elle reprend dans un Platonisme rénové la tradition de Dante. Pontano institue un type de réflexion plus spécifiquement littéraire qui met l'accent sur les figures et le sublime. Ici encore, la tradition platonicienne vient corriger l'Aristotélisme. Mais l'intermédiaire est cette fois Cicéron, dont les traités de rhétorique tendaient à concilier les deux courants. Sur le problème que nous avons posé, Horace intervient assez peu.

On aboutit, avec Fracastor, à un triomphe de l'esthétique. L'auteur du *Naugerius* affirme cette idée fondamentale: la fonction du poète est de trouver le beau.

Encore faut-il savoir ce qu'il est. Nifo et Torquato Tasso débattent de sa nature. Le premier insiste sur ses aspects vivants et charnels, le second retrouve Platon en insistant sur son mystère spirituel. A travers tant de débats sur la beauté, nous assistons aux métamorphoses de la notion de grâce, qui s'approfondit. Ficin ne la confondait pas avec le *decorum*; Nifo souligne cette conquête. Mais Tasso rappelle (avec Ficin) que le *decorum* lui-même est fleur et lumière de la beauté.

Ajoutons un dernier mot. Puisque nous parlons de Platon, d'Aristote et de Cicéron, quand il s'agit de beauté, il s'agit de l'homme. Il est vrai qu'il s'agit de l'ange aussi. Nous l'avons vu chez Ficin comme chez le Tasse. Le rôle de la beauté est double: elle retient l'homme au monde dont elle lui révèle la joie avec Aristote. Mais aussi, avec Platon, elle l'en délivre. Les deux philosophes reconnaissent dans le beau le rapport mystérieux qui existe entre la jubilation et la mélancolie. Entre l'une et l'autre, la pureté sert de médiatrice. Puissions-nous, au travers des réalités de l'histoire littéraire, avoir entrevu sa lumière.

Université de Paris — Sorbonne

Notes

1. Alain Michel, *La parole et la beauté. Rhétorique et esthétique dans la tradition occidentale* (Paris, 1982).

2. Robert L. Montgomery, *The Reader's Eye. Studies in Didactic Literary Theory from Dante to Tasso* (Berkeley — Los Angeles — London, 1979).

3. Sur *mimésis* et *diégésis*, cf. Platon, *République*, III, 392 sqq.; la théorie de la beauté est exposée dans l'*Hippias majeur* et dans le *Phèdre*.

4. Cf. Johannes Stroux, *De Theophrasti uirtutibus dicendi* (Leipzig, 1912).

5. Nous suivons: Sylvain Matton, *"En marge du 'De lumine': Splendeur et mélancolie chez Marsile Ficin,"* in *Lumière et Cosmos, Cahiers de l'Hermétisme* (Paris, 1981), pp. 31-54.

6. Sur Landino, nous renvoyons à la Conférence de M. Di Cesare, prononcé dans le présent Congrès.

7. Sur Nifo, cf. M. de Gandillac, in *Histoire de la philosophie*, t. II, Encycl. de la Pléiade, pp. 110-14. L'humaniste (et, après lui, Tasso, dans les textes que nous citerons) suit de très près l'*Hippias majeur* de Platon. La Renaissance, sans méconnaître l'ensemble de la tradition antique, revient ainsi à ses sources fondamentales.

Platina and the Illnesses of the Roman Academy

Mary Ella Milham

Bartholomeo Sacchi, known as Platina (or "the man from Piadena," outside Cremona) was a member of the eccentric Roman Academy of Guilio Pomponio Leto, was celebrated as the author of the first *Lives of the Popes* and was the first official librarian of the Vatican collections. One of his earliest writings, *De honesta voluptate ac valetudine*, was the first work on diet, food and health to be cast in print, at some time between 1470 and 1475, since an undated edition may be the "editio princeps." As I proceed toward a modern Latin edition, I find that Platina's guide to health has been ignored by most scholars, perhaps as a trifling cookery book. Only one of its sources has been traced and its nine manuscripts were long unnoted in the literature.[1] From my collations of these manuscripts and attempts to construct a stemma I have found two points at which alterations were made in the names of Platina's friends. The earliest must correspond with Pope Paul II's incarceration of Platina and others of the Academy in the so-called Conspiracy of 1468. Where identifiable, the true names will be used below. Since, however, the Academy used Latin nicknames drawn from Roman history and literature, I have not as yet identified such persons as Caelius and Cassius.

Platina was not a medical scholar but a Humanist. We know from a letter to Jacopo, Cardinal Ammanati that *De honesta voluptate* was composed in the summer of 1466 or 67 at the villa of his one-time student Francesco, Cardinal Gonzaga at Albano.[2] It combines general advice upon health and right living with a long list of foodstuffs — including herbs, spices, condiments, vegetables, fruits, nuts and meats — describing their cultivation, distribution, preparation, use and medicinal properties. The second half of the volume contains recipes, most of which Vehling proved nearly sixty years ago to be Latin translations from the Italian original of the famous cook Martinus Novicomensis,[3] extant in two copies in the United States.[4]

While most of the material in *De honesta voluptate* would need to be drawn from earlier sources, there is one kind of embellishment to his recipes, and to a few of his foodstuffs, which must be his own and which must betray his own level of medical knowledge. This is his use of personal anecdote about his friends to enliven his text.

Many of Platina's anecdotes about his circle recount food-related preferences or foibles or record happy hours spent in dining. In fact, in a single passage at the beginning of Book V, on Edible Birds, Platina praises the simple table in a brief panegyric which names eleven friends, including Giulio Pomponio Leto, the leader of the Academy, Antonio Settemuleio Campano, Nicolo Lelio Cosmico, Fabio da Narnia and Antonio dei Rossi, some of whom were within a short time to be jailed with Platina in Castel Sant' Angelo on the order of Paul II. A few anecdotes draw, however, upon medical lore to describe the kinds of illnesses his friends suffered, with suggested dietary remedies. There are in all twenty-two references in Platina to specific ills among his acquaintances, fittingly enough, mostly ills of digestion and elimination.

Four of Platina's friends are described as melancholic, that is, possessed of too much black bile according to humoral theory. Caelius must have presented a severe case because he is mentioned twice, once with the remark that he "surpasses Saturn in melancholy." For this Platina suggests that he eat elderberry blossom *torta* (VIII.32) — a *torta* is not a cake but a quiche or pie, usually with an egg-base and one or two crusts. He should also avoid venison (IV.25), which Brutus should avoid for the same reason. Platina also suggests that Pandagato da Lonigo should avoid peas in almond milk because they increase melancholy and are bad for the nerves (VII.65).

Like Pandagato, other friends of Platina are identified as each having two ills, for which a single dish is recommended or prohibited. Callimacho Esperiente, who was to immortalize himself by fleeing Rome ahead of the Pope's arrests within the Academy, presumably had weak eyes and an oversupply of passion, as a result of which Platina recommends that he not eat kid in garlic sauce, which would increase both problems (VI.25). Aristoxenus Gallus and Glaucus (Marino Coldermaro da Venezia), however, need their passions aroused, and both suffer from dysury. To Glaucus, Platina recommends turnip, pear or quince *torta* (VIII.30), while to Aristoxenus he commends white zanzarella, a sort of almond custard or trifle (VII.72). In another recipe, Archigallus, who may be the same person as Aristoxenus Gallus since he shares the same ills, should use chicken *torta* to increase fertility and stimulate his passions (VIII.47).

Digestive or urinary problems plagued other friends of Platina. Galba, who cannot control his urine, should not eat turnip casserole (VII.41) while Cassius, who suffers from colic and "the stone," should avoid gourd *torta* (VIII. 29) and, in another recipe, is enjoined to avoid roe and almond *torta* because of his colic (VIII.44). Three other associates of the Roman Academy may have suffered from gall-bladder (or kidney) problems. Voconius is bothered by yellow bile and should therefore avoid a galantine made of boiled pig's feet and egg-yolks (VI.24). Hircius's illness is not named, but pain in the side causes him to cry out in the night, perhaps with gallstones giving pain after he had eaten the evening meal (VIII.31). He is enjoined to avoid *polenta* made of cheese, eggs and pearl barley. The famous bookseller Vespasiano da Bisticci likes a two-crust pie made from vine- or rose-props and ground udder because it checks the bile (VIII.33), but Platina does not tell us whether this is precautionary or to correct a dysfunction.

A single reference describes an ordinary digestive ill: poor Caelius, who is twice cited for melancholia, is also constipated and should eat a *minutal* of herbs boiled in a little sugar as a laxative (VII.66). Pietro Marsi, on the other hand, is racked with a cough, which should be soothed by a sweetened *roux* of flour and fat (VII.40). Whether Cornelius is ill or merely cautious is not clear, but he does not eat cabbage Roman style (VII.69) because it is harmful to the head and stomach.

By modern medical standards, this sage advice of Platina's seldom has validity. We would consider melancholia and probably "passion" more psychological than physical and therefore, in conventional medical circles, relatively unrelated to diet, and we would not think avoiding kid in garlic sauce of much use in preventing weakness of the eyes. Gourds, however, like other members of the melon family, can contribute to gall-bladder problems, so that Platina's advice to Cassius to avoid gourd *torta* because of "the stone" would be considered sound. The suggestion that Caelius eat a *minutal* of herbs cooked in sugar for constipation is unclear, for some herbs are laxative, some binding, but the sugar might in any event be helpful. Some of his other suggestions cannot really be judged, for modern science, with its insistence on controlled experimentation, has little pursued the effects of specific foods on individual ills, organs or areas of the body. It is probable that Platina's friends had learned by trial and error what they ought not to eat and that he is attempting to give these discoveries quasi-scientific explanations.

It is interesting that in his discussions of ills and remedies Platina has sometimes lumped together unlike illnesses and then recommended a single dish as good or bad for them. Also he usually recommends or forbids cooked dishes which are composed of many ingredients rather than specific foodstuffs. These characteristics, as well as a lack of corresponding passages, suggest that he knew little of the great Arabic works on diet and health, which had been translated into Latin in the twelfth and thirteenth centuries, nor even the *Regimen Sanitatis Salernitanum* which had been drawn up in the Italian medical School of Salerno from Arabic sources and which suggests the medicinal properties of specific foods for specific ills.

Although he gives lip-service to the humoral theory, which came from Hippocrates and Galen through Avicenna down to the seventeenth century, Platina gives little evidence that he understands its complex logical pattern as described in the *Abengnefit* of Ibn Wafid or Avicenna's works, both translated into Latin in the twelfth century by Gerard of Cremona (Gerardo da Sabbioneta). These works had long been in Italy and might well have been available to Platina. Except for some quotations from Avicenna, they do not appear in this work.

At least one Latin translation from the Arabic, however, was used in *De honesta voluptate*; Platina's introductory precepts for good health and a few of his descriptions of foods were drawn from the *Tacuinum Sanitatis* of Ibn Butlan, which had been widely circulated in the Po Valley in an abridged version in the fourteenth century.[5]

Because I must determine Platina's sources for my new Latin edition, I have also investigated several of the herbals and agricultural writings which were well known in his time, but his headings and descriptions of plants and foods both differ from the sorts of information which are found in the *Opus Ruralium commodorum* of Pietro da Crescenzi or in those versions of the *Herbarius* which I have already seen. I have not yet examined two texts which exist only in manuscript at Paris. One is far too short to be of special significance while the other is a description of herbs and condiments translated from the Arabic by Maestro Jambobino of Cremona in the twelfth century and suggested as a source of Platina by several authors. The quotations from this work, which I have seen thus far only in secondary sources, are unrelated to Platina.

One debt of Platina's work is clear. Throughout his book he quotes frequently from Hippocrates, Galen, Varro, Cato, Columella, Palladius and Dioscorides. Furthermore, the majority of his anecdotes and illustrations, as well as his accounts of illnesses as related to diet, are drawn from ancient history. As a Humanist learned in both Latin and Greek, and as a member of an Academy so paganized as to wear togas and to celebrate Vergil's birthday, he may have rejected the intellectual ferment of his own time and scorned most of medieval and contemporary learning. Even his somewhat bizarre dietary remedies and prohibitions for the ills of his friends may be derived from an imperfect understanding of the specialized writings from the antique past.[6]

University of New Brunswick

Notes

1. M. E. Milham, "The Manuscripts of Platina 'De honesta voluptate ...' and its Source Martino," *Sc*, 26 (1972), 127-28; also excerpts in Ms. Venice: Bibl. del Museo Correr, Malvezzi 126.

2. *Epistolae et Commentarii Jacobi Picolomini Card. Pap.* (Milan, 1506), c. 140.

3. J. D. Vehling, "Martino and Platina Exponents of Renaissance Cookery," *Hotel Bulletin and Nation's Chefs* (October, 1932), pp. 192-95.

4. Milham, "The Manuscripts of Platina...", 127-28; the Pichon Ms. may now be in private hands in Cambridge, Mass.

5. Milham, "New Aspects of 'De honesta voluptate ac valitudine'," forthcoming in *Acta del Convegno di Studi su Bartolomeo Sacchi, detto il Platina* (Padua, Antenore Press, expected 1984).

6. For valuable discussion of the medical aspects of Platina's references to foods and illnesses I am indebted to Dr Thomas E. Dugan of Waukesha, WI, U.S.A., who is in no way responsible for any errors or misinterpretations of my own.

Barbaro's Themistius and Gelli's *Letture*: Philosophy Lost in Translation

Phillips Salman

This communication is concerned with an idiosyncratic problem in a text of an unusual Renaissance Italian literary critic, Giovan Battista Gelli. If my argument appears idiosyncratic, that is partly because the text has raised more problems than I have been able to solve as yet, and I would be grateful for any suggestions that would enable me to pursue my study of Gelli's works. Specifically, this communication concerns one of seven references Giovan Battista Gelli makes to Ermolao Barbaro's Latin translation of Themistius of Euphrada's paraphrase of several works of Aristotle. This interesting reference is to an image of the heart, the location of memory and imagination, as a book which the intellect reads. Gelli tells us, in his *Letture sopra la Commedia di Dante*,[1] that he is using Barbaro, and I assume that all the references he makes to Themistius are to the Barbaro translation. In effect, this paper really concerns four references to Barbaro, because Gelli, apparently by misremembering what he has read in Barbaro, extends my one reference to two others and consolidates a fourth into his argument. Most of the "philosophy lost in translation" of my title is about Gelli's apparent misremembering his neo-Latin text and its implications for his criticism. I hope to work through a small thicket of topics and references to show how Gelli transforms Barbaro's Themistius in reading two significant passages in Dante's *Divina Commedia*. My demonstrations will issue in some comments on Gelli's sense of the nature of words.

Textual history is not in point here; however, it is worth reminding ourselves that Barbaro's translation of Themistius's *Paraphrasis in Aristotelis* went through numerous editions — the British Library, for example, owns nine that were published between 1481 and 1560[2] — and that Gelli's *letture* on Dante were delivered to the Florentine Academy between 1541 and 1563. Barbaro (1453 or 1454–93) is well known for his role in *quattrocento* Venetian Humanism. Gelli (1498–1563) requires more comment because he is less well known, because use of him requires justification, and because he is surely an unusual figure. Gelli was a shoemaker in Florence, who achieved literacy; attended conversations at the Orti

Oricellari; studied with Verino; wrote plays, dialogues, and translations; and who lectured to the Florentine Academy on Petrarch and Dante. One dialogue, the *Circe*, was immensely popular and was translated and circulated in Renaissance England. Gelli is interesting as a popularizer of humanist thought and as a conservative and eclectic critic whose work raises typical critical questions, among them, some about nominalism. I am using Gelli, in fact, to ease myself into the cold bath of nominalism and realism in Renaissance critics.

The references to Themistius occur in *Lettura Decima, Lezione Secunda*, where Gelli is commenting on *Purgatorio* XVIII.49–53. It probably helps my case that Gelli slightly misquotes these lines. They are

> Ogni forma sustanzial, che setta
>   è da matera ed è con lei unita,
>   specifica virtue ha in sè colletta,
> La qual senza operar non è sentita
>   né si dimostra mai che per effetto.

In Singleton's translation,

> Every substantial form that is both distinct from matter and united with it, holds within itself a specific virtue, which is not perceived except through operation nor ever shows itself save by its effect, as life in a plant by the green leaves.

Where the text has *ogni forma sustanzial*, Gelli has *ogni sustanzial forma* and he fails to complete Dante's sentence. The quotation should end with a simile "come per verdi fronde in pianta vita."

In *Purgatorio* XVIII, Dante asks Vergil to define love for him. The answer is given in terms of the perceptual operations of the faculty psychology and the awakening of desire for an object. The lines Gelli quotes are from Vergil's resolution of further doubts. Dante wants to know how the soul can be blamed or punished for loving sinful objects if the soul is moved only by external ones. In the lines quoted, Dante has Vergil elaborate the concluding part of his first explanation, where forms are seen as imprinting on wax. Substantial forms, Vergil shows, cause effects, and the forms are not perceived except by their effects. These forms, in turn, can be sought or fled by an innate power of mind that is at once conscience and free will.

Gelli follows this principal quotation with three lines that he describes as "il secondo terzetto del nostro testo." In fact, this tercet comes from two cantos earlier in the *Purgatorio*, although from a canto that raises and anticipates the point made in Canto XVIII. In Canto XVI, where the purgation of the wrathful is described, Marco Lombardo discourses on free will. He describes the way the will becomes more sophisticated in its choice of objects as one matures. When we are children,

L'anima semplicetta, che sa nulla,
    se non che, mossa da lieto fattore
    volontier corre a cio che la trastulla. (ll. 88-90)

(The simple little soul, which knows nothing, save
that, proceeding from a glad Maker, it turns eagerly
to what delights it.)

Gelli uses this tercet to show that Dante thinks every soul has its proper operation
and that in man proper operation is by means of the will's seeking its highest good.
Gelli also uses the passage to make the point that seeking one's highest good is
a function of one's cognitive processes. The first line of this tercet, to which I will
return, recurs later as Gelli turns his discussion of cognition to questions of
nominalism and realism and shows the role of phantasmata or images in thought.

These passages form the basis of a commentary that places the quoted lines
in a context of the mind's functioning when it learns something. One move in
Gelli's strategy is a comparison of Platonic and Aristotelian positions on the way
the mind learns. Gelli first describes the Platonic theory of reminiscence, with
its notion of knowledge already present in the mind, and then refutes it and
espouses Aristotle's image of the mind as a *tabula rasa* that receives impressions
from the senses.

Our reference to Barbaro's Themistius occurs as Gelli denies that universals
exist in the divine mind are outside of our intellects. Those views, he says, are
"contrary to the doctrine of Aristotle and to truth itself." "The intellect needs,"
he continues:

> certain inherent powers in its operation. These are the memory and the phan-
> tasy. One of these reserves things understood or known through the senses,
> and the other the phantasms or images of things seen. Next the intellect,
> considering things in the memory or phantasy, in the manner of one reading,
> draws from them the universals it understands, as Themistius well explains
> in his paraphrase of Aristotle's book concerning memory and recollection,
> saying that our phantasy, which he places in the heart, is a book in which
> the intellect continually reads; and the phantasms and the images reserved
> from the phantasy are the letters.

> (Ha bisogno dunque lo intelletto, per le predette cagioni, nel suo operare,
> di alcune potenzie organiche; e queste sono la memoria e la fantasia; l'una
> delle quali riserba le cose intese o conosciute da'sensi, e l'altra fantasmi o
> vero le immagini delle cose vedute. Nelle quali dipoi risguardando l'intelletto,
> a guisa di uno che legga, ne cava gli universali che egli intende, come bene
> dichiara Temistio nella sua parafrasi sopra il libro *De la memoria e reminiscen-
> zia* d'Aristotile, dicendo che la fantasia nostra, la quale egli pone nel cuore,
> è il libro nel qual legge continovamente lo intelletto; e i fantasmi e le im-
> magini riserbate da quella sono le lettere.)[3]

Gelli refers to the *Themistii Paraphraseos De Memoria & Reminiscentia*, which we now know was not written by Themistius but by someone named at the moment, Pseudo-Themistius.

In two other *letture* Gelli brings up this striking image for the way three of the mind's faculties work, finding it in two separate places in Barbaro's Themistius, namely the paraphrases of the *Posterior Analytics* Book II.33, and of the *De Anima*, probably Book III.24. I say "probably" because the reference mentions no book or section. Like T. S. Eliot's cat, McCavity, however, the images are not there. To be sure, there are references to the intellect working on sense data in the phantasy or memory, but the specific image of the intellect reading a book does not occur. In the probable passage in the *Posterior Analytics*, the memory is referred to as a *thesaurus*, but with the exception of a reference in Pliny (*Ep.* 1. 22. 2) to *thesaurus* as a book, it seems unlikely that the word serves to justify Gelli's memory of a book image in his other two passages.

We know that all writers work from memory and sometimes get their sources wrong. There is no point in criticizing Gelli as a critic-philosopher that misremembers. The extension, however, of the book image into other sections of Barbaro-Themistius can interest us for what it does to Gelli's source and for what it does in Gelli's reading of Dante. One cannot exactly know why Gelli remembered the image in other passages, yet earlier in our *lettura* he gives a clue when he cites Aristotle's well-known image of the mind as a *tabula rasa*. The mind, he says, "is like a *tabula rasa* (to use the words of [the Peripatetics'] master Aristotle) on which nothing at all is written," and he continues:

> They do not mean, however, that the writing-tablet is like that preparation that would be in the writing-tablet and like that capacity to receive every character and every picture, as Averroes asserts Alexander held (because such a preparation as that is accident and the soul is a substance); but that it has a nature fitted to receive any sort of letter.

> (Non intendendo però che ella sia simile a quella preparazione che sarebbe in quella tavola, e a quella attitudine di ricevere ogni carattere e ogni pittura come recita Averroe che tenne Allesandro (perche cotale preparazione e uno accidente, a l'anima e sustanzia); ma ha quella natura atta a ricevere ogni sorte di lettere.)[4]

Gelli uses the analogy of the *tabula rasa* to grasp the point Averroes offers. When he adopts Averroes's refutation of Alexander and sees the problem in terms of substance and accident as well as of material and its preparation, he indicates, as we shall see again, that he considers the concrete image to be a way of knowing the immateriality of the mind's operation and nature. He uses the verbal representation of an image as if it were an image directly reported to his mind by his senses, without the mediation of Barbaro's book.

Gelli's use twice of the writing-tablet in this *lettura* must, therefore, indicate its

importance to him as a means of understanding the way the mind records sense
perception. That importance indicates why he would draw on a similar image
from Themistius on memory and it helps us see why he extends the image to other
places in Themistius. The importance of the image is further pointed up when
we look at Barbaro's Latin for the *tabula rasa* passage (*De Anima* III.31). There,
the tablet is a "litteratoria tabula in qua nihil est ascriptum simul litteras et elementa
posueris." The word *litteratoria* appears to help Gelli extend the image from the
De Memoria, since it implies and stresses, more than the word *tabula* alone, the
sense of the soul as an object capable of being written upon and therefore capable
of being read. Generally, *litteratoria* refers to a teacher of grammar and in Later
Latin *litteratoria* usually refers to something written in letters or to the erudite grammarian in the Roman sense of "philologist." A *litteratoria tabula* would be used by
the grammarian in teaching. Barbaro's warrant for *litteratoria* comes directly from
Themistius, whose Greek uses five forms of γράφειν, a piece of writing, in two
lines. One of the forms is [εν] γραμματείῳ, a writing tablet, the word originally
in Aristotle. Perhaps Barbaro wanted especially to delineate the image of the mind
reading. It is more likely that the image of the *tabula rasa* made a strong claim,
especially after having been treated by St Thomas Aquinas, and that Gelli made
the connection for himself.

To go further, it seems more likely still that Gelli had his eye on a certain critical
object that caused him to divert from the precise wording of his text and point
his auditors towards words in the mind. He manipulates his argument, that is,
so that it establishes Dante's understanding of cognitive processes largely as
Aristotelian and broaches nominalist questions. Part of Gelli's method, as I have
already suggested, is to work out major philosophical positions to connect Dante's
poetry to the background material, but there is little of such modern methods
as explication. As we have seen, Gelli merely follows his central text from Dante
with his exposition of Platonic and Aristotelian notions of cognition. Gelli is also
accustomed to stay within his text; he is even accustomed to gloss Dante with
Dante. In the *lettura* we are considering, Gelli uses the latter procedure as he works
with his point about cognitive processes. He shows the location of two of the mental
faculties in the parts of the brain and asserts that

> the intellectual soul does not know any thing by itself, nothing outside of
> the body, and that (as the Philosopher said) one does not find any thing
> in the intellect that has not first been in the senses, as our poet clearly shows,
> where he says,
>
> > It is needful to speak thus to your faculty, since only through
> > sense perception does it apprehend that which it afterwards makes
> > fit for your intellect.
>
> (l'anima intellettiva non sappia cosa alcuna da per sé, né fuori di questo
> corpo, e che (come diceva il Filosofo) nessuna cosa si ritruovi nello intel-

letto, che non sia prima stata nel senso, sì come chiaramente ne dimostra
il nostro Poeta, dove e' dice:

> Cosi parlar conveniensi al vostro ingegno,
>   Pero che solo da sensato apprende
>   Cio che fa poscia d'intelletto degno.)[5]

This passage is from the *Paradiso* (IV.40–42) and it functions as support for a point
rather than as material to be understood. It appears, therefore, that in this case
Dante's poem is not, for Gelli, poetry in any modern sense, but another instance
of a philosohical text that can be cited to develop an argument. Dante is, in fact,
Gelli's primary philosophical text.

Gelli extends his point about the intellect's dependence upon the senses by introducing a second time the tercet beginning "l'anima semplicetta" and he makes
a turn on it into the questions of nominalism and realism. Here, the first line
of the tercet is praised as poetry, and Gelli does engage in a kind of explication.
"With the greatest forethought," Gelli says,

> and with the most wonderful art, in order to express his conceit better [Dante]
> says 'that knows nothing' and he does not say, 'that does not know any thing';
> for the reason that he perhaps would have denied in the soul particularly
> cognition of *real things*, and of things that in effect are *things*, and not the
> cognition of *logical things*, which are not truly things but terms and concepts
> and names of names, found in the intellect of man so that man can know
> more clearly and easily the nature of real things.

> Dovete ancora notare, che con grandissima considerazione e con arte
> mirabilissima, per meglio esprimere il concetto suo, egli disse: *che sa nulla*,
> e non disse: *che non sa cosa alcuna*. Imperò che se egli avesse detto *che non
> sa cosa alcuna*, arebbe forse negato in lei solamente la cognizione delle *cose
> reali*, e delle cose che in effetto sono *cose*, e non la cognizione delle *cose logicali*;
> le quali non sono veramente cose, ma termini e concetti e nomi di nomi,
> trovati dallo intelletto dell'uomo per potere più chiaramente e più facilmente
> conoscere la natura delle cose reali.[6]

From this statement Gelli develops an exposition of the way knowledge is generated
in us anew and of the principles of knowledge. I cannot go into his exposition
here except to say that it is founded on a notion of terms — simple or composite —
generating notions or imaginings which are then combined into what Gelli calls
credenze, a word which perhaps could be translated as "opinions." These are the
basis for affirming or denying anything, according to Gelli, and they divide into
opinions that either can be examined further or that are self-evident. An example
of the first is the statement that the intelligences are pure act; of the second is
the statement that any whole is greater than any of its parts. The first type are
called, as in Dante, *prime notizie* or *degnita*, and elsewhere, *primi principii*, or *concetti*

communi. And these generate all other forms of cognition. This exposition concludes Gelli's treatment of the texts he started with, although it does not conclude the *lettura*, since Gelli goes on to treat the way the processes of cognition in Dante relate to faith and attempts at a knowledge of God.

Gelli says at the beginning of this *lettura* that Dante's passage on substantial form and its implications have been explained, partially at least, by *il discorso della ragione*, a phrase which appears in sixteenth-century English as "discourse of reason." It is a concept very important in Gelli's criticism generally, and in this *lettura* Gelli wants to expound it as he works on the passage from Dante. It is not true to say that Gelli expands the passage from Pseudo-Themistius to make his points on the operations of reason; rather, the image the Pseudo-Themistius uses clearly has great significance for Gelli as an occasion for explaining the thought beneath Dante's surface. Another part, therefore, of the philosophy that is lost in translation is the system within which the original operates. One bit is appropriated to support another system, almost as if the first did not exist. The system that dominates Gelli's original is the one he finds in Dante, and Dante himself, because he frequently refers to the memory as a book, predisposes Gelli to think it occurs in more than one place in Barbaro's translation. I might add that there are references in Curtius to the image and there are some references Curtius does not mention.[7] The Biblical ones could well have affected Gelli also. Especially compelling would be St. Paul's "non in tabulis lapideis sed in tabulis cordis carnilibus" (2 *Cor.* 3:3), which Curtius thinks pressed on Dante, or *Proverbs* 3:3, "et describe in tabulis cordis tui." I think Gelli's thought in this *lettura* is dominated by the topos of the book he finds in Dante. Gelli uses it as he uses the passage from the *Paradiso* we have seen.

Il discorso della ragione, according to Themistius's image, is the reading of signs. For Gelli images become words, in a sense suggested by Dante, drawing on St Thomas. In translating, Gelli makes Themistius into Dante on the nature of phantasms, a reading not justified by Barbaro's translation, although Barbaro makes his own alteration of Themistius in that direction. The not quite logical argument is logical to Gelli because he wants to see Dante's passage in terms of the concrete universal defined in his poem. Gelli's own argument is an allegory of the points he wants to make and the book image in Themistius comes naturally to mind because it expresses the exact limitations on the image pointed out by his text and because it suggests the ways words and phantasms are similar. The mind works with phantasms that it can manipulate, but it can not, as an extreme Nominalist might hold, manipulate phantasms without regard to external reality. Clearly, Gelli's literary criticism breaks no new ground. It arranges previous material to elucidate a point, in the manner of commentary. As his incarnational sense of words suggests, Gelli has his eye on the λογὸς, just as he thinks his master Dante does.

Cleveland State University

Notes

1. *Letture edite ed inedite di Giovan Battista Gelli sopra la Commedia di Dante*, raccolte per cura di Carlo Negroni (Firenze, Bocca, 1887), I, 155–56.

2. I have used the edition of 1549, Apud H. Scotum, Venetiis.

3. Gelli, II, 558–59.

4. Gelli, II, 556.

5. Gelli, II, 559.

6. Gelli, II, 560.

7. *European Literature and the Latin Middle Ages*, transl. Willard R. Trask (N. Y., Pantheon Books, 1953), pp. 304n., 307, 319, 326, and 339.

Cassandra Fidelis as a Latin Orator

Carl C. Schlam

Cassandra Fidelis (1465–1558) of Venice was famed in the last decades of the fifteenth century as *oratrix facundissima*.[1] Renaissance Humanists were most frequently known as *oratores*;[2] *oratrix* thus both denotes Fidelis's calling and indicates that consciousness of her gender was never absent. There was, early in this century, a thorough biographical study of Fidelis by Cesira Cavazzana.[3] Her career has been discussed recently by historians interested in women Humanists, most fully by Margaret King.[4] Fidelis shared in the pursuit of *eloquentia*, which she, as her fellows, saw as closely tied to *philosophia*. Her contribution to these *artes* was not momentous, and the extravagant praise she received may, as King suggests, be largely due to the wonder of men at the accomplishment of a woman. It is nonetheless appropriate for us to take some account of Cassandra Fidelis as a writer of neo-Latin.

She was from a prominent, but not aristocratic family. Her father, Angelo Fidelis, mentioned by Sansovino as a man learned in science, Greek and Latin, served the Republic in various bureaucratic capacities; her grandfather, Giovanni, a philosopher and physician, was of somewhat greater renown. Cassandra was educated by her father until age twelve, and was then entrusted to Gasparino Borro. Her work in Greek centered particularly on Aristotle. By her late teens she gave public recitations in Latin. The extant oration *de laudibus literarum*[5] was presented before the Doge Agostino Barbarigo, in the presence of the Bergamese Ambassador, who, in a letter to her, describes the occasion with great wonder.[6]

Letters and verses of several Humanists praise her outstanding combination of beauty and talent. Politian addressed an encomium to her hailing her "O decus Italiae virgo."[7] He explains, in a later letter, that he journeyed to Venice principally for the purpose of seeing her, but in her presence was reduced to silent wonder.[8] Giovanni Bellini did a portrait of Cassandra, age sixteen, now lost. A drawing probably derived from it was the basis of the carved medallion of her, long displayed on a wall in the courtyard of the ducal palace.[9]

All of the known work of Fidelis is in Latin. A collection of 3 speeches and

some 120 letters, Padua 1631, was edited by Jacopo Tomasini,[10] whose efforts
similarly preserved the bulk of the correspondence of the Brescian *oratrix*, Laura
Cereta, of whom Albert Rabil published a study in 1981.[11] Cereta's correspondence includes a letter to the older and more prominent Venetian, to which we
have no reply, and there may never have been one. Cereta elsewhere complains
of the disdain with which Fidelis regarded her.[12] The correspondence of Fidelis
includes several letters and poems addressed to her. Her letters largely express
thanks, offer or return compliments, recommend friends, and apologize for not
writing sooner. Philosophic themes are somewhat developed in 2 letters of consolation.[13] These items of standard fare serve, however, to place Cassandra in a
circle of Humanists. They also document lines of patronage, particularly with
the house of Aragon, a relationship perhaps established through Eleanor, Duch-
ess of Ferrara.[14] We also have correspondence between Fidelis and Eleanor's sister, Beatrice, Queen of Hungary.[15] Their mother, Isabella, Queen of Naples, invited Cassandra to join her court. The Senate, in 1492, forbidding her to leave
Venice, decreed that the state could not lose such an ornament,[16] though afterwards it gave her little enough support.

The early fame of Cassandra was closely tied to the oration[17] she delivered at
the graduation ceremonies of her kinsman, Bertucio Lamberto, in Padua, in 1487,
when she was twenty-two years old. It was soon published in Modena and, the
next year, in Venice.[18] Hartmann Schedel, at the time a student in Padua, sent
a copy to humanist friends in Nuremburg, where it was reprinted with fresh
tributes.[19]

Despite the glory of Cassandra's early years, the social patterns of the time left
few options open to her. She married a physician, Giammaria Mappelli, and
followed him in his career to Crete. Her occasional subsequent letters give evidence
of little professional activity. She worked on a treatise, *De scientiarum ordine*; it is
not extant and was, perhaps, never completed. She was left a widow in 1520,
in straitened circumstances, and lived on for many years with a sister and her
family. Appeals for help, including one to Pope Leo X,[20] went unanswered. In
her old age, however, an appeal to Pope Paul III, accompanied by some moving
verses, did elicit support.[21] Through his intervention Cassandra was appointed,
in 1547, at the age of eighty-two, Superiora dell'Ospitale di S. Domenico di Castello
at Venice.

In 1556 the Dowager Queen of Poland, Bona Sforza, daughter of Isabella of
Aragon, came through Venice. Her son, Sigismundo II, married, with her great
disapproval, a noblewoman, widow of a Lithuanian, and the Queen Mother was
retiring to her mother's territory, the Duchy of Bari. The senate decreed an
elaborate naval procession to honor the queen. The welcoming party, led by Doge
Francesco Venier, included Luigi Grota who spoke in Italian. Fidelis, at the head
of a group of women, delivered a Latin oration.[22] The drama of the occasion has
been recorded. The queen was so moved by her address that she took off the jeweled
chain she was wearing and put on the *oratrix*. The next day Fidelis presented it

to the Senate as an adornment more suited to their dignity than to herself, who had never cared for gold or gems.[23]

I have studied the prose artistry of two complete orations, *Pro Bertucio* and *Pro Adventu ... Reginae*, one of Cassandra's youth and the other of her extreme old age. There is, I was disappointed if not surprised to learn, no marked difference in their Latinity. I will speak further here only of the first, and treat in detail only its *exordium*.

The oration *Pro Bertucio* consists of seventy-five sentences — distinctly articulated groups of cola — even if they do not always conform to modern conventions of punctuation. These are organized into five major sections. The transitions are clearly marked in simple declarative sentences. We will return shortly to the first, the *exordium*. Cassandra announces the second section with the statement that she will turn to her proper subject, the praise of her kinsman. She will follow the tripartite scheme handed down by Cicero, Plato and the Peripatetics, of according praise to the goods of the spirit, the body and those ascribed to fortune. The virtues and accomplishments of Bertucio add glory to the splendor of his birth, and the beauty of his form is matched by the sanctity of his character. Stress is repeatedly put on his youth, which suggests he may be receiving a first degree rather than a doctorate.

"But let me proceed from lighter to more serious matters." Fidelis thus begins the third section, an *amplificatio* of the statement that the goods of the body and fortune are transitory. She displays her learning in a series of rhetorical questions — where are the rich and mighty of the past? — framed around a diversity of classical *exempla*. Only the accomplishments of virtue and ability are of use to those who come afterwards. The speaker now returns to *hic noster*, who, outstanding in ability and memory, with complete dedication to study, flourishes in eloquence. This theme is elaborated in this fourth and longest section in terms of the powers of speech, the unique human capacity, and the praise of philosophy, to which Bertucio has been devoted. The *conclusio* is marked by the abjuration of a longer speech. Echoing the *exordium*, Cassandra addresses the academic audience by their titles and reiterates her inability to praise them sufficiently. But her undying gratitude and prayers she can and does promise.

There is a clear balance in the composition of the speech. The sections consist respectively of 10, 12, 17, 24 sentences, thus increasing in size, and lastly a conclusion of again 12 sentences. The most frequent and elaborate periodic sentences are in the *exordium* and *conclusio*. In the central sections, periods are not absent, but there is a higher proportion of associative sequences, simple rhetorical questions and repeated constructions. Explicit quotation, even of classical authors, is, as O'Malley observes,[24] most characteristic of scholastic Latin. While Cassandra twice names authorities, she follows humanist usage in blending classical tags into the texture of her own prose.

Let us turn now to the text of the *exordium* of the *Oratio pro Bertucio Lamberto*:

1. Si forti animo incipienti timere decorum esset,
      amplissimi patres, academiae moderatores, vosque viri ornatissimi,
         cum ego sim coram tanto virorum consessu,
      TITUBARE AC MINUS MINUSQUE MIHI CONSTARE DEBEREM.

2. Sed hoc minime fortissimum decere cognovi.

3. TIMIDITAS ITAQUE FINEM ACCIPIAT,
      etsi non dubitem
         plerisque vestrum facinus audax videri posse
         quod ego et virgo
                  et cui per aetatem altior nulla eruditio contingere potuit,
            neque mei sexus, neque ingenii memor,
               in tantam eruditorum hominum lucem,
               et praesertim in ea urbe,
                     in qua his temporibus (ut olim Athenis) liberalium artium
                        studia florent,
            oratura processerim.

4. ME TAMEN NECESSITUDINIS CONSANGUINITATISQUE
   VINCULUM,
      quod mihi cum Bertucio intercedit,
   INVITAM HOC ONUS SUBIRE COEGIT,
      ut potius nimiae audaciae accusari malim
         quam in necessarium instantem pietate, studio, observantia,
            operam meam denegando esse durior.

5. Accedunt alia
         quae a principio deterrere videbantur,
               nunc vero maxime ad laborem subeundum hortantur atque impellunt.

6.   Singulari enim mansuetudine vestra inauditaque clementia freta,
   AD DICENDUM PRODIRE SUM AUSA,
         quam mihi veniam omnino daturam,
            si quid minus eleganter et erudite inter agendum nobis excidisset,
         non dubitabam;

7. Quamvis   non hac tantum virtute   sed reliquis omnibus   vos praeditos esse
   compertum habeam.

8. DE QUIBUS ALIQUID CERTE ATTINGEREM
      nisi verita essem
      ne
         defessos diutius longiore detinere oratione parum prudentis foret
         et audacis nimium existimare posse quantum deberem vestras
            virtutes laudare.

9. Itaque illud unum, ad quod eram vocata, non sumam, sed delibabo quidem, quando vestrarum laudum mihi difficilius est exitum quam principium invenire.

10. His igitur cohortamentis novo exemplo vela ventis pandere constitui.

I have analyzed the prose *per cola commataque* and have so typed the text, with the main clause of the longer, periodic sentences in capitals. While there are problems concerning some of the terminology to be used and disagreement, surely, on some of the specific divisions I have indicated, there is, I think, little question that the rhythm and arrangement of phrases is an essential part of prose artistry. Setting out the text in this fashion, which has been used recently in the study of Cicero,[25] can help us perceive some of the qualities which made Cassandra's eloquence impressive. We can thus more easily carry the study of *elocutio* beyond matters of diction and the *figurae* to a consideration of the patterns and variety of composition. Some of the sentences are fully periodic, those in which a series of cola are arranged in a bound and interlocking structure. Others, not less artfully, follow a more open form, *oratio perpetua*. This term can be applied not only to passages, such as several in the middle sections of the speech, characterized by parataxis, but also to relatively brief sentences in which, despite some subordination, the cola express a simple sequence.

Of the ten sentences which comprise the *exordium*, five are periodic, five are not. Numbers 2 and 10 are technically "simple"; 5, 7, and 9 are syntactically "complex"; for they include subordinate clauses, but in them the cola are not arranged in a bound and interlocking structure. In no. 5, for example, the dominant antithesis makes it virtually a compound rather than a complex sentence.

In the following scheme, I label these five N, so as to show the pattern of varied alternation between periodic (P) and non-periodic (N) constructions:

P N P P N P N P N N
1 2 3 4 5 6 7 8 9 10

Sentence one is virtually a paradigm of a period: four cola, each about the length of a hexameter, with the main clause in the final position. In the succeeding sentences the number of cola and the relationship of the main clause to the subordinate membra is varied. In sentence no. 3, the main clause begins the period; in no. 4 the main clause is again initial, but divided by a short adjectival colon. Let me translate sentence no. 6:

For relying on your singular civility and unmatched graciousness, I have dared to come forward to speak — which (graciousness) I have no doubt will grant me complete pardon, should anything be said less than elegantly and learnedly in our speech.

Here the main clause is in a medial position. It is bracketed by subordinate cola which are tied together, since the following *quam* refers back to the *clementia* of the initial participial colon.

In sentence 3, we have a nice use of the nesting of cola in the second half of the sentence. Again, I translate:

> Let there be an end, then, to fear, although I have no doubt that it may appear to many of you a bold action that I, a young woman and one to whom at her age no very lofty learning can have come, mindful neither of my sex nor of my ability, should come forward to address so brilliant an assembly of learned men, and above all, in this city, in which at this time, as long ago in Athens, the study of the liberal arts flourishes.

In the Latin, of course, the *oratura processerim* closes the period. There are two relative clauses, each part of a pair: "et virgo, et cui per aetatem altior nulla eruditio contingere potuit," then following the *memor* colon, "in tantum eruditorum hominum lucem, et praesertim in ea urbe, in qua his temporibus (ut olim Athenis) liberalium artium studia florent." The relative clauses are pendants; they balance each other, and are of almost the same number of syllables (24, 26).

We have precise isocola in the last periodic sentence, no. 8, in the chiastically arranged phrases of the *ne* clause:

> I would certainly say something about these (virtues), if I
> were not afraid that
> to hold you further, fatigued, with a longer speech, would be
>   a mark of poor prudence,
> and one of excessive pride, to think myself able to praise your virtues
>   as fully as I ought.
> DE QUIBUS ALIQUID CERTE ATTINGEREM
>   nisi verita essem
>   ne
>   defessos diutius longiore detinere oratione parum prudentis
>   foret
>   et audacis nimium existimare posse quantum deberem vestras
>   virtutes laudare.

The final semi-colon is tripartite, with the last comma longest; but the two full cola are of equal number of syllables, 20 + 7, 7 + 20, held together by brachylogy, understanding *foret* with the second.

Let me learn from Cassandra: to keep you with too long an address would not be a sign of good sense. And this kind of thing is, shall we say, an acquired taste. Yet let me close with an echo of A. E. Douglas;[26] it would be a shame if techniques of detailed verbal analysis were applied only to poetry, and not to the genre which so many writers of both palaeo- and neo-Latin considered the highest form of artistic expression.

Ohio State University

Notes

1. The abbreviation *T.* refers to Tomasini's edition; see below n. 10. The phrase occurs, for example, in the salutation of a letter addressed to Fidelis by Lodovico da Schio, *T.* ep. XCVIII. The prominence of Fidelis is noted by M. Lowry, *The World of Aldus Manutius* (Ithaca, 1979), p. 189.

2. H. Gray, "Renaissance Humanism: The Pursuit of Eloquence," *JHI*, 24 (1963), 500.

3. C. Cavazzana, "Cassandra Fedele: erudita veneziana del rinascimenta," *AtV*, 29 (1906), ii, 73–91, 249–75, 361–97, hereafter abbreviated *Cav.*

4. M. L. King, "Thwarted Ambitions: Six Learned Women of the Italian Renaissance," *Soundings*, 59 (1976), 280–304; "Book-lined Cells: Women and Humanism in the Early Italian Renaissance," in P. Labalme, ed. *Beyond Their Sex: Learned Women of the European Past* (New York, 1980), pp. 66–90.

5. *T.* 201–07.

6. *T.* ep. XCI.

7. *T.* ep. CI; Vergil, *Aen.* XI.508.

8. *T.* ep. CIV.

9. *Cav.*, 87^2, describes the medallion as on display with an inscription, but neither of these is now in the place designated.

10. Cassandra Fidelis, *Epistolae et Orationes*, J. Tomasinus ... recensuit (Padua, 1636).

11. A. Rabil, Jr., *Laura Cereta: Quattrocento Humanist* (Binghamton, 1981).

12. Rabil (above n. 11), 83–84, 89–90.

13. *T.* ep. XXXVI and XLVII.

14. *T.* ep. CV.

15. *T.* ep. XXI, LXXI, LXXIIX.

16. *Cav.*, 263; *T.* ep. X–XIII, LX.

17. *T.* 193–201.

18. *Cav.*, 255^2.

19. *Cav.*, 257. A copy of this edition is in the Morgan Library, New York.

20. *T.* ep. CXXIII.

21. *Cav.*, 365–66.

22. *Pro Adventu Serenissimae Sarmaticae Reginae, T.* 207–10.

23. *Cav.*, 368–70; *T.* 36.

24. J. O'Malley, *Praise and Blame in Renaissance Rome* (Duke University Press, 1979), p. 40.

25. H. Gotoff, *Cicero's Elegant Style: An Analysis of the Pro Archia* (University of Illinois Press, 1979); C. Robbins, "A Colometric arrangement of Cicero," *CJ*, 75 (1979), 57–62. H. and K. Vretska, in their edition of Cicero, *Pro Archia* (Darmstadt, 1979) print the text colometrically.

26. A. E. Douglas, "The Intellectual Background of Cicero's Rhetorica: A Study in Method," *ANRW*, 13 (1973), 99.

Francesco Florio, nouvelliste italien

Gilbert Tournoy

Au premier Congrès d'Etudes néo-latines, que nous avons organisé à Louvain, j'ai essayé de tracer les grandes lignes de mon étude consacrée à la nouvelle latine de la Renaissance. Je suis parti d'une définition assez rigoureuse du terme, en distinguant deux branches, c.-à.-d. d'une part les traductions de nouvelles écrites originalement en langue vulgaire — et en premier lieu celles de Boccace —, et d'autre part les nouvelles écrites directement en latin.[1]

Depuis lors les recherches ont progressé dans plusieurs directions. En ce qui concerne les traductions latines de nouvelles en langue vulgaire, il suffit de mentionner l'étude approfondie consacrée par Paolo Viti aux traductions du *Décameron* faites par Filippo Beroaldo.[2]

Quant aux nouvelles originales c'est surtout la fameuse histoire d'Euriale et la belle Siennoise Lucrèce, composée par Enea Silvio Piccolomini, qui a fait l'objet de nombreuses études. Les autres nouvelles originales n'ont guère pu susciter le même intérêt, non seulement à cause de leur moindre valeur artistique, mais aussi et peut-être surtout parce que leur auteur est moins renommé.

Aussi ai-je cru préférable d'examiner en détail chacune des nouvelles et leurs auteurs respectifs avant d'entreprendre une étude synthétique de la nouvelle latine.

Le terrain le plus fructueux semblait être présenté par la vie et les œuvres d'un imitateur assez fidèle de Piccolomini, à savoir le nouvelliste italien Francesco Florio. Encore en 1971 M. Lionello Sozzi s'exprima à son égard dans les termes suivants: "La figura del Florio è anch'essa del tutto oscura e meriterebbe, senza dubbio, accurate indagini."[3] Au milieu du siècle précédent, ont pouvait encore lire, dans le t. 17 (1858) de la *Nouvelle Biographie Générale* par ex., "qu'on est même allé jusqu'à nier son existence." Les rédacteurs de la *Nouvelle Biographie Générale*, comme ceux de la *Biographie Universelle*, dans laquelle la notice sur Francesco Florio apparut deux ans auparavant, ignoraient qu'en 1855 M. André Salmon avait publié une autre œuvre de Florio, le *De probatione Turonica compendium* précédée

de quelques notes biographiques, pas toujours exactes d'ailleurs.[4] Il faut attendre plus de cent ans avant que l'autre aspect des activités de Florio ne soit mis
en lumière: en 1963 M. Charles Finlayson de l'Université d'Edimbourg consacra
un premier article à trois manuscrits copiés par Florio (Edimbourg, BU, ms. 195:
œuvres de Virgile; Paris, Arsenal 1183: Décret de Gratien; Oxford, Merton
College, A.3.1.: œuvres de Sénèque). Dans un second il attira l'attention, à
juste titre à mon avis, sur la portée autobiographique de la nouvelle.[5] Après les
recherches de M. Finlayson on peut encore signaler la notice de M. Fiot à
propos de la date et de quelques termes du De probatione Turonica (1970), l'utilisation du même ouvrage par M. Sozzi pour son dossier concernant la polémique
anti-italienne en France (1972) et surtout la confrontation faite par Anneliese
Schmitt de la nouvelle latine avec la version allemande, qui date d'un siècle plus
tard.[6]

Mais tout cela n'a guère augmenté nos connaissances de la vie et des œuvres
de notre nouvelliste. On a longtemps attendu l'étude promise sur ce sujet par M.
Jacques Guignard, ancien conservateur de la Bibliothèque de l'Arsenal à Paris,
qui déjà en 1940 espérait "pouvoir bientôt publier une étude sur ce personnage."[7]
M. Guignard ayant renoncé depuis longtemps à ce projet, comme il me l'a con-
firmé il y a plusieurs années, voyons de quelles données, anciennes et nouvelles,
on dispose en ce moment pour retracer la vie de notre humaniste.

1° Premièrement, on sait que Florio a copié des manuscrits. M. Finlayson en
avait découvert trois dont seulement un, celui de Paris, était daté entre 1478 et
1480; les deux autres furent écrits à Paris à une date non précisée.

A ces trois manuscrits on peut en ajouter au moins deux autres, pourvus chacun
d'un colophon élaboré.

Le premier est un manuscrit contenant la Summe theologice prima de Thomas
d'Aquin, conservé à la Bibliothèque Municipale de Toulouse (ms. 214), transcrit
à Paris par le frère dominicain François Florio entre le 22 mai et le 28 août
1465.[8]

L'autre manuscrit, qui se trouve à la Bibliothèque Laurentienne à Florence (cod.
Med. Palat. 109), contient le Ad Herennium longtemps attribué à Cicéron et les
satires de Juvénal et de Perse.[9] Après chaque œuvre le copiste a indiqué où et
quand il avait transcrit le texte précécedent. Ainsi il finit à Paris le 17 août 1467
la transcription de Cicéron, et le 28 août 1467 les satires de Juvénal. Malheureusement la troisième partie du ms. est incomplète: manque la sixième satire de Perse,
et donc aussi le colophon que Florio y avait sans doute ajouté.

A remarquer encore que dans les deux dates il manque un C (indication de
cent) qui semble être raturé dans l'un et l'autre colophon. C'est un phénomène
qu'on rencontre aussi dans d'autres manuscrits. Parfois il s'agit d'une simple erreur imputable à la négligence du copiste; dans d'autres cas on pourrait déceler
l'intention de faire vieillir le manuscrit d'un siècle pour le rendre ainsi plus respectable. C'est le cas sans doute d'un ms. du Filocolo de Boccace, copié à Vérone en
1469, mais qui porte la date de 1369.[10]

2° Copiste de manuscrits, Florio est aussi l'auteur de quelques œuvres littéraires, qui toutes, dans une mesure plus ou moins grande, contiennent des données autobiographiques.

a) La première œuvre, aussi dans l'ordre chronologique, est naturellement sa nouvelle, la *Historia de amore Camilli et Emilie Aretinorum*, dédiée en 1467 à l'humaniste Guillaume Tardif et publiée cinq fois au quinzième siècle. J'y reviendrai tout à l'heure.

b) Vient ensuite son traité *De probatione Turonica compendium*, dans lequel il fait l'éloge de la belle ville de Tours. Ce traité, dédié à un de ses amis demeurant à Rome, Jacobus Tarlatus Castillionensis, a été publié il y a plus d'un siècle maintenant, par M. André Salmon, qui l'a daté, inexactement à mon avis, vers 1477.

c) A ces deux œuvres, utilisées par les savants qui ont pu en prendre connaissance, il faut ajouter un dernier opuscule, qui n'a jamais été publié, et pas même cité. Il s'agit de la *Visio mira super archana Francie*, "une vision merveilleuse concernant les secrets de la France." Le manuscrit somptueux, qui probablement est autographe, se trouve actuellement à la Biblioteca Nazionale à Rome, sans que l'on sache de quelle manière ou par quels détours il a pu arriver là-bas (ms. V.E. 428). Avec cette vision, dont le début rappelle la *Divina Commedia* de Dante, et qui pour le reste fourmille de réminiscences de Virgile, Horace, etc. Florio sans doute a voulu gagner la faveur royale.

La combinaison de tous les éléments contenus, soit dans les œuvres littéraires, soit dans les manuscrits copiés, nous donne la possibilité d'esquisser ici pour la première fois un tableau assez net de la vie de François Florio.

Commençons par la nouvelle, qui marque les débuts de Florio dans le monde littéraire. Il y raconte l'aventure amoureuse de deux jeunes gens d'Arezzo, Camille et Emilie, tout en suivant les traces de son prédécesseur célèbre, Enea Silvio Piccolomini, le pape Pie II, qui avait composé sa nouvelle une vingtaine d'années auparavant. En voici le contenu:

Camille, fils d'un pauvre coutelier d'Arezzo, est adopté à l'âge de trois ans par la famille très riche d'Emilie, dont le père décide d'éduquer les enfants ensemble. Les deux grandissent, toujours inséparables — précisément comme Pyramus et Thisbe — et peu à peu leur amitié s'épanouit dans une première amourette. La séparation qui leur est imposée à l'âge de quatorze ans ne fait qu'accroître leur affection. Trois ans après Emilie est mariée à un jeune homme riche de sa classe, et Camille reste seul, inconsolable. Mais bien vite les amants trouvent le moyen d'expédier l'un à l'autre des billets doux, mieux encore, de passer de nombreuses nuits dans des étreintes mutuelles.

Cela dure jusqu'au moment où un autre jeune homme, attiré par la beauté irrésistible d'Emilie, guette jour et nuit devant sa maison; et quand Camille entre furtivement, il le tient pour un voleur et donne l'alarme.

La peine de prison que l'on inflige à Camille n'éteint pas leur passion, mais augmente leur prudence. A nouveau ils sont séparés lorsqu'Emilie est envoyée par son mari à son château hors d'Arezzo, et Camille ne retrouve pas sa trace.

Mais Dame Fortune leur vient en aide: Camille est invité comme organiste dans l'église qui se trouve à mi-chemin entre Arezzo et le château, et les deux amants se rencontrent par hasard sur le seuil de l'église. Le rendez-vous qui s'en suit est interrompu par le mari revenu à l'improviste. Tandis qu'il va chercher des témoins, Camille se sauve par la fenêtre, et c'est Emilie qui seule subit la colère de son mari. Exaspérée, elle fuit à son tour. Après avoir erré dans les bois durant quelques jours, elle est découverte et on la ramène non pas chez son mari, mais chez ses parents. Le pauvre mari fait tout son possible pour regagner sa belle épouse, mais en vain: la porte d'Emilie ne s'ouvre que pour Camille. Mais lui non plus ne peut rester indéfiniment, et tandis qu'il s'adonne aux études à Florence, la peste commence à sévir à Arezzo. Emilie est atteinte, et meurt pieusement. Ayant fait célébrer quelques messes pour son âme, Camille s'en va courir le monde.

Avant de nous demander quelles données de la nouvelle peuvent servir à la reconstruction de la vie de Florio, il convient de s'attarder un moment à la date de composition de sa nouvelle. Généralement, la date de 1467 est retenue, puisque l'auteur lui-même nous l'indique dans le colophon:

> ... liber feliciter expletus est Turonis ... pridie Kalendas Ianuarii, anno domini millesimo quadringentesimo sexagesimo septimo.

Mais à la première lecture déjà, il apparaît que la nouvelle a été écrite en plusieurs phases. Si la lettre liminaire et l'épilogue peuvent bien dater de 1467, rien n'exclut d'autre part qu'une première ébauche de l'histoire ait été composée plusieurs années auparavant. En effet, avant de commencer son récit, Florio fait l'éloge de sa ville natale, Arezzo, et il mentionne non seulement François Pétrarque, Leonardo Bruni et Carlo Marsuppini (+ 1453), mais encore les frères Accolti; par opposition aux premiers nommés, ceux-ci sont représentés bel et bien vivants. L'un est *maintenant*, dit-il, chancelier de Florence, l'autre est professeur à Ferrare. Or, Benedetto Accolti, qui en 1458 avait succédé à Poggio Bracciolini en qualité de chancelier de Florence, est mort le 26 février 1464. Son frère Francesco (1416/17–88) était professeur de droit à Ferrare à partir de 1457. Mais en mai 1461 il partit pour Milan sur les instances de François Sforza.[11]

En tenant compte de ces données on pourrait situer cette partie de la nouvelle au moins entre 1458 et 1461. L'hypothèse que Florio ne serait pas très bien au courant des événements survenus dans sa patrie après son départ, n'est pas très vraisemblable, puisqu'il n'est parti pour la France qu'en 1461, comme nous le verrons tout à l'heure.

Qu'est-ce qu'on peut maintenant dégager de la nouvelle pour retracer la biographie de notre auteur?

Tout d'abord, Florio naquit à Arezzo et non pas à Florence, comme porterait à le croire le fait que lui-même se nomme "Florentinus," e. a. dans le titre de sa nouvelle où on lit: "Francisci Florii *Florentini* de amore Camilli et Emilie ..." L'un n'exclut pas l'autre, puisque la ville d'Arezzo dépendait politiquement de la république florentine depuis le siècle précédent. Plusieurs indications font pencher pour Arezzo comme la ville natale de Florio:

— dans sa nouvelle, ou mieux dans la lettre liminaire il appelle les protagonistes Camille et Emilie ses compatriotes, et dans la *Visio mira* il en fait de même pour Carlo Marsuppini (f. 4ᵛ).

— de plus sa nouvelle s'ouvre sur un bel éloge de la ville d'Arezzo, où naquirent toute une série d'hommes éminents.

Si l'on peut faire crédit au caractère autobiographique de la nouvelle, et surtout à l'identification Camille–Florio, ce dernier serait né vers 1428 environ, dans une humble famille. En effet, dans la nouvelle le père de Camille n'est qu'un coutelier très pauvre, qui n'a pas les moyens de nourrir sa grande famille. Quant à la date de naissance de Florio (1428), elle se déduit du fait que la nouvelle fut terminée le dernier jour de l'an 1467, alors que Florio d'autre part écrit dans sa lettre d'introduction que Camille n'avait pas encore atteint la quarantaine à ce moment.

Suivant la chronologie de la nouvelle, il étudia avec sa sœur de lait jusqu'à l'âge de quatorze ans, les deux dernières années étant consacrées à l'éducation musicale. Cela nous mène jusqu'en 1442–43. Les qualités musicales de Camille qui sont relevées plusieurs fois dans la nouvelle, constituent une première possibilité de connexion avec Florio. Celui-ci s'attarde en effet longuement dans son *De probatione Turonica* sur Jean Ockeghem, le Flamand qui fut nommé en 1465 maître de chapelle du roi, et qui ne cessa de l'enthousiasmer par son art.

Dans la nouvelle une séparation de trois ans est imposée à Camille et Emilie (1442/43–45/46), après quoi Emilie est donnée en mariage, mais leur relation se poursuit sans être troublée, pendant deux ans (1445/46–47/48). Alors Camille est surpris dans la maison d'Emilie et puisqu'il est "clericus," il sera jugé par un tribunal ecclésiastique. Voilà de nouveau une connexion possible avec Florio, dont déjà M. Salmon avait supposé qu'il était dans les ordres, premièrement à cause d'un passage de l'épître introduisant la nouvelle, où on lit: "Quod si non multum mee professioni dixeris convenire." Et M. Salmon continue:

Nous fortifierons cette induction en ajoutant qu'il vivait à Tours dans la maison d'un chanoine de la cathédrale, et que dans sa description de cette ville, il se complaît surtout à retracer tout ce qui se rattache aux églises et aux cérémonies du culte.[12]

Cette hypothèse est devenue une certitude par la découverte du manuscrit 214 de la Bibliothèque Municipale de Toulouse, où on lit dans le colophon:

scripta per Franciscum Florium, de provincia Romana, eiusdem almi ordinis Dominici fratrem ...

Et à la lumière de ces faits il devient clair pourquoi Florio dans son *De probatione Turonica* indique l'église de Santa Maria sopra Minerva à Rome comme "sacrarium nostrum":[13] cette église fut en effet bâtie au treizième siècle par deux dominicains florentins, fra Sisto (+ 1290) et Ristoro (+ 1284).

Retournons à la nouvelle. Trois ans après l'arrestation de Camille, le bruit court que les soldats du roi Alphonse d'Aragon vont envahir le territoire de la république de Florence. Voilà un fait historique que l'on peut situer exactement dans le temps. On connaît le traité entre Naples et Venise datant de juin 1451 et stipulant que chaque ville de son côté attaquerait Florence. Mais précisément comme écrit notre auteur: "adventus eius usque in alium annum protenderetur," les hostilités ne commencèrent que dans l'été de l'année suivante.

Camille et Emilie ne se rencontrent plus jusqu'en septembre 1451, et quand ils se retrouvent, le mari les surprend. Après le retour d'Emilie à la maison paternelle, Camille vient la voir pour quelques jours, puis s'en va continuer ses études à Florence. Et de nouveau on peut prolonger la relation Camille–Florio: dans sa *Visio mira*, Florio nous apprend en effet qu'il a suivi à Florence les cours de son compatriote Carolus Aretinus: "gignasiis Caroli Aretini compatriotae tui nutritus" (f. 4ᵛ). Ce Carolus Aretinus n'est autre que Carlo Marsuppini (1398–1453), qui enseignait à Florence non seulement le latin, mais aussi, à partir de 1451, le grec. Et de cet enseignement on discerne encore les traces chez Florio, qui mit son nom en caractères grecs sous sa *Visio mira*, mais non sans commettre quelques fautes d'orthographe: Φρανκισκωσ Φλωρηοσ Φλορεντινος.

Peu de temps après, Emilie meurt, et Camille, fortement impressionné, se décide à courir le monde, n'ayant pas encore achevé sa vingt-cinquième année. Cela concorde également avec les informations que donne Florio sur lui-même dans le *De probatione Turonica*: "Florius tuus postquam actus satis Etruriam deseruit,"[14] et un peu plus loin: "cum tamen omnem fere Europam Asiaeque partem lustraverim,"[15] et encore:

Nec mihi quis Tyburtina loca aut Tarentina praedicet, nemo laudet Thessala Tempe, cum et ego illa viderim et ista probaverim.[16]

Afin de pouvoir suivre correctement Florio dans ses vagabondages, il faut maintenant essayer de dater ce traité *De probatione Turonica*. M. Salmon en avait fixé la rédaction vers l'an 1477. Voici son argumentation (p. 88):

D'un côté il [Florio] n'eut pas manqué, en décrivant le tombeau de saint Martin, de mentionner la grille d'argent dont Louis XI le fit entourer en 1478, si ce travail somptueux et extraordinaire eût été déjà exécuté quand il écrivit son opuscule, et en second lieu si l'on suppose que Florio fut appelé en France par Jean V d'Armagnac lors de sa rentrée en grâce, à l'avènement de Louis XI en 1461, en ajoutant à cette date les seize années depuis lesquelles Florio dit avoir quitté sa patrie, on trouve encore 1477.

Malheureusement ce calcul est critiquable, même si l'*argumentum ex silentio* semble être valable pour indiquer le *terminus ante quem*. Il est évident que dans l'espace de seize ans, que Florio a passés à l'étranger, sont à situer non seulement son séjour en France, mais aussi les grands voyages qu'il a faits sans doute avant d'arriver en France à la demande de Jean d'Armagnac.

Nous proposons donc la chronologie suivante:

en 1452 Florio quittait Florence et commençait ses pérégrinations. A partir de cette date se compte son séjour à l'étranger, de sorte que le *De probatione Turonica* doit être situé en 1468. Une confirmation de cette datation peut être trouvée au début de son traité, où Florio parle du silence (*taciturnitas*) qu'il observe depuis sept ans envers son ami Jacobus Tarlatus résidant à Rome. A retrancher sept ans de 1468 on arrive à 1461, l'année où Florio probablement quittait la ville éternelle pour entrer au service du comte d'Armagnac.

Mais sa fortune auprès du comte fut de courte durée: bientôt trompé dans ses espérances, le voilà reparti à travers toute la France à la recherche d'un nouveau mécène. Il devait en trouver un à Paris, où il demeura trois ans avant de venir en Touraine, comme il nous l'apprend dans son traité:

> ut comitem Armaniacum inveniret, Gallias intravit; a quo ut comperit se delusum, totum prius Francorum regnum lustravit atque Parisiam incoluit per triennium; tandem paci ac quieti suae consulens, Turoniam sibi civitatem delegit in coloniam.[17]

La première attestation du séjour de Florio à Paris est donnée par le colophon du manuscrit 214 de la Bibliothèque Municipale de Toulouse, qui a été transcrit entre le 22 mai et le 28 août 1465 à Paris. Très vraisemblablement deux autres manuscrits, copiés à Paris et signalés par M. Finlayson, sont à situer dans cette même période: le Sénèque d'Oxford et le Virgile d'Edimbourg.

Le manuscrit de Florence finalement, contenant le *Ad Herennium* et les satires de Juvénal et de Perse, et transcrit en août 1467, marque sans doute la fin (provisoire?) des activités de Florio à Paris: presque aussitôt après il quitte la capitale pour se rendre à Tours. Il a en effet achevé sa nouvelle le 31 décembre de cette même année, au cours de laquelle il écrit dans sa lettre à Tardif que déjà sont passés quatre mois sans qu'il ait pris contact avec lui.

Un problème qui reste à résoudre est celui de la résidence de Florio à Tours. Dans le colophon de la nouvelle on lit:

> In domo domini Guillermi archiepiscopi Turonensis....

Puisque Géraud (ou Girard) de Crussol fut archevêque de Tours à partir de 1466, avant d'échanger le siège épiscopal de Tours contre celui de Valence, et que le roi nomma le 17 juin 1468 Hélie de Bourdeille, il est difficile de croire que Florio ait résidé dans le palais de l'archevêque, à moins qu'on n'accepte "Guillermi" comme une erreur de plume pour "Gerardi." Aussi M. Salmon et M. Finlayson ont-ils, indépendamment l'un de l'autre, placé sa demeure chez un certain Guillaume Larchevesque, dont on ne sait rien pour le reste.[18]

En tout cas, Florio n'y est pas resté longtemps: lorsqu'il écrivit son *De probatione Turonica*, il était déjà logé chez un chanoine fort aimable, François Thouars, secrétaire de l'archevêque. A ce moment ses difficultés semblent s'être dissipées, et Florio est déterminé à passer le reste de sa vie à Tours. Mais en fut-il ainsi?

La dernière œuvre de Florio, la *Visio mira super archana Francie* nous renseigne sur ce point. Il convient d'en examiner le contenu pour la situer dans l'espace et le temps.

Dans cet ouvrage, où s'observe un mélange très remarquable d'éléments païens et chrétiens, Florio décrit une vision qu'il a eue naguère. Dans son sommeil il faisait un voyage à travers plusieurs endroits — qui sont à identifier avec les différents stades du programme scolaire médiéval (le trivium et le quadrivium), pour arriver finalement devant le trône de Dieu lui-même. Et là, une jolie femme, qui n'est autre que la France personnifiée, se plaignait de ses malheurs. Elle peint la situation politique en France dans les années 1461–69, les actions du roi contre les pairs de France réunis dans la Ligue du Bien Public, et son attitude envers son jeune frère Charles (1447–72) qui, placé à la tête de cette Ligue, osa même lui faire la guerre.

A cette plainte de la France, Dieu répond par des propos réconfortants: Il lui promet un successeur pour le roi Louis XI, qui lui-même se reconciliera avec son frère et lui donnera le duché de Guyenne. Ces deux derniers éléments permettent une datation bien précise: à la fin d'avril 1469 le roi Louis XI réussit à faire accepter par son frère Charles le lointain duché de Guyenne au lieu de Brie et Champagne qui touchaient au territoire de son adversaire puissant, le duc de Bourgogne, et il conclut avec lui une alliance de paix éternelle. D'autre part il y a la promesse d'un successeur pour Louis XI, qui naîtra comme le futur Charles VIII le 30 juin 1470. Puisqu'il n'y est pas question des nouvelles intrigues de Charles contre son frère le roi, ni de sa mort survenue le 28 mai 1472, on peut admettre que la *Visio* date de la fin de 1469 ou du début de 1470. Florio était-il encore à Tours à ce moment?

A cette question nous sommes enclin à répondre par la négative. Bien que le début de la *Visio* soit rayé et réécrit, de sorte que l'on ne peut en déchiffrer que difficilement et à l'aide de la lampe de Wood les premières lignes, on peut découvrir qu'une nouvelle fois la Fortune s'est tournée contre Florio. Un peu plus loin, la Muse donne aussi la raison de sa disgrâce:

> Sed quid te nunc in hoc baratro detrusit, nisi inconcessa Venus, insatiabilis Iuno, honoris ac reverentiae libido? Quae te nunc super vario bellorum eventu cogunt fluctuare? Non quod ad te spectet quis fratrum victoria potiatur, sed quod ne longius tibi Cupido faveat pertimescis.

La Muse semble donc faire ici allusion à une nouvelle escapade de Florio, à la suite de laquelle il fut contraint de quitter la ville de Tours.

Est-il retourné à Paris, et a-t-il travaillé là-bas quelque temps dans une imprimerie, où il avait des amis et où il pouvait surveiller l'impression de sa nouvelle, dont l'editio princeps date de 1473 environ?

Et quand entre-t-il au service de Tristan de Salazar, archevêque de Sens depuis 1474/75 et qui normalement résidait à Paris? C'est pour celui-ci que Florio copia, de 1478 à 1480, le volumineux *Décret de Gratien*, dont le colophon, extrêmement long et instructif, constitue en même temps le dernier signe de vie de notre Florio. En voici la traduction:

> Louange et gloire à la très-haute Trinité. A l'honneur et l'utilité de chacune de ses deux églises ce décret de Gratien a été exécuté aux frais et grandes dépenses du révérend père monseigneur Tristan de Salazar, par la clémence de Dieu archevêque de Sens; mais exécuté par ma main et grâce à de très grands efforts de ma part. Moi, François Florio de Florence, j'en ai commencé la transcription à Sens le neuf juillet; à cause de la peste qui sévissait j'étais à Saint-Julien le 20 août de l'année suivante quand j'en eus fini la moitié; finalement, grâce à la faveur de Dieu, j'ai pu heureusement mener à terme ce travail 20 mois et trois jours après le commencement, c'est-à-dire à la fête de S. Grégoire, le 12 mars de l'an 1480, dans la maison du doyen de La Rivière-de-Vanne près de Villeneuve-L'Archevêque.

Katholieke Universiteit Leuven

Notes

1. G. Tournoy, "La novella latina nel Rinascimento", in *ACNL*, eds. J. IJsewijn and E. Kessler (Leuven–München, 1973), pp. 681–86.

2. P. Viti, "Filippo Beroaldo traduttore del Boccaccio," *Rin*, II, 15 (1975), 111–40.

3. L. Sozzi, "Petrarca, Tardif e Denys de Harsy (con una nota su Francesco Florio)," *SFr*, 43 (1971), 78–82 (p. 81, n. 2).

4. A. Salmon, "Description de la ville de Tours sous le règne de Louis XI par F. Florio," *Mémoires de la Société Archéologique de Touraine*, 7 (1855), 82–108.

5. C. P. Finlayson, "Florius Infortunatus," *Sc*, 16 (1962), 378–80; et "Florius Infortunatus, Scribe and Author" ibid., 19 (1965), 108–09.

6. R. Fiot, "Jean Fouquet à Notre-Dame-La-Riche de Tours," *Revue de l'Art*, 10 (1970), 30–46; L. Sozzi, "La polémique anti-italienne en France au XVIᵉ siècle," *AAT*, 106 (1971–72), 99–190 (pp. 156–61); A. Schmitt, "Camillus und Emilia. Zur Entstehung und Tradition einer Renaissancenovelle in Deutschland," in *Studien zur Buch- und Bibliotheksgeschichte. Hans Lülfing zum 70. Geburtstag am 24. November 1976*, eds. U. Altmann and H.-E. Teitge (Berlin, 1976), pp. 109–20.

7. J. Guignard, "Humanistes tourangeaux," *Humanisme et Renaissance*, 7 (1940), p. 139, n. 1.

8. Cf. *Catalogue général des manuscrits des bibliothèques publiques des départements. VII. Toulouse–Nîmes* (Paris, 1885), p. 135. Voir aussi Bénédictins du Bouveret, *Colophons des manuscrits occidentaux des origines au XVIᵉ siècle*, Spicilegii Friburgensis subsidia, 3 (Fribourg/Suisse, 1967), p. 93, n° 4263; C. Samaran-R. Marichal, *Catalogue des manuscrits en écriture latine portant des indications de date, de lieu ou de copiste*. Vol. VI, 1 (Paris, 1968), p. 397.

9. A. M. Bandini, *Bibliotheca Leopoldina Laurentiana*, III (Florence 1793), coll. 301–02.

10. Le ms. 2868 de la Bibl. civ. de Vérone. Cf. (Boccaccio), *Mostra de manoscritti, documenti e edizioni*, 2 vols. (Certaldo, 1975), I, 28–29, n° 5.

11. Pour les frères Accolti, voir les notices biographiques dans le *Dizionario biografico degli Italiani*, I (Roma, 1960), pp. 99–101 (Benedetto) et pp. 104–05 (Francesco).

12. Salmon, "Description," 86.

13. ibid., 105.

14. ibid., 91. Je cite d'après le ms.

15. ibid., 92.

16. ibid., 106.

17. ibid., 91.

18. ibid., 88; Finlayson, "Florius" (1962), 380, n. 11.

P.S. Un commentaire inédit de Florio aux comédies de Térence est conservé dans le ms. L.86 de la Cathedral Library à Hereford. Voir Claudia Villa, *La "lectura Terenti." I. Da Ildemaro a Francesco Petrarca* (Padoue, 1984), p. 292.

L O W   C O U N T R I E S

Andrea Alciati's View of Erasmus:
Prudent Cunctator and Bold Counselor

Virginia W. Callahan

On several occasions I have pointed out the influence of the writings of Erasmus, especially the *Adagia*, on the *Emblemata* of Alciati. A stemma of influences would, among others, show a straight line from the *Greek Anthology* to Alciati's work. Although this, for a number of reasons, is undeniable, many of the echoes of the *Anthology* found in the *Emblemata* came to Alciati via the *Adagia*. While thus a rich body of Erasmus-derived material can be discerned in Alciati's famous book, the "Erasmus-Alciati Friendship" more or less demands the presence of Erasmus himself in the *Emblemata*, and this is, indeed, the case. At the first Neo-Latin Congress in 1971, I noted that in Alciati's Emblem CXXXVIII, motto "Duodecim certamina Herculis," (ed. publ. Tozzi, Padua, 1621, p. 592), there was a highly suggestive correlation between the allusions to the labors of Hercules on the one hand, and, on the other, to the arduous achievements of Erasmus. Significantly, the Hercules emblem, a late-comer to the body of the *Emblemata*, first turned up in the Venice edition (1546); that is to say, at a time when the writings of Erasmus were considered as not just controversial, but as outright heretical. Accordingly, one might state that Emblem CXXXVIII, as a tribute to the life and work of Erasmus-Hercules, was a courageous act of *pietas* on the part of Alciati.[1]

In the following observations I intend to show that in two other Alciati emblems we find significant allusions to Erasmus's personality. As the title of this essay suggests, these emblems embody two closely linked aspects of Erasmus's way of dealing with the sharply conflicting views with which he was confronted in his later years. Those were the years when his support was sought by the rival factions involved in the Lutheran controversy.[2]

The first of the two emblems with which I propose to deal appeared under the motto "Optimus civis"; we find it in the editio princeps, Augsburg (Heinrich Steyner) (28 February) 1531, where it was the last of four emblems which have this in common that they lack woodcuts. One may infer from this defect that these emblems had been added at the last moment, when it was too late to commission appropriate pictures for them.[3] The epigram reads:

Dum iustis patriam Thrasybulus vindicat armis,
    Dumque simultates ponere quemque iubet,
Concors ordo omnis magni instar muneris, illi
    Palladiae sertum frondis habere dedit.
Cinge comam, Thrasybule, geras hunc solus honorem,
    In nostra nemo est aemulus urbe tibi.

Thrasybulus of Steiria, son of Lycus, had been one of the ship-captains at the Athenian naval victory at Arginusae. Banished from Athens by the Thirty Tyrants, he joined the other exiles at Phyle, and became the leader of the restored democracy in 403 B.C., after which he advised a reconciliation of all parties, thus ending civil strife at Athens.[4] No leader was more highly praised by Greek and Roman authors. Pausanias calls him the greatest of all famous Athenians before or after him.[5] The ancient references to the amnesty which he proposed and carried out are numerous. Aeschines, for example, reminded the Athenians that, when the exiled democracy came back from Phyle with Archinus and Thrasybulus as their leaders, they took an oath to forgive and forget, an act which, he maintained, won for their state "the reputation of the highest wisdom."[6]

Valerius Maximus, writing at the time of the emperor Tiberius, noted that Thrasybulus achieved a victory considerably more famous than his restoration of liberty through the praise of his moderation, for "he imposed upon the people a plebiscite, lest there be any mention of things past, and this forgetting which the Athenians called an amnesty recalled the city, shaken and falling into ruins, to its former condition.[7] It was Cornelius Nepos who recorded that in return for his having achieved peace in Athens through a law of forgetting (*lex oblivionis*), Thrasybulus was given a crown of two olive branches. Nepos further commented that Thrasybulus incurred no envy as a result of this honor, because the love of the citizens, and not force, had bestowed it, and that Thrasybulus, content with the crown, sought nothing more, thinking that no one outdid him in honor.[8]

Erasmus exhibited his familiarity with the ancient sources relating to Thrasybulus in his *Adages*. One of these is "Ne malorum memineris" (*Ad.* II.I.xciv — LB 445B), which he equates with the Greek μὴ μνησικακήσῃς. He says that it means: "Do not stir up afresh the memory of evils." The passages from Valerius and Cornelius Nepos are quoted almost verbatim. Erasmus adds that Cicero in his *First Phillippic* (I.I.1) mentioned that he had tried to achieve peace in Rome by recalling the example of the Athenians, even appropriating the Greek word which that city used to calm disagreements. In illustrating the Greek use of μὴ μνησικακήσῃς Erasmus cites a line from Aristophanes's *Plutus* (l. 1146): "If you have taken Phyle, do not recall past injuries," a clear reference to Thrasybulus's leadership of his exiled countrymen. He also cites a passage from his favorite Lucian (*Prometheus* 8) in which Prometheus remarks to Hermes that to recall past injuries (μνησικακεῖν) is not seemly for the gods and in any case not kingly. "This," Erasmus concludes, "will be the use of the proverb, if, following this shrewd advice, we admonish someone not to disturb himself with the memory of past evils, since what has been done cannot be undone."

Thrasybulus is featured in one other Adage: "Thrasybulo Dionysium dicitis esse similem" (*Ad.* II.VIII.xciii — LB 661B). Erasmus explains that this is usually said when someone compares things which differ greatly from each other. It is taken from Aristophanes, *Plutus* (l. 55). Dionysius, according to Erasmus, was commemorated as the most pestilential tyrant, whereas Thrasybulus was praised because he was "rei publicae studiosissimus."

On March 23, 1523, Erasmus wrote to Pope Adrian VI from Basel (Allen, *Ep.* 1352, vol. V, p. 257ff.) in response to the Pontiff's urging that he come to Rome to assist the Church in dealing with the Lutheran dissidents. Erasmus claimed that ill-health precluded his making the long journey, but he did presume to offer the following advice (ll. 170ff.):

> First of all, the sources whence this evil sprouted forth so many times should be explored, and these should be cured before all. Then, on the other hand, it will not be useless if impunity is again extended to those who have erred as a result of persuasion or pressure from someone else; or preferably there should be an amnesty (ἀμνηστία) of all former evils which seem to have come about through some fate. If God acts daily thus with us forgetting all wrong-doings as often as the sinner laments them, what is there to prevent God's vicar from doing the same thing?

In a letter to Ulrich Zwingli written August 31, 1523, (Allen, *Ep.* 1384, vol. V, pp. 326ff.) Erasmus mentioned this letter to the pope, indicating that so far the Pontiff had not replied (ll. 25–26). Pope Adrian died 14 September 1523. According to Allen, Erasmus's letter to him was not made public until 1529.

It is not unlikely that Erasmus's own recommendation of an amnesty would have reminded him of Thrasybulus's famous and successful application of the device. As I have said, during the last days of 1530 Alciati chose to give his Thrasybulus emblem pride of place by making it the final in the editio princeps. It is my belief that the Humanists for whom the little volume was intended would have perceived in it the image of Erasmus. The word *concors* in line two of the epigram is reminiscent of the *concordia ecclesiae* for which Erasmus so longed and to which he referred so often in his writings.[9] We should note that in the last two lines of the epigram Alciati speaks in his own voice:

> Crown your hair, Thrasybulus, you alone deserve this honor:
> in our city no one rivals you.

The name Thrasybulus means "bold counselor." The commentators speculated as to the meaning of the phrase "in our city." In the context which I am suggesting, it might well stand for the *respublica Christiana* with which Erasmus and his contemporaries alluded to the Christian community.

An interesting parallel to these last lines, which indicate that Thrasybulus was without peer, is to be found in a letter of Alciati to Erasmus written about the

end of May, 1522 (Allen, *Ep.* 1288, vol. V, pp. 71ff.). In it Alciati was attempting to persuade Erasmus that he had no need to be disturbed by recent Lutheran
attacks upon him. In concluding the letter Alciati wrote: "But you constitute the
unique ornament of our age, beyond all risk of envy" (ll. 40–41).

I cannot refrain from adding a postscript to this recounting of Erasmus's dream
of amnesty and leniency for the *Luteriani.* On January 31, 1524, he addressed
a letter to the new Pope Clement VII as a preface to his Paraphrase on the *Acts*
(Allen, *Ep.* 1414, vol. V, pp. 389ff.). In it Erasmus conjectured that old age and
ill-health had prevented Adrian VI from action. But he writes that now he has
great hopes that the new pope will conform to the name he has chosen (Clement),
and that in keeping with his cognomen (Medici) he will cure the great disease,
since it is more efficacious to cure ills than to suppress them. At the end of this
letter Erasmus reminded Clement that Luke, the author of the *Acts of the Apostles,*
was himself a *medicus,* and he concludes with the hope that the *clementia* of Christ
will keep Clement safe for a long time. The pope acknowledged the dedicatory
letter and sent a gift of money to Erasmus, but he did not respond to the suggested notion of clemency. Pope Clement VII died 25 September 1534.

Still hopeful, Erasmus wrote to Clement's successor Pope Paul III, from
Freiburg, January 23, 1535 (Allen, *Ep.* 2988, vol. XI, pp. 61ff.). As in his letter
to Clement VII, he made use of the name taken by the new Pontiff, equating
Paul with the Greek $\pi\alpha\tilde{\upsilon}\lambda\alpha$, which he said among the greeks meant peace and
tranquillity. Towards the end of this letter Erasmus again recommended an am-
nesty: "Since this plague seems to be a fatal one, it would not be useless, in conformity with the opinion of a synod, to promise an amnesty of what is past to
those who have come to their senses." In this pope at least he found an attentive
respondent. For in his reply to Erasmus (Allen, *Ep.* 3021, vol. XI, pp. 137ff.)
Pope Paul acknowledged the urgency of seeking "tranquillity" for the Church and
he expressed the hope that he might rely on the aid of Erasmus's learning and
eloquence in attempting to achieve it.

In the last two years of his life, 1548–49, Alciati added 11 emblems, bringing
his collection to a total of 212. Among these was one in which Fabius Maximus
Cunctator was the leading figure (Emblem XXVI in the 1621 edition, pp. 151–56).
The motto consists of one word: "Gramen." The later commentators were dis-
satisfied with the word as a motto and agreed that it might better be exchanged
for *tutela salusque* (protection and salvation), words found in the one but last line
of the epigram. The epigram reads:

> Gramineam Fabio Patres tribuere corollam,
>   Fregerat ut Poenos Hannibalemque mora.
> Occulit inflexo nidum sibi gramine alauda,
>   Vulgo aiunt, pullos sic fovet illa suos.
> Saturno Martique sacrum, quo Glaucus adeso
>   Polybides, factus creditur esse Deus.

His merito arguitur nodis tutela saluque:
Herbaque tot vires haec digitalis habet.[10]

Today I am chiefly concerned with the first two lines of the epigram. Quintus Fabius Maximus was the most distinguished member of a noble Roman family which proudly traced its ancestry back to Hercules. He was made dictator after the disastrous defeat of the Romans by Hannibal at Trasimene (May 217 b.c.). By a military strategy of constant delay, by avoiding being engaged in battle with the enemy, Fabius succeeded in weakening the strength of Hannibal and his army. From this came Fabius's cognomen Cunctator, which typifies him as the "one who acts with delay and hesitation." A crown of grass was traditionally given to a general who rescued others from a siege. Pliny (XXII.iv.6) tell us that it was called a siege crown (obsidionalis) since it was given when a whole camp was relieved and saved from destruction, and that it had never been conferred except upon a leader of a forlorn hope. He deemed it the highest distinction a human being could attain, and noted that it was given to Fabius when Hannibal was driven from Italy, adding as a special feature in the case of Fabius that it was the only one given by the whole of Italy.[11]

The ancient sources for the life of Fabius are plentiful. His military tactics are discussed both by Livy and Plutarch. However the most famous pronouncement on him in antiquity was a single line of Ennius:

Unus homo nobis cunctando restituit rem.[12]

The words were included by Cicero in his De Officiis (I.84) and echoed in a crucial passage in the Aeneid (VI.846). The De Officiis, I should add, was edited by Erasmus and published in Basel by Froben in 1520. Erasmus himself made use of the line in three of his Adages.

One of these is the Adage "Romanus sedendo vincit" (Ad. I.X.xxxix — LB 375F). Erasmus explains the proverb as relating to those who, although tranquil and leisurely, nevertheless accomplish what they wish, not through strength, but by stratagem (arte). He then remarks that he thinks it comes from the history of Fabius Cunctator, who, when Hannibal was gloating childishly, destroyed him by his own patience (sua patientia fregit). The other two Adages in which Erasmus refers to the delaying tactics of Fabius are "Festina lente" (Ad. II.I.1 — LB 399B) and "Qui nimium properat, serius absolvit" (Ad. III.V.lx — LB 842E).

Fabius appears in several other writings of Erasmus. We find him in two of the early educational treatises: the De Ratione Studii (LB I.524B) where the prudent delaying tactics of Fabius are suggested as a memorable historical theme to set before boys. In the De Copia, chapter 46 (LB I.135F) on varying the expression of the superlative Erasmus offers as an example from history the phrase "more cautious than Fabius (Fabio cunctior)." In The Education of a Christian Prince, written for the young Charles, Erasmus mentioned Fabius Maximus and others "who took only fame as a reward for their services to the state" (LB IV.593B). In 1531

among the *Apophthegmata* of famous personages he included eleven sayings attributed to Fabius Maximus (LB IV.254–55). The figure of Erasmus arises in
a rather bizarre episode in his career in 1535. In one of his Adages ("Myconius
calvus," *Ad.* II.I.vii — LB 409B) Erasmus, in listing a number of incongruities,
had written: "Just as if one might speak of an erudite Scythian, a warlike Italian,
an honest merchant, a pious soldier, or a faithful Carthaginian." The Italians were
outraged, and Peter Cursius wrote a fiery treatise defending their prowess as war-
riors: *Petri Cursii Defensio pro Italia ad Erasmum Roterodamum*. It was printed in Rome
in the spring of 1535. Erasmus's response in letter form and addressed to John
Choler was in fact an *apologia*; it was published in Basel no later than August with
the title *Responsio ad Petri Cursii defensionem nullo adversario bellacem*. H. M. Allen
and H. W. Garrod included it among the *Epistolae* "as biographical document of
some importance" (*Ep.* 3032, vol. XI, pp. 172ff.). Erasmus insisted that he had
been misinterpreted, that he had meant no slight to the Italian character, maintaining that to imply that a person was not *bellax* did not mean that he was un-
skilled in warfare, and as proof he cited the great Roman commander: "contator
ille Fabius, nec bellax erat, nec imbellis" (l. 90). Professor William Heckscher,
with whom I have discussed the Fabius emblem at some length, wondered if
Erasmus might not have thought of these words as a kind of portrait of himself.

Be that as it may, as early as January 20, 1523, the word *cunctator* had been
applied to Erasmus by Glareanus, a scholar who had known Erasmus for some
years. In a letter to Ulrich Zwingli in attempting to explain Erasmus's reluctance
to become actively involved in the Lutheran controversy he wrote: "Senex est;
quiescere vellet.... Timidus est, quia cunctator."[13]

In August of the same year Erasmus wrote to Zwingli:

> You call me a delayer. I beseech you, what would you have me do? Up
> to now, what I have written I have written freely, And if I am anywhere
> rather non-committal (*blandior*), I do not betray the Evangelical truth, but
> I affirm it where one can. Of the present Pope I had conceived high expec-
> tations. Now I fear that he has failed me. If you had read my letter to him
> you would say that I am not mild when the occasion offers itself. And I
> would be even freer if I saw that I was going to be successful. It is madness
> to bring ruin upon yourself, if you accomplish nothing.   (Allen, *Ep.* 1384,
> vol. V, p. 327.)

About August 1524, Boniface Amerbach, who regularly served as an intermediary
between Erasmus and Alciati, wrote to Alciati:

> Once upon a time no one was more celebrated than Erasmus; but now no
> one is more despised. As a sycophant of the Pope he is ridiculed as Balaam
> (for that is the way they put it), he is disdained as timid and him, to whom
> everyone attributed the greatest knowledge of theology, that mad gang of
> Lutherans do not blush to charge with being a mere rhetorician, and one
> who is unfamiliar with the sacred matters of theology.[14]

Alciati's reply came in a letter to Amerbach from Milan, May 7, 1525:

> I grieve for Erasmus' change of fortune, but in this respect I think it is a
> good thing, because to displease those spiritualizers seems to me to be the
> highest praise.[15]

In this paper I have tried to suggest that Alciati had intended in certain of his
emblems to celebrate the spiritual grandeur of Erasmus amidst a sea of troubles.
No more suitable vehicle for the expression of such sentiments could be imagined
than that of the rhetorical disguise which governs each of Alciati's emblem.

Howard University (Washington, D. C.)

Notes

1. Virginia W. Callahan, "The Erasmus-Alciati Friendship," *ACNL Lovaniensis*, ed.
Josef IJsewijn and Eckhard Kessler (Munich, 1973), pp. 133–41.

2. For an excellent and concise account of Erasmus's attitude toward Luther and his
followers between the years 1517 and 1524 see Craig R. Thompson's Introduction to his
edition of Erasmus, *Inquisitio de Fide* (1st ed. Yale University Press, 1950; 2nd ed. The
Shoe String Press, Hamden, Conn. 1975), pp. 1–51.

3. Woodcuts in subsequent editions: c. Wechel, Paris, 1534, p. 110, Thrasybulus, a
mail-clad warrior with spear over his left shoulder is walking towards a group of men who
are emerging from the gate of a city; the leaders of the group are holding aloft a wreath;
Roville and Bonhomme, Lyons, 1551, Embl. CXXXIIII, p. 478, Thrasybulus, standing
with spear in lowered right hand, is being crowned by two men; at the left a group of
men waving branches in acclamation; Tozzi, Padua, 1621, Emblem. CXXXV, p. 576,
Thrasybulus, clad as a warrior, is being crowned by two men in togas; in left and right
background two men with arms raised in acclamation. In none of the later editions is the
emblem the last in the collection.

4. See, for example, Xenophon, *Hellenica*, Bk. II, III–IV and Marcus Junianus Justinus,
Trogi Pompeii Historiarum Philippicarum Epitoma, Bk. V, 9–10.

5. Pausanias, *Description of Greece*, Bk. I, xxix, 3.

6. Aeschines, *On the Embassy*, III, 187.

7. Valerius Maximus, *Factorum et Dictorum Memorabilium Libri Novum*, Bk. IV, 1.

8. Cornelius Nepos, *De Excellentibus Ducibus Exterarum Gentium*, VIII, 3–4.

9. See Erasmus's letter to Peter Barbirius, Pope Adrian's chaplain, dated April 17, 1523,
in which he refers to his proposals to the Pontiff as "cohortatiuncula.... ad Christianam
concordiam," (Allen, *Ep.* 1358, ll. 3–4) and recalls the title of his work *De Sarcienda Ecclesiae
Concordia*.

10. In the woodcut in the 1551 ed., a man is being offered grass by a group of kneeling
men, at the right are the two gods Mars and Saturn, and in the foreground a lark is nested
in tall grass. In the 1621 ed., a Senator is seated on a raised platform, flanked by two
attendant figures; at the foot of the platform Fabius is raising his right hand in a gesture
of speech, while the Senator places the grass wreath on his head.

11. On the *corona obsidionalis* see also Aulus Gellius, *Attic Nights* V, vi, 8-10, and Erasmus, Adage "Herbam dare" (I.IX.lxxvii — LB 360F).

12. For the frequent citations of this line of Ennius see the Loeb edition of *Remains of old Latin*, vol. I, Ennius, Bk. XII, p. 132.

13. *Huldreich Zwinglis Sämtliche Werke* (*Corpus Reformatorum*), ed. E. Egli, G. Finsler, und W. Kohler, 1905 — VIII, Briefwechsel, II, 8, ll. 7-19.

14. *Die Amerbachkorrespondenz*, ed. a. Hartmann, vol. II (1943), p. 483, ll. 41-46.

15. *Le Lettere di Andrea Alciato*, ed. G. L. Barni, no. 36, p. 64, ll. 17-18. As always I want to express my thanks to Professor Heckscher for his kind assistance in the shaping of this paper and to Mrs Agnes Sherman of the Princeton University Library.

Luis Vives's Pacifist Sociology in *De Pacificatione*

Philip Dust

I n 1529, at Bruges, appeared Luis Vives's *De Pacificatione*, a work in sequel to his earlier and longer *De Concordia et Discordia*. Dedicated to Alfonso Manrico, it is a pacifist appeal to Spain's highest ecclesiastical authority. At the same time, it is a message to all Christians to end war. The work divides into three parts: 1) an introduction of Christian stoic principles; 2) a sociological classification; 3) a conclusion urging the establishment of the City of God in this world. The main body of the work, the classification, is an especially important sociological study.

The principle that the Christian Humanist founds his ethical actions on peace, concord, charity, and benevolence is proposed immediately in *De Pacificatione*. Impulse to such conduct comes from human nature and from the teachings of Christ.[1] Vives bases his theory of social harmony on the principle of similitude.

> For there is nothing in nature more pleasing than similitude.[2]

According to the principle, everything is ordered towards its proper object. The just man seeks justice, the temperate man temperance; they do not seek injustice and intemperance.

Stoic thought represents the ideal man as fixed and stable. If difficulties arise, the wise man will bear with them. The great man lives for the sake of others. This is the principle Vives will apply to his division of the classes of society. Lucan, citing Cato on this subject, is Vives's classical source.[3]

Christian thought too, in the example of Christ himself, is the model of pacifism. The Christian humanist synthesis is realized in the following statement about Christ:

> He is the Jupiter Savior, he is that Hercules, the adversary of evils, the tamer of monsters, the purifier of the world.

The important place that Hercules held in stoic thought is noteworthy.[4] Before Christ's coming, man had been at war with himself, with the angels, and with

God. But by his suffering and death, Christ took on man's sin of discord and enabled him to attain peaceful happiness in immortal life. Vives cites Malachias to the effect that Christ is like the fuller who burnishes and refines the dross of mankind. In the doctrine of the Mystical Body, we are made one with Christ. This Utopian ideal finds expression in the prophecy of Isaiah:

> Their swords are beaten into plowshares.

And it is also expressed in the beatitude of the New Testament:

> Blessed are the peacemakers, for they will be called the sons of God.

Vives is appealing to his audience in terms of the great reward it can expect if it pursues peace unremittingly. But he warns about the powers of discord. If those who strive for peace are the sons of God, then those who sow discord must be the sons of the author of hate, the Devil. All classes of men, therefore, are urged to work for peace.

The distinction is made between those classes of men who can work directly to achieve peace and those who can act only indirectly. The latter group aids by bearing a common will with those directly involved, by fasting, and by prayer. The former group is sub-divided into ten categories: the wealthy, the nobility, counselors, teachers, families, neighbors, friends, soldiers, priests, and bishops. The nobles are considered in relation to those they rule, in other words in terms of superiors and subordinates. And chief of all the nobles is, of course, the prince. Teachers are considered in relation to students. Families consist in the father-husband, wife-mother, children components. Priests and bishops might have been considered one class, but Vives marks out the latter as in an especially prominent position for aiding the cause of peace.

The first classification deals with wealth and Vives admits that it is an important factor in men's lives. He does not, however, approve of that importance, since wealth has an appeal only to the external senses rather than to interior judgments and reason. Wealth consists of money, possessions, servants, land, villas. The mere conservation and ostentation of possessions has no social value. It is only in relation to the ethical and social concepts of law, equity, right, and justice that they derive any worth. Ultimately these concepts are directed toward peace and concord. One thinks of the Utopian contempt for gold in More's treatise on the ideal state.[5] Social utility of wealth as opposed to the self-seeking goals is the value-giving factor.

The nature of true nobility, which was a year earlier much discussed by Castiglione, is taken up by Vives, namely as to its proper origin.[6] Nobility is not so much a matter of distinguished ancestry as of service to one's fellow men. That service does not consist in the wearing of the sword. Rather it is in the interest of justice and concord that the true noble should act. Vives introduces the concept of law as the guiding principle for suitable action. It is law which curbs the lower passions of the soul. If one's ancestors have rendered service to the law, then there is some claim to being descended from a noble line. But if they have fomented wars and discords, such will not be the case. In other words, the laws, judgments, rights and equity of the whole state are the primary concern of anyone who would merit the title of nobility.

An important distinction, as it had been for Erasmus, is that between the good king who benefits his people and the tyrant who feeds their hatreds.[7] The latter is compared to a shepherd who strangles his sheep and to the guard of the grain store who sets fire to it. The exemplar of the good king is Christ. Vives also cites Greek philosophy:

as Plato, Aristotle, and others, who distinguish the king from the tyrant, because the king cares for and cultivates peace among his citizens; the tyrant, on the other hand, irritates souls, and spreads the seeds of discord, which where they increase, he nourishes them.

The tyrant does not regard the utility of those he rules, rather he uses occasions of dissension to spoil and destroy the country.

Next to the prince is the class of counselors. Vives says that not uncommonly the counselor is more powerful than the prince himself. An analogy is drawn between the rule of the state and human psychology. The counselor is the reason of the state; the prince is its will. There are faint overtones of Hythlodaeus's diatribe in Thomas More's *Utopia*.[8] On the whole, however, Vives is kinder to counselors. He does say

A bad Prince with good counselors is to be preferred to a good Prince with bad counselors.

Very Platonic, indeed, is the function of the counselor: to bridle the will, to teach the better course of action, to stimulate in the direction of the beautiful, and to incite to honesty. But Aristotelian is the observation that wars and discord arise from perturbed affections; peace and concord from a balanced state of the reason. The major point is that a tainting of the very fountainhead of reason, of the pivotal center of the state is an evil which cannot be counteracted. Since the fount of the state is the king and his counselors, it follows that the corruption of that fount breeds wars.

A distinction is made between the public and the private when Vives turns to the class of teachers. The teacher is a

shaper of the student to modesty, moderation, temperance, humanity, that is to a certain placid tranquility of mind with sweetness and with benevolence toward others.

The obligation of the teacher is not only to foster friendship among students, but also concord in their relations to the other classes of society. Education is for a pattern of living, not for mere ostentation and factiousness. Learning is defined as a cultivation of the mind whereby we get rid of rudeness, wildness, hard, barbarous and inhumane customs; we take up civility and humanity, so that nothing is more foreign to every reason of letters and studies than dissensions, discords, hatreds, malevolence.

Turning to the family as a distinct and key social class, Vives says that it is subject to two of the most powerful affections of the mind—love and hate. These affections assert a kind of tyranny.

Love delineated with a certain sweetness and softness, hate, however, profuse with bitterness, they draw all the functions of the mind into their jurisdiction and possession, and force them to serve.

For this reason, the husband, treating his wife as an equal, will endeavor to keep from his home hatreds and animosities. Vives also employs the larger concept of the family to include servants. Plutarch is cited:

Nothing is more to be avoided and fled from by servants ... than the anger of the master; from no other perturbation of mind is there more danger to servants.

Masters are counselled to treat their servants mildly.

The classification of neighborhood for Vives has a larger extension than just a collection of houses on the same block. It includes rural areas and in an even broader way, the state itself. Vives is almost romantic in his description of the rural ideal. The beauties of the fields and meadows

> laugh, engage, call, invite, detain.

The example is used of men who have travelled all over the world and who make an end to their wanderings in order to settle back in their neighborhoods because of the peace they find there. They have learned that it is better to live among friends than to live in a kind of exile where strangers might molest them. Vives's own experience of a lifetime of continual wandering no doubt prompted his warming to this subject.[9]

A classification which has a notable tradition in ancient times involves the concept of the friend. Vives begins his discussion on a negative note, with a description of a false friend, one who enjoys seeing his professed friend upset, who does not help him in trouble, and who is not affected by his friend's adversities. We are reminded of Cicero's distinction between true and false friends in the *De Amicitia*. The implication for a doctrine of pacifism is that true friendship by virtue of its service to others fosters peace.

Although he distinguishes between brave men and soldiers, brave men not being really directed toward war, Vives, as Erasmus in his *Colloquies*, is very hard on professional soldiers.[10] He says that there are two kinds: those who follow the standards for the sake of gain and those who seek asylum and immunity from their crimes in the military camp. But there is yet a further classification:

There are others, although rare, nevertheless some, who from a certain truer and better notion of the military, have devoted their hands, arms, bodies to the safety of the state and the prince.

Only these few, the truly brave and selfless men, fulfill their Platonic function as guardians of the state.

Priests, as the Apostle Paul says, are coadjutors with Christ himself. But Christ's work was to preach a gospel of peace to the world. If Christ as the head of the Mystical Body dissuaded from dissensions and persuaded to harmony, his followers can do no better than to imitate their master. Priests are rebuked from inciting to wars in their sermons and exhorted to meditate, discuss, persuade, impel others to peace. They should search for good arguments for peace in order to reach the very souls of those who listen to them.

Bishops, the class which possesses the fulness of the power of the apostles and who are so influential in the political world, have an especially significant role in the pursuit of peace. By virtue of their authority and dignity, they are obligated to their flocks to work for peace. Objections that they will displease the nobility, that war must be conducted to maintain economic balance, are ruled out for episcopal authorities. Their first duty is to a God of peace.

Ultimately the object of Vives's investigations into a sociology of pacifism has been the same as had been those of Socrates—to determine what constitutes the nature of the good man. Vives invokes the example of the great Greek philosopher. His argument is that Socrates as a pagan was more in accord with the will of God than many so-called Christians. Lacking the certainty of faith as he did, Socrates was convicted as a criminal for acting as Christians should act. The reproach to Christians is that in an age in which they are in positions of power, they do not perform the proper duties implied by their social standing in pursuit of peace.

But Vives's pacifism is most solidly based on the foundation of Christ's example. He reiterates, in a modified form, the classification he has made of society as in need of Christ's help:

the Prince, the subject, the father, the son, the teacher, the student, the lord, the servant, the powerful, the weak, the wealthy, the needy.

This summary involves more than the initial classification. It outlines the clear dependence of certain segments of society on others, if the peace is to be maintained. Such is the relationship of Christ to his Church. Vives says

that was not enough for Him, to clothe Divinity in a human face, but He surrendered Himself to poverty, want, hunger, thirst, labors, sweats, tears, ignominy, crucifixion.

Christ's passion was meant as an example for men of all social classes to follow. It was an example of service to others above all else.

The final peroration of *De Pacificatione* rings with the concept of St Augustine's

City of God already being set up within the city of man. God's kingdom on earth has been founded and all classes of men are subject to it. The new society comprising all classes is united under the Prince, Christ. Relegation to separate classes is transcended. Vives asks

> Do you wish those to be separated who are of the same flock, college, brotherhood, pursuits, arts? Do you demand that friend hate friend, teacher hate student, or, on the other hand, that the student hate the teacher, that brother persecute brother, that a mother wish badly for her own son?

God is the common father of all mankind. The point is the same which Erasmus makes about the doctrine of the Mystical Body in *Dulce Bellum Inexpertis*.[11] This doctrine which teaches that class is mystically transcended, at the same time teaches that all classes of men in this world are united in a common brotherhood of mutual interest — peace.

Northern Illinois University

Notes

1. The view expressed here is in disagreement with the otherwise excellent study of Vives by Carlos G. Norena, *Juan Luis Vives* (The Hague, Martinus Nijhoff, 1970), pp. 200-27. Norena admits the "humanistic synthesis of Christian theocentrism and Greek rationalism" in Vives's method, but he says that the emphasis is on the naturalistic rather than the Christian. If anything, in the *De Pacificatione*, it is the other way round.

2. All translations and analyses based on them are from Gregorio Majensio, ed., *Joannis Ludovici Vivis Opera Omnia* (Valentiniae, In Officina Benedicti Monfort, 1784), V, pp. 404-46.

3. *Pharsalia*, II, ll. 307-13 in the Loeb edition. Vives's use of Cato's incitement of younger men to war is ironic.

4. See B. L. Ullmann, *Colucii Salutati De Laboribus Herculis* (Turici, In Aedibus Thesauri Mundi, n.d.), vols. I and II.

5. Edward Surtz, S.J. and W. H. Hexter, eds., *The Complete Works of St Thomas More* (New Haven, Yale Univ. Press, 1965), IV, 169-71; 151-53.

6. Lewis, Count of Canossa, says he would have the "Courtier a gentleman borne and of a good house." L. Gaspar Pallavicino disagrees: "I say (in mine advise) that nobleness of birth is not so necessarie for the Courtier." See *The Book of the Courtier by Count Baldassare Castiglione Done into English by Sir Thomas Hoby* (London, J. M. Dent, n.d.), pp. 31, 33ff.

7. Lester K. Born, transl., (New York, Octagon Books, 1965), p. 166.

8. *The Complete Works of St Thomas More*, pp. 101-03.

9. Norena, p. 17 and *passim*.

10. Craig R. Thompson, transl., *Erasmus: Ten Colloquies* (Indianapolis, Bobbs–Merrill, 1957), pp. 113-19.

11. Margaret Mann Phillips, transl., *Erasmus On His Times* (Cambridge, England, Cambridge Univ. Press, 1967), p. 122.

Hugo Grotius, Poet and Man of Letters

Arthur Eyffinger

The impact of Grotius's work and thought, it is generally recognized, tells first of all in the juridical and theological fields: he has been hailed as the father of international law and the zealous champion of ecclesiastical unionism. Some dramatic episodes of his life did much to focus attention on his political and diplomatic career too. But the high esteem Grotius drew from his achievements as a philologist, man of letters and poet in the judgment of his contemporaries, has been reduced by time to a much smaller circle of readers. Most neo-Latinists will be acquainted with his three dramas on biblical themes, the *Adamus Exul*, the *Christus Patiens* and the *Sophompaneas*, be it only in the broader context of vernacular literatures and due to the intermediary function of poets such as Milton, Opitz or Vondel. Only a few will have perused Grotius's *Poemata*. And the same holds good for the historian: it was with his *Annales et Historiae* that Grotius cherished hopes of eternal fame. As confident as any Humanist would claim, as modest as befitted the Christian scholar and remonstrant. History, though, judged otherwise: the *Annales* did not meet with lasting international applause and soon passed into oblivion.

And yet, much of the fame the legal and theological treatises actually acquired may have been due to Grotius's eminence as a man of letters. Scholars have been puzzled by the immediate and lasting success of these works. It is argued, and quite legitimately, that despite the credit their author is entitled to, they did not clearly outclass the competing publications of the day as far as contents are concerned. Nor did they suggest brand new ideas or lines of research. Suarez, Gentili and Puffendorf may well have developed more coherent systems or at least set out their ideas more systematically. Orthodox theologians probably surpassed Grotius's efforts in their highly technical dogmatizing pamphlets full of hairsplitting subtleties. Dutch historians of the day offered a more detailed, possibly even a more trustworthy picture of the Dutch Revolt. Still, the influence, the impact of Grotius's works on his times has been definitely more impressive.

Two arguments may be put forward to explain this. The first may be the wide horizons that are opening up to the reader of any of these works of Grotius, the "all-compassing" which impresses one. Grotius indeed was a specialist in any of the fields mentioned, that is, taken in the sense of being fully aware of the state of research and perfectly capable of handling the tools of the trade. But he never let himself be restricted by the limits of the specialism. He would introduce any piece of knowledge relevant to the argument at hand and apart from that, he would make ample use of two inexhaustible resources: classical literature and biblical and patristic documents. The second aspect concerns the actual style. Not the elaborate product of artificial refining, but one that goes along with natural eloquence. The result of these qualities put together accounts for much of the success of Grotius's works in the *respublica literaria*. Specialists were compelled by the vast amount of erudition, non-specialists were pleasantly surprised by the total absence of dogmatism, technical jargon and futile stressing of system or form. Enlarging on whatever topic, Grotius was above all the universal scholar and man of letters, and his work within one discipline permeated his publications in other fields.

And yet these literary preoccupations had their distinct restrictions too, sometimes even surprising ones. Indeed Grotius's talents did not show to full advantage in some rather common literary provinces of the age. His correspondence, for instance, forms an impressive and, for the genesis of his works, highly instructive monument of over 7,500 letters. However, not even 100 of them bear a distinct literary character or pretention, and most of these were written before 1608, to close friends like Heinsius. Afterwards Grotius would only rarely find occasion or feel the need to style his letters. They are marked by a clear directness and simple elegance in impeccable Latin but make for dull and formal reading. They are unmistakably prompted by the expressive wish to inform, and to inform only. The careful formulation bears witness to an analytical mind at work, never risking redundancy at the cost of precise meaning and proper sense. The same holds good for the genre of speech, the *oratio*. No editor ever appeared to collect Grotius's letters or speeches for strictly literary purposes as was the common practice of the day, and admittedly only a handful of them would be worth the trouble.

Let us now turn to the poetry. As stated before, three biblical tragedies and a survey volume of minor poems are nearly all that is left, and certainly the most that is generally known of Grotius's poetical efforts, which indeed is a pity. I would not say that the poetry preserved is not fairly representative of the poet, but it certainly suggests an incomplete picture and the scant secondary literature available actually does much to distort its historicity. In fact, to judge Grotius on the strength on his extant poetry implies the neglecting of twenty-five years of hard labour and the disregard of the outspoken objective and intention of the author.

Two categories of poetry should be discerned in Grotius's *œuvre*, the so-called original poetry and the translations and paraphrases. Though not without certain qualifications, both categories can be considered to reflect quite distinct periods: the first one reflecting the youth, the latter the adult, or — in biographical context — the first one Grotius's Dutch years, the second his stay in exile in France and Germany.

The original poetry consists of verse written in Latin, Greek and Dutch, the Latin poetry being predominant by far. Greek poetry amounts to 361 lines exactly, whereas the vernacular poetry, running to some 9,000 lines, was all written within two years. Now, as to the Latin poetry, approximately 5 to 10 percent of Grotius's Latin verses are no longer extant. The total amount of poems preserved runs to nearly 25,000 lines, over 650 poems of various length generally understood to be the result of 50 years of poetical efforts. Over 80 percent of these, however, were written virtually before 1610, in the first twenty-five years of his lifetime and the first fifteen of his poetic activity, Grotius being born in 1583. Of the remaining 20 percent, over 10 percent were composed before 1618 and only slightly over 2,500 lines were written after Grotius's escape from Loevestein Castle in 1621. So the total number of lines written in the last twenty-five years of Grotius's life equals the *yearly* production of any year between 1600 and 1610. And of these 2,500 lines the tragedy *Sophompaneas*, dating from 1635, accounts for half the number. One cannot but conclude therefore, that as early as 1610 Grotius practically lost his appetite for this kind of poetry.

Now, at the end of 1616 a first survey volume was edited, the previously mentioned Leyden *Poemata*. Actually it had only been preceded by two major publications in the field, the juvenile *Sacra* containing the *Adamus Exul* in 1601, and the *Christus Patiens* of 1608. The survey volume of 1616 comprised some 11,500 lines, which implies nearly 50 percent of all poetry written up to that moment, as can be verified from a manuscript preserved at Leyden University Library comprising over 300 poems. Being an authorized edition, the *Poemata* should be considered the poetical legacy of Grotius's youth. The volume saw four enlarged reprints (which, incidentally, is not too many, given the celebrity of its author), none however authorized. The first appeared in circles of William Laud in 1639 (being, like more imprints, the result of the increased interest with Grotius in Britain, due to his polemics on Maritime Law with Selden) and was issued without any previous knowledge of the author, whereas the second, published incidentally in the same year at Leyden was edited against Grotius's express wishes, previous negotiations between author and editor having resulted in a complete deadlock. The third reprint occurred in 1645, again without the author's involvement and meant, as was his firm impression, to compromise his unionistic efforts. The last edition appeared in 1670 posthumously and should be termed a simple reprint.

As for the contents of these reprints, our previous survey reveals that no substantial enlargements could be made, Grotius's vein having practically dried up around 1610: however, three additions should be mentioned, all of the utmost value: an eulogy on the deceased French historian J. A. de Thou (1621), a Latin version of his Dutch poem on Christian Baptism (1635) and the *Sophompaneas* (1635). These additions indeed represent the best of Grotius's production in the field over his last twenty-five years and yet the title of the 1645 and 1670 reprints (*Poemata Om-nia*) suggests an essentially false impression of his poetical activity. A brief survey of Grotius's production and intentions will help to elucidate this.

During his teens and early twenties Grotius fervently indulged in every kind of poetry that crossed the path of the eager student. Most of the poems were inspired by the political events of the day, Maurice of Orange's campaigns in particular. Grotius's juvenile poetry definitely and predominantly bears a social stamp. The verses reflect the ambitious youth witnessing the miracle of a society in complete change. The expansion of learning at Leyden University founded in 1575 and favoured by the influx of intellect from the Southern Provinces in chaos, opened the far horizons of Humanism to the hitherto relatively backward provinces. The newly launched East Indian Company revealed worlds never dreamed of and riches unparalleled, and truly inspired economy. The military successes stirred both national pride and private confidence enormously.

The significance of these events for the mental development of the young Grotius cannot be overestimated. All this is reflected in the brilliance, genius and exuberant wit bestowed upon the poetry, matched in prose only by an ambitious socio-political comparison of the Athenian, Roman and Dutch Republics, the so-called *Parallela* (first draft ca. 1602), of which the better half has been lost unfortunately. The *literary* value of these juvenile poems is not too impressive though. At best they still should be typified as occasional poetry pursued in the traditions of *imitatio*. I cannot refrain from inserting here some comments, however brief, on a more literary level: Grotius's juvenile poetry is particularly distinguished by its self-imposed restrictions. This applies equally to genres and metres and consequently to imitation. First, a marked preference is to be noted for the epic genre and the epigram: panegyrics, epithalamia and epitaphs on the one hand and short epigrams especially in connection with engravings are predominant by far. Accordingly, the hexameter, the elegiac distich, the iambic trimeter and, up to a certain point, the hendecasyllabic prevail, the hexameter for instance even in the psalm paraphrases. Horatian metres will be searched for in vain in the volume, having incidentally been handled by Grotius with appropriate subtlety in his teens. Love poetry, which — of all genres — must be considered a Dutch neo-Latin province by tradition (represented by Janus Secundus, the Dousa's and Daniel Heinsius), is practically non-existent with Grotius, and his juvenile poetry must surely not be termed "tender" or "elegant" in the first place.

Parallel restrictions hold good for *imitatio*. In every other field of research Grotius bears witness to his vast erudition, referring to and quoting classical authors from any period, including the church fathers. In his poetry, though, one will look in vain for reminiscences of any but a mere handful of authors, excluding even classics such as Vergil, or for that matter, contemporary or Italian Renaissance models. Claudian is his favourite, and the others in question actually confirm his quite outspoken views in these matters: Statius, Lucan, Manilius and Sidonius for the *Silvae*, Martial for the epigram, Seneca for the drama and Tacitus for the *Annales et Historiae*. The Silver Age apparently sufficed for Grotius!

You may forgive these described deficiencies, for after all the poems are described as *lusus*, and after 1610, when (past the age of twenty-five) earnestness breaks through for good, the impulses fail to come spontaneously and that means the abrupt end of the genre. The fast intellectual development Grotius went through resulted quite naturally in the alienation of his juvenile trifles. Once having married in 1608 and his public career becoming established, the more sedate scholar emerges who found little time and even less interest in occasional poetry. In the subsequent years the darkening horizon of home politics could only prompt these developments. Once the truce with the Spanish concluded in 1609, the inner controversies around the Remonstrance broke free with appalling intensity, leading up to civil war within a few years. No poetry of any significance has been preserved over the years 1610–17. Why then, one wonders, a survey volume in 1616?

The first time such an edition was ever considered occurred in 1602–03, on the instigation of prominent men of letters at Leyden. "Not yet," Grotius must have argued that time. He was spurred on once again in 1608 by his friend Heinsius: "Not any more" he objected firmly this time: "viro silere quam balbutire satius!" And yet, as late as 1616 he consented. Not wholeheartedly though. And in the introductory letter to the volume he extensively dilates on the subject, apologizing over and over: the excessive imitation, the fierce tone of the *Patria*, the merriment of the *Nuptialia* and the lack of poetical vein in the *Sacra*, the frequent references to pagan deities and the changed feelings towards former friends, but most of all the fact that the poetry dated back a long time, had been conditioned by the moment and was therefore less suited for publication. It was the urgent requests of friends, though, and the regular appearance of his verses in mutilated form, sometimes even without reference to his authorship, or the virtual absence of his verses in anthologies such as the *Delitiae* (1614) by Gruterus that brought him round at last to accept the offer of his younger brother and trusted friend Vossius to provide an edition.

It did not take him long to regret this decision. The outcome actually was a bitter disappointment to everyone involved. The volume has been printed without due care. Many unevennesses and irregularities in the pagination disgrace the outer appearance. Not all of these deficiencies are to be blamed on the printers though. However, halfway through the printing Grotius seriously considered withdrawing the commission and surely *he* would never have contemplated a reprint on his own initiative. No reprint, it should be noted, ever appeared in France or Germany where Grotius had the best of relations, and a first attempt initiated in 1625 by a Leyden printer foundered since at the first notice of a slight disagreement Grotius broke down negotiations. The 1639 London edition displeased him and at the appearance of the Leyden reprint Grotius was even positively upset. He was firmly opposed to it and actually tried hard to impede this renewed publication of eulogies on former relations who had treated him so badly (like Maurice of Orange) and of poetry that he felt lacked literary merits at that.

It was this reprint indeed that made him decide in the fall of 1639 to publish an edition of poetry to his heart's content and at his own initiative. This volume, to be called *Poemata Nova*, should reflect twenty-five years of serious concern with poetry. As the result of a series of events Grotius, despite many efforts bestowed upon the project over more than five years, never succeeded to bring about this volume. This failure should be deeply regretted indeed, for most of the poetry concerned actually got lost in the following decades. Fortunately, substantial evidence from his correspondence enables us to reconstruct Grotius's intentions and to fill up this gap of twenty-five years. For this much must be taken for certain: Grotius said farewell to occasional poetry after 1610, only to concentrate on what he thought of more essential value ever since. We shall have to consider this period now.

In August 1618 the blow fell that abruptly ended five years of hectic activity, the end of a series of politico-religious treatises. Within six months solitary detention in Loevestein enclosed him: it meant a period of reflection ... and energetic study, his attention after nearly ten years once again directed to philology and poetry. But not to occasional poetry this time. It is in these months of imprisonment, and solely in this period, that Grotius composed poetry in the vernacular. Nearly all *Nederduytsche* (Dutch) poems preserved date from these days. The second decade of the century witnesses the steady growth of recognition gained by the mother tongue in Holland. The publication of Heinsius's *Lofzangen* on Christ and Bacchus edited by P. Scriverius in 1616 at Leyden, the reactionary bastion of classicism, may be seen as a landmark. Grotius's Dutch poems from the days of his confinement may well have been inspired by these developments; at least his correspondence with the Dutch poet P. C. Hooft in these days confirms this impression.

Whereas therefore available data compel us to consider Grotius's phase of *Nederduytsche* poetry a mere interlude, the same cannot be said about his Latin poetry. It was in these specific fields that Grotius during his very confinement designed a highly ambitious programme that was not to leave him for the rest of his days, viz. the effort to keep the remnants of the Greek poetical heritage within the reach of contemporary European Humanism by means of integral Latin translations. Men of letters like Erasmus, Budé and Buchanan had preceded him in this endeavour. The parallels, incidentally, between Grotius's efforts and Buchanan's achievements are apparent in many fields and very worth notice.

Grotius designed his basic conceptions at Loevestein castle: once he had reached Paris, he put them into effect with redoubled energy. As early as 1623 he published a textcritical edition with integral Latin translation of all poetical fragments in Stobaeus's *Florilegium*, a fifth-century anthology of Greek classical poetry, and included treatises by Plutarch and Basilius Magnus on the use of Greek poetry in pedagogy, thus illustrating that his aims were not exclusively literary. Only three years later, one year after his masterly *De Jure*, the *Excerpta tragicorum et comicorum* appeared, Grotius's personal choice of the *sententiae* of the Greek dramatists. The gleams of wisdom of the classical poets and philosophers, Grotius thought, could be of good help to Christian pedagogy.

The *Excerpta* also mark his growing interest in classical drama, especially tragedy. His subsequent publications confirm these signs. In 1630 he edited the text and an integral Latin translation of Euripides's *Phoenissae* with *prolegomena* that constitute a masterfully written treatise of prime interest for the history of literary criticism. Five years later a third tragedy of his own invention was to follow, the well-known *Sophompaneas* (1635). The theme of Joseph in Egypt, one of the popular stories of sixteenth-century school drama was actually recommended by Heinsius in his *De Tragoediae Constitutione* as the only theme in the realm of biblical literature properly fitted for being dramatised in harmony with the aristotelian ideas of *anagnorisis* and *peripeteia*, at least as he interpreted these. It is not unlikely, moreover, that the theme of Joseph who received full rehabilitation abroad for the injustice done to him at home, appealed to the author who the year before had accepted the honorable embassy on behalf of the Swedish Crown at Paris.

Even afterwards Grotius occupied himself quite intensively with Greek drama. He twice again translated plays by Euripides, the *Supplices* and *Iphigeneia Taurica*, and was engaged on Sophocles in his last years. All these translations were meant to appear in the *Poemata Nova* that failed to be issued. Apart from the *Phoenissae* that appeared in separate print they have all been lost.

From the beginning around 1618 Grotius must have had a clear idea in mind of how to accomplish these successive publications. In his correspondence he repeatedly refers to the successive "steps, stages." The final stage and the conclusion of the programme was meant to be the integral translation of the *Anthologia Graeca*. And Grotius did indeed succeed in achieving this gigantic labour, a task undertaken previously by many prominent Humanists but never accomplished for obvious reasons. Grotius worked on it at intervals for over twenty years ... but the voluminous size and Grotius's specific demands as to the typeface and layout plus his request for full registers surpassed the technical abilities and financial funds of all publishers applied to and eventually caused publication to be postponed. It would take an early nineteenth-century admirer of Grotius to finish the work and accomplish the issue.

The final conclusions to be drawn from this long tale can be formulated rather briefly. The first one is this: literary interests and strict philological and poetical activities have been a lifelong occupation to Grotius, which actually permeated his thinking and other activities and can therefore be coined essential to his personality. Second: these interests have grown more intense with the years and were ever more restricted, covering all genres at first, concentrating on epigram and drama after 1618. Third: after 1618 these interests were made subservient to the ultimate object to graft biblical drama on the classical tree and to revive the Greek literary legacy.

Verbal Subordination in the Vulgate and in Erasmus's First Version of the New Testament as Sampled in Acts 15 (1506–09)

Henri Gibaud

In a number of verses, Erasmus (E) and the Vulgate (V) are identical in the way they subordinate verbs:

2 *statuerunt ut ascenderent* (object clause),

4 *Qum venissent autem* (adverbial clause of time),

21 *Moses ... habet qui eum/ipsum predicent*, i.e., men qualified for preaching him (relative clause of consequence or purpose in the subjunctive),

31 *Quam qum legissent* (connecting relative clause embedded in adverbial clause of time),

38 *Nolebat ut is qui defecisset ... adiungeretur* (relative clause within object clause).

I will discard these instances as they are by far the less frequent and the less interesting from our point of view; instead I shall concentrate on the occasions where Erasmus's constructions differ from the Vulgate's. There are two classes of examples: on the one hand, a group of twenty in which the Vulgate has a non-finite construction, whereas Erasmus has a finite (in fifteen cases) or else another non-finite construction (five cases), and, on the other hand, a small group of random differences. I shall address myself to the latter category first, so as to expatiate more leisurely on the larger one. This prompts me to arrange my paper in two parts, that I will designate by A and B.

A1

In the Greek of Acts 15, *hoti* occurs four times, in verses 1, 5, 7, 24. This conjunction introduces either an adverbial clause of cause — of which there is no occurrence in this chapter — or an object clause. The treatment of the construction by the *Vetus Interpres* is fairly regular: he gives *quia*, as in 1, 5, 24, with an occasional *quoniam*, as in 7: *scitis quoniam ... Deus ... elegit*. E's translation complies with the Latin idiom: it suppresses all equivalents of *hoti* in direct speech (1) and consistently uses *quod* in indirect speech (5, 7, 24).

A2

Then comes the problem of sequence of tenses. E uses the subjunctive more often than the Vulgate: *Quia oportet* (5), says the Vulgate (and henceforth I shall give the Vulgate's translation first, then Erasmus's), *quod oporteret* says Erasmus; v. 13, we find *postquam tacuerunt* versus *postquam conticuissent*. In 5 and 24, E logically uses the pluperfect when the Vulgate has the preterite: *qui crediderunt/qui crediderant*, *non mandauimus/non mandaueramus*, and in 14, the future perfect of E replaces the perfect of V: *visitauit/visitauerit*.

A3

In two cases in Acts 15, — of the likes of which I have not spotted more than half a dozen in the whole New Testament — a subordinate clause of V (here a relative clause) is replaced in E by a noun in the ablative. This is the case in both verses 22 and 37: the past participle *kaloumenon* is rendered by a relative clause: *qui cognominabatur* in V and a noun: *cognomento* in E.

So much so for the lesser and more heterogeneous category of subordinate clauses. The larger one could be grouped under the heading "non-finite vs finite": in ten cases, V presents a participle and in another ten an infinitive, whereas E, more often than not, uses a finite subordinate construction. I shall select first the participial clauses.

B1
Present participle in V/finite mode in E

In 1 and 17, *descendentes* and *faciens* of the Vulgate are rendered by relative clauses in E: *qui descenderant, qui facit*. *Fide purificans* of 9 has for equivalent an adverbial clause of time: *qum fide purificauerit*. V29, *custodientes vos* becomes *si conseruaueritis vosipsos* (adverbial clause of condition/hypothesis). In all these cases, the Greek also has a present participle. Slightly different is the case of *annunciantes* (4). The Greek has the aorist tense, but for some reason, the *Vetus Interpres*, who seemed to have a liking for non-finite modes, forsook his other penchant for a word-for-word translation. Erasmus restored the "veritas graeca" by means of the corresponding perfect: *annunciaueruntque*.

B2
Present participle/past participle

Scribentes per manus eorum (23) is replaced in E by an ablative absolute: *missis per manus eorum literis*. Another related case is found in 24, where *exeuntes* is replaced by a past participle form, but with an active meaning (deponent verb): it becomes in E *egressi*. In both cases, the Latin verb actually corresponds to the verbless preposition *ex*.

B3

Past participle/various finite constructions

2:the equivalent in E of the ablative absolute in the Vulgate: *Facta ... seditione* is *Qum orta esset seditio*. In this verse, the locution *Et disceptatio*, which follows *seditio*, figures in the Greek, and was introduced as recently as 1979 by *Nova Vulgata*, the official Vatican version.

29 Corresponding to the single Greek word *eidôlothutôn* (= idol sacrifices), we find *ab immolatis simulacrorum* in V, and *ab his que sunt immolata simulacris* in E.

33 offers matter for some reflection. V has, here again, an ablative absolute: *Facto ... aliquanto tempore*, while the Greek has an active present participle: *poièsantes de chronon*. Erasmus, who avoids *facere* whenever possible, uses another deponent that will be less banal and will fit perfectly into the context: *Commorati ... aliquantum temporis*, with the accusative of duration.

B4

Infinitive/*vt* + subjunctive construction

This occurs in vv. 6, 7, 10, 14, 22, 37, 38, to which we could add a *ne* + subjunctive construction (*ne* = *vt non*). Here is one example to illustrate the eight cases. (6) *Conueneruntque ... videre*, says V; this becomes in E: *conueneruntque ... vt dispicerent*, with a change of verb into the bargain.

18–20 and 25 are two erratic cases after this long series. In 19–20, E replaces the infinitive by a gerundive. *Censeo non inquietari ... sed scribere* is expressed in E as follows: *censeo non obturbandum esse ... sed scribendum*. And in 25 the infinitive becomes a past participle: *eligere/dilectos* (later corrected into *delectos*, as in 22).

At the term of these considerations, though it is impossible indeed to draw any conclusion valid for the whole NT, one feature is striking: in faithful, if not servile accord with the Greek, V has many non-finite constructions (twenty in this chapter), where E prefers to use finite clauses (fifteen cases), which are more in conformity with the genius of the Latin tongue. In order to reach general conclusions, many more studies like this one would be necessary. Who will volunteer to conduct them?

Université Catholique de l'Ouest, Angers

Histoire d'un opuscule d'Erasme: La *Brevissima maximeque compendiaria conficiendarum epistolarum formula*

A. Jolidon

L a *Brevissima maximeque compendiaria conficiendarum epistolarum formula*,[1] c'est-à-dire la "recette très courte et très condensée pour faire des lettres," au titre paradoxalement interminable, est l'un des textes d'Erasme les moins connus aujourd'hui, en dépit du grand nombre de ses éditions au seizième siècle (cinquante-trois de 1520 à 1579).[2] En effet elle n'a été incluse ni dans les *Omnia opera* de Bâle (1540), ni dans les *Opera omnia* de Leyde (1703), ni dans le *Supplement* publié par Wallace K. Ferguson (1933). Et elle n'a pas encore fait l'objet d'une étude approfondie.[3]

C'est aussi l'un des textes les plus énigmatiques de l'illustre Rotterdamois. On ne sait avec certitude ni ce qui est réellement de sa plume dans cette plaquette, ni son rapport exact avec le *Libellus de conscribendis epistolis* de 1521 et avec l'*Opus de conscribendis epistolis* de 1522, ni quelle en est l'édition originale, ni qui a été le responsable de sa première publication en 1520. Nous ne prétendons pas résoudre définitivement ces différents problèmes, mais nous essaierons de les poser correctement. Pour cela nous étudierons successivement les témoignages externes sur les circonstances de la composition de l'ouvrage, son contenu, et l'histoire de sa publication.

Pour déterminer la date et les circonstances de la rédaction de la *Formula*, nous disposons avant tout de trois textes d'Erasme: la préface des *Progymnasmata quaedam primae adolescentiae Erasmi* (Louvain, Martens, mars(?) 1521);[4] la postface du *De puritate tabernaculi sive ecclesiae Christianae* (Bâle, H. Froben et N. Episcopius, 20 fév. 1536);[5] et la postface du *Eiusdem argumenti ... compendium* faisant suite au *De conscribendis epistolis libellus vere aureus* de J. L. Vives (Bâle, T. Flatter et B. Lasius, mars 1536).[6]

Première surprise: les propos de 1536, apparemment, contredisent ceux de 1521. En effet le plus ancien de ces textes a tout l'air d'un désaveu de paternité. "La pire impudence, s'y écrie Erasme, c'est d'attacher mon nom à des niaiseries commises par d'autres. Dans cet ouvrage (notre opuscule), à part un tout petit nombre de formules furtives, il n'y a rien de moi" ("praeter pauculas voces furtivas, nihil est meum"). Cette déclaration semble péremptoire. Mais en quoi consistaient donc au juste ces "formules furtives"? Erasme considérait-il comme étant ou n'étant pas de lui les citations, si nombreuses dans la *Formula* qu'elles constituent près de la moitié du texte? Dans le second cas la part du texte authentique serait malgré tout considérable. L'auteur ne nous donne qu'un exemple précis de la falsification: l'invention du nom du dédicataire, donné comme un certain "Petrus Paludanus." C'est bien peu de chose. La colère même qui semble animer ici l'humaniste a pu le pousser à exagérer beaucoup l'inauthenticité du texte qui nous occupe. Rappelons-nous qu'il a d'abord nié avec presque autant de vigueur avoir composé celui des *Familiarium colloquiorum formulae*.

Toujours est-il que quinze ans plus tard, en 1536, Erasme s'exprime fort différemment au sujet de notre *Formula*, sans faire référence à sa condamnation de 1521, qu'il a manifestement oubliée. Ce petit ouvrage, nous dit-il, "a été extrait par amputation" ("truncatim decerptum est") d'un recueil de notes assez élémentaire rédigé en deux jours et destiné à un élève anglais "peu futé" ("crasso"). Cette fois-ci la part du texte due à Erasme est donnée comme au moins égale, voire très supérieure, à 50%: "il a tiré certaines choses de ce manuscrit" ("quaedam decerpsit") "et y a mêlé certaines autres de son cru" ("sua quaedam admiscuit"), écrit l'auteur dans la postface au *De puritate*. "Il a extirpé (du manuscrit primitif) la plupart ("pleraque") des éléments de l'opuscule et leur a ajouté un bon nombre d'autres de son fonds," confirme-t-il dans l'adresse au lecteur du "Compendium."

Erasme parle aussi, dans les deux postfaces, de l'addition au texte original d'une lettre à un certain Fabricius, "lettre insignement plate et sans rapport avec le sujet" de l'opuscule, "où il n'y a pas un mot qui soit de lui." Il semble bien que l'humaniste, dont la mémoire, longtemps étonnante, commençait peut-être à baisser, considère ici l'auteur de la lettre comme étant aussi responsable de la remise du manuscrit de la *Formula* à un éditeur en 1520. Nous savons aujourd'hui que c'est impossible, puisque l'édition originale, quelle qu'elle soit, contient en appendice, non pas la lettre à Fabricius, mais deux lettres de Pline le Jeune. Nous reviendrons plus loin sur l'auteur de cette lettre, et nous chercherons à identifier le détenteur du manuscrit primitif de la *Formula* quand nous aurons déterminé quelle en a été l'édition originale.

Voyons maintenant à quelle date et dans quelles conditions ont été composées les parties authentiquement érasmiennes de notre opuscule.

On ne peut pas tirer grand-chose du "ante annos quadraginta" de la postface du *De puritate* (1536), ni du "annis abhinc ferme triginta" de la lettre-préface de 1522 à Nicolas Bérauld, ni du "ante annos ferme triginta" de l'*Appendix de scriptis Clichtovei* de 1526, ni du "ante annos viginti quinque" du chapitre IX du *De conscribendis epistolis opus* de 1522. Quarante, trente, et même vingt-cinq, sont des chiffres ronds, très certainement exagérés, l'auteur souhaitant souligner sa jeunesse à l'époque de la première rédaction pour excuser l'imperfection de son travail. Mais si l'on rapproche ces dates des trois textes déjà sommairement analysés et de l'*Exemplum epistolae mixtae* du *Libellus de conscribendis epistolis*, lettre adressée à un certain Robert qui devrait être Robert Fisher, et puisque le *Libellus* représente probablement le deuxième état de l'ouvrage d'Erasme sur l'art de rédiger des lettres, on est conduit à penser que la *Formula* est sans doute, au moins partiellement, le premier état de cet ouvrage,[7] et qu'Erasme l'a composé vers le mois de novembre 1498, à Paris, pour ce même Fisher, à la hâte, plus précisément en deux jours, après deux semaines et demie de préparation, parce que son disciple se disposait à partir pour l'Italie et qu'il avait supplié Erasme de le munir d'un aide-mémoire lui permettant de bien tourner les lettres (surtout les lettres de sollicitation, peut-on penser).

Voyons à présent ce que nous apprend le texte lui-même.

La *Formula* est une petite plaquette, de quinze à vingt-cinq pages en moyenne, que les éditeurs ont généralement étoffée au moyen d'appendices divers (lettres de Pline le Jeune, lettre "à Fabricius," autres traités portant sur le même sujet).

Elle comprend, après une lettre dédicatoire à un certain Petrus Paludanus, une définition du genre épistolaire, puis une série de trois chapitres numérotés de I à III contenant des remarques générales sur l'éloquence, et enfin une autre série de quatre chapitres non numérotés qui répartissent en trois groupes les différentes espèces de lettres.

La préface a été publiée dans le tome XI des *Erasmi epistolae* (Appendix XXVI). Sa forte ressemblance avec la préface du *Libellus* de Siberch, adressée à Robertus (sûrement Robert Fisher), a été maintes fois relevée.

Le texte du *Libellus* est à coup sûr plus élégant, plus ample, plus imagé. Les coéditeurs du dernier tome de la correspondance d'Erasme, H. M. Allen et H. W. Garrod, en déduisent que la dédicace de la *Formula* n'est qu'une reprise abrégée, et même mutilée, de la dédicace authentique. Mais Erasme ne nie pas avoir écrit la préface de la *Formula*, puisqu'il l'appelle "veterem praefationem," et on peut très bien supposer que cette préface est la première version du texte, et celle du *Libellus* une révision de ce dernier. Le passage de "sed" à "at," de "vis?" interrogatif à "vin?," la suppression de phrases enchevêtrées ("quantis me calumniis" $\longrightarrow$ "quantis calumniis me"), l'introduction d'hyperbates ("neque alienis inhaesurum vestigiis"), le souci plus grand de la variété du vocabulaire (trois "dicere" devenus respectivement "dicere," "scribere," "respondere") sont tout à fait conformes à ce que nous savons des habitudes d'Erasme quand il se corrige. Le P. du début ("humanissime P."), qui a donné l'idée d'appeler Petrus Paludanus le destinataire, pourrait avoir été l'initiale de "Piscator," traduction latine de "Fisher."

Le long titre de la *Formula* ("Brevissima maximeque compendiaria conficiendarum epistolarum formula") n'est probablement pas d'Erasme, qui ne mentionne jamais son (?) opuscule sous ce nom, préférant l'appeler "libellus," "opusculum," ou "compendium." Il a manifestement été emprunté à la fin de la lettre dédicatoire. Mais son caractère redondant ("brevissima," "maxime compendiaria," "formula") pourrait bien faire allusion malicieusement au désir, exprimé sans doute avec beaucoup d'insistance par Robert Fisher, d'avoir un manuel court et pratique, lui permettant de passer le moins de temps possible à acquérir une culture littéraire. Erasme fait justice, dans son *Opus* de 1522, de ces étudiants pressés, amateurs de savoir en pilules (ASD 12, p. 228, l. 1 à 12). La dernière phrase de la préface n'est d'ailleurs pas complètement dépourvue d'insolence: "Convainc-toi avant tout de ceci," écrit l'auteur à son disciple. "Les lettres requièrent non seulement du vocabulaire, mais de l'art" ("non verbis tantum, sed arte etiam indigere"). Fisher attendait sans doute de lui un simple recueil de formules, comme en offraient les "artes dictaminis" du Moyen Age.

Le chapitre qui vient ensuite est intitulé "Epistolae definitio." C'est incontestablement le mieux venu de tous. Partant de la belle formule du rhéteur Libanios: "La lettre est une conversation à distance" ("absentis ad absentem colloquium"),[8] l'auteur y insiste sur la nécessité que le style épistolaire soit dépourvu d'emphase, simple, savamment négligé, qu'il évite les mots rares. Et il condamne ceux qui, encore de son temps, sertissent une lettre autour d'un joli mot, au lieu de mettre les mots au service de la pensée.[9]

A part quelques répétitions de mots, ce chapitre est tout à fait digne de la plume d'Erasme. Les phrases sont amples, le vocabulaire riche et varié, le style imagé. Notons les néologismes ("grandiloquentia," "balbuties"),[10] les diminutifs ("negligentiusculus,[11] vocula"), les tours pittoresques ("verba repetita ex Aborigenum saeculis";[12] "verborum aucupes atque anxii captatores"; "palmarum fructum reperisse"), les heureuses alliances de mots ("est quaedam negligentia diligens";[13] "suam barbariem ac balbutiem";[14] il y a dans ce dernier cas à la fois allitération, homéotéleute et paronomase). Les citations, explicites ou implicites, d'Horace, de Cicéron, de Quintilien, l'utilisation de "porro," emprunté sans doute à ce dernier, l'admiration exprimée pour Pline le Jeune, tout cela est bien conforme aux habitudes et aux préférences du Rotterdamois. Et l'utilisation du mot "colloquium" fait penser aux *Colloquia familiaria* qu'Erasme avait en tête à Paris vers la même époque.[15]

Les trois chapitres suivants ("De exercitatione et stylo"; "De imitatione"; "De judicio," où nous reconnaissons la fameuse triade *Ars, imitatio, exercitatio* ne procurent assurément pas le même plaisir. Le premier, le dernier et le début du second consistent presque uniquement en une paraphrase de l'*Institution oratoire* de Quintilien (X.3 et 7 pour le premier chapitre; X.2 pour le deuxième; X.2, II.11, II.13, II.12 pour le troisième). La suite des idées est souvent peu nette: le sujet, la façon d'écrire des lettres, est pratiquement perdu de vue dans le premier chapitre, au début du second, et au début et à la fin du troisème. Et un sous-titre vient bizarrement couper en deux morceaux le chapitre II "De imitatione": "Circa imitationem exactissimo judicio opus est." Cette série de recommandations générales s'appliquerait certes aussi bien ou mieux à un apprenti orateur qu'à un épistolier.

Tout est dans la disposition de la matière, est-il d'abord affirmé. Il ne faut pas se tracasser pour le vocabulaire, qui vient naturellement. Il faut s'exercer à écrire le plus souvent et le plus soigneusement possible, pour acquérir de l'assurance et de l'abondance. Il faut écrire lentement d'abord, beaucoup lire, fuir une facilité superficielle; l'aisance viendra peu à peu. Mais l'excès de scrupules aussi est un défaut.

Choisissons avec soin, dit le deuxième chapitre, les modèles à imiter, les meilleurs étant, en ce qui concerne la correspondance, Cicéron (pour les qualités naturelles), Pline le Jeune (pour l'art), Politien (pour l'originalité des idées et pour la minutie), et avec des réserves Sénèque au style trop heurté, mais très moral et brillant. Au reste ne nous contentons pas de lire des lettres; abordons aussi d'autres genres littéraires, en lisant par exemple toute l'œuvre de Cicéron, qui est si variée.

Le dernier chapitre, qui est le plus long, est aussi le plus désordonné. Il s'intitulerait mieux, à tout prendre, "De arte."

Quelques lignes, d'abord, qui seraient mieux à leur place à la fin du chapitre précédent, développent à nouveau l'idée que l'imitation suppose du discernement, et que si on suit Cicéron, on progressera à la fois pour l'expression, pour la recherche des idées et pour la détermination du plan. Pourtant l'imitation ne suffit pas; on ne peut pas se contenter de singer autrui, car il y a dans toute éloquence une part qui n'est pas imitable. Outre l'entrainement à parler ou à écrire, outre la pratique de l'imitation, il faut des connaissances théoriques. On nie parfois qu'il y ait un art, une technique de la rédaction des lettres. Certains soutiennent même qu'il n'existe pas à proprement parler d'art d'écrire. Il serait pourtant étrange qu'il n'y ait pas de technique du langage, alors qu'il y en a pour tous les arts de la matière, art de forger, tissage, poterie. On dit aussi que les lettres familières et improvisées se passent de la rhétorique, et qu'il y faut seulement de l'esprit d'à-propos. Certes il est bon de s'écarter parfois de l'ordre traditionnel d'exposition, l'intérêt personnel vaut toutes les règles et tous les professeurs du monde. Pas de plan passe-partout dans les lettres: sujet, destinataire, circonstances, tout est toujours différent. Il y faut donc du bon sens, "praesens consilium." Tout dire ou tout écrire conformément au même modèle serait une contrainte insupportable. Mais ne jamais suivre de règles serait aussi peu raisonnable. La culture ralentit la plume, mais elle corrige les défauts. L'ignorant est un violent et non un homme fort.

Cette série de chapitres, qui n'évite pas toujours les banalités, prête donc le flanc à la critique, et on pourrait être tenté de penser qu'elle n'est pas d'Erasme. Ce n'est pas impossible, évidemment. On retrouve pourtant par endroits[16] la belle langue imagée du début de la *Formula*: "Celui qui s'est donné Cicéron comme chef et comme porte-enseigne." "Il faut donc du discernement, le compagnon ou le père de l'art lui-même; la même hardiesse néologisante ("promptitudinem"; "effunditant"); la même vigueur critique, par exemple lorsque l'auteur condamne, comme Heinrich Bebel à la même époque, ceux qui pensent que tout l'art épistolaire consiste à décomposer les lettres en "salutatio," "exordium," "narratio" et "conclusio."[17] Ajoutons que la connaissance étendue de Quintilien que supposent ces chapitres ne surprend pas chez un admirateur de Valla tel qu'Erasme, pas plus que la citation de Pline le Jeune ou l'enthousiasme manifesté pour Politien[18] parmi les modernes. Et les deux vers, des sénaires iambiques catalectiques, qui agrémentent le chapitre "De judicio" ("quo se cunque rapit impetus sequuntur / percurruntque velut effusis habenis") ne détonnent pas chez un poète humaniste tel qu'Erasme en 1498.

Les chapitres suivants, au nombre de quatre, esquissent un classement des diverses espèces de lettres.

Le premier, intitulé "De tribus generibus causarum," est à la fois l'annonce du plan de la fin de l'opuscule et une transition par rapport aux chapitres précédents: si l'on veut découvrir l'art caché dans les lettres de l'Antiquité et suivre des règles plutôt que son instinct, l'on remarquera que les lettres peuvent se classer comme les discours en trois groupes: démonstratif, délibératif, judiciaire.

Le chapitre suivant traite du genre "démonstratif," qui consiste à louer ou à blâmer. La louange (ou le blâme) peut être morale, physique, ou concerner des biens extérieurs à la personne proprement dite. L'auteur s'appuie encore une fois sur l'*Institution oratoire* (III.7 et IX.4) et analyse deux lettres de Pline le Jeune, dont l'une fait l'éloge du philosophe Euphrates (I.10) et l'autre celui du magistrat Munitius (I.14). Les descriptions abondent dans les lettres de ce genre. Les lieux communs y sont l'aspect et l'utilité. Le style de ces lettres supporte fort bien les ornements, même poétiques. Car il y a, comme le dit Quintilien (IX.4, 19) deux styles de discours: l'un serré, l'autre plus lâche; et c'est du second que relèvent les lettres et la conversation, sauf quand elles portent sur des sujets élevés. Dans les descriptions de lieux, il faut imiter Tite-Live et Salluste; dans les autres (animaux, végétaux, etc.) Pline l'Ancien, qui est à lire tout entier à cause de sa variété.

L'auteur parle ensuite du genre délibératif, en suivant de très près, au début du moins, le chapitre 8 du livre III de l'*Institution oratoire*. Appartiennent à ce genre les lettres qui persuadent ou dissuadent, exhortent ou découragent, demandent, donnent des avis, expriment l'amour. Elles considèrent les points de vue de l'utilité, de la moralité et de la possibilité, la moralité étant le point de vue essentiel. L'auteur rattache à cette catégorie la lettre de recommandation, parce qu'on ne peut recommander quelqu'un sans démontrer que la recommandation est justifiée. Il est bon d'user d'un préambule modeste pour susciter la sympathie du destinataire avant d'énumérer les qualités de la personne recommandée, et d'insister sur l'importance et la facilité du rôle de la personne sollicitée. Mais il faut éviter de recommander des gens ... peu recommandables. Enfin il est parlé brièvement de la lettre de demande, qui doit toujours offrir une contrepartie de la faveur demandée.

Passant enfin au genre judiciaire, le rédacteur de notre plaquette, s'inspirant encore de Quintilien (surtout III.9, III.10, et IV.1), distingue ses deux aspects opposés, l'attaque et la défense, et énumère parmi les lettres qui attaquent la lettre d'accusation, la lettre de reproche, la lettre de blâme, la lettre de contre-accusation. Il est difficile de formuler ici des principes généraux à cause de la variété des sujets: l'un des moins discutables est qu'il faut grossir les faits quand on accuse et en masquer la gravité quand on excuse. La lettre de ce type peut prendre un caractère passionné et contenir des souhaits, des exécrations, des supplications, tout comme un discours. Dans un bref exorde (dont Erasme ou le pseudo-Erasme donne un modèle), le rédacteur doit insister modestement sur sa faiblesse et sa timidité. Il doit alors s'exprimer le plus simplement possible, en évitant de paraître partial et méchant. Les considérations relatives à la jeunesse ou à l'âge avancé de celui qui écrit sont ici très efficaces.

Au total, si l'on considère les sources de la *Formula*, c'est de très loin Quintilien que l'auteur sollicite le plus. Outre les emprunts massifs que nous avons déjà signalés, nous en avons décelé çà et là une foule d'autres, concernant les chapitres I.2; II.13; II.17; VI.3; VII.2; XI.1, l'épître à Tryphon, et surtout le prologue du livre VIII de l'*Institution oratoire*; et nous sommes persuadé qu'il en reste encore à découvrir.

Viennent ensuite Pline le Jeune, plusieurs fois nommé, et cité pour les lettres I.5; I.10; I.14; II.13; Horace, pour ses Epîtres (I.1; I.9; I.18; I.19) et son *Art poétique*; le chant I de l'*Enéide* de Virgile, deux fois cité, Sénèque pour sa fameuse lettre sur les esclaves. Aristote et Politien sont mentionnés, mais sans précision; Cicéron aussi, mais de façon très générale également.[19] Le commentaire de Lorenzo Valla sur l'*Institution oratoire*[20] a été utilisé au moins à deux reprises[21], ce qui est en faveur de l'authenticité de la *Formula*, puisqu'Erasme, grand admirateur de Valla, possédait cet ouvrage dans sa bibliothèque.[22]

Le Rotterdamois affirme, dans sa préface, qu'il "ne marchera sur les traces d'aucun de ses devanciers." Nous avons effectué, pour contrôler cette affirmation, un rapide survol des traités d'art épistolaire parus entre 1470 et 1500,[23] et nous ne pouvons pas la démentir totalement. L'auteur reprend bien certaines idées de Perotti, mais jamais littéralement. Il emprunte beaucoup de qualificatifs aux classifications de Filelfo et de Negro, mais il en élimine beaucoup aussi. Il doit sans doute à Sulpizio ou à Dati l'idée de répartir les lettres en trois grandes classes identiques à celles des discours; mais il est le seul, par exemple, à mentionner la définition de Libanios.[24] Le recours à Quintilien est constant, il est vrai, mais ce dernier n'ayant pas, ou presque pas, parlé des lettres, Erasme pouvait ne pas le considérer comme un devancier.

Nous avons déjà parlé du style de la *Formula*, en particulier à propos de son premier chapitre, si érasmien d'allure. Mais nous pourrions encore relever, comme signes possibles d'une paternité érasmienne, les formes de démontratifs "hii" et "hiis," fréquentes dans les textes les plus anciens de notre humaniste; les mots "scopus," "usqueadeo," et le tour "ut ita dixerim," familiers à Erasme; la forme surcomposée "versati fuerint"; et plusieurs images et expressions pittoresques: "le remords est le compagnon d'une telle recommandation," ou "de vieux routiers de l'éloquence." En revanche nous avons été surpris de ne jamais trouver ni "nec … quidem," si courant dans la première version des "Antibarbari," ni "alioquin" devant consonne, ni "verum etiam" au lieu de "sed etiam." Mais les dimensions réduites de l'opuscule rendent ces absences peu probantes.

Reste la question du rapport entre la *Formula*, le *Libellus* de 1521, et l'*Opus de conscribendis epistolis* de 1522, question qui est fort délicate.

Constatons d'abord, et la chose est troublante, qu'en dehors de la préface il n'y a pas de reprises de développements, ni même de paragraphes ou de phrases de la *Formula* dans les deux autres versions du *De conscribendis epistolis*. Alors que l'*Opus* dérive manifestement du *Libellus* complètement remanié dans sa première partie et fortement augmenté dans la seconde, il n'y a qu'un assez vague rapport de plan entre *Formula* et *Libellus*. Le *Libellus* ne contient pas de définition de la lettre, contrairement à la *Formula*; en revanche son premier chapitre, intitulé "Cuiusmodi esse debeat epistolaris character, et in ea quid fugiendum, quid sequendum," développe l'idée qu'il faut bannir la grandiloquence, comme la fin du premier chapitre de la *Formula*; mais il s'achève sur un développement relatif à la "salutatio" qui n'existe pas dans la *Formula*. Et il n'y a rien de comparable, dans le *Libellus*, aux chapitres "De exercitatione et stile," "De imitatione," "De judicio." Comme la *Formula*, le *Libellus* classe ensuite les lettres en trois groupes, mais elle place en seconde position le "demonstrativum genus" et ajoute un quatrième groupe de lettres, les "extraordinaria genera." Et sauf pour le "demonstrativum genus," l'étude des diverses espèces de lettres y est beaucoup plus développée.

Les rapports entre *Formula* et *Opus*, assez curieusement, paraissent un peu plus grands: le chapitre "Peculiaris epistolae character" de l'*Opus*, donne une définition de la lettre attribuée à Turpilius, mais fort semblable à celle de Libanios dans la *Formula*; et le titre au moins du chapitre "Exercitatio et imitatio" fait penser aux chapitres "De exercitatione et stilo" et "De imitatione" de la *Formula*. Erasme revient sans doute dans l'*Opus* à son plan initial, celui esquissé dans la *Formula*, tandis que le *Libellus* de Siberch, peut-être à cause d'une grosse lacune au début du texte, se réduit presque uniquement à une classification des lettres.

On pourrait être tenté de conclure de ces dernières constatations que la *Formula* n'est pas d'Erasme. Tel n'est pourtant pas notre avis, car, nous l'avons vu, une étude minutieuse du style de l'opuscule conduit à la conclusion inverse.

Nous pensons en définitive que le Rotterdamois a écrit vers la fin de 1498 un texte bâclé et médiocrement original que lui a littéralement arraché Robert Fisher et qui n'était pas très différent du texte paru en 1520 (un peu plus long pourtant, puisqu'Erasme parle de mutilation: "truncatim," "detruncavit"); que deux ans plus tard, déçu du peu de reconnaissance de Fisher à son égard et cherchant d'autres mécènes, il a refondu entièrement (cf. le mot "retractanti") le texte primitif pour le rendre plus présentable, voulant le dédier à Mountjoy ou à Adolphe de Veere; qu'en mars 1521, furieux de voir ressurgir, avec la *Formula*, un texte médiocre qu'il espérait bien avoir gommé à tout jamais grâce à la refonte de 1500, il s'est efforcé de faire croire, en exagérant beaucoup, que la version de 1498 n'était pas de lui; que la publication par Siberch en octobre 1521 de la version de 1500, mutilée elle aussi, l'a obligé à reprendre son texte pour en donner une édition définitive, le "De conscribendis epistolis opus"; et qu'en février et mars 1536 enfin, sans plus se souvenir de ses dénégations de 1521, il a décrit de façon correcte la *Formula* comme un extrait de l'aide-mémoire ("commentarius") primitif.

Nous ne pouvons qu'esquisser l'histoire assez complexe de la publication de la *Formula*. La collation des éditions est un travail amusant à faire, mais beaucoup moins amusant à exposer. Nous nous contenterons donc ici, sans entrer dans tout le détail de la démonstration, d'indiquer les résultats obtenus sur trois points particulièrement intéressants: la détermination de l'édition originale, la personnalité d'un certain "Hugualdus," et le travail de révision d'Erasme reconnaissant enfin son enfant en mars 1536.

Au début de notre enquête, trois éditions pouvaient prétendre au titre d'édition originale: une publiée par Johann Schoeffer à Mayence en septembre 1520; une autre due à Valentin Schumann à Leipzig, en 1520 également; une dernière composée à Erfurt par Matthes Maler, toujours en 1520. Les éditions de Schoeffer et de Schumann sont de belles éditions en caractères italiques, très soignées. Mais c'est certainement l'édition de Maler qui est l'originale, bien qu'elle soit typographiquement horrible (gros caractères romains tassés, lignes de texte parfois brisées, absence de ponctuation presque complète, le début des phrases étant simplement marqué par des majuscules, abréviations multiples, fautes d'impression grossières, comme "jubes" pour "habes," "facultete" pour "facultate," "commendos" pour "commendas," "pernullarius" pour "parmularius"). Citons seulement, parmi une foule d'autres, un argument qui démontre de façon particulièrement probante que Schumann a travaillé à partir du texte de Maler, un autre qui prouve qu'il en va de même pour Schoeffer, et un dernier qui nous confirme que l'édition d'Erfurt est bien l'origine commune des deux autres.

Dans le chapitre "Deliberativum genus," le texte de V. Schumann présente un très étrange et inintelligible λυηατον (ou λυχατον) au lieu de δυνατον. Or on s'aperçoit, quand on se reporte au texte de Maler, que ses très bizarres caractères grecs comportent un delta minuscule à longue queue, inspiré du delta majuscule, qui ressemble fort à un lambda, et que son nu minuscule, réduction lui aussi du nu majuscule, est assez semblable à certains êta ou kappa minuscules. Il est évident que le typographe de Schumann, ignorant le grec, a cru reproduire ainsi au mieux le texte de Maler.

Quant à la postériorité de la première édition de J. Schoeffer (Mayence, septembre 1520) par rapport à celle de Maler, elle est démontrée par exemple par la présence du mot "panagiricis" dans le chapitre "Demonstrativum genus" de Maler et de Schumann,[25] convenablement corrigé en "panegyricis" dans l'édition de Schoeffer. Cette correction est tout à fait naturelle de la part d'un prote un peu frotté d'humanisme comme devait l'être celui de Mayence. Et inversement la régression de "panegyricis" à "panagiricis" est absolument invraisemblable. Ajoutons que jusque dans les premières années du seizième siècle Erasme n'avait de la langue grecque qu'une connaissance très médiocre, et que les fautes de ce genre ne sont pas rares dans la première version des "Antibarbari."[26]

Enfin dans le même chapitre, quatre lignes plus bas, Maler écrit: "Poetice[27] quid ut ..." en laissant entre "quid" et "ut" la place d'une lettre qui a été oubliée par le typographe. Or Schoeffer transcrit servilement, sans s'apercevoir que son texte est inintelligible: "Poetice quid, ut...." En revanche Schumann, tenant compte de la lacune évidente, corrige intelligemment en: "Poetice quidem ut...."

C'est à la même conclusion que nous conduisent les divergences sur le nom du destinataire de la première des deux lettres de Pline le Jeune ajoutées au texte d'Erasme: Maler lit Aerio, Schumann Berio et Schoeffer Atrio!

Il n'est pas outre mesure étonnant que la *Formula* ait paru pour la première fois à Erfurt, principal foyer européen de l'érasmophilie, ou plutôt de l'érasmolâtrie ou de l'érasmomanie, à partir de 1517. Erasme lui-même eut d'ailleurs plus d'une fois à réfréner, et en particulier en 1520, lors de sa controverse avec Edward Lee, la vigueur immodérée de ces partisans trop enthousiastes qu'étaient Eoban Hesse, Euricius Cordus, Petreius von Eberbach et tant d'autres. Dans un pareil contexte, le moindre rogaton érasmien ne pouvait qu'être chaleureusement accueilli, et plus de 50% de la production de Maler tourne alors autour d'Erasme et de ses amis.

Est-ce l'un de ces nombreux amis erfurtiens du Rotterdamois venus le visiter à Louvain qui a remis à Maler le manuscrit de la *Formula*? Ou faut-il penser à un acte de piraterie littéraire commis par un spécialiste de la chose tel qu'Augustin Vincent Caminade (s'il était encore en vie) ou le mystérieux William Thale, ou par quelque ami anglais de Robert Fisher? A cette question, hélas, nous ne pouvons pas répondre actuellement. Notre excuse est qu'Erasme lui-même ne le pouvait pas en 1521 (puisqu'il dit: *"nescio quis ... libellum emisit"*) et que c'est à tort, très probablement, qu'il a cru pouvoir l'identifier en 1536 (cf. "quis sit hic artifex ... facile divino").

En tout cas le texte de Maler a bientôt pris son vol vers l'est (Leipzig) et vers l'ouest (Mayence), et c'est de l'impression de Schoeffer dans cette dernière ville que dérivent à leur tour presque toutes les éditions ultérieures à Cologne, Paris, Bâle et aussi à Landshut, Augsbourg, Lyon, Venise et de nouveau Leipzig. Nous n'avons pu examiner l'édition de Cracovie (1527), dont il est légitime de supposer qu'elle dérive, elle, d'une impression de Leipzig.

Parmi ces éditions plus tardives, qui témoignent de la brillante carrière de l'opuscule au seizième siècle, celle d'Adam Petri, parue à Bâle en septembre 1521, retient particulièrement l'attention, car elle substitue aux deux lettres de Pline à l'aide desquelles Maler avait étoffé le texte d'Erasme, une lettre de sept pages et demie intitulée: "Fabricio suo H." suivie d'une postface au lecteur. Le mystérieux H. se révèle dans le cours de la lettre être un dénommé "Hugualdus," et ce dernier, que nous avons vu Erasme exécuter si sommairement (rappelons-nous le "insigniter insulsam"), mériterait pourtant d'être l'objet d'une petite monographie. L'une de ses infortunes est d'avoir été confondu avec un autre humaniste bâlois presque contemporain, un historien celui-là, dénommé H. Mutius,[28] très certainement parce que dans la *Bibliotheca universalis* de Conrad Gesner (1545), l'article concernant Mutius suit celui très court consacré à Hugualdus sans que l'alinéa soit bien marqué. A cause de cela l'érudit suisse Conrad Lycosthenes dans son *Elenchus scriptorum omnium*, (1551), puis les érudits allemands Struve et Mueller ont fabriqué un personnage imaginaire dénommé Huldreich Hugwald Mutius, dont les catalogues de la Bibliothèque Nationale et de la British Library ont ensuite entériné l'existence.

La production littéraire d'Udalricus (ou Huldrichus) Hugualdus Durgeus, c'est-à-dire d'Ulrich Hugwald du Thurgau, pour lui rendre sa véritable identité, semble avoir été tout entière éditée par Adam Petri, dont Hugwald était probablement le correcteur. Elle s'étale sur deux ans seulement, de 1520 à 1522, et ne comprend que quatre ou cinq titres. Ce sont, dans l'ordre chronologique probable de parution: en septembre 1520, un *Dialogus, studiorum suorum prooemium, et militiae initium*, en 1521, une édition d'un ouvrage de Luther, la *Tesseradecas consolatoria pro laborantibus et oneratis*, en septembre 1521, une édition de la *Formula* d'Erasme, suivie, comme nous le disions, d'un texte original de Hugwald, une lettre à un certain Petrus Fabricius sur la rhétorique (et contre la dialectique syllogistique); composée en 1521, à Schonenberga (?), et publiée ultérieurement par un certain Johannes Peterus à qui Hugwald avait laissé tous ses papiers en quittant Bâle, une *Lettre à la sainte Eglise de Zürich*, où il se déchaîne contre les "doctorculi theologastri," c'est-à-dire les scotistes, et contre les "Romanenses," c'est-à-dire les papistes. Enfin Gesner donne comme parue en 1522 (à Bâle d'après Lycosthenes) une "Epistola ad omnes qui Christum ex animo quaerunt" qui est probablemnt distincte de l'"Epistola ad sanctam Tigurinam ecclesiam" que nous venons de mentionner. Il semble qu'Hugwald soit retourné vers 1522 dans son Thurgau natal, et sans doute est-il mort assez jeune puisque Gesner le qualifie d'"adolescens."

L'énumération de ses œuvres suffit à nous montrer qu'il s'agissait d'un luthérien fervent. Son admiration allait à des hommes comme Claude Chansonnette, Beatus Rhenanus, Conradus Pellicanus (dont il dit: "un moine certes, mais un homme fort pieux et fort instruit"). Il est probable que c'est à son instigation qu'Adam Petri est devenu le grand éditeur luthérien de Bâle. Si Hugwald s'est intéressé (fugitivement) à Erasme, c'est sûrement parce qu'il voyait en lui un esprit ouvert, apparemment acquis aux idées nouvelles en théologie, et parce qu'il partageait son mépris pour la dialectique scolastique.

Dernière étape importante dans l'histoire des éditions de notre *Formula*; la décision prise par Erasme de donner à ses lecteurs un texte revu et corrigé de l'opuscule.

Malgré les efforts, souvent heureux, des divers éditeurs, ce texte restait grevé de nombreuses fautes. Ne pouvant plus en empêcher la diffusion, l'humaniste confia à deux éditeurs débutants, Thomas Platter et Balthasar Ruch, dit Lasius, les successeurs d'Andreas Cratander, le soin de publier l'édition définitive, qui parut en mars 1536.[29] Le texte d'Erasme, intitulé *Compendium*, y est précédé, ce qui est un très heureux parti, du *De conscribendis epistolis libellus vere aureus* de Vives, déjà paru à Anvers chez Hillen en 1534. Et il est suivi de la postface "Quando typographorum" que nous avons sommairement analysée au début de notre article.

Le travail de révision, quoique important, laisse pourtant subsister d'assez lourdes erreurs. Erasme a bien corrigé un "cum" en "tamen," un "itaque" en "ita," un "ac etiam quos" en "ac eorum quos" et un inintelligible "aperta ad favorem emerentia" en "apta ad favorem emerendum," comme il se devait, mais il a laissé subsister au moins cinq fautes graves[30] qui défigurent sa pensée. La vieillesse commençait à peser sur lui, et sans doute aussi n'a-t-il pas consacré toutes les forces qui lui restaient à cet ouvrage mineur.

En dernière analyse, il nous paraît que la *Formula* est pour une bonne part une production authentique d'Erasme, (composée à un moment de sa carrière où il se passionnait pour Quintilien), et qu'elle mérite pour cette raison une attention plus grande de la critique contemporaine, bien qu'il s'agisse d'un travail peu soigné et sans commune mesure avec le *De conscribendis epistolis opus* né en quelque sorte de ses cendres. La publication de cette plaquette à Erfurt en 1520 est l'une des multiples manifestations de l'activité pédagogique du jeune humanisme réformateur en Allemagne, illustré aussi par les grands noms de Mosellanus, de Melanchthon et de Hegendorf. A cette époque, humanisme et réforme religieuse marchaient encore de pair, et Erasme était considéré, bien naturellement, comme un des champions de cette sainte alliance.

Université de Rennes

Notes

1. L'édition originale est consultable à Louvain.
2. Cf. Appendice.
3. Seuls cinq auteurs, à notre connaissance, ont parlé de la *Formula*. Ce sont:
—P. S. Allen, *Erasmi epistolae*, IV (1922), 456; XI, (1947), 286–90 et 366–67.
—A. Gerlo, " 'L'ars epistolica' et le traité d'Erasme 'De conscribendis epistolis'," *Les études classiques* (avr. 1969), pp. 98–109.
—J. D. Tracy, "On the composition dates of seven of Erasmus' writings," *BHR*, 31 (1969), 358–59.
—J. C. Margolin, Introduction au *De conscribendis epistolis*, *Opera omnia Desiderii Erasmi Roterodami*, I, 2 (1971), 157–203 et surtout pp. 160–61 et 174–75.
—J. Chomarat, *Grammaire et rhétorique chez Erasme*, (1981) pp. 1003–05.
4. Cf. P. S. Allen, *Erasmi epistolae*, IV, 456, ll. 1–7.
5. ibid., XI, 287–88, ll. 19–28.
6. ibid., XI, 286–87, ll. 1–14.
7. P. S. Allen, (*Erasmi epistolae* IV, 456, 5n) prétend avoir trouvé dans les brouillons de Basile Amerbach conservés à Bâle la mention d'un "Modum conficiendarum epistolarum Moguntiae" dont la parution aurait décidé Erasme à revoir une dernière fois le texte du *De conscribendis epistolis* et à le publier en août 1522. Malheureusement nous n'avons pu retrouver le passage en question. Si Allen ne s'est pas trompé, il s'agirait évidemment d'une des deux éditions Schoeffer de la *Formula* (septembre 1520 et février 1522).
8. Cette citation des Ἐπιστολιμαῖοι χαρακτῆρες de Libanios, inconnue des devanciers d'Erasme, fait problème, car c'est seulement le 29 mars 1499, chez Alde Manuce, à Venise, qu'ils ont paru pour la première fois, dans un volume intitulé: Ἐπιστολαὶ ζιαφόρων φιλοσόφων, ῥητόρων, σοφιστῶν, ἐξ πρὸς τοῖς εἴκοσι ... Erasme a-t-il découvert ce passage dans un manuscrit? Ou a-t-il revu ultérieurement son texte de 1498?
9. Qui l'auteur vise-t-il par cette allusion? Ce n'est pas facile à deviner.
10. Ce mot est familier à Erasme, qui l'a peut-être forgé. Sans beaucoup chercher, nous l'avons rencontré à cinq reprises dans le reste de son œuvre: dans la lettre n° 61, l. 251

(août 1497); dans le *Libellus de conscribendis epistolis*, f. XXXIX^r (texte de 1500?); dans le *De copia*, LB, I 8 C 1 (1512); dans la deuxième version du *De ratione studii*, ASD, I,2, p. 146 l. 16 (1512); dans la *Ratio seu methodus compendio perveniendi ad veram theologiam*, Holborn, p. 181 l. 29 et LB, V 77 F 7 (1518).

11. Un hapax.

12. J. D. Tracy note avec raison que ce tour se rencontre dans la lettre n° 47, l. 53 (8 novembre 1495).

13. Un emprunt à Cicéron (*Orator*, 78), qui s'est lui-même inspiré de Térence (*Andr.*, 20–21).

14. Il y a dans ce dernier cas à la fois allitération, homéotéleute et paronomase.

15. Point également noté par J. D. Tracy.

16. Nous ne nous occupons pas, bien entendu, des innombrables citations, empruntées surtout à Quintilien.

17. Erasme ne dit rien de la "petitio," souvent mentionnée pourtant.

18. L'allusion appuyée à Politien fournit un "terminus post quem" intéressant pour la datation de notre plaquette, car les lettres de Politien ont paru pour la première fois dans ses *Opera omnia* chez Alde Manuce à Venise, en juillet 1498; et la correspondance d'Erasme vers cette époque témoigne aussi de son admiration pour l'humaniste florentin (cf. la dédicace des *Adagiorum collectanea* à Mountjoy, lettre n° 126 de juin 1500, l.133).

19. Nous n'avons repéré dans la *Formula* que deux citations textuelles de Cicéron. L'une d'elles (*De oratore* I, 150) a été manifestement empruntée à l'*Institution Oratoire* (X, 3, 1). L'autre, déjà signalée dans la note 12, peut provenir du *Scribendi orandique modus* de Mancinellus (Venise, 1493).

20. Première édition: Venise, Peregrinus de Pasqualibus de Bononia (1494). Le commentaire de Valla y est joint à ceux de Pomponius et de Sulpitius. Nous n'avons pas retrouvé la trace d'une édition de 1488 signalée par J.-C. Margolin (ASD, I 2, p. 103 n. 99).

21. 1°) A propos de III, 8, 30. Texte de Valla: "Servi apud priscos poena capitali a re militari, ut scribit Martianus XL de re militari: Ab omni militia, inquit, servi prohibentur; alioqui capite puniuntur." Texte correspondant de la *Formula* (chap. "Deliberativum genus"): "cum servi tamen poena capitali a re militari arcerentur, authore Marciano jurisconsulto."

2°) A propos de III, 9, 1. Texte de Valla: "Intentio est oratio crimen debitumve alicui objiciens. Depulsio est oratio qua crimen debitumve objectum repellimus." Texte correspondant de la *Formula* (Chap. "Judiciale genus"): "Intentionem nunc dicimus accusationem, cum crimen reo intenditur. Depulsionem, cum reus objectum crimen defendit et a sese procul amolitur."

22. C'est le n° 119 du catalogue publié par F. Husner (Gedenkschrift, 1936).

23. Il n'existe encore aucun travail important sur les traités d'art épistolaire de la fin du quinzième et du début du seizième siècle. Le court article d'A. Gerlo est beaucoup trop sommaire. Voici, dans l'ordre chronologique de parution, une première liste, certainement très incomplète, de ces traités:

1468: Niccolò Perotti, *Rudimenta grammatices* (ch. "De componendis epistolis").

1470: Agostino Dati, *De variis loquendi regulis orandique modis*.

1475 (?): Antoine de Haneron, *De epistolis brevibus edendis*.

1475 (?): Pseudo-Poggio Bracciolini, *Modus epistolandi*.

1476: Carolus Virulus (= Menniken), *Epistolares formulae*.

1477 (?): Giovanni-Mario Filelfo, *Epistolare*.

1480 (?): Guilelmus Sophonensis, *Modus epistolandi*.

1485 (?): [Anonyme], *Ars epistolandi* ["Qui petis absentis ..."].

1486: Poncius, *Rhetorica*.

1486: Paul Lescher, *Rethorica*.

1488: Francesco Negro, *Opusculum scribendi epistolas.*

1489: Giovanni Sulpizio, *De componendis ornandisque epistolis.*

1492: Conrad Celtes, *Tractatus de condendis epistolis.*

1493: Antonio Mancinelli, *Scribendi orandique modus.*

1495: Niccolo Ferreto, *De elegantia linguae latinae servanda in epistolis et orationibus componendis.*

1496: Johannes Ursinus (= Baer), *Modus epistolandi.*

1500 (?): Heinrich Bebel, *Commentaria epistolarum conficiendarum.*

(avant 1501): [Jacobus Presbyter], *Ars Tulliano more epistolandi.*

1501: Josse Bade, *De epistolis componendis compendium.*

1503: Lorenzo Valla, *De conficiendis epistolis opusculum.*

1506: Marinus Becichemus Scodrensis, *Ars de componenda epistola.*

1509: Jean Despautère, *Ars epistolica.*

24. Qui dérive elle-même de celles de Cicéron (*Rep.* III, 3; *Phil.* II, 7).

25. Outre la position géographique d'Erfurt entre Mayence et Leipzig, plusieurs raisons s'opposent à ce que Schoeffer ait travaillé sur l'édition de Schumann, et en particulier le nombre de cas, une dizaine au moins, où Maler et Schoeffer offrent une même variante, différente de celle de Schumann, et surtout le fait que l'accord entre Schumann et Schoeffer contre Maler est exceptionnel (deux cas seulement).

26. Que Silvano Cavazza date de 1500 environ, c'est-à-dire d'une époque très proche de celle présumée pour la composition de la *Formula.* Cf. *Rin*, 15 (1975), 141-79.

27. "Poeticȩ": faute pour "Poetice."

28. Auteur, en 1539, de *De Germanorum prima origine, moribus, institutis, legibus et memorabilibus pace et bello gestis omnibus omnium saeculorum usque ad mensem Augustum anni 1539 libri chronici XXXI* (Bâle, Heinrich Petri).

29. Deux éditions de la *Formula* sont parues à Bâle en 1536: la première en mars, celle que nous décrivons; la deuxième en août, qui joignait au *Libellus* de Vives la *Methodus* de Celtes, et celle de Hegendorf.

30. l. 152-53: "pernullarius" (au lieu de: "parmularius"); l. 218: "et a corporis" (au lieu de: "ut a corporis"); l. 245: "poetice quid?" (au lieu de : "poetice quidem"); l. 37: "prohibete et mala. Te ..." (au lieu de: "prohibete mala, et: Te ..."; l. 398 "quanquam" (au lieu de: "quamque"). Nous doutons d'autre part que le "qualem commendas" de la citation d'Horace à la l. 335 soit bien imputable, comme le prétend Erasme dans la postface de 1536, à la négligence des éditeurs, et nous l'attribuerions plutôt à l'infidélité de la mémoire de l'auteur, et au laxisme de sa syntaxe vers 1498.

Appendice: Liste des éditions de la *Brevissima ... formula.*

— Erfurt, M. Maler (1520).

— Leipizig, V. Schumann (1520).

— Mayence, J. Schoeffer (septembre 1520).*

— Cologne, C. Caesar (12 janvier 1521).

— Paris, N. Desprez (juin 1521).

— Anvers, M. Hillen (23 juillet 1521).

— Bâle, A. Petri (septembre 1521).

— Landshut, J. Weyssenburger (1521).

— Leipzig, N. Schmidt (1521).

— Cologne, P. Quentel (1521).

— Mayence, J. Schoeffer (février 1522).

—Paris, S. de Colines (octobre 1522).
—Paris, P. Gromors (mars 1523).
—Augsbourg, S. Grim (5 août 1523).
—Paris, S. de Colines (novembre 1526).
—Cracovie, M. Scharffenberger (1527).
—Paris, C. Wechel (1530). [In: C. Hegendorf, *Methodus conscribendi epistolas*].
—Paris, S. de Colines (1532).
—Strasbourg, J. Albrecht (mars 1534). [In: Erasmus, *De conscribendis epistolis opus.*]
—Paris, P. Gaudoul (1534). [In: C. Hegendorf, *Methodus conscr. ep.*]
—Bâle, T. Platter et B. Lasius (mars 1536) [In: J. L. Vives, *De Conscr. epistolis libellus....*]
—Bâle, B. Lasius et T. Platter (août 1536). [In: J. L. Vives, *De conscr. epistolis libellus...*]
—Wittenberg, J. Klug (1536). [In: J. L. Vives, *De conscr. epistolis libellus....*]
—Leipzig, N. Schmidt (1536). [In: J. L. Vives, *De conscr. epistolis libellus....*]
—Cologne, J. Gymnich (1537). [In: J. L. Vives, *De conscr. epistolis libellus....*]
—Venise, ? (1537). [In: J. L. Vives, *de conscr. epistolis libellus....*]
—Bâle, B. Lasius (mars 1539). [In: J. L. Vives, *De conscr. epistolis libellus....*]
—Paris, S. de Colines (1539).
—Paris, C. Wechel (1541). [In: J. L. Vives, *De conscr. epistolis libellus....*]
—Bâle, R. Winter (1541). [In: J. L. Vives, *Linguae latinae exercitatio.*]
—Lyon, S. Gryphe (1542).
—Paris, S. de Colines et F. Estienne (1543).
—Cologne, Haeredes J. Gymnich (1544). [In: J. L. Vives, *De conscr. epistolis libellus....*]
—Bâle, N. Brylinger (1545). [In: A. Brandolini, *De ratione scribendi epistolas....*]
—Zürich, C. Froschauer (s. d., vers 1545). [In: J. L. Vives, *De conscr. epistolis libellus....*]
—Mayence, I. Schoeffer (1547).
—Cologne, M. Gymnich (1548). [In: J. L. Vives, *De conscr. epistolis libellus....*]
—Bâle, J. Oporinus (1549). [In: A. Brandolini, *De ratione scribendi epistolas....*]
—Mayence, I. Schoeffer (1550).
—Bâle, J. Oporinus (mars 1552). [In: Sambucus, *Epistolarum conscribendarum methodus.*]
—Bâle, N. Brylinger (1555 ?).
—Mayence, G. Wagner (1556).
—Cologne, P. Horst (1557).
—Paris, T. Richard (1557). [In: A. Brandolini, *De ratione scribendi epistolas....*]
—Bâle, J. Oporinus (mars 1558). [In: Sambucus, *Epist. conscribendarum methodus.*]
—Bâle, N. Brylinger (1561). [In: Erasmus, *De conscr. epistolis opus....*]
—Cologne, P. Horst (1563).
—Anvers, P. Nuyts (1565).
—Bâle, N. Brylinger (1567).
—Cologne, P. Horst (1569).
—Cologne, A. Birckmann (1573).
—Londres, H. Middleton (1573).
—Cologne, P. Horst (1579).
—Copenhague, H. Waldkirch (1602).

* Le baron Siegfried von Scheurl a eu l'extrême courtoisie de nous faire parvenir un microfilm de ce rarissime volume.

Les *Adages* d'Erasme et la Censure Tridentine

Christiane Lauvergnat-Gagnière

La sévérité de l'*Index* romain à l'égard d'Erasme est bien connue. L'édition de 1564 énumère les œuvres interdites, tels *Colloquiorum liber*, *Moriae encomium*, et subordonne celles qui traitent de la religion à un examen des théologiens de Paris ou de Louvain. Pour les *Adages*, la lecture en sera autorisée dans l'édition que prépare Paul Manuce; en attendant sa parution, on pourra utiliser les textes qui se trouvent sur le marché, après en avoir supprimé les passages jugés suspects par des institutions qui font autorité dans le monde catholique.[1]

Onze ans devaient s'écouler avant qu'on pût disposer d'une édition "romaine" des *Adages*, parue à Florence en 1575. Elle est l'œuvre d'Eustachio Locatello, évêque de Reggio d'Emilia, qui y avait travaillé à la demande de Thomas Manriquez, comme nous l'apprennent les pièces liminaires du recueil.[2] Tous deux avaient été procureurs de l'Ordre des Dominicains. Tous deux étaient bien en cour à Rome: Locatello avait été choisi par Pie V pour être son confesseur; et Manriquez, avec le titre de Maître du Sacré Palais, avait la haute main sur "l'imprimatur." Il ne se contentait pas toutefois de lire les ouvrages soumis à son jugement, puisqu'on lui doit, entre autres ouvrages, une édition complète de l'œuvre de Saint Thomas revue et corrigée, et celle des gloses du droit canon.[3] Ce spécialiste de la censure était sans doute trop occupé par ses responsabilités et ses travaux pour pouvoir se charger d'établir un texte des *Adages* conforme aux directives du Concile; il confia donc cette tâche à Locatello, qui l'avait achevée en 1573, quelques mois avant la mort de Paul Manuce. Le volume vit enfin le jour sur les presses florentines des Giunti, dont Alde le Jeune était le gendre et l'associé.[4]

Quelques années auparavant, un imprimeur parisien avait entrepris le même travail. La correction du texte avait été confiée à deux de ses amis que rien ne permet d'identifier;[5] nous savons seulement qu'ils étaient "fort experts aussi bien en théologie qu'en Belles-Lettres."[6] Ils achèvent leur tâche avant le Dominicain de Rome, ce qui ressemble fort à une opération commerciale réussie: l'édition parisienne des *Adages*, revus et corrigés, paraît en 1570 et connaît d'emblée un beau succès, puisqu'on en connaît cinq éditions entre 1570 et 1572, partagées entre deux libraires, Nicolas Chesneau et Michel Sonnius.

A partir de 1575, on dispose donc de deux versions nouvelles des *Adages* d'Erasme, dont la comparaison n'est pas dénuée d'intérêt. Dans l'attente d'un dépouillement complet des volumes, nous proposons ici l'étude de la quatrième Chiliade.

La page de titre de l'édition italienne, placée sous l'autorité du Pape, fait disparaître le nom d'Erasme et présente l'ouvrage comme un recueil des proverbes publiés jusqu'à ce jour. Elle annonce cependant que le texte a été expurgé de toutes les erreurs qui pourraient offenser un lecteur pieux et dévoué à la cause de la Vérité catholique; on a également supprimé les fausses interprétations et quelques digressions longues et inutiles.[7]

L'édition parisienne laisse à son auteur la paternité de l'ouvrage, qui a été "corrigé avec soin" et enrichi des remarques d'Henri Estienne.[8] La lettre du typographe au lecteur s'ouvre sur un éloge d'Erasme, avant de reconnaître que ce grand esprit avait ses faiblesses (*naevus*) qui pourraient offenser ou même blesser le lecteur pieux; il se plaisait à mêler le sacré et le profane, à parsemer ses écrits de propos sur la religion qu'il aurait mieux valu tenir en d'autres lieux plus appropriés ou passer sous silence. Le travail des censeurs à donc consisté à n'ôter du texte que ce qui est généralement contraire à la pureté de notre religion et à celle des mœurs.[9] Il faut protéger la jeunesse des audaces de jugement et de style dont Erasme s'est parfois rendu coupable; car l'érudition n'a rien à voir avec la religion, surtout lorsqu'on en parle avec la passion d'une âme blessée. Quant aux propos lascifs qu'on a supprimés, tels qu'une citation de Pétrone ou d'Aristophane, Saint Paul les a bannis; et de plus, ils n'éclairent en rien les adages où ils se trouvent. Tout semble se passer comme si l'imprimeur parisien cherchait à justifier la censure qu'Erasme à subie, mieux même à se disculper, attitude peu fréquente en semblables circonstances.

Lorsqu'il ouvre l'édition florentine, le lecteur habitué à feuilleter les *Adages* constate avec surprise que la division du texte en chiliades et centuries a disparu, ainsi que la numérotation des différents articles. A l'examen, il apparaît que ces omissions ont été nécessitées par l'élimination de nombreux proverbes (quatre-vingt-dix-huit pour la quatrième chiliade), généralement très courts.

Mais ces suppressions sont loin d'être toutes fondées sur des critères évidents. On comprend que les censeurs aient préféré faire disparaître des adages où Erasme fait état de l'impossibilité d'expliquer la généalogie du Christ (3. 70) ou des désaccords des exégètes lorsqu'il s'agit d'identifier les aveugles et les boîteux de l'Evangile (5. 47). La présence des monastères parmi les maisons qui dégénèrent sous de mauvais maîtres explique que l'adage "O domus antiqua ..." (7. 65) n'ait pu être conservé; il en est de même pour le commentaire de "Porrigere Manus" (9. 8), où la connaissance des langues est présentée comme l'auxiliaire de la théologie.

Mais rien, ni le sens de l'expression, ni les commentaires d'Erasme, ne peuvent expliquer la disparition de nombreuses rubriques, par exemple "Utrumque" (2. 37), qui se dit de ce qui peut avoir plusieurs sens; "Suspensa manu" (4. 2), qui s'applique à un travail fait d'une main légère et donc peu soigné; "Nihil simile" (4. 18), qui s'emploie pour une comparaison injustifiée; "Subinde alius" (4. 18), pour un homme soudainement changé; "Pedem conferre" (4. 48), synonyme de "se rapprocher," etc. La nécessité d'alléger le texte original pour pouvoir ajouter d'autres proverbes à ceux d'Erasme n'est pas une explication qui résiste à l'examen; dans les volumes imprimés à Paris, on peut lire des extraits de divers autres recueils contemporains sans que pour autant le texte d'Erasme ait été amputé.

Une autre forme de la censure, moins apparente au premier abord, mais plus révélatrice, est commune aux éditions parisiennes et florentines: l'adage est conservé, mais on en supprime certaines phrases, parfois quelques mots seulement.

La disparition du nom d'Erasme sur la page de titre de l'édition italienne entraîne logiquement la nécessité d'éliminer toutes les interventions personnelles de l'auteur. On remplace alors "opinor" par "opinamur," "arbitror" par "arbitramur," etc.; on supprime ici un "ni fallor," là un "nisi nasus me fallit." Les rares allusions qu'Erasme se permet à des souvenirs personnels disparaissent aussi, qu'il s'agisse d'une simple phrase, telle "Ego novi divites ..." (6. 70), d'un long développement consacré à la Hollande (6. 35), ou même de l'anodin récit d'un voyage à cheval où Erasme s'est perdu dans la forêt (8. 27). Tous ces passages sont, fort logiquement, conservés dans les éditions parisiennes.

La même divergence s'observe lorsque le texte comporte des allusions à l'Italie, que les Dominicains trouvent souvent désobligeantes. Parfois, il est vrai, Erasme attaque l'Eglise en parlant de Rome (1. 53 par ex.) ou se montre peu respectueux du prestige de la ville (8. 29). Mais les censeurs pontificaux sont parfois d'une susceptibilité qui fait sourire. Ils n'acceptent pas qu'Erasme déplore la disparition des vignobles célèbres dans l'antiquité et de leurs crus, tels ceux de Phalerne ou de Sorrente (8. 14) ou qu'il compare Venise à Corinthe pour ses courtisanes (3. 68). On le laisse critiquer les exhibitions d'ours et de singes savants qu'on peut voir en Angleterre, mais on supprime les lignes où il réprouve les spectacles donnés par des enfants bien dressés, dont il voit l'origine en Italie (4. 54), tout comme une plaisanterie sur les courses de taureaux à Rome (4. 29).

Face à ces censures anodines, des préoccupations plus sérieuses se manifestent: il faut faire disparaître des *Adages* tout ce qui porte la marque d'une époque désormais révolue, celle du début du siècle où bien des libertés de langage étaient permises. Sur ce terrain, Parisiens et Romains se rejoignent parfois, avec cependant de notables différences.

Les uns et les autres éliminent les allusions que fait Erasme à son édition du Nouveau Testament (5. 24) ou aux démêlés qui ont opposé Reuchlin aux Dominicains de Cologne (5. 64). Ils suppriment également les critiques trop virulentes des hommes d'Eglise: abandon des préceptes de l'Evangile ou des décrets des premiers Papes comme s'il s'agissait des vestiges d'un âge révolu (4. 29), faste des gardes du corps dont s'entourent les Pontifes d'aujourd'hui à l'image des Princes d'autrefois alors qu'ils n'en ont plus besoin pour assurer leur sécurité (5. 14), prétention à être les héritiers des ermites Paul ou Antoine même lorsqu'on vit en vrais Sardanapales (7. 28), débauche des chrétiens pour qui l'adultère est devenu un jeu et qui n'hésitent pas à violer des vierges (6. 25).

Mais l'édition de Paris conserve plus d'un passage qui ne trouve pas grâce aux yeux des censeurs romains. C'est ainsi qu'elle seule laisse subsister des critiques du clergé bien connues des lecteurs d'Erasme: les évêques sont souvent indignes de leurs fonctions (2. 86); les prêtres sont souvent ignorants (3. 4); pontifes, cardinaux et moines n'hésitent pas à prétendre que leurs discours sont la parole même de Dieu (5. 35). Des vieillards briguent le chapeau de Cardinal pour le seul plaisir de pouvoir inscrire leur titre sur leur tombeau (9. 6). Ceux qui font commerce des reliques se soucient moins de la piété que des profits qu'ils pourront réaliser (8. 55); tout aussi cupides sont les prêtres qui réclament de l'argent pour célébrer les offices ou administrer les sacrements (8. 48). L'Eglise est devenue un moyen de parvenir aux honneurs du Monde, et ses dignitaires ne se différencient guère des Rois et des Princes; c'est pourquoi Erasme les associe souvent dans sa réprobation (4. 3 par ex.); il n'hésite pas à rappeler que des évêques se font courtisans tout comme certains savants (5. 73), ou à dénoncer le pouvoir de l'argent qui sert à acheter des titres ecclésiastiques aussi bien que des trônes (6. 37). Les passions humaines l'emportent, et la rigueur évangélique exige désormais trop d'efforts pour être respectée: "quod volumus sanctum est" (7. 16).

Même la critique des Princes est souvent censurée plus sévèrement par les Dominicains de Rome, qui font disparaître la réprobation d'Erasme à l'égard des prodigalités des grands qui exploitent leurs peuples (5. 16) ou une rapide réflexion sur les troubles qui ravagent les Etats gouvernés par des souverains trop jeunes (5. 54). On les surprend même à remplacer le mot "monarcha" par un simple démonstratif lorsqu'il s'agit de dénoncer les abus de pouvoir (6. 11, Paris: "quadrabit in monarchas ..."; Rome: "quadrabit in eos quibus promptum est facere quicquid animo allibitum fuerit, sive jure, sive injuria").

Parmi les textes qu'il cite, Erasme n'hésite pas à faire appel à l'Evangile. C'est encore une occasion pour les Dominicains d'exercer leur censure rarement prise en défaut,[10] affirmant ainsi la nécessité de protéger la lecture de l'Ecriture contre tous les dangers de l'érudition profane, où cependant les Pères de l'Eglise gardent droit de cité. Par là sans doute s'explique aussi la suppression du commentaire de l'adage "Tam perit quam extrema faba" (4. 72) qui subsiste dans l'édition de Paris: "c'est comme si on disait que la théologie périt comme l'extrémité de la fève pour être traitée par des profanes et des hérétiques," ou quelques mots dirigés contre les vieux "scotistes" (3. 93).[11]

Le traitement subi par le premier adage de la quatrième chiliade, le célèbre "Dulce bellum inexpertis," illustre à merveille, les principes qui nous semblent avoir guidé les censeurs et les révèlent, pour ainsi dire, au premier coup d'œil.

L'édition florentine ne laisse subsister de ce long adage que quelques lignes.[12]

Certes, les censeurs de Paris ont, eux aussi, supprimé avec soin plusieurs passages de ce texte enrichi par Erasme à plusieurs reprises: l'attaque dirigée contre les princes grossiers de notre temps (l. 336–39); la dénonciation des prédicateurs qui justifient la guerre du haut de la chaire en détournant de leur sens certains textes de l'Ecriture (l. 351–86); la longue invective contre ceux qui mettent les écrits d'Aristote au-dessus de l'Evangile et contre le pouvoir temporel des évêques (l. 624–70); une critique de la notion de guerre juste (l. 791–805); celle du clergé corrompu par l'argent qui prêche la guerre contre les Turcs, alors que les Infidèles sont sans doute beaucoup plus proches du Christ que beaucoup d'entre nous (l. 1006–45); la mise au grand jour de l'ambition des Princes qui utilisent la guerre pour exploiter leurs peuples (l. 1070–74) et de la mauvaise foi des théologiens et des jurisconsultes (l. 1095–97); enfin, l'appel à la tolérance (l. 1080–85).

Mais si la virulence du propos d'Erasme est quelque peu atténuée, le sens de l'adage demeure: les Chrétiens ne peuvent légitimer la guerre qu'en étant infidèles au message du Christ dont ils se réclament. L'Evangile ne peut triompher par une trahison aussi flagrante, même si des prélats devenus princes temporels savent justifier leurs entreprises par des arguments spécieux. La guerre contre les Infidèles ne peut être acceptée au nom de la religion, qui ne gagnera pas de nouveaux adeptes par la force. Quant aux hostilités qui opposent des pays limitrophes, elles sont au service de l'ambition des grands, engendrent la corruption morale et la décadence des belligérants et mettent aux prises des hommes qui tous se proclament disciples du Christ, ce qui est le comble de l'absurdité.

Quelques lignes choisies parmi tant de pages conservées par l'édition parisienne suffiront à prouver que le texte d'Erasme n'a rien perdu de sa force: "On soupçonne d'hérésie celui qui prêche avec véhémence contre la guerre; et ceux qui … énervent l'enseignement évangélique et fournissent aux princes l'occasion de satisfaire leurs désirs sont orthodoxes et docteurs en piété chrétienne. Un docteur vraiment chrétien n'approuve jamais la guerre; il la permet peut-être dans certains cas, mais contre son gré et avec douleur" (l. 815–20).

Au terme de ce rapide examen, dont les conclusions devront être confrontées avec celles qu'imposera le dépouillement du recueil des *Adages* en son entier,[13] il apparaît que, si les censeurs parisiens ont bien supprimé les audaces de langage les plus hardies d'Erasme, sa pensée n'en est pas profondément altérée. Et peut-être l'éloge qui est fait de lui dans l'épître au lecteur prend-il alors tout son sens: les recommandations du Concile ont été respectées, mais Erasme continuera à être lu grâce à cet ouvrage protégé, en quelque sorte, par sa facture érudite.

Rien de tel avec le recueil révisé par les Dominicains de Rome, qui ont voulu supprimer jusqu'au nom d'Erasme. Avec eux, les *Adages* ne sont plus qu'un morne dictionnaire de citations sans nerfs ni sang.

Son usage fut limité, semble-t-il, à la Péninsule, sans y connaître un grand succès; on n'en compte que trois éditions pendant le dernier quart du siècle. L'édition parisienne eut plus de succès, sans toutefois franchir les frontières, les pays germaniques restant fidèles à l'édition originale de Bâle.[14]

C'est dire que le travail des censeurs ne nous apparaît plus aujourd'hui que comme un accident dans la tradition des *Adages*. Leurs efforts ne parvinrent pas à étouffer une pensée déjà trop largement répandue dans les milieux intellectuels européens pour être réduite au silence.

Université de Saint-Etienne

Notes

1. "Desiderii Erasmi Roterodami *Colloquiorum liber, Moria, Lingua, Christiani matrimonii institutio, De interdicto esu carnium,* ejusdem *Paraphrasis in Mattheum* quae a Bernardino Tomitano in Italicam linguam conversa est. Caetera vero ipsius opera in quibus de religione tractat, tamdiu prohibita sint quamdiu a facultate theologica Parisiensi vel Lovaniensi expurgata non fuerint. Adagia vero ex editione quam molitur Paulus Manutius, permittentur; interim vero quae jam edita sunt, expunctis locis suspectis judicio alicujus facultatis theologicae universitatis catholicae vel inquisitionis alicujus generalis, permittantur." Cité d'après Reusch, *Die Indices librorum prohibitorum ...* (Tübingen, 1886) (Reprint, Nieuwkoop, 1961), p. 259.

2. "Ego frater Eustachius Locatellus ordinis praedicatorum, Episcopus Regii, attestor quatenus precibus Reverendi Fratris Thomae Manrique, olim Magistri sacri Palatii, Adagia Erasmi perlegi et castigavi, et ea ab omnibus quae religionem Christianam et pias lectoris aures offendere poterant expurgavi, et sic castigata et expurgata eidem Reverendo Magistro Sacri Palatii ostendi; quae demum ipso approbante Paullo Manutio excudenda tradita fuerunt." Cité d'après F. Van der Haeghen, *Bibliotheca Belgica,* rééd. par M. Th. Lenger (Bruxelles, 1964), p. 315.

3. *D. Thomae Aquinitatis opera tomis XVII comprehensa* (Rome, 1570). *Censura in glossas et additiones juris canonici omnibus exemplaribus* (Rome, 1572). Cf. Echard J., *Scriptores ordinis praedicatorum ...* (Paris, 1721), T. II, 230.

4. La déclaration de Locatello (citée n. 2) est datée du 27 février 1573, l'autorisation d'imprimer, du 15 mars de la même année. C'est donc bien la mort de Paul Manuce qui a retardé la parution de l'ouvrage, comme l'explique son fils dans sa dédicace au Pape Grégoire XIII.

5. L'un d'eux pourrait bien avoir été Claude Mignault, qui a complété le recueil de 1570 par un choix d'adages "ad studiosorum commoditatem," précédé d'une préface (datée de septembre 1570). Dans ce même recueil figure une ode latine de Mignault.

6. "... a duobus amicis, in theologia egregie versatis et politioribus litteris apprime eruditis, contendi ut et Consilii Tridentini decreto et studiosorum voluntati facerent satis." ("Typographus lectori.")

7. *Adagia quaecumque ad hanc diem exierunt Paulli Manutii studio atque industria, doctissimorum Theologorum consilio atque ope, ex praescripto Sacrosancti Consilii Tridentini, Gregorio XIII Pont. Max. auspice, ab omnibus mendis vendicata quae pium et veritatis Catholicae studiosum lectorem poterant offendere. Sublatis falsis interpretationibus et nonnullis quae nihil ad rem pertinebant longis inanibusque*

digressionibus. C'est le titre de l'édition de 1585. Pour la description précise de l'édition de 1575, cf. *Bibliotheca Belgica*, p. 307 et sq.

8. *Adagiorum Des. Erasmo Roterdami Chiliades quator cum sesquicenturia; magna cum diligentia maturoque judicio emendatae et expurgatae, quibus adjectae sunt Henrici Stephani Animadversiones, suis quaeque loci sparsim digestae.* (Titre de l'édition de 1579; les éditions recensées par la *Bibliotheca Belgica* y sont décrites en détail.)

9. "… jam diu neglectam ab aliis provinciam lubenter susceperunt, susceptamque ita obiverunt nihil ut resecandum putarent praeter ea quae religionis nostrae sinceritati et integritati morum officere solent."

10. La perspicacité semble parfois faire défaut aux censeurs romains. L'adage 6. 51, "Sacer manipulus," cite Athénée selon lequel il s'agissait d'un corps d'armée où étaient réunis amants et aimés qui puisaient dans leur attachement mutuel une grande force et le mépris de la mort. Erasme ajoute: "On pourra en user en disant que la cause de la chrétienté dépend aujourd'hui des moines comme d'un manipule sacré." L'édition parisienne préfère supprimer ce commentaire, que le Dominicain de Rome conserve pour n'en avoir sans doute pas vu la perfidie.

11. Contrairement à l'édition de Paris, celle de Florence supprime toutes les citations de l'Ecriture, sauf en 8. 27 où est conservée la maxime du *Livre de Sira* ou *Ecclésiastique*.

La suppression de la référence au Symbole d'Athanase, dont l'orthodoxie était suspectée, nécessitait une correction du texte, absente de l'édition florentine où l'adage commence par les mots "huis simillimum" qui ne renvoient plus à rien. Les censeurs de Paris remanient le texte pour lui laisser un sens.

12. Nous utilisons ici l'édition qui en a été donnée par Y. Rémy et R. Dunil-Marquebreucq, "Latomus" (Bruxelles, 1953).

13. M. Jolidon nous a fait remarquer qu'à son avis, d'après l'étude de l'adage "Scarabeus," l'édition de Paris est attentive à ne pas conserver les critiques des Princes.

14. Cette édition ne cesse d'être lue sans doute, puisque le *Novissimus librorum prohibitorum et expurgandorum Index,* édité à Madrid en 1640 (qui reproduit l'Index dit "de Plantin" daté de 1570), donne la liste des passages qui sont à supprimer dans le texte original des *Adages.* On s'en tient ici à l'essentiel; six articles seulement doivent être expurgés: le "dulce bellum," réduit à quelques lignes (jusqu'à "cunctationem"), les adages 5. 24, 7. 28, et 7. 64, censurés dans les éditions que nous avons étudiées, et deux titres censurés sans la seule édition dite "Manuce": 7. 16, qui a le droit de conserver une phrase de plus, et 8. 48.

Scaliger et Erasme

Michel Magnien

V*anus ac mendax, parricida, monstrum, labes, Furia*, telles sont, parmi tant d'autres, les épithètes que Scaliger lance contre Erasme après qu'il a publié son *Ciceronianus*.[1] Pourquoi tant de violence? Ce médecin, encore obscur, souhaite arracher au prince de l'humanisme, si prompt à la réplique, une de ces *antapologiae* qui mettrait aussitôt son nom en lumière. Il provoque donc.

Mais le pamphlétaire a trop souvent masqué le théoricien qui entend, face à Erasme, affirmer sa conception de l'imitation, voire de l'humanisme. Aussi, sans nous laisser arrêter par sa réputation de scandale, nous chercherons dans un premier temps à dégager les lignes de force de l'*Oratio pro M. Tullio Cicerone*; puis nous examinerons la réaction d'Erasme face à cette attaque; nous nous interrogerons enfin sur le sort fait à Erasme dans l'œuvre de Scaliger.

L'*Oratio prima* est avant tout une réponse au *Ciceronianus*, que Scaliger, malgré les affirmations de son fils,[2] a lu et bien lu: nous n'y avons pas relevé moins de 170 citations ou allusions au dialogue d'Erasme. Malgré l'annonce d'un plan (f. Avii^v), le discours semble constitué d'une série de remarques faites au fil de la lecture, qui s'enchaînent sans autre lien logique que le texte qu'elles contredisent de bout en bout. Ce décousu permet à Scaliger d'aborder, non sans ostentation, les disciplines les plus diverses, la rhétorique, la métrique, la philologie, bien sûr, mais aussi la médecine, l'histoire naturelle et la philosophie. L'Agenais affirme ainsi son savoir, face aux erreurs qu'Erasme aurait commises en ces domaines. Mais chemin faisant, il répond aussi aux deux principales questions soulevées par Erasme dans le *Ciceronianus*: éloquence et imitation, éloquence et religion.

Erasme avait montré qu'il n'existe pas de modèle parfait, et que Cicéron, le meilleur d'entre eux, n'est pas exempt de défauts difficilement évitables. Il invitait donc ses contemporains à choisir, à l'image du peintre Zeuxis, plusieurs modèles, afin de retenir chez chacun d'entre eux ce qu'il y a de meilleur. Scaliger admet cette démarche; mais il existe selon lui un état idéal de la langue, rejoint à la fin de l'ère républicaine, "elegantissima aetas" (f. Eiiii^v). Le choix s'opérera dans ces limites temporelles précises: Caelius, Brutus, les contemporains de Cicéron (f. Dii^r–Dii^v).

Toutefois, le plus sage sera encore de choisir un seul auteur parfait, pour s'épargner des peines inutiles (f. Dviii^v). Et l'imitation du "censeur de la langue romaine" (f. D^v) sera moins le respect de la lettre que de l'esprit cicéronien: il existe des barbarismes à rejeter, cependant Cicéron, par son exemple, nous invite à élargir notre vocabulaire (f. Dii^v–Diii^r).

Scaliger va plus loin: renoncer à un modèle unique, c'est renoncer à se donner un idéal; se complaire dans la *varietas*, c'est en définitive sombrer dans le pyrrhonisme et aboutir à l'échec (f. Gviii^v). Erasme affirmait dans le *Ciceronianus* qu'il ne faut jamais forcer son talent; or cette nécessité de garder intact son *genius* est un leurre, puisqu'une trop forte conscience de ses limites, le manque d'audace stérilisent l'individu. La métaphore médicale relevée dans le *Ciceronianus* le prouve: Erasme redoute l'excès de santé par crainte de la maladie;[3] il ne visera donc pas à la perfection par peur de l'échec.

Et l'Agenais scelle son opposition farouche à ce qu'il considère comme une école de découragement dans un long éloge des études presque provocateur dans sa revendication de la souffrance (f. Gii^v–Giii^v). On ne naît pas orateur, on le devient (f. Fiii^r); la vertu n'est pas un état statique, c'est une marche vers la perfection. La perfection du style exige de grands sacrifices, une longue ascèse; elle est une conquête héroïque sur l'angoisse de la mort: notre effort ne sera-t-il pas récompensé par l'immortalité de notre gloire? Nous devrons ainsi par tous les moyens tenter d'atteindre à la pureté cicéronienne.

Rien, en dépit des affirmations d'Erasme, n'empêchera un Chrétien d'imiter Cicéron. L'Arpinate était un esprit universel, qui sut adapter ses talents oratoires à tous les types d'expression; si nous l'imitons, nous parviendrons, comme lui, à parler de manière adéquate à la dignité de notre sujet, fût-il théologique. Rien ne nous interdira, tout en conservant les noms et les titres de la religion chrétienne, d'habiller d'une éloquence classique et cicéronienne les vérités exprimées jadis dans un latin raboteux et barbare (f. Fvi^r–Fvi^v). Les mots ne sont pas par eux-mêmes chargés de valeur morale et il ne saurait exister une subordination de l'élocution à l'invention, comme le prouvent les éloges paradoxaux, dont les auteurs ne manquent pas d'éloquence. Refuser d'imiter Cicéron dans la rédaction de textes religieux revient à priver la religion de toute éloquence; un Cicéronien possédera une force de persuasion inégalée pour démontrer la grandeur de la foi, à l'exemple de Paul, qui n'a pas hésité à recourir aux procédés de la rhétorique païenne pour convaincre son auditoire (f. Bv^v).

Erasme ne cessait de souligner dans le *Ciceronianus* la coupure entre pensée antique et révélation chrétienne; il y condamnait les conceptions qui tendaient à ne faire de la religion chrétienne que le prolongement de la philosophie païenne. Scaliger rappelle de son côté la dette de Thomas et de Duns Scot à l'égard d'Aristote (f. Gviii^r); la philosophie chrétienne et la philosophie antique sont pour lui comparables sur le plan de l'éthique; et les spéculations des philosophes anciens sont nécessaires aux chrétiens dans l'affermissement de leur foi. Pensée chrétienne et pensée païenne doivent donc cohabiter, puisque complémentaires. D'où la nécessité d'une connaissance approfondie de la réflexion et des mœurs antiques, apportée même par des objets aussi dérisoires qu'une stèle ou qu'une pièce de monnaie.

Le beau plaidoyer que l'Agenais prononce en faveur de l'archéologie et de l'épigraphie (f. Giii^v-Gvi^r), face au dédain d'Erasme pour ces disciplines, marque ainsi que le culte exclusif du Christ ne saurait emplir notre vie. Car l'existence est une succession d'activités bien distinctes, toutes pareillement respectables. On ne saurait pour tous privilégier la prière et la méditation au détriment du commerce ou de l'agriculture (f. Gvii^r-Gvii^v). Scaliger dénonce par là une attitude qui, sous prétexte de sainteté, pourrait nous ramener à la barbarie; il renvoie la balle dans le camp d'Erasme, qui, sous couvert du Cicéronianisme, voyait pointer le paganisme. Bref, le christocentrisme érasmien, dans sa volonté d'imposer à tous et partout la parole et le culte du Sauveur, risque d'aboutir à une dévaluation du sentiment religieux. L'existence de plusieurs centres d'intérêt fera ressortir la prééminence du divin. Car mettre le Christ partout, c'est ne le placer nulle part (f. Gvi^v).

On voit avec quelle force Scaliger affirme son orthodoxie, nous serions tentés de dire son conservatisme. Outre son rejet de la philosophie scolastique, il reproche encore à Erasme de critiquer les ordres religieux ou d'appliquer la philologie à l'écriture, ce qui l'amène à remettre en question les institutions et les dogmes de l'Eglise (f. Ciii^v, Cvi^v). Dans cette dénonciation d'une pensée qui tend à ne plus faire allégeance à Rome, Scaliger rejoint ses compatriotes Italiens. L'Agenais combat donc aussi sur un plan idéologique. Le *Ciceronianus* visait, selon lui, à la remise en cause de la suprématie romaine dans la *translatio studii*; et il n'a pas de mots assez durs pour flétrir l'ingratitude d'Erasme à l'égard des savants italiens qui lui ont fait partager leur savoir, et sa jalousie face à l'éloquence romaine, encore éclatante après quinze cents ans.

Ainsi s'explique, en matière religieuse comme en matière littéraire, cette volonté affirmée de nier toute solution de continuité entre passé et présent: la gloire de la Rome antique lui fournit, malgré tous les démentis, une raison d'exalter la puissance de la Rome papale. Au nom du primat latin, du dogme chrétien et de l'évangile cicéronien, Scaliger part en guerre contre la *Barbaries* du Nord et contre celui qui, à ses yeux, l'incarne, "le Pape de Bâle" (f. B^v).

Joignant sa voix aux adversaires les plus tenaces d'Erasme, Cajetan ou A. Pio, Scaliger fait à son tour de l'humaniste de Bâle le disciple, ou plutôt le maître, du théologien de Wittenberg. Par l'*Eloge de la folie*, où l'on découvre un irrespect tout lucianique pour l'Eglise et ses institutions, par les *Paraphrases* ou les *Colloques*, Erasme a ouvert dans l'édifice de la religion chrétienne une brèche où s'est engouffré Luther. A tout moment Scaliger rappelle la condamnation de ces ou-

vrages par la Sorbonne (f. Aii^v, Av^r, Avii^v, Cviii^v...); il en loue les professeurs
(f. Fviii^v); il évoque la liesse de la population parisienne devant le bûcher où
brûlent les ouvrages condamnés (f. Fvii^v); si bien qu'Erasme ira imaginer que
Noël Béda a "déversé un peu de son venin" (Allen, 2635, 41) dans le pamphlet.
Et il ne manquera pas, avec ses disciples parisiens, de mettre en relation la parution dans la capitale, à quelques mois d'intervalle, des *Censures* de la Sorbonne
et de l'*Oratio* de Scaliger (Allen, 2579, 33–36; 2613, 36–42).

Erasme ne prend pas connaissance de ce texte, malgré les affirmations de l'Agenais,[4] avant son impression. Scaliger, après avoir dédié son discours aux étudiants de Paris, afin de lui donner le plus de retentissement possible, en avait
envoyé le manuscrit, vers la fin de 1529, au Collège de Navarre; et l'on sait qu'il
y disparut. Mais personne n'en fit alors parvenir copie à Erasme, puisque le Rotterdamois n'en fait aucune mention dans sa correspondance avant novembre 1531,
date à laquelle B. Amerbach lui en transmit un exemplaire qu'il venait de re-
cevoir de Paris.

La réaction d'Erasme fut immédiate: dans les prises de position anti-luthé-
riennes, dans les allusions à son séjour vénitien, il reconnut, et il l'affirme à plus
de quinze reprises, la plume du "scurra mitratus" (Allen, 2577, 23), de Jérôme
Aléandre, dont "il ne connaissait pas moins le style que le visage" (Allen, 2581,
5–6; 2613, 43–45). Le légat du Pape désirait, selon Erasme (Allen, 2565, 13–18;
2682, 50–54), se venger par là des attaques que ce dernier avait, à mots couverts,
lancées contre lui dans son *Apologia ad Albertum Pium*; et il publiait ce "libellum
plusquam famosum ac simpliciter furiosum" (Allen, 2620, 32) en s'abritant sous
un nom d'emprunt.

Indigné de tels procédés, Erasme tentera d'interrompre par voie de justice la
diffusion de ce brûlot. Dès la fin de novembre 1531, il écrit à Jean Morin, qui
avait signé le privilège imprimé à la fin du libelle, pour lui ouvrir les yeux: soit
ce privilège est un faux, soit le lieutenant de baillage a été abusé, car cet ouvrage
diffamatoire ne méritait aucune autorisation; dans les deux cas, il faut punir les
scélérats qui sont à l'origine de cette publication illégale (Allen, 2577). Et comme
le conservateur des privilèges se montre rétif, demande des gages à Erasme par
l'intermédiaire de Jacques Omphalius, le Rotterdamois lui envoie une seconde
lettre (Allen, 2635) pour le rassurer et l'inviter à agir sans tarder. Il semble bien
cependant que les partisans d'Erasme aient pris les devants et se soient attachés
(comme l'affirme Rabelais dans sa fameuse lettre adressée au Rotterdamois) à
faire disparaître les exemplaires du discours en les brûlant.

Un autre moyen de faire tomber le pamphlet dans l'oubli était de feindre de
l'ignorer, même si Erasme, malgré ses affirmations réitérées de mépris ("nondum
perlegi" Allen, 2682, 23; 2736, 12; 2810, 83–84), a bien lu le discours.[5] Ainsi
s'ourdit parmi les Erasmiens une conjuration du silence; puisqu'il se refuse à
répondre, le Rotterdamois invite ses *famuli* et ses correspondants à ne pas cé-
der à la provocation: "nullum videtur aptius ultionis genus quam silentium."[6]
Et lorsqu'un partisan trop zélé, Jacques Jaspar, dit Danus, décochera quelques

épigrammes vengeresses à Scaliger, Erasme s'en plaindra amèrement: "non est movenda Camarina" (Allen, 2792, 56; v. aussi 2736, 12–13).

Par la suite, Erasme feindra de même d'ignorer toutes les diatribes suscitées par la publication du *Ciceronianus*. Seul Pietro Corsi se verra honoré d'une réponse, et encore s'était-il attaqué aux *Adages*, non au fameux dialogue. Pourquoi cette réserve, alors qu'Erasme est si prompt à la riposte? Il a bien répondu à la Sorbonne, mais il se déclare trop offensé pour répliquer à de telles attaques (Allen, 2690, 29–33). Est-ce bien là la raison? Les *Censures* de la Sorbonne ou les œuvres d'A. Pio, comme nous le verrons, n'étaient guère plus amènes que ce pamphlet. Faut-il voir dans ce mépris affiché le signe d'une lassitude, après tant d'années de combat? A moins qu'Erasme n'ait pressenti que cette polémique littéraire, engagée par des inconnus, était — à la différence des attaques en matière de religion — sans danger pour son autorité et son prestige, et que la violence de ces "jeunes Italiens" les discréditait assez, sans qu'il fût besoin de perdre son temps et son énergie à les combattre.

Aussi, il nous paraît bien hasardeux de voir dans *Opulentia sordida* une réponse détournée aux insinuations de l'Agenais. Publié en septembre 1531, avant même qu'Erasme ait eu connaissance du pamphlet de Scaliger, ce Colloque, dans sa description de l'avarice d'Asulanus, semble pourtant bien faire écho à la dénonciation par l'Agenais de la goinfrerie et de l'ivrognerie d'Erasme, ravalé pour la circonstance au rang de correcteur d'imprimerie. Mais toutes ces accusations se trouvent déjà dans l'œuvre posthume d'Alberto Pio, parue au début de 1531.[7] C'est donc au Prince de Carpi que répond Erasme dans *Opulentia Sordida*, d'autant plus qu'il n'hésitera pas, dans un autre colloque paru la même année, *Exsequiae seraphicae*, à dépeindre son agonie et son inhumation avec une ironie grinçante.

Lorsque l'on sait que le père de Scaliger, le miniaturiste Benedetto Bordone, a, comme A. Pio, fréquenté l'Académie Aldine, la convergence des témoignages devient troublante et amène à penser que l'attitude d'Erasme, s'isolant dans sa chambre pour y déguster de copieux repas, avait profondément froissé les susceptibilités vénitiennes.

Malgré le démenti formel donné par Aléandre (Allen, 2638 et 2639), malgré les informations fournies par Rabelais (Allen, 2763) sur ce médecin agenais qu'il dit bien connaître, Erasme continuera longtemps de dénier toute réalité à Scaliger. Et lorsqu'il aura fini par admettre l'existence d'un auteur portant ce nom, qui publie en 1533 un recueil d'épigrammes,[8] il en fera un jouet entre les mains d'Aléandre, un des multiples conspirateurs du complot cicéronien, tendant à susciter au sein de la République des Lettres des dissensions aussi tragiques que celles causées par les Luthériens dans la Chrétienté (Allen, 2600, 22–23; 2682, 11–13; 3005, 9–11).

Erasme rattache donc sans cesse Scaliger à cette "factio qui fervet apud Italos" (Allen, 2599, 65–66), à cette troupe de "juvenes male feriati," prétendument menée par Aléandre, dont les menaces — réelles ou imaginaires — assombriront les dernières années de son existence, et où le vieillard moribond verra finalement

la main du Diable (Allen, 3127, 48–50). Est-ce un hasard, si, lorsqu'Erasme rédige la dernière lettre que nous possédons de lui, il manifeste encore ce sentiment
d'être poursuivi de la haine inexpiable d'Aléandre, et si le nom de Scaliger revient une dernière fois sous sa plume (Allen, 3130, 16–17)?

En dépit de sa volonté, les sentiments d'Erasme furent en définitive révélés
à l'Agenais, alors qu'il desespérait d'obtenir jamais réponse, quatre longues années après la parution de l'*Oratio prima*. Une lettre d'Erasme, adressée à deux correspondants italiens (Allen, 3005) lui parvint en effet par le circuit des libraires:
le Rotterdamois l'y accusait d'avoir "chaussé le soulier d'un autre," et ne voyait
dans le discours que mensonge, impudence et folie furieuse. Piqué au vif, Scaliger prit aussitôt la plume pour revendiquer la paternité du discours et déverser
sur Erasme une nouvelle série d'invectives, moins rhétoriques, sans doute, que
les premières.[9]

Il avait naguère opéré une critique serrée du *Cicéronianus*, il va maintenant
disséquer la lettre d'Erasme, qu'il placera au devant de son discours, comme
un trophée arraché à l'ennemi. Ulcéré, Scaliger feint d'exulter: il a enfin obtenu
réponse et Erasme a changé de langage; après avoir décrié les Cicéroniens, il
clame maintenant son amitié pour Bembo ou Sadolet. Mais ce qui irrite le plus
l'Agenais est de ne pas deviner qui Erasme a bien pu mettre derrière son nom
(f. F^v–F2^r).

Ce deuxième discours, plus injurieux que le premier, présente moins d'intérêt
pour notre sujet, puisque Scaliger y fournit de nombreux détails biographiques,
afin de prouver son existence et la réalité de ses travaux; il ne fait surtout qu'y
réaffirmer les conclusions de l'*Oratio prima*, sans approfondir les positions théoriques adoptées alors: Erasme veut détruire le prestige de Cicéron pour faire va-
loir à sa place sa *varietas* et sa *copia*; or son latin est relâché, son style ambigu et
obscur; ses œuvres sont le fruit de l'improvisation, quand ce n'est pas de la compilation; Erasme, à la différence de Longueil,[10] se refuse à tout effort pour con-
quérir l'éloquence romaine. Le culte du travail et de l'effort se manifeste ici à travers l'évocation du passé militaire de Scaliger, contrepoint au pacifisme érasmien,
et période préparatoire aux souffrances endurées par l'humaniste.

Les lettres que Scaliger adresse à son ami A. Le Ferron,[11] après que ce dernier lui a reproché de partir de nouveau à la charge, sont encore plus violentes.
Il est irrité de voir l'un de ses proches tenter de prendre la défense d'Erasme.
L'invective est alors à son comble: dans aucun domaine, Erasme n'a renouvelé
la connaissance; tout ce qu'il a apporté de neuf, c'est une "nova theologiae facies"
et une "nova loquacitas."

Malgré ce que son fils a pu faire croire à beaucoup,[12] la mort d'Erasme ne
changera rien aux sentiments de Scaliger, seul le ton s'apaisera un peu. Ainsi,
il semble bien avoir relancé, en 1537, ses amis parisiens, pour obtenir l'impression de l'*Oratio secunda*, elle aussi retardée; et il continuera de s'en prendre à l'humaniste défunt dans une œuvre parue deux ans plus tard, le *De Comicis dimen-*

sionibus.[13] Ce traité de métrique est, d'un bout à l'autre, une attaque en règle d'Erasme, sur l'un de ses terrains de prédilection. Pied à pied, vers après vers, Scaliger y marque son désaccord avec les options prises par l'auteur du *Convivium Poeticum* ou par l'éditeur des œuvres de Sénèque et surtout de Térence. C'est en effet une édition du dramaturge latin, parue en 1532, où Erasme avait en marge indiqué le type de mètre employé dans les échanges et éclairci les difficultés de scansion, qui est la cible particulière de Scaliger. Après avoir dénié toute valeur théologique aux travaux d'Erasme, il tentait là de détruire sa réputation de grammairien.

Si l'on en croit ses affirmations renouvelées, Scaliger aurait d'ailleurs rédigé, entre les deux discours publiés, une troisième harangue, où il prétendait démontrer à quel point Erasme avait desservi les Belles-Lettres. Comme l'on connaît son habitude de remodeler continuellement ses œuvres, d'en modifier les titres et la destination, afin de gonfler artificiellement sa bibliographie, on est en droit de se demander si le *De Comicis dimensionibus* n'est pas — avec un commentaire des *Adages* auquel il fait par ailleurs allusion[14] — un fragment de cette troisième harangue, que Scaliger serait parvenu à faire publier, en masquant son contenu réél sous un titre anodin.

Et dans le *De Causis* ou la *Poétique*, naturellement,[15] mais même dans des œuvres aussi éloignées des préoccupations d'Erasme que ses commentaires sur les traités d'Aristote et de Théophraste ou les *Exercitationes*,[16] Scaliger ne manquera jamais une occasion de relever ce qu'il appelle "les erreurs du Batave." Vivant de sa plume Erasme a, selon lui, été contraint de produire une quantité d'œuvres énorme, qui portent toutes la marque de l'improvisation et de l'inachèvement.[17] Doué d'un esprit et d'une capacité de travail remarquables, cet auteur brouillon s'est complu dans les disciplines du *Trivium*: il n'a jamais été pour l'Agenais qu'un *grammaticus* (*Or. I*, f. G^r ou Bviii^v).

Aussi, Scaliger semble vouloir mettre les générations futures en garde contre le mirage érasmien: si le Rotterdamois pouvait pallier un certain manque de travail par ses facilités (*ingenii magnitudo: Poétique*, p. 364), trop de gens ont cru pouvoir l'imiter, sans posséder ses ressources; seuls le travail et l'effort apportent la gloire, lorsque l'on n'a pas à sa disposition les charmes de la "mirifica latinitas" érasmienne, contre lesquels Scaliger met son fils aîné en garde (*ibid.*, p. 176D').

Rival de Gorgias (*Or. I*, f. Bvii^v), Erasme s'est fait fort d'aborder tous les sujets; trop fidèle à ses chers Grecs, il en adopté tous les travers: si le Rotterdamois avait opposé sophistique païenne et philosophie chrétienne, Scaliger voit bien en lui le prototype du sophiste chrétien.

Le fossé est large et profond: d'un côté le Rotterdamois, dont on peut se demander s'il a jamais réellement vu quelqu'un d'autre qu'Aléandre derrière le nom de Scaliger, de l'autre, l'Agenais qui, à travers son œuvre, a voulu dénoncer les faux-semblants de l'œuvre érasmienne. Et pourtant la postérité, Joseph Scaliger le premier, s'est ingéniée à combler ce fossé, à gommer l'antagonisme.

Tant de pages écrites par Scaliger contre Erasme semblent dès lors s'effacer derrière deux témoins d'une fugitive et peu sincère palinodie: une lettre à Jacques Omphalius, exprimant le désir d'une réconciliation, un court tombeau à la gloire de l'humaniste défunt.[18] Et les auteurs qui évoqueront le différent entre les deux hommes considéreront tous l'épitaphion de Scaliger comme son dernier mot.

Comment ne pas voir ici le désir de réconcilier, malgré le poids des textes, deux grands esprits dont l'affrontement dut paraître incongru aux générations ultérieures; désir manifesté par l'insertion, dans le recueil que Paul Mérula publie en hommage à Erasme, du tombeau composé par Scaliger,[19] par l'impression de la même pièce en tête d'une édition hollandaise des Colloques,[20] jadis si décriés par l'Agenais, ou par la réunion, côte à côte, de l'effigie des deux humanistes dans le cabinet de travail d'un Guy Patin?[21]

Pau

Notes

1. Dans l'*Oratio pro M. T. Cicerone contra Des. Erasmum Roterodamum*, Paris, Pierre Vidoue, s.d. (privilège *in fine*, daté du 1er sept. 1531), in-8° de 62ff. non chif. (nous renvoyons à cette édition entre parenthèses pour nos citations).

Nous préparons actuellement une édition des deux discours (1531 & 1537) de Scaliger contre Erasme, qui formera un des prochains volumes de la Collection des "Travaux d'Humanisme et Renaissance" de la maison Droz, à Genève. Nous y renvoyons le lecteur, qui trouvera là tous les éléments appuyant notre démonstration, que nous n'avons pu, faute de place, donner ici.

2. "Peut-être mon Pere n'avoit pas lû ou n'entendoit pas Erasme." *Scaligerana*, Cologne, Scagen, 1667, p. 73.

3. *Ciceronianus* (éd. Gambaro, Brescia, 1965), ll. 1445–1450; v. la longue argumentation de Scaliger, f. Fiii^v–Fv^v.

4. Scaliger prétend en effet dans deux lettres (*Epistolae aliquot nunc primum vulgatae*, Toulouse, R. Colomiez, 1620, ep. II & XII, p. 10 & 25) que les étudiants parisiens ont intercepté son discours pour le transmettre à Erasme. Sur les déconvenues connues par Scaliger lors de l'impression de ses deux discours contre Erasme, v. notre art. *BHR*, XLIV, 2 (1982), pp. 307–29.

5. Les citations qu'il fait de l'*Oratio I* à ses correspondants (Allen, 2577, 6–12; 2581, 7–11; 2682, 25–49), sont en effet puisées dans des passages répartis sur l'œuvre entière.

6. Allen, 3127, 39–40; la formule s'applique à Dolet. Mais cette conviction est partagée par tous les admirateurs d'Erasme, de B. Amerbach, qui ne montrera le discours de Scaliger à personne (Allen, 2564, 5–6: il le reçoit depuis Paris de J. Sphyractès et non de Ph. Montanus; 2574, 2), à G. Morrhe, qui approuve avec tous ses amis parisiens la méprisante réserve d'Erasme (Allen, 2633, 33–36).

7. M. Mann Phillips l'a naguère démontré: *The Adages of Erasmus*, Cambridge, 1964, pp. 62–66.

8. C'est M. de Vascosan qui se chargea d'imprimer les 36 ff. du *Novorum epigrammatum liber unicus*; Erasme en informe, dès mai 1533, W. de Zwichem, en citant non sans ironie, la préface où Scaliger justifie l'adjectif *"nova"*: "Praefatur in his nihil esse dentis, quod ingenium ipsius semper abhorruerit ab omni mordacitate." (Allen, 2810, 81–82).

9. Achevé le 25 sept. 1535, le second discours ne paraîtra que deux ans plus tard: *I.C.S. adversus Des. Erasmi Roterod. Dialogum Ciceronianum Oratio secunda*, Paris, P. Vidoue, 1537, in-8° de 42 ff. non chif.

10. Nous voyons en effet surgir dans l'*Oratio II* (f. c^r & F4^v) la figure de Longueil, totalement absente de l'*Oratio I*. Est-ce la lecture de Dolet (*De imitatione Ciceroniana ... pro C. Longolio*, Lyon, Gryphe, 1535) qui a ouvert les yeux de Scaliger?

11. *Ep.* XIII, XIV & XV, pp. 27–54 de l'éd. citée; le passage évoqué se situe p. 42.

12. V. A. Flitner, *Erasmus im Urteil seiner Nachwelt, das literarische Erasmus-bild...*, Tübingen, 1952, pp. 96–98.

13. *Liber de comicis dimensionibus*, Lyon, S. Gryphe, 1539, in-8°, 56 p. Ce traité sera, avec quelques légères variantes, entièrement retranscrit au dernier livre de la *Poétique* (Lyon, A. Vincent, 1561, pp. 350–64).

14. V. *Exercitationes*, Paris, Vascosan, 1557, *ex.* CI, § 19: "Et tu (= Cardan) nobis Erasmum facis autorem, quem totius ignarum fuisse naturae, cum alibi (= son commentaire de l'*Histoire des Animaux* d'Aristote), tum eo demonstravimus commentario quem de ejus fecimus Chiliadibus."

15. V. *De Causis Linguae Latinae*, Lyon, Gryphe, 1540, l. II, ch. LX, pp. 105–06 ou l. V, ch. CXIII, p. 233; *Poétique*, éd. cit., outre les quinze dernières pages (cf. note 13), pp. 176 C'-D', 308 B, 337 C.

16. V. In *libros de Plantis, Aristoteli inscriptos, commentarii*, Lyon, G. Roville, 1556, p. 39; *Commentarii et Animadversiones in sex libros de Causis Plantarum Theophrasti*, Lyon, G. Roville, 1566, p. 217; *Exercitationes*, CI § 19, CXLII § 6, CCXXXIX; *Aristotelis Historia de Animalibus, J.C.S. interprete ...* Toulouse, J. Colomiez, 1619, l. I, ch. 98; l. IV, ch. 8.

17. Ce leit-motiv de l'*Oratio I* est repris dans la conclusion du *De Comicis dimensionibus*, et par là-même, de la *Poétique*. Le P. A. Possevino ne manquera pas de relever la dure formule qu'y emploie Scaliger ("Erasmi nomen maius futurum, si ille minor esse voluisse") dans son réquisitoire contre les œuvres du Rotterdamois: *Apparatus sacer*, Cologne, J. Gymnicum, 1608, p. 418.

18. Pour la lettre à Omphalius, v. *ep.* XVII, p. 55–59 de l'éd. cit.; elle est datée du 4 mai 1536. Le tombeau d'Erasme, souvent reproduit, fut publié pour la première fois en 1539, dans le recueil *Heroes* (paru à Lyon, Gryphe, p. 23), à une place de choix: entre le poème consacré à Virgile et celui qui prête la parole à Cicéron.

19. *Vita Des. Erasmi Rot. ex ipsius manu fideliter repraesentata ...* Leyde, Th. Basson, 1607, p. 57.

20. *Des. Erasmi Roter. Colloquia nunc emendatiora.* Leyde, Elzevir, 1643, in-16, 672 p.; le tombeau est reproduit parmi les pièces liminaires (f. 4^r non pag.).

21. Dans une lettre à son ami Falconet, du 2 déc. 1650 (*Lettres*, éd. Reveillé-Parise, Paris, Baillière, 1846, t. II, p. 571), Patin décrit son cabinet de travail, qui contient une véritable galerie de portraits; les trois premiers qu'il évoque sont ceux "d'Erasme et des deux Scaliger."

The Date of the *Opuscula varia* of J. L. Vives

Constant Matheeussen

The *Opuscula varia* of Joannes Ludovicus Vives were printed at Louvain by Dirk Martens. They have no date on the title page nor at the end. Modern scholars have proposed three solutions: 1519, 1520, 1521.[1]
The *Opuscula varia* are a collection of fifteen small works by Vives, which however were not all *editiones principes*. In several cases, a dedicatory epistle introduces two works, so that, actually, the fifteen items can be reduced to ten units, the dedications of which bear a date. Some of those dates are incomplete ones, such as "Louvain 1518," or "April 1519." Sometimes too, there is uncertainty in this sense, that it is not obvious which dating style Vives had in mind. So, e.g., "February 1519" could actually stand for "February 1520," if Vives referred to the Easter Style. As a matter of fact, one of the arguments for dating the *Opuscula varia* in 1520 is precisely connected with the assumption that Vives used the Easter Style when he dated *In Pseudodialecticos* "February 1519."

In discussing this problem, I will first sum up the theoretical possibilities concerning the dating style in the Louvain situation.[2] They are three in number: 1) Louvain *University* used the Christmas Style; in this hypothesis "1518" (e.g.) covers the period from Christmas 1517 until December 24, 1518. In the *Opuscula varia* Vives and/or Martens could have used that style, since Martens was the printer to the University, and since Vives had a lot of connections with the University; 2) On the other hand, the *town* of Louvain, belonging to the duchy of Brabant, used the Easter Style, beginning the year at Holy Saturday. Since the *Opuscula varia* were printed at Louvain, the hypothesis of Easter Style dating cannot be excluded *a priori*; 3) From the Middle Ages onwards, private people kept using the New Year Style or Circumcision Style (that is the style we use today), even if a given institution or political entity used officially a different style.

Those three possibilities are extant in the case of the *Opuscula varia*. In most cases however, the Christmas Style is of minor importance, since the difference is reduced to a single month (December) or even week (the week from December 25, to December 31). As a matter of fact, the hypothesis of the Christmas Style is of no actual importance for the dating of the *Opuscula varia* as a whole, although for some items it results in an alternative, which one should mention, since there is no real proof in the *Opuscula varia* to exclude the possible use of that style.

As to the Easter Style, it is obvious that the problematic period here is much longer, since it covers several months (January to March/April). I shall indicate below that the *Opuscula varia* have several items in which there is a high probability that Vives did not use the Easter Style. This involves the need of strong positive arguments for the assumption of the Easter Style having been used in one or another work of the *Opuscula varia*. In other works, the burden of proof of inconsistency in the *Opuscula varia* lies with the assumption of the Easter Style.

Let me deal now with those items or units in the *Opuscula varia* that are relevant to the date problem.

To begin with, the *Christi Iesu Trimphus* and the *Virginis Dei Parentis Ovatio* are joined together by a dedication to Bernardus Mensa, bishop of Elna.[3] There are several interesting problems here. Both works had been previously printed in a Paris edition of 1514, an edition that already had the dedication to Bernardus Mensa. But in the *Opuscula varia*, Vives reworked both the works themselves and the dedicatory epistle. Indeed, in 1514 Mensa was not yet bishop of Elna (which he did not become until January 12, 1517), but bishop of Tripoli. Notwithstanding, the subscription of the letter to Mensa in the *Opuscula varia* is: "Paris, April 1514." Thus the very important verification can be made, that Vives in his later version of the letter added the date (in 1514 there was only: "Vale. Ex Academia nostra Parrhisiensi"), but that this date remained the original one (id est: 1514), although the letter was adapted (i.a. concerning the ecclesiastical title of Mensa) to the modified circumstances.

But what is the exact meaning of the incomplete date "April 1514"? Since we know that Vives's stay in Paris was from March until June 1514,[4] we can say that what is meant here, is indeed 1514. I should stress also that this item, dated 1514, is in the *Opuscula varia* preceded by a work of 1518. In other words, the arrangement of the items in the *Opuscula varia* is not chronological. This can be strengthened by other works in the *Opuscula varia*: indeed, also *De initiis, sectis et laudibus philosophiae* (dated 1518) comes next to a unit dated April 1, 1519 (*Veritas fucata* and *Anima senis*).

The second unit to be discussed has also two works: *Veritas fucata* and *Anima senis*. The dedication to Joannes Curvimosanus is dated April 1, 1519. In Easter Style, the year 1519 is from April 23, 1519 to April 6, 1520. In other words, there is no first of April in the Easter Style year 1519 during our year 1519! Thus, in the hypothesis that the date under discussion is given in Easter Style, it means actually April 1, 1520!

Now, for two reasons April 1, 1520 is rather difficult to accept: a) A Canterbury letter of Thomas More to Erasmus, dated May 26, 1520, proves that More at that time had read at least two works of the *Opuscula varia: In Pseudodialecticos* and *Aedes legum*.[5] If then by April 1, 1520 the *Opuscula varia* were not yet printed, the lapse of time from the printing of the book to its arrival at Canterbury is rather short; b) In April 1520, Jean Briard of Ath was already dead (January 8, 1520).[6] Now, the *Opuscula varia* have a work dedicated to him, the *Genethliacon Christi Iesu*. If the book was printed after April 1, 1520, one should expect an allusion to Briard's death. Then, as one will remember, the letter to Bernardus Mensa in the *Opuscula varia* clearly proves that Vives adapted an older letter to new circumstances.

This *Genethliacon* demands some more attention in regard to the date problem. Its dedication to Briard has no date, but Vives says that the book is meant as a gift on the occasion of the Kalends of January. Unfortunately, the phrasing of this letter does not permit the inference that Vives here used the New Year Style.

Which first of January is meant, can not be said exactly; but, as I already mentioned, there is no allusion at all to the death of Briard (January 8, 1520). Bearing in mind Vives's habit of adapting a dedication, one should conclude that by January 8, 1520 the *Opuscula varia* were printed, or at least the printing was so far advanced as to make an adaptation of this letter impossible.

The next unit is the *Aedes legum*-group,[7] dedicated in "April 1519" to the Valencian *iurisconsultus* Martinus Pontius. In the hypothesis of the Easter Style this means April 23 to April 30, 1519; or: April 1 to April 6, 1520. For the reasons already given, April 1520 is really impossible. This holds good as well for the *Pompeius fugiens*, which is also dated "April 1519."

Finally, I have to deal with the *In Pseudodialecticos*, which is the last item of the *Opuscula varia*, and is dated February 13, 1519. I will further on discuss the arguments advanced by modern scholars to prove that actually 1520 is meant here, in other words: that Vives here uses the Easter Style.

Before discussing however the theories of modern scholars on the date of the *Opuscula varia*, I shall summarize the facts that can be derived from a closer inspection of the *Opuscula varia*: a) the latest date appearing in the *Opuscula varia* is April 1519; b) the *Opuscula varia* have no chronological arrangement; c) three letters in the *Opuscula varia* are most probably not dated according to Easter Style (letter to Joannes Curvimosanus; letter to Martinus Pontius; dedication of *Pompeius fugiens*); d) the letter to Jean Briard makes it very probable that on January 8, 1520 the *Opuscula varia* were printed.

I shall now review briefly the different proposals to be found in modern studies on the date of the *Opuscula varia*.

Of course, initially 1519 was accepted. But even after other solutions had been proposed by such authorities as Allen and De Vocht, so excellent a Martens specialist as the late Reverend Father K. Heireman kept dating the *Opuscula varia* in 1519, I think since he could prove that Martens in his second Louvain period (1512–29), more precisely in a book of 1523, did not date according to Easter Style.[8]

The hypothesis of 1520 was adopted ultimately by Allen in the fourth volume of the *Opus epistolarum Erasmi*; De Vocht, in the second part of the *History* of the

Louvain *Collegium Trilingue*, followed Allen. Allen gives two arguments:[9] 1) A letter of Vives (dated June 4, 1520) shows that in May 1520 Vives was not quite sure that *In Pseudodialecticos* was already known in Paris, although he expected that it was the case; furthermore, a letter of Thomas More proves that in May 1520 he had recently become acquainted with *In Pseudodialecticos* and *Aedes legum* in England (see above); 2) The second argument has to do with the fact that *In Pseudodialecticos* appears as the last item of the volume; this work is dated February 1519, but is preceded by two works dated April 1519; in other words, Allen seems to accept a chronological arrangement, and so accepted the Easter Style dating for *In Pseudodialecticos*.

I think that those arguments are not convincing. There is no chronological arrangement in the *Opuscula varia*. The other argument works with a rather elastic and unprecise conception: the recent appearance of the *Opuscula varia* in May 1520 for French and English readers. If one supposes that the *Opuscula varia* were printed after (or even in) April 1519, one can easily accept that in May 1520 the book could be considered as a recent one in Paris or Canterbury. Moreover, there are arguments against a conversion of 1519 into 1520, this conversion implying the use of Easter Style. This now is at least not so in some other works of the *Opuscula varia*; so, accepting the use of Easter Style needs a stronger argumentation to counterbalance the following facts: a) the University of Louvain did not use Easter Style; b) Martens certainly did not use at least once in those years the Easter Style; c) Vives in three letters of the *Opuscula varia* did not use that style; d) in the letter to Briard there is no trace of a reworking which alludes to the death of Briard, whilst Vives in the *Opuscula varia* clearly did not hesitate to adapt such letters to modified circumstances.

Finally, the third hypothesis is 1521.[10] The argument here is that the *Aedes legum*-group was dedicated to Martinus Pontius, who came to the Netherlands in September 1520 as a member of a Valencian embassy to the Court of the Emperor Elect Charles. Now 1521 is impossible, since there is clear evidence that in May 1520 the *Opuscula varia* were known to More. Furthermore, the *Aedes legum*-group has no allusion to the embassy of Pontius nor to the civil war situation at Valencia, which was the reason for that embassy. Thirdly, to prove that a dedication to a Valencian does not need the presence of that Valencian in the Netherlands, I can say that another work in the *Opuscula varia* is dedicated to a Valencian too (Serafín, count of Oliva). This work, *De tempore quo natus est Christus*, is dated December 1518. It speaks of the *pax Romana* after a period of horrible civil wars. Now Serafín was one of the noblemen that paid for the embassy of Pontius and an allusion to the Valencian civil wars would have been very easy to introduce. But Vives does not speak at all of the Valencian civil war (in which furthermore an uncle of Vives played a role).[11]

So I come to some conclusions:

1) In general, no one has thus far produced anywhere a convincing argument

for the use of the Easter Style in the fixing of any of the available dates for the *Opuscula varia*.

2) In view of the preceding, the latest date in the *Opuscula varia*, April 1519, is the *terminus post quem* for the book.

3) Of course, there can have been a lapse of time prior to the actual printing of the book. But the absence of an allusion to the death of Jean Briard makes January 8, 1520 an all but certain *terminus ante quem*. This *argumentum e silentio* is in my opinion persuasive when one remembers two things: first, that Vives clearly reworked a dedication-letter (the one to Bernardus Mensa) as a result of modified circumstances; and secondly, that after January 8, 1520, a reworking of the dedicatory epistle to Jean Briard accompanying the *Genethliacon* would also have been necessary. However that may be, an absolutely certain *terminus ante quem* is May 26, 1520, the date of More's letter to Erasmus mentioning two works of the *Opuscula varia*.

4) These considerations lead to me to conclude that the most likely date for the appearance of the *Opuscula varia* in print was also no later than 1519 (between April 1519 and the beginning of January 1520).

Universitaire Faculteiten Sint-Aloysius, Brussels

Notes

1. I have written a complementary article for the *Liber amicorum L. Voet*; it will appear under the title "De omstreden datering van een Leuvense Martens-druk: J. L. Vives' *Opuscula varia*" in *De Gulden Passer*, 1985. A technical description of the *Opuscula varia* is to be found in W. Nijhoff and M. E. Kronenberg, *Nederlandsche bibliographie van 1500 tot 1540*, I ('s-Gravenhage, 1923), number 2172.

2. E. I. Strubbe and L. Voet, *De chronologie van de Middeleeuwen en de Moderne Tijden in de Nederlanden* (Antwerpen–Amsterdam, 1960), p. 96 and p. 494; H. Grotefend, *Taschenbuch der Zeitrechnung des deutschen Mittelalters und der Neuzeit*. Zehnte erweiterte Auflage, herausgegeben von Th. Ulrich (Hannover, 1960), p. 11 and p. 13.

3. J. IJsewijn, "Zu einer kritischen Edition der Werke des J. L. Vives," *Juan Luis Vives. Arbeitsgespräch in der Herzog August Bibliothek Wolfenbüttel vom 6. bis. 8. November 1980*. Vorträge herausgegeben von A. Buck. *Wolfenbütteler Abhandlungen zur Renaissanceforschung*, 3 (Hamburg, 1981), pp. 23–34.

4. J. IJsewijn, "J. L. Vives in 1512–1517. A Reconsideration of Evidence," *HL*, XXVI (1977), 82–100; and: J. IJsewijn, art. cit., *Juan Luis Vives. Arbeitsgespräch...*, p. 32, n. 12.

5. P. S. and H. M. Allen, *Opus epistolarum Des. Erasmi Roterodami*, IV (Oxonii, 1922), ep. 1106.

6. H. De Vocht, *History of the Foundation and the Rise of the Collegium Trilingue Lovaniense 1517-1550*, I (Louvain, 1951), p. 302, n. 7.

7. This group contains: a dedicatory epistle to M. Pontius, the *Praefatio in Leges Ciceronis*, the *Aedes legum*. See my article "Das rechtsphilosophische Frühwerk des Vives" in

Juan Luis Vives. Arbeitsgespräch..., pp. 93–106. See also, Io. Lod. Vives Valentinus, *Praefatio in Leges Ciceronis e Aedes legum. Edidit Constantinus Matheeussen. Bibliotheca scriptorum Graecorum et Romanorum Teubneriana* (Leipzig, 1984).

8. *Tentoonstelling Dirk Martens 1473–1973* (Aalst, 1973), number A 300 and number A 344.

9. P. S. and H. M. Allen, *Opus epistolarum Des. Erasmi Roterodami*, IV (Oxonii, 1922), ep. 1108, l. 7 (note); H. De Vocht, *History of the Foundation...*, II, p. 3, n. 3.

10. A. Bonilla y San Martin, *Luis Vives y la filosofía del Renacimiento*, III (Madrid, 1929), p. 183 (also vol. I, p. 104).

11. On the Valencian civil war (known as *Germanía*): A. Ebert, *Quellenforschungen aus der Geschichte Spaniens* (Kassel, 1849), pp. 43–224; M. Danvila y Collado, *La Germanía de Valencia. Discursos leídos ante la Real Academia de la Historia* (Madrid, 1884); on the embassy to the Netherlands: Danvila y Collado, op. cit., p. 104; and Bonilla y San Martin, op. cit., p. 93 and pp. 103–04.

Eloquentia, Eruditio, Fides: Erasmus's Life of Jerome

John C. Olin

Erasmus's *Life of Jerome* is the first critical biography of the saint. It is also one of Erasmus's most interesting and important compositions, and as an extended historical work it stands alone among his writings. Erasmus was not an historian, but in this instance he wrote history, and he wrote it well.[1] His *Life of Jerome* however is not simply an historiographical tour de force. It was written as an introduction to the great edition of Jerome's works which Froben first published in 1516, and it shares in the purpose of that undertaking as well as in the broader reform goals of Erasmus. And it bears a particularly personal stamp because of Erasmus's devotion and scholarly attachment to the saint. The work thus has dimensions other than the purely historical and displays a distinctly rhetorical character wherein purpose and style as well as scholarship and historical accuracy are dominant features. *Eloquentia, eruditio, fides* combine to make it a singular achievement.

The historicity of the work however is the first quality that strikes the reader. In the opening pages of the life — in the exordium — Erasmus sets down the critical standards that will guide him in his narrative. It is a unique statement in the literature of that time of a critical historical method and of the need for truthfulness and accuracy in the writing of history. He disavows the use of the "noble" or Platonic lie, the practice of inventing stories and telling fictitious tales about the past for a good purpose,[2] and he affirms that he will give an honest account of Jerome's life. "I think that nothing is better than to portray the saints just as they actually were," he writes, and he continues: "Truth has its own power matched by no artifice." He criticizes the medieval lives of Jerome which, curiously, he attributes to one man whom he severely berates. "In these writings," he tells us, "you would find neither erudition, nor eloquence, nor prudence, nor diligence, and beyond all this you would find least of all what in historical writing is the prime desideratum, namely trustworthiness." Erasmus thereby enumerates the basic qualities of good history, observing their absence in the earlier hagiographic accounts. He then describes his own methodology and approach:

In good faith and with all possible care I have constructed the life of the great saint from Prosper, Severus, Orosius, Rufinus, calumniator though he is, and from such other authors whose credibility should not entirely be disregarded, but above all I have based my inquiry into Jerome's life on the works of Jerome himself. For who would have a better knowledge of Jerome than Jerome himself?... I therefore have looked into all of Jerome's works and have reduced to narrative form the material I was able to gather from scattered parts of his writings. In doing this I invented nothing because to me the greatest miracle is the miracle of Jerome as he expresses himself to us in his many works of lasting and preeminent quality.

What follows this incisive introduction is the chronological narrative of Jerome's life. That narrative, as we might expect, is the longest part of the biography.[3] It is not without shortcomings and obscurities, but it is nevertheless an excellent biographical sketch, a work of serious scholarship and ample documentation generally faithful to the principles Erasmus set down.

The critical approach Erasmus outlined and followed was clearly an aspect of his Humanism, and the life he wrote is a prime example of the development of modern historical method within the context of Renaissance Humanism. Its importance on this score cannot be exaggerated. Humanism, as we know, embodies an historical consciousness—a perspective on the past, an awareness of distance from it, a desire to recapture it. This explains of course the Humanists' emphasis on the study of the ancient languages and the recovery of ancient texts. They sought accurate historical knowledge, and their return to the sources and their linguistic and philological method were the means of attaining it. Erasmus's *Life of Jerome* demonstrates the sense of history inherent in Humanism more fully and effectively than any other work of the period—at least of which I am aware.

The Humanists however were not historians in a narrow academic sense. Following classical models they saw history as coming under the aegis of rhetoric and as having a didactic function.[4] It was the *magistra vitae,* and it taught by examples. This view by no means ruled out a critical approach or the desire to uncover the truth. Cicero in his *De Oratore* had written that the first law of history was to tell the truth, and Lucian in his essay on the writing of history stressed truthfulness above all else.[5] Difficulties indeed could arise in this area, for tension may well exist between historical accuracy and a didactic aim. However a balance can be struck, and certainly the critical disposition of the true scholar will impel him to achieve it. In addition history must be written with skill and eloquence. Cicero, Quintilian, Lucian make this crystal clear. Humanist history thus in accord with the classical tradition was closely linked to rhetoric. Purpose and style as well as truthfulness were of its essence. Erasmus shared this concept of historical writing, and the *Life of Jerome* illustrates it in a striking way.[6]

This brings us to the second quality of the work that can be emphasized, its rhetorical character. The most manifest sign of this is its general thrust and structure. The life is a combination of the panegyric and forensic types of rhetorical composition. It was written in praise of Jerome and in his defence. The two types or modes overlap, indeed intertwine, but there is no mistaking their distinctive as well as complementary presence. The narration of the life is full of praise, and Jerome is held up as an example and ideal. By the same token opponents of Jerome's way of life (and also of Erasmus's way of reform) are rebutted. Then Jerome himself is staunchly defended against two principal bands of critics: scholastic theologians who refuse to acknowledge his status as a theologian and certain humanist detractors who find fault with his style. This defence segment which forms the third major part of the biography follows in logical order after the introduction and the narrative account, and the latter in turn is the proof and confirmation for the defence Erasmus will make. The whole is extremely well structured and developed and conforms to the formal divisions of the oration as both the ancients and Erasmus describe them.[7] There is an exordium, a statement of facts or narration, an argumentation consisting of proof and refutation, a peroration. And the work also complies with rhetorical precepts in its more detailed arrangements and style.[8]

In the architectonics of rhetoric form follows function. It was Erasmus's purpose in presenting Jerome and arguing his case that gave shape to the work and determined its specific character and thrust. As Monsignor Coppens points out, the *Life of Jerome* is above all a plea in behalf of the ideas and reforms Erasmus held most dear.[9] Jerome thus appears as an exemplar, a model to be followed. He is the ideal Christian scholar, the right kind of monk, the true theologian. To tell his authentic story and defend him against his critics is to argue the case for the reforms in theology and religious life that Erasmus sought. Indeed Erasmus identified with Jerome, and the life in many respects is his own justification and defence, an *apologia pro vita sua*. We love those in whom we see our own resemblance, Erasmus realized.[10] But even as a personal projection — an aspect of the life that should not be overemphasized — Jerome is an historic model and his portrait embodies a program and a plea for humanist reform. That fundamental concern clearly controls the work.

It is interesting to observe how Erasmus accomplishes his purpose. In his narrative of Jerome's life the focus is on the saint's education and study, that is, on his preparation to be the great scholar, writer, and theologian he will become. Erasmus tells of his early training at home, his classical schooling in Rome, his concentration on rhetoric so that he might eventually enhance theology with "dignity of style."[11] Then came travel and further study and finally Jerome's decision to enter upon a monastic life in the East. He took his library with him to Syria, his studies continued, he learned Holy Scripture word for word, and "as from the purest springs he drew the philosophy of Christ." He read all the authors pagan or heretic, he despoiled the Egyptians,[12] he learned Hebrew and Chaldee. Finally he could take his place as a superb Christian scholar and theologian.

The import of this portion of the life is obvious. Erasmus is asserting that this kind of training is essential for the theologian and is giving us Jerome as the model to imitate. He is also asserting that theology is the study of Holy Scripture and requires every talent, every skill, and he is defending this thesis against his scholastic opponents who had a very different concept of that sacred discipline. We are here at the heart of Erasmus's reform Humanism: his aim to revitalize theological study, to restore the true theology — the *vera theologia* — of the early Church. In this endeavor Jerome led the way and represented the goal.

The third major part of the life which takes up the defence of Jerome against his critics continues this central theme. The chief of these critics are the *barbari*, the anti-humanist scholastic theologians who disapproved of Jerome's learning and denied him the status of a theologian. Erasmus derides them for taking the so-called dream of Jerome seriously[13] and attacks them for not recognizing in Jerome the hallmarks of a genuine theologian. "Who had a more thorough knowledge of the philosophy of Christ?" he asks. "Who expressed it more forcefully in his writings or in his life?" The rhetorical questions Erasmus poses at this point constitute the climax of his *Life of Jerome*. They define the theologian, and they elevate Jerome to that rank. At the same time they underscore the connection between Jerome and the Greek and Latin New Testament which Erasmus edited and Froben published earlier that same year.[14] They let us know that Jerome's writings are the great companion piece of Holy Scripture itself.

There is a second group of critics at the other end of the spectrum against whom Erasmus also defends Jerome. They are excessively humanist and pedantically critical, and they include those who feel that Jerome was not Ciceronian enough in his style. The charge is paradoxical in view of the story of the dream. Erasmus refutes their remarks and sharply attacks the notion that the Christian author must speak exactly as Cicero did. "Cicero himself would have had to change his language if he were Jerome," he declares. His argument here foreshadows the longer attack he will make years later in his *Ciceronianus*. It is characteristic that Erasmus fights both extremes — those who exaggerated the demands of *bonae litterae* as well as those who ignored them entirely — in the name of effective humanist reform.

The criticism may be made that Erasmus's *Life of Jerome* is too partial, too apologetic and that in presenting his subject Erasmus sometimes departs from the historical accuracy that had been his boast. In a strict sense perhaps this is true — he exaggerated Rufinus's culpability, he is over-defensive about Jerome —, but Erasmus was not striving for a complete or totally objective picture of the saint. He was giving us Jerome as an exemplar, selecting his details accordingly, and arguing the cause of a humanist theology. Along these lines the validity of his portrait — its *fides* — is certainly sound.[15] And indeed its historicity extends still further. Erasmus did break with the earlier hagiography of the saint and attempt to reconstruct his life accurately on the basis of the historical evidence. In this endeavor and achievement lies the most striking characteristic of the *Life*. And that so authentic a portrait emerged in the context of Erasmus's reform purpose is a measure both of his historical perception and his rhetorical skill.

Fordham University

Notes

1. Peter G. Bietenholz, *History and Biography in the Work of Erasmus of Rotterdam* (Geneva, 1966), pp. 90-92. A collated Latin text of Erasmus's *Life of Jerome* is in *Erasmi Opuscula*, ed. Wallace K. Ferguson (The Hague, 1933), pp. 134-90. It was originally published in the early Erasmus editions of Jerome's works and separately in 1517 and 1519. It is curious it was not included in the Leyden *Erasmi Opera Omnia* (10 vols., 1703-06). On the *Life* see Joseph Coppens, "Le portrait de Saint Jérôme d'après Erasme," *Colloquia Erasmiana Turonensia*, ed. J.-C. Margolin, 2 vols. (Toronto, 1972), pp. 821-28 and J. B. Maguire, "Erasmus' Biographical Masterpiece: *Hieronymi Stridonensis Vita*" *RQ*, 26 (1973), 265-73.

2. Cf. Sissela Bok, *Lying* (New York, 1978), chap. 12: "Lies for the Public Good." On the broader question of truth in history as Erasmus perceived it, see J.-C. Margolin, "Erasme et la vérité," *Recherches érasmiennes* (Geneva, 1969), pp. 45-69.

3. There are three main divisions in the *Life*:

   1. the introductory excursus on historical method (ll. 1-135 of the text in *Erasmi Opuscula*)
   2. the narrative account of Jerome's life (ll. 136-1125 of same)
   3. the defence of Jerome against his critics (ll. 1126-1533 of same)

4. Myron P. Gilmore, *Humanists and Jurists* (Cambridge, 1963), chap. 1: "The Renaissance Conception of the Lessons of History"; Felix Gilbert, *Machiavelli and Guicciardini* (Princeton, 1965), chap. 5: "The Theory and Practice of History in the Fifteenth Century"; and Donald J. Wilcox, *The Development of Florentine Humanist Historiography in the Fifteenth Century* (Cambridge, 1969).

5. *De Oratore*, 2. 15 and Lucian's "How to Write History."

6. See J. IJsewijn and C. Matheeussen, "Erasme et l'historiographie," *The Late Middle Ages and the Dawn of Humanism outside Italy* (Louvain, 1972), pp. 31-43.

7. Cf. Quintilian, 3. 9 and Erasmus's *De copia*, CWE, 24, p. 648.

8. Cf. Quintilian, 3. 7. 10-08 and Margaret Mann Phillips, "Erasmus and Biography," *UTQ*, 42 (1973), 190-91.

9. Coppens, p. 822.

10. *De ratione studii*, CWE, 24, p. 686. See also Jacques Chomarat "Grammar and Rhetoric in the Paraphrases of the Gospels by Erasmus," *Erasmus of Rotterdam Yearbook*, One (1981), 65-66.

11. Cf. Diana Webb, "Eloquence and Education: A Humanist Approach to Hagiography," *JEH*, 31 (1980), 19-30.

12. The metaphor is from Saint Augustine's *De doctrina christiana* 2. 40. 60. Erasmus discusses it in the *Antibarbari*, CWE, 23, pp. 97-98.

13. For the account of the dream see Jerome Ep 22. 30. Jerome years later in his polemic with Rufinus minimized its importance.

14. Erasmus first used the term "the philosophy of Christ" in the *Paraclesis* or introduction to his New Testament of 1516. His use of it in the *Life of Jerome* also links the two editions.

15. Cf. Margolin, "Erasme et le vérité," pp. 62–65.

Literary and Philosophical Aspects of Lipsius's *De Constantia in Publicis Malis*

P. H. Schrijvers

The celebrated Lipsius dialogue *De Constantia in Publicis Malis* (1584) could be called a dialogue of conversion for two reasons. Lipsius describes his transition to the doctrine of steadfastness as well as his "conversion" from philology and letters to philosophy in general.

The first twelve chapters on travel, adversity, hypocrisy, patriotism and pity are of a more literary character in general, as is the introduction on gardening and the garden in Book II and the final section on adversity in the past. This more light-hearted matter forms the framework of two principal sections on dogma, that is on providence, fate and free will (I.13–21) and on God's goodness and the evil in this world (II.6–18). In these two central sections in particular Lipsius tries to combine stoic and Christian doctrines.

Up to now it is mainly the relationship between Lipsius and Seneca that has been examined in great detail.[1] But as to form and content of this dialogue another author of late Antiquity has been of equal importance (at least), although he is hardly ever mentioned as a source of inspiration for Lipsius. This is Boethius, who wrote *De Consolatione Philosophiae*.[2] In the central sections of *De Constantia* Lipsius was sometimes inspired by Books 4 and 5 of Boethius's *Consolatio* in great detail.[3] In his comparisons too borrowed from for instance medicine, navigation, battle, light and darkness Lipsius often followed Boethius.[4] In *De Consolatione Philosophiae* the philosophical observations are interspersed with poems by Boethius himself for the sake of variety. Fortunately Lipsius had sufficient self-knowledge in literature to restrict himself to one poem of his own included at the very end, which has no literary value and seems to serve mainly to illustrate his own religious devotion. Moreover we may conclude from this poem that Lipsius tended to consider his bad health as a *publicum malum*. With Lipsius the many poetic quotations, striking comparisons and the prose hymns inserted have the same function of varying the philosophical discourse. The introductory passages of both dialogues very clearly echo each other:[5] when Boethius sits down, in low spirits and not knowing what to say, his interlocutor in this conversation, Lady Philosophy, softly lays her hand on his breast to console him; when Lipsius has arrived at Liège greatly confused and despondent, Langius, who embodies stoic philosophy, encouragingly pats him on the breast. Lipsius seems to have deliberately concealed Boethius's influence in his dialogue in order to make his originality stand out the more.[6] In his letters to Coornhert he advances in defense of his doctrine of fate his conviction that he does not give new insights but only reflects the views that had been accepted long ago by the most learned theologians and scholastics (read Boethius and Thomas Aquinas). Also the wording of "relative necessity" occurring in these letters comes straight from the fifth book of Boethius's *Consolatio*.[7]

Although Lipsius's journey to Vienna is historical fact, the dialogue itself in the form here presented has certainly been invented. It has been chosen for didactic, literary as well as strategic reasons. This manner of presentation enabled the author to put his possibly offensive opinions in the mouth of canon Langius, who had died in 1573 and was thus out of reach of the Inquisition—on earth that is. The biographical data about the interlocutor Langius does not in any way suggest that he had been such an enthusiastic follower of the Stoa.[8] If the actual journey to Vienna took place in the autumn or winter of 1571,[9] the dialogue contains as a matter of fact some references to historical events which took place in 1572 (the Massacre of St Bartholomew).[10] Lipsius's personal interest in the Stoa and the shift of his attention from matters of philology and textual criticism towards practical philosophy seems to stem from the early eighties. Thus in his commentaries on Tacitus's *Annals* and *Histories* of 1581 and 1585 respectively we find highly personal panegyrics on the Roman stoics Thrasea Paetus and Helvidius Priscus, two symbols of *constantia*; their fate is also mentioned in the final section of his dialogue.[11] Also in those years Lipsius writes a satire on philologists.[12] In the argument put in the mouth of Langius about patriotism and punishment we meet with motives which return in more elaborate form in Lipsius's *Politica* of 1589.[13] In other words, autobiographical data and personal aspects of the author have been introduced in both interlocutors (young Lipsius and canon Langius).

In his *Praescriptio* added to the second edition of *De Constantia* of 1585 Lipsius speaks of some five objections which are said to be made by the critics. Generally his tract showed too little Christian spirit; they protested especially against his glorification of right reasoning (*recta ratio*), against his views on fate and free will, against the idea that the ungodly are punished "for their own good" and against denouncing the emotions. Before discussing these five objections briefly I must point out that the publishing history of *De Constantia* knows two major stages. In the second edition of 1585 Lipsius has been conciliatory towards objections from Christian critics by a few additions to his text and by writing an apology in the preface, (the so-called *Praescriptio*). These additions are lacking in the late sixteenth-century translations and their modern reprints. In the last edition, prepared by the author himself in 1599, a limited number of passages in the dialogue is again deleted; or changed (that is: mitigated). The edition of 1599 forms the basis of the text that is printed in the seventeenth-century *Opera Omnia* editions. Modern critical studies on Lipsius and the Neo-Stoa generally start from the *Opera Omnia* edition within reach, that is to say from a text of *De Constantia* which has been mitigated somewhat in philosophical, theological and political respects as compared to the first and second edition.[14]

The dialogue's reception was dominated by the question whether a synthesis of the Stoa and Christianity was possible. Lipsius passes over differences of principle and dogma, which had been mentioned by Erasmus for instance in the preface to his second edition of Seneca's works (1529),[15] by either smoothing them over or being quiet about them or by defining them as theological problems outside the domain of philosophy and by warning continually against man's dangerous curiosity as to divine matters. Only in his discussion of pity and of fate does he sum up some differences between Christian views and the Stoa's.

Concerning attempts in the sixteenth and seventeenth centuries to combine stoic and Christian ethics into a synthesis, we are to start with the question: which ranked first in the presentation, paganism or Christianity? The difference in emphasis is clearly illustrated when we compare Lipsius's dialogue with the tract of the Leyden family doctor Petrus Geesteranus (Pieter van der Geest) entitled *De Constantia Christiana* which appeared posthumously in 1679 and one copy of which is kept in the Amsterdam University Library. Lipsius's dialogue, especially in his first unchristianised edition is clearly marked by antique paganism. The Scriptures are not quoted; the reference to Adam's Fall is worded so vaguely that the sixteenth-century translator Sir John Stradling (1594) seems not to have understood what the text was about.[16] The author will have shocked some of his readers especially by everything he did not include: in his dialogue there was no mention of the Bible, faith, grace and the figure of Christ. Illustrating his doctrines Lipsius moreover referred to classical heroes, such as Cato, Brutus, Regulus and others; Job and Christian saints and martyrs were not mentioned. But the family doctor Petrus Geesteranus does refer continually to the gospels, the Pauline epistles, biblical examples. There follow in his case some stoic texts at the end taken from Seneca, Epictetus and Lipsius himself. Not until 1679 did *De Constantia Christiana* appear, more than forty years after the Leyden family doctor had died. This posthumous publication at a remarkably late date may be explained by the fact that in 1675 a new Dutch translation of Lipsius's dialogue appeared done by François van Hoogstraeten at Rotterdam. It seems possible that the Christian camp reacted by wanting to have a *constantia christiana* published.

The second objection Lipsius had to defend himself against was that he was excessive in his praise of right reasoning,[17] just like classical authors. His defence in the second edition of the dialogue was limited to a few soothing words in his *Praescriptio* and the addition of "and God" in some places where he mentions right reasoning as his starting point. When I consulted Lipsius's own copy of the first edition of *De Constantia* at the Leyden University Library, it was rather exciting to note how the author scribbled *ac Deus* next to the word *ratio*, as he had unfortunately forgotten to do in the first edition. At the time he seems to have preferred changing the pagan plural *Superi* (the gods) into a dogmatically more correct singular *deus*.[18]

The Index of books prohibited for Spanish Catholics of 1667 orders Lipsius to be read with great caution in everything he tells us on fate (*caute legendus!*). Especially chapter 20 of Book I (Lipsius's own so-called doctrine of fate) was severely criticised. Because of this the author tinkered with the text in the various reprints that have been found. In his discussion of true fate, which he also calls moderate or pious fate, Lipsius wants to hold on to the Latin word *fatum* following Boethius in order to be able to distinguish between each man's individual fate and God's universal providence.[19] In keeping to the word *fatum* he counters the views of among others Augustine, Thomas Aquinas (as well as Calvin), who all preferred to avoid the term considering its pagan (stoic) associations.[20]

To maintain man's free will as opposed to universal divine providence, Lipsius derives the idea of "secondary causes" (place, time, order) from the Stoa (Chrysippus), which man can realize according to his wishes. More important for him is that man acts from necessity from the divine point of view, but in freedom from the human point of view. This conception leads to the phrase highly criticised by Coornhert: "man necessarily sins in full freedom."[21] In this theory of divine and human perspectives Lipsius follows Boethius and Thomas Aquinas, as he reluctantly admits in his letters. After his death some defenders also referred to Thomas Aquinas in this respect.[22]

Whereas Lipsius's exposition on fate and human will evoked much criticism towards the end of the sixteenth century, there is as far as I know hardly any contemporary criticism in reaction to his attempts to reconcile God's goodness and providence with the existence of evil in this world in Book II of *De Constantia*. The Index was not critical either. This reticence illustrates in how far his views on adversity as punishment for sin or as natural necessity were shared at the end of the sixteenth and for the greater part of the seventeenth centuries. To defend the idea of God's goodness and to justify his involvement in evil Lipsius often uses stoic concepts which greatly influenced Christian views as to the theodicy as well of among others Augustine, Boethius and Thomas Aquinas. Lipsius follows Seneca for instance who emphasized that physical harm is a means for Divinity to educate human beings. Aside from that he also introduces the cosmological arguments which the Stoa and Christianity used in their theodicy: the world forms one organic whole and complete order is often achieved only at the cost of several parts; the world is a beautiful work of art and there is no beauty without variety, no light without shadow. Such totalitarian concepts lead to a denial of the value of the individual, also characteristic of Lipsius. The problem of Albert Camus's *Les Justes* our Justus never posed.

Lipsius's justification of God's goodness in Book II of *De Constantia* can be considered a precursor of the theodicy discussions that broke out in Western Europe especially in the eighteenth century. It is to be regretted that in twentieth century surveys "on the problem of evil in West European philosophy" Lipsius's contribution has completely passed into oblivion.[23] His "theodicy" resembles to a certain degree the famous *Théodicée* by the German philosopher Leibniz, especially the more ethical and pragmatic parts which in their turn have been strongly influenced by stoic and Thomist views.[24] As we know, the optimism of philosophers like Leibniz and the Englishman Shaftesbury made Voltaire write his satiric novel *Candide ou l'Optimisme*. The character of doctor Pangloss in this novel is a caricature of Leibniz, but as a type he is in some ways also a second Lipsius. Voltaire's satire on optimism characterized by Candide as "the folly of maintaining that everything goes well when everything is going wrong" also presents us with the best indirect answer to Lipsius's concepts as to the theodicy. The cosmological and totalitarian views which are characteristic of this so-called optimism are being exposed by Voltaire. It is remarkable that the notorious concept of "man sinning necessarily in freedom" is parodied by Voltaire also.[25]

The difference between Lipsius and Voltaire is also illustrated by the way in which both philosophers have used the favourite symbol of the garden to give expression to their world view and to their ideal of "The Happy Man." Lipsius (II.3) sees the garden as the ideal microcosm, to which he retires for rest and seclusion to think, to read and to write; what happens in the wide world outside is of no concern to him: "I sojourn inside myself."[26] On the other hand Lipsius draws us a picture in *De Constantia* II.11 of the wide world as a garden, "as a plantation where God is the most accomplished planter; here he snaps off a few top-heavy twigs of some families, there he picks some leaves, some people. This helps the trunk." As we know, Voltaire's novel ends with a scene in the garden and shows those who live there working without reasoning in order to make life bearable. When doctor Pangloss starts again about this "best of all possible worlds," Candide answers: "This is excellently put but let us work in our garden."

The last objection that Lipsius quotes in his *Praescriptio* was that he wanted to restrain the emotions too much. Throughout the ages protest was heard against the stoic ideal of the superhuman Sage without emotions. I need only mention Erasmus's criticism of Seneca in *In Praise of Folly* and Pascal's criticism of the diabolical pride shown by the philosopher Epictetus.[27] Pascal as well as our Leyden family doctor Petrus Geesteranus points out that the stoic ideal of ἀπαθεῖα is incompatible with Christ's anguish and grief in the Garden of Gethsemane. I like to think that in his *De Constantia* edition of 1599 Lipsius has actually toned down his views on the emotions.[28]

His ideas on the stoic Sage as Übermensch are also expressed in the dialogue itself. In Book II (chapter 3) Langius describes how in philosophical ecstasy he seems to shed everything that is human and to ascend to heaven on the fiery chariot of Wisdom. Irresistibly and paradoxically the image suggests the prophet Elia. Lipsius answers to this (II.4): "How happy you are in peaceful as in troubled times! Your life is one that is hardly human." In his commentary of Tacitus, Lipsius uses the same phrase to praise the Roman stoic Thrasea Paetus. In Book II, chapter 20 Lipsius describes himself as a man among men and asks for medicine that is somewhat more human. To our (modern) surprise this seems to consist of a series of terrifying disasters from the past, the so-called honey of historical examples. Never does Lipsius state explicitly that the stoic Sage is God's equal, but he suggests a divine dimension by the religious imagery he uses in connection with Constantia, called "a goddess" (II.5) and Langius's study, called "a temple with an altar" (II.5). Their conversations were called "a mystery ritual" (end of the dialogue). Highly characteristic is the final scene in which Langius imagines himself leading his pupil to the summit of Mount Olympus to show him the past, present and future of this world. A Christian reader might be reminded of the temptation scene between Christ and the devil on top of a high mountain!

These short remarks on literary and philosophical aspects of *De Constantia* take me to two desiderata: a new edition of the Latin text of *De Constantia* with variant readings; a comprehensive and profound commentary on this dialogue, that collects many earlier beams and itself has known a wide emanation. The historical value of the dialogue is not under discussion, but it has been variously judged and this will probably remain so.

Leyden University

Notes

1. See T. M. van de Bilt, *Lipsius' De Constantia en Seneca*, diss. Nijmegen, 1946. Unfortunately J. L. Saunders does not discuss *De Constantia* in his book *Justus Lipsius, The Philosophy of Renaissance Stoicism* (New York, 1955).

2. The influence of Boethius has been grossly underrated by van de Bilt, op. cit., 66.

3. Cf. especially *Consolat. Philosoph.* IV, ch. 4, 6, 7, V, ch. 1-5.

4. *Consolat. Philosoph.* I, ch. 5 (esp. pp. 38-42 ed. Peiper), ch. 6 (pp. 52-59), II, ch. 1 (pp. 52-53), ch. 2-3, III, ch. 1.

5. *Consolat. Philosoph.* I, ch. 2 (pp. 8-10 ed. Peiper) "Cumque me non modo tacitum sed elinguem prorsus mutumque vidisset, admovit pectori meo leniter manum"; *De Constantia*, I, ch. 3 "hostem reperies apud te et in isto (pectus mihi concutiebat) penetrali."

6. An explicit reference to Boethius in a note to the *Praescriptio* of the second edition (1585) has been deleted in later editions of *De Constantia*. I suppose Lipsius will not have appreciated that Coornhert stopped his translation of *De Constantia* and published a Dutch translation of *Consolat. Philosoph.* in the same year (1584). The diminishing interest in Boethius's *Consolation* during the seventeenth century (noticed by Courcelle in R. R. Bolgar ed., *Classical Influences on European Culture A.D. 500-1500*, Cambridge Univ. Press, 1971, p. 138) may have been caused as well by the popularity of Lipsius's dialogue.

7. Cf. Lipsius's second and third letter to Coornhert (9th and 15th April 1584, Burmannus, *Sylloge*, I, pp. 178, 179) and *Consolat. Philosoph.* V, ch. 6 (esp. pp. 101ff., ed. Peiper).

8. See the article "Delanghe" in *Biographie Nationale de Belgique*, 5, pp. 310-15.

9. See Justus Lipsius, *Von der Bestendigkeit [De Constantia]*, ed. by L. Forster (Stuttgart, 1965), Anmerkungen 3*-4*.

10. See *De Constantia* II.24 and also I.16 (marginal note "anno LXXII" on *sidus exortum hoc ipso anno*).

11. See Lipsius's commentaries on Tacitus's *Annals* (ed. 1581, p. 474) and *Histories* (ed. 1585, p. 61) and in general P. H. Schrijvers, "Justus Lipsius, Grandeur en misère van het pragmatisme" in *Voordrachten Faculteitendag 1980*, Rijksuniversiteit Leiden, 1981, pp. 46-54. In *De Constantia* II.25 Lipsius quotes Tacitus, *Agricola*, ch. II.

12. Cf. C. H. Heesakkers on Lipsius's *Lusus in nostri aevi Criticos* (1581) in *Lampas*, 12 (1979), pp. 315-39.

13. See on the relationship between *De Constantia* and the *Politica* G. Abel, *Stoizismus und frühe Neuzeit* (Berlin-New York, 1978), pp. 78ff.

14. The most relevant alterations in the successive editions are noted in my Dutch translation of *De Constantia*, entitled "Over standvastigheid bij algemene rampspoed" (Ambo, Baarn, 1983). Since the second edition (1585) ch. II, 14 was divided in two separate chapters (not without errors in the numbering of the chapters in the second edition: II.14, 15, 15, 16, 18). In later editons II.16-26 corresponds to II.15-25 of the first edition. In the edition of 1599 Lipsius's stylistic *brevitas* has been mitigated as well, mostly by the addition of forms of the verb *esse*.

15. Allen, *Opus Epist. Erasmi*, 2091.

16. Cf. Stradlings translation of the phrase (*De Constantia* II.17) *peccavimus enim et rebelles magno huic regi fuimus in uno omnes*: "for we have transgressed and rebelled against this mighty king every one of us" (*Two Books of Constancie*, repr. New Brunswick, 1939, p. 173), and the correct rendering by Mourentorf: "Wij hebben alle gader in éénen mensch ghesondicht" (*Twee Boecken vande Stantvasticheyt*, repr. Amsterdam-Antwerp, 1948, p. 103).

17. See in general R. Hoopes, *Right Reason in the English Renaissance* (Cambridge, Mass., 1962).

18. These alterations occur in II.3 and II.16 (17) respectively; compare the alteration in the *dedicatio*: "Sapientiae viam ... quae sola possit ducere" (1584[1]), and "quae cum divinis litteris conjuncta possit ducere ad Tranquillitatem et Quietem" (1585[2] and later editions).

19. *Consolat. Philosoph.* IV, ch. 6.

20. See also van de Bilt, op. cit., 87 and note 6; in Lipsius's marginal note at I.19, the reference to Thomas Aquinas's *Libellus de Fato* is extremely misleading, because Thomas disapproves in fact the use of the term *fatum*.

21. See Coornhert, *Brieven-boeck*, I, nn. 88.

22. Cf. the remarks of P. Bayle in *Dictionnaire historique et critique* (Amsterdam, 1740[5]), 3, p. 125.

23. See studies like R. P. Sertillanges, *Le problème du mal* (Paris, 1948-51), Fr. Billicsich, *Das Problem des Übels in der Philosophie des Abendlandes* (Wien, 1952, 1955).

24. See F. Kuhn, *Die historischen Beziehungen zwischen der stoischen und Leibnizischen Theodicee*, diss. Leipzig, 1913, H. Koppehl, *Die Verwandtschaft Leibnizens mit Thomas v. Aquino in der Lehre vom Bösen*, diss. Jena, 1892. Leibniz mentions Lipsius as his source for stoic philosophy in *Théod.* E III.331, 332, 378 (cf. E. Hagemeier, *Die ethischen Probleme der Leibnizischen Théodicée und ihre hauptsächlichsten Vorarbeiten in der Geschichte der Ethik*, diss. Münster, 1929, 14).

25. Cf. Voltaire, *Candide ou l'optimisme* (1759), ch. 4 (*in fine*), 19, 22 (pp. 193, 205, 206, ed. Pléiade), ch. 5 (*in fine*): "la liberté peut subsister avec la nécessité absolue; car il était nécessaire que nous fussions libres; car enfin la volonté déterminée ..."

26. During the discussion after the communication Professor Forster pointed out that in the dialogue young Lipsius is praising (real) gardens for the wrong reasons (as a place of flight); in Langius's reply the use of a garden is for modest recreation (See also L. W. Forster, "Meditation in a Garden" in *German Life and Letters* [October 1977], 23-35.) For my view on the garden, considered also in *De Constantia* as symbol of the world and of

life, see the final phrase of II.1, "in exiguum hunc locum Natura conclusisse" and the repetition in II.2, "vide hunc morientem subito, alium subnascentem" and "modo ad hunc occidentem, modo ad illum exorientem manum vultumque circumferre."

27. Cf. Abel, op. cit., pp. 305ff.

28. See the alterations in the text of the *capitula* I.12 on *miseratio*: *eam* ⟨*nimiam*⟩ *in vitio esse*; I.13 on *mala*: *nec gravia* ⟨*nimis*⟩ *nec nova*; and in I.13 *imo* ⟨*fortasse*⟩ *impius*; I.22 *ne* ⟨*nimis*⟩ *adfligere*, alterations from ἀπάθεια to μετριοπάθεια.

Sebastián Fox Morcillo's
De regni regisque institutione (Antwerp, 1556):
Humanist Approaches to Empiricism

R. W. Truman

For centuries, treatises *de regimine principum* were seen as being concerned, in effect, with the issue of the translation of principle into practice. It was through the prince that principle, whether grounded in the will of God, the nature of the universe and man, or the teaching of the Church Fathers or that of Classical Antiquity, became embodied in the practice of government. It is notorious that Machiavelli turned this assumption into an acutely painful question. However, in his recent remarkable work *The Foundations of Modern Political Thought*, Professor Quentin Skinner has argued that "it is ... appropriate to regard the political theory of the northern Renaissance essentially as an extension and consolidation of a range of arguments originally discussed in *quattrocento* Italy."[1] That is to say, the sixteenth-century North European Humanists took a still more idealistic view of the nature and function of the ruler than the main run of Italian Humanists had done in the preceding century. Skinner quotes Erasmus's *Institutio principis christiani* to the effect that the duty of the prince is at once to promote and embody virtue in the highest degree.[2] That virtue, the northern Humanists agreed, included the virtue of godliness. They were critical of tendencies among Italian Humanists to regard war as part of the necessary and legitimate order of things and "to endorse the morally ambivalent notion of 'reason of state.'"[3] Into his account of North European Humanism Skinner brings Spanish practitioners of the *de regimine principum* genre, on the grounds that he finds a basic identity of approach in the two cases.[4] This provides the context for the remarks that will follow here; because some Spanish authors of treatises on kingship belonged to northern Europe in the obvious sense that they lived and wrote there; and of these Sebastián Fox Morcillo (not mentioned by Skinner) was one.

Born at Seville in the late 1520s into a family of prosperous *converso* artisans, Fox Morcillo came to Louvain in 1548 to study at the Collegium Trilingue.[5] In 1550 he published his first book, and over the next seven years more than a dozen others followed, presenting a familiar humanist pattern of interest: a compendium of moral philosophy, a treatise on history, another *De imitatione*, another

De honore, two others on dialectic, commentaries on Plato's *Timaeus*, *Phaedo* and *Republic*. The *De regni regisque institutione* was among the last of Fox Morcillo's works, being published at Antwerp in 1556. By then he held the post of Master of the King's Pages, at Brussels.

At the very outset, in his preface, Fox Morcillo makes it clear that this is to be a treatise *de regimine principum* with a difference. The kind of king he portrays here will not be the sort portrayed by philosophers of old, whiling away their time in their Schools ("non qualem philosophi veteres in angulis scholarum per otium depinxere" … "non ut antiquorum plerique"); rather, he will be the kind of king required at the present day ("quem nostra desiderent tempora").[6] It seems, then, that we are promised something quite different from, say, Francesco Patrizi's *De regno et regis institutione*, written a century before and still being printed in Fox Morcillo's own day. Casting his work in the form of a dialogue, he gives one Aurelius the task of describing the relevant ruler.

And yet his *introductio ad rem* has the familiar character of the old idealizing manner. He begins by talking about Philip II, who had just succeeded to the throne:

> Cum tantam itaque in hoc uno rege vitae praestantiam virtutumque omnium specimen animadvertam, rarum profecto, atque excellentem quendam principem eum ipsum esse arbitror, ut quoties regem aliquem omnibus numeris quaeram perfectum, in illum tanquam in formam absolutissimam, & quasi Idaeam cogitatione mentis adumbratam animum convertam (sig. A7ʳ).

This prompts a notably sour response from the other interlocutor, Antonius. It seems to him that in every age such a range of excellence as that, all in one man, has been something to be desired rather than found. This was no less true in their own day, when many were called kings who were in fact tyrants, caring only for their own personal advantage, selling public office to the unworthy for profit, and handing themselves over to flatterers who merely multiplied the tyranny. In the mouths of such people, the actions of greed and self-seeking were disguised in the terminology of virtue and public concern, and—he adds—Aurelius himself was not innocent of such flattery (sigs. A7ʳ-B2ʳ). Aurelius, for his part, observes that Antonius had spent much time in Italy and Switzerland and had studied the government of Venice, Genoa, Siena, and the Swiss Cantons, with the result that he had become a convinced republican. He (Aurelius) will therefore make it his aim to defend monarchical rule and show it to be superior to any other form of government (sig. B3ʳ-4ᵛ). Such an aim was, of course, far from original; but what is of interest here is how Aurelius sets about it and what Fox Morcillo himself thinks of his performance.

Most of the book is taken up with Aurelius's account of what the king should be like. His scheme of exposition is familiar from Italian Renaissance treatises on the subject. Book I is on the education of the prince—physical, moral and intellectual—with a large debt to Plato's *Republic*. Book II sets out at considerable length the qualities requisite in a prince, and these are presented in terms of the four cardinal virtues, with their many subordinate virtues. It is only after all this, in Book III, that Aurelius undertakes to show that monarchical rule is better than any other form of government.

His account (despite what we read in Fox Morcillo's preface) has an obviously idealizing, humanist aspect. Time and again in the account of the princely virtues, examples and exemplars are drawn in typical humanist fashion from the writers of Classical Antiquity. It is clear that Fox Morcillo was deeply attached to the Renaissance humanist belief in the importance of bringing the world of daily living into relation with the world of moral ideals and principles presented by the Ancients. And so it is not surprising that the other speaker, Antonius, should repeatedly find grounds for protesting to Aurelius that he is describing an ideal ruler of a kind that has never existed and never will in the world of reality. As he says at the start of Book III:

> Fingat sibi quidquid velit ipse, instituat arbitratu suo principem iustum, prudentem, fortem, moderatum, omnibus denique officiis virtutum instructum, nihil sane effecerit: quando nec tales unquam principes sunt inventi, & ea praeceptis describi oporteat, quae homines aliquando re ipsa consequi possint (sig. V6^r).

He later charges Aurelius with having forgotten his own promise to portray not a "perfect king" but one suited to the needs of the present time (sig. X6^v).

But this, as we have seen, was precisely the distinction and the aim that Fox Morcillo had set out in his own preface to the work. Do we conclude, therefore, that he is allowing Antonius, the republican, seriously to suggest that he, the author, has not fulfilled his stated purpose in writing? In other words, does Antonius serve here to express a doubt, a degree of self-questioning, in Fox Morcillo's own mind as to his own procedure and the value of what he gives Aurelius to say? This involves a prior question: is Antonius speaking here out of mere republican *parti pris*? How far has he taken account of what Aurelius has in fact been saying? This is something that needs to be looked into rather more closely.

It is true that Aurelius's whole account of kingly conduct is cast in the form of an extended exposition of the virtues. But one of the most striking features here is the extent to which he relates these virtues to the world of daily affairs, the practical tasks of government, and also to the prince's own position as regards his subjects. For example, when discussing commutative justice, he is led on to currency questions (sig. O3^v–5^r). For the sake of trade, the prince must not manipulate currency values but hold them constant throughout his realms. But this involves taking due account of money values in other countries; otherwise currency will find its way abroad. (Fox Morcillo notes how little of the gold and silver brought to Spain from the New World has stayed there.) Therefore officials must be appointed to oversee these matters. Again, when Aurelius speaks of *magnificentia* as a part of justice, one finds him moving on to the subject of how the prince can prevent food-shortages, especially of grain (sigs. P7^v–Q1^v). He has "often been amazed," he says, by the fact that such shortages are far more frequent in Italy and Spain than in northern Europe, even though the southern countries are, in his view, more fertile. However, "having (he says) looked closely and at length into the matter," he has found the explanation. "Cuius rei causa, mihi, accurate id inquirenti, ac percunctanti, sępe videtur quod ..." in the north, unlike the south, the supply of grain is not in the hands of a few people only. When the few have control, they will hold back supplies in order to drive up prices. Once again, officials must be appointed to prevent this, just as measures have been taken in England by Sir Thomas More (as Fox Morcillo thought) to limit the number of sheep and cattle that any one man may own. Or again, in the case of Spain and her trade with the rest of Europe, remedies must be applied to a situation where primary commodities are exported cheaply while unnecessary luxury goods are imported at a high cost (sig. Q2^{r-v}). This was a point being urged on the Crown at precisely this time in Spain. In a number of ways, Fox Morcillo's treatise expresses the kind of concern being expressed there at what was a time of severe financial and economic crisis.[7]

On the other hand, the fact remains that the form and character of his discussion here did not altogether lend themselves to the discussion of such issues. It is striking that several times, after discussing such topics at some length and with obvious interest, Aurelius feels it necessary to offer an apology for the fact that, as he says, he has digressed from his subject — digressed, that is, from his account of this virtue or that. Having got on to the question of currency in the course of expounding commutative justice, he remarks: "Sed nimis exilia persequor, a communi ratione longe digressus. Redeam ad caetera commutationis officia ..." (sig. O5^r). A similar remark occurs later in his treatment of the same cardinal virtue of justice when he has been discussing princely *magnificentia*. This, as we have seen, leads him to consider questions of food-supply and international trade. But from that he goes on to urge the importance of not allowing large numbers of the population to be idle: "nec tantam mancipiorum copiam in Hispania vituperare non possum, quia multis hoc modo otiandi vagandique datur occasio" (sig. Q2^v–3^r). Fox Morcillo is moved here by the awareness that such people can give rise to civil commotion. Nevertheless, at the end of this series of wholly practical observations, Aurelius echoes his earlier apology: "Sed nimis exilia consector, & longe ab instituto digressus sum" (sig. Q3^r). One senses at such moments that Fox Morcillo's interests repeatedly tend in a direction that he could not wholly justify to himself in terms of the kind of exposition he had chosen to adopt. That is to say, when Aurelius, expounding his kingly virtues, gives them a notably practical application, this is not straightforwardly the intended outcome of the stated aim of Aurelius and of Fox Morcillo himself — the aim, that is, of portraying a ruler "such as the present times require." And that, in turn, gives sharper edge to Antonius's criticism of Aurelius for adopting an excessively theoretical approach to his subject. Antonius does seem to be expressing doubts lurking in Fox Morcillo's mind as to his own approach, at least so far as formal categories are concerned. Nevertheless, Fox Morcillo still feels bound to these, even if the framework that they establish for his discussion proves somewhat constrictive for what he in fact wishes to talk about.

His bi-focal view of princely rule makes itself apparent in a particularly interesting way when Aurelius talks about war. In the section on "military fortitude" he insists on the traditional criteria of the "just war." The prince will not wage war to satisfy his own greed, ambition, or anger, to extend his kingdom, or for the sake of his "glory" (sig. R4^v-5^v). Nevertheless, when discussing the virtue of prudence, Aurelius urges the study of the art of warfare (sig. K2^v-4^r). The prince should learn to look at terrain with the eye of a general, and he should take some figure of great military renown as a model for himself: as Caesar took Alexander, Alexander Achilles, and as Scipio took Cyrus. In this way the prince will emulate Philopoemen, the Achaean soldier and statesman "who reportedly did not consider any time of peace so tranquil that he should cease to reflect often on matters of war" (sig. K4^r). All this, of course, comes from Chapter 14 of Machiavelli's *Prince*. There are other borrowings; for example, from Chapter 3, from which Fox Morcillo takes over substantial elements from Machiavelli's advice on how the prince should establish his power and authority in newly conquered dominions (sig. L6^v-8^r). Beyond that, it seems clear that Fox Morcillo owes to Machiavelli his interest in the question of sedition and how the prince shall forestall it. In itself, it is not surprising to find Fox Morcillo taking over material from *Il Principe*. After all, the distinction between useless and useful treatises on kingship which he makes in his preface has obvious resemblances to a famous passage in *Il Principe* itself. It is, nevertheless, of interest to find this happening in a work that largely holds to the humanist idealizing manner and, more especially, in a lengthy section, stresses in a distinctly Erasmian fashion the prince's duty to promote godliness and genuine Christianity on the basis of sound learning and a respect for the Scriptures (sig. I1^r-6^r). Fox Morcillo's treatise is, so far as I know, the earliest Spanish work in which one finds borrowings from Machiavelli's *Prince*. Perhaps because Fox Morcillo nowhere mentions either the name of Machiavelli or the title of *Il Principe*, this has gone unnoticed, as it seems, in studies of reactions to Machiavelli's thought in sixteenth-century Europe.

But if Fox Morcillo takes over some elements from *Il Principe*, he rejects others. As we have seen, he excludes the pursuit of "glory" as a legitimate ground for war. Still more emphatically, he repudiates the view that the ruler need not keep good faith. That he has Machiavelli in mind here is clear from the fact that he echoes his praise for the way in which Pope Alexander VI succeeded in his aims by never keeping faith with anyone (sig. N8^v). Fox Morcillo comments: "Quorum opinione quid turpius, absurdius, aut perniciosius? quid enim aliud est, fidem non servare, quam pietatem ac religionem deserere? quam omnem naturae legem violare?" (sig. O1^r). It will, of course, be "necessary" (as he puts it) for the ruler sometimes to hide his thoughts, to feign one thing and do another. But Fox

Morcillo is at pains to establish a moral distinction between dissembling and the breaking of faith. And so we see that, while he has shown some intellectual initiative, even boldness, in borrowing from a work such as *Il Principe*, he remains attached to traditional attitudes when it is a matter of fundamental principles.

As already mentioned, it is in Book III that Aurelius at last addresses himself directly to the task of arguing for the superiority of monarchy over all other forms of government, and particularly over the republicanism favoured by Antonius. And it is here that one is most sharply aware of intellectual tensions: tensions, that is, between the *a priori*, theoretical conceptions of kingship to which Fox Morcillo remains attached, and, on the other hand, the empirical view of government as a functioning system which had established itself as an important element in his thinking. This has much to do with the fact that Antonius is now allowed to say something on his own account and challenge a number of Aurelius's assertions. As we have seen, he opens Book III by rejecting Aurelius's whole manner of proceeding so far. In what follows, much time goes on claim and counter-claim between the two speakers regarding what one can hope for, and what one must fear, from monarchical or from republican government alternatively. Each speaker is allowed to make effective points against the other, and on largely empirical grounds. It is not the case that Aurelius emerges as clearly right and Antonius as clearly and wholly wrong. Antonius makes points about the difficulties of monarchical rule in practice that seem obviously to bear on what Aurelius has himself said earlier, in Book II, when talking about the various matters requiring government management and control in his own day. But it is particularly interesting to see what happens, in this final book, to the various theoretical statements about monarchical rule to which Aurelius now has recourse.

First, there is Aurelius's attempt—his first attempt—at a teleological presentation of the function of government. This, he argues, exists to uphold law and thereby promote peace. Peace promotes the *commoditas publica*, from which follows a "recta vitae institutio virtuti congruens," while the end or goal of that is the "ultimum illud bonum quo cuncta referuntur" (sig. Y3^r). Aurelius stresses the interconnectedness of these different things and, of course, believes that monarchy is the form of government best able to lead men on from the one to the other. But his terminology here, although clearly owing something to Thomistic argument, is notably summary and imprecise and there is no attempt to show how it all comes to pass. However, he soon reinforces this view of government with another, where he argues for kingship—specifically—in terms of the whole constitution of the created order. "Videmus quacunque in re bene constituta ordinem omnem ab uno veluti capite, cui reliqua subiiciantur, proficisci, idemque caput optimum esse, quia reliquis praesit" (sig. Z1^r). But since, he continues, earthly things are images of the heavenly, which are ordered by God himself ("eaque unius Dei nutu regantur"), "shall we not say that monarchy is the best form of rule?" (sig. Z1^v). It was with this highly traditional view of monarchy (much beloved of those writers of the past whom he speaks of as tucked away "in angulis scholarum") that Aurelius had opened his whole discourse in Book I (sig. B5^r-6^v), before developing it in the way we have seen. Clearly, it was a way of looking at things that still held appeal for Fox Morcillo. At this point in Book III, however, Antonius simply ignores such argument and brings the conversation down to earth: one man cannot deal with all the business of government by himself; one man "cannot always be good," as he says; and so on (sig. Z3^{r-v}). The great conception of kingship adumbrated by Aurelius is left hanging in the air. At the end, however, when Aurelius returns to the topic, Antonius does voice his dissent. Aurelius eloquently evokes the principle of unity that sustains all things: there is one ruler of the universe ... one sun in the heavens ... one final end (sig. Aa6^{r-v}). Therefore he would like to see, here on earth, one single supreme ruler, to whom all other princes would be subject. The advantages of this, he contends, have already been shown by the Roman Empire. All this brings to mind Dante's idea of a world-ruler, a "curator orbis," as described in the *De monarchia* (I.xiv; III.xvi). Frances Yates has reminded us of the appeal that Dante's vision had for those in the sixteenth century whose aspiration was to see such an order of things actualised under the Emperor Charles V.[8] But Antonius is unimpressed. He simply tells Aurelius that he is talking like Gorgias or Thrasymachus, "dum non tam rationum acumine quam ubertate dicendi nos vis obruere" (sig. Aa3^r, 7^r). As for the Roman Empire, it did not cover even one tenth of the globe; and, he adds, by no means all nations will be persuaded to accept kingly rule when they have known republican liberty.

With this their discussion comes to an end: to an end rather than a conclusion, for the final words of Antonius are worth noting: if there were time, he says, "multa quae tu pro veris & exploratis constituisti, vocaram in dubium iterum" (sig. Aa7^v-8^r). Aurelius has failed to convince him. More importantly, the work as a whole leaves the reader with the impression that Antonius has some good reasons for not being convinced. It also leaves the impression that Fox Morcillo recognised this, despite Aurelius's role as spokesman for Fox Morcillo's own views. Machiavelli, in his *Prince*, was able to make a clear mental distinction between "la verità della cosa" and "l'immaginazione di essa." For Fox Morcillo things were more complex. The interest of his treatise has much to do with the way in which it shows the divergent and even self-questioning movements of his own mind.

The appeal, in broad terms, that the anti-authoritarian, empiricist approach held for him is indicated by remarks of his in other works. In his *De historiae institutione* he makes mocking mention of those "qui eisdem semper vestigiis insistentes, naturam rerum ipsam non contemplentur, non animi sui aciem exacuant & intendant...." As far as he is himself concerned (as he writes in the preface to his commentary on Plato's *Republic*), "certe apud me pluris est veritatis ... examinatae au[c]toritas quam vel doctissimi viri ... defensio." But such remarks perhaps suggest a more radical approach than his writings in fact show. As we have seen, similar remarks are found in the preface to his *De regni regisque institu-*

tione, whereas his approach to empiricism in the work at large is by no means straightforward.

Taken as a whole, its character presents marked similarities to the "Commonwealth" literature of Early Tudor England as described some years ago by A. B. Ferguson.[9] It is Ferguson's contention that the authors of the works to which he refers, while recognising the moral basis of society, were not content to talk only in ethical terms. They showed an interest in tracing economic cause and effect, and desired legislation embodying practical policies and capable of remedying the ills of society.[10] This does not mean that they made a clean break with old habits of thought. They still saw society in terms of the analogy of the human body; their formal ideal of society was still a static one. However, as Ferguson puts it, in the interests of an essentially conservative ideal they invoked a creative policy.[11] If their work indicates a move towards empiricism, it remains the case that "their empiricism was undoctrinaire, all but unformulated."[12]

As regards Fox Morcillo's treatise, we have seen that its author declares at the outset an interest in approaching his subject with an eye to the needs of his own day, avoiding what is excessively theoretical and out-of-date and concerning himself with what it is reasonable to hope for. As the work progresses, an interest in government as a matter of practical management of public affairs — financial, economic, military, political (in the narrower sense) — repeatedly emerges. At such times one is likely to feel that this is carrying him beyond the ambit of the basic terms in which he envisages kingly rule. These terms, however, are such as still to give a central position to the personal concept of government and to moral categories and ideals of conduct. The greater part of the treatise takes the form of an account of the education the prince must receive and the virtues he must practise. It is in Fox Morcillo's defence of monarchy as the most desirable form of government that the tension, if not actual conflict, between the aprioristic and the empirical approaches to the central issues of his discussion most clearly shows. In the work as a whole it appears not only in the explicit and permitted disagreement between the two contending interlocutors but also in the corresponding oscillation in the approach of Fox Morcillo's own spokesman to his theme. These features of the work can perhaps be seen as giving it a characteristically sixteenth-century stamp. They also suggest that Fox Morcillo deserves to be seen as a figure of some significance in the context of the political thinking of the sixteenth-century North European Humanists of whom Professor Skinner writes. Juan Luis Vives was not the only Spaniard actually writing then in northern Europe to have things of interest to offer here.[13]

Christ Church, Oxford

Notes

1. *Foundations of Modern Political Thought*, 2 vols. (Cambridge, 1978), I, 244.
2. id., I, 231.
3. id., I, 246, 248.
4. id., I, 198, n. 2; 213–14.
5. See Henry de Vocht, *History of the Foundation and Rise of the Collegium Trilingue Lovaniense 1517–1550*, 4 vols., *HL*, 10–13 (Louvain, 1951–55), IV, 438–41. See also Ruth Pike, *Aristocrats and Traders. Sevillian Society in the Sixteenth Century* (Ithaca and London, 1972), pp. 144–47.
6. sig. A3^{r-v}, 4^{v}. I follow here the Antwerp 1566 edition published by Jean de Laet. The foliation of this is identical to that of the Speelmans first edition (Antwerp, 1556).
7. See Marjorie Grice-Hutchinson, *The School of Salamanca. Readings in Spanish Monetary Theory 1554–1605* (Oxford, 1952), p. 89; also by the same author, *Early Economic Thought in Spain 1177–1740* (London, 1978), pp. 127–29.
8. "Charles V and the Idea of the Empire," in *Astraea. The Imperial Theme in the Sixteenth Century* (London, 1975), pp. 1–28 (pp. 20–26).
9. "Renaissance Realism in the 'Commonwealth' Literature of Early Tudor England," *JHI*, 16 (1955), 287–305. See also Skinner, I, 223–28.
10. Ferguson, pp. 291–93.
11. id., p. 293.
12. id., id.
13. After this treatise was first brought out by Speelmans in 1556, there seem to have been two further Antwerp editions in 1566, a second one by Speelmans as well as that of Laet. In the early seventeenth century the work appeared twice more, on each occasion being printed along with Scipione Ammirato's *Discorsi sopra Cornelio Tacito*, in the Latin version of Christoph Pflug, and the latter's own *Digressiones politicae ex Tacito excerptae* (Frankfurt, 1609 and 1618), "ob argumenti similitudinem summamque operis elegantiam." Palau notes only the 1566 editions.

The Unsuspected Source of Eobanus Hessus's
Victoria Christi ab Inferis

Harry Vredeveld

When Eobanus Hessus, the Erfurt Humanist, proposed in his brief epic *Victoria Christi ab Inferis* to sing of arms and the man who triumphed over infernal Jove and rescued from limbo the patriarchs of old, he invoked for his adventurous song the aid of the conquering hero himself.[1] But alas for brave words and noble sentiments! For it was not to be Christ, not that heavenly Muse, who inspired our human, all too human Humanist here. Indeed, the things that Eobanus intended to pursue had often been attempted before him, in prose and rhyme, in adaptations famous and obscure. And from the latter — *miserabile dictu* — he took one long forgotten to his bosom and nurtured it and brought it out again as his own.

It was early 1517, the halcyon days of northern Humanism before the storms of the Reformation. The Reuchlin-affair was ending in the apparent victory of humanist enlightenment over scholastic obscurantism; the Erfurt *sodalitas*, from whom the first volume of the *Epistolae Obscurorum Virorum* had sprung just the year before, was still gloating over the *coup de grâce* it had given the forces of darkness. And at the head of these Humanists was the acknowledged poet-king, Helius Eobanus Hessus, even then — as the first *poeta* to hold that post in Erfurt — being appointed professor of rhetoric and poetics.

Thus, his mood euphoric, exuberant, and triumphant, Eobanus quite naturally found himself attracted once again to the congenial and appropriate theme of Christ's triumph over the darkness of hell. Twice before he had adapted the story: once, in the *Heroidum Christianarum Epistolae* of 1514, where Mary of Magdala writes to the distant beloved, the risen Lord, and recounts the harrowing of hell after the manner of the apocryphal Gospel of Nicodemus; and again, in 1515, in the *Hymnus Paschalis*, where he pointedly associates Christ's triumph with that being won by Reuchlin. And now, at Easter 1517, still in high spirits at Humanism's apparent victory, he approaches the theme again, this time in the epic hexameter.

The poem opens, as we saw, with the standard *propositio* and *invocatio* to the heavenly Muse and proceeds to introduce the subject proper with an account of the Creation and man's fall. Five thousand years have since passed; and in the gloom of limbo the righteous await their Redeemer. They will not have long to wait. For now Christ, having died on the Cross, descends into hell while all Nature grieves and groans for its Creator. Deep in the bowels of Stygian darkness the master of hell, Dis, looks out from his castle's ramparts and anxiously watches Christ's drawing near. Terrified at the prospect of another defeat at Christ's hands and fearful of losing even this infernal home-away-from-home, he speaks manfully to his minions: they are to defend the fatherland! And off they scurry, like so many howling wolves, to take up their battle positions, while the cowardly Dis retreats to the safety of his fortress. Hell's gates are barred and barricaded—much more heavily, says the poet, than when those ancient heroes Hercules, Theseus, and Aeneas made their katabases. Then, behold! a wondrous light shines in the darkness. All are stunned, the tormentors and judges no less than the damned. Even Charon stops his work and attempts to hide his skiff in the reeds. But the legions of devils, not daring to stand in the way of Him who calls on the gates to raise their heads, flee in mass panic as Christ breaks down the outer gates and enters limbo. The righteous, of course, are jubilant. One by one, Adam at their head, they proceed to welcome their Redeemer. Christ responds with kind words. Thereupon He breaks down the inner gates of hell, the gates to Dis's castle, and finding the ancient serpent cowering in his hiding place binds him with adamant chains. The victory gained, Christ raises the standard of the Cross and conducts the throng of the righteous to heaven. Then he descends once more in rapid fall to earth, to Jerusalem, where His body is still being guarded by Pilate's soldiers. Now it is Easter morning. Christ rises from the dead, and Nature rejoices at His return. And as the Lord appears to many of His followers, the faith begins to spread. Only the tribe of the circumcised remains unregenerate, which is why it is condemned to wander forever over the face of the earth. But Christ ascends to heaven where even now, sitting at the right hand of God Almighty, He rules the earth and commands the obedient stars.

If I have retold at such length so familiar a tale, it is to demonstrate that in this entire poem there is not a single motif, not a single thought that cannot readily be traced to earlier adaptations of the theme. Nor does one expect, or miss, originality of invention in a reworking of the traditional story of the harrowing of hell. What one looks for here is the force and elegance of the diction, the clarity and energy with which the well-known plot is unfolded. And by that standard, it would seem, Eobanus's *Victoria Christi* rates quite high, if one is willing to forgive its occasional lapses into involuntary humor. The essential point for now, however, remains this: there appears to be no problem whatsoever with Eobanus's narrative sources. He knew the apocryphal Gospel of Nicodemus well. Variations on that familiar tale in the *Victoria Christi* can easily be accounted for by reference to medieval and Renaissance adaptations. For instance: Nicodemus speaks of two rulers of hell, Satan and Hades; Eobanus knows of only one, Dis. But that is a common variant at least since Carolingian times, recurring also in the humanist reworkings of the theme—in Erasmus's version for example (which Eobanus did not know), or in Macarius Mucius's *Triumphus Christi* (which he did know and use). Likewise, when Eobanus employs antique colors and pagan myths to depict the Underworld, he is following the old Christian-poetic tradition of using Vergil and Ovid, Statius and Claudian for breathing a measure of life into the abode of the dead.

With the problem of narrative sources, for all I knew, solved, indeed no problem at all, I set out to reread the Christian poets for parallels of phrasing, imagery, and motifs. And as I was making my way through Migne's *Patrologia Latina* and had just finished Juvencus's *Historia Evangelica* (*PL* 19), I came across a little poem ascribed to Juvencus, entitled "Triumphus Christi heroicus," an interesting, forceful epyllion on the harrowing of hell.[2] The poem is certainly not by Juvencus. Most likely it is the work of a late-medieval poet steeped in Vergil and the early Christian poets. So correct in metre and diction is the poem that—were it not for a few ecclesiastical medievalisms—it could well be mistaken for the product of a Christian Humanist of the High Renaissance.

Eobanus Hessus appears to have thought so too. In fact, he thought it so good that he took the obscure and widely forgotten poem and gave it a wider circulation—under his own name, of course. For when one compares the "Triumphus" with Eobanus's *Victoria* one will quickly realize that the Humanist has borrowed nearly every one of the medieval poem's first eighty lines, amplifying each line or group of lines into an epic totalling 487 verses. To the source's narrative frame he has prefixed an introduction of fifty-eight lines containing the *propositio* and *invocatio*, as well as the account of the Creation and of man's blessed state and dismal fall, until one greater Man should come to redeem us. Then comes the main narrative section, the very skeleton of which is formed by the medieval "Triumphus Christi heroicus." Here Eobanus contents himself with endowing those bare bones with the flesh and sinews of his erudition.

This is not the place to analyze Eobanus's techniques of amplification, to dissect the plagiarizer's art of swelling up one's model in order both to hide one's tracks *and* ease the pangs of conscience by the rationalization that one is, after all, improving on the source. A few examples will suffice. Both the "Triumphus" and Eobanus's *Victoria* describe how all Nature grieves at the death of its Creator. But where the source is content to leave well enough alone and stops the description with the sixth line: "Et quid opus multis? lugebant cuncta creata," Eobanus feels compelled to add that the moon too blushed and turned red at the sight of Christ's death—a baleful sight indeed! But this, our Christian *poeta doctus* continues, was not the blush that Luna displayed when enjoying the *dulcia furta* with her beloved Endymion. Or again: Where the source recounts in seven lines how the Gorgons and Harpies, the "Ultrices Dirae, Furiae, Parcaeque sorores" are stunned by Christ's illumination of the world of darkness, Eobanus expands the list of infernal beings by adding the names of the judges of the Underworld, as well as those of the damned. Not content with mere name-dropping, he also tells us what it is that each of them in their sudden amazement do or fail to do. Thus Aeacus, disgusted at being the only one left in his hall of justice (the others having disappeared to see the miraculous sights), himself decides it is time to adjourn. Rhadamanthus and Minos too leave their chambers. But those old wretches Tantalus, Ixion, Sisyphus, and Prometheus all enjoy a moment of respite from their torments — as did many other such mythical figments of a foolish age, so the Christian Humanist assures us. By now, however, the source's seven lines have been expanded to thirty.

Sed quid opus multis? Everywhere Eobanus contents himself with a mere swelling up of the source by the inclusion of more or less relevant, more or less poetic material, be it by adding descriptions of such places as limbo (in part after Vergil and his own heroic epistle) or of Paradise (after the *Phoenix* ascribed to Lactantius and after Baptista Mantuanus), or by adding similes of sometimes gargantuan proportions. Only once does he transpose a group of lines, and that only because the source had awkwardly inverted the chronological sequence of events and had then to backtrack with a *prior* (l. 30). Elsewhere Eobanus has faithfully plagiarized his model, pausing only to expand it and retard to a degree the forward flow of its narrative.

How or where Eobanus discovered the obscure poem I do not know. It must have been in some manuscript, for it was first published in 1537, in the appendix to Poelmann's edition of Juvencus which appeared in Basel. How unknown the "Triumphus Christi heroicus" was, may be gathered also from a letter of Mutian Rufus's to Lange, April 21, 1517. There Mutian praises Eobanus's *Victoria Christi ab Inferis* as a marvellous, powerful poem, and quotes a few lines from it as especially good examples of his friend's art. Little did Mutian know that of the four lines he cites two and a part of the third actually stem, nearly word for word, from the medieval "Triumphus"![3] Thus, as long as the anonymous poem lay forgotten by all except Eobanus, his guess that no one would ever find out remained a fairly safe bet. And indeed, had it not been for Poelmann's mistaken attribution of the poem to Juvencus and for the subsequent reprintings of the epyllion by Arevalus in the late eighteenth and by Migne in the nineteenth century, Eobanus's source might even now be entirely unsuspected.

Still, "in the end truth will out." So too here. And when we now read Eobanus's *Victoria* we may well agree with Mutian and with Ellinger that this is an attractive, readable, energetic little epic. But our admiration will henceforth be severely tempered by the realization that the energy here displayed is not at all Eobanus's own, but rather that of the anonymous poet of the "Triumphus Christi heroicus." Not from that heavenly Muse which he so earnestly invokes at the outset did Eobanus derive his inspiration, but rather from that Stygian anti-muse, Plagiary.[4] In this humanist harrowing of hell, one is tempted to conclude, Satan at last obtained a measure of revenge.

The Ohio State University

Notes

1. *Victoria Christi ab* | *Inferis.* | *Carmine Heroico Helio* | *Eobano Hesso Authore* | Colophon: *Impressum Erphordie per Mattheum* | *Maler anno domini. 1. 5. 17.* | 12 leaves, 4°. The text of the epyllion is to be reprinted, together with a German translation, in volume II of my edition of Helius Eobanus Hessus's poetic works in the series *Ausgaben deutscher Literatur des XV. bis XVIII. Jahrhunderts* (Berlin, de Gruyter).

2. Migne, *Patrologia Latina*, 19, cols. 385–88. See also Arevalus's introduction to Juvencus, *PL* 19, cols. 19 and 36–37, for bibliographical details.

3. See Karl Gillert, ed., *Der Briefwechsel des Conradus Mutianus*, Geschichtsquellen der Provinz Sachsen und angrenzender Gebiete, herausgegeben von der Historischen Commission der Provinz Sachsen, achtzehnter Band, zweite Hälfte (Halle, Hendel, 1890), p. 241. Mutian cites ll. 219–22 as follows:

> Nec mora, cardinibus postes cecidere solutis
> Cum sonitu magnamque dedit prolapsa ruinam
> Ianua, non aliter quam si Iovis igne repente
> Tacta cadat sonitumque trahat super equora rupes.

The corresponding lines in the "Triumphus Christi heroicus," ll. 27–29, are

> Nec mora, cum sonitu postes cecidere solutis
> Cardinibus, magnamque dedit collapsa ruinam
> Janua, et admittunt concussa palatia Christum.

It should be noted that Mutian must have read Eobanus's work in manuscript form, since the printed version has changed *magnamque* (l. 220 of the *Victoria* and l. 28 of the "Triumphus") to the more Vergilian-sounding *ingentemque*.

4. Of course Eobanus was by no means the only German poet of the time to engage in plagiarism. Tilonin, for instance, is often characterized, by Mutian and others, as a literary thief and a plagiarizer; probably he is the one whom Mutian labels "pestilens fur ... et plagiarius Ovidii" (Gillert, *Briefwechsel*, erste Hälfte, p. 137). And Conrad Celtis's plagiarism of a hymn to the Virgin Mary by Gregorius Tifernus and of poems by Bohuslaus von Hassenstein also quickly came to light; on this see Gustav Bauch, *Die Universität Erfurt im Zeitalter des Frühhumanismus* (Breslau, Marcus, 1904), pp. 122–23, and Lewis W. Spitz, *Conrad Celtis, The German Arch-Humanist* (Cambridge, Harvard University Press, 1957), pp. 8–10.

F R A N C E

Du Bellay, Turnèbe and Montaigne

Dorothy Gabe Coleman

During the 1550s and up until the outbreak of Civil War in 1562 Paris experienced the youthful surge of vernacular literature and knew the heyday of Latin scholars like Turnèbe, Muret, Dorat, Scaliger, Denys Lambin and so on. The printing, scholarly, Classical world interacts with the world of creative vernacular writing throughout the Renaissance but we have been slow to react to it. It is a well-known fact that Muret gave a course of lectures on Catullus, a course that Ronsard and Du Bellay followed with great eagerness in 1552. Yet, with the exception of Mary Morrison's two articles in the *Bibliothèque d'Humanisme et Renaissance* (1955 and 1956) and Trinquet on Montaigne (*passim*), very little work has been done on Muret and we still have only the *Scripta Selecta* which came out in Heidelberg in 1809 as a "modern" text. Everyone has known that the secret of Ronsard and Du Bellay lay in the hands of Dorat, their great Classical teacher, but even Quainton in his recently produced book on Ronsard does not mention Dorat. However, in 1979 Madame Demerson published a very fine edition of *Les Odes latines* of Dorat and through these odes we can live in the world of Henri II and his sons, Marguerite de Savoie, the cardinal of Lorraine and almost participate in the public events of that period. Other scholars (for instance Françoise Joukovsky in her *Montaigne et le problème du temps*, 1972) make admirable use of commentaries and sixteenth-century editions of Classical writers. And this is one of the biggest tasks that French Renaissance scholars have to do, that is to look closely at the Classical texts in editions of the period — otherwise we cannot even start to assess the Classical influences on vernacular literature. A number of Classical scholars (for instance Kenny and Pfeiffer) have studied some of them but from the point of view of textual criticism, the technique and art of restoring a text to its original state. Our task is different: we want to read them in their sixteenth-century context. It is crucial that the commentaries, the *adversaria*, the *variae lectiones*, the *annotationes* (and even the *annotatunculi!*) and *recensatio* — these are the terms given for a scholar's interpretation — of all the editions of the sixteenth century be worked on. For it is useless consulting the most recent Oxford text of Horace when we are describing Montaigne's use of him.

I want to pick out today several tiny threads from this silk-spun bilingual web and I shall take Turnèbe as my textural centre with Du Bellay and Montaigne as subtly-woven fabrics in the loom of creative writing.

Du Bellay had already shown himself as a translator of Books 4 and 6 of the *Aeneid*; the *Quatriesme Livre de l'Eneide* was published in 1552 by Vincent C(*sic*)ertenas. The Rome milieu accounts for his publishing in 1558 his neo-Latin *Poemata*. It is the milieu also that matters when he returns to France in 1557. He enters the circle of Féderic Morel, a circle full of eminent Latinizers such as Dorat, Macrin, Buchanan, Michel de l'Hospital, Lancelot de Carle, Guillaume Aubert, Sainte-Marthe and Turnèbe.[1] At his death on January 1, 1560 a neo-Latin *tombeau* was compiled for him by Turnèbe, Claude d'Espence and lesser figures like Claude Rouillet, Hélie André and Léger du Chesne. Turnèbe had been the *lecteur royal* since Toussaint died in 1547; he taught in Latin; at first he had a dislike for everything in the vernacular but was soon won over by the Pléiade and was present at the production of Jodelle's *Cléopatre* in 1553. He edited in 1552 and 1555 several works of Plutarch; in 1552 he published seven plays by Aeschylus; the victory of the French over the English at Calais in 1558 had him writing a "Panegyricus de Calisio capto," while Du Bellay wrote first in French "L'Hymne au Roy sur la prinse de Callais" and then in Latin "In laudem Francisci Lotareni Guisorum ducis." Turnèbe and Du Bellay knew and admired each other and so it is no surprise that the latter translates a poem of the former in 1559, "Nouvelle Maniere de faire son profit des Lettres."[2] The circumstances around this neo-Latin poem — such as the fact that it was a satire directed against Pierre de Paschal — are well known and can be read in Chamard's edition of Du Bellay's works.[3] He was the ideal person to translate the quips at the Italianisms the court lapped up so that,

> Censeo in Italiam, trans & gradiaris ut Alpes.
> Hinc pretiosa venit merx, quae nos ducit hiantes
> Defixosque tenet ...   (ll. 24–26)

becomes

> Tu dois veois l'Italie, & les Alpes passer:
> Car c'est de là que vient la fine marchandise
> Qu'en bëant on admire, & que si hault on prinse ... (ll. 34–36)

And a little further on he translated Turnèbe's phrase *namque solet cumulare profectio Musas* (l. 34) as

> Car aux Muses souvent profite un long voyage.

But there is irony here: the epistle is satirising Paschal and his dishonest life as a literary courtier; underlying the first meaning there is, surely, the fact that Du Bellay's own career has so brilliantly demonstrated in 1558 with the publication of four of his collections of poetry—Italy is good for a poet. It inspired him to turn his gaze to satire, to irony, to Rome—its grandeur through the Latin poets and its decline in the present time—thereby establishing his immortality on subjects that had not been dealt with by Ronsard.

In fact in Turnèbe's epistle the lines before the "Voyage of the Muses" are redolent of Du Bellay's own poetry. *Si Romam strepit ore* (l. 28) becomes,

> S'il sçait, parlant de Rome, un chacun estonner ...

and both *Les Regrets* and the *Antiquitez de Rome* have talked about the eternal city. He avoids translating accurately *strepit ore*. The next line *Undivagos & si Venetos, atque Appula rura*, becomes,

> Si des Venitiens que la mer environne ...

and brings clearly to our minds sonnet 133 of *Les Regrets* where he had so brilliantly brought to life the sounds and views of Venice,

> Il fait bon voir (Magny) ces Coions magnifiques.

When Turnèbe says of Italy,

> Est illic Helicon, illis Parnasia laurus,
> Et fons Pegaseo quem protulit ungula cornu ...   (ll. 43–44)

Du Bellay has to bring in the name of the country,

> Doncques en Italie il te convient chercher
> La source Cabaline, & le double rocher,
> Et l'arbre que le front des Poëtes honore ...   (ll. 61–63)

And finally, the advice given by Turnèbe to an aspirant second-rate Court poet,

> Sed quaesita tibi sit opinio fraude, tuenda
> Arte, subinde aliquid non magnum scribe sagaci ...   (ll. 78–79)

is nicely rendered as,

> Il te fault quelques fois, soit en vers, soit en prose,
> Escrire finement quelque petite chose
> Qui sente son Virgile, & Ciceron aussi ...   (ll. 107–09)

If one takes this out of its context, is it not the innutrition theory that Du Bellay promoted himself in the *Deffence & Illustration de la poësie française*?

Du Bellay died on January 1, 1560 and Turnèbe in 1565. Montaigne admired them both, particularly Turnèbe. We cannot say that he knew Du Bellay—there is too little evidence of Montaigne's activities between 1546 and 1555—but he certainly knew and respected Turnèbe. In "Du pedantisme" (I.25) they are both mentioned: his hatred of pedants is supported by Du Bellay—"tesmoing nostre bon du Bellay" and then he quotes the line,

Mais je hay par sur tout un sçavoir pedantesque ...   (*Les Regrets*, 68)[4]

The example Montaigne gives of a gentleman who was not a pedant was Turnèbe and we may look at his description,

> comme *j'ay veu* Adrianus Turnebus, qui, n'ayant faict autre profession que des lettres, en laquelle c'estoit, à mon opinion, le plus grand homme qui fut il y a mil 'ans, n'avoit toutesfois rien de pedantesque que le *port de sa robe*, et *quelque façon externe*, qui pouvoit n'estre pas civilisée à la courtisane ... Car au dedans c'estoit l'ame la plus polie du monde. *Je l'ay souvent a mon esciant* jetté en propos eslongnez de son usage, il y voyoit si cler, d'une apprehension si prompte, d'un jugement si sain, qu'il sembloit qu'il n'eut jamais faict autre mestier que la guerre et affaires d'Estat. Ce sont natures belles et fortes ...   (vol. I, p. 139; the italics are mine)

At what date did Montaigne know Turnèbe? Trinquet's hypothesis[5] — though it be attractive — that Montaigne was in Paris from 1549 to 1556(?), is rather rash. I am going to put forward a suggestion that is backed by some facts. We know for certain that Montaigne was in Paris for seventeen months from 1561-62; he was twenty-eight years old and could consult Turnèbe more easily than at fourteen — the latest date if he sees him in Toulouse in 1547, the date Turnèbe left to settle in Paris permanently; he has several books from Turnèbe's press in his library;[6] and we have one extra fact. There is in Libourne's Municipal Library a copy of Philibert de l'Orme's *Nouvelles inventions pour bien bastir et a petits fraiz*, with the autograph of Montaigne cut out. Presumably it was cut out after Montaigne's *Essais* had been put on the Index by a decree of 12 June 1676. Now the fascinating thing about this copy — apart from Montaigne's interest in a pioneering book of architecture — is the date and the publisher: *A Paris, De l'Imprimerie de Federic Morel, rue S. Iean de Beauuais au franc Meurier. M.D.LXI. Auec priuilege du Roy.* It is Du Bellay's printer: Fédéric Morel, surnamed the Elder (1523-83) set up in business in 1557 and was made printer to the king in 1571. Morel not only printed practically all of Du Bellay's circumstantial work in 1559 but was going to, for instance, bring out in 1569 an edition of *Les œuvres françoises* of the poet. The cénacle of Morel is going strongly in 1561; it still counts Turnèbe as a faithful client; could it be that Montaigne entered that cénacle? Could it be that he bought the Philibert de l'Orme straight from the Morel press? When he paid another trip to Paris in 1571-72 he saw to it that it was Morel who published the *Vers françois* of La Boétie. If it is assumed that he frequented the Morel cénacle several things emerge. Montaigne is much more of a scholar than he would like us to think. I have several pieces of evidence to "prove" this.

In the 1550s scholars produce editions of Classical writers which are far more erudite and careful; collating manuscripts is on the go. Examples such as Muret's *Catullus* (1554 and 1559), Charles Estienne's *Cicero* (1554) and later in the 1560s Lambin's *Horace* (1561) and *Lucretius* (1563 — dedicating the second book to Ronsard). And we have a term meaning literary criticism — *animadversio*.[7] It appears first in 1553 in a book by Turnèbe entitled *Leodegarii a quercu animadversiones in Rullianos Petri Rami commentarios* ... against Ramus's teaching (Léger du Chesne being merely a pseudonym for Turnèbe). We see the word later on in Scaliger, Justus Lipsius, Didier Hérauld and Isaac Causabon.[8] We find the word in the *Essais* (III.9, II.946) "la justice a cognoissance et animadvertion aussi sur ceux qui chaument" with the usual meaning of censure. Where we really see it in the meaning of literary criticism is in the *Journal de Voyage en Italie*[9] which Montaigne did not publish and did not intend it ever to be published. He uses twice the word *animadversion* in the meaning of literary criticism. The first time (pp. 115–16) is in the context of a scholarly discussion,

> Disnant un jour à Rome avec nostre ambassadur, où estoit
> Muret et autres sçavans ...

Muret had been a tutor in the collège de Guyenne when Montaigne was a pupil there; his enthusiasm for Roman poetry and his enlightened literary criticism are obvious to anyone who has read his commentary on Catullus; it would have been obvious to a man like Montaigne. The whole company converses on the worth of Amyot (who was himself a pupil of Lambin and Cujas) interpreting Plutarch via his translation to French of the *Œuvres morales & meslées* and the *Vies des hommes illustres*. Montaigne maintains that Amyot is an excellent translator,

> Que où le traducteur a failli le vrai sans de Plutarque, il y en a substitué
> un autre vraisemblable et s'entretenant bien aus choses suivantes et pré-
> cédentes.

But the scholars are opposed to this and they produce,

> l'animadversion (which they attribute) au fils de M. Mangot, avocat de Paris,
> qui venoit de partir de Rome ...

Eventually, having considered the different meanings around the words chosen by Amyot and Henri Estienne to translate the Greek, Montaigne says,

> j'avouai de bone foi leur conclusion

We see here Montaigne the scholar giving in to other scholars whereas in the *Essais* he can remain convinced that his esteem, nay adoration, of Amyot for himself, that is, for Michel de Montaigne, the non-pedant and non-academic, is just.[10]

The second time he uses *animadversion* is even clearer. Montaigne's own copy of his *Essais* had been taken from him (together with a number of books) to be read by the Papal court in Rome. They are given back to him "chastiés selon l'opinion des docteurs moines." First of all they had to use an interpreter. Secondly, the *Maestro del Sacro palasso* listens to Montaigne's arguments kindly,

> et se contantoit tant des excuses que je faisois sur chaque article d'animad-
> version que lui avoit laissé ce François, qu'il remit à ma consciance de ra-
> biller ce que je verrois estre de mauvès gout.   (p. 121)

But Montaigne fights back in support of the Frenchman's translation,

> Je le suppliai, au rebours, qu'il suivît l'opinion de celui qui l'avoit jugé,
> avouant, en aucunes choses, comme d'avoir usé de mot de fortune, d'avoir
> nommé des poètes haeretiques, d'avoir excusé Julian, et l'animadversion sur
> ce que celui qui prioit devoit estre exempt de vitieuse inclination pour ce
> tamps ... que c'estoit mon opinion, et que c'estoit choses que j'avois mises,
> n'estimant que ce fussent erreurs.

On the other hand he sees how some of his words have been misinterpreted,

> à d'autres niant que le correcteur eust entendu ma conception.

Thirdly, Montaigne can see in intellectual terms that it is a game; the Italian
is a *habil'home* and can use arguments — "pledoit fort ingénieusement" — to support
any case. Montaigne can seem to agree to the Papal censure but in fact does not
alter any statement in the *Essais* of which the Papal court disapproved.

Besides this one fact of influence via contemporary Classical scholars on the
way Montaigne can use the term *animadversion*, the *Journal de Voyage* is steeped
in learned, theological and erudite events, acquaintances, discourses and conversations. I have time for only a few instances. His Classical learning is profound:
thus he has just left Spoleto behind and sees a village which is nowadays called
Monteleone Sabino,

> Servius dict sur Virgile, que c'est *Oliviferaeque Mutiscae*, de quoi il parle liv. VII.
> Autres le nient et argumantent au contrere.   (p. 138)

Not only does Vergil come to mind when he is riding on his horse, but Servius's
commentary of Vergil and what is more, other scholars who argue in an opposite
direction. Montaigne is using the methods of scholars: one opinion against another;
one annotation against the other; the *variae lectiones* of the world.

The people he likes are also scholarly. For instance, while in Rome,

> Le 29 de decembre M. d'Abein, qui estoit lors ambassadeur, gentil homme
> studieux et *fort amy de longue main de Montaigne*, fut d'avis qu'il baisast les pieds
> du pape.   (p. 97; my italics)

This man, a pupil of Joseph Scaliger, was very erudite; he corresponded with
the Florentine philosopher Vettori and took lessons from Muret in Rome. On
first coming to a village or town Montaigne at once makes for a theologian — be
he a Lutheran, Zwinglian, Benedictine, Jesuit — and it comes as a surprise that
he likes particularly the Jesuits. For instance, being in Rome during Lent Montaigne can indulge himself with a good supply of sermons — both from Jews and
from Christians; especially Padre Toledo,

(en profondeur de sçavoir, en pertinance et dispostion, c'est home très rare);
un autre très éloquent et populere, qui prechoit aux jesuites, non sans
beaucoup de suffisance parmi son excellence de langage; les deux derniers
sont jesuites. (pp. 122–23)

Immediately following this comes a paragraph of enthusiastic admiration for the
Jesuit Order, complimenting them on their efficient services and ending up by
saying,

C'est celui de nos mambres qui menasse le plus les hérétiques de nostre
tamps. (p. 123)

The military precision of the Society, the high average of intelligence in a large
body of men and the firmness of their institution would be approved of in a time
of Religious Wars. In addition Montaigne visited the Vatican Library: he saw
the famous Bible in four languages printed by Plantin, a printer of many books
in Montaigne's own library.[11] He makes a good comment on the Vergil copy
there,

Ce Virgile me confirma, en ce que j'ai tousjours jugé, que les premiers vers
qu'on met en Aeneide sont ampruntés: ce livre ne les a pas. (p. 115)

In this, he was right. Altogether, Montaigne reveals himself in the *Journal* as
learned, erudite, intellectual, scholarly and interested in everything as Turnèbe
was.

Finally, the vocabulary that Montaigne uses in the *Essais* is heavily dependent
on Latin. Carol Clarke in her book *The Web of metaphor* (Lexington, 1978) made
the point of the concrete quality of Latin which Montaigne channels into French.
I have elsewhere[12] examined style in the Renaissance and shown that the Latin
force of masculinity, the muscular imagery, the intellectual character of virility
dominated the poetics of the writers both in France and England. The concept
of *masle virilité* of language was commonplace but it is worth seeing it in two authors,
Turnèbe in Latin and Montaigne in French.

In 1564 Turnèbe published his *Adversaria*.[13] This book is dominated by close
and careful scholarship but the general taste and liveliness of its author mean that
it is delightful to read. And in particular, the language and literary criticism are
very thick and dense. For example, after quoting two lines from an Epistle of
Horace,[14]

An tacitum sylvas inter reptare salubres,
Curantem quicquid dignum sapiente bono-
que est?

the language he uses is very concrete,

sub ipso verborum *tectorio* ... Et ut *sub putamine nucleus* latet, ita quoque sub
ipsa *velut nuce*, quae frangenda est, quiddam tanquam salubre, *eduleque* recon-
ditur. (the italics are mine; p. 12)

Phrases like *sub tectorio, sub putamine nucleus* and *edule* are metaphors calling up *tego* and *sermo verbis tectus* (Cicero, *Fam.* 9. 22. 1); the shell and kernel phrase seems rare in Classical writers who used the words only in a literal sense and the *edulium* calls to the metaphor of food. Turnèbe uses the weaving, the interweaving, the interlacing and intertwining metaphor many times (e.g., f. 128ᵛ *retexebat omnia* or p. 203 *annotationibus intexere.*) Both Montaigne and himself may have had in mind the famous phrase of Seneca (*Ep.* 33) *Contextus totus virilis est; non sunt circa flosculos occupati* (*Essais* vol. II.873) which Montaigne uses in his most dense piece of literary criticism. He makes the important statement a little further on,

> Le maniement et emploite des beaux esprits donne prix à la langue, non pas l'innovant tant comme la remplissant de plus vigoreux et divers services, l'estirant et ployant.

Are not the dislike of innovation and the spirit of criticism here the same as Turnèbe's attitude to emendation? Hear him on f. 100ʳ,

> Ut moribus antiquis stabat res Romana, sic Romana lingua stat antiquis exemplaribus, à quibus cum recedunt editiones, merito doctis suspectae sunt, & prope falsi condemnantur. Etsi enim aliquid plerunque non incommode fingunt, novitium tamen id est & nuperum, non cana illa vetustate venerandum. Itaque etiam cum minus fidem facit antiquitas, tamen eam quoquo pacto possumus, interpretari & retinere malumus, quam quicquam innovare ...

Words like *tissure* (used only twice by Montaigne)[15] and *nerveux* (a neologism of Montaigne in Robert's dictionary: the example he gives is,

> un parler succulent et nerveux, court et serré, non tant délicat et peigné comme vehement et brusque ...   (vol.I.171)

and *succulent* are grooved into French by Montaigne. They may be compared to a passage such as this one in Turnèbe,

> Est ut longa iam maturitate victorum fructuum, ac conditaneorum ipsa temporis diuturnitate rugosorum iucundissimus succus: ita vetustissimorum scriptorum suavissimus gustus, habetque, ut vinum vetus gratam palato salivam, sic antiquitas saporem quendam intelligentibus suavem. (f. 195ʳ)

His delight in savouring, digesting, relishing Classical texts may be compared to Montaigne who *rumine* words from Vergil and Lucretius in his essay *Sur des vers de Virgile: la gaillardise de l'imagination* dominates both writers. The words of the Classical texts for both of them *signifient plus qu'elles ne disent*.

Turnèbe gives the world good texts of Classical writers but the heyday of the scholarly, printing world is over when he dies in 1565. The world of the Renaissance, eager to possess Classical texts, is satisfied; from this time onwards, it will only be Classical scholars who will go on collating the texts, emending the words and reviewing past texts. Vernacular literature has won the day; Montaigne, as Eliot saw — but did not mention his name — made French prose mature, expressive and sophisticated. He admires above all the Gascon dialect,

à la vérité un langage masle et militaire plus qu'autre que j'entende ...

He compares it with French, to the latter's delicate floweriness,

autant nerveux, puissant et pertinant, comme le François est gratieus, delicat et abondant.

But Montaigne's language is both sinewy, manly, fleshy and delicate, full and gracious. Claude Expilly writing a sonnet to praise the great man starts with the line,

Que tu es admirable en ce masle langage ...

and ends with,

Les siècles à venir chanteront à bon droit,
Montaigne par lui-mesme ensigna comme on doit
Et bien dire et bien vivre, et bien mourir encore.

(Appeared for the first time in the 1595 edition of the *Essais*)

Let me end with an English example of praise for Montaigne. John Locke in his *Journal* in 1685 wrote,

Montaigne, by a gentle kind of negligence, clothed in a peculiar sort of good language, persuades without reason: his Essays are a texture of strong sayings, sentences, and ends of verses, which he so puts together, that they have an extraordinary force upon men's minds.

University of Cambridge

Notes

1. This learned circle was of the same type as the one he had been in at Rome. After all, Ariosto had died in 1533, Bembo in 1547 — both good poets whereas the circle that Du Bellay circulated in consisted of Annibal Caro, Basilio Zanchi, Lorenzo Gambara, Bailleul, Bizet, Gohorry, Lestrange, Antoine Caracciol, Gordes and Panjas. Several sonnets of *Les Regrets* are dedicated to one or other of this group: for example, no. 30. "Quiconque (mon Bailleul) ..."; no. 53. "Vivons (Gordes) vivons ..."; no. 72, l. 3 "Si est-ce (Gohory) qu'icy ..." and no. 143. "Bizet, j'aymerois mieux faire un boeuf d'un formy."

2. I am using the B.N. editions, which are *De nova captandae utilitatis e literis ratione epistola ad Leoquernum* (Parisiis, apud viduam P. Attaignant, 1559) (Ye.8716) and *La nouvelle manière*

de faire son profit des Lettres: traduitte de Latin en François par I. Quintil du Tronssay en Poictou. Ensemble le Poëte courtisan (Poitiers, 1559) (Rés.Ye.1710).

I have not taken notice of the *v* and *u* in the Latin: the quotations are done in a way that should be familiar to readers and not according to the text. I have not used the ligatures in the Latin. This is in conformity with what classicists do nowadays.

3. H. Chamard, *Œuvres poétiques, Discours et Traductions*, vi, i (Paris, 1931).

4. Villey-Saulnier's edition of the *Essais* (Paris, 1978), 2 vols., I, 133.

5. Roger Trinquet, *La jeunesse de Montaigne* (Paris, 1972).

6. Here are a few books from Turnèbe's press that are in Montaigne's library: *Apollinaire*. Ex bibliotheca Regia, Parisiis, 1552, apud Adr. Turnebum typographium regium; *Philon*. Philonis Judaei in libros Mosis de mundi opificio, historicos, de legibus. Ejusdem libri singulares. Ex bibliotheca regia, Parisiis, ex officina Adriani Turnebi typographi regiis typis, 1552; *Synesius*. Parisiis, 1553. Ex officina Adriani Turnebi, typographi Regii, Regiis typis.

7. Littré gives under the word *animadversion*: a sixteenth-century neologism, meaning a criticism, or observation or attention. Cotgrave (*A dictionarie of the French and English Tongues*, 1611) says that it is "a marking, or heeding; a consideration; a judgement." The O.E.D. mentions that the French neologism may have been the immediate model and gives as one of its meanings "a criticism, comment, observation, or remark (usually, but not always, implying censure)," and gives an example from Thynne, *Animadversion* 2. "My petye animadversions upon the Annotations and Corrections ... delivered by master Thomas Speghte upon the last edition of Chaucers Workes."

8. J.-C. Scaliger, *Animadversiones in historias Theophrasti*, apud Ioannam I. Iuntae F. Lugduni, 1584; Justus Lipsius, *Ad. Velleium Paterculum animadversiones*, 2 pt. in officina H. à Porta apud fratres de Gabiano; G. Iullieron pr. Lugduni, 1592 and another edition in 1594; Didier Hérauld, *Animadversiones ad libros xii epigrammat. M. Val. Martialis*, apud C. Morellum, Parisiis, 1600, and Isaac Casaubon, *Animadversionum in Athenaei diphosophistas libri XV*. A. de Harsy; G. Iullieron pr.: Lugduni, 1600, fol.

9. ed. Maurice Rat, Classiques Garnier (Paris, n.d.).

10. He does not alter the eulogy of Amyot that he had already written in 1580 after hearing the discussion in Rome. It remains the same,

> (car on m'en dira ce qu'on voudra: je n'entens rien au Grec, mais je voy un sens si beau, si bien joint et entretenu par tout en sa traduction que, ou il a certainement entendu l'imagination vraye de l'autheur, ou, ayant par longue conversation planté vivement dans son ame une generale Idée de celle de Plutarque, il ne luy a aumoins rien presté qui le desmente ou qui le desdie) ...   (II.4, vol I, p. 363)

This suggests that Montaigne had already had scholarly discussions on the worth of Amyot during his several visits to Paris.

11. Among the autographed book there is, of course, the famous Caesar with its commentary which was published by Plantin in 1570. Plantin was also the printer of Justus Lipsius whom Montaigne compared to *mon Turnèbe*.

12. See my *Gallo-Roman Muse. Aspects of Roman literary tradition in sixteenth-century France* (Cambridge, 1979).

13. *Adriani Turnebi Regii philosophiae graecae professoris adversariorum. Tomus primus duodecim libros continens. Cum Indice copiosissimo*. Parisiis, Ex officina Gabrielis Buonij in clauso Brunello, sub signo D. Claudij. 1564. Cum privilegio regis.

14. *Epistles*, I, 4.

15. See Roy E. Leake, *Concordance des Essais de Montaigne* (Geneva, 1981), 2 vols.

Du recours à l'histoire comme argument linguistique dans deux œuvres latines du seizième siècle

Colette Demaizière

I l est difficile de nier l'influence de certains événements historiques sur les questions linguistiques: le français compte des mots d'origine francique parce que le monde gallo-romain fut ébranlé par les invasions germaniques et que, parmi elles, celle des Francs aboutit à la conquête et à l'établissement du pouvoir politique; les guerres d'Italie que firent Charles VIII, Louis XII et François Ier permirent aux Français de découvrir les merveilles artistiques de la Renaissance italienne et d'acquérir des mots nouveaux pour parler de musique, de peinture ou d'architecture. Ces faits sont reconnus, mais le seizième siècle présente un autre aspect du rôle de l'histoire dans la linguistique: pour pallier l'insuffisance de connaissances scientifiques, notamment dans le domaine de la phonétique historique, de nombreux auteurs raisonnent sur l'histoire elle-même et y recherchent directement des arguments pour fonder leur théorie sur l'origine de telle ou telle langue. C'est le fonctionnement et les limites de cette méthode que nous nous proposons d'étudier.

Notons d'abord que cette attitude n'est pas générale et qu'Henri Estienne, par exemple, appuie sa démonstration sur des comparaisons linguistiques. Poursuivant son effort pour hausser le français au rang de la langue grecque, il utilise en 1565 dans le *De latinitate falso suspecta*[1] et en 1582 dans ses *Hypomneses de gallica lingua,*[2] comme dans ses œuvres françaises de la *Conformité*[3] et de la *Précellence,*[4] des arguments tirés de la comparaison entre les mots et les tournures syntaxiques, pour montrer la parenté directe du français avec le grec ou l'héritage grec par l'intermédiaire du latin. Ainsi, pour les mots du vocabulaire médical: la *dose*[5] de δόσις et les noms de maladies *pleurésie, paralysie, apoplexie*[6] etc., ou, pour les variations orthographiques des adverbes français: *jusque* devant consonne et *jusques* devant voyelle comme en grec ἄχρι et μέχρι devant consonne ἄχρις et μέχρις devant voyelle.[7]

En revanche, d'autres auteurs comme Joachim Périon et, à un degré moindre, Charles de Bovelles s'efforceront d'étayer leur thèse sur des arguments tirés de l'histoire, avant de se livrer, en guise de complément et de confirmation, à des rapprochements linguistiques.

Les deux ouvrages qui retiendront notre attention en ce domaine sont les *Dialogues*[8] de J. Périon et le *Liber de differentia*[9] de Bovelles. Les références historiques s'y rattachent à trois sources: la source biblique et principalement noachique, la source hellénique: guerre de Troie et descendance de Priam, enfin César.

Suivant une démarche qui doit nous aider à mieux comprendre les préoccupations et les hésitations de Périon, nous examinerons ces trois sources dans un ordre opposé à celui de la chronologie, ce qui nous conduit à commencer par César.

L'œuvre de César est très connue au seizième siècle. Le géographe italien Raymond Marliani (Marlianus), que citent Bovelles et Périon, a fait une édition des *Commentaires*, suivie d'une table de noms géographiques, qui a eu un immense succès et connut, après sa mort, de très nombreuses réimpressions dans les principales villes d'Europe.[10] Charles de Bovelles ne cache pas son admiration pour César qui, dit-il, "soumit les Gaulois jusqu'alors invaincus" et il rapporte complaisamment ce vers louangeur: "celui-là seul a vaincu les Gaulois qui vainquit aussi le monde."[11] L'autorité de César est telle que l'on tire même argument de ses omissions ou que, du moins, on essaie de les expliquer. Ainsi, Bovelles considère comme une preuve que la Flandre était inhabitée le fait que César, dans ses *Commentaires*, ne mentionne absolument aucune ville de Flandre.[12] Périon, qui a lu dans Strabon que l'on étudiait les lettres grecques à Marseille, s'étonne que César n'en ait pas parlé, mais il en voit la raison dans le fait que Marseille se trouvait dans la province romaine pacifiée, territoire qui n'est pas touché par la guerre des Gaules.[13]

Le premier argument linguistique tiré de César (*BG* VI.14) repose sur cette indication: les Druides estiment que la religion interdit de confier cela (il s'agit de textes religieux appris par cœur) à l'écriture, alors que, pour le reste en général, pour les affaires publiques et les comptes privés, ils se servent de l'alphabet grec ("litteris graecis utantur"). Bovelles, qui fait un contre-sens sur ce point en interprétant: les Druides usaient dans leurs mystères de la langue grecque, en conclut à l'existence en français de très nombreux mots venant du grec.[14] Périon, quant à lui, fait bien la différence entre "graecis litteris" et "graeco sermone uti," mais, dit-il: "si enim graecis litteris in omnibus fere rebus publicis privatisque rationibus, ut ait Caesar, utebantur, quid est causae quin graeco sermone eos usos concludamus?"[15] Il se livre alors à une sorte de commentaire de textes sur les lignes de César, pour expliquer "ea quae Caesar obscure dicit." Pour lui, les affaires publiques, ce sont les assemblées politiques, la justice, la religion; les comptes privés, ce sont les contrats, achats, locations, emprunts et aussi les jugements, plaidoiries, d'où cette conclusion que les Druides prononcent les sentences en langue grecque et que les avocats plaident dans la même langue.[16] Cette pratique du grec en Gaule leur paraît à tous deux confirmée[17] par un autre passage de César (*BG* I.29) disant qu'après la victoire de Montmort sur les Helvètes, on trouva dans leur camp des tablettes écrites en caractères grecs "litteris graecis confectae." Ces tablettes, qui furent apportées à César, contenaient la liste nominative des émigrants en état de porter les armes et aussi une liste particulière des enfants, des vieillards et des femmes. Bovelles, qui s'en tient à la thèse du français venant du latin et contenant, de surcroît, un certain nombre de mots d'origine grecque, ne tire aucune autre conséquence de ces deux passages du *De bello gallico* mais Périon, qui veut expressément démontrer la parenté de la langue française avec la langue grecque, poursuit son examen du texte. Or, au livre V, ch. 48, il a noté que César avait envoyé à Quintus Cicéron, assiégé par les Nerviens, une lettre écrite en caractères grecs pour qu'elle ne puisse être comprise de l'ennemi, si elle était interceptée. Périon rapporte ce fait, en reproduisant textuellement les mots de César: "hanc graecis conscriptam litteris mittit, ne intercepta epistula, nostra ab hostibus consilia cognoscantur" et, comme il l'a déjà fait, il pense que non seulement la lettre est écrite en caractères grecs mais en langue grecque. Pourtant César précise que Cicéron, ayant reçu la lettre, en donne lecture devant ses troupes et qu'elle excite chez *tous* les soldats la joie la plus vive "maximaque *omnes* laetitia afficit"; il n'est pas vraisemblable que *tous* les soldats de Q. Cicéron aient compris le grec mais cette nuance a échappé à Périon. Quoi qu'il en soit, ce passage du livre V détruit, en grande partie, son argumentation précédente car, si on écrit une lettre en grec pour qu'elle ne soit pas comprise par les Gaulois qui pourraient l'intercepter, c'est la preuve que ces Gaulois n'ont pas la pratique courante du grec, contrairement à ses déductions. Sans se laisser décontenancer, Périon va trouver, selon son sentiment, l'explication chez César, lequel, au livre VI, ch. 13, a dit que la société gauloise comptait deux classes d'hommes considérés: les Druides et les chevaliers. Ainsi, estime-t-il, on peut penser que si les Druides savaient le grec, il n'en était pas de même des chevaliers qui ignorent le grec mais dont beaucoup savent le latin, à cause de leur longue habitude de la guerre.[18] On peut remarquer que ces raisonnements n'ont rien de linguistique, qu'ils reposent même plutôt sur des erreurs de traduction et que, de toutes façons, ils ne sont guère convaincants, d'où la nécessité de les renforcer par le recours à d'autres sources, comme la source hellénique.

Dans le désir de trouver des ancêtres illustres et, autant que possible, des héros éponymes, on remonte, par les chemins de l'Enéide et de l'Iliade, jusqu'à Francus, fils d'Hector. Si l'on en croit Ronsard, dans sa préface de la *Franciade*,[19] c'était une légende communément adoptée à son époque: "Voyant que le peuple français tient pour chose très assurée selon les Annales que Francion, fils d'Hector, suivi d'une compagnie de Troyens, après le sac de Troie, aborda aux Palus Méotides[20] et, de là, plus avant en Hongrie, j'ai allongé la toile et l'ai fait venir en Franconie à laquelle il donna le nom, puis en Gaule fonder Paris, en l'honneur de son oncle Pâris." C'est là démarche de poète qui n'hésite pas à avouer qu'il a "allongé la toile," le poids historique de cette référence est bien faible, aussi on remarquera que cette source hellénique, seule, sera peu exploitée. Bovelles rappelle[21] que les Francs ont échappé à la ruine de Troie, se sont établis en Pannonie puis ont occupé une région voisine du Rhin et il ajoute que c'est Francus, leur roi de cette époque, qui leur fit préférer le nom de Francs à celui de Sicambres qu'ils portaient précédemment. C'est la seule conséquence linguistique que Bovelles tire du nom de Francus. Périon, lui, va se livrer à des déductions: "si ce fameux Francus, qui était troyen, a eu tant d'influence chez les anciens Gaulois qu'il y a conquis le pouvoir royal, penses-tu (Périon dialogue avec son neveu Pierre) qu'il soit parvenu, seul, en Gaule? Non, dit celui-ci, surtout du fait qu'il était le fils du roi Priam. Il est vraisemblable que ceux qu'il avait commandés à la guerre de Troie, délivrés du danger de la guerre et chassés du royaume, sont finalement venus avec lui en Gaule. Or, puisqu'il usait de la langue grecque, n'est-il pas vraisemblable que … beaucoup de mots grecs se soient mêlés à la langue gauloise?"[22] L'argument n'est pas bien fort et il remonte à un fait en apparence beaucoup moins sûr que ceux relevés par César qui les avait observés lui-même. L'idéal serait donc de pouvoir appuyer le raisonnement sur les textes sacrés et ce sera le recours à la source biblique qui, nous le verrons, va parfois curieusement rejoindre la source hellénique.

L'évocation des textes sacrés est fréquente, ainsi Claude Mitalier[23] renvoie, dans sa lettre *De vocabulis quae Iudaei in Galliam introduxerunt*, aux souvenirs de Luc dans les *Actes des Apôtres*: "Il a été consigné dans les ouvrages anciens que, peu après (la Pentecôte), on vit des Juifs dans les Gaules où ils vivaient." De cette présence, il tire argument pour attribuer une origine hébraïque à des mots comme *satin, perruque, jardin* ou *guerre*. Bovelles rapporte[24] l'épisode sur la prononciation de *Sibolet* et *Shibolet* emprunté au *Livre des Juges* (XII.4–6) pour montrer que la prononciation d'un même mot change selon les régions et il fait plusieurs fois référence au mythe de Babel comme au passage de la *Genèse* (II.19–20) où l'on voit Dieu laisser à Adam le soin de nommer tous les animaux créés.[25] C'est la thèse bien connue de la monogenèse du langage et le mythe de Babel, que Périon utilise beaucoup, lui aussi, traduit ce que R.-L. Wagner a appelé "une sorte de recours désespéré à l'histoire pour minimiser le scandale de la polyglottie."[26]

Périon se fait, auprès de son neveu Pierre, l'écho de la tradition selon laquelle la première langue des hommes était l'hébreu: "sermo is quo tum homines utebantur Hebraicus fuisse dicitur,"[27] puis, il y a eu le déluge et Babel et cette langue unique s'est divisée en langues multiples et variées "unum sermonem quem nonnullis Hebraicum fuisse placet in multos variosque (Deus) divisit atque distinxit."[28] Périon ne veut pas reprendre à son compte l'idée que la première langue était l'hébreu car, du moment qu'après Babel les hommes ne se comprenaient plus, rien, à son avis, ne permet de dire si la première langue était l'hébreu, le grec, le latin "aut alius atque diversus"[29] et lorsque, un peu plus loin dans leur dialogue,[30] son neveu lui dit: "eos quidem reprehendebas qui hebraicam linguam caeteris antiquitate antecellere judicant," il répond "ita est." Ainsi, Périon a le mérite de critiquer la thèse de l'hébreu langue-mère, mais il n'échappe pas complètement au désir de relier l'idiome à la parole révélée, en remontant du français au grec et en cherchant des liens avec une ascendance noachique. Il annonce (p. 21) qu'il s'inspire de l'historien Bérose, mais il présente deux versions "bérosiennes" de la descendance de Japhet. Celle que nous a transmise Flavius Josèphe[31] lui attribue sept fils parmi lesquels Gomares ou Γαμέρ, qui fut à l'origine des Gomariens, ensuite appelés Gaulois. Ce personnage est aussi nommé en latin Gomerus ou Comerus Gallus; il représente une tradition plus ou moins influencée par la Kabbale. Il est cité dans le *Candélabre* de Guillaume Postel et Bovelles évoque,[32] lui aussi, cette filiation, à propos du nom de la commune de Gauville dont il écrit: "elle a un nom tiré de Gallus, le premier fondateur des Gaulois ... comme si c'était, par hasard, cette région qui ait, la première, offert l'hospitalité à Comerus Gallus, ancêtre des Gaulois, comme le veut le Babylonien Bérose." Réfutant le rapprochement qu'il estime injustifié entre le mot "gaulois" et γάλα le lait,[33] Périon voit en ce *Gallus* un héros éponyme, comme *Juda* pour les Judaei, *Hispal* pour les Espagnols ou *Italus* pour les Italiens. Cependant, les conclusions linguistiques sont bien minces car, avoue Périon,[34] dans cette confusion des langues (en hébreu: babel) on ne peut dire quelle était celle de Japhet "nec quo Iapetus ipse in illa confusione perturbationeque linguarum sermone uteretur dici potest."

Périon développe, en outre,[35] une seconde filiation qui, toujours selon Bérose, attribue à Japhet huit enfants. Il reconnaît que les noms des sept autres ne concordent pas tous avec cette version et n'indique pas où il a trouvé cette interprétation "bérosienne." Or, il est évident que c'est celle d'Annius de Viterbe.[36] En effet, non seulement la descendance est exactement celle que donne Périon mais, de plus, on trouve, à la suite, un supplément à Bérose par Manéthon, Xénophon *De aequivocis* et *Catonis fragmenta de Originibus*, toutes œuvres auxquelles Périon se réfère. De plus, certains passages sont absolument identiques dans les termes eux-mêmes, ainsi Périon, p. 26[v] et Annius de Viterbe, p. 35[v]. Cette descendance de Japhet (ce qu'Annius de Viterbe appelle le troisième arbre) comprend: Comerus ou Gomerus (primogenitus), Medus, Magogus, Samothes Dis ou Ditis, Tubal et Jubal, Moscus et Thira. Seuls Gomerus, Magog, Tubal et Thira sont communs aux deux descendances, celle donnée par Flavius Josèphe et celle de Bérose selon Annius de Viterbe. Bizarrement, alors que nous retrouvons bien Comerus ou Gomerus Gallus, c'est vers Samothes surnommé Ditis que va se porter, cette fois, tout l'intérêt de Périon. On comprendra pourquoi, en voyant qu'il rattache ce passage à César (*BG* VI.18): "Tous les Gaulois se prétendent issus de Dis Pater; c'est une tradition qu'ils disent tenir des Druides. C'est pour cette raison qu'ils mesurent le temps par le nombre des nuits et non par celui des jours." Le texte de César étant incontestablement ce que Périon considère comme le plus sûr en matière historique et peut-être aussi parce qu'il a des doutes sur l'authenticité des indications fournies par Annius de Viterbe (en effet, contrairement aux autres, c'est une source qu'il ne cite pas expressément), pour ces raisons, il donne l'impression d'être, en quelque sorte, rassuré de pouvoir relier ce Samothes, surnommé Ditis (Pluton) à une tradition druidique, connue grâce à César. Cette correspondance d'une religion à l'autre ne peut nous surprendre et, de la même façon, chez Annius de Viterbe, Noé est soit Noa, soit Ianus, soit Caelum, son épouse Titea, Vesta ou Terra. Samothes est, selon Périon, le premier qui ait fondé des colonies chez les Celtes, c'est-à-dire, précise-t-il, "iis in locis quae Celtae, id est Galli incolant."[37] Annius de Viterbe dit à peu près la même chose: "Celtas sive Gallos Francigenas condidit Samothes"[38] et, après cela, il appelle les Gaulois Samothei. Parmi les descendants de Samothes, Druides a donné son nom aux Druides car c'est lui qui aurait dirigé une sorte de collège de druides fondé par son père Saron. Là encore, Périon voit une confirmation dans César (*BG* VI.13) qui écrit: "His autem omnibus Druidibus praeest unus qui summam inter eos habet auctoritatem." Cette habitude du commandement unique lui paraît héritée du premier chef d'école: Druides. Ensuite, après un certain Bardus, doué pour la musique et les vers, vient un Celtes ou Celta qui, bien sûr, a donné son nom aux Celtes, nom sous lequel, dit-il, "les anciens Grecs comme Platon et Aristote incluent tous les Gaulois."[39] Voilà donc une filiation noachique jusqu'aux Gaulois mais le problème linguistique n'est pas pour autant résolu car Périon avoue qu'il ne sait pas plus quelle langue parlait Samothes que Japhet "nec quem (sermonem) Samothes proferret dici potest."[40]

Alors, par une sorte de bifurcation vers une autre branche de la maison de Noé, nous rejoignons Hercule de Lybie, que l'on rencontre également chez Lemaire de Belges. Selon Annius de Viterbe, dans la postérité de Cam, il y a un Osiris, qui a engendré un Lybius "cognomine Hercolem."[41] Ce dernier, quittant la Celtibérie (après l'épisode des bœufs de Géryon) se dirige vers l'Italie à travers le pays des Celtes. Il traverse donc la Gaule, y fonde Alesia et est aimé d'une princesse du pays, une Galatée, qui lui donne un fils Galates, lequel obtient le pouvoir royal après la mort de Celta. C'est ainsi que nos ancêtres, d'abord appelés Samothéens, puis Celtes, se nomment enfin Gaulois.[42] En dépit de cette nouvelle filiation, le problème linguistique reste entier et Périon est obligé de reconnaître, vers la fin de son premier livre, qu'il peut seulement dire que les premiers habitants de la Gaule ont usé d'une langue née au moment de la diversification des langues, mais "quo usi sint, dici non potest," et il ajoute "id doceri posse a nemine."[43] Il pense que les premiers éléments du grec et du latin sont nés après Babel et que les deux langues ont été perfectionnées par la suite, mais il répète encore "nihil enim certum de primo sermone qui naturalis est, pronuntiare possum."[44]

On peut se demander pourquoi, ayant suivi un chemin si compliqué et abouti à si peu de certitudes, Périon a jugé bon de nous faire part de ses recherches et de ses doutes. Notons à son bénéfice qu'il montre une grande honnêteté intellectuelle en n'essayant pas de dissimuler les textes qui le gênent comme l'épisode de la lettre à Q. Cicéron; il révèle également sa clairvoyance en repoussant très nettement l'hypothèse de l'hébreu langue-mère du français: "conclusum est ... primum sermonem non fuisse eum qui hebraicus nominetur. Ex quo etiam illud vis effici, caeteras linguas ex ea ortas non esse: quo posito atque concluso, illud sequi video, Gallicum nostrum ab eo non habuisse originem."⁴⁵ Il a une conviction personnelle: la grande parenté du français avec le grec, il essaie de montrer historiquement cette parenté et, dans son désir de conférer à la langue vulgaire une généalogie aristocratique, il utilise abondamment l'histoire, de la plus sûre pour lui (César) à la plus discutée (Annius de Viterbe). A la différence de Bovelles qui n'a recours à l'histoire qu'à titre d'exemple, selon la tradition rhétorique, ou à des moments bien précis de son raisonnement, lequel demeure essentiellement linguistique, Périon consacre deux livres sur les quatre de ses *Dialogues* aux recherches évoquées ci-dessus et la façon spontanée, voire désordonnée, dont il livre le cheminement, parfois tortueux, de sa pensée est un gage de sa sincérité. Ainsi, interrogé par son neveu sur la probabilité d'un Pluton, ancêtre des Gaulois (p. 15), il répond tout d'abord "non credo ... fictaque omnia esse puto poetarum licentia aut furore potius quae de isto Dite patre, id est Plutone traduntur,"⁴⁶ mais nous avons vu qu'ensuite il développe le thème de Samothes en se référant à cette origine plutonienne des Gaulois. L'histoire ne lui a donc pas permis d'aboutir à une démonstration linguistique décisive; à partir de la p. 41 du second livre, il cherchera des preuves dans des comparaisons de vocabulaire, mais, lorsque (p. 105ᵛ) il nous dit que *tenser* est un mot grec parce que, si on considère ἐπιτιμῆσαι, qu'on enlève la préposition ἐπί, qu'on change i en e, qu'on supprime η, *tenser* "fere manebit," ne vaut-il pas mieux l'entendre disserter de César et de Bérose?

Ainsi, l'histoire, lorsqu'elle est sollicitée, non seulement pour fournir des exemples rhétoriques mais aussi des arguments linguistiques ne peut suffire à la démonstration. Cependant, s'il est certain que la philologie, la grammaire comparée, la phonétique historique sont des facteurs indispensables dans l'étude d'une langue, il est également vrai que cette étude ne peut être complètement détachée de l'histoire, même événementielle et politique. Celle-ci nous le rappelle chaque fois qu'elle intervient directement dans les problèmes de langue comme François Ier le fit par l'édit de Villers-Cotterets.

Université de Lyon III

Notes

1. *De latinitate falso suspecta* (Parisiis, H. Stephani, 1576).
2. *Hypomneses de Gallica linqua, peregrinis eam discentibus necessariae, quaedam vero ipsis etiam Gallis multum profuturae* (1582), Slatkine reprints 1968.

3. *Traicté de la conformité du langage françois avec le grec* (Paris, chez Iaques du Puis, 1569).

4. *La précellence du langage françois,* 1ère éd. (Mamert Patisson 1579); éd. Feugère (Paris, Delalain, 1850).

5. δόσις, portion, dose chez Dioscoride, *dosis* en latin médical.

6. cf. *De Latinitate*, f. 95.

7. cf. *Hypomneses*, f. 72.

8. J. Périon, *Dialogorum de linguae gallicae origine eiusque cum graeca cognatione libri quattuor* (Paris, Sebastien Nivelle, 1555).

9. Charles de Bovelles, *Liber de differentia vulgarium linguarum et gallici sermonis varietate* (Parisiis, R. Stephani, 1533), éd. commentée avec traduction, C. Dumont–Demaizière (Paris, Klincksieck et Société de Linguistique picarde, 1973).

10. La table de Marlianus a pour titre: *Veterum Galliae locorum, populorum, urbium, montium ac fluviorum alphabetica descriptio, eorum maxime quae apud Caesarem in Commentariis sunt et apud Cornelium Tacitum,* auctore Raymundo Marliano, viro clarissimo et sui temporis eruditissimo.

En témoignage de son grand succès, on peut relever les éditions suivantes des *Commentaires* de Marlianus aux quinzième et seizième siècles: Mediolani 1478, Tarvisii 1480, Venetiis 1494, Lugduni 1508, Venetiis 1513, Florentiae 1514, Venetiis 1517, Lugduni 1519, Basileae 1528, Lugduni 1538, Parisiis 1543, Lutetiae 1544, Antverpiae 1570, Lausannae 1571, Lugduni 1572, Antverpiae 1574, Venetiis 1575.

Bovelles, comme Périon, se réfère à Marlianus en citant César.

11. cf. *Liber de differentia*, ch. IX.

12. ibid.

13. cf. Périon, *Dialogorum*, f. 39ᵛ.

14. cf. *Liber de differentia*, ch. I.

15. traduction: si, en effet, comme le dit César, ils se servaient de caractères grecs dans presque toutes les affaires publiques et les comptes privés, quelle raison y a-t-il pour nous empêcher de conclure qu'ils se servaient de la langue grecque? *Dialogorum*, f. 33 et 33ᵛ.

16. ibid., f. 35.

17. cf. *Liber de differentia*, ch. XXXIV et *Dialogorum*, f. 37ᵛ.

18. cf. *Dialogorum*, f. 37 et 37ᵛ.

19. Préface de 1572, au lecteur.

20. Les *Palus Méotides,* où se jette le Don, c'est l'ancien nom de la mer d'Azov.

21. cf. *Liber de differentia*, ch. VII.

22. cf. *Dialogorum*, f. 32 et 32ᵛ.

23. Claude Mitalier, juge royal de la province de Vienne, écrit cette lettre au lyonnais Jérôme de Castillon. Le texte de la lettre est publié, à la suite des *Hypomneses* d'Henri Estienne, ed. de 1582, Slatkine reprints 1968. Elle occupe onze pages.

24. cf. *Liber de differentia*, ch. II. C'est un épisode de la guerre entre Ephraïmites et Galaadites. La tribu de Galaad occupe les gués du Jourdain et tue tous ceux qui prononcent *Sibolet* au lieu de *Shibolet,* terme qui désigne à la fois l'épi et le cours d'eau.

25. cf. *Liber de differentia*, ch. LII et LIII.

26. R.-L. Wagner, *Contribution à la préhistoire du Romanisme,* in Conf. de l'Institut de linguistique de l'Université de Paris, 1951, p. 117.

27. cf. *Dialogorum*, f. 3ᵛ.

28. ibid.

29. ibid. f. 4.

30. ibid. f. 6ᵛ.

31. Flavius Josèphe, *Antiquités judaïques,* I, ch. 3, cite, à propos du déluge, le récit de Bérose le chaldéen.

Bérose est un prêtre babylonien, astronome et historien, qui vécut à l'époque d'Alexandre le Grand; il écrivit une histoire babylonienne que nous connaissons uniquement par des intermédiaires comme Flavius Josèphe, Clément d'Alexandrie, Eusèbe ou Alexandre Polyhistor (Syncelle).

Sur Gomares et les autres fils de Japhet, cf. Flavius Josèphe, *Antiquités Judaïques*, Livre I, ch. 6.

32. cf. *Liber de differentia*, ch. VII.

33. cf. *Dialogorum*, f. 26 et 26^v.

34. ibid. f. 29^v.

35. ibid. f. 22^v et 23.

36. Annius de Viterbe (Nanni Giovanni) est un dominicain né à Viterbe vers 1432 et mort en 1502. Il a publié à Rome en 1498 *Antiquitatum variarum volumina XVIII* cum commentariis Fr. Ioannis Annii Viterbiensis, dans lesquels il prétend apporter des inédits de Bérose, Fabius Pictor, Caton, Manéthon, Archiloque etc. Il fut très violemment critiqué dès le seizième siècle et on se demanda s'il fallait le considérer comme un faussaire ou comme un homme trop crédule. Ses *Antiquités* connurent un très grand nombre d'éditions, en 1509 à Paris, 1510, 1511, 1512, 1515, toujours à Paris, en 1530 à Bâle, 1545 à Anvers. Lemaire de Belges lui-même en était nourri.

Nous avons consulté l'édition d'Anvers, 1545: *Berosi sacerdotis chaldaici, antiquitatum libri quinque*, cum commentariis Ioannis Annii Viterbiensis sacrae theologiae professoris, nunc primum in antiquitatum studiosorum commoditatem, sub forma Enchiridii excusi et castigati.

37. cf. *Dialogorum*, f. 22^v.

38. op. cit., f. 36.

39. cf. *Dialogorum*, f. 25^v.

40. ibid., f. 29^v.

41. op. cit., f. 18 et 18^v.

42. cf. *Dialogorum*, f. 26.

43. ibid., f. 29^v.

44. ibid., f. 30.

45. ibid., f. 9.

46. ibid., f. 15.

Présence de Virgile chez Du Bellay

Geneviève Demerson

Roma ingens periit: uiuit Maro doctus ubique. (Joachim Du Bellay)

L orsque Du Bellay compare les productions de son ami Ronsard à celles du "divin" Maro

Omnia diuino digna Marone sonas   (p. 445)[1]

on ne sait auquel des deux il fait le plus d'honneur. Le nom du "savant Maro" est, en tout cas, le premier qui se présente à l'humaniste quand il oppose la déchéance des ruines romaines à la vitalité permanente et universelle de la poésie latine: "uiuit Maro doctus ubique" (p. 436).

On conçoit que l'élève de Dorat ait été séduit par la science de ce poète divin, mais pour lui, comme pour Ronsard, comme pour leur maître,[2] l'expression de l'infinie variété de la Nature est le premier critère de l'agrément, et c'est par là que Virgile plaît, précisément:

Sic *uariat* uultus laeta Camoena tuos.[3]

...

Hac iuuat et ... spectare
... magni grande Maronis opus   (p. 456).

Ainsi Du Bellay, lecteur, mais aussi traducteur de Virgile, a si intensément médité sur cette variété sublime, que son œuvre latine révèle une très profonde intimité avec le poète de Mantoue: notre propos est d'essayer de retrouver cette présence de Virgile chez Du Bellay, en allant de la surface du texte vers ses profondeurs.

Du point de vue formel, et déjà au niveau des mots, la présence de Virgile est insistante. Nous ne tenterons pas de dresser ici une liste exhaustive des "larcins"—dont il n'est pas sûr, du reste, qu'ils soient reconnus comme tels—mais plûtot de mettre en évidence une typologie de ces emprunts.

Il apparaît tout de suite qu'un certain nombre d'énoncés sont passés tels quels dans l'œuvre du poète français: ils proviennent généralement de passages très connus du texte de Virgile. Ce sont, souvent, des débuts d'hexamètres: *Vere nouo*

(*G*. 1. 43 et p. 455), *Nuda genu* (*En*. 1. 320 et p. 440), souvent aussi des fins d'hexamètres: *ordine longo* (*En*. 1. 395; 703 et p. 450), *sedesque beatas* (*En*. 6. 639 et p. 519), *prata recentia riuis* (*En*. 6. 674 et p. 434). Peu s'en faut, une fois, que le vers ne se retrouve en entier:

<blockquote>Nox erat, et placidum carpebant cuncta soporem   (p. 495),</blockquote>

mais le texte d'*En*. 4. 522 donne *fessa*, non *cuncta*.

Il arrive aussi que deux énoncés virgiliens soient intimement amalgamés. Ainsi la séquence *lumine cassus* (p. 532) est suscitée par *cassum lumine* (*En*. 2. 285), mais le rythme est celui d'*aethere cassis* (*En*. 11. 104).[4]

Du Bellay se souvient également de Virgile lorsqu'il distribue les épithètes de nature, du type *lasciua capella* (*B*. 2. 64 et p. 451), *curuus arator* (*B*. 3. 42; *G*. 2. 189 et p. 452), ou d'excellence — *gelidi fontes* (*B*. 10. 42 et p. 434), et c'est à sa suite qu'il nomme Théocrite "le pasteur sicilien" — *pastor Siculus* (*B*. 10. 51 et p. 457). Parfois, une fine connaissance de la langue de Virgile se révèle dans telle acception spécifique d'un mot, par exemple *fuga* (p. 444 et *En*. 1. 317).

Mais Du Bellay ne se contentait pas de lire Virgile des yeux: il en possédait aussi la matière sonore. On retrouve en effet, sous sa plume, des hexamètres qui reproduisent le rythme de son "modèle." On pourrait, sans doute, considérer que c'est là un hasard,[5] mais une telle conclusion est difficile à admettre lorsque les deux textes sont liés aussi par une analogie thématique. Ainsi, l'admirateur de la statuaire romaine, qui cherchait à évoquer le *Laocoon* a écrit:

<blockquote>Ān pătrĭs implēxōs // squāmōsīs ōrbĭbŭs ārtūs   (p. 434).</blockquote>

Cet énoncé, contrairement à ce qu'on pourrait croire, ne doit pas grand'chose à *En*. 2. 204.[6] Du Bellay, en fait, s'est reporté à un autre texte, qui traite lui aussi de serpents

<blockquote>Squāmĕŭs iñ spīrām // tractū sē cōllĭgĭt añguĭs   (*G*. 2. 153)</blockquote>

et ce qu'il en a retenu, c'est un rythme.[7] On peut faire un rapprochement analogue à propos de l'évocation du Tibre, entre

<blockquote>Īlle ĕgŏ sūm[8] Tўbrīs, // tōtō ñotīssĭmŭs ōrbĕ   (p. 438),</blockquote>

et

<blockquote>Cāĕrŭlĕŭs Tҳybrīs // cōelō grātīssĭmŭs āmnĭs   (*En*. 8. 64).</blockquote>

Du Bellay, au reste, avait été à bonne école, car Dorat liait indissolublement la musique et la poésie.[9]

Mais le poète néo-latin se joue volontiers des fausses similitudes, et le nouveau message est, en fait, une déformation de son "modèle," au niveau des sons comme à celui du sens.

La paronymie — qui suppose la complicité la plus attentive du lecteur — procure à ce dernier l'agrément de la surprise.[10] Ainsi, tout le monde connaît la formule par laquelle Virgile admet l'infériorité artistique des Romains

Excudent alii spirantia mollius aera   (*En.* 6. 847),

mais Du Bellay, reprenant les deux derniers pieds, les a transformés en *mollius aere* (p. 524), avec un ablatif complément du comparatif, alors que, chez Virgile, ce complément était implicite. Ailleurs, ces mots *spirantia* ‾˘˘ *aera* sont devenus *spirantia* ‾˘˘ *ora* (p. 472). La déploration du jeune Marcellus par son ancêtre — *tu Marcellus eris* (*En.* 6. 883) — se transforme, par un changement de temps, en celle du bon pape Marcel — *tu Marcellus eras* (p. 509).[11] Par le même procédé le prodige de *B.* 4. 28 — *flauescet campus arista* — devient une évocation bien réelle des champs blondissants de l'Anjou — *flauescit campus aristis* (p. 451).[12] La suprême habileté consiste à maintenir le rythme virgilien, tout en déformant l'énoncé, notamment par la paronymie

Nix umeros infusa tegit   (*En.* 4. 250).
Nox oculos infusa tegit   (p. 468),

alors que Du Bellay, comme Virgile, parle d'Atlas.

Parfois, ce qui était une évocation très concrète est pris par Du Bellay dans un contexte métaphorique. Ainsi, c'est le concours de tir des jeux en l'honneur d'Anchise (*En.* 5. 502–04) qui, avec une légère modification de la syntaxe, sert à montrer l'Amour perçant le cœur de poète:

neruo stridente sagittam
Infixit   (p. 486).

Mais les mêmes mots ne veulent pas toujours dire les mêmes choses. Ainsi le *furtiuus amor* de Didon (*En.* 4. 171) était une passion qui se dissimule, même à celle qui la subit, tandis que les *furtiui amores* (p. 489) de Joachim et de Faustine seraient "furtifs" parce qu'ils seraient des ébats nocturnes au fond d'un couvent. Et lorsque l'exilé déclare que Ronsard "habite"[13] les forêts où les Nymphes le protègent

Ille colit uestras, tutissima numina, syluas   (p. 444),

il reproduit, en le dénaturant, le début d'un vers où *colere* signifie "veiller sur," mais le rythme est identique, et il n'est peut-être pas indifférent que l'emphatique *ille*, dans le texte ancien, représente Jupiter:

Ille colit terras, illi mea carmina curae   (*B.* 3. 61).

Les cercles romains amateurs de centons virgiliens n'eurent sans doute aucun mal à repérer les "larcins" opérés par Joachim[14] à des fins satiriques pour évoquer le nom des divers *papabili* au conclave de 1559:

Mantua me genuit,[15] Iudicium Paridis,[16]

/ ... /

> ... Deus aethere missus ab alto[17]
>
>   (Mss. Dupuy 736, f. 253[r]).

Quant à l'épigramme "In Didonem dormientem" (p. 461), qui est une *ekphrasis* et se veut "antivirgilienne" — puisque Virgile, lui, a peint Didon insomniaque (*En.* 4. 529 et suiv.), elle met en œuvre une technique insolite de centon, puisque Du Bellay y a repris des énoncés virgiliens pour les nier.[18]

Mais Du Bellay a emprunté au "divin Maro" autre chose que des mots, fussent-ils dénaturés: il a une prédilection pour nombre de thèmes virgiliens.

La tentation, pour un humaniste averti comme l'est Joachim, est d'intégrer, par le biais de la comparaison, quelques-unes des précieuses paillettes de "l'or de Virgile."

Or il peut arriver que la comparaison, légitime en elle-même, finisse par apparaître un peu forcée, parce qu'elle tourne au développement autonome. Tel est le cas, nous semble-t-il, du rapprochement opéré par Du Bellay — au moyen de *sic* (p. 518) — entre le sort des Français morts à Saint-Quentin et celui d'Hector: la déploration de ce dernier fait oublier, un temps, les victimes tombées à la "route Saint-Laurent" sous les coups de l'armée impériale. Au reste, l'idée de cette lamentation d'Andromaque est probablement née du discours que lui prête Virgile au chant 3, lorsqu'Enée la rencontre au cénotaphe d'Hector, mais l'essentiel du propos tenu par le poète français est d'opposer l'état lamentable du cadavre d'Hector à sa gloire récente: "*Heu qualem aspicio ... At non talis eras*" (p. 519). C'est précisément ainsi que Virgile a conçu l'apparition d'Hector à Enée lors de la dernière nuit de Troie:

> Hei mihi, qualis erat, quantum mutatus ab illo
> Hectore   (*En.* 2. 274–75).

Comme Virgile, Du Bellay insiste sur la poussière sanglante qui souille le corps, sur les pieds gonflés — *quam foedos puluere crines / ... / quam tumidosque pedes* (p. 519).[19] A cette horreur, l'Andromaque de Du Bellay oppose le souvenir du glorieux épisode du chant 15 de l'*Iliade*

> Cum flammam Argolicis puppibus iniiceres   (p. 519)

comme l'avait fait Enée lors de l'apparition nocturne.[20]

Le poète français, soucieux de reprendre le fil de son propos résume le développement et enchaîne

> Gallia *sic* forsan pignora chara gemit   (ibid.),

mais la présence de l'adverbe *forsan* révèle qu'il a des doutes sur la crédibilité de la comparaison.

Tel n'est pas le cas lorsque le succès de Ronsard est comparé par son fervent ami à l'admiration que la foule des âmes ressent en présence d'Orphée:

Elysiis *qualem* mirantes Orphea campis
Hinc atque hinc densae suspiciunt animae   (p. 444).

Virgile est intensément présent ici. Il avait, en effet, déjà noté que les âmes n'ont pas de demeure fixe,[21] que Musée dépasse de toute la tête la foule qui l'entoure,[22] et il fait se promener au milieu des bienheureux

Le grand prestre de Thrace au long sourpely blanc.[23]

Du Bellay n'a pas cessé de travailler en français[24] sur les énoncés de ce motif qui lui est particulièrement cher.

Mais la sympathie de Joachim pour son "modèle" peut s'exprimer directement, sans passer par la comparaison. Ainsi pour l'exilé romain, l'amour de la patrie, du minuscule royaume,[25] se traduit par le motif virgilien du toit qui fume:[26]

Quando erit, ut notae fumantia culmina uillae
Et uideam regni iugera[27] parua mei   (p. 446).

On peut voir ici qu'un motif, même peu étoffé, révèle une constellation de souvenirs virgiliens.

Du Bellay, sans doute, avait d'excellentes raisons pour évoquer l'accueil fait par le dieu du Tibre à l'ambassadeur du roi de France,[28] mais le cadre de cet épisode est, d'abord, somptueusement développé pour lui-même, et les couleurs sont très virgiliennes. Ce dieu Tyberinus, avec ses cheveux blonds ceints de feuillage, son vêtement agrafé par un roseau

humeris aptabat arundine uestem,
Cinxerat et flauas fronde uirente comas   (p. 436)

ressemble bien au Tiberinus d'*En.* 8. 31-34, mais si le poète néo-latin a repris nombre de détails de son "modèle," il les a utilisés à des fins différentes. Ainsi, chez Virgile, les feuillages servaient de cadre à l'apparition du dieu, le roseau couvrait ses cheveux. L'évocation de la grotte fraîche — *antrum* (p. 436) — où des nymphes fileuses sont assises sur des sièges de cristal, a bien été suggérée à Du Bellay par celle de la demeure — *thalamos* — de Cyrène (*G.* 4. 333 et suiv.). La finale de l'hexamètre *impulit aures* (p. 437 et *G.* 4. 439), et les mots *uitreisque sedilibus* (p. 436 et *G.* 4. 350) en témoignent avec éclat,[29] mais les toisons — *-uellera* (*G.* 4. 334) — sont devenues des poids de laine — *pensa* (p. 436); la notation de la couleur est différente — *Assyrio ... saturata ueneno* (ibid.);[30] la mention de la chevelure, incidente chez Virgile (*G.* 4. 337), est ici développée pour elle-même (p. 437). Pourtant, les différentes occupations des nymphes sont présentées ici comme celles des âmes rencontrées par Enée — *pars* (*En.* 6. 642; 644 et p. 437), et si le Nar sulfureux — *sulfureus Nar* (p. 436) — n'est pas mentionné parmi les fleuves qui prennent leur source dans l'antre qu'admire Aristée, l'indication qui le concerne est virgilienne (*En.* 7. 517).

Ainsi donc il apparaît que le poète français a, d'une part, souhaité attirer l'attention sur sa dette multiple en la soulignant, chaque fois, par une signature précise, mais que, d'autre part, au moment où il emprunte des thèmes, il prend le plus grand soin de cultiver les plus subtiles différences.[31]

La dette du poète néo-latin à l'égard de Virgile, tant du point de vue formel que du point de vue thématique est donc considérable, mais plus encore que la parenté de goût, que la parenté spirituelle, ce qui a fait que Du Bellay s'est tourné vers Virgile, c'est qu'il s'est cru investi d'une mission analogue à celle du chantre d'Auguste et de la paix romaine.

Virgile a proclamé qu'il aurait l'audace d'ouvrir les fontaines sacrées et d'aller chanter par l'Italie un poème ascréen.[32] Dès lors Du Bellay se sent le devoir, bien qu'il soit français—et précisément parce qu'il l'est—de composer à Rome, en latin, et d'ouvrir, lui aussi, les fontaines sacrées: ce sont les dieux qu'il prend à témoins:

> Sit mihi fas, Gallo, uestros recludere fontes   (p. 436).

Son rapport à Virgile est bien celui de l'émulation nationale. Sincèrement, il peut prétendre relayer l'auteur de l'éloge de l'Italie, non seulement quand il se fait le laudateur de la Rome éternelle, mais aussi quand il admet les séductions de la cité fangeuse de Romulus. La manière dont est présentée la *Romae descriptio* ne peut laisser aucun doute: même si Chamard a jugé sévèrement ce texte,[33] la technique est bien celle de l'illustre morceau de *Géorgiques* 2, la composition "en boule de neige." Pas plus que Virgile, Du Bellay n'a reculé devant des termes comme *adde* (p. 433 et *G.* 2. 155), *quid referam* (p. 433 et *G.* 2. 158), *quid memorem* (p. 434) et *an memorem* (*G.* 2. 161).

Ce rôle, virgilien par excellence, Du Bellay le tient une seconde fois lorsqu'il met dans la bouche du Tibre, accueillant M. d'Avanson, un nouvel éloge de l'Italie, et même si l'exilé romain était sujet, parfois,[34] à émettre des réserves, comment le Tibre ne montrerait-il pas l'Italie sous son plus beau jour? Dans ce morceau, on retrouve l'artifice de présentation *quid memorem, adde* (p. 438), mais Du Bellay y pratique aussi, à la suite de Virgile, l'éloge négatif:[35]

> Quod si *nulla* meo splendescat littore gemma   (p. 438),

en opposant dans un second temps—*tamen*—les éléments qui fondent la vraie gloire.

Mais un sujet du roi de France conscient de ses devoirs ne peut que reprendre à son compte l'idée de louer la patrie, et proclamer que cette France peut rivaliser même avec l'Italie antique. Aussi, après avoir évoqué, dans sa nostalgie, les rives de la Loire, les forêts chevelues et le gras terroir de l'Anjou, Du Bellay conclut-il pour justifier ses états d'âme:

> Quae lacte et Baccho, flauentis et ubere campi
>   Antiquae *certant* laudibus Italiae   (p. 446).

En fait, si Du Bellay se prend à assumer le rôle politique de Virgile, c'est que, désormais, c'est à la France et à son roi qu'il appartient d'imposer l'ordre aux nations. Détournant de son sens originel la périphrase *Mauortia tellus* (*G.* 4. 462), il l'applique à la France, et l'intègre dans une ample salutation qui éveille forcément des échos:

> Magna uirum, frugumque parens, Mauortia tellus,
> Gallia   (p. 455).

Et le fait est d'autant plus significatif que le texte est dédié à un Italien, Annibal Caro.

Mais il est bon de rappeler, et en particulier au milieu des épreuves, le grand destin réservé à la France. Comme Enée avait reçu des lèvres du dieu Tibre lui-même des assurances sur l'accomplissement de sa mission (*En.* 8. 35–65), ce même dieu vient déclarer à l'ambassadeur du roi la grandeur qui sera celle de son maître: avec une tranquille certitude, il annonce que le coq éloignera les limites de l'empire, tandis que la corneille se verra arracher les plumes d'aigle qu'elle avait usurpées:

> Tum raptas Aquilae fallax cornicula plumas
> Exuet, at Gallus proferet[36] imperium   (p. 439).

Ces indicatifs futurs sont un écho de ceux de Virgile, et le poète français conclut en rappelant, lui aussi,[37] le caractère vaticinant de ce discours: *Haec* cecinit *Tybris* (p. 440).

Mais le lecteur ne doit pas s'y tromper: si le dieu pouvait dire à Enée: *Hic locus urbis* erit (*En.* 8. 46), les temps sont accomplis, et ce même dieu avertit aussitôt l'ambassadeur français que Rome est bien morte:

> Quemque uides campus, maxima Roma *fuit*[38]   (p. 438).

Si le procédé de présentation est le même, Du Bellay a voulu aussi que toute l'aura des héros virgiliens vînt nimber leurs héritiers, le roi et son ambassadeur qui le représente ici. Avanson, comme Enée, est l'homme que le "Latium" attendait; il y sera chez lui, tout étranger qu'il est,[39] et l'impatience du Tibre, enfin satisfaite, est celle d'Anchise à l'arrivée de son fils:[40]

> Venisti tandem, aruis expectate Latinis,
> ...
> ... et tibi certa domus   (p. 438).

Même les nymphes des Laurentes, auxquelles Enée adressa une prière (*En.* 8. 71), sont là pour accueillir l'ambassadeur par leurs danses:

> Nymphae Laurentes instituuntque choros   (p. 439).

D'ailleurs, Rome pourra reconnaître la belle prestance d'Enée dans celle du nouvel orateur:

Te similem spectans os humerosque deo[41]   (p. 439).

Au-delà de l'apparente flagornerie, le propos est bien réellement politique par les échos qu'il éveille. Avanson est, de fait, le digne serviteur de son maître, cet Henri puissant aux armes—*armipotens* (p. 439)—épithète dont Virgile a qualifié Achille (*En.* 6. 839), et Mars lui-même (*En.* 9. 717). Ce prince, à l'imitation de M. Claudius Marcellus,[42] suspendra en l'honneur de Quirinus les enseignes prises à l'ennemi:

Captaque suspendet signa, Quirine, tibi   (p. 439).

Or ce Marcellus avait été surnommé "l'epée de Rome": l'allusion n'est pas gratuite, et Du Bellay ajoute carrément, à l'usage de l'Espagnol:

(Rex)
Auertetque procul Romanis arcibus hostem   (ibid.).

Au reste, de même qu'Enée avait promis d'instituer des fêtes en l'honneur de Phébus,[43] Rome le fera ... en l'honneur d'Henri:

Henrici festos instituetque dies   (p. 440).

Quant à l'actuel détenteur de la puissance impériale, Du Bellay l'invite poliment à mettre bas les armes, le premier, dans les termes mêmes qu'Anchise a employés pour dissuader Jules César de continuer les guerres civiles:[44]

Tuque prior, Caesar, proiice tela manu   (p. 441).

Du Bellay, sans doute, prétend bien considérer comme "civiles" les guerres entre princes chrétiens, mais, ici, les deux tronçons d'hexamètres virgiliens sont reconstitués en un pentamètre, avec, entre les deux, en relief à la césure, ce titre dont l'humiliante défaite devant Metz a fait une dérision.[45]

Mais en attendant que la couronne et le globe reviennent au roi de France, celui-ci est en mesure de tenir le rôle augustéen, et son poète met dans la bouche véridique du Tibre le programme de cette résurrection. Henri, en effet, n'a plus qu'à réaliser le modèle: tout a été fait seize siècles plus tôt, et un grand poète en a porté témoignage.

D'abord, le roi de France rétablira le Paix et, comme Auguste, il fermera les portes du temple de Janus:

... *iterum* ... claudet penetralia Iani   (p. 439).

Après avoir dépeint les joyeuses festivités où Galatée,[46] éclatante de beauté, sèmera des fleurs dans les rues, Du Bellay évoque encore une fois le retour—triomphal—du destin d'Auguste:

Sic *iterum* antiquos spectabit Roma triumphos   (p. 440).

Le pluriel a son prix, et il procède encore d'un souvenir virgilien.[47]

Enfin, le roi sera en mesure de parachever cette action et, comme l'avait espéré Virgile,[48] on reverra sur terre le bonheur du règne de Saturne:

Hisque *iterum* campis reddens Saturnia regna (ibid.).

Par la magie des vocables virgiliens, la *translatio imperii* va totalement s'accomplir.

Ainsi, comme on pouvait s'y attendre de la part du traducteur de deux chants de l'*Enéide*, la lettre même du texte de Virgile est extrêmement présente dans les poèmes latins de Du Bellay, qu'il s'agisse d'une rédintégration pure et simple ou, plus volontiers, d'énoncés dénaturés par la paronymie ou le changement d'acception.

Sans doute, un certain nombre d'énoncés sont pris là où l'on pouvait s'y attendre, mais si le "Votum rusticum," par exemple, emprunte beaucoup aux *Bucoliques*, le souvenir de l'*Enéide* n'est pas absent. En effet Du Bellay, s'il a repris les motifs virgiliens qu'il aimait, s'il a volontiers, non sans coquetterie, souligné son "larcin," a sans cesse opéré une cristallisation qui révèle sa science — une qualité virgilienne, qui procure au poème néo-latin la grâce d'une variété dont Virgile est, précisément, le modèle.

Il existait, bien sûr, une parenté entre ces doux poètes, l'exproprié qui chante son inquiétude au bord du Mincio et l'Angevin nostalgique. Pourtant, jamais ce dernier n'en a fait état, alors qu'il se plaisait à rapprocher son destin de celui d'Ovide.[49] Cela tient à ce que, d'homme à homme, son rapport à Virgile est bien différent: c'est, si l'on peut dire, un rapport idéal. Du Bellay, cependant, ne se "guinde" pas pour tenter de ressembler à son "modèle," mais lorsqu'il assume le rôle poétique et politique du Mantouan, notre tendre poète, dans la langue de l'Europe humaniste, exprime les espoirs de la France et de son roi par un riche réseau de connotations subtiles, où presque tout est virgilien.

Centre de Recherche sûr l'Antiquité Classique
Université de Clermont–Ferrand II

Notes

1. Tout naturellement il souhaite que son ami dépassse "le grand Virgile" — *magnum praestare Maronem* (p. 459). Nous renvoyons, avec la seule indication de la page, à l'édition Courbet, *Poésies françaises et latines de J. Du Bellay* (Paris, Garnier, 1919), t. 1.

2. Dorat voit dans la Nature une magicienne, qui varie infiniment ses productions et, de ce fait, ne peut jamais être parfaitement imitée (*Poëm. lib. V*, p. 156, in *Poëmatia*, Paris, Linocier, 1586). Pour Ronsard, l'infinie variété de la Nature est source de beauté (*Au Lecteur*, STFM, I, 47).

3. Du Bellay s'adresse au poète romain Basilio Zanchi.

4. Dans un vers tel que "Dum tenui paruam meditaris arundine Musam" (p. 457), Du Bellay amalgame *B.* 1. 2 et *B.* 6. 8 (Virgile s'imitant lui-même).

5. La probabilité de reproduction du rythme d'un hexamètre est, théoriquement, de 1 sur 16, mais certaines structures sont plus fréquentes.

6. L'emploi d'*orbibus*, à la même place.

7. Cf. aussi *Sit mihi fas, Gallo, uestros recludere fontes* (p. 436) et *G.* 2. 175 (cf. ci-dessous, p. 324); cf. encore *Argento e nitido spirantia Palladis ora* (p. 472) et *En.* 4. 847.

8. Mais *ego sum* rappelle *En.* 8. 62 (c'est le Tibre qui parle).

9. Cf. par ex. F. Le Duchat, *Praeludiorum lib. III* (Paris, Caveillier, 1554, f. 31).

10. Cf. Cicéron, *De or.* 2. 255.

11. Du reste, le rapprochement est explicite: *Marcellum cecinit diuini Musa Maronis* (p. 510).

12. Du Bellay oppose au contraire, en jouant sur le mode, le vœu d'Iolas — *Nullaque per segetes* sterilis dominetur auena (p. 451) à la réalité de *G.* 1. 154.

13. Sur la traduction de ce vers, cf. Geneviève Demerson, "Joachim Du Bellay traducteur de lui-même," *Neo-Latin and the Vernacular in Renaissance France*, ed. Grahame Castor and Terence Cave (Oxford, Clarendon Press, 1984), p. 115.

14. Dans l'autre version (Mss. Dupuy 697, f. 371ʳ) ce texte est anonyme.

15. Sur le "tombeau" de Virgile; le cardinal est Mantua.

16. Cf. *En.* 1. 27; M. de Paris est le cardinal Jean Du Bellay.

17. Cf. *En.* 4. 574; il s'agit du cardinal Santangello.

18. Cf. par ex. l'arrivée de Mercure annulée par *frustra*, la fuite d'Enée et la mort de Didon par *nec*. Du Bellay, en outre, s'ingénie à varier les détails de l'énoncé: *iussa superba* (p. 461) / *horrida iussa* (*En.* 4. 378); *morituram linqueret hospes* (ibid.) / *moribundam deseris, hospes* (*En.* 4. 323) et *frustra moritura relinquat* (4. 415).

19. Cf. *aterque cruento / Puluere perque pedes traiectus lora tumentes* (*En.* 2. 272-73); *concretos sanguine crines* (op. cit., 277).

20. Cf. *Vel Danaum Phrygios iaculatus puppibus ignes* (*En.* 2. 276).

21. Cf. *En.* 6. 673.

22. Cf. op. cit., 667-68.

23. *Regrets*, 10, fin; cf. *En.* 6. 645.

24. Cf. op cit., en n. 13.

25. Cf. *mea regna* (*B.* 1. 69).

26. Cf. *Et iam summa procul uillarum culmina fumant* (*B.* 1. 82).

27. Cf. *pauca ... / iugera* (*G.* 4. 127-28).

28. Cf. ci-dessous, p. 00.

29. Mais le rythme est différent.

30. Cf. *hyali saturo fucata colore* (*G.* 4. 335).

31. Par ex., l'évocation du dieu levant la tête au-dessus de l'eau — *ac summo sustulit amne caput* (p. 437) — ne doit rien à *G.* 4. 352, ni à *En.* 1. 127.

32 Cf. *sanctos ausus recludere fontes / Ascraeumque cano Romana per oppida carmen* (*G.* 2. 175-76).

33. "La composition est très défectueuse" (*Joachim Du Bellay 1522-1560*, repr. Genève, 1969, p. 287, n. 4).

34. Mais parfois aussi à admettre les séductions de Rome; *Forsan et est Romae ... / ... uiuere dulce mihi* (p. 446).

35. *Haec loca* non *tauri* (*G.* 2. 140) / ... / sed (op cit., 143).

36. Cf. *En.* 6. 795: (*Augustus Caesar*) *Proferet imperium*.

37. *Haud incerta cano* (*En.* 8. 49).

38. C'est avec ce même verbe que Virgile donne acte de la mort de Troie: *fuit Ilium* (*En.* 2. 325). Dans le "Tumulus Romae ueteris" (p. 505), Du Bellay paraphrase la formule de Virgile sur la grandeur de la Ville aux sept collines (*G.* 2. 535), qui devient dérisoire,

puisque ces sept collines sont maintenant sept tombeaux.

39. *Exspectate solo Laurenti aruisque Latinis* (*En.* 8. 38); *certa domus* (op. cit., 39).

40. *Venisti tandem* (*En.* 6. 687).

41. *Os humerosque deo similis* (*En.* 1. 589).

42. *Tertiaque arma patri suspendet arma Quirino* (*En.* 6. 859).

43. *Instituam festosque dies de nomine Phoebi* (*En.* 6. 70).

44. *Tuque prior* (*En.* 6. 834); *Proiice tela manu* (op. cit., 835).

45. *Virtus inuicta* (F. de Guise) / ... / *Exitium portat, Carole uicte, tuum* (p. 441).

46. Le nom de *Galatea* est, lui aussi, virgilien. Signe des temps, elle est ici accompagnée de Parthenope et de Flore. D'autre part, la princesse dont l'union avec Hercule permet, selon Annius de Viterbe, de donner aux Gaulois une glorieuse origine mythique portait ce nom.

47. *At Caesar* triplici *inuectus ... triumpho* (*En.* 8. 714).

48. Espoir trop précoce (*B.* 4. 6), mais exprimé ensuite avec assurance (*En.* 6. 792–94).

49. Cf. Geneviève Demerson, "Joachim Du Bellay et le modèle ovidien," in *Actes* du colloque de Tours, *Présence d'Ovide*, pp. 288–93.

Peregrinations of the Kiss:
Thematic Relationships between Neo-Latin and French Poetry in the Sixteenth Century

Ellen S. Ginsberg

In 1558 after his return from Italy, Joachim Du Bellay published four volumes of poetry, the result of his four-year sojourn in Rome. Three are in French: the *Antiquitez*, the *Regrets* and the *Divers Jeux rustiques*; one in Latin: the *Poemata*.[1] In this latter volume, Du Bellay has violated his own principle (as expressed in the *Deffence et Illustration de la langue francoyse*) concerning the importance of writing in one's own language and the impropriety of writing poetry in a foreign tongue.[2] Some of these Latin poems were translated by Du Bellay in various forms in the three collections of French poems, thus violating another of his principles that poetry cannot be translated.[3] While working on the section of Latin poems called the *Amores*, I noticed that one of these poems, the "Basia Faustinae," reappears in the *Divers Jeux rustiques* as "Autre Bayser," and has furthermore been retranslated back into Latin as "Basium Juliae"[4] by Marc-Antoine de Muret, an important French Humanist contemporary with Du Bellay. My paper concerns the transformations of the three versions of this poem.[5]

The origins of the genre of the kiss poem are well known.[6] They go back to the *Greek Anthology*, Catullus and the Latin elegiac poets. The same genre or theme is also found in medieval poetry, was picked up by neo-Latin poets in Italy, France and the Low Countries, with Joannes Secundus's *Basia* being the best known version, and then transposed into the vernacular. In France, Ronsard led the way by including several "Baisers" in his *Odes* of 1550 and his *Folastries* of 1554. One in particular, "Des Baisers de Cassandre," from the *Odes* shows considerable similarities to Du Bellay's poem and would merit a comparative study.[7]

I

BASIA FAUSTINAE, Joachim Du Bellay (1558)

Cum tu ad basia nostra sic reflectis
Cervicem niveam, Columba, poeti

Molle et nescio quid natent ocelli,
Prae desiderio mihi liquescit
Ipsa pene anima, in tuumque sensim   5
Prorsus exanimis sinum relabor.
Admotis sed ubi hinc et hinc labellis,
Udo tramite mutuum recursant
Linguae, et ambrosios anhelo ab ore
Flores carpere mi licet beato,   10
Tunc mi, tunc videor Jovis tonantis
Assidere epulis, sacrumque nectar
Haurire intrepide, Deum sodalis.

Si summis bona proxima, ô Columba,
Praebes tam facilis beato amanti,   15
Cur tu summa negas misello, et una
Misellum facis, et facis beatum?
Num forsan metuis Deus fruendo
Ipse ne efficiar, velimque solus
Te sine Elysios videre campos?   20
Hunc, hunc pone metum, venusta, bella,
Vitae dimidium meae, Columba:
Nam quaecunque oculos tuos tenebit
Sedes, illa mihi domos Deorum,
Et campos referet beatiores.   25

Du Bellay's Latin poem combines and tranposes several themes from Secundus's *Basia*, published in 1539, either as a result of direct knowledge of these poems or through Ronsard's version. Yet a close reading shows that the poem is not a mere translation or transposition of Secundus or Ronsard.

Du Bellay's poem, "Basia Faustinae," is composed of twenty-five hendecasyllabic verses, divided into two parts (by the printer or the poet) of thirteen and twelve lines respectively. It forms part of a cycle of love poems dedicated to Faustina, the woman he had loved in Rome. It comes immediately after the poem celebrating the return of Faustina after her forced separation from her lover. It celebrates the renewal of their love in intimate, personal terms. The name of the lady, or rather her nickname, Columba, is mentioned three times. She is addressed directly and their passionate kiss is described. The vocabulary used is partially a repetition of that used in the other poems to Faustina, thus creating a continuity within the cycle.[8]

The first section describes the kiss of the lovers and its effect on him. He mentions her bent snowy neck and her langorous eyes, which cause him to faint with desire. The actual kiss, the joining of their lips, and especially the action of their tongues, revives him, allowing him to pluck the ambrosial flowers of her breath, and makes him feel the equal of the Gods, sipping their sacred nectar.

Up to this point Du Bellay has combined two passages from Secundus: (1) *Basia*
V.1–12 (a description of a passionate kiss);[9] (2) *Basia* IV.8–10 (the suggestion
that the lover becomes like a God thanks to these kisses).[10] Although the general
development of the themes is similar, Du Bellay does not simply copy or paraphrase
Secundus. He leaves out details and introduces new ones (perhaps borrowed from
other Secundus poems). But he creates a different effect by using different vocabulary, by increasing the number of rhetorical figures, and by ordering the elements into two logical, chronological, parts: (1) at the approach of the lady, he
faints in her bosom, overcome by desire; (2) her passionate kiss revives him and
elevates him to companionship with the Gods.

But the poem has a second part which introduces a new note. The lover asks
the lady why she does not yield the ultimate favor to him since she has yielded
that which is a prelude to it — a kiss. This theme of the "fifth point of love,"[11] to
which the kiss is only a prelude, does not exist in Secundus's *Basia*, but it also
has a long history. Theocritus, the *Greek Anthology*, Ovid, the troubadours and
trouvères, the Italian and neo-Latin poets, Jean Lemaire de Belges and Clément
Marot among others used this theme. Du Bellay may have borrowed it in this
particular instance from another well-known neo-Latin author of kiss poems,
Nicolas Bourbon, whose *Nugae* were first published in 1533. In the second edition
(1538) appears the following poem which is the likely source for this passage in
Du Bellay:

> Si das, Rubella, basium
> Libens, et ultro cur mihi
> Negabis illud quod sequi
> Solet? cuiusque basium
> Quoddam est velut praeludium?
> Hem? quid, Rubella, mussitas?[12]

Though the ideas are very similar to those in Du Bellay's poem, the vocabulary
is different except for the verb *nego* ("negas/negabis"). Bourbon's poem is no more
than a brief epigram, urging the lady to go beyond the kiss since it is only a prelude
to what should follow.

Du Bellay makes this theme follow logically upon the description of the tongue
kiss, the "baiser à l'italienne" as he calls it in the French "Bayser" which immediately
precedes "Autre Bayser" in the *Divers Jeux rustiques*. The tongue kiss or what is
usually called the French kiss, is indeed an act of intimacy that symbolizes passion and penetration. The next step is to replace this kind of penetration by the
complete act of love-making, and so the second part of the poem is a request for
"le dernier point" or "le dernier degré" of love.

The last eight lines of Du Bellay's Latin poem respond in advance to the argument of the lady, namely that the lover might truly become a god if he were to
attain such ecstasy and thus leave her behind. He swears that the home of the
Gods is wherever she is and that he will not forsake her. In presenting this argu-

ment, Du Bellay again alters his source. Secundus's fourth *Basium* ends with the lover declaring that he should become immortal if Neaera were to give him many kisses such as he has just described. He asks her to be sparing of such gifts or else become a Goddess with him, for without her, he cares not for the tables of the Gods, even if he were to replace Jove as the ruler of the heavenly realm. Du Bellay transforms this notion by turning it into an argument which the lady advances indirectly (ll. 18–20) and to which he responds by declaring that the true realm of the Gods is the one over which she reigns, so that he is content to remain on earth with her (ll. 21–25). He thereby admits that his declaration that he is become like a God is nothing but a metaphor or symbol for the real happiness he wishes to enjoy with her on earth. This argument and counter-argument are presented in a lively manner through the hypothetical dialogue which Du Bellay has created.

II

AUTRE BAYSER, Joachim Du Bellay (1558)

Quand ton col de couleur de rose
Se donne à mon embrassement,
Et ton oeil languist doulcement
D'une paupiere à demy close,

Mon ame se fond du desir   5
Dont elle est ardentement pleine,
Et ne peult souffrir à grand'peine
La force d'un si grand plaisir.

Puis quand j'approche de la tienne
Ma levre, et que si pres je suis,   10
Que la fleur recuillir je puis
De ton haleine Ambrosienne:

Quand le souspir de ces odeurs
Ou noz deux langues qui se jouënt
Moitement folastrent et nouënt,   15
Evente mes doulces ardeurs,

Il me semble estre assis à table
Avec les Dieux, tant suis heureux,
Et boire à longs traicts savoureux
Leur doulx breuvage delectable.   20

Si le bien qui au plus grand bien
Est plus prochain, prendre on me laisse,

> Pourquoy ne permets-tu, maistresse,
> Qu'encores le plus grand soit mien?
>
> As-tu peur que la jouissance   25
> D'un si grand heur me face Dieu,
> Et que sans toy je vole au lieu
> D'eternelle resjouissance?
>
> Belle, n'aye peur de cela,
> Par tout ou sera ta demeure,   30
> Mon ciel jusq'à tant que je meure,
> Et mon paradis sera là.

Du Bellay has succeeded in combining, transposing and varying several themes common to the *Basia* genre to create a new poem, different from all previous ones on the same subject. He obviously thought well enough of his poem to translate it into French and publish it again among the *Divers Jeux rustiques* as "Autre Bayser." The twenty-five hendecasyllables of the "Basia Faustinae" become thirty-two octosyllabic verses organized into quatrains with "rimes embrassées" or enclosing rhymes regularly alternating between masculine and feminine.[13] It is an ode or "odelette." The content remains essentially unchanged, though some amplification occurs, and some condensation as well. The structure also remains much the same, with the break between parts I and II coming after l. 20 in the French poem. The changes that we shall note are mostly stylistic.[14]

Let us begin with the title. The Latin poem mentioned the name of the lady, Faustina, and used the word "Basia" in the plural. The French title, "Autre Bayser," eliminates the personal reference to the name of the lady, links the poem to the previous poem in the *Divers Jeux rustiques*, entitled "Bayser," and uses the generic name "Bayser" instead of the plural "Basia" which refers to actual kisses. In Du Bellay's French collection "Autre Bayser" becomes a specific example of the "baiser à l'italienne" which the lover had requested in the preceding poem, but it is no longer part of a cycle of love poems.[15]

If we look further in the poem, we note that all references to Faustina or Columba have been systematically eliminated or replaced by the words "maistresse" or "belle." Thus, despite its intimate subject, the poem loses something of its personal flavor in French. In l. 2, "cervicem niveam" becomes "col de couleur de rose." Line 3 eliminates "ut nescio quid" as too vague and translates "ocelli" (a plural diminutive) as "ton oeil." The image "poeti natent ocelli" is replaced by "ton oeil languist." The Latin image in ll. 5–6 of the lover sinking back lifeless in the bosom of his lady is eliminated in favor of a more general and vague expression in ll. 7–8 of the French poem: "Et ne peult souffrir à grand'peine / La force d'un si grand plaisir." Several emphatic repetitions are eliminated in the French: l. 7, "hinc et hinc"; l. 11, "Tunc ... tunc"; l. 21, "Hunc, hunc." Stanza 3 (ll. 9–12) contains several more examples of synecdoche as Du Bellay changes plurals ("labellis" and "flores") to singulars ("la tienne / Ma levre"; "la fleur").

In stanza 4 Du Bellay resorts to amplification in his attempt to convey the actions of the lovers' tongues: "nos deux langues qui se jouënt / Moitement folastrent et nouënt," while dropping "Udo tramite" and transferring "ambrosios flores" to the previous stanza. Lines 7–10 have been amplified to 8 lines in the French text. In ll. 11–13, "Jovis tonantis" along with "Deum sodalis" are replaced by "avec les Dieux," less specific and less pagan. Du Bellay also substitutes "à table" for "epulis." In ll. 12–13, "sacrumque nectar / Haurire intrepide" becomes "boire à longs traicts savoureux / Leur doulx breuvage delectable," although he keeps "ambrosios flores" which becomes "la fleur de ton haleine Ambrosienne."

The opposition "beato/misello" which occurs twice in the Latin ll. 14–17 is totally eliminated in the French. The "Elysios campos" of l. 20 is replaced by "lieu / d'eternelle resjouissance" — again a vaguer and less pagan description. Most of the apostrophes addressed to his mistress in ll. 21–22 ("venusta, bella, / Vitae dimidium meae, Columba") are deleted. Only "belle" remains. The metaphor of "quaecumque oculos tenebit sedes" is dropped in favor of "Par tout ou sera ta demeure," which is more banal. Also removed is the repeated mention of the lady's eyes (cf. l. 3 of the Latin) with its reminiscence of their effect on him. And finally "domos Deorum" and "campos beatiores" are replaced by the less pagan "ciel" and "paradis," a similar repetition of terms.

Du Bellay's French version reveals a tendency toward simplicity, as repetitions, metaphors, images, antitheses, paraphrases and apostrophes are suppressed, and simultaneously a tendency toward amplification, as the author attempts to convey the sensations or emotions attendant on the actions of the poem. There is also a tendency toward a more impersonal, less sensual, tone, which is at the same time less pagan and more modern. As for the vocabulary, Du Bellay avoids neologisms, latinisms and other recherché expressions in favor of common usage which, alas, is subject to monotony, cf. repetitions of certain words, such as "Doulcement," "Doulx ardeurs," "Doux breuvage"; "grand'peine," "grand plaisir," "plus grand bien," "le plus grand," "grand heur."

III

BASIUM IULIAE, Marc-Antoine de Muret (1576)

Cum roseam inflectens cervicem, ad basia torques,
    Et tibi iam poeti molle natant oculi,

Prae desiderio prope tum mi anima ipsa liquescit,
    Vixque potest tanti vim tolerare boni.

Post, ubi iam licet, admotis utrinque labellis,   5
    Ambrosium suavis sugere florem animae;

Tum mihi, tum videor Divorum accumbere mensis,
    Atque haurire avide nectareos latices.

Iulia, flos aevi, cum quae sunt proxima summis
    Tam facilis dones, cur modo summa negas?   10

An metuis, Deus efficiar ne fortè fruendo,
    Et sine te sedes evolem ad aetherias?

Pone metum, formosa: tuos quaecunque tenebit
    Ora oculos, semper caelum erit illa mihi.

This is not the end of our poem. In 1576 Marc-Antoine de Muret published his *Hymnorum Sacrorum* along with *Alia Quaedam Poematia*, which included a fourteen-verse Latin poem in elegiac couplets called "Basium Juliae," a retranslation (without acknowledgement) into Latin of Du Bellay's poem. The circumstances in which this poem was composed by Muret are, alas, unknown.

The relationship between Du Bellay and the French Humanists such as Dorat, Muret, Turnèbe, has not been examined in depth. Ample documentation exists concerning the close relationship between Muret and various other members of the "Brigade" (as Ronsard called the future Pléiade) between 1551–53, when Muret was lecturing in Paris. Du Bellay may have studied under him during this period, and must surely have known him, as Ronsard mentions both Muret and Du Bellay frequently as members of the "Brigade." But there does not seem to have been a warm relationship between Muret and Du Bellay, as we have no poems in Muret's *Juvenilia* (1552) for Joachim, and no poems for Muret among Du Bellay's poetry of those years. Yet they certainly did know each other, for according to Scévole de Sainte-Marthe, Muret, Du Bellay and Pierre Fauveau had engaged in a poetic competition in Poitiers in 1546, where both Muret and Du Bellay had gone to study law.[16] All three had composed an amorous epigram which Salmon Macrin judged. He awarded the prize to Fauveau. Unfortunately none of these epigrams survive and we do not even know in which language they were composed — though probably Latin. This early competition between Du Bellay and Muret foreshadows their later rivalry in composing Latin poems, although there seems to be no direct relationship between the two events.

Muret was well qualified to translate Du Bellay's poem back into Latin, both by profession and inclination. He was one of the best known French Humanists of his time, and during the period when he was in close contact with the Pléiade he was chiefly known for his lectures on Latin poetry. Ronsard confirms this impression in his poem "Les Isles Fortunées" by describing Muret reading the Latin poets to the happy band setting sail for the fortunate isles:

Divin Muret, tu nous liras Catulle,
Ovide, Galle, et Properce, et Tibulle,
Ou tu joindras au Sistre Teïen
Le vers mignard du harpeur Lesbien:[17]

In his *Juvenilia*, Muret published a number of amatory poems in "neo-Catullan" style and later published editions with commentaries of Catullus, Tibullus and Propertius. There is no doubt but that he was well-versed in the Latin tradition of love poetry. He also wrote the commentary on Pierre de Ronsard's *Amours* for the 1553 edition, explicating difficult passages and indicating sources.

In 1553 Muret left Paris for Toulouse and then went to Italy, where, except for a brief period in 1561–62, he remained for the rest of his life. Of course, it is not necessary to postulate personal contact between the two. Muret could easily have known Du Bellay's French and Latin poetry which had been published in 1558 and widely diffused. A study of Muret's Latin poem shows that he made use of both the Latin and French versions of Du Bellay's poem.

Muret succeeds in reducing Du Bellay's twenty-five line Latin poem and thirty-two-line French poem to fourteen lines, i.e., seven elegiac couplets, a veritable tour de force of reduction, if not of poetry. In so doing, he shows us that Du Bellay's poems were amplified and repetitious, and that Latin is a more concise language than French.

Muret's poem follows the same order as Du Bellay's. Although the poem is written in elegiac couplets, the structural organization of the content makes it closely resemble a sonnet. In general Muret used the vocabulary of Du Bellay's "Basia Faustinae," but even in the passages which are closely copied, there are some important differences.[18]

The first four lines resume ll. 1–6 of Du Bellay's Latin poem: however, "cervicem niveam" becomes "cervicem roseam" (from the French poem), and the diminutive "ocelli" becomes "oculi." Muret eliminates "ut nescio quid" and the image of the lover sinking back on the bosom of his mistress (as did the French poem) in favor of a more neutral expression: "Vixque potest tanti vim tolerare boni," which owes its origin also to Du Bellay's French poem (ll. 7–8).

Lines 5–8 condense ll. 7–13 of Du Bellay's Latin poem. There is considerable repetition of similar or identical expressions: "admotis labellis: ambrosios / Flores" vs. "Ambrosium florem"; "licet"; "Tunc" vs. "tum"; "videor"; "nectar / Haurire" vs. "haurire nectareos." However, Muret removes the passage on the "Italian kiss" (in effect he eliminates stanza 4 of Du Bellay's French poem), but adds the notion of inhaling his mistress's soul ("suavis sugere animae") which he borrows directly from Secundus (*Elegiae* I.v) or from classical sources. Muret follows Du Bellay's French text more closely as he replaces the expression "Jovis tonantis / Assidere epulis" by "Divorum accumbere mensis" (cf. "Il me semble estre assis à table / Avec les Dieux"). The first eight lines of Muret's poem thus divide clearly into two quatrains as to content, while each elegiac couplet resumes one quatrain of Du Bellay's French "odelette."

The same system operates in the second half of Muret's poem, which may be divided into a couplet followed by a quatrain, or into three couplets, each of which again resumes one quatrain of Du Bellay's French poem, while still closely following the vocabulary of the "Basia Faustinae."

In ll. 9–10, Muret introduces the name of his lady, Julia, and adds the expression "flos aevi," found in neither of Du Bellay's texts, but which has solid classical antecedents and which suggests an allusion to the *carpe diem* theme. Muret deletes the opposition "beato/misello" as Du Bellay's French version had done, but faithfully reproduces the content and most of the vocabulary of the lines Du Bellay had invented based on Bourbon's epigram: "quae sunt proxima summis, / Tam facilis dones, cur modo summa negas?"

In the following couplet (ll. 11–12), Muret responds to the supposed fear of the lady that he will really become a God and go to the Elysian fields without her. He uses the expression "sedes aetherias" rather than "Elysios campos," closer to the French than to the Latin. Muret avoids the repeated exclamations and apostrophes of ll. 21–22 of Du Bellay's Latin poem, replacing them by the simple "formosa," a direct translation of the French "belle." He repeats Du Bellay's image: "tuos quaecumque tenebit / Ora oculos," but simplifies the final images by substituting "caelum" for "domos Deorum" and "campos beatiores" (a direct translation of the French "ciel").

Whereas Du Bellay had practiced "contamination" of several Secundus poems, combined with amplification and a generous use of rhetorical figures, Muret succeeds in practising "contamination" of two Du Bellay poems and concision at the same time, while maintaining intact and even tightening the structure of the poem. Muret deletes several of the more sensual and erotic parts of Du Bellay's poems, but substitutes in one case another, the soul kiss for the tongue kiss. He follows Du Bellay's French version by deleting mythological references to thundering Jove and the Elysian Fields, and a number of the rhetorical figures prominent in Du Bellay's original version. It is not surprising that Muret's Latin poem seems superior to Du Bellay's.

IV

A fascinating epilogue may be added to the discussion of Muret's poem. A later edition of the same poem with a different title, "Ad Fulviam Puellam," contains variants, several of which are relevant to our study.[19] In line 6, "sugere" is replaced by "carpere," as in Du Bellay's poem, and two additional lines are found after l. 6:

> Udoque errantes colludunt tramite linguae,
> Dulcis et ardores ventilat aura meos:

These two lines provide a version of stanza 4 of Du Bellay's French poem, the description of the tongue kiss, and thus turn Muret's poem into a sixteen-line poem, each couplet of which is equivalent to one of Du Bellay's quatrains. In l. 9, "Julia" is replaced by "Fulvia," as in the title. Finally, line 14 becomes: "caeli mi vice semper erit," a prudent effort to diminish the possible religious tonality of the expression.

It is difficult to know to whom to attribute these variants, as it is even difficult to examine the different editions of Muret's works. The first appearance of this revised version of the poem, to my knowledge, is in the 1729 Verona edition where it is described as a manuscript version, although the provenance is not made explicit.[20] The editor of that edition seems unaware that the poem appeared in an earlier version during Muret's lifetime. Perhaps it will always remain a mystery, but I suspect that further research into the works published by Muret, into his letters and into archival sources would reveal much more material on this very interesting Humanist, poet, and dramatist, and on his relationship to sixteenth-century literature.

V

The poems we have examined are specimens of the art of translation, imitation and contamination as practiced during the Renaissance. Each author follows a literary fashion, uses specific models, yet creates something personal. Du Bellay is certainly the better-known and more important figure as far as French literature is concerned. Muret has been less studied, as is generally the case with authors whose works are mainly in Latin and whose influence has been underrated.

Du Bellay's Latin poem is of interest to us as an example of the neo-Latin vogue for ardent, sensual, erotic poetry, rather uncharacteristic of what he had previous written in French. He lives up to his anti-Petrarchan stance of "Contre les Pétrarquistes" by imitating the neo-Latin *Basia* of Secundus and Bourbon rather than Petrarch. But his Latin poem contains a number of the rhetorical techniques which are equally prominent in his French poetry of the period: repetition, antithesis, enumeration, as well as "neo-Catullan" mannerisms such as diminutives and endearments. Du Bellay's imitation is not a translation, as there are considerable differences in vocabulary, images and rhetorical devices between his poem and his likely "sources." He has adapted his sources to his own purposes and to the context in which the poem is situated as part of a cycle of Roman love poems.

The French version of the poem, "Autre Bayser," undergoes a considerable sea-change. Certains elements which are quite suitable for a Latin poem disappear, such as the mythological expressions, and other rhetorical figures are simplified or eliminated. Du Bellay is more intent on conveying the impressions or emotions associated with the passionate kiss he is describing and less concerned with the formal, stylistic elements. His French poem is simpler, more direct, more successful. Du Bellay is more at home in French than in Latin.

Muret took upon himself the task of retranslating and condensing Du Bellay's poem. It was perhaps no more than a game for him, but it was a common practice among men of letters of the period and often meant as a compliment. Muret's pared-down version, whether in the original fourteen-line, or the later sixteen-line version, combines much of the vocabulary of Du Bellay's Latin poem with images and expressions taken from his French poem to create a tight-knit composition. He follows Du Bellay's French version in reducing the number of obvious rhetorical devices and yet avoids the diffuseness of the French. And yet Muret's compact composition is more like an intellectual exercise than a work of imagination. It is more composition than poem. Although its logical and psychological development is impeccable, it has lost its ability to move us. To clarity of development and expression, it does not join richness and variety, essential elements of a successful poem. Muret's Latin poem is a better poem *qua* Latin poem, than Du Bellay's Latin poem, but is it really a good poem? Or should we not be willing to recognize that Du Bellay is rightly considered a superior poet, at least in French, while Muret must remain for us chiefly a Humanist, teacher, commentator of texts and excellent Latinist?

Notes

1. See H. Chamard, *Joachim du Bellay, 1552–1560* (Geneva, Slatkine Reprints, 1969), p. 394, and V.-L. Saulnier, *Du Bellay* (Paris, Hatier, 1968), p. 116.
2. Joachim Du Bellay, *La Deffence et Illustration de la langue francoyse*, ed. H. Chamard (Paris, Didier, 1948), Book I, passim.
3. op. cit., I, vi.
4. The texts of these three poems are taken from the following modern editions, but have been checked against the original editions: *Póesies françaises et latines de Joachim Du Bellay*, ed. E. Courbet (Paris, Garnier Frères, 1918), I, 497–98 and *Ioachimi Bellaii, Andini Poematum, Libri Qvatvor* (Paris, Federic Morel, 1558). Joachim du Bellay, *Œuvres poétiques*, ed. H. Chamard (Paris, Hachette, 1923), V, 91–93 and *Divers Jeux rustiques, et autres œuvres poëtiques* ... (Paris, Federic Morel, 1558). Marc-Antoine de Muret, *Opera omnia* (Geneva, Slatkine Reprints, 1971), II, 431, and *Hymnorum Sacrorum Liber ... Eiusdem alia quaedam Poematia* (Paris, Mamert Patisson, 1576).
5. The chronology of Du Bellay's two poems is doubtful. Both Chamard and Saulnier have tended to view the French poem, "Autre Bayser," as the translation of the Latin "Basia Faustinae," although Saulnier admits that it is not impossible that Du Bellay wrote the French poem first and translated it into Latin, and that the French poem was first addressed to Olive or some other lady. See Joachim Du Bellay, *Divers Jeux rustiques*, ed. V.-L. Saulnier (Geneva and Paris, Droz and Minard, 1947), p. xiv, note 1. I shall assume for the purposes of this paper that the Latin poem came first.
6. See Paul Laumonier, *Ronsard, poète lyrique* (Paris, Hachette, 1923), pp. 514–18; Du Bellay, *Divers Jeux rustiques*, ed. V.-L. Saulnier, pp. xxix–xxxii, and Nicolas J. Perella, *The Kiss Sacred and Profane: An Interpretative History of Kiss Symbolism and Related Religio-Erotic Themes* (Berkeley and Los Angeles, University of California Press, 1969), passim.
7. Pierre de Ronsard, *Œuvres Complètes*, ed. P. Laumonier (Paris, Hachette, 1914), I, 197–99. An interesting comparison could be made between Ronsard's "Des Baisers de Cassandre" and Du Bellay's "Basia Faustinae," for they are both heavily though not exclusively based on the same two Latin poems of Joannes Secundus, *Basia* IV and V. Ronsard's version of the poem, however, never varies much from the original passages of Secundus, except in its transposition of elements.
8. See my paper on "The *Amores* of Joachim Du Bellay," in *Acta Conventus Bononiensis:*

Proceedings of the Fourth International Congress of Neo-Latin Studies, edited by R. J. Schoeck (Binghamton, Medieval & Renaissance Texts & Studies, 1985).

9.   Dum me mollibus hinc et hinc lacertis
            Astrictum premis, imminensque toto
            Collo, pectore, lubricoque uultu,
            Dependes humeris, Neaera, nostris,
            Componensque meis labella labris,
            Et morsu petis, et gemis remorsa,
            Et linguam tremulam hinc et inde uibras,
            Et linguam querulam hinc et inde sugis,
            Aspirans animae suavis auram
            Mollem, dulcisonam, humidam, meaeque
            Altricem miserae, Neaera, vitae,
            Hauriens animam meam caducam...
                                    (Secundus *Basia* V.1-12)

10.   Quae si multa mihi uoranda dentur,
            Immortalis in iis repente fiam,
            Magnorumque epulis fruar deorum.
                                    (Secundus *Basia* IV.8-10)

Isidore Silver, "Du Bellay and Hellenic poetry, IV. Imitations of the Greek Lyric Poets," *PMLA*, 60 (1945), 953-54, suggests that the origin of this notion may be found in Sappho, *Lyra Graeca*, I, 186.

11. Laumonier, *Ronsard, poète lyrique*, pp. 514-16, quotes the following passage from Jean Lemaire de Belges, *Illustrations de Gaule*, I, ch. xxv: "Les nobles Poëtes disent que cinq lignes y ha en amours, c'est-à-savoir le regard, le parler, l'attouchement, le baiser: Et le dernier qui est le plus désiré et auquel tous les autres tendent, pour finale resolution, c'est celuy qu'on nomme par honnesteté Le don de mercy." Cf. E. R. Curtius, *European Literature and the Latin Middle Ages* (New York and Evanston, Harper and Row, 1963), pp. 512-14.

12. Nicolas Bourbon, *Nugarum libri octo* (Lyon, S. Gryphe, 1538), VI, 42. My text comes from *Les Bagatelles de Nicolas Bourbon*, ed. V.-L. Saulnier (Paris, J. Haumont, 1945), p. 42.

13. Paul Laumonier has shown in his *Ronsard, poète lyrique*, pp. 93-99 that Ronsard impressionistically imitated the Latin hendecasyllables of Catullus, with their characteristic rhythms, mannerisms and tricks of style. Like Ronsard, Du Bellay imitates the Latin hendecasyllable by employing a short simple meter which allows him to develop his thought freely, but he does not use astrophic couplets as Ronsard did. Cf. Mary Morrison, "Ronsard and Catullus," *BHR*, 28 (1956), 240-74.

14. Cf. Michel Glatigny's article on "Du Bellay, traducteur dans les *Jeux Rustiques*," *IL*, 18 (1966), 33-41, for an overview of Du Bellay's techniques as a translator.

15. See Helen O. Platt, "Structure in Du Bellay's *Divers Jeux rustiques*," *BHR*, 35 (1973), 19-37.

16. *Elogia*, art. Petrus Fulvius, ed. of 1616, pp. 72-74.

17. Ronsard, *Œuvres Complètes*, ed. P. Laumonier, V, 188.

18. Exactly 50 percent of the vocabulary of Muret's poem is taken from that of Du Bellay's Latin poem.

19. Muret's revised poem appeared in the 1729 Verona edition of his *Opera*, IV, 239-40.

20. See Muret, *Opera Omnia*, ed. D. Ruhnkeniius (Leiden, 1789), IV, 615. A footnote gives the above-noted variants with the following remark: "Hanc Elegiam, acceptam a Petro Catarino Zenone, sub titulo *Ad Fulviam puella*, pro inedita protulit Editor Veronensis Operum Mureti, Tom. IV, pag. 239." I have not been able to trace this version back to an earlier edition.

Text and Argument in Descartes's First and Second Meditations

Robert Ginsberg

The first sentence of Descartes's first Meditation sets forth the *project*, *problem*, *background*, *prerequisite*, and *occasion* of the Meditations. That is a great deal for one sentence to do, and it requires sixty-four words to do it.[1] All the Meditations spring from the germ of the first Meditation, and it springs from the germ of its initial sentence. Since all is latent in the beginning then the truth is self-revelatory. It unwinds from recognition of what we have. Like the layers of an onion, the Meditations are the layers of the truth already held in hand. Each peel must be examined in turn, but the generative core sustains them all.

This discussion of the Meditations is about thinking, that is, the development of the argument. But it is also a discussion about writing, that is, the presentation of the text. How are text and argument related? The text is not merely the container of the argument, the neutral packaging of the thinking, but the thinking itself is a textual strategy. What is the importance of the Meditation for the Cartesian thinking in the *Meditationes*? Let us explore the question by explicating a few passages in the first and second Meditations.

Returning to the first sentence, the *project* is to reconstruct knowledge or the sciences in a firm and stable way from the foundation. The *problem* is that there is something deficient in the sciences, understood in that broad sense of organized knowledge, namely their lack of firmness and stability. The weakness in the structure of knowledge is attributed, by implication, to something rotten at the foundation. Structures whose foundations are weak may come tumbling down any moment although they seem sound.

Is the project really for a reconstruction of the sciences rather than merely for the reconstruction of Descartes's own knowledge? Are we dealing with a psychological rather than an epistemological question? Because the Meditation is written as the intimate thought of a single subjectivity, we may be tempted to view the project as a private one. But if that were so then we could propose as remedy to Descartes the study of the sciences, those public bodies of knowledge that would provide answers to the unsure individual. Yet the very unreliability of public knowledge is the *background* to the present project. What he had been taught turned out false; what he built upon dubious. Thus, the obstacle to genuine knowledge is what passes for knowledge. There is a paradox in the crisis. The apparent solution to the problem of deception is itself the problem: the deceptive state of knowledge. Hence the problem is radical; its remedy must be radical.

The *prerequisite*, then, to building knowledge from secure foundations is to dismantle the present faulty structure of science, that is, to rid oneself of what is merely opinion. Elimination of the unreliable clears the ground for construction upon the truly reliable. Thus, the advancement of knowledge in a fundamental way is attached to the rejection of what is not knowledge.

The initial sentence introduces the *temporal dimension* of the project. There are four stages mentioned: (1) the mistaken learning, since youth, of opinion under the appearance of knowledge; (2) the recognition, quite a time ago, of the mistake; (3) the postponement of the project until a more mature age; and (4) the concession that there is not enough time left for further postponement. In the next two sentences, completing the paragraph, the further temporal note is sounded: (5) now is the time to come to the aid of one's understanding. What is puzzling is the postponement. Why rely for such a long time on what one recognizes to be unreliable? Why put off seeking the remedy to a pervasive fault? In part it is due to the project itself: its radical nature, its inherent difficulty; in part to the nature of the mind: its attachment to habit, its disinclination to change fundamental commitments.

Does Descartes confess intellectual cowardice? The task he long has recognized should be done he puts off doing as long as possible. The comfortable circumstances he now enjoys have been won at the expense of a life lived in darkness. "I would not have sought such delays," so may think the reader. But the suspicion has been planted that what the reader takes for knowledge may also be deceptive. Yet rare is the reader who acknowledges lack of intellectual maturity to deal with the project.

Thus, Descartes's opening wins the reader not only by its candor and its sympathetic note of human frailty, but also by its skillful opening of the reader's experience so that the reader may join in the enterprise. The Meditations lack autobiography, idiosyncrasy, or personal confession. Yet they begin with an intimate tone as the inner voice speaks; we are listening to the echoes that sound from the bedrock of subjectivity. The inner voice thereby becomes our own. Hence, thinkers may return to the Meditations to rethink them from the start. Even as the paths of our thinking diverge, we share with Descartes the opening sentence. The method of imitation already is implied in that opening. By thinking about thinking one comes to the truth.

What a great deal of thought has gone into that opening sentence. The style has a disarming naturalness that succeeds in drawing us along without our being fully aware of what we are led through. It is the narrative opening of a storyteller.

The presence of a live human is immediately sensed; this is not an abstract treatise. There is a person of flesh and blood who is the thinker. The rambling structure of the sentence itself suggests the passage of time, the twisting and turning of the problem, and the interconnectedness of a number of things. We could have our undergraduates rewrite the sentence in five simple sentences, each making one clear point. But for Descartes these are not separate points; they are the uncoiling of the same point. By its artful construction and its artless appearance the first paragraph catches us up in the coils. We have joined the project.

Let us turn to the next paragraph. One more essential of our work is needed: the *method*. There are two negatives offered concerning procedure. It will not be necessary to show that things are false in order to reject them; it will suffice to show them doubtful. But it will also not be necessary to show each item to be doubtful in order to reject it; it will suffice to show as doubtful the principles upon which various categories of things are based. In other words, in order to seek something that is certain we do not need to be certain about the falsity of things. Doubt is the name of the game. And the endless task of examining everything is reduced to the feasible task of examining a few principles.

The method, then, is one of critical elimination. By locating that which can be placed in doubt (cf. the heading given the first Meditation), we reject it in our search for the best candidate for the foundation to knowledge. The winning candidate would be precisely that principle which was not subject to doubt. But doubting is both the way of discovering the doubtful and the indubitable, for the indubitable is what cannot be doubted. If, then, we can find any doubt whatsoever in the candidate it is rejected; if, on the other hand, it resists every effort at doubt then it is indubitable. Doubting is the acid test for certainty.

Notice how the method of doubt springs out of the coil which is the problem: the doubtfulness of knowledge. The prerequisite of the project, to dismantle doubtful knowledge (the image of buildings is strong in this second paragraph) is served by methodological doubt. What had been the great annoyance turns into the easy way of ridding oneself of the annoyance: that which is evidently doubtful is expeditiously disposed of. Thus, doubtful knowledge brings its own downfall. But the project to build science anew from the foundation is also served by this application of doubt, for the perfect foundation would resist doubt. Disposing of what has annoyed us clears the ground so that we may find the remedy to further annoyance. Doubt cures itself. While there were delays in starting the project, for there were doubts about one's readiness, there need be no delay in performing the work, now that one is in readiness to doubt. Categories of knowledge built on dubious principles will swiftly tumble. Doubt is a great timesaver.

The two paragraphs stand together, linked verbally by the closing line of the first and the opening line of the second. They accomplish huge reversals of ironic nature, for they build a project out of a problem, turn a hindrance into a strategy, overcome time by shortcuts, and link a prerequisite to a final test. All the rest of the Meditations stand apart from this beginning. What follows is application. Both the successes and the failings are tied to what has been laid down at the beginning.

Doubt is the beginning. Descartes's reasoning springs from a principle which gives its own justification by throwing light on itself. It is not a mere tautology in a closed system, like a mathematical axiom. Note the necessary relationship between the pairs | True | False | and | Doubtful | Indubitable | . Something may be true yet doubtful: we do not know that it is true. Though something doubtful may be true, it may also be false: we do not know which. Therefore, to build on the doubtful, even if true, is always to take a risk. The edifice of knowledge would be an unsure structure. But consider something that is indubitable: it must be true. There is no doubt about it. So truth may be arrived at by exercising doubt until something indubitable is disclosed. Hence, the pairs of terms have to be recast as interpenetrating: Indubitable

$$
\begin{array}{c}
\text{T} \\
\text{r} \\
\text{u} \\
\text{e} \quad\quad \text{Doubtful} \quad\quad\quad \text{False}
\end{array}
$$

The indubitable crosses over from merely being the opposite to the doubtful and enters in its entirety into the domain of the true. There is a breakthrough to truth by the force of methodological doubt.

In the third paragraph Descartes brings forth the first candidate for testing: the senses, upon which all his previous knowledge was based. Since the senses are sometimes deceptive they admit of doubt, hence they and everything built upon them is dispatched. The method operates with elegant efficiency. It takes but one sentence in one small paragraph to dispose of the usual foundation to our knowledge. There is something startling, awesome, frightening in the clean-cut action of the method at work: something radical has been lost. Our knowledge has been cut down to the ground. The brevity of the paragraph emphasizes the power of the method, the clarity of its use, and the profundity of our error.

Since we have spent so much time on the opening paragraphs of the first Meditation, let us attend to the closing paragraph.[2] It is the longest one in the Meditation, ponderous in style and content. Descartes acknowledges the huge realm of the doubtful. It is necessary to make extraordinary efforts to be on guard against deception and the illusions that may spring from an evil genius. But he totters under the weight of the task; he is drawn back to ordinary life. We see now why the great project had been postponed while one lives with faulty knowledge: the work is hard, the outcome is not guaranteed, and the attractions are strong of those things which may in principle be doubted but which in habit we have accepted. The last sentence is a long one that weighs us down with a forceful image of the prisoner who dreams of freedom and resists awakening. It is one thing to doubt whether we are awake or dreaming, it is another to wish to awake from a bad dream, but it is even more unnerving to desire not to awaken from a dream because we recognize the reality of the waking state to be unbearable. We close on a profound sense of subjectivity at a loss.

The scorecard for the first inning: 0. We have suffered thorough reversal. Not only has no candidate passed the test for the reconstruction of knowledge, but the method has been so devastatingly effective in eliminating all likely candidates that there is nowhere to turn for an answer. The project was to free us from servitude, but the project itself comes to overwhelm us. The method was to make things easy, but it worked so well that our difficulty of continuing is compounded. The first Meditation, then, is a masterpiece of doubt, one of the mind's greatest achievements in epistemic purgation. It is as thorough an intellectual enema as one can find.

But why does the Meditation end here? Why not continue for a few pages in order to draw the ego out of the hat or introduce the *deus ex meditatione*? Descartes has opted for a dramaturgy to the Meditations. If the first ends in terror at the absence of knowledge, the second will end in a relaxed confidence in the acquisition of a certitude, and the third concludes on the note of deep spiritual joy in the contemplation of God's existence. We have stages in the mind's progress to God. The Meditations are plural; each has its layer of the onion of truth to peel.

No matter how far we are able to follow in the Meditations, we must acknowledge that Descartes has made the experience of doubting a shattering one. It is not simply that claims to knowledge are calmly shattered by an intellectual method; rather, our calm as intellects is also shattered. The method shakes up the mind that uses it. This is a genuine crisis of being. But a genuine crisis of being can only be suffered by a being, which is the solution discovered in the second Meditation.

In this study of openings and closings, we need to look at the beginning of that second Meditation, for it explicitly reflects upon the whole of the first Meditation.[3] The doubts raised by that effort are unforgettable. And one's head is full of them. There is no way evident to escape them. Another forceful image is brought to mind with nightmare quality: one is adrift in a sea of doubts, unable either to touch bottom with one's feet or swim to shore. *Terra firma* is beyond one's grasp, and the terror of drowning overwhelms one.

Yet Descartes will set out again. Any hint of cowardice the reader detected in the first paragraph of the preceding Meditation is replaced here by admiration for intellectual heroism. We too wish to follow, for our own integrity is at stake in the second Meditation. To change the metaphor, we are in the same boat with Descartes. This is one of the noblest moments of philosophy. Having suffered the deepest disappointment in the search for knowledge, one simply tries again. It is a rebirth of the Socratic recognition of one's ignorance that nonetheless leads to continued searching for wisdom. The quest for knowing is stronger than the suffering of doubt. While one cannot be sure that something certain can be found, yet one at least may know through one's continued efforts nothing certain can be found. The consolation of failure is in knowing that we cannot know. But even this cannot be known unless we continue to try. So the answer to the first Meditation is not to give up the project but to reaffirm it. We begin again.

The solution is reached in another page or so: the proposition, *"Ego sum, ego existo," quoties a me profertur, vel mente concipitur, necessario esse verum.*[4] My thinking reveals that I exist. But what is it that I am? asks Descartes in a paragraph of startling brevity.[5] *Res cogitans*: a thing which thinks, a thinking thing. That is almost tautological. To think is to be something that thinks. But what is a thing which thinks? asks Descartes. He provides an enumeration of what constitutes a thing which thinks, and the first item is doubting. This is a landmark paragraph as the definition of thinking being.

In the next paragraph an affirmation is made of the definition as befitting Descartes, by means of a rhetorical question: "Am I not this same one who doubts nearly everything...?" What is the evidence for this claim? The first Meditation. There is no doubt about it. The first Meditation, so shot through with doubt, stands as solid testimony of what is recognized in the second Meditation as a mode of thinking—and hence of being. The first Meditation, then, is not the total loss we felt it had been, but a superb positive gain. Revise the scorecard to read: 1. One certain thing is all that we needed as foundation for our project. There are other kinds of thinking that take place in that Meditation, such as imagining, which also serve as evidence in the application of the definition, and these demand separate study.

Let us stick with doubt and apply it methodologically, in the spirit of the first Meditation, to the discovery in the second Meditation. That is, I doubt that "I think." But doubting, by definition, is a kind of thinking, so that if I doubt then I think. Let us go back one step further in our rigorous effort to apply the Cartesian method to the Cartesian principle, for doubt is the rock bottom. To doubt that I doubt is to oblige the method to face itself as well as to force the problem to face itself. If I succeed in doubting that I really doubt, then I have put doubt in jeopardy as truth. One could argue that everything is doubtful, even that one doubts. But if one does doubt that one doubts, then one *is* doubting. There it is: the foolproof self-evidence at the core of the onion. The sea of doubt opens to an island of certainty. Whichever way we entertain the candidate of doubt, either doubting it or not doubting it, we are, in effect, doubting. Doubt, then, is indubitable. Whatever we must suffer in our first Meditation in the name of doubt, we profit from in our second Meditation in the name of thinking.

It is possible to reach further back, conceiving the possibility that we have fooled ourselves somehow, and try to doubt that "I doubt that I doubt." And so on *ad infinitum*. In other words, one can always try to raise a further doubt about the alleged doubting one engages in. But at every raising of further doubt one perforce is also doubting. Hence, the regress is an infinite confirmation of the existence of thinking. There is something wonderful—filled with wonder—in doubt, for though it may constantly put everything in question, it is also perpetually affirmative.

If doubting doubt is the clincher latent in Descartes's argument, even if he did not work it out fully in those terms in the Meditations, then we must also point out the fallacy unnoticed by Descartes in his argument which reduces it to something highly dubious. In all these claims of "I doubt," "I think," and "I am," what has been smuggled into the premise is exactly that which is aimed for in the conclusion, namely the "I". An identity of selfhood is assumed. This is open to considerable doubt, as philosophers such as Hume have shown. We need to doubt that "*I* doubt." Who is to do that doubting if not I? But this question presumes that a mind exists which is I, and that is the very thing to be proven. The "I think" would have to be reformulated as "thinking is going on." Therefore, Descartes's argument reduces to: "doubting is occurring, therefore thinking is taking place, since thinking is defined to include doubting, and hence something is thinking." Yet that "something" is assumed as correlative to the activity of thinking. Strictly speaking, *thinking* is thinking, or thinking is being *thought*. By throwing doubt upon the pronoun, doubt is also being thrown upon the mind and the existent. Sterile tautology then taunts us — if we may still speak of "us."

Descartes's metaphysics or *prima philosophia* comes tumbling down as absolute science. Certainty is unavailable as an Archimedean point for knowledge. One's existence is not known with certainty by thought. Those who look for the core of the onion find tears in their eyes. That does leave a useful though uncertain grounding for all the branches of knowledge: one account among others, probabilistic and corrigible. Thus, the project does have reasonable success, but all human knowledge may be faulty.

We may wonder why Descartes missed the *petitio principii* in the argument. Is selfhood so persuasive that one cannot think without the certainty that one is thinking? Is the presumption in favor of the "I" psychological, ontological, or grammatical? The fallacy occurs in the Discourse as well, whose Latin translation by de Courcelles (1644) of Descartes's French (1637) has bequeathed to us the best-known phrase of neo-Latin: *cogito ergo sum*. But the very structure, format, and styling of the Meditations serve to conceal the error in thought. The meditative mode takes place within the mind. The commitment to existence of one's thinking is made before the Meditations open, for the unspoken prerequisite of this kind of work is that there is a mind through which — in which — the work will be presented. Thus, the opening sentence is made possible only by a mind already existent. As that sentence unfurls we readers are caught up in it so that two things seem beyond question: (1) that we are following the thinking of a mind; and (2) that we are a mind following that thinking. As readers of the Meditations it seems unthinkable that we are not thinkers.

The impression of selfhood is persuasive in a literary way. Powerful images bind us to the plight of a person. Language retains the feel of the human speaker. We are so keenly aware of the struggle of an identity throughout the first Meditation that we do not even bother to ask if it is necessarily the same identity which opens the second Meditation the next day. The matching of consciousness at the opening of the second to the closing of the first foreshadows the art of consciousness that connects chapters in the novels of Henry James. If the Cartesian Fallacy of the Existent Mind is committed before the first Meditation opens, then it is also committed in that space between the first and second Meditations. What happens between them is the presumed continuity of an existent self as thinker. The linking presumption is present within the first Meditation as paragraphs lead to one another, and as sentences lead to one another in those paragraphs. From the first sentence on the Meditations are grounded in the existence of a thinking subject. The error is embedded in the initiation and entirety of the work.

The Cartesian Fallacy is one of the most brilliant and persuasive errors in the history of thought. After all, we all have a certain interest at stake in presuming our existence as thinking selves. What makes the error so successful—that is, so disguised—in large part is the art of the Meditations as a neo-Latin literary work.

Notes

1. Descartes, *Meditationes de prima philosophia* (1641), in *Œuvres*, eds. Charles Adam & Paul Tannery (Paris, Léopold Cerf, 1897–1913), VII, 17:

> Animadverti jam ante aliquot annos quàm multa, ineunte ætate, falsa pro veris admiserim, & quàm dubia sint quæcunque istis postea superextruxi, ac proinde funditus omnia semel in vitâ esse evertenda, atque a primis fundamentis denuo inchoandum, si quid aliquando firmum & mansurum cupiam in scientiis stabilire; sed ingens opus esse videbatur, eamque ætatem expectabam, quæ foret tam matura, ut capessendis disciplinis aptior nulla sequeretur.

The duc de Luynes in translating Descartes's text into French (1647) was obliged to employ ninety-eight words, spilling the content over into a second sentence, IX, 13.

2. ibid., VII, 22–23. Cf. the French, IX, 17–18, which breaks the paragraph into two.
3. ibid., VII, 23–24.
4. ibid., VII, 25.
5. ibid., VII, 28.

La Rome de Virgile et celle du seizième siècle dans "Ad Ianum Avansonium apud summum pont. oratorem regium, Tyberis" de Joachim Du Bellay[1]

James S. Hirstein

Vers la fin de la *Deffence et Illustration de la langue francoyse* (1549), Du Bellay essaie d'encourager ses compatriotes à employer la langue vernaculaire en les décourageant d'écrire en grec et en latin. Il fait allusion au grand nombre d'écrivains qui l'ont déjà emporté dans ces domaines:

> Les larges campaignes Greques et Latines sont déja si pleines, que bien peu reste d'espace vide. Ja beaucoup d'une course legere ont attaint le but tant desiré. Long temps y a que le prix est gaigné.[2]

Du Bellay devait pourtant ressentir lui-même un manque d'espace littéraire pendant son séjour à Rome de 1554 à 1558 où il écrivait ses propres vers néo-latins. Nous mettrons l'accent aujourd'hui sur la question d'espace textuel en ce sens que le poète, même en imitant des modèles, a besoin d'un espace de signification libre. Dans les six vers sur lesquels nous allons nous pencher, de ce poème de cent cinquante-deux vers en distiques élégiaques, il sera question d'un espace de signification qui est intertextuel.[3]

Cet espace de signification est intertextuel dans la mesure où le poète nous renvoie du corps de son propre poème à des textes antérieurs, que l'on appellera des intertextes. Il nous y renvoie au moyen d'un fragment de l'intertexte qu'il aura monté et le plus souvent transposé dans son poème; on appellera ce fragment un renvoi intertextuel. Le renvoi intertextuel arrêtera le lecteur qualifié en pleine lecture du texte en question, le contraignant à se rappeler l'intertexte. C'est dans le mouvement entre les deux textes, où en tenant compte de leurs contextes et des changements que le fragment de l'intertexte aura subis, que le lecteur arrivera à une lecture intertextuelle qui sera unificatrice sur le plan des moyens, même si elle finit par séparer davantage le texte de l'intertexte.[4] Du point de vue du poète qui déclenche cette rencontre entre les deux textes, c'est dans cet espace intertextuel qu'il trouvera son espace de signification libre.[5]

L'écriture intertextuelle exige deux opérations essentielles de la part du poète car le fait de renvoyer à des intertextes peut produire un effet à double tranchant.

D'une part, si le poète ne transpose pas le renvoi intertextuel selon ses propres besoins, l'intertexte, qui sera très bien connu dans la plupart des cas, pourrait bien s'emparer de son texte en le vidant de sa signification grâce à sa notoriété; d'autre part, l'introduction des renvois intertextuels risque de détruire l'équilibre de son texte comme totalité structurée de sorte qu'il doit bien monter les renvois dans son texte.[6] En passant donc par ces deux opérations, la transposition et le montage des renvois intertextuels, on examinera la façon dont Du Bellay se crée un espace intertextuel afin d'y former une vision de Rome parmi celles d'autres poètes tels que Virgile ou ceux qui, comme lui-même, évoquaient la ville éternelle à travers les murs croulants et les colonnes brisées du seizième siècle.

Jean de St Marcel, Seigneur d'Avanson, ambassadeur du roi de France Henri II auprès du Saint-Siège est arrivé à Rome à la fin du mois de mars 1555.[7] Si l'on fait confiance aux temps des verbes du narrateur de ce poème, il a été écrit après l'arrivée d'Avanson. "Ad Ianum Avansonium ..." se divise en trois parties. Dans la première (vv. 1–50) un narrateur anonyme dépeint le Dieu fluvial Tibre et sa cour. A droite du Tibre se tient la rivière Anio, à gauche le Nar soufré, eux et quarante autres rivières qui le servent. Ensuite il y a des groupes de nymphes qui l'entourent: il y a une section "travail" où l'on tisse, une section "beauté" où l'on se pare, et une section "musique" où l'on joue de la lyre; pendant que les nymphes s'occupent de leurs devoirs, le Tibre les encourage. Puis est venue la nouvelle de l'arrivée d'Avanson de sorte que le Tibre s'est réjoui de voir venir le libérateur de l'Italie.

Dans la deuxième partie du poème (vv. 51–88) le Tibre adresse la parole à Avanson en l'accueillant et en lui parlant de Rome. C'est cette partie-ci qui va nous intéresser.

La troisième partie présente des louanges d'Avanson de la part du Tibre et de grandes prédictions sur ce que sera son succès auprès du Saint-Siège et des députés du Saint Empire romain germanique. On lit par exemple que grâce aux conseils d'Avanson:

> Tunc raptas Aquilae fallax Cornicula plumas
> Exuet, at Gallus proferet imperium: (vv. 113–14)

et plus loin:

> Hisque iterum campis reddens Saturnia regna,
> Littoribus condes aurea secla meis.   (vv. 145–46)

Le narrateur revient aux quatre derniers vers pour clore le poème en décrivant le départ du Tibre sous les eaux.

Il y a donc trois personnages dans ce poème, le narrateur, le Tibre, et Avanson. Avanson ne parle pas, ce qui fait que les descriptions du narrateur font un tiers du poème alors que les deux autres tiers comprennent le discours du Tibre. Le narrateur commence le poème au passé tout en décrivant la cour du Tibre au présent. Puis il présente le discours du Tibre et le clôt au passé tandis que le discours lui-même est au présent, en discours direct.[8]

Du Bellay donne à la deuxième partie un cadre virgilien. Dans le huitième livre de l'*Enéide*, Enée, s'étant endormi tout inquiet de la guerre contre Turnus et les Latins, rêve du Dieu Tibre. Le Dieu fluvial lui conseille d'aller chercher l'aide d'Evandre, le roi d'Arcadie. En le saluant le Tibre lui parle ainsi:

> "O sate gente deûm, Trojanam ex hostibus urbem
> Qui revehis nobis, aeternaque Pergama servas,
> Exspectate solo Laurenti arvisque Latinis,
> Hic tibi certa domus, certi, ne absiste, Penates;"[9]   (VIII.36–39)

Le Tibre de Du Bellay se sert de quelques-unes de ces expressions:

> Venisti tandem, arvis expectate Latinis,
>   O patriae columen, praesidiumque tuae:
> Venisti, et magnae spectas iam moenia Romae,
>   Dulcis ubi statio est, et tibi certa domus.   (vv. 51–54)

Enée et Avanson sont tous les deux attendus des champs latins de même qu'il y a pour tous les deux une demeure assurée en Italie. De Virgile à Du Bellay le Tibre semble rester le même, c'est la personne à qui il s'adresse qui change. Avanson se substitue à Enée, un changement certainement flatteur pour le Français.

Le parallélisme entre les deux textes continue. Après s'être rendu en Arcadie, Enée trouve Evandre, fondateur de la cité romaine, qui lui montre les lieux où sous Saturne l'on a vécu l'âge d'or. Il lui indique des édifices renversés—monuments à des héros anciens—de même que le Tibre montre à Avanson les restes poudreux de la Rome des Césars.[10] C'est ici dans le poème de Du Bellay que la situation semble exiger des vers chargés de renvois intertextuels, les vers 61–66.

Evandre montre à Enée le Capitole qui sous son règne est en plein éclat, mais qui n'était pas toujours ainsi:

> Aurea nunc, olim silvestribus horrida dumis.   (VIII.348)

Le Tibre de Du Bellay, qui remplace Evandre comme guide, transpose ce vers de Virgile et l'applique à toute la ville. Il commence par s'affirmer et par désigner la plaine vide:

> Ille ego sum Tybris toto notissimus orbe,
>   Quemque vides campum, maxima Roma fuit.
> Nunc deserta iacet sylvestribus horrida dumis,   (vv. 61–63)

Si l'on place le vers de Virgile et les vers similaires de Du Bellay l'un au-dessus des autres comme le poète nous y incite implicitement, on peut voir que le Tibre résume la grandeur passée de Rome dans l'hémistiche du vers 62, mais emploie tout le vers 63 pour décrire sa chute. Il y a de plus un mouvement chiastique des éléments temporels: le "nunc" de Virgile se transpose dans le "fuit" de Du Bellay et le "olim" de Virgile s'inverse dans le "nunc" de Du Bellay. Pour souligner en passant la tradition néo-latine italienne de ce poème, il y a une transposition similaire de ce même vers de Virgile chez Poggio Bracciolini (1380–1459) où l'on trouve "Aurea quondam, nunc squalida spinetis vepribusque referta".[11]

On pourrait dire pour autant que les vers de Du Bellay parodient le vers de Virgile, conformément à l'étymologie du mot "parodie" rappelée par Gérard Genette dans son livre *Palimpsestes*, "le fait de chanter à côté, donc de chanter faux ou dans une autre voix, en contrechant — en contrepoint — … déformer donc ou *transposer* une mélodie."[12] Etant donné la signification ordinaire du mot "parodie," M. Genette suggère pour décrire une parodie sérieuse le terme "transposition," d'où mon emploi du verbe "transposer."[13]

En tenant compte du contexte du fragment virgilien dans le poème de Du Bellay et de son intertexte, l'*Enéide*, on conçoit que la Rome du Tibre du seizième siècle soit retournée à un état postérieur à l'âge saturnien mais antérieur au règne d'Evandre, un état sauvage, mais bien capable de reconstruction. C'est une Rome qui attend encore une fois son Evandre et son Enée ou le cas échéant, son Avanson.

Il y a un autre renvoi intertextuel dans le pentamètre du même distique:

Nunc deserta iacet sylvestribus horrida dumis,
    Nec bene quae fuerit tanta ruina docet.   (vv. 63–64)

L'intertexte ici est une formule de l'époque de Du Bellay, "Roma quanta fuit ipsa ruina docet" dont se servaient des peintres et des dessinateurs "ruinistes."[14] Elle surmonte par exemple un dessin de Marten Van Heemskerk (1498–1574) où sont représentés la pointe sud du Palatin et le Septizonium. On voit à l'arrière-plan, à gauche et au centre, des squelettes des bâtiments du Palatin ouverts au ciel et puis au premier plan à droite une portion du Septizonium qui reste encore debout.[15] On a l'impression que la formule en haut à gauche témoigne de l'échec du dessinateur qui aurait aimé tout dessiner, mais qui, faute de modèle, a dû faire appel à des mots afin de combler le vide.

Le Tibre, en réponse à cet effort pour suppléer ce qui manque, fait entendre que c'est peine perdue. Ce n'est pas à partir de ses décombres que l'on peut imaginer ce que fut Rome.

Ces transpositions d'un vers de Virgile et d'une formule du seizième siècle représentent le renversement de la ville ancienne. Il y a, si vous voulez, un mouvement mimétique — ville renversée — vers inversé. On peut penser aussi à la *via negativa*, on ne peut décrire Rome qu'en rappelant ce qu'elle n'est plus. Toutefois, le contexte virgilien de cette partie de "Ad Ianum Avansonium …" fait qu'elle est très positive. Enée, avec l'aide d'Evandre pourra réaliser son rêve. Il est le commencement d'une ligne qui sous César Auguste ramènera un nouvel âge d'or. Avanson, et à travers lui, son roi, est censé être le même commencement.

Ainsi le distique suivant fait-il apparaître un début de résurrection romaine:

> Roma tamen superest: Capitoli immobile saxum
>   Restat, et ingentis nominis umbra manet. (vv. 65–66)

Rome survit; sa tête, le Capitole, reste encore debout et l'ombre, la survivance d'un grand nom, demeure. Il y a dans le pentamètre un fragment dont l'intertexte semble être la préface d'Erasme à une édition des *Historiae Augustae scriptores* qu'il a dirigée. La préface, adressée à l'électeur Frédéric et au duc Georges de Saxe, date du 5 juin 1517. Après avoir passé en revue le grand nombre de mauvais empereurs romains et le petit nombre de bons, Erasme s'étonne de la franchise des historiens romains, vu qu'il y a toujours des gens de son époque qui exigent que l'on parle des empereurs, même les plus scélérats, avec déférence. Mais il trouve plus grave encore que l'on ne considère que le nom de l'Empire, "nomen illud imperii," sans tenir compte de ses origines tout à fait criminelles. En parlant de ce nom d'Empire, il dit qu'il fut autrefois inviolable et saint dans le monde et que même encore maintenant il est respecté et vénérable aux yeux de beaucoup de gens alors qu'il ne survit à peu près rien que l'ombre vaine de ce grand nom, "cum nihil fere supersit praeter inanem magni nominis umbram."[16] Plus loin il parle de l'inutilité d'une renaissance de l'ancien empire, d'une *monarchia orbis*, pour nous diriger vers le Christ, qui est le seul *monarcha orbis*.[17] Mais de même que le nom de l'Empire était toujours vivant, de même l'idée de cette monarchie universelle avait toujours ses partisans à l'époque, qui se disputaient, d'ailleurs, à propos du prochain héritier de l'Empire, la question de la *translatio imperii*.

Le Tibre, pour transposer le jugement d'Erasme, semble reprendre le verbe "supersum" au vers 65 et puis au vers 66 il laisse tomber l'adjectif défavorable "inanis." Tout cela pour nous faire savoir que la ville et le nom de l'Empire demeurent tous les deux (la chose et le mot, si vous voulez) et que malgré les dangers d'un nouvel *imperium*, ils pourraient bien renaître, surtout (ceci étant sous-entendu à cet endroit du poème) si le coq gaulois en était le chef.

Quant au montage des renvois, l'élément maître est le rapport entre eux et la voix principale du poème, celle du Tibre. En tant que celui qui parle, le Tibre est le principe d'unité et de continuité. Il monte les divers renvois intertextuels dans son discours en servant de toile de fond et de porte-parole en même temps. Il est créateur de continuité en tant que personnage historique évoqué par Virgile aussi bien que par Du Bellay. Témoin de toutes les métamorphoses qui se sont produites sur ses rivages, lien entre le "olim" et le "nunc," il n'a pas changé, une constance qui fait rappeler la fin du troisième sonnet des *Antiquitez de Rome*:

> Le Tybre seul, qui vers la mer s'enfuit
> Reste de Rome. O mondaine inconstance!
> Ce qui est ferme, est par le temps destruit,
> Et ce qui fuit, au temps fait resistence.[18]

Si l'on revient aux six vers étudiés, on se rappellera que le Tibre a commencé sa description chargée de renvois intertextuels en disant "Ille ego sum Tiber." On a l'impression qu'il s'affirme d'emblée comme principe unificateur contre les mots des autres poètes qui suivent ce vers.[19]

Après avoir examiné les procédés intertextuels du poète, il nous reste à parler, d'une façon très générale, de la motivation d'une telle sorte d'écriture. Sur le plan du poème, on se demande si ce n'est pas la question de Rome qui a provoqué tant de renvois intertextuels dans la description que donne le Tibre. La question romaine était épineuse à cause de son caractère politique. Aux vers 113–14 cités au début de notre exposé où sont nommés les trois oiseaux — la petite corneille perfide qui représenterait le Saint Empire romain germanique, l'aigle romaine, et le coq gaulois — on voit bien le problème: si l'Empire romain est toujours vivant, lequel des pouvoirs de l'époque le réincarnera-t-il?[20] Encore une fois, la question de la *translatio imperii* se pose, mais c'est à un Tibre francisé d'y répondre.[21]

A Rome où se pratiquait une politique de bascule, la façon dont on représentait la ville n'était pas sans intérêt. Trancher la question nettement n'aurait pas été bien sage. Mieux valait dire pour Du Bellay que c'était un Français qui allait ramener l'âge d'or à travers des renvois intertextuels dans un cadre italien; il ne faut pas oublier que c'est le Tibre qui parle. Une écriture intertextuelle peut être donc utile devant une situation ambiguë. On présente, tout en les transposant, des jugements antérieurs de sorte que l'on peut s'exprimer à partir des autorités, sagement et discrètement.

Utiliser les autorités, surtout les autorités littéraires, pose un problème plus large, celui de l'imitation des modèles. Comment les imiter, les respecter, mais en même temps les surpasser?[22] Après des modèles tels que Virgile, comment trouver un espace d'écriture? Lui, ou bien ceux qui se sont inspirés de lui, n'ont-ils pas tout dit? Surtout, parler de Rome ouvre la porte à des *topoi*, à des lieux communs qui encombrent le texte du poète de leur passé riche en signification.[23] Le processus intertextuel fait pourtant que l'on peut reconnaître ses prédécesseurs tout en les changeant ou comme le dit plus radicalement Julia Kristeva, "le texte poétique est produit dans le mouvement complexe d'une affirmation et d'une négation simultanées d'un autre texte."[24] Le poète donc, en transposant et en montant des lieux communs à sa façon, peut les récrire dans l'espace de signification créé entre l'intertexte et son propre poème.

Université d'Orléans
Université de Virginie

Notes

1. Toutes les citations de "Ad Ianum Avansonium ..." sont tirées de l'édition établie par E. Courbet, *Poésies françaises et latines de Joachim Du Bellay avec notice et notes par E. Courbet* (Paris, Garnier Frères, 1918), I, 436–40. Il se trouve à la biliothèque municipale d'Orléans un exemplaire de l'édition de 1558 de chez Frédéric Morel qui ne semble pas différer de celui dont Courbet s'est servi. Je tiens ici à remercier le personnel de la bibliothèque aussi bien que Mme J. Gallier et Mlle T. Pellicane, mais je suis surtout reconnaissant à M. et Mme J.-C. Thiolier qui ont très gracieusement revu avec moi le texte néo-latin de Du Bellay et mon propre texte; je suis pourtant seul responsable de ce qui suit.

2. Joachim Du Bellay, *La Deffence et Illustration de la langue francoyse*, éd. Henri Chamard (Paris, Didier, 1948), p. 190 (livre II, chap. xii). Cf. également la page 188 (livre II, chap. xii), "ou pour estre opprimé de l'infinie multitude des autres plus renommez, il [le nom de celui qui écrit en grec ou en latin] demeure quasi en silence et obscurité."

3. Mis à part les problèmes d'espace littéraire sous la Renaissance, je pense aux mots de Julia Kristeva dans *Sèméiôtikè: Recherches pour une sémanalyse* (Paris, Seuil, 1969), p. 255: "Le signifié poétique renvoie à des signifiés discursifs autres, de sorte que dans l'énoncé poétique plusieurs autres discours sont lisibles. Il se crée, ainsi, autour du signifié poétique, un espace textuel multiple dont les éléments sont susceptibles d'être appliqués dans le texte poétique concret. Nous appellerons cet espace intertextuel." Voir aussi Harold Bloom, "The Breaking of Form," dans *De-Construction and Criticism* (New York, Seabury Press, 1979), p. 6 et p. 18 où il parle de la création de l'espace "imaginatif" ou "poétique."

4. Chez Michael Riffaterre, "La Trace de l'intertexte," *la Pensée* (Oct. 1980, no. 215), 5, il est question d'une "double lecture—textuelle et mémorielle."

5. Sur le plan critique, il faut distinguer la critique des sources et l'intertextualité. Laurent Jenny, "La Stratégie de la forme," *Poétique*, 27 (1976), 262, écrit: "Contrairement à ce qu'écrit J. Kristeva, l'intertextualité prise au sens strict n'est pas sans rapport avec la critique "des sources": l'intertextualité désigne non pas une addition confuse et mystérieuse d'influences, mais le travail de transformation et d'assimilation de plusieurs textes opéré par un texte centreur qui garde le leadership du sens." Je ne suis pas tout à fait convaincu que la critique des sources soit "une addition confuse et mystérieuse d'influences," mais je veux souligner avec L. Jenny que l'on met l'accent sur la transposition et le montage des textes antérieurs plutôt que sur l'origine tout court de tel ou tel fragment.

6. Cf. Laurent Jenny, ibid., p. 259 et p. 267.

7. Voir Joachim Du Bellay, *Œuvres poétiques*, éd. Henri Chamard (Paris, Edouard Cornély, 1910), II, 45, où Du Bellay dédie les *Regrets* à Avanson.

8. Voir par exemple vv. 49–51 de "Ad Ianum Avansonium ...": "Demulcensque manu concretam uligine barbam,/Hos placido laetus reddidit ore sonos:/Venisti tandem ..."

9. Virgile, *Œuvres de Virgile, traduction nouvelle accompagnée du texte latin*, 2 vols., 3ᵉ éd., trad. Emile Pessonneaux (Paris, Charpentier, 1865).

10. Cf. dans le texte de Virgile, l'*Enéide*, VIII, 312 "virûm monumenta priorum," et 356 "Relliquias veterumque vides monumenta virorum."

11. Poggio Bracciolini, "De Varietate fortunae," dans *Latin Writings of the Italian Humanists*, éd. F. A. Gragg (New York, Charles Scribner's Sons, 1927), p. 112: "Hic Antonius, cum aliquantum huc illuc oculos circumtulisset, suspirans stupentique similis, 'O quantum,' inquit, 'Poggi, haec Capitolia ab illis distant, quae noster Maro cecinit, "Aurea nunc, olim silvestribus horrida dumis"! Ut quidem is versus merito possit converti: Aurea quondam, nunc squalida spinetis vepribusque referta.'"

12. Gérard Genette, *Palimpsestes: la littérature au second degré* (Paris, Seuil, 1982), p. 17. C'est G. Genette qui souligne.

13. ibid., p. 36. Bien que M. Genette distingue "intertextualité" et le champ de son étude, "hypertextualité," ses termes nous sont utiles.

14. Roland Mortier, *La Poétique des ruines en France: ses origines, ses variations de la Renaissance à Victor Hugo* (Genève, Droz, 1974), p. 23, n. 3.

15. ibid., gravure IX.

16. Erasme, *Opus epistolarum* éd. P. S. Allen (Oxford, Clarendon Press, 1906-65), II, lettre 586, lignes 126-27. Voir à ce propos Augustin Renaudet, *Etudes Erasmiennes (1521-1529)* (Paris, Droz, 1939), p. 67, n. 2 et p. 75; et *Erasme et l'Italie* (Genève, Droz, 1954), p. 184. Cf. également Gilbert Gadoffre, *Du Bellay et le sacré* (Paris, Gallimard, 1978), p. 99.

Lors d'une discussion après ma communication, Mme G. Demerson, qui prépare l'édition critique des *Poemata*, m'a indiqué un autre intertexte pour ce renvoi de "Ad Ianum Avansonium ...", celui de Lucain, *La Guerre civile*, 135 I, où il est dit de Pompée "Stat, magni nominis umbra." Voir, à ce propos l'article de Frank Chambers, "Lucan and the *Antiquitez de Rome*," *PMLA*, 60 (1945), 937-48 où parmi des renseignements très utiles, l'auteur parle incorrectement, à mon avis, de l'influence de Lucain au vers 63 de "Ad Ianum Avansonium ..." (p. 939) où se trouve l'hémistiche de Virgile dont j'ai déjà parlé.

17. Allen, op. cit., lignes 186 et 231.

18. L'édition de J. Jolliffe et M. A. Screech, 2e éd. (Genève, Droz, 1974).

19. Cf. Harold Bloom, *The Anxiety of Influence* (London, Oxford Press, 1973), p. 72: "Strong poets are wrestlers with the dead."

A propos de cet hémistiche, M. J. IJsewijn, après ma communication, m'a indiqué des vers d'Ovide où se trouvent les mots "Ille ego sum," *Tristia*, IV, x, 1 et *Ex Ponto*, IV, iii, 11, 13, 15, 16, et 17.

20. Voir l'interprétation que donne Gilbert Gadoffre, op. cit., p. 96, du 17e sonnet des *Antiquitez* où il est question de la "corneille Germaine" et de l'"aigle Romaine." Voir aussi les notes de Screech, op. cit., pour ce sonnet.

21. Voir à ce propos Gadoffre, ibid., pp. 90-99.

22. En ce qui concerne le surpassement de ses modèles, voir Quintilien, *The Institutio Oratoria of Quintilian*, trad. H. E. Butler (Boston, Harvard University Press, 1922), IV, p. 77 (Livre X ii 4-7) et Jacques Peletier (*Art Poëtique*, éd. André Boulanger (Paris, Les Belles Lettres, 1930), p. 96.

23. Voir Terence Cave, *The Cornucopian Text: Problems of Writing in the French Renaissance* (Oxford, Clarendon Press, 1979), p. xix, où il parle de la répétition et du déplacement des *topoi*. Il souligne, comme c'est certainement le cas dans le poème de Du Bellay (cf. par exemple dans notre exposé l'emploi que fait le Pogge du même vers de Virgile dont se sert Du Bellay), que le fragment intertextuel renvoie à tous les emplois antérieurs du fragment, pas uniquement à celui de l'original."

24. Julia Kristeva, op. cit., p. 257.

Fatum in the Writings of Etienne Dolet

K. Lloyd-Jones

Recent publications by Emile Telle and Claude Longeon have served to focus attention on the life and thought of one of the most intriguing figures of the French Renaissance, Etienne Dolet, and to open up once again not only the specific question of Dolet's own religious stance, but also the more far-reaching issue of the position of the so-called "paganizing" Humanists in the religious debates of their time. It will be remembered that, following his condemnation for heresy, Dolet was executed after an extraordinarily strenuous series of attempts by the Sorbonne to silence him, including a first arrest in 1542 (resulting in his freedom thanks only to the personal intervention of the king), a second arrest in 1544 (from which he escaped), and a third arrest later that year. This led to his incarceration in the dungeons of the Châtelet, and, in August 1546, to his death in the Place Maubert.

While he had enjoyed the favor and, at times, the protection of some of the great figures of his day, his killing of a man in self-defence (1536) had not helped matters, nor had the publication of his *Poemata* two years later. These were denounced as heretical by the authorities in Lyon, who were troubled by his personal re-wording of certain Christian precepts, and by his treatment of the concept of *fatum*.

More than any other publication, however, it was his highly polemical answer to Erasmus's criticism of Ciceronianism that must have kept his name before the authorities as someone to watch. Erasmus, in his *Ciceronianus* (Basel, 1528), had condemned the cult of Ciceronian style as being, *inter alia*, little more than a cover for paganizing, and Dolet's violent rebuttal (*De Imitatione Ciceroniana*, no doubt composed as soon as Erasmus's text was known to him, but not published until 1536 in Lyon), was to espouse the defence of a literary style whose doctrinal implications were, at that particular moment, dangerous.

It may perhaps no longer be possible to identify Dolet's intimate convictions with certainty, and we may never know whether he was indeed a martyred freethinker, or simply a hapless victim of the contemporary French church's unwillingness to distinguish between rhetorical style and conceptual substance. Nevertheless, one line of inquiry lies in the consideration of certain of his writings published first in Latin and then in French. The examination of his own self-translations is particularly instructive, and takes us to the heart of the question of the relationship between faith and Ciceronianism, and — perhaps — toward a clearer understanding of his own religious stance. It is revealing to compare both his *Genethliacum Claudii Doleti* and the corresponding *Avant Naissance de Claude Dolet* (both Lyon, 1539), and his *Gallorum Regis Fata* and the corresponding *Gestes de Françoys de Valoys, Roy de France* (Lyon, 1539 and 1540), particularly insofar as each text raises the question of the extent to which human life is pre-ordained. The Latin originals point to the recourse to stoicism as a means of dealing with vicissitudes, while the French texts urge the virtue of humility in accepting God's will. Equally, Dolet develops a notion of the classical *fatum* in the Latin texts, in terms which essentially preclude its assimilation with the providential God of Christian orthodoxy to be found in the French versions. Dolet seems systematically to dilute the stoic sense of determinism in the Latin by the declaration of infinitely less dangerous beliefs in the French.

It is of course at this point that we must confront the question of Dolet's Ciceronianism. Can it not be argued that we are dealing here with essentially stylistic rather than conceptual distinctions? For many Humanists, it was perhaps more a matter of semantic code than anything else; writing in Latin committed one to a certain set of values, writing in the vernacular to another. And yet, even if we concede that the shifts we have noted above stem from stylistic or philological reasons, not from reasons having to do with Dolet's personal beliefs, we are still faced with the fact that, permeating much of his other Latin writings, there are positive elements which might well be judged "pernicious to Christian belief," and which none of his French writings match in their penetration or in the depth of their conviction. It is in this context that certain of the articles to be found in the two massive volumes of his *Commentarii Linguae Latinae* (Lyon, 1536 and 1538), which Dolet himself considered to be his major claim on the attention of posterity, merit our consideration.

It is instructive to compare the entries in the *Commentarii* under *fortuna* and *fatum*, two rubrics which would no doubt echo, for Dolet's contemporaries, much of the current free-will–predestination debate. In spite of the fact that the *Commentarii* are essentially philological compilations, Dolet's voice is clearly to be heard deriding the idea of *fortuna* as a cover for our own weakness and ineptitude, whereas he approvingly quotes a purely Ciceronian understanding of the idea of *fatum*. If we turn to the rubric *virtus*, traditionally both the classical and the Christian remedy against the vicissitudes of fortune, we find once again a purely Ciceronian reading of the idea: Ciceronian *recta ratio* in place of "faith, hope and charity."

When we set this notion of *virtus* against the idea of *fatum* mentioned above, it seems difficult to avoid the conclusion that the Church's identification of Dolet's unorthodoxy was fundamentally accurate: he seems to argue that we triumph, not by the free choice of moral options, but by the attitudes we hold toward events owing nothing to a morally ordered structure.

It must however be conceded that such an interpretation depends on the extent to which we assume an element of personal conviction in his philological enterprises, and this is something we cannot be entirely sure of. Certainly, nothing more succinctly points out, or sums up, the problem of the relationship between faith and language in the broader context of Renaissance Humanism, as well as in Dolet's own case, than the complaint of the authorities with regard to the Latin original of the *Gestes de Françoys de Valoys*, to the effect that he had availed himself of the word *fatum* "non comme devoit faire ung chrestyen, mays en celle signification que le prenoient les anciens philosophes, voulant aprouver la predestination."[1] Although the fateful word *predestination* had not yet fully assumed the dogmatic status it was soon to acquire, the point of the authorities' concern is clear: in the collision of Ciceronian *fatum*, Lutheran Christian determinism and an Erasmian free-will granting God, Dolet's position is necessarily ambiguous in its articulation if not in its conviction. The evidence we have brought forward is persuasive, if not conclusive.[2]

Trinity College, Hartford, Conn.

Notes

1. *Documents d'archive sur Etienne Dolet*, ed. C. Longeon (Saint-Etienne, 1977), p. 26.
2. This is a considerably abridged version of both my paper and the article that grew out of it; the latter, containing complete textual and bibliographical information, and re-titled "Orthodoxy and Language: Dolet and the question of Ciceronianism in the Early Reformation" appeared in *Classical and Modern Literature*, 2 (1982), 213–30.

Cohérences d'Etienne Dolet

Claude Longeon

Depuis quelques années on assiste à un renouveau des études dolé-tiennes, dont l'initiative revient en grande partie à Emile V. Telle, éditeur stimulant de l'*Erasmianus*.[1] L'érudition s'est intéressée à divers aspects de l'humaniste: le traducteur, l'historien, le philologue, l'homme de lettres, le propagandiste ...[2] Plusieurs textes, un peu oubliés, ont été réédités et sa bibliographie a été refaite.[3] Aujourd'hui l'occasion nous est offerte d'une pause pour présenter une image globale de Dolet, assez différente sans doute de celle qui prévalait depuis les travaux très méritoires de Richard Copley Christie.[4]

Longtemps l'Orléanais fut présenté comme un être à la destinée complexe, fait d'engagements et de repentirs soudains, un être pétri de contradictions irréductibles, dont la logique de la pensée et de l'action se laisse mal saisir ... Comment comprendre que celui qui professe un grand mépris pour les querelles théologiques et qui refuse de prendre parti, soit amené bientôt à éditer des textes d'inspiration de plus en plus nettement évangélique? Comment expliquer que cet humaniste, zélateur de Cicéron et qui ne jure que par les lettres latines, ait pris la brusque décision d'écrire et de publier en français? Comment expliquer ce souci d'instruire le plus grand nombre, ce besoin de multiplier l'amitié avec ce sentiment aigu de la persécution et cette méfiance soupçonneuse, cette soif de jouissances immédiates et cet esprit d'ascèse, cette revendication de liberté et cette tentation de s'abandonner à la rassurante facilité de l'Inévitable?...

C'est à ces questions que nous voudrions tenter de répondre.

De l'enfance de Dolet, nous ne savons rien, si ce n'est les sarcasmes de ses camarades toulousains sur la modestie de ses origines et de vilaines rumeurs sur le sort qu'aurait connu son père ... Quoi qu'il en soit (et la légende s'est emparée de cette zone obscure de son existence), toutes les conduites de Dolet montrent à l'évidence qu'il avait une revanche à prendre: disgrâce physique, famille désunie, timidité excessive ... Il se sent rejeté de la communauté des hommes et à plusieurs reprises il exprime sa hantise de terminer ses jours à la façon d'un animal. L'image de la déchéance le poursuit et la terreur de l'anonymat prend le visage d'un échec insoutenable. Plus qu'un autre sans doute, il lui faut être remarqué, reconnu, célébré, aimé; il lui faut tenir un rôle, si possible le premier.[5]

Ce qui lui impose d'abord de s'affranchir des autorités qui tiennent l'individu en tutelle. Chose aisée en paroles: Dolet n'a pas de mots assez violents pour condamner ces maîtres qui exploitent leurs serviteurs (les ambassadeurs et leurs secrétaires, les imprimeurs et leurs ouvriers, les princes et leurs courtisans...); il milite pour la liberté totale de l'écrivain, à la seule réserve que son intention ne soit pas de porter atteinte à la Religion ou au Souverain: "Tel effort d'esprit doibt estre libre, sans aulcun esgard, si gens mal pensants veulent calumnier ou reprimer ce qui ne leur appartient en rien. Car si ung autheur a ce tintoin en la teste que tel ou tel poinct de son ouvrage sera interpreté ainsi ou ainsi par les calumniateurs de ce Monde, jamais il ne composera rien qui vaille [...] ne fault par apres que lascher la bride à la plume, ou aultrement ne se mesler d'escrire";[6] il déplore la versatilité des princes qui souvent rejettent ceux qu'ils ont favorisés; il se moque des grammairiens qui prétendent imposer à la langue des normes abstraites; il repousse certaines pratiques religieuses qui font du chrétien une mécanique ... Voilà ce qui chez Dolet a pu passer pour une affirmation agressive des droits de l'individu.

Mais il n'est pas un individualiste, au sens strict du mot. Sa revendication de liberté s'accompagne de la recherche avide d'une autorité et d'une commmunauté où ou sur laquelle elle s'exerce. Nous ne parlons pas ici de l'autorité de l'Eglise à laquelle il faut affirmer sa soumission pour s'épargner les tracas, ni de celle du Roi dont il faut capter les faveurs pour assurer sa subsistance. Mais de cette autorité plus profonde, plus intériorisée, que Dolet, dès qu'il est en âge de former sa personnalité, place en Cicéron et dans les maîtres qui le lui ont fait connaître, Nicolas Bérault, Christophe de Longueil et Simon de Villeneuve. C'est la seule qu'il accepte totalement, lointaine, silencieuse et exigeante, au point d'engager la polémique avec Erasme sur ce nom. Sa démarche est plutôt de s'investir d'une autorité au sein d'une communauté qu'il a choisie ou qu'il s'est imposée: Orateur de la Nation française à Toulouse, un des premiers parmi les imprimeurs lyonnais ... Se plaçant ainsi en point de mire, il tiendra tous ses maux de cet appétit de puissance.

Un Pouvoir que Dolet a toujours proclamé vouloir mettre au service des autres, la petite élite des "litterati" d'abord, la jeunesse ensuite, l'ensemble de la communauté chrétienne de langue française plus tard. Son désir de jouer un rôle social, d'influer sur les affaires de son temps, de transmettre ce qu'il sait relève bien évidemment de la tradition déjà solide de l'humanisme moderne, mais aussi, plus personnellement, de son obsession de la mort et de sa recherche haletante de la gloire. Plus qu'un autre, Dolet eut le sens d'une triple vocation personnelle, professionnelle et nationale. Dans le temps même où il s'efforçait d'imposer ses mérites et son nom, il prit une certaine mesure de l'importance qu'acquérait progressivement l'opinion publique, capable en retour de reconnaître et de faire accepter, contre tous les pouvoirs, celui qui l'a servie. Nous verrons ainsi comment Dolet fit violence à sa réserve et à son aristocratisme d'esprit pour devenir un propagandiste déterminé.

L'Orléanais n'est pas homme à renoncer aux apparences, disons aux marques concrètes de la gloire, puisque la gloire est ce qui donne forme à sa vie. Aussi, sans pour autant la nier, ne parie-t-il pas pour la renommée posthume. Cet appétit de louanges tangibles, qui lui inspire plusieurs textes audacieux, joint à un souci de préserver la coexistence de la foi et de la raison, proche par certains aspects de la théorie de la double vérité exposée dans les écrits padouans,[7] l'amène dès ses premiers textes à distinguer soigneusement l'ordre humain de l'ordre spirituel, celui de la foi (qu'il affirmait avoir et que nous ne mettrons pas en doute) de celui des raisons naturelles.[8] Dolet a toujours marqué la plus grande aversion pour les théologiens, professionnels ou amateurs, qui, parfois au mépris de leur vie mais toujours au détriment de la paix civile et de l'harmonie des consciences, débattent de questions qui ne sont que l'enveloppe verbale de la religion. Et sa méfiance s'étend bientôt à ces humanistes qui ramènent tous leurs mots à la vie chrétienne. C'est pour dénoncer ce piège tendu par le spirituel, où chacun perd sa liberté, et qui détourne la foi de sa sublime retraite que Dolet s'en prend à Erasme avec la violence que l'on sait. Opération publicitaire, destinée à faire connaître bruyamment le nom de celui qui osait s'attaquer au monument de l'Europe humaniste, mais dans laquelle on aurait tort de ne voir que positions excessives et injustes. Il y a dans l'*Erasmianus* de 1535 plus de vrai Dolet que dans bien de ses écrits postérieurs. On y lit un plaidoyer pour une sagesse humaine, pour une liberté morale de l'écrivain, une condamnation de la "garrulitas" théologique qui oublie que la Parole du Christ se passe de tout commentaire, l'affirmation que la foi est du domaine de la conscience et qu'il est ridicule d'en vouloir mesurer la profondeur aux bavardages sur la religion. Lorsqu'il en parle, c'est pour dénoncer les pratiques superstitieuses, les rites païens, les excès et les pompes: ses préférences vont nettement à une religion dépouillée et intériorisée, mais point en rupture avec les traditions. Nous voici à l'opposé de tout fanatisme, laïque ou religieux, dans la conviction d'un homme qui a mis tous ses espoirs et toutes ses craintes dans l'usage des mots.

Etienne Dolet sait combien est ambitieux son programme de vie; mais c'est dans la mesure où il aperçoit devant lui cet idéal presque inaccessible, qu'il se sent digne de l'humanité qu'il porte en lui en voulant l'atteindre. L'une des critiques les plus vives qu'il adresse à Erasme est d'avoir choisi une certaine "mediocritas" et de s'être abandonné aux facilités de sa nature. Car, même s'il reconnaît que le désir d'émulation est inné, Dolet refuse à la nature une confiance aveugle. Si, comme il le croit, le sort "hic et nunc" de chacun dépend de soi-même, il faut se fixer un idéal rigoureux et mettre ses efforts inlassablement à l'atteindre. Travail, persévérance, conquête héroïque sur soi-même, sacrifice, discipline, enthousiasme, Dolet a retenu quelque chose de ce "climat" stoïcien qui entoure les œuvres padouannes. Doit-il à la lecture du *De Fato* l'importance qu'il accorde au destin? En tout cas ce thème central de son œuvre n'est qu'en apparence incompatible avec ce volontarisme conquérant; car Dolet est bien placé pour constater que la détermination et le travail acharné ne conduisent pas nécessairement au succès! Et mieux vaut alors expliquer ses échecs par l'intervention commode d'un pouvoir absolument extérieur qu'en acceptant de reconnaître ses erreurs et ses limites.[9]

Les circonstances de son éducation avaient fait de Dolet un spécialiste de la rhétorique latine. C'est donc l'idéal d'un verbe exigeant et persuasif qu'il se fixe et qu'il incarne dans celui qui passait pour le meilleur orateur romain, Cicéron. Si l'on regroupe en effet toutes les convictions et les ambitions que Dolet se forge pendant les premières années de sa vie (exigence d'un idéal de rigueur, ascèse de l'être et de la forme, souci de jouer un rôle dans l'éducation de la jeunesse et le gouvernement de la cité, nécessité d'acquérir au plus vite la gloire qui l'arrachera aux ténèbres...), on constate que le métier d' "orateur" s'imposait à lui comme une évidence. Avec Cicéron, plus près avec Valla, il est convaincu que les orateurs, dont le métier est de persuader les autres, ont leur part à jouer dans la vie sociale et politique de leur temps. Ils sont tout autres que les philosophes et les dialecticiens, puisqu'ils prétendent légitimement être utiles au public, contribuer par la stratégie verbale à donner forme à quelque dessein favorable à la communauté sociale. L'orateur peut être un "dux populi" (Valla), un moteur de l'histoire, puisque cette conception "activiste" de la rhétorique donne les moyens de mieux comprendre le monde mais aussi de mieux le façonner. L'écart est faible entre cet idéal de l'orateur "engagé" et le programme de prosélytisme de la Réforme: il faut, par référence à des modèles sûrs, produire des méthodes efficaces de persuasion et d'endoctrinement. En 1535, Dolet prend bien garde de distinguer les deux démarches et de libérer l'art oratoire de tout "soupçon" religieux; il rêve d'une éloquence profane à la fois instrument et symbole d'harmonie politique, lieu d'une épuration de la forme qui est en elle-même une épreuve de la grandeur d'âme. L'orateur selon le cœur de Dolet, purgé des tentations religieuses, doit faire fi des préjugés moraux qui voulaient que le bon et le beau fussent indissolublement unis et que le "maître de bien dire" (Ramus) dût être d'abord celui qui agit vertueusement. Avec courage et insistance, Dolet proclame dans l'*Erasmianus* (1535) cette idée assez neuve et audacieuse que la beauté d'un texte et ses qualités oratoires n'ont que faire de la bonté de celui qui le prononce, en d'autres termes qu'on ne fait pas nécessairement de la bonne littérature avec de bons sentiments. Il plaide ainsi pour un orateur qui soit un authentique professionnel, défini par sa compétence dans l'art de persuader et non par ses certitudes religieuses et morales. Toujours cette distinction entre les deux ordres!

Les principes sont posés, les convictions assises; les exigences ne manquent pas, ni les ambitions. Reste à voir comment les circonstances de sa vie personnelle et publique ont permis que Dolet les exprimât.

Des années d'apprentissage, il faut retenir cette "sodalitas" de Padoue réunie autour de Simon de Villeneuve qui apprit à Dolet, disciple et ami, la pureté du style latin et l'art de la rhétorique. Dans ce milieu clos des fidèles de Cicéron, l'Orléanais mena une existence protégée favorable au travail et à l'affirmation de sa personnalité. Sur l'orateur il connut les écrits théoriques et il étudia dans leurs détails les stratégies du discours cicéronien. De ces années date son projet de *Commentaires sur la Langue latine* pour lequel il entasse des milliers de fiches où il note quel usage Cicéron fait des mots et le contexte dans lequel il les emploie; il faut avoir cela présent à l'esprit lorsqu'on lit les *Commentarii*; qui ne sont, sauf rares développements personnels, qu'un travail de philologue s'efforçant d'examiner l'usage des auteurs, et non la somme des pensées intimes de Dolet sur la providence, le destin et l'immortalité de l'âme.

Vient alors le temps de la pratique, car il est offert au jeune Dolet deux chances successives de ne pas s'ensevelir dans la poussière de l'érudition et de vérifier le bien-fondé de ses idées sur le rôle de l'orateur dans la Cité. La première expérience concrète—il fut une année le secrétaire d'un évêque ambassadeur à Venise—ne fut pas très concluante: certes il eut part à quelques activités politiques, rédigea un certain nombre de dépêches diplomatiques; mais il n'était pas le maître du jeu au sein de cette petite société de courtisans et de diplomates: on lui fit sentir l'obscurité de ses origines et de sa tâche, et il vécut mal cet état de sujétion. A contre-cœur il accepta alors d'entreprendre à Toulouse des études de droit et il s'apprêtait à "divorcer d'avec l'éloquence et dire adieu aux plus douces connaissances," lorsqu'il est choisi pour tenir le rôle d'Orateur de la Nation française: l'éloquence, objet d'études et de veilles, peut devenir mode de vie et programme d'action, Cicéron se réincarne ... Et Dolet pendant quelques semaines eut l'impression de remplir un rôle de chef, d'influer sur le cours des choses, de se battre sur le terrain contre l'ignorance et l'intolérance ... L'échec, on le sait, fut à la mesure de cet immense espoir. Tout s'effondre, même sa santé. La communauté étudiante se divise sur son cas puis le rejette; la petite troupe des humanistes toulousains se méfie de cet homme imprudent.

A Lyon, qui ne devait être qu'une étape sur le chemin de l'Italie mais où il demeurera jusqu'à sa dernière arrestation, Dolet n'abandonne rien de ses convictions ni de ses ambitions. Mais de cette expérience douloureuse il tire une double leçon:

1) un grand destin ne peut s'épanouir au sein de ces petites communautés d'humanistes et d'intellectuels, fragiles et frileuses, qui se détournent des audacieux. L'aristocratisme cicéronien qui l'avait guidé jusqu'ici ne résiste pas aux épreuves de la foule. Il faut continuer à écrire pour l'élite mais il faut se trouver de plus solides appuis, celui des grands, celui du Roi, celui de ce que nous avons appelé l'opinion publique dont Dolet, l'un des premiers, soupçonne l'importance à travers son aventure toulousaine. C'est donc à des lecteurs nouveaux qu'il lui faut s'adresser, plus nombreux et moins savants. Sans jamais renoncer définitivement au latin, Dolet met de plus en plus l'accent sur la langue français. Plusieurs de ses ouvrages paraîtront d'ailleurs dans les deux langues, comme s'il voulait se concilier les deux publics, celui qui donnera à son œuvre la respectabilité érudite, celui qui popularisera son nom et protègera sa vie.

2) une deuxième évidence s'impose à lui: jamais plus il ne lui sera offert la chance de Toulouse d'être orateur défendant une cause digne de son nom et de son maître à écrire; au reste la semaine passée en prison l'a incité à la prudence. C'est alors qu'il touche de ses mains le pouvoir extraordinaire de la chose imprimée. Il acquiert vite la conviction que le livre, c'est l'Eloquence poursuivie par d'autres moyens, que l'éditeur-imprimeur est l'orateur des temps nouveaux.

On tient là les fils qui réunissent les moments de cette courte vie: de l'étude de Cicéron au métier d'imprimeur, de l'usage exclusif du latin à l'apologie de la langue française, des discours violents de Toulouse aux prudences de ses livres, des *Commentarii Linguae Latinae* à l'édition de Marot et de Rabelais ... Un point cependant demeure obscur: on distingue mal son cheminement, de son refus catégorique de s'engager dans la querelle religieuse à la profusion d'ouvrages d'inspiration "évangélique" qu'il imprime dès 1541 et qui le conduiront au bûcher. L'affaire est plus simple qu'il n'y paraît et s'explique nullement par une brutale conversation:

1) Dolet n'a jamais prétendu qu'il ne fallait point s'occuper de religion mais le faire en laissant parler plutôt sa foi que sa plume. Ce fidéisme, hostile aux dissertations théologiques, est-il si éloigné d'une certaine forme d'Evangélisme?

2) N'est-ce point la même discipline de l'imitation qui règle la vie du bon orateur et celle du chrétien sincère? Dolet lui-même le soutient dans la préface à son édition française des *Prières et Oraisons de la Bible* d'Otto Brunfels (1542): "il fault tenir asseurement qu'en toutes choses bonnes et louables imitation a le premier lieu. Car imitation n'est qu'ung exemple des choses parfaictes et esmerveillables en leur genre: soyt art mechanicque, ou de plus spirituelle et ingenieuse vacation. Je dy cecy pour conclure à la fin que si imitation est tant bien repceuë es faicts et exercitations humaines, elle ne peult estre que bonne (ouy necessaire) es meditations et actions divines."[10] L'imitation de Cicéron ne mène-t-elle pas à l'imitation du Christ? On oublie parfois qu'Etienne Dolet fut l'éditeur et le préfacier de l'*Internelle Consolation* (1542), cette traduction paraphrasée des trois premiers livres de l'*Imitatio Christi*.

3) Enfin, dans sa recherche d'une communauté capable de le reconnaître et de le protéger, Dolet est conduit par les circonstances à élargir ses prétentions: les cicéroniens de Padoue, les étudiants de Toulouse, les imprimeurs de Lyon, le peuple de France, la communauté des chrétiens. Et quelles œuvres adresser à cette dernière si ce n'est celles qui avivent la foi en la fondant sur les Ecritures et qui professent une religion moins bavarde, plus dépouillée, plus sincère?

Quoi qu'il en soit, on ne répètera jamais assez combien les ouvrages "évangéliques" de Dolet sont dépourvus d'audace. Aucun — qu'il en soit l'auteur ou seulement l'éditeur — qui contrevienne aux dogmes fondamentaux de l'Eglise romaine: en 1542 la critique de la légalité rigide et aveugle, de certaines pratiques extérieures, de l'hypocrisie et de la sottise des théologastres était devenue banale. En vérité cette timidité n'est pas pour nous surprendre, car rien chez Dolet ne l'approche d'un révolutionnaire: il fait des études traditionnelles, il se préoccupe d'abord de

sa carrière, il professe sur la philologie, la famille et la politique des idées parfaitement conservatrices. Son originalité est ailleurs, dans cet idéalisme pragma-
tique qui dicte ses attitudes: à l'idée platonicienne que le bien et le beau sont
même chose, à laquelle Dolet souscrit naturellement, la vie oppose un doulou-
reux démenti. L'Orléanais porte trop haut l'idée même d'idéal pour souffrir de
le vivre hypocritement: s'inclinant devant les faits, il admet que, si le bien n'est
pas de ce monde, on peut néanmoins s'efforcer d'y atteindre le beau, non point
en dilettante ou en esthète, mais en professionnel qui ne sépare pas la beauté de
l'efficace. Dans cette société civile soigneusement distinguée de la société religieuse
puisqu'elles se réfèrent à des idéaux distincts, Dolet réconcilie la contemplation
et l'action et ménage à son orateur-médiateur un espace d'autonomie et de lé-
gitimité. Cette tentative de sécularisation de la morale et de l'action qui ouvrait
la voie à une nouvelle race d'intellectuels n'attira pas l'attention des censeurs tout
occupés à scruter les positions religieuses, et Dolet mourut pour tout autre chose.
On voulut en faire un théologien, alors qu'il était un idéologue, l'un des premiers
de l'époque moderne.

Université de Saint-Etienne

Notes

1. Genève, Droz, 1974.
2. Parmi les derniers travaux, citons F. Joukovsky, *La gloire dans la poésie française de
la Renaissance* (Genève, Droz, 1969), pp. 190-92; J. Céard, *La nature et les prodiges* (Genève,
Droz, 1977), pp. 106-11; M. Fumaroli, *L'Age de l'Eloquence* (Genève, Droz, 1980), pp. 110
à 115.
3. Ed. Longeon du *Second Enfer*, des *Préfaces Françaises* et de la *Correspondance* (Genève,
Droz); C. Longeon, *Bibliographie des œuvres d'Etienne Dolet écrivain, éditeur et imprimeur* (Genève,
Droz), 1980.
4. *Etienne Dolet* (Paris, Fischbacher), 1886 (dans la traduction de Stryienski).
5. Sur la période toulousaine et son influence sur la conduite de Dolet, voir l'art. de
C. Longeon, "Etienne Dolet: années d'enfance et de jeunesse" in *Réforme et Humanisme* (Mont-
pellier, 1977), pp. 37-61.
6. Epitre à Lyon Jamet en tête de C. Marot, *L'Enfer* (Lyon, Dolet, 1542), *Préfaces Françaises*, op. cit., p. 99.
7. Tout reste à dire sur les influences que Dolet subit pendant son séjour à Padoue.
8. Voir surtout le *Dialogus de imitatione ciceroniana* ... (Lyon, Gryphe, 1535), passim.
9. Sur ce thème, on peut lire C. Longeon, "Etienne Dolet historien" in *Mélanges Franco
Simone*, t. III, pp. 184-97.
10. *Préfaces Françaises*, op. cit., p. 153.

The Counter-Reformation Latin Hymn

Ann Moss

Of all forms of neo-Latin literature hymns have by far the longest history of continuous publication, and they must be the only examples of translation from neo-Latin with which non-specialist twentieth-century readers are familiar.[1] In this paper I shall attempt firstly to suggest a number of co-ordinates which I think would produce particularly interesting lines of inquiry into neo-Latin hymnology; and secondly to give a brief outline of the history of the neo-Latin hymn, with special reference to France.

Central to any study of hymn-writing in our period are the hymns of the Breviary or closely associated with it, that is to say hymns appointed to be said or sung at the canonical hours, together with the immense variety of hymns provided for special feasts of the Church and saints' days. The Counter-Reformation history of these hymns starts with a tradition and develops within a context. The tradition comprises the hundreds of hymns written since the fourth century A.D. and throughout the medieval period. One of our most fruitful fields of investigation lies here, for it is the only area of Renaissance literature in which a conscious effort was made to assimilate medieval poetry into the revolutionary style of taste and expression instigated by the Humanists. Most Breviaries of the period include at least some medieval hymns and they must have been the only regular channel transmitting medieval Latin poems to the ordinary public of early modern Europe. What is crucially interesting is how this transmission was received. For the earlier part of the sixteenth century our evidence lies where it normally does at that period: in commentaries. When we come to new hymns produced or, as also happens, old hymns rewritten in the sixteenth and seventeenth centuries we can make quite rigorous comparisons between them and their medieval counterparts because the calendar of the Breviary stays virtually the same and so the uniformity of the basic material throws differences of treatment into sharp relief. Thus we can make precise distinctions about neo-Latin linguistic usage, metrical niceties and figures of speech, as well as more general observations about modes of thought and feeling.

There are of course much broader contexts in which the hymn must be placed. Firstly there is the context of religious history and theological controversy. Then there is its connection with the genres of Latin and Greek poetry promoted by the Humanists. Because it is a short poem in lyric metre commentators and poets generally ally the Christian hymn to the Horatian ode. But most were also conscious of the more lengthy kind of hymn praising the gods and the design of nature, to which humanist theorists gave great prominence and of which the best Renaissance examples are by Marullus and Ronsard. Any study of neo-Latin hymnology has to be aware of the whole scope of style and material implied by the Renaissance concept of hymn, and of the fact that the Christian hymn comes within the purview of the precepts and common-places of epideictic rhetoric as taught and practised in the schools of the period.[2] Indeed, the history of hymns, especially of new hymns, bears upon contemporary literature in all sorts of interesting ways. There is, for example, the question of the contexts in which Breviary hymns were read or heard. For the reader may be a private individual, a priest or pious lay-person reading his breviary alone, and hymns may thus incline towards introspective meditation or interior prayer; or they may be used for communal expression, originally in religious houses and later, in the seventeenth century, by large choirs of lay-people and even congregations in churches. Hymns written in the sixteenth and seventeenth centuries disclose a sophisticated sense of their dual function and so reflect the modulation between the public and private voices of poetry which is characteristic of our period. Publicly at least the hymns were sung, and the relationship between poetry and music which plays so large a part in poetic theory in the Renaissance has severe practical implications for the writer of hymns, influencing both his rhythmical patterns and his choice of vocabulary. Finally, there are more purely aesthetic questions of style and vision, which are worth pursuing not only for the analysis of the hymns themselves, but in the context of contemporary vernacular literature. Comparisons between Latin hymns by seventeenth-century Frenchmen and translations of them which were made almost immediately show up features of neo-Latin style which translators felt inhibited about putting into the French of Boileau. Moreover the general question of the relation of style to content, *verba* to *res*, is particularly relevant when poetry is used to express religious truth and excite the profoundest spiritual and emotional fervour.

Neo-Latin hymns have a pre-history, which is to be found in humanist commentaries on the traditional repertoire. The first printed edition of hymns in which we can catch the distinctive signs of the humanist critical spirit is the collection edited by Jacob Wimpfeling, the friend of Sebastian Brant and correspondent of Erasmus.[3] The prefatory letter, dated 1494, takes us straightaway not to church, but to school. Wimpfeling assumes his readers are students of "optimae humanitatis litterae," whose standards of good Latinity have already begun to alienate them from Christian poetry. His task as editor is to conciliate the fifty or so medieval hymns he reproduces with the grammatical criteria of humanist

Latin. This he does partly by some discreet emendation, based on the assumption that if he eliminates barbarisms he will have reconstituted the original and authentic form of his texts. He is thus using the same working criteria as contemporary editors of classical writings. He also shares with them his major preoccupation, which is with metre. Few of the traditional hymns are purely quantitative in metre; most are more or less accentual. Nevertheless, it is as examples of classical metrical form that Wimpfeling hopes most effectively to recommend his hymns. He makes some corrections and not only gives detailed explanations of prosody reminiscent of his contemporary Despauterius, but lists the hymns in groups according to the standard lyric metres of antiquity. Wimpfeling presupposes that the hymn is essentially a literary genre and amenable to the normal categories which humanist scholars had evolved for the analysis of literature.

The second major commentary from the earlier part of our period was that of Jodocus Clichtoveus, the intimate associate of Lefèvre d'Etaples. His edition of the hymns of the Breviary originally formed part of an *Elucidatorium ecclesiasticum*, first published in 1516, an effort to help ill-educated priests to understand the sense of the Latin they used.[4] The context of the commentary is the programme of pastoral reform promoted by the French Evangelicals and it is addressed specifically to the clergy. Clichtoveus has two objects in view: firstly to instil some sense of correct Latin usage, and secondly to integrate the hymns very firmly into a biblical frame of reference. In his preface he defines annotation as a grammatical exercise, and he parses the Latin of the hymns, defines their metrical structure, and on occasion, like Wimpfeling he emends the text in order to regularise the metre. Unlike Wimpfeling he is very interested in the figurative language of the hymns, and makes some quite sophisticated distinctions. When explaining the literal meaning of difficult vocabulary, whether simple words or words which have acquired a figurative connotation through some form of transposition (for example, "chaos" for "night"), Clichtoveus refers for illustration to classical poets and commends his hymn-writers in terms to do with elegance and refinement. Of quite another order is metaphorical reading, which Clichtoveus always defines as taking us from the corporeal to the spiritual. To read spiritually, we must be alive to similitudes between the language of the hymns and that of the Bible. Only by picking up biblical echoes, which the writers have deliberately inserted into the hymns, will the reader recognise, for example, that Prudentius's description of the cock-crow at dawn is not only as accurate and as elegant as Vergil's and Ovid's, but that it is also a figure for Christ.[5] There is literal reading and a literal understanding of tropes, for which analogies are to be sought in classical literature, and there is metaphorical reading in the true sense, the spiritual sense, of which the Bible has the prerogative. For Clichtoveus, hymns invite both kinds of reading, without any sense of discord between them, and this approach associates his commentary with the Christian Humanism of the age of Erasmus.

The next stage in the history of neo-Latin hymns takes us from commentary to composition. It also takes us from France to Rome, where the minor adjustments with which a Wimpfeling or a Clichtoveus had attempted to accommodate medieval to Renaissance Latin seemed totally inadequate. Under the aegis of Popes Leo X and Clement VII an Italian bishop, Zacharias Ferrerius, produced an entirely rewritten hymnary in 1525, "iuxta veram metri et latinitatis normam." These hymns or "odes," as Ferrerius styles them, were meant for educated priests who apparently were prone to burst out laughing at the barbaric Latin they were asked to get their tongues around.[6] The new hymn-book is a product of a clash of Latin cultures. What emerges is a translation of the essential content of the old hymns into a radically different language. Grammatically and metrically it conforms to classical usage, embellished by some curiously non-classical sound patterns. Its vocabulary and its figures of thought are those of ancient poetry. The six days of Creation do not recall the Bible, but the works of Lucretius and Ovid; from Christ's side flows not water, but Thetis; the blessed Virgin is a nymph, a goddess; and each feast day dawns in a classical periphrasis. The amplifications and associations of Ferrerius's Latin greatly enhance the graphic qualities of these poems, but it cuts out most of the biblical reverberations on which Clichtoveus made spiritual sense depend, and, because it works with rhetorical figures which above all vary the visual presentation of the material, the reader is spectator rather than actor in the drama of salvation. There was only one edition of this elitist hymn-book and its use was certainly discontinued within ten years. After 1535 the reformed Breviaries of the Roman Church, including the Breviary authorised for universal use by the Council of Trent in 1568, reproduce a selection of the traditional hymns, and objections to their Latin were over-ruled.

Thus the initial effect of the Counter-Reformation proper on the Breviary hymns was conservative. But this did not inhibit writers from producing new hymns for private reading. The range of original hymn-writing in the sixteenth century is perhaps best illustrated as far as French authors are concerned by Salmon Macrin and Marc-Antoine Muret. Salmon Macrin, whose hymns were published in 1537 and 1540, uses the genre in a highly literary way to explore just how far the language of Christian truth and the language of pagan poetry are compatible.[7] The poems test all the varieties of neo-Latin idiom, vocabulary, metrical patterns, figures of speech and thought, as vehicles of spiritual meaning. The middle-ground between classical poetry and the traditional hymn which Macrin discovers and makes his own is a private area of domestic happiness and domestic anxiety which he reconciles with God's loving providence in very personal lyrics about himself, his wife and children. Such intimacy is totally absent from the hymns of Muret, published forty-four years later.[8] The occasions for Muret's hymns are the religious offices, not the private life and its emotions. Muret's is the collective voice of the Tridentine Church. The poems are uniform in length, taut, very logically structured, often following the pattern of a clearly argued doctrinal point; the language is emotionally restrained, a rather austere amalgam of strict classical usage with the substance of the traditional hymns which had won the day at Trent. What distinguishes Muret's compositions is intellectual rigour, expressed at its best in figures of antithesis and metaphors which are carefully sustained throughout each hymn.

Muret's hymns and other new collections suggest that the classical purists were not happy with the Gothic barbarisms foisted on them by Trent. A French edition of 1619 makes corrections to twenty-seven hymns,[9] but this was only symptomatic of an ever-growing insistence on good Latinity, a cause which was to find an unassailable champion in the pope himself. In 1629 there was a new edition of the Tridentine Breviary hymns emended by a commission of Jesuits appointed by Pope Urban VIII.[10] Nearly a thousand adjustments were made to bring the hymns into line with correct Latin and correct quantitative metre, some of them quite substantial. The whole exercise is very informative about criteria for linguistic usage at the most sophisticated stage of neo-Latin. The modernised hymns were officially incorporated into the Breviary in 1632 and for the next 250 years it was in this neo-Latin adaptation that medieval hymns were most generally known. Not universally, however, for most of the religious orders retained the old forms, and among the laity there was considerable resistance, especially from church choirs grumbling about the expense of new hymn-books and the problems of fitting new words to old tunes. This evidence about the use and abuse of hymns in public worship comes from the *Heortologia* produced in 1657 by the Jesuit Charles Guyet, an enthusiast for Urban VIII's reforms, who applied the pope's principles for correcting the standard Breviary repertoire to hymns in use locally in French dioceses.[11] Guyet also encouraged new authors and he delineates the level of style appropriate to the modern hymn, accessible to the unlearned yet essentially poetic, but not so gratuitously and self-indulgently ornate that it draws attention to its own ingenuity rather than promoting Christian piety. As a model for writing he refers to the architecture of contemporary churches, the splendour and elegance of their altar-pieces and other furnishings.

Guyet's vision of a Baroque hymn style was to be realised magnificently in France at the end of the seventeenth century. In the years between 1678 and 1739 successive archbishops of Paris authorised substantial reforms of the Breviary and Missal, and foremost among them was the introduction of a new hymnary. The impetus which this gave to Latin hymn-writing resulted in the composition of hundreds of new hymns. There are interesting extra-literary contexts to these hymns: the political Gallicanism supported by Louis XIV at the end of the seventeenth century; Jansenism; the integration of new converts following the Revocation of the Edict of Nantes. There is also the question of the new music which was written for them, and their function in the structure of the mass, now that the so-called neo-Gallican reforms encouraged the congregation to participate actively, especially by singing hymns. It is, however, the literary merits of these works which demand most attention, because as lyric poetry they are far and away superior to anything written in French at the same period.[12] The most exciting of the new writers was Jean-Baptiste Santeul, whose hymns were published in two editions, in 1689 and 1698. He is the archetypal poet of the fully developed

Baroque, a poet of vertiginous vistas, intellectually energetic, virile in sentiment. The reader's path through his hymns is by way of apostrophe, imperative, interrogation, exclamation, all figures to engender amazement, excitement and dramatic involvement. Our visual sense is stimulated by brilliant colour, purples and reds, and by refulgent light which breaks through clouds. There is a dynamic sense of physical movement between earth and heaven, which is often the product of Santeul's use of metaphor to make giddy mental leaps and identifications between seeming opposites. But even his boldest conceits do not dissipate our attention or deflect it from the focus of each hymn. Every metaphorical expression is part of a carefully coordinated pattern of meanings and sense impressions, and their point of reference is always the figurative language of the Bible and its most familiar images representing the basic paradoxes at the crux of Christian belief. Santeul's hymns are nearly all for feasts and saints' days and are most typically hymns of public praise and triumph, but they also belong to the Counter-Reformation tradition of meditative poetry. In some cases hymns for the different offices of a saint's day are in effect a powerful devotional sequence and close on the prayerful yearning of the exiled soul. It is this strain of religious experience that is most insistent in the hymns of Charles Coffin, the second major talent of this Golden Age. Coffin belongs to another generation and to the eighteenth century. His own hymns were published in 1736 and he was largely responsible for the selection of hymns for the definitive version of the Paris Breviary produced in that same year, to which he was the major contributor. Coffin's vision is more inward and more stable than Santeul's. Moral themes predominate, a consciousness of imperfections mitigated by the hope of grace, and a stress on love, both as the way the individual knows God and as the fellowship which binds together Christian society. The language too is much more sober, the syntax plainer and more relaxed, and Coffin's rather muted metaphors play a weaker part in articulating his thought than do Santeul's. Coffin's favourite device for emphasis is repetition, which tends to make his poems emotionally fervent rather than intellectually vigorous. Moreover, metaphor begins to lose its privileged position as a vehicle of spiritual sense. It is not primarily through syntheses at a figural level of discourse that Coffin relates his hymns to the language of the Bible, but through paraphrase and echoes of phraseology. Coffin's hymns set the tone for the 1736 Breviary, in which Santeul's poems appear in a somewhat emasculated version, along with some of the most intensely passionate of medieval hymns, reformed to meet modern linguistic standards, but integrated with superb artistry into the neo-Latin hymnary.

The 1736 Breviary and others modelled on it survived in use in most of France until the mid-nineteenth century, and with them the neo-Latin hymns. Numerous translations made their sense available to the congregation who sang them, but their social history remains to be written. Certainly it would be different from that of their Protestant vernacular counterparts. Santeul loved to hear his hymns performed in splendid churches by well-trained choirs; but when he overheard a cow-herd singing them in the fields, it is said that he told him not to bellow like one of his own cows, but be quiet and listen.[13]

University of Durham

Notes

1. About thirty neo-Latin hymns are regularly sung in the Church of England, and there is still useful information to be obtained from *Hymns Ancient and Modern, Historical Edition*, ed. W. H. Frere (London, 1909). There is no overall critical study of neo-Latin hymn-writing. The Counter-Reformation period is usually relegated to a deprecating appendix in histories of Latin hymns, but there is a valuable brief survey at the end of J. Szövérffy, *Die Annalen der lateinischen Hymnerdichtung*, 2 vols. (Berlin, 1964-65), II, 430-47.

2. J.-C. Scaliger conflates Christian and pagan hymns in his chapters on the genre, but gives much more prominence to the hymns of Orpheus, Homer and Marullus than to Christian hymns, of which he can find no practitioner worth citing other than himself (*Poetices*, Book III, chapters cxi-cxv). Antonio Possevino in his *Bibliotheca selecta*, a critical encyclopedia which reflects the spirit of the Counter-Reformation at the close of the sixteenth century, lists Christian poets at the end of his chapter on Horace. His selection embraces a wide spectrum, juxtaposing the traditional office hymns with neo-Latin poems on a much more ambitious scale, modelled on the Greek hymns of antiquity (1603 edition, II, 520-28).

3. *Hymni de tempore et de sanctis: in eam formam qua a suis autoribus scripti sunt denuo redacti: et circum legem carminis diligenter emendati atque interpretati* (Strasburg, 1513; other editions, 1516, and 1519). Wimpfeling had a long-standing preoccupation with the critical problems presented by hymns: see also his *De Hymnorum et Sequentiarum auctoribus, generibusque carminum que in Hymnis inveniuntur, brevissima Erudiuncula* (?Heidelberg, 1500; preface dated 1499); and his *Castigationes locorum in canticis ecclesiasticis et divinis officiis depravatorum* (Strasburg, 1513). For Wimpfeling's place in the intellectual history of the period, see A. Renaudet, *Préréforme et humanisme à Paris pendant les premières guerres d'Italie (1494-1517)*, second edition (Paris, 1953); C. Béné, "L'Humanisme de J. Wimpfeling," *ACNL Lovaniensis* (Munich, 1973), pp. 77-84.

4. The *Elucidatorium* was reprinted eight times up until 1558 and the sections on hymns and sequences separately in an abbreviated version in 1555. Clichtoveus was still being cited as an authority on hymns in the seventeenth century. For the place of the *Elucidatorium* in the context of the rest of Clichtoveus's work, see J. P. Massaut, *Josse Clichtove, l'humanisme et la réforme du clergé*, 2 vols. (Paris, 1968); for relations between Clichtoveus and his contemporaries, see A. Renaudet, *Préréforme et humanisme*.

5. "Hanc autem galli conditionem a somno excicatricem, apta metaphora accommodat hic author ad Christum, assidua admonitione scripturae nos ut a somno peccati surgamus et vigilemus excitantem" (on *Ales diei nuntius*, f. 15 of the sections of the *Elucidatorium* published at Venice in 1555, entitled *Hymni et Prosae quae per totum annum in ecclesia leguntur, cum explicatione Iodoci Clichtovei*).

6. *Zachariae Ferrerii Vincent ... Hymni novi ecclesiastici iuxta veram metri et latinitatis normam a beatiss. patre Claemente VII. Pont Max. ut in divinis quisque eis uti possit approbati* (Rome, 1525).

Ferrerius claims that the bad Latin of the old hymns was causing a scandal, "quod qui bona latinitate praediti sunt sacerdotes dum barbaris vocibus Deum laudare coguntur in risum provocati sacra saepenumero contemnunt" (f. Bii^v). For Ferrerius and subsequent developments in the Roman Breviary, see S. Bäumer, *Histoire du Bréviaire*, French translation by R. Biron, 2 vols. (Paris, 1905; reprinted Rome, 1967).

7. *Hymnorum libri sex, ad Jo. Bellaium* (Paris, 1537); *Hymnorum selectorum libri tres* (Paris, 1540). The place of Macrin's hymns in the context of the rest of his work is thoroughly documented by I. D. McFarlane in "Jean Salmon Macrin (1490–1557)," *BHR*, 21 (1959), 55–84, 311–49 (321–39).

8. *Hymnorum sacrorum liber* (Rome, 1581); Muret's exercises in religious poetry are closely allied with those of his Jesuit friends, especially Francesco Benci, who included hymns in the second volume of his *Carmina*, published in 1595.

9. *Hymnorum sacrorum, qui per Christianum orbem ab optimis latinae linguae scriptoribus compositi in S. R. Ecclesia decantari soliti, iampridem ... pravis aspersi mendis, deformes leguntur, tam ex veter. M.SS. quam recti sermonis et Poësis ratione iusta, emendatio, In integrum restitutio* (Paris, 1619).

10. *Hymni Breviarii Romani ... Urbani VIII iussu Et Sacrae Rituum Congregationis approbatione emendati, et editi* (Rome, 1629). The copy in the British Library has further manuscript corrections by the Pope himself. The editors insist that their aim is to emend, not to improve, "divinas enim Laudes, si non ornari floribus verborum, certe decenti cultu carere non convenit." Their criteria unite the principles of textual criticism with a fastidious Latinity, but they spare the 'Etruscan' rhythms and "verba non elegantissima" of St Thomas Aquinas in deference to piety and tradition. The cultural background to Urban's revision of the hymns is deftly brought to life in M. Fumaroli, *L'Age de l'Eloquence. Rhétorique et 'res literaria' de la Renaissance au seuil de l'époque classique* (Geneva, 1980), pp. 202–26.

11. *Heortologia, sive de Festis propriis locorum et ecclesiarum* (Paris, 1657). There was a reprint at Venice in 1729, in which Guyet's prescriptions for writing hymns appear on pp. 172–76 and his corrected versions of French hymns (with reference to Clichtoveus) on pp. 359–99.

12. Partisan feeling has run high on the subject of the French revisions of the Breviary and Missal, with the result that the standard histories of the breviary are too prejudiced to be very informative and the hymns of the period have been much neglected. The new breviary hymns are reproduced with useful biographies of their authors in U. Chevalier, *Poésie liturgique des Églises de France aux XVIIe et XVIIIe siècles ou Recueil d'Hymnes et de Proses usitées à cette époque* (Paris, 1913). H. Bremond made an enthusiastic attempt to rehabilitate the hymns and there are some lively and perceptive analyses in his chapter on the *Hymni Gallicani* in volume X of his *Histoire littéraire du sentiment religieux en France depuis la fin des guerres de religion jusqu'à nos jours* (Paris, 1932). There is a brief survey of the subject and some tunes in C. E. Pocknee, *French Diocesan Hymns and their Melodies* (London, 1954). The Rev. C. Johnson of Quarr Abbey is preparing a complete bibliography of the local liturgical books of the dioceses of France, which will give a proper scholarly context to further research. For the historical and social background to seventeenth-century liturgical developments, see R. Taveneaux, *Le Catholicisme dans la France classique, 1610–1715*, 2 vols. (Paris, 1908).

13. An anecdote recounted by Montalant-Bougleux, *J. B. Santeul ou la poésie latine sous Louis XIV* (Paris, 1855).

Montaigne and the Christian Foes of Tacitus

Malcolm Smith

Various writers, from very early times, have expressed hostility towards Tacitus on account of what he says about Jews and Christians. One passage which caused disquiet is the long description of the origins and beliefs and customs of the Jewish nation, in the fifth book of the *Histories* (1–13).[1] Another, and this is the one which mainly concerns us here, is the passage in the fifteenth book of the *Annals* (44) in which Tacitus relates how Nero blamed Christians for the fire in Rome in A.D. 64. Tacitus here describes Christians as "a class of men loathed for their vices," and describes their belief as a "pernicious superstition" and a "disease"; and, while he attacks Nero vigorously for his treatment of Christians, he adds that they "had earned the most exemplary punishment."

Interest in Tacitus appears to have grown rapidly in the second half of the sixteenth century.[2] As this interest grew, his admirers sought to mitigate damage to his reputation caused by his remarks about Christians. One of his defenders was Jean Bodin who, in 1566, in his *Method for easily understanding history,* refuted hostile verdicts on him by Guillaume Budé (1467–1540) and by Tertullian (c. 155–c. 222) and Paulus Orosius (c. 390–after 418).

> Budé (writes Bodin) harshly called Tacitus the most wicked writer of all, since he wrote things against Christians. And it is for this reason, in my view, that Tertullian called him a great liar, and Orosius called him a sycophant. But, just as Marcellus, the lawyer, said that a whore acted repulsively in so far as she was a whore, but did not repulsively choose to be a whore, in the same way Tacitus acted impiously, in so far as he was not a Christian, but did not impiously write against us, since he was bound by a pagan superstition. Indeed, the reason I would not call him impious is that he did hold that there was a religion which was true, and he observed that religion and sought to overthrow those opposed to it. For, at a time when Christians and Jews were being condemned daily, as being sorcerers

and tainted with every crime and scandal, what historian could refrain from insulting them? If ignorance is an excuse, then Tacitus certainly has to be excused [...]

The point of the rather unfortunate analogy between Tacitus and a whore seems to be that Tacitus was not in a position to make a free and conscious choice to adopt paganism and reject Christianity: his religion was thrust upon him by the milieu in which he found himself, and his ignorance of Christianity was not his fault.[3]

Michel de Montaigne was another French Renaissance author who felt that early Christian attitudes to Tacitus had been unjustly severe. In 1580, in the chapter of his *Essays* titled "On freedom of conscience" (II.xix) he deplored the fact that much of Tacitus's work is lost,[4] and blamed this loss on the fanaticism of early Christians:

> It is common to see good intentions, if pursued immoderately, impel men to very evil results. [...] It is certain that when our religion first began to flourish and acquire legal authority and power, zeal armed many people against all sorts of pagan books and, as a result of this, men of letters have suffered an amazing loss. In my view, this disorder wrought more damage to literature than all the flames of the barbarians. Cornelius Tacitus is a good witness to this: for, though his relative the emperor Tacitus had by special decree populated every library in the world with his books, nonetheless not one complete copy has survived the meticulous searches of those who sought to suppress him for the sake of five or six trivial clauses contrary to our faith.[5]

I have conjectured, in my book *Montaigne and the Roman Censors,* that Montaigne is here referring, allusively and discreetly, to harm caused to literature in his own day by burning of books by religious authorities.[6]

There is another sense in which Montaigne may in this passage be alluding to topical events. The third-century emperor Tacitus who, Montaigne recalls, disseminated the books of his namesake the historian, had initiated another monument to him by having a tomb built for him. Now, just as fanatical early Christians destroyed the books, a zealous Christian contemporary of Montaigne's destroyed the tomb, and this sixteenth-century foe of Tacitus was no less a person than Pope Pius V, the erstwhile Grand Inquisitor of the Roman Church.[7] It is not inconceivable that Montaigne's attack on zealous Christians seeking to stamp out the name of Tacitus is an allusion to Pius V. For Montaigne was well capable of such oblique allusions to contemporaries, and indeed he seems to have become increasingly keen that his readers should be alert to such allusions. In 1588, two-thirds of the way through the chapter "On vanity" (*Essays* III.viii), he wrote that his book contains many discreet topical allusions to contemporary people and events, and that some people will see more in these passages than others will. He added:

> I reveal here what my inclinations and feelings are in so far as I decently can; but I do this more freely and readily face to face to anyone who wants to know more.

He reiterated the point in the first posthumous edition of the *Essays* (1595). The examples I cite, he says, "[...] often refer allusively to more delicate matters, for the benefit of myself (for I do not wish to express myself more fully) and of those readers who catch what I am getting at" ("A consideration about Cicero," *Essays* I.xl).

A further indication of hostility towards Tacitus in inquisitorial circles is given in a letter written from Rome by Marcus Antonius Muretus, dated 2 November 1572 and addressed to a lawyer in the Paris *parlement* named Claude Dupuy. The letter, written in a curious mixture of Latin, Greek and French, tells a rather entertaining story:

> I hear you had a good laugh at the criticisms of Tacitus, and the story is worth telling in some detail. Just recently someone who was teaching Latin literature here, in the post which Romulus Amasaeus used to hold, left: and no-one could be found to replace him. The cardinals who are responsible for the teaching besought me, with exquisite courtesy, to take the job on. I declined. In the end, the chief priest himself summoned me. He addressed me with great kindness, and indicated that if I were to undertake that task, he would greatly appreciate it. What could I do? By asking, he compelled me, and you know what happened. I was all the more ready to yield to his request in that instead of the two hundred crowns I was earning, he raised my salary to four hundred. The next question which arose was, what book was I going to lecture on? I told cardinals Sirleto and Alciati, who are responsible for the syllabus, that I would like to lecture on Tacitus. They strongly dissuaded me, for he speaks unfavourably somewhere of Christians, and of Jews, and, in a word, they had it in mind to forbid his works. I gave many reasons why I should be released from the responsibility, but they would not yield. I feel so annoyed about this that I wish I had never started work on this author. But I cannot be frightened off loving him and reading him, and reading him assiduously.

Muretus does not tell us which "chief priest" (that is, pope) he is referring to but given the date of his letter it must be either Pius V (who had died on 1st May that year) or his successor Gregory XIII.[8] The anecdote would of course be all the more amusing if it were about Pius V, the fanatical opponent of Tacitus's renown.

Muretus's account suggests that the passages in *Histories* V and *Annals* XV, dealing respectively with Jews and Christians, formed the basis of the hostility to

Tacitus. Further possible grounds for this hostility in inquisitorial circles are indicated by a Jesuit scholar, Antonius Possevinus, who was closely in touch with
these circles at about this time and who some years later was to publish a book
titled *Materials for the history of all nations*.[9] Possevinus, besides deploring Tacitus's
allegedly "malicious" remarks about Christians, alleges that some of his own
sixteenth-century contemporaries were so besotted by Tacitus that they overlooked
what Christ says about how to administer affairs (doubtless an allusion to
"Machiavellian" politicians who turned to Tacitus for guidance[10]); he attacks
what he sees as a denial of divine providence, in the *Histories*;[11] and he objects
to Tacitus's proposed derivation for the word *Iudaeos* (from Mount Ida, in Crete:
Histories V.2) — a curious detail to single out in the long disquisition on Jews.[12]
A further possible reason for objection to Tacitus by Roman Catholic theologians,
particularly in view of the Reformation controversies on miracles, is that he records
the popular belief that the emperor Vespasian wrought miracles (*Histories* IV.81).
And a final reason might be that some inquisitors simply felt ill at ease about
such an ardent advocate of freedom of thought and of speech: for example, in
the *Annals* (IV.35), Tacitus argues firmly against the burning of books and, as
one illustrious sixteenth-century Tacitus scholar pointed out, there was a lesson
in this for the papists who used the same methods.[13]

Whatever factors may have prompted guardians of orthodoxy to destroy
Tacitus's tomb, to forbid Muretus's lectures in 1572, and to contemplate including
Tacitus in the *Index of forbidden books*, there existed other considerations militating
in favour of liberalism. One was that many of the custodians of orthodoxy were
themselves committed scholars. Pope Paul III, who founded the Roman Inquisition in 1542, was himself, according to Muretus, a constant reader of Tacitus,
and took more delight in the historian than in any other secular author.[14] And
Cardinal Sirleto, one of the two who forbade Muretus to lecture on Tacitus, actually gave considerable help to Muretus himself, and to Justus Lipsius, in ensuring they had access to manuscripts of Tacitus![15] And, as Paul Grendler has
shown in his admirable book *The Roman Inquisition and the Venetian Press*, inquisitors
were concerned not to alienate by unduly repressive measures those Catholic
scholars and printers upon whom the Church depended so much for a restoration
of its credibility and prestige in the aftermath of the Reformation. Furthermore,
Tacitus had merits which could not be gainsaid even by his Christian foes:
Possevinus, in the passage I have already referred to, cited with approval a eulogy
by Lipsius of Tacitus's prudence, his moral teaching, his love of truth, his con-
ciseness, and his aphorisms, and acknowledged for his own part Tacitus's discern-
ment and the relevance in his (Possevinus's) own day of Tacitus's judgments on
princes.[16] Indeed, these merits of Tacitus must account for the fact that one
sixteenth-century Roman Catholic index not of forbidden books but of commended
books includes the works of Tacitus![17] And a final factor which could work in
favour of liberalism (or, of course, in the opposite direction) was the individual
outlook of whoever happened to be pope. For example, the destroyer of Tacitus's

tomb, Pius V, was an utterly relentless exponent and supporter of inquisitorial methods[18]—but he was succeeded by Gregory XIII who gradually and unobtrusively relaxed a whole series of repressive measures.[19]

It may well be as a result of the increasing liberalism under Gregory XIII that in November 1580 Muretus was finally let off the leash and given permission to lecture on Tacitus in Rome. Muretus, doubtless confident that the old repressive attitudes towards Tacitus would not return, immediately spoke out freely and vigorously against Tacitus's foes. He declared, in a discourse inaugurating his lectures on Tacitus, "I shall reply to those people who are surprised at my high esteem for Tacitus, and surprised that I sought for so long and so strenuously to secure permission to expound his work publicly." And a little later in the same discourse, he adds, "I shall refute and confound a few of those objections which are rashly flung at him by the ignorant." In a second discourse, he defended Tacitus against five objections which, he said, had been made by those who had sought to prevent him lecturing on him. These five objections are (i) that Tacitus wrote about tyrannical emperors and a period of moral degeneracy, and that Suetonius is a better historian of the imperial period anyway; (ii) that Tacitus's books contain falsehood; (iii) that he was an acknowledged enemy of the Christian faith; (iv) that he is difficult; and (v) that he writes bad Latin.

The second and third of these objections are the ones that concern us here. Broaching the charge that Tacitus's work contains falsehood, Muretus, who does not elaborate on what the alleged falsehoods are, observes that the same has been said of every other illustrious historian, and there is no reason why the charge should be held to be particularly damaging when levelled at Tacitus. He then turns to Tertullian, who described Tacitus as "the most garrulous liar," and says he will answer this charge at the same time as he answers the most serious of the objections, which is that Tacitus was hostile to the Christian faith. This, incidentally, suggests that the alleged lies in Tacitus were pre-eminently his remarks about Christians. The earliest Christians, Muretus says, were so pious ("and would that we were!" he adds parenthetically and perhaps a little disingenuously) that they would hear nothing that was not Christian, and totally rejected everything that was opposed to Christianity. But if we adopted that rule nowadays, Muretus asks, what would happen? We would be obliged to refrain from reading all the ancient Greek and Latin writers. Muretus then gives a very interesting survey of ancient Greek and Latin authors, pointing out those aspects of their work which the kind of Christian who objects to Tacitus would logically be obliged to deplore. If it is argued (said Muretus: and his wording suggests it may well have been argued by some at the time) that pre-Christian Greek and Latin authors can more readily be forgiven than can Tacitus, who lived after the time of Christ, then it will still be necessary to condemn—if you are going to condemn the historian—authors like Suetonius, who refers scornfully to Christians; the younger Pliny, who actually prosecuted Christians; Plutarch, who "has the same fables about Moses and the Jews as Tacitus does"; Quintilian, who writes with scorn about

Moses; Ulpian, who wrote a book on how to punish Christians; and the philosophers Porphyry, Simplicius, and Averroes, as well as Galen; and the historians Ammianus Marcellinus, Eunapius and Zosimus. Muretus concludes:

> If, however, we do not reject them as well, why should we be more severe towards Tacitus? Is any of us so weak that there is a danger of him stumbling in his Christian faith if he were to find out that Tacitus was not a Christian? Let us rather feel sorry for him, and be grateful to God for bathing our souls in greater light.[20]

This defence of Tacitus is a shrewd one. If Muretus's argument that Tacitus is no more harmful to Christianity than other ancient writers is accepted, then the Church could not forbid him without virtually declaring war on classical literature. Clearly there was no desire for such a crusade. On the contrary, ancient texts were generally looked on with indulgence: the rules of the Council of Trent's *Index of forbidden books*, for example, stipulate only that those ancient texts which are obscene should not be used in schools.

In the same month as Muretus was eventually allowed to lecture on Tacitus, November 1580, Montaigne, who had been a pupil of Muretus's at the Collège de Guyenne in Bordeaux, arrived in Rome.[21] One aspect of Rome which interested Montaigne greatly, and which disturbed him, was incursions by the Inquisition on personal and intellectual freedom. It is clear, moreover, from a remark by Montaigne's secretary recorded in his diary, that this was a favoured topic of conversation with Montaigne.[22] We know from Montaigne's diary that he met Muretus in Rome on at least one occasion: in March 1581 he dined with Muretus and other scholars at the French ambassador's house. It is tempting to conjecture that, either at this meeting or on other occasions during his visit to Rome, Montaigne sounded Muretus out on the effects of the Inquisition on intellectual freedom: for Muretus was evidently a veritable mine of information on the subject, as Dejob showed in his book *Marc-Antoine Muret*, and his views on the subject were very similar to Montaigne's. They might indeed have discussed the specific case of attitudes to Tacitus, for Montaigne's recently published *Essays* had, as we have seen, deplored the fanatical suppression of Tacitus by early Christians — and Muretus had himself been a victim of a similar "fanatical" suppression of Tacitus.

A few days later, still in March 1581, Montaigne was himself to have the first of two encounters with the Church's censors, in fact with the two officials in charge of the censorship, Sisto Fabri and his assistant Joannes Baptista Lancius. I have described these encounters in *Montaigne and the Roman censors*. The censors were armed with a list of objections to the *Essays*, and they invited Montaigne to comment on these. Six of these objections are known, for Montaigne lists them in his diary, but he adds that there were others besides, and I have been unable to identify them. But it is highly tempting to speculate that his attack on the fourth-century Christian zealots who destroyed Tacitus's work was on the list: for the other example of excessive Christian zeal which Montaigne attacks in the very same passage, the over-hasty condemnations of the emperor Julian, was censured. Furthermore, if the passage about Tacitus's enemies was read by the censors as an allusive attack on his enemies in the sixteenth century, and notably his foes among the guardians of orthodoxy — and we have seen it can easily be read that way — this would be additional cause for objection. Whether or not this passage on Tacitus was originally censured, we know that the censors were so satisfied with Montaigne's explanations of the censured passages that they withdrew all objections — and indeed expressed great approval of that intellectual freedom which so intimately characterises Montaigne's book. I have concluded that the encounters of Montaigne and the censors illustrate the relative liberalism of the pontificate of Gregory XIII.

The 1588 edition of the *Essays* contains, for the first time, a great many first-hand borrowings from Tacitus.[23] It also contains a long passage on Tacitus which answers some sixteenth-century Christian objections to him, and this passage may be, like so many others in later editions of the *Essays*, a reply to the censors who momentarily objected to parts of his book in 1581 (though of course it is possible Montaigne encountered these objections elsewhere, e.g., through his reading of Bodin, or his meeting with Muretus[24]). In the chapter "On the art of conversation" (*Essays* III.viii), Montaigne affirms, against those who accused Tacitus of purveying falsehood, that "Those who call into question his honesty are revealing they have some other grievance against him" — and this "other grievance" is almost certainly his anti-Christian sentiment (for, the charges of being a liar and of being anti-Christian are coupled in the defences of Tacitus by Bodin and Muretus). A little further on, Montaigne answers a second objection:

> He does not need any excuse for approving the religion of his time, according to the laws which governed him, and for ignoring the true one. That is his misfortune, not his shortcoming.

We have seen similar versions of this defence of Tacitus in both Bodin and Muretus: it seems to me a fair argument, since the remarks in Tacitus which his Christian foes objected to do indeed show he had no knowledge at all of Christian belief and only heard rumour about the lives of Christians. And a third passage in this chapter "On the art of conversation" seems to rebut objections by some Roman Catholics to Tacitus: Montaigne defends him for giving accounts of apparent miracles. Miracles were being invoked then by Catholic theologians in polemic with the Reformers as a sign of divine truth: clearly it would be hazardous to concede (as Tacitus records some people did) that Vespasian, a pagan, could procure miracles. This must be the point of Montaigne's comment, which is that it is proper for historians to record what is commonly believed about alleged miracles, and that this is all that Tacitus does. Montaigne adds, and pointedly it seems, that the task of the theologian and of the philosopher is to say whether these common beliefs are correct beliefs.[25] He is delineating, judiciously, the territory of respective disciplines and firmly repelling incursions by theologians into the domain of historians.

In defence of Tacitus, Montaigne not only deals with specific issues which preoccupied theologians, he offers a full portrait of the man and his work. Unlike those early Christians whom he had castigated, in the earlier chapter "On freedom of conscience," for condemning Tacitus on the strength of "five or six trivial clauses contrary to our faith," Montaigne intended to make an equitable judgment. He carefully stresses at the beginning of his discussion of Tacitus that he has read the historian's whole extant work, and indeed that it is highly unusual for him to do this sort of thing ("It is twenty years," he says, "since I spent a whole hour on one book"). The verdict which he arrives at is a nuanced one, but as a whole overwhelmingly favourable. He commends (against Tacitus himself) the moral and political usefulness and attraction of history that deals with the lives of individuals, commends the solid arguments Tacitus deploys, his pointed and unaffected style, his sound opinions, his honesty and courage. Interestingly, this approach to an author, in which discussion of individual opinions is placed in the context of an overall appraisal of the man, an approach so characteristic of Montaigne, seems to have been that which the Roman censors themselves adopted, at least in the case of Montaigne himself.[26]

At the beginning of the chapter "On the art of conversation" and (implicitly) at the end, Montaigne stresses that he is no kind of model to be emulated or authority to be believed. Such disclaimers, in the *Essays*, are usually a sign that he is broaching moral or religious issues. The fact that these disclaimers embrace the chapter as a whole suggests that the whole chapter has something to say which might interest theologians. And indeed it has. Montaigne's point is that all intellectual encounter is about free exchange of ideas. We must be receptive to corrections, he says — but at the same time we must retain our freedom of judgment. It is a point which, in the fourth century, the fanatical Christian foes of Tacitus had forgotten: and it is a point which their sixteenth-century successors needed reminding of. This surely is why, in a chapter devoted to conversation, Montaigne includes the otherwise rather incongruous discussion of the character and work of Tacitus. It is no coincidence that the chapter on conversation, which deplores tyranny and domineering assertiveness, is also the chapter which, more fully than the earlier — and possibly censured — one, rehabilitates a historian who had himself advocated freedom of thought and expression, and who had been a posthumous victim of opponents of such freedom.

Bedford College, London

Notes

1. Other material in Tacitus which alludes to Jews is recorded and annotated in M. Stern's formidably erudite book, *Greek and Latin authors on Jews and Judaism*, 2 vols. (Jerusalem, 1976, 1980), II, 1-93.

2. P. Burke has counted four editions of the *Annals* and *Histories* in the second half of the fifteenth century, thirteen in the first half of the sixteenth, and thirty-two in the second half. In the following fifty years Tacitus was to become the most widely-published ancient historian. See "A survey of the popularity of Ancient Historians, 1450-1700," *History and Theory*, 5 (1966), 135-52.

3. The passage is from Bodin's assessment of Tacitus in chapter 4 of his *Methodus ad facilem historiarum cognitionem* (Parisiis, 1566, BL 580 g 2). For Budé on Tacitus ("vaecordium omnium scriptorum perditissimus," etc.), see J. von Stackelberg, *Tacitus in der Romania* (Tübingen, 1960), 160; for Tertullian, see his *Liber apologeticus adversus gentes pro christianis*, ch. xvi; I have not traced the allusion to Tacitus in Orosius which Bodin is referring to, despite the excellent indexes in the edition by C. Zangemeister (*Historiarum adversum paganos libri VII; accedit eiusdem liber apologeticus*, Vindobonae, 1882).

Bodin's *Methodus* was to be included in Roman Catholic lists of prohibited books in and after 1581. See F. H. Reusch, *Die Indices librorum prohibitorum des sechzehnten Jahrhunderts* (Tübingen, 1886), pp. 356, 412, 493-94, 559 (and cf. 537). A Jesuit writer on history (and on many other subjects), Antonius Possevinus, repudiated Bodin's view that Tacitus's defence of his pagan religion shows he was not impious (see Possevinus's *Iudicium de Nuae* [...], *Joannis Bodini, Philippi Mornaei et Nicolai Machiavelli quibusdam scriptis* [...] [Lugduni, 1593, BL 1492 f 56], p. 89).

4. Of the thirty books of history Tacitus is known to have written, only the first four books of the *Histories* and a fragment of the fifth have survived, and the first four books of the *Annals*, a fragment of the fifth, most of the sixth and books eleven to sixteen (though the beginning of the eleventh and the end of the sixteenth are lost).

5. Modern scholars discount the possibility of a family relationship between the historian Tacitus and the emperor. On the emperor disseminating the historian's works ("almost certainly a fabrication of the late fourth century," according to L. D. Reynolds and N. G. Wilson, *Scribes and Scholars* [Oxford, 1975], p. 29), see the life of the emperor by Flavius Vopiscus (*Historia Augusta*, ed. D. Magie, Loeb, *Tacitus* X). I do not know what Montaigne's source is for the statement blaming Christians for the loss of Tacitus's work: other sixteenth-century commentators I have read merely state that the emperor's dissemination of Tacitus's books failed to preserve them (e.g., Bodin, and F. Baudoin, *De institutione historiæ universæ* [...], published in the 1576 Basle edition of Bodin's *Methodus*, BL 580 c 9, p. 654). Nor do I know how Montaigne was able to assert that it was for "five or six trivial clauses" that Tacitus's books were destroyed (for presumably the work now lost may have contained more anti-Christian material).

6. See *Montaigne and the Roman Censors* (Geneva, 1981), pp. 53-55.

7. On Pius V destroying Tacitus's tomb, see Francesco Angeloni, *Historia di Terni* (Roma, 1646, BL 660 e 11), pp. 51-52 (Dr J. F. Killeen of the University of Galway very kindly drew my attention to this book). Contemporary apprehensiveness about Pius V's plans to destroy "pagan" remains in Rome is documented in vol. 17 of L. von Pastor's *History of the Popes* (London and St. Louis, 1951), pp. 113-14, 407.

8. For the text of Muretus's letter, see P. de Nolhac, "Lettres inédites de Muret," *Mélanges Graux* (Paris, 1884), pp. 381-403 (pp. 389-90). Unfortunately Nolhac has no infor-

mation on the nature of the criticisms of Tacitus which amused Dupuy. P. Paschini, in his excellent study "Letterati ed indice nella riforma cattolica in Italia," quotes a letter from Pier Vettori to Sirleto (19 December 1575) acknowledging "la lettera di V.S. R^ma sopra quel mio dubbio di Tacito," but does not have the text of Sirleto's probably important letter (see his *Cinquecento romano e riforma cattolica* [Romæ, 1958], pp. 237-73, 241).

9. A letter of Possevinus's to Cardinal Sirleto (undated, but probably written between 1573 and 1580) gives an interesting glimpse of his contact with Sirleto and of his zealous action against condemned books: see C. Dejob, *De l'influence du Concile de Trente sur la littérature et les beaux-arts chez les peuples catholiques* (Paris, 1884), pp. 43-45.

10. One scholar has concluded that in the Renaissance, "condemnation of Tacitus had its genesis in the fact that he was considered as the intellectual parent of the author of the *Prince*, synonym for all that was to be condemned" (J. L. Brown, *The "Methodus ad facilem historiarum cognitionem": a critical study* [Washington, DC, 1939], p. 112). This seems untenable: Tacitus was condemned on other grounds besides. On use of Tacitus by Machiavelli, see J. von Stackelberg, *Tacitus in der Romania* (Tübingen, 1960), especially 4, "Machiavelli und der Tacitismus" pp. 63-93.

11. It seems to me highly unlikely that Tacitus really is denying providence in the passage Possevinus quotes, which reads: "Never did more appalling calamities befall the Roman people, as a clear sign that the gods were concerned not to save us but to punish us" (*Histories* I.3).

12. See Possevinus's *Apparatus ad omnium gentium historium* [...] (Venetiis, BL 580 c 15), III, xiv. On this book, see note 16 below.

13. The scholar is Justus Lipsius, and the occasion was an inaugural discourse on Tacitus at Iena in 1572: see his *Orationes octo* [...] (Francofurti, 1608, BL 1090 c 7), pp. 35-36. Lipsius was later to return to the Roman Catholic faith, which accounts for the cordial tone of an exchange of letters with Possevinus (see note 16 below). Burning of books in the Reformation era was not of course the sole prerogative of Roman Catholic judiciaries: see my *Montaigne and the Roman Censors*, pp. 53-55 and 121-22.

14. See Muretus's *Scripta selecta*, ed. J. Frey, 2 vols. (Lipsiae, 1871, 1873), I, 151.

15. See J. Rysschaert, "Juste Lipse éditeur de Tacite," in *Atti del Colloquio la Fortuna di Tacito dal secolo XV ad oggi*, a cura di F. Gori e C. Questa (Urbino, 1979), pp. 47-61 (pp. 53, 54). Sirleto's tireless dedication to scholarship is chronicled in P. Paschini's excellent monograph, "Guglielmo Sirleto prima del cardinalato," in his *Tre ricerche sulla storia della chiesa nel cinquecento* (Roma, 1945), pp. 153-281.

16. Possevinus's overall verdict on Tacitus is therefore a balanced one. Interestingly, this book was extolled by no less a Tacitus scholar than Justus Lipsius. Lipsius's very cordial letter to Possevinus (29 January 1599) can be read in his *Centuriae* (III, lxii: in his *Epistolarum selectarum chilias* [Lugduni, 1616, BL 1084 h 9], p. 280) and Possevinus's equally cordial reply (24 March 1599) is in Petrus Burmannus's *Sylloges epistolarum a viris illustribus scriptarum* (Leidae, 1727, BL 636 k 16-20), II, 45.

17. The document, published in Munich, contains the tridentine *Index of Forbidden Books* together with a list of books *ex quibus integra Bibliotheca Catholica institui recte possit*, and this latter list contains the name of Tacitus. The year of publication was 1569 — during the pontificate of Pius V, the foe of Tacitus's renown! See F. H. Reusch, *Die Indices librorum prohibitorum*, pp. 329-37.

18. On the activities of Pius V (Michele Ghislieri) as inquisitor, see L. von Pastor, *The History of the Popes*, XVII (London and St. Louis, 1951). His relentless zeal was well described by Muretus in his funerary oration:

Cum autem alia in hoc viro admirabilia fuerunt, tum singulare studium conser-

vandae verae ac catholicae religionis, et adversus eos qui illam ulla ex parte labefac-
tare conarentur, implacabile odium semper eluxit. Quibus cum ille perpetuum bellum
gerens, ne punctum quidem temporis in vita ab eis vexandis et exagitandis conquievit.
[...] Qui ab ecclesia descivissent, nisi aut ipsos erroribus, aut ipsis orbem purgaret,
vitam sibi acerbam atque insuavem esse ducebat (*Oratio habita in funere Pii V. Pont.
Maximi*, Patavii, 1572, BL 4855 bb 25, pages unnumbered).
Muretus's true feelings were less enthusiastic: see the next note.

19. On 2 June 1572, a month after the death of Pius V, Muretus wrote to Claude Dupuy
contrasting the freedom of speech which prevailed in France with the "oppression" in Rome
under Pius V (this part of his letter is written — perhaps prudently — in Greek). He adds
that with the new pope, Gregory XIII, "On se promettoit quelque plus grande liberté,
mais je me doutte, qu'il n'i aura plus grand gaing au change" (Nolhac, "Lettres inédites
[...]," p. 387). But Gregory XIII did turn out to be relatively liberal: see *Montaigne and
the Roman Censors*, pp. 108, 127.

20. See Muretus's *Scripta selecta*, ed. J. Frey (Lipsiae, I, 1871), pp. 158–61.

21. On Muretus's relationship with Montaigne, see R. Trinquet, *La Jeunesse de Montaigne* (Paris, 1972), especially pp. 460–65, 488–91, 503–05 and 548–50.

22. See *Montaigne and the Roman Censors*, pp. 15–16.

23. It appears that whereas the 1580 edition had contained no material directly derived
from Tacitus, the 1588 edition contains three quotations and twenty-three borrowings from
him, and five further quotations and nine borrowings were added to the *Essays* thereafter:
see P. Villey, *Les Livres d'histoire moderne utilisés par Montaigne* [...] (Paris, 1908), p. 241.
One of the quotations from Tacitus in the 1595 edition is presented to elucidate the nature
of Christian faith: "Sanctius est ac reverentius de actis deorum credere quam scire" (*Germania* XXXIV, quoted in *Essays* II.xii).

24. Montaigne was in contact also with Justus Lipsius, who has been described (by Frank
Goodyear in his superb edition of Tacitus's *Annals*) as "First and indisputably first of all
Tacitean scholars." Three of Lipsius's letters to Montaigne have survived, though none
of Montaigne's to Lipsius is extant (they are not listed in the admirable *Inventaire de la correspondance de Juste Lipse, 1564–1606*, by A. Gerlo and H. D. L. Vervliet, Antwerp, 1968).
Montaigne borrowed copiously from Lipsius's *Politica* (a book which draws heavily on
Tacitus), and paid tribute in the *Essays* (I.xxvi) to this "learned and industrious compilation"; and he described Lipsius as "the most learned man still living, endowed with a very
fine and judicious mind" (*Essays* II.xii). Lipsius, for his part, having enjoyed the *Essays*
of the "French Thales," lavishly extolled his wisdom. See P. Villey, *Montaigne devant la postérité*
(Paris, 1935), pp. 24–26, 348–50 and especially G. Abel, "Juste Lipse et Marie de Gour-
nay: autour de l'exemplaire d'Anvers des *Essais* de Montaigne," *BHR*, 35 (1973), 117–29.
There is no echo of the contemporary debate on Tacitus in Lipsius's surviving letters to
Montaigne.

Lipsius and Montaigne had a joint acquaintance in Muretus: on Lipsius's acquaintance
with Muretus, see J. Rysschaert, "Une édition du Tacite de Juste Lipse, avec annotations
de Muret, conservée à la Mazarine," *RBPH*, 23 (1944), pp. 251–54 and especially the same
scholar's article, "Le séjour de Juste Lipse à Rome (1568–70) d'après ses *Antiquae lectiones*
et sa correspondance," *Bulletin de l'Institut historique belge de Rome*, 24 (1947–1948), pp. 139–92.

25. See also the end of chapter xxvi in Book I of the *Essays*, on attitudes of theologians
and philosophers towards reports of miraculous events. Montaigne has several judicious
passages dealing with such reports. See for example *Essays* I.xxvii, where he denounces
the folly of rashly disbelieving accounts of miracles; III.xi, where he attacks the opposite
folly of excessive credulousness; and II.xxxii, where he defends Plutarch against Bodin's

charge that he included incredible things in his history. There is an interesting discussion of Tacitus's account of Vespasian's "miracles" in Innocent Gentillet's *Discours contre Machiavel* (II.ii: pp. 163–64 in the edition by A. d'Andrea and P. D. Stewart, Florence, 1974).

26. See *Montaigne and the Roman Censors*, pp. 20, 105.

Un recueil poétique hors du commun, Le *Naeniae* de Salmon Macrin (1550)

Georges Soubeille

Les *Naeniarum libri tres* et les *Poemata uaria de Gelonide* constituent le seizième et dernier recueil publié par Salmon Macrin, en 1550, à l'occasion de la mort de sa femme Guillonne Boursault, plus connue sous son surnom littéraire de Gélonis.[1] C'est un ouvrage d'une certain importance, quantitativement (125 poèmes, plus de trois mille vers) et par la qualité des collaborateurs, Joachim Du Bellay, Jean Dorat, Mellin de Saint-Gelais entre autres. Le volume pourtant n'a guère jusqu'ici retenu l'attention et n'a pas acquis la notoriété d'autres Tombeaux plus célèbres, comme ceux du Dauphin François, de Marguerite de Navarre ou de Ronsard. Le Tombeau de Gélonis, après un renom de quelques années, tomba dans l'oubli, après avoir reçu, en 1603, de Jean Dousa le coup de grâce: "Macrini, abite, uapulate, Naeniae."[2] Ces Nénies présentent cependant une certaine originalité et différence des Tombeaux poétiques habituels; Salmon Macrin y retrouve une inspiration tarie depuis une quinzaine d'années et il échappe ainsi, du moins partiellement, aux lieux communs qui sont une loi — et une plaie — du genre.

Le recueil est organisé selon une ordonnance soignée: après deux poésies liminaires, l'une de Jacques Goupil, l'autre de Nicolas Denisot, et une dédicace à Marguerite de France, on trouve trois livres de *Naeniae*, composées par Macrin lui-même, les deux premiers regroupant les odes éoliennes, soit 1,172 vers, le troisième livre ne comprenant que des distiques élégiaques, soit 1,064 vers; enfin la partie collective du livre couronne l'édifice et comprend 1,100 vers; ce souci de l'équilibre et de la variété se retrouve dans l'organisation interne de chaque partie: le livre un, par exemple, contient 47 strophes alcaïques, 26 strophes saphiques et 278 vers lyriques de mètres divers, et le livre deux 45 strophes alcaïques, 26 strophes saphiques et 318 vers lyriques de mètres divers. Cette harmonie architecturale n'est évidemment pas due au hasard et Macrin a si visiblement structuré son ouvrage que, pour étoffer la partie collective, restée un peu maigre et disproportionnée malgré ses appels à l'aide, il l'a grossie de 238 vers de sa propre fabrication, tandis que, pour des raisons plus familiales que littéraires, il plaçait dans la partie centrale la poésie composée par Charles Salmon en l'honneur de sa mère. Une intention très nette ainsi se dessine, celle de conférer au monument *de Gelonide* le plus d'ampleur possible, selon une esthétique, non de la sobriété, mais de la surcharge, du *multa meae*, pourrait-on dire. La recherche des effets de masse et de volume traduit un désir de matérialiser l'immensité du chagrin; d'où les répétitions, les longueurs, les insistances, les détails de mauvais goût; d'où l'introduction de poésies étrangères au sujet, un "epicedion" de Marguerite de Navarre, la paraphrase d'un psaume de David sur la mort de Saül, une traduction de la "Déploration du bel Adonis" composée par Saint-Gelais, et même une Ode à la Seine, poésie encomiastique célébrant le retour à Paris du Cardinal Du Bellay, et une lettre de recommandation au juge Brinon en faveur du gendre Adrien Dreux, victime d'un procès.[3] Des matériaux d'origine diverse ont donc été ajoutés, mais pour l'essentiel le contenu du recueil peut se réduire à deux composantes: les *Naeniae*, chants d'adoration et de prière modulés par Macrin en multiples variantes; la partie collective ou *Tumulus* proprement dit, réunissant les œuvres de vingt-deux participants et ayant pour but la glorification de la défunte.

L'étude des *Nénies* exige une remarque préalable: lorsque l'on passe des strophes éoliennes des deux premiers livres aux distiques élégiaques du troisième, on ne constate aucune différence dans les thèmes abordés, Macrin reprenant souvent les mêmes sujets en les traitant sur des mètres variés, *numero modo hoc, modo illo*, selon une vieille habitude;[4] simplement les odes ont en général plus d'ampleur, un ton plus soutenu que les pièces élégiaques, plus courtes, plus intimes, plus propres aux confidences familières.[5] Mais dans toute cette poésie funèbre et lacrymatoire où les larmes coulent d'abondance, où le nom de Gélonis revient comme un refrain et un appel, le thème principal est, bien sûr, celui de l'amour en deuil, un amour qui, en prenant de nouvelles teintes, continue au-delà du tombeau; l'auteur cède souvent au plaisir amer de remâcher son chagrin ("Laetitiae mixtis infremo tristitiis," dit-il, p. 69), il cherche un réconfort dans l'évocation d'un passé heureux, ces vingt-deux ans de mariage qui lui paraissent maintenant à peine vingt-deux journées; il supplie Gélonis de revenir hanter ses rêves, lui apporter consolation et illusion, il se réfugie dans les coins les plus sauvages de la campagne loudunaise, où ses larmes inondent le gazon, et tout naturellement il se compare alors à l'archétype, à Orphée pleurant son Eurydice. La tentation du suicide lui vient même à trois reprises, mais en un réveil courageux, chaque fois Macrin se ressaisit et balaie tous ces phantasmes littéraires empruntés au néo-pétrarquisme. Ce veuf de soixante ans, qui se retrouve dans une maison bouleversée, qui a encore six enfants à élever ou à doter, n'a plus l'âge de suivre les traces de Pétrarque et de Laure. Il se libère de toutes les imitations et devient enfin lui-même; sa poésie se confond avec sa vie, c'est le tableau de Gélonis, brodant ou lisant au coin du feu, c'est la mésaventure de Timothée tombant de son berceau ou les petits malheurs de Théophile placé chez une nourrice, loin de sa mère, c'est le prochaine maternité de Camille: Macrin espère avoir une petite-fille qui ressemblerait à Gélonis et qu'on appellerait Gélonia. Les *Nénies* prennent l'allure d'un album de famille où le poète consacre une épître à chacun des siens, écrivant même à sa belle-mère[6] une lettre pleine d'humour; à tous il promet de ne pas se remarier, par fidélité et aussi pour conserver aux enfants leur héritage. Mais les affaires le rappellent bientôt à Paris; cet éloignement va-t-il faire germer un thème conventionnel, le désir nostalgique du pèlerinage sur la sépulture de la femme aimée, les roses répandues, le myrte ou le laurier que l'on plantera sur la tombe? Au contraire: Loudun fait maintenant horreur à Salmon et il voudrait ne plus y revenir; quand sonne l'heure du retour forcé, il écrit à son vieil ami Rémy Roussel qu'il ne va pas rentrer comme autrefois à tire-d'aile, emporté par l'amour, mais "Iam testudineo mi placet ire gradu," dit-il ("il me plaît d'avancer à la vitesse d'une tortue") (p. 90).

Car Gélonis n'est pas là-bas au cimetière de Loudun, elle est toujours et partout avec lui, dans sa mémoire et dans son cœur. Sans se lasser, Macrin refait le récit de la maladie de Guillonne — la tuberculose sans doute — puis de sa courageuse et chrétienne agonie. Il décrit le halètement, la toux incessante qui au dernier moment l'empêchera de saisir l'hostie, les crachements de sang, le feu de la fièvre qui peu à peu fait place au froid de la mort, l'extrême-onction, les remèdes inutiles conseillés par les trois médecins et l'apothicaire;[7] un remords ronge Salmon: sa propre absence à l'instant fatal; dans ses monologues intérieurs, il en demande pardon à Gélonis, tout en lui redisant son amour, en lui parlant de leurs enfants, en évoquant leurs jours heureux. Les vertus de Gélonis, sa beauté, sa voix mélodieuse, ses qualités de maîtresse de maison lui inspirent bien des distiques et, grâce à cette omniprésence de Gélonis, les *Nénies* constituent une suite du *Livre des Epithalames:*[8] avant de se clore à jamais, le cycle amoureux déploie encore ses mille facettes. Autre signe d'une continuité assurée par les réflexes d'un vieil humaniste, les légendes mythologiques fournissent ornements habituels, langage codé et symboles, mais ici aussi Salmon manifeste une indépendance chèrement gagnée. Si Pénélope et Laodamie lui servent, très conventionnellement, de modèles de référence, Gélonis est l'objet d'une autre comparaison, inattendue, car ses douze enfantements sont rapprochés des travaux d'Hercule, la fièvre qui la dévore et qu'elle supporte stoïquement, en cachant son mal, devient une second tunique de Nessus. Quant à Macrin lui-même, il pouvait difficilement, nous l'avons vu, échapper à la légende d'Orphée, mais il transforma le mythe; sans illusion et sachant bien qu'aucun chant ne pouvait arracher sa femme au tombeau, il s'attacha, dans les *Nénies*, en adressant des prières à Dieu et à Marie, en exaltant la piété exemplaire de Gélonis, à l'aider à obtenir son salut. C'est dans ce sens qu'il fut un nouvel Orphée, un Orphée chrétien, capable, par la puissance de sa lyre, de conférer une double immortalité, céleste et terrestre:

> Ergo pio studio nunquam est moritura Gelonis,
> uiuet et illa polo, uiuet et illa solo.[9]

Sûr de la bonté divine, convaincu que sa femme, par sa vie et par sa mort, a mérité le ciel, confiant dans ses prières et ses chants,[10] Macrin, en plus de dix passages, se plaît à imaginer le bonheur céleste de Gélonis, qui, mêlée aux chastes héroïnes, regarde jouer, sur des gazons fleuris, parmi les anges, leurs six enfants prématurément disparus, tandis que lait et miel coulent à flots et qu'elle écoute, en goûtant le nectar et l'ambroisie, des chœurs et des concerts merveilleux, conversant avec de grands poètes, Sannazar, Flaminio, Marulle ou Pontano.[11] Ces évocations font beaucoup penser aux descriptions païennes des Champs élyséens, mais s'y ajoutent des éléments qui suppriment toute ambiguïté: Gélonis est bien au Paradis chrétien puisqu'elle contemple éternellement Dieu et la sainte Trinité (p. 25; p. 76), puisqu'elle a rejoint la troupe des servantes fidèles du Christ (p. 20; p. 93). A l'idée d'un tel bonheur, Macrin appréhende un moment que Gélonis oublie son mari et leur vie passée il souhaite la rejoindre au plus vite, mais, bientôt rassuré par plusieurs apparitions nocturnes, il termine les *Nénies* par deux poèmes d'espérance et de foi: la déploration chargée d'amour charnel et humain se change en une adoration mystique et presque religieuse; sans diviniser Gélonis comme les païens faisaient de leurs grands disparus, Salmon va consacrer ses dernières années à célébrer le culte d'une épouse que la mort, à ses yeux, a transfigurée en Bienheureuse et en Sainte.[12]

Sans présenter la brillante diversité des œuvres de la quarantaine, les trois livres de *Nénies* offrent pourtant une forme très achevée du talent macrinien: une technique de versification éprouvée s'y met au service de grands mouvements affectifs. Salmon était prédisposé à la poésie funèbre; en ses débuts, au temps où il pratiquait surtout le distique élégiaque, il avait été le disciple de Quintiano Stoa, cet auteur italien qui avait accompagné la mort d'Anne de Bretagne de lamentations célèbres; puis il avait consciencieusement participé au Tombeau de Louise de Savoie et à ceux du Dauphin François; la mort de sa mère et de ses deux sœurs, emportées par la peste, lui avait inspiré, vers 1525, quatre poignantes *Naeniae*.[13] Mais l'ambition d'être l'Horace français l'avait longtemps fait s'essouffler sur les voies escarpées du grand lyrisme. La mort de Gélonis, en le rendant à lui-même, lui fit retrouver sa vraie vocation, c'est-à-dire la poésie élégiaque, un genre mineur, sans doute, *ars parua*, mais où il pouvait exprimer, en toute sincérité, ses sentiments personnels et devenir un authentique créateur. C'est le sens de son retour aux distiques élégiaques (57 élégies sur les 80 poèmes des *Nénies*) mode d'expression le mieux adapté au deuil et à la tristesse.[14]

La dernière partie du recueil, les *Diuersorum authorum poemata de Gelonide*, présente moins d'originalité. Vingt-deux amis de Macrin y unissent leur érudition et leur sensibilité pour élever à Gélonis un *Tumulus* digne d'elle, 45 poèmes au total, 32 en latin, 8 en grec et 5 en français, soit un ensemble de 1,100 vers, dont 818 vers latins et seulement 68 vers grecs; le latin, langue officielle de l'humanisme, domine largement le grec, réservé au petit nombre, et dans la plupart des cas on a jugé plus prudent d'ajouter aux poésies grecques leur traduction latine.[15] La qualité des participants doit retenir aussi l'attention; il y a d'abord le groupe des Loudunais, fidèles à leur compatriote, Adrien Dreux, Pierre Boulenger, Claude

Mangot, Jacques Goupil, Jean Sanel; leur présence prouve que toute petite ville avait ses érudits, son foyer d'humanisme. Assez curieusement, on constate ensuite que quatre médecins envoyèrent des *poemata*; à défaut de la guérison, Goupil (déjà cité), Antoine Armand, Pierre des Mireurs et Simon Vallambert offrirent à Gélonis des fleurs de rhétorique, car les médecins au seizième siècle sont aussi des humanistes. Nous trouvons même deux amis italiens, Giovanni Ferrerio et Vincent Gigliano, qui apportent au *Tumulus* une dimension internationale.[16] Mais voici le fait le plus significatif: Jean Dorat et Joachim Du Bellay, les deux poètes dont la participation est la plus abondante et la plus remarquable,[17] Pierre des Mireurs, Nicolas Denisot, Jean de Morel, Antoinette Deloynes appartiennent à la Pléiade ou gravitent autour d'elle; Macrin les avait connus à Paris, chez Morel, dont la maison réunissait les lettrés.[18] Leur collaboration au Tombeau de Gélonis ne semble pas seulement dictée par l'amitié. Sur le plan littéraire, on peut y voir aussi la preuve d'affinités et peut-être la reconnaissance d'une dette. La nouvelle école, née au Collège de Coqueret et récemment pourvue de son manifeste, la *Deffence et Illustration* de 1549, à travers son hommage à Gélonis, Muse de la poésie néo-latine, saluait celui qui, depuis plus de trente ans, travaillait à faire refleurir les lettres antiques; entre l'école de poésie en langue savante, dont Salmon était le chef, et la Pléiade, malgré l'opposition linguistique, régnait une communauté de vues dans des domaines aussi importants que l'admiration des anciens, la conception aristocratique de la poésie ou même l'esthétique.[19] Devant ce vieillard endeuillé, dont la lyre avait déjà illustré le règne de Louis XII et qui avait contribué à introduire Horace en France, la jeune génération éprouvait un sentiment de vénération et de reconnaissance filiale, que traduisent bien cette apostrophe d'Antoine Armand, "Quid fles, o uenerande senex" (p. 105), cette expression de Pierre des Mireurs, "Care pater uatum" (p. 107) ou cet hexamètre de Gigliano: "Credidimus te olim uatum, Macrine, parentem" (p. 100). Mais sous la mélancolie d'une fin de règne, perce l'enthousiasme juvénile qu'inspirent les renouveaux; Joachim Du Bellay s'écrie:

> Sus donc et qu'on essuye
> Les pleurs et le souci.
> Le beau temps et la pluye
> S'entresuyvent ainsi.
> Celui qui bien accorde
> De la lyre le son,
> Cherche plus d'une corde,
> Et plus d'une chanson   (p. 131).

Cette exhortation renferme une part de cruauté inconsciente à l'égard d'un homme qui définitivement venait de raccrocher sa lyre. Du moins, Jean Salmon Macrin avait la satisfaction, avant d'entrer dans le silence, d'avoir publié un dernier recueil hors du commun, car, dans les *Naeniae*, vibrent sans artifice les accents émouvants de la "plaintive élégie" et les *Poemata varia*, où la Pléiade décerne au vieux poète la couronne de l'honorariat, établissent la filiation des deux écoles et constituent un jalon dans l'histoire littéraire de la Renaissance.[20]

Université de Toulouse–Le Mirail

Notes

1. *Salmonii Macrini Iuliodunensis Cubicularii regii Naeniarum libri tres, de Gelonide Borsala uxore charissima, quae annos XXXX, menses II, dies XV nata, obiit XIIII Iunii, Anno Domini M.D.XXXXX. Diuersorum Authorum Poemata, Latina, Graeca, Gallica, de Gelonide.* Lutetiae, apud Vascosanum, M. D. L. (144 pp. in-8°).

2. *Iani Dousae Echo siue Lusus* (Hagae Comitis), 1603, f. 16, "In effigiem Io. Secundi … poetae unici." Dousa rejette les *Nénies* parce qu'il préfère l'érotisme des *Basia* de Jean Second.

3. [Epicedion], p. 44; [Psaume de David], p. 46; [Déploration d'Adonis], p. 141; [Ode à la Seine], p. 139; [Au juge Brinon], p. 8.

4. "Tour à tour sur tel mètre, puis sur tel autre"; sur la versification de Macrin, voir Jean Salmon Macrin, *Le Livre des Epithalames*; *Les Odes de 1530 (Livres I & II)*, éd. critique avec introduction, traduction et notes par Georges Soubeille (Université de Toulouse–Le Mirail, 1978), ouvrage couronné par l'Académie française (Prix Mgr Marcel, 1979).

5. Les odes ont une longueur moyenne de 52 vers, les élégies de 18 vers.

6. "Ad Carlottam Analdeam, Gelonidis matrem," p. 84; à la fin de l'épître, Macrin souhaite à sa belle-mère une vie aussi longue que celle d'Hécube, mais moins de malheurs….

7. Gélonis avait été soignée par Gaucher de Sainte-Marthe, ancien premier médecin de François Ier, par Jean Coyttard, doyen de la Faculté de Poitiers par Jacques Goupil, par l'apothicaire Jean Herbelin. Le traitement consistait en un régime alimentaire, des tisanes, des fumigations de médicaments en poudre et d'aromates (p. 10; p. 53).

8. Le *Carminum Libellus* de 1528 fut réédité en 1531 sous le titre d'*Epithalamiorum Liber*; les fiançailles, le mariage, la première maternité de Gélonis alimentent l'inspiration de ce recueil; on peut lire à ce sujet mon article "1528, une date importante dans l'histoire de la poésie néo-latine en France, la publication du *Carminum Libellus* de Salmon Macrin" dans *ACNL Amstelodamensis* (Munich, 1979), pp. 943–58.

9. Salmon met ces paroles prophétiques dans la bouche d'Antoinette Deloynes, qui plus prudemment, n'accordera à Macrin que le pouvoir d'immortalisation terrestre dans son "Epigramme sur le trespas de Gélonis" (p. 135).

10. Mea opinio certa est / uxorum aethereo uiuere in axe meam, p. 85; His nam conspicuam moribus aethera / admissam in liquidum incredulus haesitem? p. 12.

11. Mme Françoise Joukovsky apprécie beaucoup ces évocations (notamment An ducunt choreas Leues,… p. 23) et appelle Macrin le poète des Champs Elysées (*La Gloire dans la poésie française et néolatine du XVIe siècle* (Genève, 1969), pp. 566–67; cf. aussi p. 416).

12. Salmon fait une mise au point très nette à ce sujet; il n'est pas question pour lui de diviniser Gélonis, comme par exemple Cicéron voulut le faire pour sa fille, p. 94; p. 96.

13. Publiées dans les Odes de 1530, à la fin du quatrième livre; pour Quintiano Stoa, se reporter à Raymond Lebègue, *La Tragédie religieuse en France (1514–1573)* (Paris, 1929), pp. 129–42; 490–93.

14. On peut lire une mise au point intéressante sur la fonction primitive de l'élégie dans R. Martin et J. Gaillard, *Les Genres littéraires à Rome* (Paris, 1981), t. II, 107–09; Macrin semble être revenu aux sources du genre élégiaque. D'autre part, son inspiration s'intègre dans une veine poétique ou l'on retrouve les élégies composées par Ausone à la mort d'Attusia Lucana Sabina sa femme, certains Tombeaux de Pontano consacrés à Ariadna, la Nénie de Joachim Du Bellay intitulée "Maritus et uxoris umbra," les "Regrets et larmes funèbres sur la mort d'Aymée" de Pierre de Brach. Cette tradition est soulignée dans l'Ode "In amores coniugales Petri Brachii" composée par Jean Dousa le fils: "Plorans Amatae funera coniugis / quali Charontem carmine Thracius / uates et impexos capillis / Eumenidum stupefecit angues. / Quali Gelonis Salmonio fuit / defleta uersu; uel numeris quibus / cognominem Cressae puellam / Pierio recubans in antro / Pontanus ad caelum extulit." dans *Iani Dousae filii poemata* (Lugduni Batauorum, 1607), p. 120, vv. 29–37.

15. Sur les huit poésies grecques, deux fois l'auteur s'est traduit lui-même (p. 124; p. 125), trois fois Macrin s'est chargé de l'opération (p. 32; p. 76; p. 81), André Dampierre a traduit Daniel d'Augé, p. 104; la confection d'un *Tumulus* était vraiment un travail d'équipe.

16. Admirateur du Mantouan et de Pontano, Salmon fut toujours en amicales relations avec des Italiens, comme Théocrène, Livio Crotto, Lorenzo Toscano ou Fondullo; il était considéré avec une certaine estime de l'autre côté des Alpes; Paolo Cerrati lui dédicaça son poème *De Virginitate* (lire Jean Porcher, "Un envoi à Salmon Macrin" dans *Humanisme et Renaissance*, IV [1937], p. 80); Macrin avait édité à Paris vers 1516 le *De laudibus Diuinis de Pontano* (voir I. D. McFarlane, "Jean Salmon Macrin," dans *BHR* (XXII), 1959, 68–69) et en 1527 l'*Ars Poetica* de Vida (cf. Mario A. Di Cesare, "The Ars Poetica of M. G. Vida," in *ACNL Lovaniensis*, Munich, 1973, p. 217).

17. Jean Dorat envoya une élégie et une grande ode pindarique de six triades (rééditée et traduite par Mme Geneviève Demerson dans Jean Dorat, *Les Odes latines* [Clermont–Ferrand, 1979], pp. 68–83), Joachim Du Bellay une "Ode à Salmon Macrin, sur la mort de sa Gélonis" de 144 vers et une "Imitation de l'ode latine de Jehan Dorat sur la mort de la Roine de Navarre" de 48 vers.

18. Voir dans les *Naeniae* l'ode alcaïque que Salmon a dédiée à Morel, pp. 3–8.

19. Lire à ce sujet I. D. McFarlane, "Poésie néo-latine et poésie de langue vulgaire à l'époque de la Pléiade," *ACNL Lovaniensis*, pp. 389–403.

20. Nous ne parlerons pas du contenu de ces *Poemata varia*; il s'en dégage une consternante banalité, qui se manifeste dans l'éloge démesuré de Gélonis, dans les consolations apportées à Macrin, dans l'affirmation vingt fois répétée de l'immortalisation conférée par la poésie; l'argumentation est presque toujours la même: "Gélonis n'est pas morte, car elle survit 1) dans ses enfants 2) grâce à la gloire reçue de son mari 3) dans un lieu de béatitude;" autre type de consolation: "oui, Gélonis est morte, il faut s'y résigner, nous savions qu'elle était mortelle."

"Nobilium culpa iacent literae": Guillaume Budé and the Education of the French "Noblesse d'Épée"

James J. Supple

In a short but incisive study of attitudes towards the education of the Renaissance nobility, J. H. Hexter has drawn our attention to the fact that many of those condemning its ignorance were themselves noblemen. He argues, correctly in my view, that with men like Noël du Fail, François de la Noue, Michel de Montaigne and Jean Saulx-Tavannes demonstrating the need for the nobility to be well educated, the chorus of complaint concerning noble ignorance must have been, to some extent at least, a self-perpetuating literary commonplace which, by the sixteenth century, could no longer claim to correspond to the true realities of the situation.[1] His study suffers, however, from his failure to point out that the primary impetus inducing a move away from acceptance of the unbookish educational ideal incarnated by Chaucer's Squire came from Humanists like Jean Bouchet, Guillaume Budé, Laurent de Carle, Symphorien Champier, Josse Clichtove, Antoine du Saix and Claude de Seyssel.[2] The latter were, to some extent, inspired by the same motive as their counterparts amongst the *noblesse d'épée*: by the desire to persuade the military aristocracy that it needed to acquire a good liberal education if it wanted to increase its participation in the government of the kingdom.[3] But they were also inspired by other motives: by the need to convince the nobility that it should patronise men of letters;[4] by the desire to see that the values of Humanism should permeate the entire state;[5] and, as part of that programme, by the need to replace the archetype of the perfect man as warrior with the at times conflicting archetype of the perfect man as a scholar.[6]

Study of these motives would take us well beyond the scope of the present paper. It is interesting, however, to examine the way in which they affected the thought of the most important of the Humanists mentioned above: Guillaume Budé. The latter is, indeed, a particularly significant example since he was widely regarded as the leader of the humanist movement in France in the early decades of the sixteenth century, and was praised by his biographer, Loys Le Roy, for being the first to introduce the *literae humaniores* to the royal court: "Nec vero debetur laus parva Budaeo, qui primus bonarum artium incunabula in aulam intulit."[7] Budé himself complained in a letter to Richard Pace about "regum nostrorum principiumque [vitium], qui non tam ipsi arte doctos homines arceri ab aula sua volunt, quam semetipsi ab aula docti utro procul submoverent." Although he claims that the antipathy in question is produced "fatali nimirum aulicorum elegantiumque ingeniorum dissidio," he decided to try to find a remedy for it, as he declares in the *De philologia* (1532), where he expresses the hope that, if the court can be won over, the cause of good letters will benefit throughout the kingdom: "sua deinde vi in priscum honoris gradum opinionisque reponeretur."[8] Much of his attention is very naturally directed at the most influential figure in the royal court: the king himself. The *Institution du prince* (c. 1518–19) was written for Francis I; the *De studio literarum recte et commode instituendo* (1532) is dedicated to him; and the *De philologia* is couched in the form of a dialogue between the king and his humanist interlocutor, in which his majesty is portrayed as being exceptionally receptive to Budé's arguments concerning the advantages of study. Budé is also concerned, however, with the *noblesse d'épée*, whose ignorance he had already criticised in the *De asse* of 1515 (new style).

It is interesting to note, first of all, that Budé's prime concern is self-interested. He is furious about the way in which Frenchmen "primariae auctoritatis" insist that good scholars are to be found only in Italy. This may be a veiled reference to the Cardinal d'Amboise, who had offered Budé little recognition for his services to scholarship; and it is certainly part of the on-going debate between French and Italian Humanists concerning the alleged *translatio studii* from Rome to Paris.[9] Budé mainly views it here, however, as a pretext used by members of the military aristocracy to justify their hostile attitude towards French scholars, an attitude which they believe becomes them because it corresponds to the Second Estate's traditional reputation for despising letters: "Caput vero erroris est, quod nobilium natio indecoram esse literarum cognitionem claris penatibus ortis, semper existimavit." Budé is quite sincere when he laments the disastrous consequences which this prejudice has on the advice which noblemen, ignorant of the beneficial moral effects produced by study, give to the king:

> Nam quum primores procerum, ignorantiam literarum percupide sibi vendicent, ac nihil sui muneris esse in pacis artibus credant: evenit ut plurima aulae consulta ex paucorum commodo fiant, qui in rem ipsi suam suarumque necessitudinum concipere edicta principis consultaque didicerunt.

But he is also distressed by the effect which their attitude has on men of letters, who, not receiving the honour which is their due,[10] retire from court. Worse still, the lack of esteem shown for letters by the nobility has proved contagious, and other groups, notably the priesthood, have reacted in a similar way. Thus, letters (which should be the preserve of noble souls)[11] are cultivated only by plebeians:

> Huius igitur mali causa est nobilium institutum, qui res consentaneas & mutua ope nixas, generis claritatem, literarumque peritiam, collidi inter se

& dissidere putant: quo errore factum est, ut disciplinae olim ingenuae ap-
pellatae, ad plebem iamdiu transierint, non tantum a nobilibus sed etiam
(ô mores perditos) a sacricolis repudiatae, ne non satis generosus esse & lautus
antistitum ordo praesulumque putaretur.

This is what Budé (or more probably his publisher) is complaining about when
he writes in an abrupt marginal comment summarising this passage: "Nobilium
culpa iacent literae."[12]

One of the ways in which Budé attempts to change this situation is to attack
the view held by influential men who believe that a liberal education is not a prerequisite for those who govern the country: "literarum bonarum studium nihil
ad reipublicæ moderamen pertinere."[13] This, he claims, is obviously untrue of
the Humanists' special domain, eloquence, which should be given an eminent
role in the affairs of the kingdom: "Nam [...] olim rerumpublicarum magnorum-
que imperiorum domina [fuit] ipsa & gubernatrix eloquentia." The position in
Budé's time is quite different ("nunc vero a gubernaculis reiecta [...], e concioni-
bus enim & foris, a capitalibus periculis, controversiisque civilibus summota est");
but the inacceptability of this is only too evident to him — as, for example, in embassies to foreign nations: "Iam vero legationes apud exteras gentes maximis de
rebus obire composite, apposite & efficaciter, quis sine comitatu eius possit, vel
ea potius non præeunte?"[14] The persuasive power of eloquence can also be of
value in other contexts, of course, where, ever mindful of the militaristic outlook
of the *noblesse d'épée*, Budé insists that it can be more effective than valour. This
is why he places such emphasis on the Gallic Hercules, who was followed by a
"grant [*sic*] multitude de gens de toutes sortes qui le suyvoient comme par force,
car il les tenoit attachez tous par les oreilles à chesnes menues d'or et d'argent."
He interprets this as meaning that Hercules's great deeds were accomplished not
through great strength but through learning and eloquence.[15]

More generally, Budé tries to prove that the king and his counsellors need the
prudence to be obtained through the study of letters. He is objective enough to
admit that prudence may be a natural gift and that it can be increased by experience; but he continually stresses the key role which letters must play: "Verum
enimvero prudentia est illa quidem luculenta dos naturae atque magnipendenda,
praesertim cum adminiculis experientiae subnixa esse coepit. Sed tamen si
literarum scientia vacat & historiae antiquae cognitione, est veluti Pallas semier-
mis atque aegide sua orbata."[16] This is why he places such emphasis on the aid
given to Achilles by Minerva, the symbol of letters: "Proinde quum ille poëta fons
ingeniorum dictus [Homer], talem strenuum militem, eundemque ducem fortissimum inducat, ut nusquam ita destitutus, ita deprehensus, sit quin praesto
consilium & rationem habeat [...] planum [est] utique, qui sapientia & prudentia
careant res ab ijs maximas nec bello nec pace geri posse."[17] The same symbol,
referred to this time as Pallas, is also utilised in the *De philologia* to emphasise
the value of prudence obtained through the study of letters. The fact that the An-

cients believed that this deity was born fully armed is a symbol of a deeper truth: "artium literarumque scientiam: ex eaque prudentiam emanentem, suapte vi & consilio, copijsque proprijs instructam esse atque munitam ad se suaque tuenda domi & militiae, in hostico iuxta & in pacato." For this reason, it is essential that those in government should consult learned men whose knowledge (especially the knowledge of the past acquired through the study of history) enables them to rival the wisdom of Homer's Nestor:

> Quare & ad quieta consilia & ad bellica, primum hominum doctissimorum & dissertissimorum quasi quorundam Nestorum Homericorum sententiam exquiri opportere: eam ob rem maxime quod praeter rerum causas, quas literarum scientia tenet, etiam exemplorum eventuumque memorabilium plena est historia, plena etiam alia monumenta antiquitatis, ex quorum lectione & memoria prudentia & consilium oriuntur, aut naturae certe benignitate enata, aluntur & confirmantur.[18]

Budé is not, as one can see from his reference to "quieta consilia & bellica," solely concerned with the government of the kingdom. He is only too aware of the emphasis which the *noblesse d'épée* places on fighting, and is anxious to emphasise, therefore, the military usefulness of study. This is why he is so incensed by the suggestion that the Gauls were valiant but not well educated: he is conscious of the fact that the enemies of letters are appealing to an age-old tradition, and seeks to destroy its prestige. It is for this reason that, unlike David O. Mc-Neil,[19] he finds Strabo's testimony so relevant.[20] It provides proof that, however warlike their ancestors may have been, there is nothing in the character of the French which makes them incapable of cultivating good letters: "Nec literas Gallis Strabo, nec animum studiis liberalibus aptum promptumque negat, etiam si eis ad praelia animos gestientes tribuat." The evidence of history shows, Budé claims, that military power and dedication to study go together, as was the case with the Greeks and the Romans: "Utrunque autem imperium non minus animis excolendis, quam corporibus exercendis, quaesitum est, et retentum." The symbolic value attributed to Pallas by the Ancients proves, Budé asserts once again, that letters have a more universal application than their enemies would allow: "quippe idem numen Palladis & Minervae, & Martios animos loricatis pectoribus & togatis praecordijs aut palliatis vim iudicandi censendique inspirare creditum est." He refuses to believe, therefore, that his country's reputation for producing valiant soldiers means that it will be unable to produce wise men. This view may be widespread ("Hoc [...] vulgo nostrates homines dicunt"), but it leaves Budé indignant and incredulous: "Quasi vero vero natura dissidium inter cor & manus ingenerarit." He claims to be convinced, for his own part, that there is an indissoluble link between the mind and the body, which means that those who cultivate both arms and letters are most likely to excel: "Egovero in utranque partem vires animorum valere puto, quum recte animi ipsi formantur doctrina & institutis, & praesertim in ijs gentibus, quae naturae plena dote praeditae, & corpora & mentes ad omnia versatiles habent."[21]

Here we have a statement concerning the compatibility of military and literary accomplishments of a kind which suggests that Budé is susceptible to the appeal of the *uomo universale*, a concept the influence of which Hexter is perhaps too quick to reject.[22] In Budé's case, however, the situation is not as simple as it may appear. To begin with, he has no real sympathies for the warrior ideal. Like many of the Humanists of Northern Europe at this time, he regarded war as a terrible blight, arguing that both France and Europe in general were wasting their energies (energies which could have been better employed in the service of the Muses) in continual warfare.[23] He is especially worried by the warlike ardour of Francis I — an ardour which he does his best to nip in the bud in the *Institution* when he highlights the unfortunate fate of Pyrrhus, who would not listen to the advice of Cineas and died pursuing his insatiable desire for military aggrandisement.[24] He is particularly concerned, too, by the opposite advice given to the king by contemporaries (very probably members of the *noblesse d'épée*) who encouraged his bellicose proclivities: "Ce que peu d'hommes des plus sages luy veulent accorder & pleust à Dieu qu'aussi ne feit aucun de tous ceux qui le flattent en ceste grande alaigresse & confiance qu'il met aux armes."[25] Budé, for his part, is determined to convince the monarch that, even in military affairs, men of letters can be of more use to him than his soldiers. Again using Cineas as an example, he argues that a wise and eloquent ambassador can be far more effective than an army: "il monstra bien [...] que souvent on fait par prudence de parler et par facunde, ce qu'on ne pourroit faire ne par acier ne par guerre."[26] The fact that, faced by a seemingly impregnable Troy, Agamemnon wished that he could have ten more wise and eloquent counsellors like Nestor rather than ten more valiant soldiers like Ajax or Diomedes is also adduced to make the same point.[27]

The emphasis which Budé seems to place upon the interdependence of the mind and the body is equally suspect since he tends to regard the latter from a Platonic point of view, insisting that nothing is of more value than the mind and that the soul is corrupted by the body.[28] The episode in which Homer portrays Minerva as aiding Achilles is supposed to show that the wisdom gained through letters is both useful and necessary in war; but the episode in which Ulysses restrains the choleric young warrior is given a symbolic value by Budé which suggests that mental powers are more important than physical strength: "cum sub Achillis persona ostendere vellet, quid robur corporis summum cum animositate posset: contra sub Ulyxis, quid vis mentis & ingenij praestantis." We have seen Budé argue that prudence is an essential prerequiste in a soldier, but he also believes that prudence (which is, for him, prudence of an essentially literary kind) is superior to the soldier's art: "Quocirca peritissimos homines non paucos cum princeps maximus habuerit, tum ipse denique Palladis aegide & reverentia tutus erit, nedum Martis copijs impedimentisque succinctus." The pun on the meaning of "impedimenta" may or may not be deliberate, but Budé is in no doubt that prudence of the kind that he is recommending is of more value than military force: "Quod munimentum cum securitatem perinde ab inimicis & ab hostibus, tum ab occulta itidem oppugnatione praestat ut ab aperta."[29] It is not surprising, therefore, that he should show himself to be more concerned with persuading the king to introduce learned men into his council than in convincing the nobles already in the council that they should be better educated.[30] Budé may suggest that those with a versatile body and a versatile mind are most favoured by nature, but his concept of prudence is such that he is bound to be more concerned with cultivating the mind through study than with cultivating the body through military exercises. This is why he is so angry at the suggestion that, being gifted for war, the French nation has no talent for letters. This, for him, is the same as saying that the French are necessarily imprudent: "qui literas Gallis adimunt, non iam scientiam nobis elegantiorum artium, sed etiam prudentiam omnino quasi sensum communem [afferunt]."[31] Those who adopt this position are suggesting that, though the French excel in battle, they are unable to know when or how to wage war: "Quid enim est aliud quam Gallos ad praelia dictitare, bellis autem gerendis aut opportune suscipiendis consilium ipsis non suppetere?" Worse still, the view of the French that this implies conflicts with Budé's most basic convictions about the nature of man. For him, as for all Humanists, man is essentially a creature who excels all others because he is endowed with reason.[32] Denying this basic faculty to the French is tantamount, therefore, to denying their very humanity: "Quod ipsum quid est aliud quam hominem (ut dicitur) ex homine tollere?" As for the bodily qualities which are so obviously needed by the soldier, Budé seems ultimately to have nothing but disdain for them: "Nonne si animae principem partem [prudence] a corpore humano sustuleris: quae remanebunt, communia cum simijs nobis erunt."[33]

Budé's basic lack of interest in improving the educational standards of the soldier is further demonstrated by the fact that he gives only the vaguest details concerning the disciplines which could be of practical benefit to him.[34] This is not at all surprising in view of his hostile attitude towards war and his own prejudice in favour of the scholar. It is also noticeable, however, that, apart from history and eloquence, he gives few details concerning the precise way in which a liberal education can assist the nobleman who wishes to dedicate himself to a career in government.[35] This may well reflect his belief that the ruler should be as independent as possible and, if Claude Bontems's conclusions are correct, his conviction that the nobility should be "évincée de la scène politique."[36] It seems surprising, none the less, in an author who complains so bitterly that "homines singulari ignorantia praediti [...] summis ac multis honoribus praediti [sunt]."[37]

The explanation for this paradox is to be found, I believe, in the tensions within Budé himself, and, in particular, in his ambiguous attitudes towards the active life. Knowing that it was the widespread belief that letters could not help the man of action which was largely responsible for the disdain in which they were held, he was determined to try to explode this dangerous myth:

Quippe huiusmodi hominum opinio longe lateque pervagata, quantam calamitatem intulerit hactenus, quantam pauperiam fecerit in nomine literario, in ordine studiosorum, in natione hominum Minervae consecra-

torum, cum omnibus notum sit & manifestum, tum vero identidem queri-
tantes videmus nostrae sortis studiosos, seculorum iam aliquot iniquitate,
ignorantiaque factum esse principium & primorum, ut recta perpolitaque
eruditio e civitatum gubernaculis, e fori tribunalibus, ex cohortibus pur-
puratis ac praetextatis explosa, nec in Regum principiumque hominum con-
sulta admissa sit & retenta, ad sellularias nunc classes deiecta.[38]

He counterattacked by criticising the ignorance of one of the most important rul-
ing groups, the *noblesse d'épée*, and by embarking on public service himself, cumu-
lating posts in a way which has led F. Plaisant to describe him as "un haut fonc-
tionnaire" roughly equivalent to a "secrétaire d'état."[39]

Budé fulfilled his duties with such success that he was able to play a prominent
role in persuading the king to found the institutions which we today know as the
Bibliothèque Nationale and the Collège de France. By temperament, however,
he was a scholar who greatly resented the way in which his official tasks distracted
him from his studies,[40] and, as Mme de la Garanderie has rightly argued, a
Christian mystic who nurtured deep doubts about participating in the affairs of
a corrupt world.[41] This is why he describes himself as having been dragged to
court ("velut in aulam raptum")[42] and why he so frequently abandoned it.[43]
Eugene F. Rice, Jr. has suggested that Budé is "disturbed by the fear that he has
given too much time to the pursuit of wisdom and not enough to acquiring prudence," a virtue which Budé sees as having a more immediate practical value.[44]
It should be remembered, however, that the *De philologia* (the work to which Rice
is referring) is a *dialogue* and that the views expressed by the character "Budaeus"
are not necessarily always those of the historical Budé. The character in question
is, in fact, expressing the view of friends, relatives and indeed enemies of the author who felt that "frugiperdae" disciplines like the *literae humaniores* would not help
him increase his family's fortunes.[45] Budé, who often insists on the need for scholars to be given adequate patronage,[46] can see that they have a point; but his
heart remains with Philology, his *altera coniunx*, who will lead him to wisdom and,
with God's grace, help him to eternal life.[47] This is why he disagrees with the
view expressed by his well-meaning friends and less well-meaning enemies: "Me
ne ut Philologiae meae pertesum sit unquam aut poenitare possit? quae mihi iam
doti omnia bona sua dixit: quibus ego in bonis cornu illud copiae uberimum semper esse censui? non usque adeo sapientiam prae prudentia contemnendam esse
reor."[48] He tends, indeed, to despise "externa bona" of the kind which he is urged
to seek, and associates public life with ambition and cupidity.[49] He feels that only
those whose studies of good letters have given them the necessary moral integrity
should rule the state; but he also fears the moral compromises which personal
involvement might bring:

Equidem haud libens summum in rerum administratione locum mereri
velim, si tantum ipse munus quoquo modo obire possim, ut simile aliquod dedecus aut portentum auspiciis meis accidisse aliquando prodere-
tur.[50]

He was certainly soliciting advancement from the king when he wrote the *Institution du prince*;[51] but he was never fully committed to public service — witness his translation in 1505 of St Basil's letter *De vita in solitudine agenda* and, only one or two years after the probable date of composition of the *Institution*, the publication of the short meditation, *De contemptu rerum fortuitarum*.[52] Emphasising Budé's public career and his desire to put his learning at the service of his contemporaries, Plaisant has described him as "un homme d'action" and affirmed that his career "s'apparente plus à celle d'un Morus qu'à celle d'Erasme."[53] This is far from being an unjust assessment. It might be more accurate, however, both as concerns his own career and as concerns his attitude towards the public service owed by the *noblesse d'épée*, to describe him as hovering uneasily between the life of the public servant and the life of the scholar and mystic.

University of St Andrews

Notes

1. "The Education of the Aristocracy in the Renaissance," in *Reappraisals in History* (London, 1961), pp. 45–70.

2. Bouchet, *Les regnars traversant les perilleuses voyes des folles fiances du monde* (Paris, Antoine Vérard), n.d., f. B iii^v; Carle, *Dispute qu'il est necessaire à un grand Prince sçavoir les Lettres* (Paris, Chrestien Wechel, 1548); Champier, *Le regime d'un jeune prince* (Lyon, G. Balsarin, 1502), f. xvi^v; Clichtove, *De vera nobilitate*, ([Paris], Henricus Stephanus, [1512]), f. 38^r–40^v; Du Saix, *Lesperon de discipline*, [Paris], 1532; Seyssel, *La monarchie de France*, ed. J. Poujol (Paris, Librairie d'Argences, 1961), pp. 155–56. For Budé, see below passim.

3. Seyssel, pp. 155–56, 159; also Du Saix, f. biiij^r.

4. See below note 46.

5. Budé, *De philologia* ([Paris], Iodocus Badius, 1532), f. XXXIIII^v.

6. For a partial study, see R. E. Hallowell, " 'Prince humaniste ou prince chevaleresque': a French Renaissance Debate," *Studies in Honor of Isidore Silver*, ed. F. S. Brown, *KRQ*, 21, supp. N° 2 (1974), 173–83; also J. J. Supple, *Arms versus Letters: The Military and Literary Ideals in the "Essais" of Montaigne* (Oxford, Clarendon Press, 1984), c. 1.

7. *G. Budaei vita* (Paris, Ioannes Roigny, 1542), p. 46.

8. *Lucubrationes* (Basle, Nicolaus Episcopius Iunior, 1557), p. 242; *De philologia*, f. III^r–v.

9. D. O. McNeil, *Guillaume Budé and Humanism in the Reign of François Ier* (Geneva, Droz, 1975), pp. 31, 33.

10. *De studio* ([Paris], Iodocus Badius, 1532), f. II^r.

11. ibid.

12. *De asse* (Paris, J. Badius Ascensius, 1515), f. XII^r. I quote from the ed. by Gryphius, Lyon, 1550, pp. 63–64. All subsequent quotations are from this edition.

13. *De asse*, p. 699.

14. *De philologia*, f. XVIe, XVII^r.

15. *Institution du prince*, in *Le prince dans la France des XVIe et XVIIe siècles*, ed. by C. Bontems and others (Paris, PUF, 1965), p. 89.

16. *De philologia*, f. LXXIII^v.

17. *De asse*, pp. 62–63.

18. f. LXVII^v–LXVIII^r.

19. p. 33.

20. *Geography*, IV, 1, 5.

21. *De asse*, pp. 84–88.

22. pp. 64–65.

23. *De philologia*, f. LXXII^{r-v}.

24. p. 117.

25. *Epistre [...] Sur les choses qui luy sembloient principalement dignes de reformation en son temps* (n.p., 1562), f. c iiij^r. This is an anonymous translation of Budé's letter to Philecous (10th October [1521], *Lucubrationes*, pp. 351–56).

26. *Institution*, p. 117.

27. ibid, p. 61.

28. *De transitu hellenismi ad christianismum* (Parisiis, Robertus Stephanus, 1535), f. 1^r; *De studio*, f. X^r.

29. *De philologia*, f. LXXXIII^{r-v}.

30. ibid, f. LXXIII^v–LXXIIII^r.

31. *De asse*, p. 61.

32. For the classic statement of this view, see Pico, *De hominis dignitate*, ed. E. Garin (Florence, Vellechi, 1942–52), 3 vols., III, 104–07.

33. *De asse*, pp. 89–90.

34. The anonymous author of the *Familiere institution pour les legionnaires* (Lyon, François Juste, 1536), f. 14^r–16^r, recommends mathematics, geometry, astronomy, medicine and geography.

35. Cf. the legal studies recommended by François de l'Aloëtte (*Traité des Nobles* [Paris, Guillaume de la Noüe, 1577]), f. 16^{r-v}, and Antoine de Laval (*Desseins de professions nobles et publiques* [Paris, Abel l'Angelier, 2nd ed., 1613]), f. 101^v–03^r).

36. pp. 18–21.

37. *De asse*, p. 733.

38. *Lucubrationes*, p. 334.

39. "L'histoire antique dans l'institution du prince d'après Guillaume Budé," *Actes du IXe congrès de l' Association Guillame Budé* (Paris, Belles Lettres, 1975), II, 715–27 (p. 715).

40. McNeil, pp. 96–97.

41. "L'harmonie secrète du *De asse* de Guillaume Budé," *BGB*, 4e série, N° 4 (1968), 473–86. See, too, her longer study *Christianisme et lettres profanes 1515–1535* (Paris Champion, 1976), especially vol. II.

42. *Lucubrationes*, p. 333.

43. McNeil, pp. 13–14, 44, 93–94; also Le Roy, pp. 46–47.

44. *The Renaissance Idea of Wisdom* (Harvard U.P., 1958), p. 150. Rice admits (p. 213) that Budé also defines wisdom in other ways.

45. *Annotationes*, p. 284. Budé's father appears to have frowned on his scholarly career (McNeil, p. 12).

46. *Institution*, pp. 83, 87.

47. *De transitu*, passim.

48. *De philologia*, f. XLII^v.

49. *De transitu*, f. 2^v; *De philologia*, f. LXXI^r; *De studio*, f. X^v.

50. *De asse*, p. 747.

51. See ibid, p. 91.

52. 1520, or possibly 1521 (McNeil, p. 59, n. 56).

53. p. 718.

The *Poemata* of Théodore de Bèze

Thomas Thomson

I n the essay "De la præsumption" published in the 1580 edition of his *Essais*, Montaigne, talking of achievements in the field of French neo-Latin poetry, lists a group of "bons artisans de ce mestier-la": Jean Dorat, Théodore de Bèze, George Buchanan, Michel de l'Hôpital, Pierre de Montdoré and Adrien Turnèbe.[1] What were the achievements of Théodore de Bèze in neo-Latin poetry that allowed him to be placed amongst this constellation of stars in the literary firmament?

Nowadays, the reputation of Bèze as a writer rests mainly on his play *Abraham sacrifiant* of 1550, published two years after he had been converted to Protestantism and left Paris for Geneva. Literary historians and critics of sixteenth-century French tragedy, although rightly insisting on the importance of this play as the first French tragedy, have perhaps done Bèze a disservice, almost pinning him down to one title out of many. The true extent of Bèze's writings can best be judged by looking at the index of Frédéric Gardy's bibliography of Bèze's works.[2] Three of the rubrics of Gardy's title — the *œuvres théologiques*, the *œuvres historiques* and the *œuvres juridiques* — have occupied the attention of eminent scholars. But what Gardy calls the *œuvres littéraires* have been rather neglected, save for the popular French versions of the Psalms which completed the work begun by Marot, and the *Abraham sacrifiant*, which was given a full critical edition in 1967.[3] What has been neglected is the sizeable production by Bèze throughout a large part of his long life of poems in Latin, and, to a lesser extent, in French and Greek.

During his years in Switzerland, from his arrival in Geneva in October 1548 after his conversion to the Reformed faith until his death in 1605,[4] Bèze's interest in and practice of religious and moralising verse in Latin is seen most clearly in his Latin metrical paraphrases of the Psalms and the Song of Songs, his *Icones, id est verae imagines virorum doctrina simul et pietate illustrium ... quibus adiectae sunt nonnullae picturae quas Emblemata vocant* and his *Cato censorius christianus*. His first published group of six Psalm versions dates from 1565 or the spring of 1566, appearing in the distinguished company of an edition of George Buchanan's Psalm paraphrases.[5] He finally renders all one hundred and fifty Psalms into Latin verse and publishes them in 1579. The Song of Songs paraphrase dates from 1584. The *Icones* of 1580 contain eulogies in prose and, in some cases, in verse. After the main body of the work come forty-four emblems which are in the moralising, didactic tradition of the genre and portray *exempla* of Christian virtue. The *Cato censorius christianus*, published at Geneva in 1591, contains eighteen epigrams against different vices.

While one might expect such works from the pen of a leading figure of sixteenth-century Geneva who had received a sound classical education at Bourges and Orléans, a man known to many as the first biographer of Calvin, the logical successor to Calvin after the latter's death, and the author of a number of sermons, theological treatises and biblical commentaries that influenced the development of Protestant theology, one is perhaps surprised to see Bèze compose a not inconsiderable number of those secular poems which abound in the vernaculars, and in Latin, Greek and Hebrew, in the sixteenth and seventeenth centuries. Liminary verses, *silvae*, birthday poems, translations and adaptations of poems from the *Greek Anthology*,[6] epitaphs both serious and humorous, epithalamia, love elegies and epigrams in the Ovidian manner, and Catullan and Martialian epigrams, all are a significant part of Bèze's output as a neo-Latin poet. Given the sizeable volume of Latin verse produced by one who is not readily identified by the literary critics as a poet, and given the number of translations, adaptations and citations of his poems in English, French, German, Dutch and Italian works, the way would seem to be open for someone to edit at least some of these poems, to open up an approach to Bèze the Humanist, Bèze the *amateur des classiques*.

Work on a critical edition of Bèze's Latin poems was, in fact, begun early this century by Léopold Micheli, the then librarian of the Bibliothèque publique et universitaire of Geneva. Micheli had, as Frédéric Gardy says, "procédé à une étude approfondie des *Poemata* et comparé les différentes éditions, en notant les variantes." However, Micheli died at the age of thirty-three before being able to complete his work, and, regrettably, little editorial work on the published *Poemata* has been done since his death. It is not that Bèze's Latin poems are inaccessible or unknown: as long ago as 1879, Alexandre Machard reprinted the text of the first edition of the *Poemata*, along with a prose translation of most of the poems *en regard*;[7] and, in 1898, Louis Maigron published a Latin thesis on the *Poemata*.[8] Whilst these books have many merits, not least in that they make available to a modern audience a text and the beginnings of a commentary on the poems, they lack any assessment that must be based on a collation and study of the many stylistic and metrical variants introduced by Bèze into successive editions of the *Poemata*.

Both Machard and Maigron use only the first edition of the poems, published by Conrad Badius at Paris in mid-July 1548 when Bèze was twenty-nine, only three months or so before his arrival in Calvinist Geneva. The book is dedicated to the Protestant classical scholar Melchior Wolmar from Rottweil in Baden-

Württemberg, who had been Bèze's mentor and preceptor in Orléans and Bourges from 1528 to 1535.[9] The contents of the volume are: four *silvae* (versified accounts of the *devotio* of P. Decius Mus and of the death of Cicero, a celebration of the night of the Nativity, and a highly poeticised version of the David and Bathsheba story, intended as a "poetic preface" to the seven penitential Psalms); twelve *elegiae* (seven love elegies, a piece on *aurea mediocritas*, a poem on the common death-day of Livy and Ovid and three other miscellaneous poems); twenty-four epitaphs, five of which are *badinages*, written at the expense of their subjects; twenty-one *icones*, mostly elegiac distichs, on heroes and heroines, gods and goddesses, writers, orators and philosophers of Antiquity; and ninety-eight epigrams (twenty addressed to his poetic mistress Candida, roughly one-third drawing the reader's attention to some aspect of human folly or weakness, some encomiastic pieces and some *poésies de circonstance*). This first edition is quite inadequate as a critical text, given that another four authorised editions, with many alterations to the original poems, as well as additions and excisions, were published before Bèze's death in 1605.

A second edition appears in Geneva published by Henri Estienne in 1569, along with Latin poems by, among others, Buchanan, Poliziano, Sannazaro, Flaminio, Secundus and Estienne. Bèze had already, in the preface to *Abraham sacrifiant*, attacked secular love poetry and repented of the misuse of his God-given poetic powers before his conversion.[10] Many poems from that period are now expunged by the Protestant Bèze: most of the elegies; about one-third of the epitaphs, including, significantly, the piece on Etienne Dolet; three-quarters of the *icones*; the twenty epigrams on Candida; and all but one of those poems on what might be considered by Calvinists to be doubtful or *grivois* subjects. New poems are added which reflect Bèze's new religious allegiance. There appear a number of epitaphs commemorating mostly Bèze's co-religionists: his former teacher Melchor Wolmar and his wife; reformers such as Luther, Calvin, Melanchthon and Zwingli; such leading continental divines as Wolfgang Musculus, Andreas Hyperius, Johannes Oecolampadius and Pietro Martire Vermigli; and the Protestant heroines Claude de Rieux, wife of François de Coligny-Châtillon, comte d'Andelot and Gaspar de Coligny's first wife Charlotte de Laval. Almost one-third of the thirty-one new epigrams are vigorously anti-Catholic, as is one of the six new *icones*. In the long letter-preface to the Hungarian André Dudycz, formerly bishop of Pécs, who was converted to the Reform in 1567,[11] Bèze gives some details of the encouragement he had received from friends to publish his poems in 1548 and, more importantly, defends himself against the calumnies of his Catholic opponents who had not been slow to use the "evidence" of one of the Candida poems (epigram 90) to "prove" that he had homosexual tendencies and that Candida, whose pregnancy is alluded to in epigram 84, was in fact Bèze's wife.[12]

A third edition, without name of printer or place, but no doubt published by Estienne at Geneva, appeared in 1576. According to the title page, it contains the other poems by various hands, but in fact lacks them in most copies that

have been found.[13] The text of those poems of the first edition which remain
has hardly changed since 1569 and the 1569 preface is retained. Added to the
poems are eleven new epitaphs (five for Coligny, two for Louis de Bourbon, prince
de Condé, and one each for Heinrich Bullinger, Johann Haller, Josias Simler
and Joachim Camerarius), seventeen new epigrams and the *Abraham sacrifiant*.

There is now a gap of twenty-one years before the publication of the fourth
edition of 1597 in a fine quarto volume set in italic type and bearing the printer's
mark of the Estiennes. An expanded issue, with a revised version of the *Cato censorius christianus*, a Latin rendering by Jean Jaquemot of the *Abraham sacrifiant* and
an appendix of new poems, appears in 1598. The fifth and final authorised edition of the poems appears in sextodecimo format from the presses of the Genevan
printer Jacob Stoer and is reissued, with a slightly altered title page, in 1614.
By now, the additions made by Bèze to the five rubrics of the first edition total
over two hundred poems.

Pirate editions of the *Poemata* appear on the Continent until 1600, a sure indication of the popularity or perhaps the notoriety of the unexpurgated poems
of the first edition, on which these largely undated pirate editions are all more
or less based. Complete posthumous reprints of the first edition appear well into
the eighteenth century: one appears at London in 1713 and two appear, allegedly
at Leiden, but in fact at Paris, *chez Barbou*, in 1757 and 1779. Many of the 1548
poems are also anthologised in various collections from Duchesne's *Flores epigrammatum* of 1555 through Gruter's *Deliciae C. poetarum gallorum* of 1609 and Brunel's
Parnasse latin moderne of 1808 to McFarlane's *Renaissance Latin Poetry* of 1980.[14]

In addition to this total of five authorised editions of the *Poemata*, there is a
manuscript which belonged to a student friend of Bèze, Germain Audebert of
Orléans, dated tentatively c. 1544, which now belongs to the Bibliothèque municipale of Orléans and which contains *inter alia* a collection of poems by Bèze, many
of which are retained in the 1548 *Poemata*.[15] Two rubrics, the *epistolae* and the
eclogues, never reappear; and four poems (epigrams 13, 48, 73 and 84) reappear
only in 1569. Bèze's poems were listed, transcribed in full if they did not reappear
in any editions of the *Poemata* and published, with some annotations, by Fernand
Aubert, Jacques Boussard and Henri Meylan in 1953.[16] The editors said of these
poems:

> Ils peuvent jeter quelque lumière sur les idées et la formation littéraire du
> futur réformateur: ils fournissent en outre une base solide à qui voudra
> étudier les *Poemata*   (p. 164)

and they clearly defined the scope of any notes which they appended to the poems:

> Dans les notes qui suivent, on a renoncé à donner un commentaire philolo-
> gique qui eût exigé un recours constant aux poètes dont Bèze s'est nourri.
> On s'est borné à offrir au lecteur des précisions sur les personnages en ques-
> tion et sur les événements mentionnés qui permettent en plus d'un cas de
> dater ces pièces de façon satisfaisante.   (p. 168)

It is clear from this that the task of some *lecteur bénévole* would be to edit the 1548 *Poemata*, make a close study of them and produce some form of commentary both on the persons and events alluded to in the poems and on linguistic and metrical aspects of the poems. The late Henri Meylan next used these manuscript poems and some others first found in the first edition in an attempt to sketch the gradual conversion of Bèze to the reformed faith.[17] This article, however, although using data from the Orléans collection, brought a critical edition of the poems no nearer, since its focus of interest was *geistesgeschichtlich* rather than *textgeschichtlich*, as was his later article on the Orléans *sodalitium*.[18] In 1959 and 1960 I. D. McFarlane published a long, authoritative article on Salmon Macrin in which he cited a letter from Macrin to his friend Antoine de Lion, thanking him for the copy of Bèze's poems which he has sent Macrin and noting certain errors of quantity and commenting on the latinity of Bèze's vocabulary and on the adaptation of Greek words which he has found in the poems.[19] McFarlane was careful to relate these remarks to the variants of the 1569 edition, noting any changes which Bèze might have made in his later text as a result of Macrin's remarks. A clear impetus to a critical edition of the 1548 poems came in 1960, when Frédéric Gardy published his bibliography of Bèze's works, listing all the authorised editions and unauthorised reprints of the *Poemata*, and in 1962 in an article by the late Eugénie Droz, who added to the corpus of Bèze's poems by establishing that Bèze was the author of a *plaquette* of French and Latin verse published at Paris in 1547 by Conrad Badius.[20] The collection contains one French poem and the following Latin poems: two epitaphs for Francis I and the Dauphin François, who died in 1536, an epitaph for Charles, duc d'Orléans, who died in 1545, and verses on the funeral and burial of Francis I and his two sons at Saint-Denis on 23 May 1547. There are also two birthday odes: one (which had already appeared in the Orléans collection) for the eldest son of Henri II, and one for Henri's daughter Elisabeth; and a poem on Henri's accession to the throne. All of the Latin poems are to be found, with variants, in the 1548 edition. Mlle Droz also cited (p. 597) an earlier version of Bèze's Latin epitaph (epitaph 7) for his uncle Nicole de Bèze which had been placed in the church of Saint-Cosme et Saint-Damien at Paris in 1543. At the same time, and looking more than fifty years on in Bèze's life, Mlle Droz drew attention to a detail important for the textual history of the *Poemata*, a detail already noted by Henri Meylan in 1960.[21] In the Bibliothèque publique et universitaire of Geneva there are manuscript emendations made by the author — Mlle Droz calls them "les ultimes corrections manuscrites" (p. 598) — in a ruled copy of the 1598 issue of the 1597 edition which belonged to Bèze. This invaluable piece of information would seem to complete the canon for the textual editor, although it is interesting to note that these interlinear and marginal corrections are not incorporated into the 1599 text. An explanation for the omission of these punctilious emendations is that they were inserted into the 1597 edition because of its quarto format and wide margins, but were made only after the 1599 edition had appeared, therefore constituting an *Ausgabe letzter Hand*.

To sum up, in order to produce a critical edition of the 1548 *Poemata*, the following items must be collated against the 1548 text: a letter of December 1539 for an early state of epigram 19;[22] the earlier version of the epitaph for Nicole de Bèze; the Orléans manuscript; the 1547 *plaquette*; the editions of 1569, 1576, 1597 and 1599; and the manuscript corrections. To these must be added the letter-preface to the 1560 *Confessio christianae fidei* for a version of the epigram "Descriptio virtutis" later to become both an *icon* and an emblem entitled "Vera Religio";[23] the 1580 *Icones* for a Greek epitaph on Budé (f. T4^r), an epigram on Erasmus (f. C3^r) and the emblem "Vera Religio" (f. Pp2^v); and two other works to which Bèze contributed and which have earlier states of poems by him: André Tiraqueau's *Ex commentariis in Pictonum consuetudines sectio de legibus connubialibus et iure maritali* (Paris, 1546) for epigram 86;[24] and *Macuti Pomponii Senatoris Divionensis Monumentum. A Musis Burgundicis constructum et consecratum* (Lyons, 1578; Paris, 1580) for epitaph 11 and epigram 69. All of this work will produce a critical edition which, one hopes, may be of the same high standard as recent and forthcoming editions of works by two of Montaigne's group—Buchanan and Dorat—and will be another useful and desirable *instrument de travail* in the context of a steadily growing interest in neo-Latin poetry.

University of Dundee

Notes

1. *Les Essais de Michel de Montaigne*, ed. P. Villey (Paris, 1965), p. 661. Montaigne owned a copy of the second edition of Bèze's *Poemata* which is now in the Bibliothèque Nationale, Paris.

2. F. Gardy, *Bibliographie des œuvres théologiques, littéraires, historiques et juridiques de Théodore de Bèze* (Geneva, 1960).

3. *Abraham sacrifiant*, ed. K. Cameron, K. M. Hall and F. Higman (Geneva, 1967).

4. The standard biography of Bèze is P.-F. Geisendorf, *Théodore de Bèze* (Geneva, 1949; reprint Geneva, 1967).

5. On this edition, see I. D. McFarlane, "Notes on the Composition and Reception of George Buchanan's Psalm Paraphrases," *FMLS*, 7 (1971), 319–60 (pp. 326–28).

6. On Bèze and the Greek Anthology, see J. Hutton, *The Greek Anthology in France and in the Latin Writers of the Netherlands to the Year 1800*, second edition (Ithaca, N.Y., 1967), pp. 117–19.

7. A. Machard, *Les Juvenilia de Théodore de Bèze. Texte latin complet, avec la traduction des Epigrammes et des Epitaphes, et des recherches sur la querelle des Juvenilia* (Paris, 1879; reprint Geneva, 1970).

8. L. Maigron, *De Theodori Bezae poematis* (Lyons, 1898).

9. On Wolmar (1497–1560), see D. J. de Groot, "Melchior Wolmar. Ses relations avec les réformateurs français et suisses," *BSHPF*, 83 (1934), 416–39.

10. *Abraham sacrifiant*, ed. Cameron, Hall and Higman, p. 46. His repentance is repeated

in the letter-preface, addressed to Melchior Wolmar, of his *Confessio christianae fidei* (Geneva, 1560). For an annotated text of this letter-preface, see *Correspondance de Théodore de Bèze*, ed. H. and F. Aubert, H. Meylan, A. Dufour and others (Geneva, 1960–), III (1963), letter 156.

11. On Dudycz, see *Correspondance*, VIII (1976), 179, n. 8 and P. Costil, *André Dudith humaniste hongrois 1533–1589. Sa vie, son œuvre et ses manuscrits grecs* (Paris, 1935).

12. For an annotated text of this letter-preface, see *Correspondance*, X (1980), letter 673.

13. See I. D. McFarlane, "George Buchanan's Latin Poems from Script to Print: A Preliminary Survey," *The Library*, fifth series, 24 (1969), 277–332 (p. 314, n. 4).

14. *Flores epigrammatum ex optimis quibusque authoribus excerpti*, ed. L. Duchesne (Paris, 1555; 1560), ff. 200^r–18^r; *Deliciae C. poetarum Gallorum huius superiorisque aevi illustrium*, ed. J. Gruter, 3 vols. (Frankfurt, 1609), III, 587–743; J. Brunel, *Le Parnasse latin moderne ou choix des meilleurs morceaux des poètes latins qui se sont le plus distingués depuis la renaissance des lettres, avec la traduction française et des notices biographiques*, 2 vols. (Lyons, 1808), I, 40–51; and I. D. McFarlane, *Renaissance Latin Poetry* (Manchester, 1980), p. 34.

15. For a description of the manuscript, see J. Boussard, "Le MS. 1674 de la Bibliothèque municipale d'Orléans," *BHR*, 5 (1944), 346–60. It also contains a version of Buchanan's *Pro lena apologia* (see I. D. McFarlane, *Buchanan* [London, 1981], p. 112) and two poems by Salmon Macrin, on which see G. Soubeille, "Deux épigrammes manuscrites de Salmon Macrin," *Pallas*, 22 (1975), 71–78.

16. F. Aubert, J. Boussard and H. Meylan, "Un premier recueil de poésies latines de Théodore de Bèze," *BHR*, 15 (1953), 164–91 and 257–94.

17. H. Meylan, "La Conversion de Bèze, ou les longues hésitations d'un humaniste chrétien," *Genava*, new series, 7 (1959), 103–25 (= H. Meylan, *D'Erasme à Théodore de Bèze. Problèmes de l'Eglise et de l'Ecole chez les Réformés* [Geneva, 1976], pp. 145–67).

18. H. Meylan, "Bèze et les *sodales* d'Orléans, 1535–1545," in *Actes du congrès sur l'ancienne université d'Orléans* (Orléans, 1962), pp. 95–100 (= *D'Erasme à Théodore de Bèze*, pp. 139–44).

19. I. D. McFarlane, "Jean Salmon Macrin (1490–1557)," *BHR*, 21 (1959), 55–84, 311–49 and 22 (1960), 73–89. The only extant poem from Bèze to Macrin is the seventy-four-line elegy "Salmonio Macrino Iuliodunensi, Querela peste laborantis anno Domini 1551" (*Poemata*, 1569, pp. 77–80). With his letter to Antoine de Lion Macrin enclosed an epigram for Bèze which is now lost.

20. E. Droz, "Notes sur Théodore de Bèze," *BHR*, 24 (1962), 392–412 and 589–610. For a close bibliographical investigation of the two states of this text, see D. J. Shaw, "Les *Tumuli Francisci Primi* de Théodore de Bèze," *BHR*, 40 (1978), 567–73.

21. *Correspondance*, I, 10, n. 1.

22. *Correspondance*, I, letter 5.

23. See *Correspondance*, III (1963), 48–49.

24. The text is given in *Correspondance*, I, 194.

Classical and Neo-Classical Influences in the Life and Essais of Michel de Montaigne

Ian J. Winter

It was the fortune of Michel de Montaigne to be born in a decade when esteem for Latin language and culture in France, and indeed in all Western Europe, had reached one of its highest points. In 1529, four years before Montaigne's birth, Erasmus had published his *De pueris statim ac liberaliter instituendis*, which stressed direct exposure to ancient tongues from the age of two or three years (i.e., *statim*), as well as the delivery of this instruction by the pleasantest of methods (i.e., *liberaliter*). Pierre Eyquem, father of the future essayist, anxious to bestow on his eldest son the best fruits of enlightened scholarship, not only hired for him a distinguished Latin tutor from Germany, but decreed that Latin alone should be spoken in the presence of the child. In undertaking this radical approach, Montaigne's father probably received advice from Erasmians at the newly established College of Guyenne, who could cite the success of the Estienne family in Paris with young Henri, Robert and Catherine.[1] Yet, whatever encouragement and direction he may have received from others on this matter, Pierre Eyquem must be congratulated on the thoroughness of its implementation because, by the age of four or five, although he knew no French nor Gascon, young Montaigne thought and spoke in the language of ancient Rome, and up to the age of thirteen he was to use Latin almost exclusively for both speaking and writing.

In preference to a school, Erasmus had counselled education in the home and Montaigne was later to endorse this notion when he gave comprehensive instructional control to a private tutor "qui eust plutost la teste bien faicte que bien pleine" (I.26.149).[2] We can therefore only speculate about the reasons why, at the age of six, his father sent him to the College of Guyenne in Bordeaux. The Erasmian enthusiasts who gave the original advice had no doubt departed, and Andreas Gouvéa, the new principal, had every interest in enrolling a pupil who had been the subject of such an unusual linguistic experiment and whose fluency in Latin was to astonish his teachers. George Buchanan, a member of the College staff, later informed Montaigne that he intended to include this successful experiment in learning Latin as a model in his own projected treatise on education (I.26.173).

We must assume some exaggeration on Montaigne's part when he states that, once in college, his Latin rapidly degenerated, and that he derived no benefit at all from this stage of his education. His father having made special arrangements, he had as private tutors Grouchy, Guérente, Buchanan and Muret, who were among the leading scholars and educators of that time. When these academics authored Latin tragedies Montaigne was given leading roles to play, and performed them very creditably. The liberal influence of Erasmus is also seen in the flexibility of one of his other tutors, who permitted Montaigne to pursue readings in Ovid's *Metamorphoses*, Vergil's *Aeneid*, and the plays of Terence and Plautus, even at the expense of the regular syllabus. Acting in Latin plays and secret readings in the classics are Montaigne's best memories of college life. Due to these experiences he survived secondary education with his appreciation of Latin literature still intact.

We may again question Montaigne's insistence that, on leaving college, he lost all use of Latin through lack of practise (I.26.175). Elsewhere he states that one never loses what is natural to oneself, confessing that, whenever he is surprised or shocked, it is Latin rather than French that comes first to his lips (III.2.788). When in his late twenties he formed a deep friendship with Etienne de la Boétie, mutual love of antiquity sealed the bond, for La Boétie was a neo-Stoic, a scholarly writer of Latin poetry, a man "moulé au patron d'autres siècles que ceux-cy" (I.28.193). There is little doubt that in this close association Montaigne's interest in classical literature and philosophy was rekindled, fortified, and broadened.[3] On the early death of La Boétie Montaigne was heart-broken, but the exemplary nature of this death and the final exhortations of his friend were continually to inspire the younger but less resolute survivor.

Montaigne's decision to retire from the Bordeaux Parlement to his ancestral château at the early age of thirty-eight can be explained, at least in part, by the loss of La Boétie. At this point he carefully arranged publication of all his friend's works, and added to his own collection of books the numerous volumes which La Boétie bequeathed to him. The library, established on the third floor of his now famous tower, was dedicated to his friend as a centre of enjoyment and immersion in Greek and Latin literature. As Montaigne began to make the jottings which he was soon to call "essays," these influences are abundantly apparent. Less obvious, but always hovering in his literary and emotional background, is the neo-classical figure of La Boétie. Had La Boétie lived, Montaigne might have written letters, perhaps in Latin. In the solitude in which he finds himself he treats the subjects and authors of antiquity which they would have discussed together. The fact that La Boétie knew him better than anyone else may have inspired Montaigne to undertake the self-portraiture which would become the central theme of the *Essais*, but in this, as in their friendship, the classical tone remains all-pervasive.

In Montaigne's time the library in the tower reflected, much more than at present, his dedication to the ancient world. The beams and rafters with their intervening spaces were covered with fifty-seven classical and biblical quotations, thirty-two in Latin, twenty-five in Greek. Even the doors and the vertical edges of the book-shelves, long since burned as firewood, were carved out in this manner. What is sometimes forgotten, in considering the environment in which Montaigne wrote, is that he had the entire interior of the tower decorated in 1572 or 1573 by an unknown nomadic artist. Little remains today of the efforts of this painter, but we know from the reports of seventeenth- and eighteenth-century visitors that, whereas the lower floors of the tower were treated fairly soberly, in the library study, which was Montaigne's inner retreat, the walls were covered with colorful scenes recalling the legends of antiquity, Ovid's *Metamorphoses* being especially well represented.[4] One painting, "Mars and Venus surprised by Vulcan," was so audacious that one of Montaigne's more sanctimonious successors felt obliged to retouch certain of the figures. This explicit portrayal could, nevertheless, have inspired the daring essay on love, "Sur des vers de Virgile" (III.5). Another painting, "Venus lamenting the death of Adonis," reminds us of Montaigne's preoccupation with death, especially in the first two books of the *Essais*.

Perhaps it is more than a coincidence that these paintings were being completed just as Montaigne began his fine essay "De l'amitié" (I.28). As he watched the artist at work he discovered a manner of imitation applicable to his writing. Around each major composition his painter wove strange grotesque shapes which, claimed Montaigne, more exactly resembled what he himself was accomplishing in the nascent essay form. How could he hope to match, or even imitate, the ancient masterpieces, or indeed the early *Voluntary Servitude* of La Boétie, which was to be the main ornament of the essay in hand? Montaigne thus proceeds with his "crotesques," his self-denigration, his apparent disorderliness, digressiveness and ambiguity; but at the same time he never loses sight of the main picture, invariably a classical theme which he expects his reader to recognize, and to which he is content to refer, at varying intervals, by an echoing phrase, an associative allusion, a subtle indirection. Needless to say, as Montaigne presents his own painter, we cannot help but recall the opening lines of Horace's *Ars poetica* where the *pictor* is ridiculed who paints grotesque forms. Montaigne draws the same parallel between art and literature, but his inspired imitation emerges with a novel form and style which lead him towards an original theme.

Of the one thousand volumes that lay on Montaigne's shelves only two hundred and fifty can now be identified with certainty, and of these, one hundred and forty, or three out of five, are in Latin. If Montaigne wished access to Greek thought it had to be through a Latin translator or interpreter, his own knowledge of Greek being less than adequate. As for contemporary works, he considered them to be of insufficient weight. Montaigne's Latin texts, from which he quoted so massively, and often obliquely, gave him access to the three principal classical schools of thought and these provided him with abundant and stimulating commentary on all humanistic questions. From these schools Montaigne derives his impetus and upon them his thinking pivots, seeking its own originality. His assessment, assimilation and adaptation of the different modes of classical thought show him to be a master in the art of creative imitation.

If the theme of death assumes the proportions of an obsession in the first two books of the *Essais*, this would appear to be attributable to a quotation from Cicero, "Tota philosoforum vita commentatio mortis est."[5] Montaigne merely alludes to this statement of Cicero in the opening sentence of an early chapter "That to philosophize is to learn how to die" (I.20), saving the full citing of it until some fifteen years later towards the end of the third book (III.12.1028). Between these two references occurs a continuous and exhaustive *commentatio* as to the relative importance we should attach to the manner of our death. In effect, it is stoicism that is being analysed, firstly from an impersonal point of view, latterly, and with increasing critical intensity, from a personal angle.

"Qui mori didicit, servire dedidicit," writes Seneca to Lucilius.[6] "Qui a apris à mourir, il a desapris à servir" echoes Montaigne (I.20.85), as if the thought were his own, and in the earliest essays he seems little disposed to challenge any major tenet of the Stoic school. "Meditare mortem" is assiduously undertaken as he consults the past to examine the manner of death of a vast range of personalities. He appears to embrace the notion that a combination of Senecan moral tension and personal familiarization with death can overcome its terror and thus place man above the human condition. "Vir fortis ac sapiens non fugere debet e vita, sed exire," is Seneca's advice to Lucilius.[7] Stoical ataraxy, concludes Montaigne, involves a reasonable and reasoned exit from life, with special attention given to the last moment, for this moment confirms the virtue of all previous moments.

Montaigne's lengthy and passionate presentation of the Stoic case has been frequently discussed and no doubt his allegiance to the memory of La Boétie was a major factor in its persistence. Suffice it to say that, through his own experience and familiarity with authors other than Seneca, Montaigne finally develops severe criticism of the stoic ideal, finding that moral tension is a false route to ataraxy. On the positive side, he gladly seizes upon the stoical concept of time, which concentrates on the present and abandons problems past. More importantly, as the study of death directed his attention to the human condition, it also led imperceptibly towards self-study, which would become his principal preoccupation.

In contrast to Seneca and the dogmatic theories of the Stoics, Montaigne was greatly attracted to the new wave of sceptical philosophy which had circulated in France since the middle of the century. Thinkers such as Ramus, Talon and Brués had presented the arguments of the Academic sceptics in order to encourage a multiplicity of points of view,[8] but they did not have access, as did Montaigne, to radical Pyrrhonism as detailed in Sextus Empiricus's *Hypotyposes*, published in Latin translation by Henri Estienne in 1562. This text included the *Life of Pyrrho*, by Diogenes Laertius, with its useful summary of Pyrrhonism, but he could equally well have consulted this in the Latin translation of Diogenes's *Lives of Eminent Philosophers*, published with regularity since the end of the fifteenth century. On scepticism Montaigne also possessed Cicero's *Academica* (Vettori's edition of 1536), but readily available were commentated editions by Talon (1547), Turnèbe (1553), Léger Duchesne (1558), and Lambin (1565–66). The influence of Sextus Empiricus on Montaigne appears most strongly in his "Apologie de Raimond Sebond" (II.12), an essay which, in Popkin's words, "became the *coup de grâce* to an entire intellectual world," and "was also to be the womb of modern thought."[9] Brilliantly adapting the sceptical tropes listed by Sextus, Montaigne assaults all aspects of human knowledge and cognition until no area of certainty remains. To support the text of the "Apologie" he draws liberally upon the Latin poets. Vergil, Horace, and Ovid are well represented, but the essayist found Lucretius's *De Natura Rerum* the most appropriate for his purposes, especially Books 3 and 4, where psychological questions are treated, and Book 5, where the subject is the creation of man. At this time, to show his adherence to perfect suspension of judgement wherein the Pyrrhonist achieves his ataraxy, Montaigne coins his celebrated motto "Que sçay-je?"

Many of Montaigne's interpreters consider Pyrrhonism to have been his principal philosophy, yet the unequivocal defense of faith in the "Apologie" demonstrates that, like Henri Estienne and Gentian Hervet, Montaigne is no total Pyrrhonist, but rather a fideist. Even if we lay aside the religious question, Montaigne's statements on education, esthetics, friendship and especially on the quest for self-knowledge, are of too positive a nature to have been proposed by a true Pyrrhonist. On the other hand, the relativism and diversionism of his later works, his interest in following custom, nature, and the legendary middle way, denote that the lessons of systematic doubt remained with Montaigne. They became a characteristic of his method, if not his final philosophy.

A sharp increase, towards the end of his writings, in references to his daily habits, tastes and pastimes has encouraged the theory of an epicurean Montaigne. His readings in Diogenes Laertius, Cicero's *De Finibus Bonorum et Malorum*, and particularly in Lucretius's *De Natura Rerum*, had familiarized him with the philosophy of Epicurus, but there is no solid indication that Montaigne sought ataraxy in liberation from Nature's laws any more than in total submission thereto, as in the case of the Stoics. For moral stimulation he still turns to Seneca's *Epistulae*, but his warmest words are for those among the ancients who interpreted the human condition with moderation and who possessed the eclecticism of "un' ame à divers estages" (III.3.799). Socrates becomes his principal model, whilst the peripatetic sect is praised for giving equal consideration to mind and body. Among authors quoted in the final additions of the *Essais*, Cicero predominates by far, with the *Academica*, *De Natura Deorum* and *De Senectute* being especially favored. Finally, the neo-Latin translator of Plutarch, Jacques Amyot, had placed at Montaigne's disposal an unending wealth of historical and philosophical information on the Greek and Latin civilizations.[10] At various points in the *Essais* Montaigne records his full sympathy with Plutarch's eclectic philosophy, method, and style, as interpreted in Amyot's text (II.4.344; II.32.704; III.5.852–53; III.12.1017).

It is thus apparent that Montaigne's facility in Latin, promoted by a far-seeing parent, bore rich fruits, firstly by bringing him into contact with Humanists such as La Boétie, Amyot, Turnèbe, Brués and the members of the Pléiade;[11] secondly, by providing him with ready access to the rapidly growing repertory of newly published ancient masterpieces. Deferential towards these in his early writings, Montaigne rapidly achieved a maturity where the ancient themes, skillfully interwoven into his text, assumed new and revitalized forms. The result is an *imitatio* of such dimensions and originality that the *Essais* themselves have become the object of endless admiration and imitation. Born at a privileged moment, Montaigne was as successful as any other writer of his generation in presenting a sense of the beauty and vitality of classical thought, literature and language.

University of Wisconsin

Notes

1. See Roger Trinquet, *La Jeunesse de Montaigne* (Paris, Nizet, 1972), pp. 235, 243.

2. References to the *Essais* are in the text and indicate book, chapter and page in *Œuvres complètes*, ed. Thibaudet and Rat (Paris, Gallimard, 1962).

3. See Pierre Villey, *Les Sources et l'évolution des Essais de Montaigne*, 2 vols. (Paris, Hachette, 1908), I, 43–44.

4. See Jacques de Feytaud, "Une Visite à Montaigne" in *Le Château de Montaigne* (Paris, Société des Amis de Montaigne, 1971), pp. 45–46.

5. *Tusculanes*, I, XXX.

6. *Ep.* 26, 10.

7. *Ep.* 24, 25.

8. See Charles B. Schmitt, *Cicero Scepticus* (The Hague, Nijhoff, 1972), pp. 91, 107.

9. See Richard H. Popkin, *The History of Scepticism from Erasmus to Spinoza* (Berkeley, University of California Press, 1979), p. 54.

10. Listed among books possessed by Montaigne were *Les Vies des hommes illustres* (Paris, Vascosan, 1565) and *Œuvres morales* (Paris, Vascosan, 1572), both translated by Amyot.

11. See Trinquet, *La Jeunesse de Montaigne*, pp. 563–64.

Etienne Dolet: From a Neo-Latin Epic Poem to a Chronicle in French Prose

Valerie J. Worth

In August 1539 a short neo-Latin epic poem by Etienne Dolet, entitled *Francisci Valesii Gallorum Regis Fata*, was printed in Lyons. The following year there appeared from Dolet's own press a French version of the same work, this time in prose, *Les Gestes de Françoys de Valois Roy de France*; several re-editions were printed in Dolet's lifetime.[1] Both the Latin and French texts are composed of three books, in each case the first and second being substantially longer than the third; in more or less chronological order Dolet gives an account of events in the history of France from 1513–39 (or 1513–44 in later French editions), with his readers' interest focused upon the fate of the king, Francis I. A forthcoming article by C. Longeon[2] discusses Dolet's motives for compiling a history of his times and raises the problem of contemporary historical documentation to which he may have had access. The present article will assess the importance of a literary rather than a historical source, namely Vergil's *Aeneid*. An analysis of the first book of the *Francisci Valesii Gallorum Regis Fata*, which spans the period from 1513 to 1525, closing with the capture of Francis I at Pavia, will demonstrate the influence of the classical epic firstly as regards the structure and presentation of Dolet's account and secondly with respect to certain features of his poetic style. Dolet's ardent defence of Cicero as the only worthy model for Latin prose is well known;[3] far less attention has been paid to his admiration of Vergil. In 1540 Dolet's press published the complete works of the Latin poet, and in a dedicatory letter to Guillaume Bigot Dolet claimed that Vergil's mastery of Latin eloquence was second only to that of Cicero.[4] It is thus hardly surprising that the *Aeneid* should have supplied the model for Dolet's own epic poem. Yet, after obtaining permission to establish his own printing press in 1538, he also showed a growing interest in the development of the vernacular as a literary language; to his roles of neo-Latin author, and commentator and editor of classical Latin texts, he added that of translator. The brief theoretical treatise, *La Maniere de Bien Traduire d'une Langue en Aultre*,[5] appearing the same year as *Les Gestes de Françoys de Valois Roy de France*, demonstrates Dolet's awareness of the problems involved in transposing ideas from one cultural and linguistic medium to another. An analysis of the principles he follows in translating passages inspired by Vergil into French will raise a question fundamental to our understanding of the assimilation of classical literary influences within the vernacular tradition: how far might readers of the French version have been expected to recognise the debt to the classical text? The answer will be important in our evaluation of the status of the French text.

From the structure of the first book of the *Francisci Valesii Gallorum Regis Fata* it is evident that Dolet is writing an epic poem on a historical subject, not a full, historically accurate chronicle. In the first seven pages he discusses the role of Destiny and sings the praises of Francis I, only then turning to the history of France from 1513. Following the model of classical epic Dolet presents a series of tableaux of major events. Throughout, the emphasis is heavily weighted on episodes of particular importance to the king;[6] historical details which are only indirectly relevant to Francis I's career are reduced to a minimum or totally omitted. Thus the last two years of the reign of Louis XII are dismissed in less than two pages, while events surrounding the battle of Marignan and the account of the battle itself occupy some sixteen pages; similarly, the years 1516–21 receive just one page of comment, while the siege and fateful battle of Pavia are accorded eight pages.

Dolet's imitation of classical epic conventions is evident from the opening line of his Latin text:

> Fata cano Regis Galli, fata aspera fata:

Speaking in the first person, the poet is echoing the opening of the *Aeneid*, "Arma virumque cano ..." Like Vergil, too, he then gives a brief opening sketch of his hero before calling on the Muses:

> Non res parva agitur: Musae, contendite mecum
> Numine dignum opus Aonio praestare canentes.   (p. 9)

This invocation is justified by the claim "Non res parva agitur," where the figure of litotes underlines the serious nature of his subject, worthy of epic treatment. At the start of the French version, however, the Vergilian overtones are absent:

> Ce qui m'a induict d'intituler ce present Oeuvre en Latin FATA, qui en nostre langue veult aultant dire, que destinées, est, que par sus tout ordre, et pouvoir humain ay veu advenir au Roy tout ce qu'il a souffert d'infortune en aulcunes entreprises de ses guerres.   (p. 13)

The language here reflects the process of logical thought necessary to the translator and chronicler, rather than the inspiration of the epic poet. After this opening divergence, the French version follows the broad outlines of the Latin text; further substantial differences between the two versions occur almost exclusively in narrative sections where Dolet chooses to insert additional details in the vernacular chronicle. Such elaborations, often drawn from *La Mer des Histoires*,[7] tend to be of a prosaic nature: the exact number of men involved in a battle; the various diplomatic and military preparations preceding major encounters; or domestic and foreign affairs less directly related to Francis I himself. Had they occurred in the epic poem, they would have distracted the focus of attention away from the hero, but they are consistent with the conventions of a prose chronicle. The narrative sections of the Latin text owe relatively little to the model of the *Aeneid*; the speeches of the heroes and the extended similes to illustrate the action or characters concerned are, on the other hand, closely imitative of Vergil's technique. They are also the passages most faithfully reproduced in the French version, and will thus provide most of the material for our subsequent comments.

The speeches are important in influencing the readers' perception of the hero. After his initial eulogy of Francis I, Dolet is not effusive in his praise of the king, but the latter's speeches serve to reinforce the parallel between his conduct and that of Aeneas. The implied comparison has historical precedents: it has been demonstrated that Octavien de Saint-Gelais's translation of the *Aeneid* was intended to flatter Louis XII in the same way.[8] Dolet's flattery relies on the readers' recognition of words and phrases characteristic of Vergil's hero. For example, in imitation of Aeneas (*Aeneid* I.198) Francis I is made to address his troops as "Socii" (p. 18) before the battle of Marignan. Although the rest of the oration is not drawn from any one particular speech by Aeneas, the arguments and key words used by the French king still recall the general mood of Vergil's epic: "honos" and "gloria" must be preserved; the men should be spurred on, "amor si nominis ullus/ Vos tangit"; and the king concludes his speech with the proud rhetorical question:

> Scilicet in genus indomitum Gallum Helvetius vim
> Fecerit impune, et Regem cum gente domabit?   (p. 19)

In the French translation, Dolet attempts to convey the same parallels with the *Aeneid*, adhering closely to the structure and figures of speech of the Latin text. Thus, although the French reader does not have the direct prompt of certain Latin words to confirm the association with the Vergilian model, he still might appreciate the creation of a situation similar in spirit to Aeneas's address to his men.

An element of the structure of the *Aeneid* which proved more difficult for Dolet to imitate was the skilful Vergilian balance between the role of the heroes and that of the gods. While at the end of Dolet's poem we are left with the impression that by 1539 Francis I was in a relatively favourable position, there can be no dramatic conclusion on the scale of the death of Turnus at the hands of Aeneas. In the first book, moreover, Dolet faces the serious problem of recounting the ignominious defeat and capture of his hero at Pavia. As Dolet hoped that the king would read his work,[9] it was essential that he should exculpate him as far as possible. It thus suited both Dolet's personal ambitions and the epic structure of his work that he chose to regard the defeat of the French at Pavia as the result of Fate, a force which, he emphasised at the start of his book, is beyond human control.[10] Francis I is therefore presented as the victim of Fate, exonerated from any share of responsibility in his own capture and defeat. In Vergil the outcome is ultimately controlled by the will of Jupiter: other gods may delay Aeneas's victory; the human characters certainly affect the speed at which the conclusion is reached, but the final result is decided from the start. Vergil makes us aware of the role of the gods in a series of conversations between several of them which punctuate the action on the human level. Since Dolet is concerned with recently attested history, rather than the shadowy area of mythology, the regular intervention of Jupiter would not have been in keeping with the choice of a contemporary subject. Thus, at the outset he prefers to speak of the role of "fata," divorced from any mythological associations.[11] Towards the end of the first book, after a passage of fairly precise details on the situation of both armies preceding the battle of Pavia, Dolet does however introduce one mythological scene, in order to illustrate the overpowering decision of Fate. When the battle seems equally poised between the French and Imperial troops, it is Jupiter who decides to turn the scale against Francis I, in order that no mortal shall be too great. Two mythological tableaux show Jupiter explaining his decision to Mars, and then Mars descending to the Underworld to seek the help of the three Furies, who are to spread terror among the French army. Although the convenience of this figurative explanation is obvious, and the scenes among the gods are colourfully portrayed, the passage nevertheless fits awkwardly into the work as a whole, since the reader is quite unprepared for the abrupt transition from precise military details to a scene from Roman mythology. It is noticeable that Dolet introduces no other such passages, and these scenes are totally omitted from the French prose translation where they would have seemed even less apt. There adverse fortune alone is held responsible for the king's defeat; the echoes of the Vergilian model are thus again removed from the vernacular text.

If certain general features of the Latin text recall the *Aeneid*, a study of Dolet's poetic style, in particular his figures of speech, confirms his close acquaintance with Vergil's poem. The areas in which Dolet uses the *Aeneid* as his stylistic model are numerous: the following examples are therefore intended to illustrate the general pattern of Vergilian influence. We have already seen that the words of Francis I before the battle of Marignan evoke a parallel with the speeches of Aeneas. Similarly, in the description of the siege of Pavia,[12] the narrative is reminiscent of the description by Vergil of the siege of Troy (*Aeneid* II.438ff.). For example, Vergil uses the figurative expression of ladders sticking to the walls, "haerent parietibus scalae" (II.442); Dolet uses the same verb in "Scalae haerent muris," but his French translation, "Les ungs plantoient eschelles au pied des murailles," changes the image conveyed by the verb, and disguises its debt to the Latin source.

A second example of Dolet's imitation of Vergil's poetic style is the use of periphrasis in many phrases suggesting the passage of time, particularly night and day. Dolet introduces this figure of speech in several places in his Latin text, especially at strategic moments, where it may reinforce the impression that his poem follows in the line of a celebrated epic tradition. Thus, Dolet commences his narrative of events on the day of the battle of Marignan:

> Iam Sol per medium Coeli traiecerat axem,
> Oceanumque amplum spectans vergebat in umbras
> Humentes umbras noctis.   (pp. 16–17)

The pairing of "umbras humentes" may recall, for example, *Aeneid* IV.7, where Vergil speaks of "humentemque ... umbram." In the French translation the figure is discarded, perhaps because Dolet considered it inappropriate for a historical narrative in prose. Instead he supplies precise details which would have been equally misplaced in an epic poem:

> Le quatorziesme jour de Septembre 1515, environ 3 ou 4 heures
> apres mydi ...   (p. 26)

There is one characteristic figure of classical epic which Dolet does systematically retain in the French translation — the extended simile. Of the thirteen examples of this figure in the first book of Dolet's Latin text, most are imitated from Vergil: sometimes he borrows only the theme, but occasionally he inserts entire phrases or lines from Vergil into his own poem. The most extreme example is the comparison between a wounded snake and the Swiss struggling to escape after the battle of Marignan.[13] Dolet imitates Vergil almost *verbatim*: he transcribes *Aeneid* V.273–79, changing only one word, and then adds two further lines of his own invention. Such wholesale plagiarism is unlikely to have escaped the more astute of Dolet's readers: indeed, it seems quite probable that he hoped they would recognise the source of his simile, for by incorporating Vergil neatly into his own work he might win some reflected glory. Like most of the other extended similes, it is translated into French with careful attention to detail.[14] In this instance Dolet may have expected even readers of the vernacular version to admire his extensive borrowings from the Latin poet. The retention of this essentially poetic figure in a prose chronicle is an interesting illustration of the assimilation of classical models into vernacular writing transcending the barriers of literary genres.

In many passages *Les Gestes de Françoys de Valois Roy de France* are thus an imitation, by translation, of an imitation. Yet the French version is published and indeed reprinted several times on its own. For all its literary (and historical) limitations, it breaks new ground in the development of humanist vernacular writings; refashioned in a traditional chronicle form, it still retains elements of a classical heritage. Almost a decade before the publication of Joachim Du Bellay's *Deffence et Illustration de la Langue Françoyse* Dolet demonstrates that "à un chacun sa Langue puysse competement communiquer toute doctrine"[15] — even when the translation must bridge the gap between a neo-Latin epic poem and a chronicle in French prose.

St. Anne's College, Oxford

Notes

1. For details of first and subsequent editions of both the Latin and French versions see C. Longeon, *Bibliographie des Œuvres d'Etienne Dolet* (Geneva, Droz, 1980), pp. 46–47 and pp. 75–81. All page references following quotations in this article refer to the 1539 edition of the Latin text and the 1540 edition of the French text.

2. C. Longeon, "Etienne Dolet historien," to appear in the *Mémorial Franco Simone*. I am indebted to Professor Longeon for kindly allowing me to consult his article before it appears in published form.

3. See especially S. Doletus, *De Imitatione Ciceroniana* (Lugduni, S. Gryphius, 1535).

4. "Alterum meum in eloquentia Latina deum (nam Ciceronem omnibus antepono) Pub. Vergilium Maronem typis nunc meis excudo," Vergilius Maro, *Opera* (Lugduni, S. Doletus, 1540).

5. *La Maniere de Bien Traduire d'une Langue en Aultre D'advantage. De la punctuation de la langue Francoyse. Plus. Des accents d'ycelle* (Lyons, E. Dolet, 1540).

6. In his study, *The Historical Epic in France 1500–1700* (Oxford University Press, 1973), D. Maskell proposes three broad categories of historical epic poems in this period: annalistic (a sequence of events relating to one person or nation), heroic (following for the most part the career of a single hero) and romanesque (the variety of material precluding any strict unity of action). Clearly Dolet's work would fall into the "heroic" category.

7. Dolet's use of this source will be discussed in the forthcoming article by C. Longeon, see note 2.

8. See C. M. Scollen, "Octavien de Saint-Gelais' Translation of the *Aeneid*: Poetry or Propaganda?" *BHR*, 39 (1977), 253ff.

9. Dolet composed a prefatory epistle and poem addressed to the king for both the Latin and French versions. He spoke of his desire to serve the French nation by recording the deeds of Francis I for posterity, and hoped that his work would please the king:

> Fuit illud meum semper institutum, Rex regum re omni praestantissime, fuit istem meorum mihi studiorum iam inde usque ab adolescentia propositus omnino fructus, ut, quam eloquentiae facultatem tum ingenii felicitate, tum assiduo, diuturnoque labore aliquando consequerer, eam omnem in Gallia illustranda consumerem, perficeremque mea tandem industria, ut, quantis virtutibus excellas, nationes omnes cognoscerent: neque in posterum reticeretur, tanta diligentia, tanta prudentia à te administratam Galliam, tanta animi altitudine toties ab hostium impetu defensam.
>
> (p. 3)

10.   Est Fatum divina propago Iovis, bona quaeque,
            Vel mala concilians, pro sollicitante Deorum
            Imperio Humani haec subeunt, tolerantque coacti
            Ordine perpetuo rerum: quo nomine recte
            Fata voces: Fata est rerum immutabilis ordo.   (p. 9)

11. Admittedly, in the Latin text "Fatum" is referred to as "divina propago Iovis" (p. 9), but this reference to Jupiter seems no more than a figurative expression of supreme divine power. This argument is borne out by the French translation, "Destinée est une fille de Dieu omnipotent" (p. 14), which could be interpreted as a reconciliation of Christian and pagan terminology.

12. *Francisci Valesii Gallorum Regis Fata*, p. 29, and *Les Gestes de Françoys de Valois Roy de France*, p. 43.

13.   Qualis saepe viae depraensus in aggere Serpens,
               Aerea quem obliquum rota transiit: aut gravis ictu
               Seminecem liquit saxo, lacerumque viator:
               Nequicquam longos pugnans dat corpore tortus,
               Parte ferox, ardensque oculis: et sibila colla
               Arduus attollens: pars vulnera clauda retentat
               Nexantem nodis, seque in sua membra plicantem:
               Sensim utcunque tamen latebris allabitur imis
               Effugiens hostem, saxis qui fervidus instat.   (p. 23)

14. En la sorte qu'ung Serpent se trouvant au chemin, si quelcque charrete luy
    passe par dessus: ou si quelcque voiageur le persecute de coups de pied, et
    le laisse demy mort, bien en vain allors il commence de se contourner, ouvrir
    ses yeulx ardantz plus que devant, et siffler a toute oultrance, haulsant le col
    plus que de mesure. La partie blessée retarde son effort: et a la fin est con-
    trainct tellement quellement trouver refuge en son pertuis, et eviter l'instance
    du voiageur.   (pp. 32–33)

15. J. Du Bellay, *La Deffence et Illustration de la Langue Françoyse* (Paris, 1549), I, x.

GREAT BRITAIN

Humanism and Politics in English Royal Biography: The Use of Cicero, Plutarch and Sallust in the *Vita Henrici Quinti* (1438) by Titus Livius de Frulovisi and the *Vita Henrici Septimi* (1500–1503) by Bernard André

C. W. T. Blackwell

Although it has been generally recognized that rhetoric transformed the writing of history between the fourteenth and sixteenth centuries, how it came to inform the material of history is less understood than one might expect. Two works examine the question in some detail, Kessler's book on Petrarch's *De viribus illustribus* and Black's article on Accolti.[1] The two biographies studied here used rhetoric in very different ways and illustrate two periods in humanist imitation of classical historians. Although the authors wrote the official lives of English kings, they were foreign Humanists specifically hired for the task; nevertheless their works have been major sources for historians of the reigns of Henry V and Henry VII. How their information should be evaluated has been a question about which there has been some debate and no answers. By attempting to identify some classical sources and how each historian used these sources perhaps the genre of each Humanist can be better understood and the historical material within the biographies can be identified. Titus Livius de Frulovisi wrote when the translations of Plutarch's *Lives* was still in progress[2] and when the practical application of a rhetorical humanist education was just being adapted for the education of a Prince.[3] Bernard André, over sixty years later wrote when imitation of classical historians was established and rhetorical analysis of classical texts quite common. By the end of the fifteenth century the humanist education of a prince was no longer a novelty, questions about how to adapt the techniques of an orator to the Prince had given way to questions about how to teach rhetoric and grammar to the Prince.[4]

Of the two, Titus Livius de Frulovisi of Ferrara had the better classical education. A former student of Guarino Veronese, trained in Greek as well as Latin, he studied at the University of Padua, then worked as a notary and wrote plays in imitation of Plautus and Terence in Venice until 1433.[5] It is his Ciceronian dialogue the *De Republica* (1433) and his life of Henry V, *Vita Henrici Quinti*, which will concern us here.[6] Frulovisi came to England at the suggestion of a fellow student of Guarino Veronese, Piero Del Monte who was Papal Collector.[7] Frulovisi held the post of secretary to Humphrey, Duke of Gloucester, from 1436–38, when Gloucester, the great Royal patron of Italian humanist scholarship in England, was collecting new translations of the Greek classics. In his capacity as secretary Frulovisi corresponded with Piero Candido Decembrio while Decembrio was translating Plato's *Republic* for Gloucester and with Leonardo Bruni when Bruni was dedicating his translation of Aristotle's *Politics* to Gloucester. It was at this time that Lapo da Castigionchio sent his translations of ten of Plutarch's *Lives* to Gloucester.[8]

Can it be said that Frulovisi was in any way influenced by these new translations? We do know that according to Piero Del Monte, Frulovisi read at least one of Plutarch's *Lives* but there is no evidence he read the new translations of Plato and Aristotle. The information about Frulovisi's knowledge of Plutarch comes from a letter by Del Monte in which he advised Frulovisi to imitate the behaviour of Pericles whose life Del Monte says Frulovisi had read. It can be assumed that Del Monte is referring here to the translation by Lapo da Castigionchio of Pericles's *Life* which had been sent to Gloucester two years before.[9] The letter tells us more than the fact that Frulovisi read one work of Plutarch. When Del Monte says to Frulovisi he is to endure all types of injuries patiently and should practice philosophy as Pericles had done, he is instructing Frulovisi in moral philosophy.[10] It is a truism that the genre of the life of a famous man was allied to moral philosophy. While to the best of my knowledge there is no direct evidence that Frulovisi quoted from Plutarch's *Lives* in either his plays, the *De Republica* or the *Vita*,[11] both examined the correct conduct of a prince — the *De Republica* in dialogue form and the *Vita* as a life of a famous man. The *Vita* was written not just as a piece of political propaganda for Humphrey, Duke of Gloucester's French policy but to transform Henry V into a model of the virtuous active life.[12] In its way the *Vita* imitated the way Plutarch's *Lives* were meant to be read, not the way they were written. The reason was quite simple, the way the *Lives* were written had yet to be remarked upon and therefore they could not yet be stylistically imitated.

A short digression into the history of comments about Plutarch's *Lives* between 1404 and 1444 will illustrate my point. Frulovisi's teacher, Guarino Veronese, was one of first translators of Plutarch's *Lives* to describe how a history should be written. Yet if we read his correspondence we see just how slowly Guarino came to articulate generalized statements about the *Lives* as either examples of moral philosophy or as examples of historical style. By 1416 Guarino had translated the *Lives* of Flaminius, Marcellus, Alexander, Caesar, Coriolanus, Dion, and Brutus and yet in his dedicatory letters he said little about the works themselves. In 1417 in his dedicatory letter to Carlo Zeni, Guarino began a theme which he and others developed over the century, that the life illustrates how a prudent man has acted in a virtuous way despite the vagaries of fortune.[13] In 1418 Guarino began to use the *Lives* as material for moral philosophy. In a letter to Corbinello he defends marriage on the grounds that Cato, Gracchus, Scipio, Cicero, Brutus,

Caesar, Socrates and Solon had all been able to pursue the study of philosophy despite the fact that they were married.[14] It can be assumed that since Frulovisi and Del Monte studied with Guarino during those years this is the view of Plutarch's *Lives* they would have received. It is not until 1435, when Guarino wrote a dedicatory letter to Leonello Este about his translation of *Lives* of Lysander and Sylla and his letter to Poggio that the theme of morality and style is developed further. Yet when Guarino quoted Plutarch's *Life of Alexander* on the stylistic differences between a life of a famous man and history it was not to analyse biographical style but to defend his own factual inaccuracies in his praise of the virtues of Alexander and Caesar.[15] The letter to Tobia in 1444, six years after Frulovisi started his *Vita Henrici Quinti*, does break new ground; yet even here Guarino omitted from his adaptation of Lucian's *De scribenda historica* the careful distinctions Lucian had made between panegyric and history, poetry and history and Lucian's criticism of poetic language.[16]

Thus Frulovisi can not be expected to have known Plutarch's technique of historical writing; but that does not mean that the *Vita* was constructed without care. It took oratory as its key, but oratory was only used as an organizing device in the dedicatory letter. The dedicatory letter was a model prooemium, carefully designed to make the reader or listener receptive to the *Vita* and well disposed to the author and his patron. The letter opens with a description of Frulovisi as a child in Italy learning about the exploits of the famous Henry V of England. This has the immediate effect of making the reader interested in the author of the life and has the added affect of turning Henry V into an international historical figure only twelve years after his death. Frulovisi then goes on to make Humphrey, Duke of Gloucester, into an attractive figure by likening him to Lycurgus, the famous Spartan law-giver who guarded his nephew's son's right to the throne.[17] By associating the person who commissioned the work with the just Lycurgus, Frulovisi implied that it was commissioned by a man who was not self-seeking and that the purpose for which the life was written was what he claimed; to provide the story of Henry V's life so it could serve as a model for his son, Henry VI. Factually the case was far different, the author had been hired to write the *Vita* by Gloucester to publicize the Duke's military successes in the French wars. Despite the propaganda function of the *Vita* Frulovisi did turn the character of Henry V into a model of virtue in action. Within the text the Ciceronian ideal of the orator-philosopher acting as a ruler became a dominant influence in the construction of the "persona" of Henry V.

In his Ciceronian dialogue, *De Republica*, written in 1433 Frulovisi discussed in some detail the way a Prince might use the techniques of the orator without losing his air of authority, how a Prince should administer justice and what his attitude should be toward good and bad fortune. His source was in part Cicero's *De Officiis* I.xxxv–xxxviii and I.xxv–xxvi. The discussion of how a Prince should use oratory is an adaptation of the techniques developed for the servant of the state, to the ruler of the state. Frulovisi warned that because the Prince was the

will and power of the Republic, he should be careful not to lower himself by using judicial oratory as a prince should not attack or defend anyone, nor should
he use demonstrative oratory because it was not his job to praise himself or to
attack someone else. It is conceded, however, that there are times when a Prince
must use eloquence. He should use deliberative oratory to urge his troops into
battle, and judicial oratory when faced with conspiracy.[18] Frulovisi then lists a
series of Roman leaders who used oratory in this way; the examples he chose he
took from Livy. Frulovisi in the *De Republica* makes a distinction between
deliberative oratory and "sermo." While he does not make this distinction in the
Vita, he does follow Cicero's advice that anger must be avoided at all times, even
if someone must be castigated.

If one examines when, why and how Henry V speaks, it is clear that the king's
speeches use deliberative oratory to great dramatic effect. His entry as a character
in the *Vita* is as a young prince leading soldiers against the rebellious Welsh. Hit
by an arrow he heroically demands to be carried to the front so his men will not
fear the enemy and flee.[19] After the English success at Hereflete again the king
dramatically urges his men to march through France to Calais so that they can
demonstrate to the French that they do not fear them.[20] His most famous speech
given before the Battle of Agincourt on hearing that he is badly out-numbered
was the ringing line: "Verum nollem huic exercitui meo solum virum addi."[21] His
emotional range all during this time fluctuated between absence of fear when urging
his troops into battle and absence of anger when deliberating how the enemy should
be attacked or treated after surrender.[22]

Essentially what Frulovisi did was to superimpose on the chronicle information taken from the *Brut*, oral information from Humphrey, Duke of Gloucester,
and some public records, as well as a Royal "persona" constructed with Cicero's
definition of the wise orator-philosopher in mind. In the *De Republica* Frulovisi
combined *De Officiis.I.xxv* and *I.xxvi* into one paragraph:

> Sed istud eo velim, *ut qui rei publicae praesunt leges* imitarentur *ad puniendum*,
> quae non iracundia sed aequitate ducuntur. Sapientissimeque factum
> putarem in omni fortuna, *in rebus prosperis et ad nostram* utilitatem *fluentibus*,
> si *fastidium, superbiam, arrogantiam* vitaremus; nec in *adversa* frangeremur nimis.
> Optima igitur est *aequabilitas in omni vita*, ut *idem* sit *semper vultus, eadem frons*,
> et idem animus in homine gravi et sapienti semper maneat.[23]

Although the details of Henry V's administration of the defeated French after
the battles for Harefleet, Caen and Bayeux were different, his approach was the
same. He quelled opposition when necessary, killed rebellious leaders without
hesitation when appropriate, but never used force unless he had to. After the fall
of Harefleet, he permitted those French who would be loyal subjects to come and
go as they pleased and he supervised the equitable distribution of booty among
his own troops after the battle.[24] Caen had been more rebellious and received
harsher treatment, Bayeux, because it yielded to the English without a battle,

was immediately given fair civil law and just government.[25] The church property was scrupulously guarded throughout the campaign.[26] The king was as controlled in his reactions to victory as he was to battle. After his great defeat of the French at Agincourt, he returned to England and made a magnificent victory progress first in London and then throughout the country. According to Frulovisi, he refused to have any praises sung to his name; God alone, he claimed, was to be credited with the English victory. However, his refusal to wear battle scarred armour in his royal triumphs seems a gesture of ostentatious modesty.[27] He truly followed Frulovisi's description of a just prince "ut qui rei publicae praesunt leges imitarentur ad puniendum, quae non iracundia set aequitate ducuntur." It is a bit ironic that this most English of English kings should have begun his strut upon the stage of history as a character constructed out of Cicero's *De Officiis* in a biography written by an Italian Humanist.

The way classical historians were read and imitated changed considerably between 1438 when Frulovisi wrote his *Vita Henrici Quinti* and 1500–03 when Bernard André wrote his *Vita Henrici Septimi*. While this is not the place to rehearse the history of the recovery and translation of Greek historians during the fifteenth century or the growing interest in the writing style Latin classical historians, one Humanist and his comments on one key Roman historian must be remarked upon. The Humanist is Lorenzo Valla and the historian on whom he wrote a commentary is Sallust. Sallust was a model for historical style to Bernard André, as he was for many others in the fifteenth century. Although there is no direct evidence that André read Valla's commentary, their approaches to style are so similar it is striking. They both saw Sallust's prooemium as a locus for historical style, they described the prooemium in rhetorical terms which focused on the orator-historian, they emphasized Sallust's "brevitas" and they both were interested in the correct stylistic use of digressions.[28]

The rhetorical approach to history is signalled by Valla's opening comment which paraphrases Quintilian x.1.101–2:

> At non historia cesserit Graecis, nec opponere Thucydidi Sallustium verear, neque indignetur sibi Herodotus aequari T. Livium, cum in narrando mirae iucunditatis clarissimique candoris, tum in contionibus supra quam enarrari potest eloquentem; ita quae dicuntur omnia cum rebus tum personis accommodta sunt; adfectus quidem, praecipueque eos qui sunt dulciores, ut parcissime dicam, nemo historicorum commendavit magis.[29]

Valla underlines the function of the prooemium by saying:

> At mihi quidem: nunc captat benevolentiam ab incommodis suis. Nam, ut ait Cicero, a nostra persona benevolentiam colligimus, si nostra incommoda proferemus.[30]

About Sallust's "brevitas" Valla comments:

Absoluam paucis: Historiam Catilinae perficiam paucis verbis et attentionem captat ab auditoribus, quia dicit breviter se historiam Catilinae esse peracturum et de re magna et ingenti dicturum: exponit etiam, quibus de rebus dicturus sit.[31]

Finally to explain the function of the digression within an historical narration Valla used the terminology of Cicero's discussion of the three types of "narratio."

Sicut apud Ciceronem est, tria sunt genera narrationum de quibus orator sumit rationem suae causae: primum oratorium quo oratores utuntur vincendi causa secundum, digressorium, tertium, poeticum. Sed digressorio secundo genere narrationis utitur Salustius quod intercurrit non nunquam aut fidei, aut criminationis, aut laudationis, aut alicuius apparationis causa. Nam digreditur Salustius ab historia quam superius coeperat, ad seditionem scilicet Catilinae et ad mores civitatis narrandos pervenit. Fit autem haec digressio, laudationis, vituperationis, et apparationis causa. Laudationis ut maiores et priscos illos laudibus exornet, qui rem publicae non conservarunt modo moribus optimis, verum etiam conservatam auxerunt. Vituperationis causa, ut homines aetatis suae vituperet, qui non virtutibus sed malis moribus dediti sunt, et rem publicam a maioribus stabilitam ac firmatam labi et ad interitum pervenire patiantur. Apparationis causa fit, ut se praeparet ad id quod dicturus est. Nam de corruptione civitatis et ab initio urbis Romae narrare incipit, quomodo populus Romae se domi militaeque habuerit et in praesenti habeat. Ut his cognitiis, versisimile fiat, in tanta morum corruptione animum ad rempublicum capiundam intendisse Catilinam.[32]

The history of the influence of this commentary has yet to be written; it was first printed in 1492 and printed in Paris in 1497. Stylist descriptions of history writing was common during the 1490's in Paris, influenced either directly or indirectly by Italian humanist teaching. Filipo Beroaldo's inaugural lectures to his courses at the University of Bologna were edited in Lyons by his student, Jodocus Badius Ascensius in 1492.[33] A careful reading of Erasmus's prefatory letter (1495) to Robert Gaguin's history, *De origine et gestis francorum* reveals that Erasmus described the work using rhetorical terminology. Style, not factual objectivity, was the standard by which Gaguin is judged. The character of the historian, not his historical methodology, is the subject of a long description. The orator in the prooemium becomes a "vir bonus," a truthful reporter.[34]

In the *Vita Henrici Septimi* the historian-orator becomes a personality in the history itself commenting on the action, on his own knowledge of the historical incidents and on his writing style. It is not the first time an historian intruded himself/herself into the text of a work, but it is one which does so following the stylistic forms taken from Sallust. The tone is set in the prooemium. At first glance this seems a mere compilation of quotations; and so it is. But the quotations are selected and modified in such a way as to indicate that André selected them with care.

The first quotation identified the genre, the life of a famous man, the second ties fame with being written about by a famous author, the third testifies to the authority of Sallust as an historian and the last quotes Sallust, selectively, to establish how history should be written. The quotations are familiar ones. André begins with Plutarch's comment on the difference between a life of a famous man and a history. Unlike the time Guarino used the quotation, this time the quotation is clearly selected to establish the genre of the work.[35] André then quotes from Cicero's *Pro Archia* x.24 on Alexander's comments on fame when he passed the tomb of Achilles. Citing Augustine on the superiority of Sallust as an historian, André then quotes from Sallust's prooemium on how to write history. First he quotes the passage on how difficult it is to write believable history and then the passage in which Sallust described his attitude of mind when writing the history and his style. André amended this to say that he would select those incidents which occur to his mind without any instruction which seem worthy of record. His mind will be free; he omits Sallust's comments that it will be free from hope, and fear and partisanship. André had established earlier that he is writing the praise of the king. André, like Sallust states that they will write as "verissime" and "paucis" as they can.[36]

Thus André introduced the *Vita* with an adaptation of Sallust's prooemium and then carefully wrote the body of the work as if it were an orator's "narratio." There was nothing new in thinking of the body of an historical text as rhetorical "narratio;" Guarino, Valla and Erasmas had already done so. It must be remembered that the "narratio" had three qualities: "brevis," "dilucide" and "veri similis." It is the concept of "veri similis" which has caused so much difficulty, for it is not always clear to the contemporary reader of a Renaissance text when "veri similis" is being used and when the "truth" is being described. To write with verisimilitude, as Black has pointed out, does not mean that the author's goal is to write objective truth, as a nineteenth- and twentieth-century historian would conceive of it, rather that the historian's goal was to write something convincing and believable.[37] The *Vita* is replete with dialogues which are written as "verisimilitude." Henry VI is given a saintly oration on fate,[38] Richard III the necessary evil oration illustrating his immoral motives for retaining the crown,[39] and Henry Richmond, the appropriate speech which denied any personal ambition for his attempt to overthrow Richard III at Bosworth Field, like Henry V he placed his possible success in the hands of God.[40] Historians to this day debate the possibility these scenes might or might not be accurate, they debate the historical truth of the recognition scene in which Henry VI prophesies the accession of Henry Richmond to the throne and the dialogue between Margaret Beaufort and the Duke of Pembroke over the safety of the young Henry Richmond. The Henry VI scene echoes a similar scene in the *Vita Henry Quinti* in which Richard II prophesies the accession of Henry V,[41] the second underlines the importance of Margaret Richmond to the accession of her son and her power at court during his reign.[42] What we have here is "verisimilitude." Exactly how and when Renaissance historians distinguished between objective truth and "verisimilitude" needs a good deal of study. For André the characterization of leading historical figures and the illustration of their motives for acting in a particular way at a particular time in history seems to be based on a pre-established ethic. This ethic is the one which should have governed their behaviour if one were to take a particular apologists point of view. Here it is to defend the usurpation of Henry VII.

If "verisimilitude" governed the orations and dialogues in the *Vita* "brevitas" governed André's writing style. From the first page of the *Vita* he points to his own use of it. In his description of the king's descent from the early kings of Britain he says:

> Atque, ut sui genitoris ab antiquis Britannis regibus descensum breviter attingam, Sancti Cadvaladri, cui post longa temporum intervalla idem Henricus legitime successit, et Cadvalonis praefati Cadvaladri genitoris, si pauca de multis illorum praeclarissimis gestis attigero, priores Britonum reges, ne historiae modum excedam, a quibus idem rex originem duxit, praesens in tempus omittam.[43]

He jumps elegantly from the Saxon kings to the Yorkist reign on the next page to leave plenty of space of the genealogy of Margaret Beaufort, through whom Henry VII claimed the throne.[44] He combines "brevitas" with his pose of the "vir bonus" when he says he will not write of the Battle of Bosworth.[45]

"Brevitas" and selection of facts suitable to the writing of a famous man's life were complementary. André reminds the reader that because he is writing a life and not a history he will not write events in order.[46] André also uses "brevitas" in part to have room for a digression or two. The dramatic and moral center of the *Vita* is a digression in which André comments on the death of the saintly Henry VI.

This section includes a paragraph in which the author exclaims to God about the cruel death of Henry VI in a section André named: "Auctoris lacrymosa exclamatio."[47]

The story of how rhetorical terms were understood and how they infused historical works is a long and complex one. The evidence presented here is just one part of the story. It might seem that since these biographies are so highly rhetorical that there is nothing of historical worth in them. It is not the intention of this article to imply that. Rather it is hoped that when the intentions of the biographers are better understood and the genre of the works examined it will be possible to know what type of evidence a reader can expect to find in them. Thinking historically (objectively) was never the aim of Renaissance biographers. For those writing for Royal patrons their necessary bias is obvious. However, these works do have much to tell us about the courts of the time, the way of recording activities, the difficulties of characterization, as well as the style in which people wished to be remembered.

Notes

1. E. Kessler, *Petrarca und die Geschichte* (Munich, 1978), pp. 19-33 and R. Black, "Benedetto Accolti and the Beginnings of Humanist Historiography," *EHR*, 96 (1981), pp. 36-57.

2. For Humphrey, Duke of Gloucester's translations of Plutarch's *Lives* see: A. Sammut, *Unfredo duca di Gloucester e gli umanisti italiani* (Padua, 1980); V. R. Giustiniani, "Sulle traduzioni latine delle ((Vite)) de Plutarco nel Quattrocento," *Rin.*, s. II, 1 (1961), pp. 3-62; see also n. 8.

3. Titus Livius de Frulovisi had a program for the education of a prince although we have no evidence that he ever used it for teaching. See: *De Republica, Opera hactenus inedita*, ed. C. W. Previté Orton (Cambridge, 1932), pp. 352-53.

4. For André see: G. Tournoy, "Two Poems written by Erasmus for Bernard André," *HL*, 27 (1978), pp. 45-51; also see my forthcoming article in *HL*, "Humanism in England, 1495-1500, Bernard André, Giovanni Tortelli, Cristoforo Landino and Pico della Mirandola."

5. For Frulovisi see: R. Sabbadini, "Tito Livio Frulovisi umanista de sec. xv," *GSLI*, 103 (1934), pp. 55-81.

6. The *De Republica* was in Humphrey, Duke of Gloucester's collection, Sammut, (n. 2), p. 81 and first printed by Previté Orton in 1932 (n. 2). The *Vita Henrici Quinti* was first printed by T. Hearne (Oxford, 1717).

7. For Piero Del Monte see: *Piero da Monte: ein Gelehrter und Apostlicher Beamter des 15. Jahrhunderts, seine Briefsammlung*, ed. J. Haller (Rome, 1941) reprint (Turin, 1971). Haller does not reprint Del Monte's two letters to Frulovisi printed by Sabbadini.

8. These seem to be the first translations of Plutarch's *Lives* to reach Humphrey, Duke of Gloucester. Antonio Pacini did not dedicate his translation of the *Life of Marius* before 1437, Antonio Beccaria dedicated his translation of the *Life of Romulus* between 1438 and 1443, the Duke of Gloucester also owned Bruni's translation of the *Life of Marcus Antonius*, see Sammut (n. 2) pp. 28, 21-22, 14. On Decembrio and Plutarch see Sammut (n. 2), pp. 37-38. For the introduction of Plutarch translation in the late fourteenth century, see A. Luttrell, "Coluccio Salutati's Letter to Juan Fernandez de Heredia," *IMU*, 13 (1970), pp. 235-43.

9. Sammut (n. 2), p. 170.

10. Sabbadini (n. 5), pp. 76-77.

11. *Vita Henrici Quinti* (n. 6), p. 2.

12. The classical allusions in the *De Republica* come from Cicero, Livy, Plautus Terence and Walter Burley's *De vita et moribus philosophorum*.

13. *Epistolario de Guarino Veronese*, ed. R. Sabbadini (Venice, 1915), I, 136-38.

14. Guarino (n. 13), I, 214.

15. ibid.

16. This important letter has yet to be analyzed in detail either for Guarino's translation of the Greek text and for the transformation of Lucian. Although Guarino does quote Cicero's *de or.* II.62: "... primam historiae legem esse ne quid falsi audeat dicere, ne qua suspicio gratiae sit in scribendo, ne qua simultatis," his reworking of Lucian's criticism of poetry introduces the term "versimilis" which does not mean truth. He says "Haec enim vel intempestive laudare et plusquam verisimilia licenter (profere) profitetur et alatos equos effingere et in deos mortales vertere nil veretur." For Guarino history was moral philosophy: "Primus namque historiae finis et unica est intentio utilitas, scilicet quae ex ipsius veritatis

professione colligitur, unde animus ex praeteritorum notitia scientior fiat ad agendum et ad virtutem gloriamque imitatione consequendam inflammatior aliaque huiuscemodi ...” Guarino (n. 13), II, 461–62.

17. *De Republica* (n. 3), p. 339.

18. *De Republica* (n. 3), p. 329.

19. “ ‘Quonam,’ inquit, ‘animo reliqui pugnabunt si me principem, regis filium pavore cedentem ex acie videbunt? Ducite me sic vulneratum ad primos, ut ego commitiones nostros non verbo, sed factis ut principem decet accebdam.’ ” *Vita Henrici Quinti* (n. 6), p. 3.

20. “Non minimum ... laude maxime triumphantes.” *Vita Henrici Quinti* (n. 6), p. 12.

21. *Vita Henrici Quinti* (n. 6), p. 12.

22. Sometimes Henry V’s attitude toward fear is transmitted in speeches to his troops. His reaction to the French delegation is a classic Stoic response, as is his response to the surrender of Rouen. *Vita Henrici Quinti* (n. 6), pp. 23, 14, 67.

23. *Off.* I xxv and xxi, cf. *Vita Henrici Quinti* (n. 6) pp. 14, 23, 67.

24. *Vita Henrici Quinti* (n. 6), p. 11.

25. *Vita Henrici Quinti* (n. 6), p. 40.

26. *Vita Henrici Quinti* (n. 6), p. 00.

27. *Vita Henrici Quinti* (n. 6), pp. 22–23.

28. Sallust, *Bellum Catalinum*, cum commentio L. Valli (Venice, 1492), sig. a ii.

29. Valla (n. 28), sig. a iii[r].

30. Valla (n. 28), sig. a iii[v].

31. Valla (n. 28), sig. a iv[r].

32. ibid.

33. Filipo Beroaldo, *Orationes*, ed. B. Ascensius (Lyon, 1492). The comments on Livy can be found in “In enarratione Titi Livii ac Silii italici continens historiae laudationem,” sigs. b ii[r]-b v[r], Sallust in “In enarratione Iuvanalis atque Salustii,” sigs. c iii[v]-c v[r].

34. The way an orator might win the good will of his listeners was discussed in *Auct. ad Her* I.iv.8. Quint. was explicit see IV.1.6-7. Here Quintilian emphasized that an orator must not only secure the general good will of the audience but give the appearance of a “vir bonus.” For Erasmus on Gaguin see: Erasmus, *Opus Epistolarum*, ed. P. S. Allen (Oxford, 1906), I, 149-52.

35. Bernard André, *Vita Henrici Septimi*, ed. James Gairdner, *Memorials of Henry the Seventh*, Rolls Series 10, (London, 1858), p. 6.

36. André (n. 35), pp. 7-9. André makes the same association between Augustine and Sallust as does Beroaldus (n. 33), sig. c v[r].

37. *Auct. ad Her.* I.viii.13, cf. Black (n. 1), Erasmus (n. 34), pp. 00-00, Valla (n. 31).

38. *Vita Henrici Septimi* (n. 35), pp. 25-26. “Haec est illa dies, misericordissime....”

39. *Vita Henrici Septimi* (n. 35), pp. 30-31. “Non ferro, non igne ...”

40. *Vita Henrici Septimi* (n. 35), pp. 14, 16.

41. *Vita Henrici Septimi* (n. 35), p. 14, cf. *Vita Henrici Quinti* (n. 6), p. 3.

42. *Vita Henrici Septimi* (n. 35), pp. 15-16.

43. *Vita Henrici Septimi* (n. 35), p. 9.

44. *Vita Henrici Septimi* (n. 35), p. 11.

45. *Vita Henrici Septimi* (n. 35), p. 32. André gives this the subtitle: “Auctoris excusatio.”

46. *Vita Henrici Septimi* (n. 35), p. 19.

47. *Vita Henrici Septimi* (n. 35), pp. 20-23.

Fuitne Thomas Morus in Aulam Pertractus?

Germain Marc'hadour

Few statements of Erasmus have been so often bandied about as the one asserting, nay assuming and almost taking for granted, that his friend Thomas More had allowed himself to be dragged into Henry VIII's court. In the verb he uses, *pertraho*, the suffix of intensity suggests some violence. An old Calepinus defines it as "To drawe by force, to trayle by the ground." Now, a number of modern historians, especially G. R. Elton and John Guy,[1] contend that, far from dragging his feet against a mighty suction from the center of Tudor power, More was all too willing, indeed rather eager to enter royal service. A closer look at the text and context of Erasmus's statement can, I believe, yield a balanced estimate both of what happened when More, over the years 1517 and 1518, resigned his post of Undersheriff to become a full-time *aulicus*, and of what impression Erasmus made on his correspondents when he used the terms *pertrahere, pertractus*.

Our major document is Erasmus's letter of 23 July 1519 to the German Humanist Ulrich von Hutten, published in the *Farrago nova epistolarum Erasmi* (Basle, Froben, October 1519, pp. 329ff.), and carefully retouched for inclusion in subsequent volumes of Erasmus's correspondence (1521, 1529). In the first *Vita Mori* which this epistle truly is, Hutten, who had been harsh on kings' courts in *Aula Dialogus* (1518), is told that More too had "formerly been rather disinclined to a Court life and to any intimacy with princes,"[2] so much so that even into such a court as Henry VIII's "he could not be dragged without much ado: nec in Henrici octaui aulam pertrahi potuit, nisi multo negocio" (ibid., line 91). The keyword recurs three times in the letter. After describing More's performance of his duties "as judge in civil causes" at City level (Under-Sheriff, 1510–18), Erasmus writes:

> He had made up his mind to be contented with this position, which was sufficiently dignified without being exposed to serious dangers. He was twice thrust into embassies ("semel atque iterum extrusus est in legationem," ibid.,

p. 20/215), and he evinced such extreme shrewdness in the discharge of the job that Henry VIII would not rest until he had dragged the man into his Court ("non conquievit ... donec hominem in aulam suam pertraheret," ibid., p. 20/216). Why should I not say, indeed, "dragged"? No one was ever more ambitious of being admitted into Court than this man was anxious to escape it.[3]

Towards the end of the letter, the word is repeated in such a way that More's reluctance to hold political office looks less exceptional and appears to be a normal stance with Humanists, whose hearts are naturally in their books:

> Such are the men whom a most shrewd king not only admits, but rather invites into his household, and into his very chamber; nor does he merely invite them, he even drags them ("nec inuitat modo verumetiam pertrahit," p. 22/777).

Thus More is not alone in dragging his feet while the sovereign tugs at him: we reckon that a measure of half-heartedness was expected of and expressed by everyone of England's educated courtiers whose names Erasmus lists at the end of this same letter: Mountjoy, Linacre, Pace, Colet, Stokesley, Latimer, Tunstal and Clerk. (Of these eight, Mountjoy alone is a layman.)

To broaden our field of inquiry, and discover the key to Erasmus's insistent repetition of this *pertractio*, we might begin at A. D. 1517, the year in which More seems to have made up his mind about royal service. Dedicating his *Complaint of Peace* to Bishop Philip of Burgundy, who was himself the holder of high office in secular government, Erasmus wrote:

> Plato, vir exquisitissimi planeque diuini iudicii, non alios existimat ad rempublicam gerendam idoneos quam eos qui huc nolentes pertrahuntur (Allen 3, ep. 603, p. 15/7) (Plato reckons nobody fit to rule a body politic save those who are dragged to it against their wills.)[4]

Plato's view was in full consonance with the philosophy and spirituality of medieval Christendom. Since More belonged to Lincoln's Inn first as student, then as teacher and administrator, I'll take an example from the life of St. Hugh, bishop of Lincoln (and Henry II's "friend"), after whom the district and the Inn were named. While Hugues d'Avalon was undergoing his monastic formation in the Grande Chartreuse, the abbot asked him how he felt about Holy Orders. The young man answered he would love to be ordained, and received this stern rebuke: "How often you have read that he who does not receive the priesthood unwillingly receives it unworthily!" This posture of humble recoiling from any lofty post of responsibility was so axiomatic that a bishop-elect was enjoined by the rubrics of the ordination ritual to utter a double *no* before yielding to his ready consecrators, although it was no secret to anybody that he had already paid for the pope's bulls. More's indulgent laugh at this *Nolo episcopari* scene constitutes an aside to the comedy played by "the Protector" when he pretended to be forced to the throne by the Londoners' "great shout, crying King Richard King Richard!" More's ox-ymorons: "compelled thereunto by his own will," and "nolentem velle,"[5] written precisely at the period of his own decision-making, are illuminating, and invite us to see nothing incompatible between his acceptance to "play at kings' games ... for the more part played uppon scaffolds" (as he says in the same paragraph) and his determination to "make a part of his own."[6]

Was More's demurring, then, a sacrifice to convention, a pose which did not even care to deceive, an avowed piece of make-believe? He was a gleeful feigner, when it came to literature, a "poet" as several of his enemies said in order to discredit his theology by referring or alluding to his *Utopia*.[7] I think we have abundant evidence of the sincerity of his reluctance, and I will adduce some after a further look at the occurrences of *pertraho* in the Latin writings of his own circle during the early years of his political career. His *Utopia* uses the verb at least three times.[8] In Book I, a counsellor of Francis I recommends that some members of the rival court "be drawn to the French alliance by a fixed pension: in suam fac-tionem certa pensione esse pertrahendos" (p. 88/10). The baits of France are "fair words and sweet promises" according to Henry VIII's complaints, quoted by Father Surtz, who sticks to the rather mild rendering *drawn* in the other instances. Thus, in Book II, where Raphaël Hythlodaeus reports on the eudemonism of his islanders, he says that in their view man's aim on earth is *bona, honesta felicitas,* to which "our nature is drawn by virtue itself: naturam nostram ab ipsa uirtute pertrahi" (p. 162/18). One can, I suppose, imagine nature recoiling from that hap-piness out of some perversity resulting from original sin or from a wrong educa-tion. In the book's last and longest chapter, "De religionibus Utopiensium," we learn of the Utopians' conviction that only a glad death is a good death, because "God will not be pleased with the coming of one who, when summoned, does not gladly hasten to obey but is reluctantly dragged against his will: inuitus ac detrectans pertrahitur" (p. 222/26).

Where Surtz uses *drawn* to render *pertractus*, R. A. B. Mynors and D. F. S. Thomson, in *The Correspondence of Erasmus*, twice show More "being haled to court" (*CWE* 5, 829/6 and 832/38): no pretence can be suspected in these two letters of April 1518, because Erasmus is writing to More himself and to Cuthbert Tunstal, More's closest friend at court. His only comfort at "poor More's bad luck" is that, with such a king served by so many educated ministers, the Court of England is "more a shrine of the Muses than a court" (Allen 3, p. 295/4 and p. 303/35). The *Mouseion* phrase Erasmus repeated in a letter of 26 July 1518 to Paolo Bombasio—another *humaniste engagé*—, adding for good measure: "quas tu Athenas, quam Stoam, aut quod Lyceum eiusmodi praetuleris aulae?" (Allen 3, p. 357/46).

On 13 Nov. 1518, Johann Froben dedicated to More, the budding councillor, the Basle edition of Hutten's *Aula*, using terms that were no doubt inspired and perhaps directly prompted by Erasmus: "quoniam nuper Musis suam vicem in-consolabiliter dolentibus in aulam inuictissimi Regis tui pertractus es."[9]

May I take you now to France, where More's opposite number was Guillaume

Budé, also a married man, also drawn into his king's household. Budé's grumpy character made him express his reluctance in louder terms than More would ever use. We find Erasmus, in August 1519, reasoning away the Parisian's qualms: There is no danger lest you be suspected of base ambition; you are a gentleman with a coat of arms, you are well-to-do, you are a literary celebrity, and it has taken some tugging to get you into Court, and the quality of that court too makes a world of difference ("in aulam es cooptatus ... Permagni refert in quam aulam immigres ... Tu et clarus imaginibus et re lauta et literarum stemmatis nobilissi- mus, nec venis nisi rogatus ac pertractus," Allen 4, p. 30/127–145). More en- dorses this view in a 1520 letter to Budé "nunc in Christianissimi Regis negocia pertracto."[10]

Erasmus, though a jealous lover of his own freedom, was not proof against be- ing drawn or dragged. Believe him or not, what with an element of Wanderlust, what with the foretaste of England given him in Paris by Thomas Grey and other British students, what with the persuasive power of young William Blount, fu- ture Baron Mountjoy, the temptation to cross the Channel in the summer of 1499 proved irresistible: "tandem a Guilhelmo Montioio discipulo pertractus in An- gliam" (Allen 11, p. 177/200). And ten years later, a similar pull from England wrenched him from a Rome he had meant to make his home, "nisi promissis aureis in Angliam fuissem retractus verius quam revocatus ... Aegre et inuitus reliqui Italiam" (ibid., p. 177/207, 227). During Erasmus's first visit, More, still a stu- dent, took him for a stroll to the Eltham residence of Henry VII's children: "Per- traxerat me Thomas Morus ... vt animi causa in proximum vicum expatiaremur" (Allen 1, p. 6/9). If the word were to carry tyrannic connotations, we should thus find the earliest Maecenas of Erasmus and his truest friend among the accused; and he would accuse himself of violence where he proudly recalls the 150 florins he forced upon Johann Froben: "compulsus est a me accipere florenos...," magnopere reluctans ... sed tamen compulsus est" (ibid., p. 45/21).[11] Why do so many assume that Erasmus fully disapproved and bitterly More's entangle- ment in the aulic net? Erasmus himself had accepted Chancellor Le Sauvage's invitation to become Counsellor of Charles.[12] Though he was careful to safeguard his freedom, he had not sided with Raphaël Hythlodaeus's *philosophia scholastica* against More's *philosophia civilior* (*Utopia, CW* 4, p. 98/6f.). In 1519 he urged Hut- ten to imitate More the courtier (Allen 4, p. 22/285), and Budé not to turn his back on the marvellous opportunities offered by a position of honour and influ- ence: "Dabit hoc aulae dignitas, vt nunc magis prodesse queas honestissimis stu- diis ... An tu mediocre praesidium existimas paratum nostris studiis posteaquam Morus et Ricardus Pacaeus regio famulitio sunt asscripti?" (ibid., p. 40/130f.). An enlightened court is intellectually more stimulating than college life; it prods one to cultivate the Muses: "calcar additum ad culturam Musarum"; to such a court Erasmus would go in person (ibid., p. 40/141f.). Not that all scholars should grace royal households, but the corporation needs a number of representatives in them, he says to P. Zutpenius: "Omnibus itaque qui studiorum sacra colunt, expedit tui similes aliquot in aulis versari" (ibid., p. 41/24f.).

More's own attitude to political involvement appears clearly in his letter of February 1516 to Erasmus (Allen 2, ep. 388). Warham, he writes, has at last been allowed to resign the burden of the chancellorship (p. 195/86); Tunstal, after only ten days squandered on a bothersome, disgusting review of all the details of his mission, is being shoved back again (*retruditur*) on another embassy, much against his will "idque ... inuitissimus" (p. 196/102f.).[13]

Eighteen months later, at the close of his own second embassy, More wrote to Erasmus:

> I am sure you are right to wish not to become immersed in the busy nothings of princes, and you show your affection for me in hoping that I may be released from them; for you cannot believe how unwillingly I spend my time on them, nor could anything be more tedious than my present mission.[14]

Yet, the king's service also meant judiciary and administrative functions at home, and in September 1521, when More had risen to Under-Treasurer, Erasmus felt proud, and gave full credit to his friend's judgment and foresight: "Sicut in caeteris omnibus, plus vidit Morus quam ego" (Allen 4, p. 584/37).

Marcantoine Muret, in a letter quoted by Malcolm Smith, explained his acceptance of a post in Rome by saying: "the pope's invitation is not as easily turned down as that of bishops." John Guy, in his *The Public Career of Sir Thomas More*, writes that "royal recruitment of outstanding lawyers was by command rather than invitation" (pp. 7–8), adding that, for the author of *Utopia*, a call from above, from the Lord's anointed, "should be heeded on grounds of public duty and moral responsibility" (p. 11).

More, as a classical scholar, had pondered the precedent set by Cicero and Seneca; as a committed Christian, he took the parable of talents seriously; with "an holy ambition," he was prepared "gladly to bear his purgatory here"[15] through a measure of self-sacrifice for the public weal. Erasmus, for all his regret whenever a *felix ingenium* is lost to literature — *litteris ademptus* (Allen 3, p. 295/4) — exhorts several scholars, if not to seek, at least not to dodge princely favor: office gives them a long arm for the defense and promotion of culture, and demonstrates to the budding intelligentsia of Christendom that *bonae litterae* are not synonymous with beggary.

More's first taste, almost foretaste, of royal service came through embassies which, to this lover of home, resembled exile. In 1515 he needed all the charm and affection of Peter Gillis to assuage the keen nostalgia that threatened his composure and serenity: *patriae desiderium, ac laris domestici* (*CW* 4, pp. 48–49). In 1517 he went to Calais with utter loathing for the kind of work that awaited him; paradoxically, it was Erasmus who expressed delight at the prospect that More would soon be on the Continent, "with us" (Allen 3, ep. 637 and 643). In letters to old friends like Tunstal and John Fisher, his fellow crewmen on the same ship of state, with no temptation of posing as a Stoic philosopher to edify posterity,

More writes: "Much against my will did I come to court, as everyone knows, and as the king himself in joke often throws up in my face," adding that his master's daily progress in learning and virtue makes his service less and less uncongenial.[16]

Erasmus, More's shrewdest observer, dedicating an edition of Aristotle to More's son and heir, in a preface which was for all the world to read, including More's peers, and his enemies (and he had many by 1531), construed More's acceptance of England's Chancellorship in terms which, had he not known them to be true, would have been cruelly ironic: "Quod [munus], nisi prorsus ignoro naturam illius, perlubenter recusatus erat, si vel phas iudicaret vsquam non morem gerere Regis optimi voluntati, vel pium existimaret patriae concordibus suffragiis ac publica voce huc vocanti pernegare obsequium" (Allen 9, p. 140/315f.). The two motives are clearly hinged on the words *fas* and *pium*: a sacred duty not to say no to one's natural lord, and not to ignore a wide consensus of the nation. Though allowance should be made for the voice of friendship, what historian of today can claim a better knowledge of the man and the circumstances?

I think one can safely conclude that More's enlistment by Wolsey and Henry implied no undue pressure, no bullying, only lots of friendly persuasion, with perhaps a promise not to infringe overmuch on his freedom, and with at any rate a pledge never to violate his conscience: this we know from his later concern to remind the king of it. Much as he had yielded to paternal pressure when first taking to the study of common law and had come to terms with a profession rich in personalities and in opportunities, he allowed himself to be included in the cast that was to perform kings' games, "for the most part played upon scaffolds," although "the wise" won't "step up and play with them" (*CW* 3, p. 81). For his compliance, and more so for the limits he put to it, he knew he would be reckoned "among the fools, and so reckon I myself, as my name is in Greek" (Rogers, p. 519/189). This allusion to Erasmus's *Encomium Moriae* indicates that St. Thomas More saw his career as a vocation, his life and death as a liturgy whose rubrics were for no human master to dictate, his decisions as fully engaging his soul, which he never intended "to pin at another man's back" (Rogers, p. 521/251). At every stage, when he seized with some misgivings on the baits of office, while he sat uncomfortably in the saddle of precarious power, when he obtained permission to dismount, and when he proved his loyalty by a refusal branded as treason, More somehow managed to remain his own master, perhaps better than the more cautious, less foolish scholar who in 1509 had praised him through praising Folly.

Angers

Notes

1. G. R. Elton, "Thomas More, Councillor" in *St. Thomas More: Action and Contemplation*, ed. R. S. Sylvester (New Haven and London, Yale U. Press, 1972), 85–122; John A. Guy, *The Public Career of Sir Thomas More* (Brighton, Harvester Press, 1980).

2. P. S. Allen, *Opus epistolarum Des. Erasmi*, Oxford 1906ff., vol. 4, ep. 999, p. 15, line 87: "Ab aula principumque familiaritate olim fuit alienior." References to this work are here in shorter form, thus: Allen 4, 999, p. 15/87. In the *Collected Works of Erasmus* (Toronto, U. Press), the volume containing this epistle (no. 7) has not appeared yet. We quote from that collection under the siglum *CWE* with volume, page and line. The 1519 letter to Hutten is available in a neat English version by John C. Olin: *Thomas More: A Portrait in Words by his Friend Erasmus* (New York, Fordham U. Press, 1977) which I shall be echoing on occasion, though I claim responsibility for every word and title of the translation offered here. The "thèse complémentaire" for my "Doctorat ès Lettres" was a bilingual (Latin and French) edition of the letter: *Thomas More vu par Erasme*. Only 100 copies were produced (Angers, *Moreana*, 1969) and it was not commercialized.

3. "Cur enim non dicam *pertraheret* (my italics)? Nullus vnquam vehementius ambiit in aulam admitti quam hic studuit effugere" (ibid., p. 20/218). John Olin had rendered the earlier *pertrahi* with "tempted." Here, Erasmus's explicit admission that he is using a strong word has prompted our Fordham colleague to use "dragged."

4. *CWE* 5, p. 23/12 somewhat softens the verb: "who are brought to do it." It repeats Allen's references to Plato's *Republic* 1. 347 and 7. 520. *Querela Pacis* was published in 1517: the dedicatory letter is not dated.

5. *The History of King Richard III*, ed. R. S. Sylvester, vol. 2 in *The Complete Works of St. Thomas More* (New Haven and London, Yale U. Press, 1963), p. 80/27f.: "For at the consecration of a bishop, every man woteth well, by the paying for his bulls, that he purposeth to be one … And yet must he be twice asked whether he will be bishop or no, and he must twice say nay, and at the third time take it as compelled thereunto by his own will." Compare More's *Richardus Tertius*: "Nam & eum qui creatur Episcopus bis rogari num velit, bis postquam sancte negare, tertio vix adduci posse, vt dicat nolentem velle, quum interim …. ambitum pene declarant emptae Pontificis bullae" (ibid., p. 80/28f.). I have modernised the spelling of the English as R. S. Sylvester himself did when re-editing *Richard III* in the "Selected Works of St. Thomas More" series (Yale, 1976), p. 83.

6. W. Roper's words about More as a young page in Morton's household, often used as a parable of More's character and career: *The Life of Sir Thomas More*, ed. E. V. Hitchcock, *EETS* (London, 1935), p. 5/8.

7. Tyndale followed by Frith, and Foxe, see Rainer Pineas, *Thomas More and Tudor Polemics* (Bloomington, 1968). Cf. Warren Wooden, "Thomas More in Hostile Hands," *Moreana*, XIX 75–76 (Dec. 1982), 77–87.

8. *A Concordance to the "Utopia" of St. Thomas More*, ed. Ladislaus J. Bolchazy (Hildesheim and New York, G. Olms, 1978) is conveniently keyed to the Yale edition (*CW* 3), ed. Edward Surtz and J. H. Hexter (1965), from which I shall quote here. It does not include the parerga, but I have searched More's two letters to Giles.

9. *The Correspondence of Sir Thomas More*, ed. Elizabeth F. Rogers (Princeton U. Press, 1947), p. 133/18.

10. ibid., p. 245/4. E. F. Rogers, in *St. Thomas More: Selected Letters* (Yale U. Press, 1961), p. 144, englishes this *pertracto* as "engaged," repeating the version of Phillip E. Hallett in his 1928 translation of Thomas Stapleton, *The Life of Sir Thomas More*, ed. E. E. Reynolds (London, 1966), p. 80.

11. For other terms of compulsion and coaction in not always unpleasant contexts, see Allen 1, p. 3/31; 4/12, 37; 7/24; 9/16; 50/93, 114; 273/10. And as free as Erasmus wants religion to be, he praises Jean Vitrier for "dragging" a number of his fellow Franciscans along his own spiritual path: "Pertraxerat aliquot et e sui gregis sodalibus" (Allen 4, p. 511/122). In Acts (16:15), where Lydia prevails on St Paul to stay at her house, the Vulgate uses "coegit nos," and Erasmus "adegit nos."

12. "Invitatus in aulam Caroli nunc Caesaris, cui consiliarius factus est" (Allen 1, p. 15/131).

13. My translation reflects that of E. F. Rogers, *Selected Letters,* pp. 68–69. Cp. *CWE* 3, pp. 233–34: "Tunstal … is posted off again suddenly…, and most reluctantly (as I know full well)."

14. *CWE* 5, p. 158. Here is the Latin (Allen 3, 111/13): "Tuum consilium probo, qui non vis principum negociosis nugis implicari: et me plane amas, quum iisdem optas vt extricer, in quibus haud credas quam inuitus versor; neque potest quicquam esse odiosius quam haec est legatio."

15. The phrase echoes More's translation of Pico's *sancta ambitio* (*English Works*, London, 1557, p. 16) and his autograph prayer (*CW* 13, p. 226).

16. Rogers, ep. 17, p. 75: "mihi non modo non ambienti, sed abhorrenti quoque ab auctoramentis aulicis"; ep. 57, p. 111: "In Aulam (quod nemo nescit, et Princeps ipse mihi ludens interdum libenter exprobrat) inuitissimus veni … Caeterum tanta est virtus et doctrina Regis et in vtroque quotidie velut de integro inualescens industria vt … minus minusque sentiam aulicam hanc vitam mihi ingrauescere."

17. More himself, when in disgrace, through letters that he knew the king might read—and no doubt hoped he would—quotes "the first lesson that his Grace gave me what time I came first into his noble service: that I should look first unto God and after God unto him" (To Dr Wilson, Rogers p. 534/26f.). These assurances, "the king's good servant" had already mentioned in a letter to Thomas Cromwell (Rogers, p. 495/124f.), and would repeat from the Tower to Margaret Roper as late as June 1535 (Rogers, p. 557/51). As proof that More never meant "to serve two masters," they are quoted in Roper's *Life of More* (*EETS*, p. 50/3f.) and in Harpsfield's *Life of More*, ed. E. V. Hitchcock and R. W. Chambers (*EETS*, p. 23/30f.).

Mendacium Dicere and *Mentiri*: A Utopian Crux[*]

Elizabeth McCutcheon

We are becoming increasingly aware of just how allusive, ambiguous, and devious a Renaissance humanist text often is.[1] Words elude our attempts to define them, the syntax refuses to stay put, the point of view shifts, and meaning collapses or reverses just as we think we finally have made sense of the text. More's *Utopia*, long the subject of demonstrably contradictory interpretations,[2] is a particularly compelling instance of the ways in which the "subterranean forces of language" are exploited.[3] It resists attempts at translation or paraphrase to excercise the mind, imagination, and conscience of the reader. Because the *Utopia* insists upon its plainness, simplicity, and candor, it is also a particularly devious example.

When the reportorial More discusses his text, he is quick to claim a "neglectam simplicitatem" (38/13)[4] for his discourse and for that of the presumed narrator, Raphael Hythlodaeus. This throwaway line mimics its own artful artlessness at the same time as it allows More to align his text with the plain style. For "neglectam simplicitatem" echoes a major motif in a long passage on Attic oratory in Cicero's *Orator* that (with the Socratic philosophical *sermo*) became the central source for the Renaissance view of the plain style.[5] Subsequently glossed as "homely, playne, and simple speche" in Robynson's sixteenth-century English translation,[6] these words conveyed ideas of sincerity and truth and a concern for thought rather than words to the Renaissance reader.

Yet everything we discover about the language of *Utopia* compels us to reject this claim of simplicity and plainness as too-simple generalization. Creating shifting patterns of dialogue and *sermo* at the larger rhetorical level, and transforming an enormous stock of *topoi* at the verbal level, the text repeatedly frustrates our efforts to define it or to read it simply or straightforwardly, even as it paradoxically encourages us to do so. It is obviously impossible to discuss all of the *Utopia's* incongruities, discontinuities, and oscillations in one brief paper. In fact, it has taken me a monograph to explore More's verbal strategies in just the short letter to Peter Giles which precedes the *Utopia* proper.[7] Here, then, I want to concentrate upon what seems to be a crux for both the prefatory letter and the *Utopia* as a whole. I shall be empirical, because I believe that More wants us to play with — at times wrestle with — his text and that we need to become more aware of the intricate process this involves. But I am interested in general questions too; I hope to show how an aesthetic for the *Utopia* is adumbrated by this particular play of and with language and meaning.

The crux appears in the middle of the letter which More addressed to Giles and added to the *Utopia* by September 3, 1516, when he wrote to Erasmus that he was sending him his " '*Nowhere*' which is nowhere well written."[8] Speaking as the reporter of another's *Historia*, More explains that he shall take the greatest care lest anything in the work be false. But if anything were "in ambiguo, potius mendacium dicam, quam mentiar, quod malim bonus esse quam prudens" (40/28–29). That is, "if anything should be in doubt, I'd rather tell a lie than lie, because I'd rather be honest than clever."[9] What we seem to be given then, and from one point of view *are* given, is a distinction between two kinds of lies.

Our response to this distinction is complicated almost immediately by a cryptic marginal gloss, which is peculiarly important as the first one in the letter and, by inference, all of *Utopia*. It directs us to note the "theological distinction" between "mentiri & mendacium dicere" (40/25–26). The inversion of the words as we move from text to gloss may or may not be deliberate; if More had a hand in the glosses, usually thought of as the work of Giles and Erasmus,[10] it almost surely is. Certainly the note perplexes and misleads. Father Surtz could not find the difference it insists on "in moral guides by Aquinas, Antoninus, and Silvester, or even by a later authority like Alphonsus Ligouri" (n. 40/28–29, p. 291). I doubt that it is findable, at least in this form, since the usual noun for *lie* is *mendacium*, the usual verb *mentiri* in such standard theological sources as Augustine and Aquinas.[11] The note is either a deliberate red herring or a calculated half-comic, half-serious mirroring of More's sophisticated game, or both, as well as a sly humanistic hit at late scholastic theologians, with their overly fine quibbles. Ambiguously calling the reader's attention to the text and initially misdirecting us, it obliquely asks us to consider the meaning behind the words, rather than in them.

In any case, despite the marginal note, the context for *mendacium dicere* and *mentiri* is not theological, but rhetorical and ethical. The text is a reworking and a condensation of two *sententiae* from a passage in the *Attic Nights* where Aulus Gellius cites Publius Nigidius on the difference between "mendacium dicere et mentiri."[12] This distinction depends upon the all-important moral question of deceit; the one who lies (*mentitur*) is not himself deceived but tries to deceive someone else, while the one who tells a lie (*mendacium dicit*) is honestly mistaken or deceived. More knew the passage well, and will return to it in a later, controversial work, the *Debellacyon of Salem and Bizance*, commenting that "I remember that there is a difference put between *mentiri et mendacium dicere*, that is as we myght say betwene hym that wittingly lyeth, and hym that telleth a lie wening y^t it were true," before he ironically describes his opponent, who claims to "speake nothing but that I thought was true," as a "good" man who lies (and should know better).[13]

In its present Utopian context, the distinction allows More to dramatize his performance as a truthful reporter. Though he might tell a lie under certain special circumstances, he would do so only because he misremembered, not because he wished to deceive anyone. To the extent that he *is* simply recounting things as he remembers them, moreover, he can hardly be said to lie by the most stringent theological definition. As St Thomas Aquinas noted, echoing a popular bit of medieval etymology, the term *mendacium* is derived from the idea that a lie is spoken "contra mentem."[14] This conditional statement of doubt, then, so solemnly and convincingly asserted, sustains the image of the honest, plainspoken man who would rather be "bonus" than clever or prudent and the compelling fiction of the mere reporter who has only his memory to rely upon that More builds up throughout the letter as an introduction to his larger Utopian fiction.

In fact, the reporter's memory has served him well, though we only discover how well after reading the whole of *Utopia*. Notwithstanding the recollection of the young John Clement, which has thrown him into such *great* uncertainty or perplexity ("magnam dubitationem"), More is right about the length of the bridge over the river Anydrus—one of two points questioned in the course of the letter. As Nagel's fine detective work has shown, More here balances "the specifying and the suppression of detail."[15] If the river is five hundred yards wide at the city of Amaurotum (118/4–5), which we learn in Book II, then the bridge must be at least five hundred yards long, as More said, rather than three hundred yards long, as John Clement suggested (41/24–28). Similarly, if we were to plot the location of Utopia in accordance with information that Raphael Hythlodaeus gives and the reportorial More duly relays, we would find that it approximates the antipodes of Europe and probably England[16]—appropriately enough, since Utopia is an inversion of the inverted world *topos* and thus a reversed mirror image of Great Britain.[17] The authorial More is engaged in a playful parody of legal wit, using the same evidence to confirm the assertion (as assertion) and the evasiveness of the witness (some part of himself). He is clearly playing a subtle game, too, for he could have checked his own text more easily than we can.

As we ponder the implications of these same details, we can discover just how subtle More's play of mind and imagination is. From one point of view, his doubts and worry are needless; the reporter has remembered the facts he questions correctly. But puzzles which the narrative solves, on the one hand, are insoluble, on the other. How long *is* a bridge over a river called Waterless? Where is Noplace? These riddles and insolubles signal a double consciousness on the part of the author and alert us as readers to the necessity to see and read the text in two different ways. The reportorial More (like Raphael Hythlodaeus, the fictional narrator) is speaking from within the frame of a larger fiction written by the authorial More.

At this point we can return to the text's future less vivid condition, "si quid sit in ambiguo," seeing in what is expressed as a small "if" with respect to two great doubts about which the reporter did not need to have any doubts at all an extreme instance of grammatical ambiguity or amphibology. The assertion is contrary to fact in two different and contradictory ways. We no longer have just a future less vivid condition, in other words, which is resolved by the internal consistency of the details questioned: we can also find an implied counter-statement about the ambiguity and conditionality of the work as a whole. In a story about "Vtopiana republica," *everything* is in a hypothetical and conditional form and "in ambiguo," in doubt, uncertain, or in a state of going at least two ways, to follow the root meaning of the word *ambiguus*, upon which the authorial More must be playing.

He may also be dramatizing the implications of a passage which immediately follows Publius Nigidius's bravura turns on *lying* in the *Attic Nights*: a discussion of ambiguity which preserves part of the pre-Aristotelian debate on the nature of truth and falsehood.[18] To the Stoic Chrysippus's claim that "every word is by nature ambiguous, since two or more things may be understood from the same word," Diodorus responds that "No word is ambiguous and no one speaks or receives a word in two senses; and it ought not to seem to be said in any other sense than that which the speaker feels that he is giving to it." But, in a hypothetical concession, Diodorus admits that ambiguity could occur when "he who speaks it [the word] expresses two or more meanings."[19] Certainly More accomplishes a comparable feat here by exploiting differences between an authorial and a reportorial perspective.

But we cannot overturn the "if" or conditional part of More's period without rethinking the "potius quam" clause which follows it. And as we do so, we realize how More's text plays upon its own antitheses and leads us to collapse the very distinction between kinds of lies that it insists upon. If everything is conditional or hypothetical from the author's point of view, then the distinction between *mendacium dicere* and *mentiri* is scarcely clear-cut. Though a reporter could, theoretically, be misled by a narrator or misremember, the authorial self is not copying his text but composing it, and the question of his having been deceived or of his telling a lie which he believes to be true becomes irrelevant. The alternative question, of his having deliberately lied to or deceived his auditors or readers, remains, of course, and some readers have used words like deceptive about the *Utopia*. But since More's text indirectly signals its own duplicities, misleading and confounding us on the one hand, but allowing us to make corrections and adjustments on the other, I prefer what Malloch calls a "show of deceit to force the reader to uncover the truth,"[20] although I should change the verb "force" to "invite."

If we accept More's present invitation and reconsider *mendacium dicere* and *mentiri*, we find that there is little distinction we can make between them, except grammatically, as soon as the context supplied by Aulus Gellius ceases to be relevant. In one case we have the usual noun for *lie* joined to a verb of saying, in the other the usual verb form; both constructions share a reference to the mind, *mens*. In the light of the author's concealed relationship to the text there is an equivocation, moreover, upon the idea of the writer as liar: feigning, or telling stories, is ambiguously suggested. So what is presented in the text as a genuine antithesis, and *is* one from the point of view in Aulus Gellius, but begins to be undermined by the putative reporter (who is himself engaged in a show of deceit which raises questions about his own insistent claims), collapses altogether as we shift our focus to the author's point of view. The worlds fold in upon each other across a void or chasm and the claim momentarily becomes a tautology—I should rather lie than lie—and then a pun. We are no longer concerned with passive copying or with lying as a moral problem, in other words, but with the telling of "lies" or fictions in a hypothetical work.[21] Neither *mendacium dicere* nor *mentiri* delineates the author's situation, then, despite the insistent claims made for the former."[22] But the play between them allows us to infer what we could call a style and aesthetic of honest deception.

Thus the author indirectly addresses that "movement from fact to fiction, from actuality to imagination, from life to art," which from Plato through the Renaissance was so inextricably connected with the problem of lying that fact and fiction were thought of as opposites, and the Renaissance defence of poetry became a defence of fiction or the "right to feign, to 'make thing up.'"[23] And this prefatory letter deserves a place in the literary history of what C. S. Lewis has called "the difficult process by which Europe became conscious of fiction as an activity distinct from history on the one hand and from lying on the other."[24] But More identifies neither the question nor the answer as such. And his language is feigned, concrete, lucid yet ambiguous, actively resisting efforts to turn it from the specific to the abstract, appropriately so since the question is the nature of a literary work, and fiction should resist abstraction. Hence the difficult job facing translators of More's text here. If they stress the antithesis between kinds of lies by drawing a contrast between *telling* or *repeating* a lie and *making* one, they may make the antithesis too complete—as with the difference between "objective falsehood" and "intentional lie." If they rely on a paraphrase of the idea of the truthful historian, they oversimplify and stabilize a fluid text, depriving More's language of its potential for ambiguity.[25] Somehow, the text needs to be allowed to suggest its own oblique duplicities.

At this point we need to step back from the text, however, and articulate the freewheeling and partly comic variation of the Liar paradox which More has concealed so artfully through this crux on lying. This paradox, which involves a "self-contradictory proposition about itself" and raises urgent questions regarding self-referential assertions of truth or falsity, attracted much attention throughout the later Middle Ages and the early Renaissance.[26] In its most economical medieval formulation it was the *insolubile* of the man *qui se mentiri dicit*, but medieval logicians constructed much more intricate instances of interdependent self-referentiality.[27] With the sixteenth century, classical authorities became newly important. Now Cicero and Aulus Gellius became major sources,[28] as did Lucian, who exploits the paradox for his own satiric purposes at the beginning of his *True History*, where he mocks the poets, historians, and philosophers for the tall tales and elaborate lies they tell but pass off as mere reporting. A disregard for the truth is common, he grants, even among philosophers, and he too is a liar. But he is a much more honest one, for he will admit that he is lying: "The one and only truth you'll hear from me is that I *am* lying.... Well, then, I'm writing about things I neither saw nor heard of from another soul, things which don't exist and couldn't possibly exist. So all readers beware: don't believe any of it."[29]

More's agile convolutions between truth and falsehood glide from one to another of these authorities, evading systematic classification. In the *Utopia* we are in a world of fiction and the possible or probable, not systematic philosophical thought, and so closer to the *Attic Nights* and Lucian and to the play and drama of ideas and values. But More's own logical subtleties echo, albeit allusively, the medieval tradition behind him.[30] And More's variation of the Liar paradox is far more fully imagined and developed than anything we can find in Aulus Gellius or even in Lucian. For Lucian is his own narrator and hyperbolically flaunts his comic adaptation of the Liar paradox. But More, straight-faced, disclaims any role as author or narrator to create the even straighter-faced Raphael Hythlodaeus. And he ironically half-reverses Lucian's already witty reversal, as reporter claiming to tell as true what are — as his authorial self signals — fictions, if not impossibilities, which, for all their humor and absurdity, surpass Lucian's tall tales in their ultimate seriousness and relevance to life. Like Lucian, then, the More of the *Utopia* is a trickster,[31] finding in that role a way to entertain and yet question the unexamined life, the conventions, hypocrisy, distorted values, madness, and absurdity of the actual world. But his text makes more demands upon the reader, and the consciousness and conscience behind it are more subtle than Lucian's. No matter how deeply we probe More's text, in fact, it seems inextricably self-reflexive and paradoxical, its forms hypothetical and fictive, its expression at once playful and serious, its language that of generative self-contradiction, by analogy with the Liar paradox it so cunningly reshapes and half-conceals.[32]

In his *Dialogue Concerning Heresies* (1529) More defends what he ironically calls the "paynted wordes" of the poets, which, he says, "moche helpe the iudgement" and quicken and develop "a good mother wyt" through the mental exercise they provide.[33] This Utopian crux on lying is a particularly good example of what he means. Defying translation because of its equivocations, wordplay, shifts in meaning, and play with levels of abstraction, the crux mimes its own duplicities and invites the reader to search for the truth while it protects the authorial self.[34] As a "show of deceit" it adumbrates an aesthetic of honest deception, or dissembling and feigning, that illuminates the workings of More's intellect and imagination, clarifies complex relationships among the writer, work, world, and reader, and allows us to see More's prefatory letter to Peter Giles as an *ars poetica* for the *Utopia*, if and as we participate in the lively exercise of wit it offers its readers.

University of Hawaii

Notes

*Much of the research on which this article is based was made possible by a Guggenheim Fellowship for 1979–80, for which I am most grateful.

1. The issue is brilliantly stated by Terence Cave in "Translating the Humanists: Erasmus and Rabelais" in *Comparative Criticism: A Yearbook*, ed. E. S. Shaffer (Cambridge, Cambridge Univ. Press, 1981), pp. 279–93. See too Terence Cave, *The Cornucopian Text: Problems of Writing in the French Renaissance* (Oxford, Clarendon Press, 1979).

2. Frank E. Manuel and Fritzie P. Manuel's *Utopian Thought in the Western World* (Cambridge, Mass., Harvard Univ. Press, 1979) surveys the "later fortune of *Utopia*," pp. 117–49; see also Judith Paterson Jones's "Recent Studies in More," *ELR*, 9 (1979), 442–58.

3. Cave, "Translating the Humanists," p. 292.

4. For the Latin text of the *Utopia* and related material I am using *Utopia, The Complete Works of St. Thomas More*, 4, ed. Edward Surtz, S.J., and J. H. Hexter (New Haven, Yale Univ. Press, 1965).

5. Compare Cicero's "non ingratam neglegentiam" and two other variations upon the idea; cited from *Brutus*, transl. G. L. Hendrickson and *Orator*, transl. H. M. Hubbell, Loeb (Cambridge, Mass. and London, Harvard Univ. Press and Heinemann, 1942), p. 362 (xxiii.77 and 78). Background materials include Wesley Trimpi, *Ben Jonson's Poems: A Study of the Plain Style* (Stanford, Stanford Univ. Press, 1962), pp. 3–91; the essays of Croll, in particular his "'Attic Prose' in the Seventeenth Century," *Style, Rhetoric and Rhythm: Essays by Morris W. Croll*, ed. J. Max Patrick and Robert O. Evans, with John M. Wallace and R. J. Schoeck (Princeton, Princeton Univ. Press, 1966); George Williamson, *The Senecan Amble: A Study in Prose Form from Bacon to Collier* (1951; rpt. Chicago, Univ. of Chicago Press, 1966); E. Catherine Dunn, "Lipsius and the Art of Letter-Writing," *SR*, 3 (1956), 145–56; Gary R. Grund, "From Formulary to Fiction: The Epistle and the English Anti-Ciceronian Movement," *TSLL*, 17 (1975), 379–95; and William J. Kennedy's study of a new sixteenth-century ironic style in *Rhetorical Norms in Renaissance Literature* (New Haven, Yale Univ. Press, 1978).

6. Citations from the first and second editions of the Robynson translation (1551 and 1556) refer to *The Utopia of Sir Thomas More*, ed. J. H. Lupton (Oxford, Clarendon Press, 1895). For Robynson's marginalia, omitted by Lupton, I have used the facsimile of the second edition (Menston, 1970); the gloss in question is on p. 2.

7. Forthcoming as *My Dear Peter: More's "Ars Poetica" and Hermeneutics for "Utopia,"* Mor Monograph No. 2 (Angers, 1983). The present study condenses and reworks some of the material to appear in this monograph.

8. *St Thomas More: Selected Letters*, ed. Elizabeth Frances Rogers (New Haven and London, Yale Univ. Press, 1961), p. 73.

9. Translation mine; p. 95 in *My Dear Peter*. Cf. the Yale *Utopia's* "Just as I shall take great pains to have nothing incorrect in the book, so, if there is doubt about anything, I shall rather tell an objective falsehood than an intentional lie — for I would rather be honest than wise" (41/31–35), and Robynson: "For as I will take good hede that there be in my booke nothyng false, so if there be anythynge in doubte, I wyll rather tell a lye then make a lye; bicause I had be good then wise rather [first ed.] (rather be good than wilie [second ed.])" (p. 6). His alternative renderings usefully call attention to the inherent ambiguity of the text.

10. See the Yale *Utopia*, pp. 280–81, n. 22/21, and clxxxvi. For an overview of the notes see Dana G. McKinnon, "The Marginal Glosses in More's *Utopia*: The Character of the Commentator," *Renaissance Papers* (1970), ed. Dennis G. Donovan (Durham, North Caro-

lina, The Southeastern Renaissance Conference, 1971), pp. 11-19. The more I work with the *Utopia* the more I wonder about the part More himself may have played in these glosses; "mentiri & mendacium dicere" is a particularly telling instance of how carefully they are adjusted to the text.

11. The titles of Augustine's treatises speak for themselves: *De Mendacio* and *Contra Mendacium*, both in *Patrologia Latina*, vol. 40; Aquinas, *Summa Theologiae*, 2a 2ae. 100. Sisella Bok, *Lying: Moral Choice in Public and Private Life* (N. Y., Random House, 1978) examines the ethical background involved.

12. *The Attic Nights of Aulus Gellius*, transl. John Rolfe, Loeb 2, 325 (XI.xi.1). In "More's Attic Nights: Sir Thomas More's Use of Aulus Gellius' 'Noctes Atticae,'" *RN*, 13 (1960), 127-29, R. J. Schoeck shows More's familiarity with Gellius in works other than *Utopia*. For Aulus Gellius in *Utopia* the indices in the Yale *Utopia* and in *L'Utopie de Thomas More*, ed. André Prévost (Paris, Mame, 1978) are helpful.

13. Citation from *The Workes of Sir Thomas More* (1557), facsimile ed. introduced by K. J. Wilson (London, Scolar Press, 1978), p. 1032A; see too Germain Marc'hadour, "Translating Thomas More and Translator Thomas More," *Mor*, No. 11 (1966), 72.

14. *Summa Theologiae*, 2a 2ae. 110,1.

15. Alan F. Nagel, "Lies and the Limitable Inane: Contradiction in More's *Utopia*," *RQ*, 16 (1973), 178.

16. Yale *Utopia*, 52/2, 108/1-2, 196/29-31, and n. 52/2, p. 305. George B. Parks, "More's Utopia and Geography," *JEGP*, 37 (1938), 224-36 plus 3 figs., argues that More worked with existing geographical theory to arrive at his antipodeal location, taking wholly seriously what I would take more playfully as a sign of More's interest in paradox and opposites. See too Arthur E. Barker, "Review Article: Clavis Moreana: The Yale Edition of Thomas More," *JEGP*, 65 (1966), 325 and 328; Hans Ulrich Seeber, "Hythloday as Preacher and a Possible Debt to Macrobius," *Mor*, No. 31-32 (November, 1971), 71-86.

17. See Rosalie L. Colie, *Paradoxia Epidemica: The Renaissance Tradition of Paradox* (Princeton, Princeton Univ. Press, 1966), pp. 14 and 42; Darko Suvin, *Metamorphoses of Science Fiction: On the Poetics and History of a Literary Genre* (New Haven and London, Yale Univ. Press, 1979), with its discussion of the utopian genre as a "possible impossible."

18. For antinomies among pre-Aristotelian thinkers see William Kneale and Martha Kneale, *The Development of Logic* (Oxford, Clarendon Press, 1962), p. 16. Cf. Quintilian, *Institutio Oratoria* 3. 153 (VII.viii.7): "I turn to the discussion of *ambiguity*, which will be found to have countless species: indeed, in the opinion of certain philosophers, there is not a single word which has not a diversity of meanings."

19. Aulus Gellius, 2. 325, 327 (XI.xii.1-3). On Gellius's role as "a Cicerone to the ancient treasures"—seen here—consult Hans Baron, *From Petrarch to Leonardo Bruni: Studies in Humanistic and Political Literature* (Chicago and London, Univ. of Chicago, 1968), pp. 196-215.

20. A. E. Malloch, "The Techniques and Function of the Renaissance Paradox," *SP*, 53 (1956), 192.

21. Thus More himself anticipates the many recent theoretical discussions of the *Utopia* or the utopian form as inherently hypothetical, written in the subjunctive, and a related concern with fictional modes of presentation. See, for example, Nagel; Suvin; Harry Berger, Jr., "The Renaissance Imagination: Second World and Green World," *CR*, 9 (1965), 36-78; Alexandre Cioranescu, *L'avenir du passé: Utopie et littérature* (Paris, Gallimard, 1972); Walter R. Davis, "Thomas More's *Utopia* as Fiction," *CR*, 24 (1980), 249-68; Michael Holquist, "How to Play Utopia: Some Brief Notes on the Distinctiveness of Utopian Fiction," *YFS*, No. 41 (1968), 106-23; Philip W. Porter and Fred E. Luckermann, "The Geography of Utopia" in *Geographies of the Mind: Essays in Historical Geography in Honor of John Kirtland Wright*,

ed. David Lowenthal and Martyn J. Bowden (New York, Oxford Univ. Press, 1975), pp. 197–223; Raymond Ruyer, *L'Utopie et les Utopies* (Paris, Presses Universitaires de France, 1950), pp. 8–26; R. S. Sylvester, " 'Si Hythlodaeo Credimus': Vision and Revision in Thomas More's *Utopia*," *Soundings*, 51 (1968), 272–89.

22. Because of the many verbal transformations, I would qualify the claims made for *mendacium* by Nagel, p. 180, and Prévost, p. 349.

23. Berger, p. 39, citing C. S. Lewis, and Lewis, *English Literature in the Sixteenth Century, Excluding Drama* (Oxford, Clarendon Press, 1954), p. 318.

24. Lewis, pp. 318–19. William Nelson's *Fact or Fiction: The Dilemma of the Renaissance Storyteller* (Cambridge, Mass., Harvard Univ. Press, 1973) traces the history of this dilemma in detail.

25. Cf. n. 9, above, for two examples of the first type of translation; Robynson was followed by Burnet (1684) and Arthur Cayley (1808). For an example of simple paraphrase see Ramón Pin de Latour's translation (Barcelona, 1957), or Paul Turner's rendering for Penguin Books (Harmondsworth, 1965). Luigi Firpo's "... preferirò dire cosa non vera piuttosto che una menzogna ..." *Utopia*, 2nd ed. (Napoli, Guida editori, 1979), p. 53, seems to me to be one of the more successful translations.

26. The history of the Liar paradox can be traced through the index in Kneale, *The Development of Logic*; other studies consulted include Colie, *Paradoxia Epidemica*, and Gregory Bateson, *Steps to an Ecology of Mind* (New York, Chandler, 1972), whom I cite (p. 184). For more specific evidence of the popularity of this paradox in the Middle Ages and Renaissance see Paul Vincent Spade, *The Medieval Liar: A Catalogue of the "Insolubilia" Literature* (Toronto, Pontifical Institute of Mediaeval Studies, 1975), which contains an inventory of seventy-one discussions; Francesco Bottin, *Le antinomie semantiche nella logica medievale* (Padua, Antenore, 1976); and E. J. Ashworth, "The Treatment of Semantic Paradoxes from 1400 to 1700," *Notre Dame Journal of Formal Logic*, 13 (1972), 34–52.

27. Kneale, pp. 227–28; cf. Ernest A. Moody, *Truth and Consequence in Mediaeval Logic* (Amsterdam, North-Holland Publishing Co., 1953), pp. 101–10.

28. Cicero, *De Natura Deorum Academica* II.xxix–xxx; Aulus Gellius, XVII.xii.1–3 and XVII.ii.10–11. Ashworth lists still other classical examples. Professor Jozef IJsewijn has called a philological reference to my attention: Nonius Marcellus, *De Compendiosa Doctrina*, a linguistic encyclopedia used by Vives, includes *mendacium dicere* and *mentiri*.

29. From *Selected Satires of Lucian*, ed. and transl. Lionel Casson (1962; rpt. N.Y., Norton, 1968), p. 15. Roy Arthur Swanson's "The True, and False, and the Truly False: Lucian's Philosophical Science-Fiction," in *Science Fiction Studies*, No. 10, 3 (1976), 228–39, includes a brief discussion of the comic paradox on p. 228; cf. Nelson, *Fact or Fiction*, pp. 11–12. Douglas Duncan, *Ben Jonson and the Lucianic Tradition* (Cambridge, Cambridge Univ. Press, 1979), devotes its first chapter to Lucian, pp. 9–25.

30. Cf. Malloch, who argues more generally for a connection between the *quaestio disputata* and the Renaissance paradox and dialogue, pp. 196–202.

31. See Duncan, pp. 67–76.

32. Cf. Erasmus's Moria, who also exploits the Liar paradox; E. H. Gombrich, *Art and Illusion: A Study in the Psychology of Pictorial Representation* (London, Phaidon Press, 1972), pp. 200–03, discusses the "perplexing effect of self-reference" and its analogies to the Cretan liar.

33. *The Complete Works of St Thomas More*, 6, ed. Thomas M. C. Lawler, Germain Marc'hadour, and Richard C. Marius (New Haven and London, Yale Univ. Press, 1981), p. 132.

34. In this connection see Leo Strauss's *Persecution and the Art of Writing* (Glencoe, Illinois, The Free Press, 1952), pp. 22–37; More is discussed briefly on p. 35.

Neo-Latin Sources in Robert Burton's
Anatomy of Melancholy

John Mulryan

Northrop Frye describes Robert Burton's *Anatomy of Melancholy* as "the most comprehensive survey of human life in one book that English literature had seen since Chaucer...."[1] He defines it as a Menippean Satire or Anatomy, a cousin to the novel. Where the novelist analyzes or anatomizes human relationships or social information, the anatomist or Menippean satirist "shows his exuberance in intellectual ways, by piling up an enormous mass of erudition about his theme or in overwhelming his pedantic targets with an avalanche of their own jargon."[2] It is the purpose of this paper to discuss Burton's creative use of sources, particularly neo-Latin sources, and a sense of what Burton was attempting to accomplish when he wrote his great *Anatomy* in 1621 is essential before we begin.

Although the *Anatomy* presents itself as a learned treatise on an important subject, it would be futile to apply modern standards of scholastic accuracy to the text. Burton is interested in presenting his subject fairly and accurately, but he is writing primarily for effect, and if a distorted version of a particular source will help him to make his point more readily, that is the version he will provide for his reader. Judith Kegan Gardiner notes that Burton is more interested in "the overall approach" of his work than in the accuracy of individual quotations — he often alters the facts and the wording of his sources to make his point, to convey an aesthetic impression, or even to add to the symmetry of his work.[3] J. B. Bamborough[4] and Robert M. Browne[5] also comment on Burton's haphazard methods of citation. Browne suggests that Burton may be "quoting either from an indifferent memory or from bad notes."[6] He speaks of Burton's "haphazard use of authorities"[7] and tendency to quote at secondhand. Where Browne suggests that Burton knew no Italian, although he cites Italian authors, Bamborough states that Burton uses French authors only for their translations of Latin works, and that French writers per se are never drawn upon in the *Anatomy*.[8] According to Sir William Osler, Burton sometimes cites sources we are reasonably sure he could not have obtained in England, and he makes a number of references to medical treatises he probably did not consult.[9] David Renaker, in his "Robert Burton's Tricks of Memory,"[10] remarks on Burton's habit of identifying the source of his quotations as the book of the writer being quoted, instead of the author of the compilation where he read the quotation. For example, Burton quotes Varro from L. G. Giraldi's *Historia* (1548), but he lists as his source Varro himself.[11] Similarly, in the section on Religious Melancholy, a list of authorities is given for the absurd multiplicity of the pagan gods, a list which could have come from Giraldi's *Historia* or some other compendium, without the need for independent reading in the sources themselves. The citation of such a string of authorities is more of an exercise in *copia* than a careful assessment of individual sources.[12]

Perhaps the greatest distortion of an author's thought by Burton has been documented by David Renaker, who claims that Burton totally distorted the work of the neo-Latin writer Petrus Ramus for his own ends, concentrating on Ramus's method, to pinpoint ideas through a symbolic application of the geographical sense of place, and ignoring what Ramus was actually trying to do: "Everything Ramus sought to banish: digressiveness, inconsistency, *copia*, the fusion of rhetoric with dialectic — ran riot over and through the meticulous pattern of the 'method.' "[13]

The problem is compounded by the lack of a good edition of the *Anatomy*. Burton increased the size of the work by a fourth in the second edition (1624), and even the first posthumous edition, the sixth (1651), is supposed to have been carefully corrected and annotated by the author. He did not bother to establish internal consistency in the work, many marginal notes are partially lost or ambiguously altered in the later editions, and we cannot really be sure of the author's final intention.[14] Nicholas Kiessling of Washington State University, U.S.A., is preparing a new edition, and he plans to employ batteries of scholars from the different humanistic disciplines to assist with the annotations, and computers to establish the text.[15] In the meanwhile, we must struggle along with the corrupt nineteenth-century edition of Alan Shilleto, with its misprints, and reprinting of errors from previous editions.[16] I might add that twentieth-century editors have almost destroyed the rhythm of Burton's sentences by translating all of his Latin quotations, or by inserting "correct" readings of his sources, particularly in places where he has intentionally distorted the original readings in order to make his point.[17]

The contents of Burton's personal library do not afford us much help either. Of the books that Burton willed to the Bodleian and Christ Church libraries, the vast majority are in Latin, with a substantial number of titles in English. There are two or three in Greek, one or two in Italian, perhaps one in French. It should be remembered, however, that these books represent only a fraction of the reading that went into the *Anatomy*, which consisted, as Halam crudely put it, of "a great sweeping of miscellaneous literature from the Bodleian library."[18] The books that survive from his library are no more helpful than the list, for Burton annotated very few of them (most of the rare notes are in the margins, and occur more frequently in the medical literature); nor did Burton keep a commonplace book based on his reading.

As we have noted, Burton had, with the exception of English books, hardly any books in the European vernacular languages in his library.[19] Yet, he cites a number of vernacular sources, including Leone Ebreo and Vincenzo Cartari, the first, the author of the famous love treatise, the *Dialoghi d'Amore*, and the other, of the famous mythography, the *Imagini*. But if we look closely at Burton's methods of reference, we will see that he is often citing a neo-Latin source (as he did with Giraldi), while claiming to use a vernacular source. For example, after a long diatribe against polytheism, Burton suggests that the reader consult two other sources: "... see more in Carterius and Verdurius of their monstrous forms and ugly pictures."[20] The form "Carterius" should alert us that Burton is using a Latin translation of the *Imagini*, in fact the one translated by Antoine du Verdier, here termed, as he is on the title page of that edition, as Verdurius. But Burton is referring to him here as an independent author, not as the translator of the *Imagini* — thus a Latin translation of an Italian book is expanded to appear to contain the sober pronouncements of not one but two Humanists.[21]

Much of the section on love theory in the *Anatomy* is drawn, directly or indirectly, from the work of another neo-Latin author, Marsilio Ficino's commentary on the *Symposium*. The remainder is drawn from the work already mentioned, the *Dialoghi d'Amore* of Leone Ebreo (1535). This work was available in a Latin translation in 1564 (*De Amore dialogi tres*, Venice), which was reissued in 1587. Although the Italian original was available in Burton's library, Burton probably used this translation for his lengthy borrowings from Leone. The examples drawn from classical mythology by Leone himself to demonstrate his view of love and wisdom, in the persons of Philo and Sophia, are to be found in another neo-Latin treatise, the *De Genealogia* of Giovanni Boccaccio.[22] When Burton adds a myth or a mythical example to the ones provided by Leone, he invariably looks to Natale Conti's *Mythologiae* (1581), Giraldi's *Historia*, or Cartari's *Imagini* in the Latin version (*Imagines Deorum*, 1581).

Frye noted the intellectual cast of the *Anatomy*, its use of "an enormous mass of erudition" to overwhelm "pedantic targets with an avalanche of their own jargon." Rabelais would be the obvious stylistic model in vernacular literature for such an approach, but I find just one reference to the great French author in the entire *Anatomy*. However, two neo-Latin models have been suggested for Burton's satiric mode and tumbling prose style. Rosalie L. Colie sees Burton's use of irony, paradox, and *copia* (Frye's "enormous mass of erudition") as distinctly Erasmian, and his informal, loose prose style as developing from the example of Erasmus. Indeed, Erasmus uses the figure of Democritus in his *Encomium Moriae*, as Burton did in his persona of Democritus Junior: Erasmus in his letter of dedication to Thomas More,[23] Burton in his preface to the reader. Most recently, Bamborough has suggested that a major influence on the style and theme of the *Anatomy* was the work of the sixteenth-century Italian physician and scientist Jerome Cardan.

Cardan, who wrote some 138 books, with another 98 unpublished in manuscript, also tries to overwhelm his readers with his erudition, in the Burtonian manner, and he was as solipsistic and egocentric as Burton himself.[24] He is at the same time one of the most frequently cited authors in the *Anatomy*, and one of the most obscure of Burton's sources.

These are some specific examples of the impact of neo-Latin literature on Burton's *Anatomy*; it would also be possible to produce equally potent examples of the influence of Chaucer or Ovid. However, taken as a single body of literature, there are more quotations, paraphrases, and allusions to neo-Latin literature in the *Anatomy*, than there are to either classical or medieval literature, even if the vernacular literatures are included in the survey.

The most exhaustive survey of Burton's sources has been compiled by Paul Jordan–Smith. He rounds off the number of authors referred to in the *Anatomy* at 1,000, and provides a list of the 122 authors most frequently cited by Burton. Of these, 50 are writers on medical topics, stretching from antiquity to Burton's lifetime.[25] Jozef IJsewijn, in his *Companion to Neo-Latin Studies*,[26] lists 21 of these as neo-Latin writers. If one includes all of the relatively obscure medical writers, 57 of the 122 qualify as neo-Latin authors. One important neo-Latin author not mentioned by IJsewijn but who appears in the Jordan-Smith list, is Ludovicus Coelius Rhodiginus, a sixteenth-century antiquarian whose enormous *Lectionum Antiquarum Libri Triginta* (last edition, 1599) covered every aspect of classical culture and had a profound impact on the development of the mythological tradition during the Renaissance. Other important neo-Latin authors in the list include the two Scaligers; the emblem-writers Joachim Camerarius and Paulus Jovius; the philosopher Ludovicus Vives; the poets Jovaninus Pontanus and Johannes Baptista Montanus; the educational theorist Melanchthon; the political writers Justus Lipsius and Thomaso Campanella; and of course the aforementioned Erasmus, Ficino, Cardan, and Boccaccio. Even if we exclude the writers on medicine from the canon of neo-Latin authors, it is clear that Burton derived many of his ideas and much of his aesthetics from the neo-Latin canon. Julius Caesar Scaliger is constantly cited on matters of style and literary theory; Ficino and Campanella provide Burton with much of his material on the philosophy of love and political theory; and the man we have come here to honor, the Scottish poet George Buchanan, is quoted extensively in the sections of the *Anatomy* that deal with love melancholy, as one of the modern poets who best epitomize the vagaries of that emotion.

To conclude: Burton, who wanted to write the *Anatomy* in Latin, but who could find no publisher to take it in that language, did the next best thing; he made his work into an anthology of quotations, mostly from Latin authors, with a substantial percentage from neo-Latin authors. Thus there is no question that Burton was familiar with neo-Latin literature, respected it as authoritative, and employed it copiously in his great *Anatomy*.

St. Bonaventure University

Notes

1. Northrop Frye, *Anatomy of Criticism: Four Essays* (Princeton, Princeton University Press, 1957), p. 131.

2. ibid.

3. Judith Keagan Gardiner, "Elizabethan Psychology and Burton's *Anatomy of Melancholy*," *JHI*, 38, 3 (July–Sept., 1977), 384–85.

4. J. B. Bamborough, "Burton and Cardan," in *English Renaissance Studies Presented to Dame Helen Gardner in Honour of Her Seventieth Birthday* (Oxford, Clarendon Press, 1980), pp. 190–93.

5. Robert M. Browne, "Robert Burton and the New Cosmology," *MLQ*, 13 (1952), 131–48.

6. Browne, p. 142.

7. ibid., p. 136

8. Browne, p. 142; Bamborough, p. 189.

9. Sir William Osler, "The Library of Robert Burton," in *Oxford Bibliographical Society: Proceedings & Papers, 1, 1922–26* (Oxford, Oxford Univ. Press, 1927), p. 187.

10. David Renaker, "Robert Burton's Tricks of Memory," *PMLA*, 87 (1972), 391–96.

11. Renaker, p. 392.

12. "... see the said *Lucian de Dea Syriâ, Mornay, cap. 22. de veritat. relig. Guliel. Stuckius Sacrorum Sacrificiorumque Gentil. descript. Peter Faber Semester.* l. 3, c. 1, 2, 3. *Selden de diis Syris, Purchas'* Pilgrimage, *Rosinus* of the *Romans*, and *Lilius Giraldus* of the *Greeks*." Rev. A. R. Shilleto, ed. *The Anatomy of Melancholy*, 3 vols. (London, George Bell and Sons, 1896). This quotation is found in vol. 3, p. 405.

13. David Renaker, "Robert Burton and Ramist Method," *RQ*, 24 (1971), 220.

14. Sir William Osler, "The Library of Robert Burton," pp. 184, 191.

15. Nicholas Kiessling, "*The Anatomy of Melancholy*: Preparation for a New Edition," *Literary Research Newsletter*, 4.4 (1979), 181–89.

16. Both Kiessling and Osler point up the deficiencies of the Shilleto edition.

17. See, for example, the edition by Floyd Dell and Paul Jordan-Smith (New York, Tudor Publishing Company, 1927). The subtitle reads: "Now for the first time With the *Latin* completely given in translation And embodied in an *All-English* text." Burton would not have been pleased.

18. Cited in Osler, "Robert Burton, His Book," p. 175.

19. Osler, "The Library of Robert Burton," p. 186. The bequests to the libraries are given in the same issue of the Oxford *Proceedings*: "Lists of Burton's Library," pp. 222–46.

20. Shilleto ed., vol. 3, p. 408.

21. See my article, "Translations and Adaptations of Vincenzo Cartari's *Imagini* and Natale Conti's *Mythologiae*: the Mythographic Tradition in the Renaissance," *CRCL*, 8, n. 2 (Spring, 1981), 272–83.

22. There is a modern edition, indeed the only modern edition of any of the Renaissance mythographers [ed. Vincenzo Romano (Bari, Laterza, 1951)].

23. Rosalie L. Colie, "Some Notes on Burton's Erasmus," *RQ*, 19 (1967), 337–39.

24. Bamborough, pp. 180–89.

25. Paul Jordan-Smith, *Bibliographia Burtoniana: A Study of Robert Burton's The Anatomy of Melancholy. With a Bibliography of Burton's Writings* (Stanford, Stanford University Press, 1931), pp. 59–60.

26. Jozef IJsewijn, *Companion to Neo-Latin Studies* (Amsterdam, North Holland Publishing Company, 1977), "Index Nominum" pp. 355–70.

Thomas Ruddimans *Grammaticae Latinae Institutiones*

Raimund Pfister

F ür die Lebensgeschichte Thomas Ruddimans kann auf eine neuere Monographie verwiesen werden;[1] für die Einordnung in die wenig bekannte Geschichte der Grammatik ist das Buch freilich unzureichend. Ruddiman wurde i.J. 1674 in Schottland auf einer Farm in Raggel (parish Boyndie, county of Banff) geboren, studierte in Aberdeen, war dann Hauslehrer und Dorfschulmeister und schließlich seit dem Jahre 1702 in zunächst schlecht bezahlter Stellung an der Bibliothek des Iurisconsultorum collegium in Edinburgh (heute National Library of Scotland). Gleichzeitig war er Verleger, Drucker und Buchhändler. I.J. 1714 veröffentlichte er *The Rudiments of Latin Tongue*. Dieses Buch wurde, z.T. in verschiedenen Überarbeitungen, für eineinhalb Jahrhunderte eine in Schottland und auch anderswo verbreitete Schulgrammatik; die letzte Auflage ist wohl die dreißigste (Baltimore, 1867). Es ist jetzt in einer microfiche-Ausgabe wieder zugänglich (Menston, 1970). I.J. 1715 gab er die *Opera omnia Georgii Buchanani* heraus. Von seinem Hauptwerk, den *Grammaticae Latinae Institutiones*, erschien der erste Band (Etymologia, d. h. Morphologie) i.J. 1725, der zweite (Syntaxis) i.J. 1731. Er starb am 19. Januar 1757.

Die Umstände, die die Erarbeitung des großen Werkes ermöglichten, werden aus dem Vorwort von 1725 ersichtlich. Ruddiman widmete es "amplissimo ac florentissimo quod in Scotia est iurisconsultorum collegio." Die etwas devote Widmung gibt Einblick in die sozialen Verhältnisse der Zeit. Ein Wissenschaftler ohne Vermögen war abhängig vom Patronat von Gönnern, die hier charakterisiert werden als "viri nascendi conditione supra vulgus elati, omni doctrinarum genere exculti et perpoliti, opibus denique, gratia et auctoritate pollentes." Die hochgestellten iurisconsulti haben diese Grammatik nicht nur dadurch ermöglicht, daß sie ihrem Bibliothekar die nötige Freizeit ließen, sondern auch dadurch, daß sie reiche Mittel für ihre Bibliothek zur Verfügung stellten. Diese war "omnibus fere bonis auctoribus, iis praesertim qui Humaniores vulgo insigniuntur, refertissima." Ruddiman hat aber auch eigene Bücher benützt, "quos aliunde nancisci poterat."

Ruddiman, ein bescheidener Gelehrter, der auch zum Understatement hinsichtlich seiner eigenen Leistungen neigt, zeigt sich besonders dankbar, weil er es wagen durfte, die *iurisconsultos* "a gravioribus curis atque a maximarum et rei publicae utilissimarum occupationum fastigio ad grammaticas hasce, quales a plerisque habentur, tricas et quisquilias devocare." Denn, wie er fortfährt, "grammatico quidem, nisi alia et altiora respiciat, in tenui (i.e., in tenuibus rebus) ... labor ac pertenuis gloria est." Doch ist er sich der Bedeutung der Grammatik durchaus bewußt: "si penitius rem intuebimur, hanc artem inveniemus, ut in se non ignobilem, ita ceterarum omnium et fundamentum et ianuam esse. — Iurisprudentia, sive causarum orandarum facultas tam arcto cum ea necessitudinis vinculo connexa ac colligata est, ut hac e rebus humanis sublata illam quoque una everti labefactarique prorsus necesse sit." Diese Warnung vor einer Geringschätzung der Grammatik kann wohl auch für die neulateinische Philologie gelten.

Dieses kurze Referat setzt sich vor allem zwei Ziele: einmal soll darauf aufmerksam gemacht werden, daß die wenig beachtete Entwicklung der lateinischen Grammatik — um nur einige Namen zu nennen — von Laurentius Valla und Nicolaus Perottus in Italien über Antonius Nebrissensis und Franciscus Sanctius in Spanien, Thomas Linacre in England, Petrus Ramus und Iulius Caesar Scaliger in Frankreich, Despauterius in Flandern, Melanchthon in Deutschland und Gerardus Ioannes Vossius in den Niederlanden bis zu unserem Ruddiman, der diese Epoche abschließt, dem Neulateiner ein reiches Betätigungsfeld bietet. Eine zweite Absicht liegt darin, bei den Schotten etwas Stolz auf ihren Landsmann zu erwecken und den Wunsch vorzutragen, es möge die Möglichkeit für einen Reprint dieser Grammatik geprüft werden.

Zielsetzung und Anlage des Werkes ergeben sich schon aus dem umfangreichen Titel: *Grammaticae Latinae Institutiones*, facili atque ad puerorum captum accommodata methodo perscriptae. Additae sunt in provectiorum gratiam notae perpetuae, quibus non solum Latini sermonis praecepta plenius explicantur, sed et ea pleraque omnia, quae a summis grammaticis aliisque ad hanc artem illustrandam sunt observata succincte simul perspicueque traduntur. Perfecit et suis animadversionibus auxit Thomas Ruddimannus A. M. Pars I Edinburgi, in aedibus auctoris, MDCCXXV. 8. min. (Cont. pag. 330). Pars II. Ibid. MDCCXXXI. 8. min. (Cont. pag. 388). Dieser Titel wurde in der von mir benützten, von Gottfried Stallbaum bearbeiteten Ausgabe (Leipzig, 1823) geändert in *Institutiones Grammaticae Latinae*; denn als Schulgrammatik war das Buch damals nicht mehr geeignet, das schon zur Zeit seines Erscheinens die Schüler durch seine Stofffülle überfordert haben dürfte. Das Werk ist zweigeteilt in Textteil und Anmerkungsteil. Der für die Schüler bestimmte Textteil wurde ohne die umfangreichen Anmerkungen in Fußnoten in einer editio minor gesondert herausgegeben und erschien bis zur 14. (15.?) Auflage 1804. Diese editio minor ist für uns wichtig; denn Ruddiman hatte für sein großes Werk einen III. Band *De orthographia* und einen IV. Band *De prosodia* (mit Metrik) vorgesehen. Diese Bände sind nie erschienen, aber Ruddiman hat seine Vorarbeiten in die entsprechenden Appendices der 4. Auflage der editio minor (1740) eingebracht. Diese Appendices sind auch in der Ausgabe von Stallbaum abgedruckt.

Der Textteil bringt zunächst jeweils hexametrische Versregeln. Diese haben eine alte Tradition, insbesondere seit dem *Doctrinale* des Alexander de Villa Dei (um 1200). Wieweit Ruddiman diese Versregeln neugestaltet hat, habe ich nicht gründlich untersucht. Sie sind oft schwer verständlich und werden deshalb durch einen knappen Prosatext erklärt und in der Syntax durch für Schulkinder geeignete Belegstellen illustriert. Die Belege gehen von Plautus und Terenz, Cicero und Sallust über die augusteischen Dichter und die silberne Latinität (dabei auch Plinius Nat. Hist. und Columella) mit Florus und Juvenal bis ins zweite Jahrhundert. Cäsarstellen sind ganz selten. Die Beispiele zeigen zumeist eine erfreuliche Einprägsamkeit, Anschaulichkeit und Buntheit. Die Langweiligkeit der Grammatiksätze kommt, jedenfalls in Deutschland, mit dem Klassizismus im 19. Jahrhundert.

Für uns sind bedeutsamer die nur für den Lehrer gedachten Anmerkungen, die den Umfang des Schülertextes oft weit übersteigen. Sie sind es vor allem, was einen Reprint, insbesondere der Syntax, wünschenswert erscheinen läßt. Diese Anmerkungen bringen eine Fülle weiterer Beispiele, vereinzelt auch aus Neulateinern wie Buchanan. Insbesondere sind sie das Ergebnis eines umfangreichen Studiums der grammatischen Literatur sowohl des Altertums wie der Neuzeit seit Valla. Nach D. Duncan hat Ruddiman über siebzig Grammatiken durchgearbeitet. Die Ansichten der zitierten Grammatiker werden oft auch ohne weiteres Nachschlagen klar; es finden sich auch längere wörtliche Zitate. So entstand — unter Ausschluß des damals nur in Handschriften zugänglichen Mittelalters — ein Kompendium der grammatischen Forschung bis zu Ruddimans Zeit, das bis heute von niemandem übertroffen wurde. Er war für diese Arbeit besonders geeignet, weil er, anders als etwa der arrogante Sanctius oder der bissige Scioppius, die Verdienste seiner Vorgänger neidlos anerkannte, die eigene Person nicht in den Vordergrund stellte und recht konservativ war.

Der Stand der Grammatik zur Zeit Ruddimans weicht von unserer heutigen Grammatik erheblich ab, auch wenn man die moderne Linguistik beiseite läßt. Trotzdem kann man die stoffreiche Grammatik Ruddimans auch heute noch durchaus mit Gewinn benützen. So wird man eine Liste mit etwa 220 Adjektiven, die mit dem Genitiv verbunden werden, mitsamt den Belegstellen dankbar entgegennehmen, da sie weit übersichtlicher ist als die im wesentlichen wohl aus ihr geschöpfte Darstellung bei Kühner-Stegmann. Aber man wird nicht weniges vermissen oder als verfehlt ansehen und gelegentlich Verständnisschwierigkeiten haben.

Es ist noch viel Mittelalterliches da, das inzwischen aus der Grammatik verschwunden ist. Mittelalterlich ist die Haupteinteilung der *syntaxis regularis* in *concordantia* und *regimen*, worauf die *syntaxis irregularis* oder *figurata* folgt. *Subiectum* und *praedicatum* erscheinen nur anmerkungsweise als *Termini* der Dialektiker (II.404). Die *essentiales sententiae partes* (II.404) werden *nominativus et verbum* oder nach mittelalterlicher Manier *suppositum* und *appositum* genannt. Für die *accidentales sententiae partes* ist ein terminologisches System noch nicht entwickelt. Das schon von Scioppius gebrauchte *obiectum*, das vereinzelt in den Anmerkungen erscheint, ist noch kein syntaktischer *Terminus* (II.155.35 *tamquam finis vel obiectum*). Die *analysis syntactica seu sententiarum* (das "Konstruieren") erfolgt wie im Mittelalter durch die Verwandlung des in den Texten vorliegenden *ordo artificialis* (in der modernen Linguistik Oberflächenstruktur, *surface structure*) in den *ordo naturalis* (eine Art Tiefenstruktur, *deep structure*): zuerst das Subjekt (*nominativus vel quod eius loco ponitur*) mit seinen Erweiterungen, dann das *finite Verb* in der Mitte, dann die Ergänzungen und näheren Bestimmungen des *Verbs*. So wird der Satz "Senectus ipsa est morbus" folgendermaßen erklärt (II.9): "Verba substantiva ... habent utrimque nominativum ad eandem rem pertinentem." — Bei der Kongruenz in "Dos ... est decem talenta" (II.10) wird nicht vom Subjekt gesprochen, sondern vom *nominativus, qui natura prior est.*

Eine klare Trennung von Haupt- und Nebensatz und eine systematische Lehre von den Nebensätzen gab es weder im Altertum noch im Mittelalter noch in der Zeit Ruddimans; sie kommt erst gegen Ende seines Jahrhunderts. In der Sache ist freilich manches bekannt. So erscheinen unser Subjektsinfinitiv und unser Subjektsatz in folgender Form: Verbis tertiae personae saepe aut infinitivus aut oratio aliqua loco nominativi praeponitur (II.6). Das Beispiel "Incertum est, quam longa nostrum cuiusque vita futura sit" zeigt, daß das praeponitur für den zugrunde liegenden ordo naturalis, die Konstruktionsordnung, gilt. Die Tempus- und Moduslehre der Nebensätze erscheint sehr knapp unter der constructio constructionum; das findet sich so noch bis weit in das 19. Jahrhundert. Zu den spezifischen Besonderheiten der Grammatik Ruddimans schreibt J. Golling, daß Ruddiman "auf rationelle Begründung der Syntax vollständig verzichtet."[2] Das hat Golling einem Understatement der Einleitung Ruddimans entnommen; er hat aber offenbar das Buch nicht gründlich gelesen und wird ihm mit seiner Bewertung nicht gerecht. Ruddiman wollte ein Buch für die Schüler schaffen, die das Latein erst lernen sollen. Dieser Zweck erforderte eine *grammatica civilis*, wie man es damals nannte, und nicht eine *grammatica philosophica*, wie sie Sanctius und sein späterer Herausgeber Perizonius, Scioppius und zuletzt Georgius Henricus Ursinus aus Regensburg i.J. 1701 geboten hatten. Besonders letzterem verdankte Ruddiman, nicht zum Schaden seines Buches, viel. In der rationalistischen *grammatica philosophica* wurden die *causae linguae Latinae* untersucht. Dabei stand im Vordergrund die syntaxis naturalis, "quae (nach damaliger Auffassung) ex ipsa vocum natura profluit, ac in omnibus fere linguis est eadem." Vernachlässigt wurde, wie Ruddiman sagt, die *syntaxis arbitraria*, "quae ex arbitrio auctorum linguae alicuius oritur, ac in variis linguis varia est" (II.1). Ruddiman bringt diese aus Ursinus übernommene Einteilung, die bei der Ausführung der Grammatik kaum zum Tragen kommen kann, um zu zeigen, daß in der Sprache nicht alles rational erklärbar ist. Damit nimmt er die künftige Entwicklung der Grammatik vorweg. Aber er arbeitet, vor allem in den Anmerkungen, gelegentlich aber auch im Textteil für die Schüler, durchaus auch mit den rationalen Erklärungen seiner ihm wohl vertrauten Vorgänger, insbesondere mit den Ellipsen, durch die Sanctius zuerst berühmt und dann berüchtigt wurde. Für die zugehörige Terminologie des *exprimi* (in der Oberflächenstruktur vorhanden) und des *supprimi, reticeri* u.ä. (in einer Tiefenstruktur zu denken, in der Oberflächenstruktur getilgt) haben wir heute im Zeitalter der generativen Grammatik mehr Verständnis als das 19. Jahrhundert. Ruddiman gibt zur Forschungsgeschichte auch eigene Stellungnahmen und versagt in manchen Fällen dem Sanctius ausdrücklich die Gefolgschaft.

In Sandys, *History of Classical Scholarship* wird aus Chalmers, dem alten Biographen Ruddimans, zitiert: "He was one of the best men who ever lived." Mögen ihn deshalb seine schottischen Landsleute nie vergessen!

München

Notes

1. Douglas Duncan, *Thomas Ruddiman. A Study in Scottish Scholarship of the Early Eighteenth Century* (Edinburgh–London, 1965).

2. J. Golling, in seiner Einleitung in die *Geschichte der lateinischen Syntax* (= *Historische Grammatik* der lateinischen Sprache, hrsg. Gustav Landgraf, III, 1, [Leipzig, 1903], p. 57).

Nominalism in the Moral Teaching of Hobbes

Peter A. Redpath

P aul Kuntz describes Montaigne as, among other things, seeming to be "an eclectic who combined this and that which seems wise without any consideration of the cosmos that would lead us to consider man in the cosmos as did Plato and Aristotle."[1] The contrast between the philosophical character of Montaigne, as described by Professor Kuntz, and the philosophical character of Thomas Hobbes, as we have come to understand him, is pronounced. They appear to us to be at opposite ends of the nominalistic world in their consideration of man in relation to the cosmos. For, unlike Montaigne, to Hobbes the functioning of the cosmos is all-important for understanding the functioning of man. Thus at the very beginning of his most celebrated work, *Leviathan*, Hobbes writes:

> Nature, the art whereby God hath made and governs the world, is by the *art* of man, as in many other things, so in this also imitated, that it can make an artificial animal. For seeing life is but motion of limbs, the beginning whereof is in some principal part within; why may we not say, that all *automata* (engines that move themselves by springs and wheels as doth a watch) have an artificial life? For what is the *heart*, but a *spring*; and the *nerves*, but so many *strings*; and the *joints*, but so many *wheels*, giving motion to the whole body, such as was intended by the artificer? *Art* goes yet further, imitating that rational and most excellent work of nature, *man*. For by art is created that great LEVIATHAN called a COMMONWEALTH, or STATE, in Latin CIVITAS, which is but an artificial man;...[2]

In the way he understands the relationship of man to nature, then, Thomas Hobbes resembles any number of Ancient, medieval, and Renaissance thinkers who see man as a mirror of the universe. Like the Montaigne of Professor Kuntz, Hobbes, to us, is, in addition, an eclectic, with both Stoic and Epicurean moments, but he is an eclectic for whom a systematic body of truths has not ceased to be a live option.[3]

While doing research for this paper, we have seen Hobbes described as a "materialist" and as a "sceptic," as a "rationalist," and even, by one thinker, as a "scholastic." (See Michael Oakeshott's "Introduction" to his Blackwell edition to *Leviathan*, p. xxi.)[4] Such descriptions show, we think, that Hobbes was, indeed, eclectic, but that he was a scholastic is something about which we have our doubts. Certainly we do not think Hobbes would relish such a description of him, and, given the emphasis put by scholasticism upon the *quaestio* and upon the text, we suspect that not too many scholastics would consider Hobbes to be one of their fold.

Still, Oakeshott's description can help us to understand the mind of Thomas Hobbes. For while Hobbes might not be a scholastic, he does resemble a medieval philosopher who has been transplanted to the seventeenth century. He is, in a sense, what is left of a medieval scholastic after he has lost his substantial form, most of his accidents, his books, and has met up with Galileo, Newton, Descartes, Luther, and Humanism.

In addition, the cosmos in which Hobbes lives resembles the medieval world transplanted to the seventeenth century. It looks to us like the carcass of the world of Avicenna. Gone are the Intelligences moving the planets. In their place is the law of gravitation and inert bodies, but, still, the motion of the planets influences the movements of man.

Given his interest in the order he sees in the cosmos, unlike Montaigne, Hobbes lays emphasis upon systematic philosophy. Yet, just as Montaigne, he does not seek to become wise within the systematic philosophy of a medieval schoolman. Also, just as Montaigne, Hobbes turns to epistemology as the starting point for his philosophy, and to nominalism as his tool.

Yet the nominalism of Hobbes is not "schooled in the concrete thought of the ancients," nor does it employ "grammar to cull expressions of wisdom."[5] Rather, it is schooled in the concrete thought of the moderns, and it employs speech to gather wisdom. And the nominalism of Hobbes is not a humanistic nominalism, at least not in the classical sense of the Humanism of the Renaissance, but, we think, more exactly speaking, a voluntaristic nominalism.

We do not think, in describing Hobbes thus, that we are doing him any injustice. Yet to demonstrate the suitability of our description of Hobbes, we will examine his nominalism within the context of parts of his *Leviathan*. Since, for Hobbes, "the end of knowledge is power," and since, for him, "the scope of all speculation is the performing of some action, or thing to be done," we think such an examination might prove most fruitful.[6] For given the stress which Hobbes places upon the relationship between speculation and action, one might reasonably expect him to take the utmost care to give a clear articulation of his philosophical character in a moral teaching like *Leviathan*.

Indeed, Hobbes himself stresses the intimate relationship between philosophy and the moral life in a telling passage from his *Elements of Philosophy*. In attempting to explain the utility of philosophy by contrasting the goods enjoyed by mankind in Europe, Asia and parts of Africa to those enjoyed by Americans and by those who live near the Poles, Hobbes says:

> Now, the great commodities of mankind are the arts; namely of measuring matter and motion; of moving ponderous bodies; of architecture; of navigation; of making instruments for all uses; of calculating the celestial motions, the aspects of the stars, and the parts of time; of geography, etc. By which sciences, how great benefits men receive is more easily understood than expressed. These benefits are enjoyed by almost all the people of Europe, by most of those of Asia, and by some of Africa: but the Americans, and they that live near the Poles, do totally want them. But why? Have they sharper wits than these? Have not all men one kind of soul, and the same faculties of mind? What, then, makes the difference, except philosophy? Philosophy, therefore, is the cause of all these benefits. But the utility of moral and civil philosophy is to be estimated, not so much by the commodities we have by knowing these sciences, as by the calamities we receive from not knowing them. Now, all such calamities as may be avoided by human industry, arise from war, but chiefly from civil war; for from this proceed slaughter, solitude, and the want of all things. But the cause of war is not that men are willing to have it; for the will has nothing for object but good, at least that which seemeth good. Nor is it from this, that men know not that the effects of war are evil; for who is there that thinks not poverty and loss of life to be great evils? The cause therefore, of civil war is, that men know not the causes neither of war nor peace, there being but few in the world that have learned those duties which unite and keep men in peace, that is to say, that have learned the rules of civil life sufficiently. Now, the knowledge of these rules is moral philosophy.[7]

In addition to the stress which Hobbes puts upon the intimate relationship between philosophy and the moral life, there is another point of emphasis which he makes which suggests that *Leviathan* is a good work to consider for one who wishes to understand the philosophical character of Hobbes. This point of emphasis is that of the reason why men have not learned the rules of civil life.

> But why have they not learned them (i.e., the rules of civil life), unless for this reason, that none hitherto have taught them in a clear and exact method? For what shall we say? Could the ancient masters of Greece, Egypt, Rome, and others, persuade the unskillful multitude to their innumerable opinions concerning the nature of their gods, which they themselves knew not whether they were true or false, and which were indeed manifestly false and absurd; and could they not persuade the same multitude to civil duty, if they themselves had understood it? Or shall those few writings of geometricians which are extant, be thought sufficient for the taking away of all controversy in the matters they treat of, and shall those innumerable and huge

volumes of *ethics* be thought unsufficient, if what they teach had been certain and well demonstrated? What, then, can be imagined to be the cause that the writings of those men have increased science, and the writings of these have increased nothing but words, saving that the former were written by men that knew, and the latter by such as knew not, the doctrine they taught only for ostentation of their wit and eloquence?... Now that which is chiefly wanting in them, is a true and certain rule of our actions, by which we might know whether that which we undertake be just or unjust. For it is to no purpose to be bidden in every thing to do right, before there be a certain rule and measure of right established. Seeing, therefore, from the not knowing of civil duties, that is, from the want of moral science, proceed civil wars, and the greatest calamities of mankind, we may very well attribute to such science the production of contrary commodities.[8]

Hobbes's *Leviathan* is, as we see it, an attempt to show the consistency of human nature and civic duty through an articulation of the right method of moral philosophy (pp. 460–68). It is an attempt to explicate the true and certain rule of actions discoverable by a clear and exact method. Hence by following the development of the relationship between Hobbes's nominalism and his method of doing philosophy in *Leviathan*, we should get a fairly clear picture of the role played by nominalism within his moral teaching.

Hobbes says in his "Introduction" to *Leviathan* that to be wise a man must *read* himself (*nosce teipsum*) (p. 6). In Part 1 of *Leviathan* he begins his self-reading with an examination of sensation (p. 7).

As Hobbes sees it, all knowledge begins with sensation. And sensation, for him, is a "seeming" or "fancy" discerned in us by "feeling." That is, as he understands it, sensation is a phantasm which results from contrary motions generated by the pressure of matter upon an organ. What exists outside the sensing subject is body and motion (pp. 7–8) (motion being a succession of parts relative to place, and body being that to which quantity belongs).[9] Motion pressing on an organ generates a counter-motion in the sensing subject. (In "Elements of Philosophy," Hobbes calls these counter-motions "endeavours," that is, a small beginning of motion before motion appears in some visible action.)[10] Sensation, thus, it seems, is, for Hobbes, the feeling of an original fancy or phantasm, which is generated by contrary endeavours within an organ (*Leviathan*, p. 31).

The qualities discerned by this feeling are:

but so many several motions of matter, by which it presseth our organs diversely. Neither in us that are pressed, are they any thing else, but divers motions; for motion produceth nothing but motion. But their appearance to us is fancy, the same waking, that dreaming. And as pressing, rubbing or striking the eye makes us fancy a light; and pressing the ear produceth a din; so do bodies also we see, or hear, produce the same by their strong, though unobserved action. For if those colors and sounds were in bodies, or objects that cause them, they could not be severed from them, as by glasses, and in echoes by reflection we see they are; where we know the thing we see is in one place, the appearance in another. And though at some certain distance, the real and very object seem invested with the fancy it begets in us; yet still the object is one thing, the image or fancy is another. So that sense, in all cases, is nothing else but original fancy, caused, as I have said, by the pressure, that is, by the motion, of external things upon our eyes, ears and other organs thereunto ordained.   (pp. 7–8)

The description which Hobbes gives of sensation appears to us to be quite revealing. For it seems to us to suggest that Hobbes is seeking to articulate his clear and exact rule of knowledge through a voluntarism which he will use in a fashion analogous to Descartes's rationalism. Descartes's method is to identify the reality of an object with a clear and distinct idea of it. From such ideas Descartes deduces the world.[11] Hobbes's method, as we see it, is to identify the reality of an object with a clear and distinct sensation, or perhaps better, feeling, of the object, and to deduce the world from clear and distinct sensations, or feelings, to the extent that these sensations or feelings are rightly defined in speech.

To make our interpretation of Hobbes more plausible, however, it is necessary for us to allow him to develop his thinking more fully. After defining sensation, therefore, Hobbes proceeds to explain what is meant by imagination and memory. Both he defines as "decaying sense," but in diverse ways. That is, "imagination" is decaying sense considered as signifying the fancy which is decaying (p. 18). While "memory" is decaying sense considered as signifying the fading of a fancy (id.).

Besides memory and imagination, Hobbes explains the meaning of "experience" and understanding. Experience, he says, is "much memory, or memory of many things" (id.). And understanding, he says, is "imagination that is raised in man by words or other voluntary signs...." (p. 13)

This kind of understanding, he adds, "is common to man and beast. For a dog by custom will understand the call or the rating of his master. And so will many other beasts. That understanding which is peculiar to man, is the understanding not only his will, but his conceptions and thoughts, by the sequel and contexture of the names of things into affirmations, negations, and other forms of speech...." (id.)

Hobbes immediately follows his consideration of understanding with an examination of "Consequence or Train of Imagination." He does this in order to make intelligible what he means by understanding "the sequel and contexture of names of things into affirmations, negations and other forms of speech...." As Hobbes sees it, thoughts do not appear in the imagination at random. Rather, they follow each other in orderly succession, resembling the succession according to which they first appeared in sensation (pp. 13–14).

This train of thoughts, he says, is of two sorts: regulated and unregulated. A regulated train of thoughts, for him, is a train of thoughts in which some desire is present. It is a train of thoughts in which there is some "passionate thought, to govern and direct those that follow, to itself as the end and scope of desire." The presence of this passionate thought within a train of thoughts gives a train of thoughts design and prevents it from wandering (p. 14).

With respect to a regulated train of thoughts, Hobbes, likewise, considers these to be of two kinds: one, common to man and to beast, in which from an imagined effect we seek the causes, and the other, proper to man alone, in which from "imagining any thing whatsoever, we feel all the possible effects, that can by it be produced; that is to say, we imagine what we can do with it when he have it" (pp. 14–15).

The latter regulated train of thoughts Hobbes calls "seeking," or the "faculty of invention." And with respect to "seeking," or to the "faculty of invention," Hobbes distinguishes two sorts: one he calls "remembrance," or "calling to mind," and the other he calls "prudence," "providence," or "foresight" (pp. 15–16).

Remembrance is scanning of one's past images, a seeking with intent, just as, Hobbes says, "a spaniel ranges the field, till he find a scent." Prudence, however, is a seeking about the future. It is a guessing about the future, a guessing, as Hobbes says, by means of signs; signs which, for Hobbes, are what we might call "hints," or "clues," or "images of the future." For Hobbes states, "The best prophet naturally is the best guesser; and the best guesser, he that is most versed and studied in the matters he guesses at: for he hath most signs to guess by" (p. 15).

In calling a sign a hint, clue, or image of the future, however, we are not being precise enough. For Hobbes wishes to suggest something more than these by the word "sign." For him a sign is the mark of an order. It calls to mind not simply an image, but a succession. Thus Hobbes says, in language which might make even the stuffiest of scholastics wince: "A *sign* is the evident antecedent of the consequent; and contrarily, the consequent of the antecedent, when the like consequences have been observed, before: and the oftener they have been observed the less uncertain is the sign" (p. 16).

So, Hobbes adds, the more experience a person has the better he is at identifying signs. For the more experience he has, the more succession he has witnessed in his train of thoughts (id.).

Now while the notion of a sign, which Hobbes takes trouble to make clear, might not appear *prima facie* to be of major importance to understanding his moral teaching, to us this notion is indispensable. For Hobbes tells us that speech is a connection of signs, and that not only is it "the most noble and profitable invention of all other," but that "understanding is caused by speech" (pp. 13, 18).

Given the importance which Hobbes places upon measuring knowledge by its practical effects, such remarks about the importance of speech do not seem to us to be offhand hyperbole. No, Hobbes seems to mean exactly what he says.

The problem we have to consider at this point, however, is what signs contribute to speech, and why Hobbes puts such an emphasis upon the practical nature of speech.

Regarding signs, Hobbes explains these in relation to marks whereby we recall our thoughts. Marks, he contends, are sensible notes of remembrance which enable us to "register" our thoughts in their order of appearance. Marks, that is, are memory devices by means of which we file or record our thoughts for future use. They are not simply devices for distinguishing thoughts. They are, in addition, and more importantly, devices for ordering our thoughts (pp. 18–19).

Marks differ from signs, Hobbes tells us, by their use. Both, that is, are marks. But signs are what we might today call "social marks." That is, marks which are used by many people in the same order and connection to signify to one another what each person conceives, thinks, or feels about something, are signs. But marks which are used by one person to register his thoughts and feelings are ordinary marks (id.).

Both sorts of marks, however, are what Hobbes calls "names" (pp. 19–20). And it is the ordering of names in verbal discourse which Hobbes calls "speech," "the mother," he says, "of all inventions":

> ... the most noble and profitable invention of all other, was that of SPEECH, consisting of *names* or *appellations*, and their connexion; whereby men register their thoughts; recall them when they are past; and also declare them one to another for mutual utility and conversation; without which, there had been amongst men, neither common wealth, nor society, nor contract, nor peace, no more than amongst lions, bears, and wolves.   (p. 18)

"The general use of speech," as Hobbes sees it, "is to transfer our mental discourse into verbal; or the train of our thoughts into a train of words...." (id.). In doing this, speech serves a practical function. Speech, for Hobbes, is an invention, not a discovery. And it is an invention of the will designed to transfer one manner of registering our images into another manner of registering them. Thus, in speech we do not name things for ourselves, but we transfer to others our fancies. That is, by commonly agreed upon signs we transfer to others feelings we have about things, about things which neither we nor anyone know nor understand. Speech is a social invention by means of which people commonly agree to name their feelings in a definite way (pp. 18–19).

What is of utmost importance to us about the way Hobbes understands speech is the degree to which he makes it depend upon the agreement of human wills. Names, for Hobbes, are voluntarily erected.[12] The social activity of naming is, also, voluntarily erected, but this is speech, and upon it depends truth and understanding. Understanding, Hobbes says, is "nothing else but conception caused by speech" (p. 24). And truth, he states, "consisteth in the right ordering of names in our affirmations...." (p. 21) Hence, for Hobbes, truth and understanding depend upon an agreement of human wills.

Given the central place occupied by speech in Hobbes's thinking, one can anticipate what he will consider to be the major obstacles to the right method of philosophic thinking. For Hobbes, to be complete, philosophy must be practical. Hence the proper method of doing philosophy requires not only agreement of wills in naming things, but also agreement of wills in doing things. The proper method of philosophic reasoning, that is, requires both right definition and power.

Hobbes says, "The first cause of absurd conclusions I ascribe to want of method; in that they begin not their ratiocination from definitions; that is from settled significations of words: as if they could cast account, without knowing the value of the numeral words, *one*, *two*, and *three*" (p. 28).

Further, Hobbes states that, of all men, those most subject to absurdity are philosophers because "there is not one of them that begins his ratiocination from the definitions, or explications of names that they use; which is a method that hath been used only in geometry; whose conclusions have thereby been made indisputable" (p. 27). For him, therefore, geometry is the only science "that God hath pleased hitherto to bestow on mankind," since in it "men begin at settling the significations of their words; which settling of significations they call *definitions*, and place them in the beginning of their reckoning" (p. 21).

As Hobbes sees it, it is not possible for anyone to acquire science without right definition. For right definition raises natural sense and imagination to a level of truth and of understanding:

> So that in the right definition of names lies the first use of speech; which is the acquisition of science: and in wrong, or no definitions, lies the first abuse; from which proceed all false and senseless tenets; which make those men that take their instruction from the authority of books, and not from their own mediation, to be as much below the condition of ignorant men, as men endued with true science are above it. For between true science and erroneous doctrines, ignorance is in the middle. Natural sense and imagination are not subject to absurdity. Nature itself cannot err; and as men abound in copiousness of language, so they become more wise, or more mad than ordinary. Nor is it possible without letters for any man to become either excellently wise, or, unless his memory be hurt by disease or ill constitution of organs, excellently foolish. For words are the wise men's counters, they do but reckon by them; but they are the money of fools, that value them by the authority of an Aristotle, a Cicero, or a Thomas, or any other doctor whatsoever, if but a man.   (p. 22)

Just as philosophy, or science, is, for Hobbes, the knowledge of consequences, so, for him, moral philosophy is "the science of what is *good* and *evil*, in the conversation and society of mankind" (p. 104). That is, just as, for Hobbes, there is no truth or understanding in natural speech and imagination (that is, prior to the social act of naming things in speech), so there is no moral good or evil apart from social agreement in speech (pp. 93–95, 461). And just as, for Hobbes, there is no true science without power to effect one's will, there can be no true moral philosophy without effecting in practice the true commonwealth (pp. 104–05).

Thus, as Hobbes sees it, in a state prior to commonly agreed upon definitions of obligation which can be enforced by a common will, there is no injustice. Because prior to commonly agreed upon definitions there is nothing a person is obliged to do or not to do. In a state of nature a man's right is co-equal to his liberty. And a man's liberty is co-equal to his strength to enforce his will (pp. 84–86).

Moral obligation begins, for Hobbes, not with the presence of rights, but with the renouncing of them through signs, words, and actions, and through the binding of multiple individual wills to one sovereign will. As Hobbes says,

> where there is no coercive power erected, that is, where there is no commonwealth, there is no propriety; all men having right to all things: therefore, where there is no commonwealth there is nothing unjust. So that the nature of justice, consisteth in keeping of valid covenants: but the validity of covenants begins not but with the constitution of a civil power, sufficient to compel men to keep them: and then it is also that propriety begins. (p. 94)

What joins together moral obligation and sovereign will is, as we see it, the nominalism of Hobbes. The human will, in order to maintain itself in act, invents speech, and through speech, a commonwealth. Thus, as we see it, the nominalism of Hobbes is an outgrowth of a voluntarism appropriate to an original thinker like Hobbes. And while we do not agree with his views, we do not think that Hobbes was either an atheist or a sceptic, which is the way some people might look at him. Rather, we think that Hobbes was a scientific and religious reformer who, in the desire to separate faith from reason, theology from philosophy, and religion from civil power, synthesized a religious reformer's view of the will and reverence for the written word with a scientific reformer's view of method and reverence for matter and motion.

St. John's University

Notes

1. Paul G. Kuntz, "Montaigne's Humanistic Nominalism," a paper delivered at the Fifth International Congress of the IANLS at St. Andrews, Scotland.

2. Thomas Hobbes, *Leviathan*, ed. Michael Oakeshott (Oxford, Basil Blackwell, 1946), p. 5. Further references to this text are given in the main text.

3. Kuntz, art. cit., p. 1.

4. Michael Oakeshott, "Introduction" to Thomas Hobbes, *Leviathan*, op. cit., p. xxi.

5. Kuntz, art. cit., pp. 1–2.

6. Thomas Hobbes, "Elements of Philosophy," in *Hobbes: Selections*, ed. F. J. E. Woodbridge (New York, Charles Scribner's Sons, 1949), p. 7.

7. ibid., pp. 7–8.

8. ibid., pp. 8–9.

9. Thomas Hobbes, "Elements of Philosophy," pp. 48 and 77.

10. ibid., pp. 107–08.

11. René Descartes, "Discourse on Method," in *Essential Works of Descartes*, transl. Lowell Blair (New York, Toronto and London, 1961), pp. 1–47.

12. Thomas Hobbes, "Elements of Philosophy," pp. 12–17.

A Neo-Latin Version of Robert Henryson's
Testament of Cresseid

Lawrence V. Ryan

Perhaps the best, and certainly the most highly praised, narrative poem in English between the works of Geoffrey Chaucer and Christopher Marlowe's *Hero and Leander* is *The Testament of Cresseid* by the fifteenth-century Scots author, the so-called "schoolmaster of Dunfermline," Robert Henryson.[1] Very little is known of the personal life of this elusive figure, not even whether he studied here at St Andrews or received his degrees somewhere abroad. His literary fame, nevertheless, is secure through his accomplished verse fables, his version of the tale of Orpheus and Eurydice, and mainly, his continuation of the story of the heroine of Chaucer's *Troilus and Criseyde*. Where his predecessor had left off with the death of the young Trojan lover after his lady had deserted him to become the mistress of the Greek Diomede, Henryson carried on, in the same verse form as Chaucer, the account of Cresseid's misfortunes through her rejection by Diomede, her decline into prostitution, her punishment with leprosy by the planetary gods for blaming her miseries on their malign influence, her pathetic last encounter with Troilus in which she is so disfigured and purblind because of her disease that neither of the former lovers recognizes the other, and her final testament and death.

In the sixteenth century, Henryson's poem became fixed as an essential part of the influential legend of Troilus and Cressida. It was printed in all of the early black-letter editions of Chaucer's poems, beginning with that of William Thynne in 1532. Thynne's version presents the oldest extant text of the narrative[2] and probably established it in many minds as having come from the English poet's own hand, even though Henryson explicitly mentions in the opening passage how he got the idea for his continuation from reading the original Chaucerian story:

> I tuik ane Quair, and left all vther sport,
> Written be worthie Chaucer glorious,
> Of fair Cresseid and worthie Troilus.[3]

He then claims, since Chaucer had contented himself with depicting Troilus's "cairis," that he took up another "Quair" by a different author, and

> fand the fatall destinie
> Of fair Cresseid, that endit wretchetlie.   (ll. 62-63)

Having come upon this other book, he wonders "gif all þat Chauceir wrait was trew?" (l. 64) and, in keeping with a venerable medieval poetic convention, pretends that he is merely the copyist of his second "authority," offering to his readers the "wofull end of this lustie Creisseid" (l. 69). Unlike Chaucer, Henryson, who apparently not so conversant with courtly love traditions, regarded the lady as a sinner deserving of her horrible fate even though, like Chaucer, he also manifests considerable sympathy, especially in her final speeches, for her plight. Yet it was this assumption of her "lustiness" and eventual promiscuity, this disapproval of her going

> amang the Grekeis air and lait,
> So giglotlike, takand thy foull plesance!   (ll. 83-84)

that helped to make the name of Cressida a byword for wanton womanhood and prepared the way for such unfavorable representations of her as the coquettish heroine of the play by Shakespeare.[4]

This viewpoint was shared by a seventeenth-century English author who rendered *The Testament of Cresseid* into Latin and whose version is the subject of this essay. On 2 April 1640, the minor Caroline poet Sir Francis Kynaston completed his translation of all five books of Chaucer's poem and immediately turned to the task of doing the same for what he entitled "The Sixt & Last Booke of Troilus and Creseid Written by M[r] Robert Henderson [sic] and called by Him the Testament of Creseide." To this work Kynaston says he was particularly attracted because of its "most elegant" mythological descriptions of Saturn and the other planets, who come to Cresseid in a dream to judge and punish her for having blasphemed in blaming them rather than her own lewd conduct for her fall.[5] Thus, in a prefatory note that also contains a scatological, and probably apocryphal, anecdote about the Scots poet, Kynaston reveals his own bias against Cresseid's character by remarking that "This M[r] Henderson ... takes vppon him in a fine poeticall way to expres the punishment & end due to a false vnconstant whore, which commonly terminates in extreme misery."[6] How this disapproving attitude may have affected the tone and diction of his translation will be glanced at presently.

Kynaston was born at Oteley, near Ellesmere in Shropshire, about 1587. In 1601 he matriculated at Oriel College, Oxford, and commenced bachelor of arts from its "satellite," St Mary's Hall, in 1604. Transferring to Trinity Hall, Cambridge, he took the master's degree in 1609, but in 1611 returned to Oxford and was also incorporated master of arts there. In 1618 he was knighted and in 1621 represented his home county in Parliament. In 1633 was printed *Corona Minervae*, a masque that he had presented before the children of Charles I; in the same year he provided English translations for a volume of Latin verse by the Scottish poet Arthur Johnston.[7] During these years he served both the royal court, as an esquire to the body of King Charles, and the University of Cambridge, where he was appointed a proctor in 1635. He also founded in London the Museum Minervae, a kind of academy or finishing school to prepare gentlemen in languages and noble exercises requisite for cutting a proper figure in their foreign travels.[8] In 1635 he published a Latin version with facing English text of the first two books of Chaucer's *Troilus*. In the preface to that work he promised eventually to produce an annotated rendering of the entire poem. Between 21 August 1639 and 4 May 1640, he accomplished this labor, along with his translation of Henryson's *Testament*. Kynaston died in 1642; in that year Richard Hearne brought out at London a volume containing his heroic romance *Leoline and Sydanis* and his amatory lyrics under the title *Cynthiades*.

Although a note at the end of the manuscript contains an *imprimatur* by Thomas Wykes, licenser to the Oxford University Press, Kynaston's complete translation of Chaucer's poem has never been printed. It exists in a unique copy in the Bodleian Library (MS Additional C. 287). His version of *The Testament of Cresseid* also survived only in the Oxford manuscript until G. Gregory Smith included it in the first volume of his edition of Henryson's works. Yet if scant attention has been paid to Kynaston's renderings of either poem, they are of considerable interest and significance because they constitute a unique experiment in neo-Latin versifying, and are quite successful attempts at transmuting the originals into a poetic language of so different a genius from Middle English or Middle Scots. If translation of the great classics into the vulgar tongue was a flourishing enterprise during the Renaissance, then Kynaston's performance represents a calculated reversal of the process. It is, moreover, a rather amusing reversal, since Chaucer had disingenuously claimed that he too was functioning simply as a translator of the story of Troilus:

> of no sentiment [poetic invention of my own]
> I this endite
> But out of Latyn in my tonge it write.   (Bk. II, ll. 13–14)

Kynaston, because he is, truthfully, doing the opposite, converts these words to

> nihil propriâ scripserim inventione,
> E nostro in Latium sed verterim sermone.

His reasons for doing so, he explains in the dedication to the published partial translation, is to preserve this "jewel of a poem" from "oblivion," and to assure its author's fame abroad by turning it into a language that would be comprehensible to foreigners.[9] For even though Chaucer's "honos & existimatio" is so great among Englishmen that he may be called "huius Insulae ornamentum & Poeseos decus egregium," his work is in danger of being forgotten because of his archaic language. In order, therefore, "aeternae suae memoriae conservationi prospicere," Kynaston has undertaken, not to modernize Chaucer's English, which itself is subject to alteration by time, but rather "illum novâ linguâ donare, & novato rythmi & carminis genere decorare; eumque perenni Romani eloquij columna fulcire, & per omnia saecula (quantum in nobis est) stabilem & immotum reddere."[10]

The same intention would have held, *a fortiori*, for Kynaston's later translation of the *Testament* which, although he did call it "The Sixt & Last Booke of Troilus & Creseid," he was the first in England to identify explicitly as Henryson's work. For if to foreigners and even to most of his seventeenth-century compatriots Chaucer's language would have proved difficult to understand, how much less intelligible to them might have been a poem in the dialect of his northern neighbors. This was true even though in all early printings of Chaucer's works, including the 1598 edition by Thomas Speght upon which Kynaston based his translation,[11] the *Testament* had appeared so much "anglicized" that it could have passed for a compostition by a Middle English, rather than a Scots, author.

As a translator Kynaston conscientiously tried to reproduce not only the sense but also the "feeling" of his originals. Thus, in explaining his procedure with the first two books of the *Troilus*, he says that he wanted to make certain not to tamper with Chaucer's meaning (a principal motive for his having decided on a translation rather than a modernization).[12] Further, though the practice was unusual, he chose to imitate, as closely as the different geniuses of the two languages made doing so possible, the original rhyme scheme and meter. In other words, instead of using, say, quantitative elegiacs for what he himself labeled a "poema eroticum," he produced in Latin an equivalent to rime royal, the accentual seven-line pentameter stanza employed by both Chaucer and Henryson.[13]

Rhyming itself presented no great difficulty, but the difference, he noted, between monosyllabic English and polysyllabic Latin, with its preponderance of words having feminine endings, made it impossible for him to generate in the latter tongue accentual iambic pentameter lines that were decasyllabic. His solution was to settle upon an eleven-syllable line containing five regular iambic stresses, a solution that he justified upon the authority of those modern vernacular "classics," Ariosto and Tasso. He argued that since intricately rhymed stanzas in non-quantitative hendecasyllables had been used successfully in recent Italian, Spanish, and French narrative poetry, they could be accommodated in Latin, from which, after all, these vulgar tongues had evolved.[14] He expressed the hope, therefore, that readers would not find displeasing these "leonine verses" upon which he had decided for his translation.

What he remarked of Chaucer held true five years later for Henryson, the sense of whose narrative Kynaston wished to preserve too in unchanging Latin rather than in the unstable vernacular. How he solved the prosodic challenge may be illustrated by one or two selections from his version of the *Testament*:

> O faire Creseid, the floure & a per se
> Of Troy & Greece, how were thou fortunate
> To change in filth all thy feminite,
> And be with fleshly lust so maculate.
> And go among the Greekes early & late,
> So giglotlike, taking thy foule pleasaunce!
> I have pite thou shouldst fall such mischance.

This stanza, in perfectly regular iambic pentameter, Kynaston renders as follows:

> Ŏ Créssĭdá, flŏs Troíaĕ sínĕ párĕ
> Ět Graéciaĕ, ŭt fŭísti ĭnfórtŭnátă
> Sĭc sórdĕ púdĭcítiăm cómmŭtárĕ
> Lĭbídĭné cărnálĭ mácŭlátă
> Ět íntĕr Dánaŏs fróntĕ pérfrĭcátă
> Quŏtídĭe írĕ, foédaĕ vólŭptátĭ
> Dédĭtă, dóleŏ vícĕs túĭ fátĭ.[15]

It is patent that Kynaston is writing accentual iambic verse. In the third line, for example, the quantities — "Sĭc sōrdĕ pŭdĭcĭtĭăm cōmmūtārĕ" — make it difficult to conceive the line as a classical hendecasyllable; the ear hears the beat of the five accents unequivocally. In order to achieve this measure, however, the translator has been forced to take certain liberties with Latin syllabification. While normal elision may account for some of this accommodation, one notes instances where dissyllables must become monosyllables to make the meter come out, as in the instances of "Dánaŏs," "dóleŏ," and "púdĭcítiăm."

This becomes standard practice with Kynaston, an even more evident example of it being the opening stanza:

> A doly season till a carefull dite
> Should correspond & be equivalent.
> Right so it was when I began to write
> This Tragedy; the weder right fervent,
> When Aries, in the middes of the lent,
> Showres of haile gan fro the North descend,
> That scantly fro the cold I might me defend.[16]

> Tĕmpéstăs trístĭs árgŭméntŏ maéstŏ
> Vĭdétŭr áptă, béne & cónvénírĕ.
> Sĭc érăt, quándŏ scríberĕ érăm praéstŏ
> Trăgoédiăm hánc, ĭnclémĕns coélŭm mírĕ,
> Cŭm grándinĕs áb Ăriétĕ quí prŏdírĕ
> Sólĕnt coĕpérŭnt Bóreă síc dĕscénderĕ
> Vt víx ă frígorĕ pótuĭ mé dĕféndĕrĕ.

Here the translator not only compresses dissyllables, as in "Trăgoédiăm," "Ăriétĕ," "Bóreă" and "pótuĭ," but he also completely elides internal unstressed syllables, as in "grándinĕs" and "frígorĕ" and, most conspicuously, in the endings to third conjugation verbs such as "scríberĕ," "dĕscénderĕ," and "dĕfénderĕ." The consequence is almost unvarying regularity in his iambic pentameter hendecasyllables. Yet if to the ear the rendering seems at times too "spare" and the beat too monotonously regular, almost jingling, Kynaston has composed his stanzas skillfully to maintain the movement, approximately line-by-line — as well as the compression and fluid ease — of Henryson's narrative. Had he employed quantitative elegiacs, he might have fallen into prolixity, as sometimes happened when Renaissance writers produced Latin versions or imitations of vernacular poems. The discipline of the rhymed stanza enabled him to keep matters under control. When one reads the entire translation, after familiarity with Henryson's original and without prejudice against the use of accentual measures when employing the tongue of the Romans, one is impressed with Kynaston's achievement.[17]

Although approximating the "feeling" of the original was one of Kynaston's objectives, he was equally, perhaps even more, concerned with preserving its meaning from distortion by such rapid linguistic shifts as the vernacular had been undergoing over the preceding centuries. That there were compelling reasons for his concern may be exemplified by the description of the attire of Saturn:

> Attour his belt his liart lockes lay
> Felterd vnfaire, ouer fret with frostes hoare;
> His garment and his gite full gaie of gray;
> His widdred weed fro him the wind out wore;
> A boistrous bowe within his hond he bore;
> Vnder his girdle a flash of felone flaines,
> Federed with ice, & heeded with holstaines.

A literal modernization of this stanza would read:

> Around his belt his matted dark grey locks, grizzled with hoary frosts, lay disorderly; his garment and his dress of grey were very handsome; the wind caused his tattered clothing to flutter; in his hand he bore a sturdy bow; under his girdle a quiver of deadly arrows, feathered with ice and pointed with hailstones.

Kynaston solves the problem of translating the passage as follows:

> Cincturam circum furui stant capilli
> Incomptis nodis, cana quos velabat
> Pruina; vestis vilis erat illi;
> Attritum tegmen ventus lacerabat;
> Robustum arcum laeua is gestabat;
> Sub zona dirum fascem sagittarum,
> Nix pluma grando cuspis erat quarum.[18]

Except for his turning the ironic "His garment and his gite full gaie of gray" into the straightforward "vestis vilis erat illi," he has rendered nicely both the sense and the feeling of Henryson's graphic description.

Throughout Kynaston shows excellent comprehension of Scottish dialect, even though he had before him only the anglicized versions of the Chaucerian editions. For instance, the line "With golden listes gilt on every geare" becomes "Cum stola aureis clauis fimbriata."[19] Again, where Speght and other editors of Chaucer in the description of Mars have an impossible reading "Right tulsure like," Kynaston emends correctly to "Right tulliure like" and appropriately translates the phrase "Sicarijs simillimus," since the Scots word *tulliure* meant a "quarreler."[20] As a courtier to a Stuart monarch, of course, and especially as a friend to the Scottish royal librarian Patrick Young, to whom he had dedicated the first book of his version of *Troilus and Criseyde*, he would have had access to experts on Henryson's dialect when such a crux occurred for him. His own linguistic knowledge and sensitivity, however, are evident in his solutions to other problems of translation.

For words current in Middle English but obsolescent in his own time he carefully searches out Latin equivalents. Thus, "wanhope" (l. 47), the old noun for *despair*, becomes the adjective *desperatum*. The phrase "none is to wite [blame] but thou" (ll. 134–35) becomes "solus tu pro istis / Culpandus es"; "frownced" (for *wrinkled*, l. 155), *Rugatus*; "stevin" (for *voice*, l. 468), *voce*; "brutlenes" (for *frailty*, l. 86), *imbecillitatem*; "roun" (for *whisper*, l. 506), *mussitare*. A special case is the clause "within mine orature / I stood" (ll. 8–9). Kynaston rightly supplies for this "meo steti in-conclavi" since Henryson was using the word in the rarer sense of "chamber" rather than a place of private prayer. Words derived centuries earlier from French for which meaning had altered or the origins become obscure are also properly translated. For example, "jolly verse" (l. 59) becomes "verbis ... camoenis" (approximating the sense of French *joli*), while the phrase describing nightfall in l. 10, "scyled under cure" is deftly paraphrased "Subduxerat sub noctis umbra graui" to reflect the relation of *cure* to *cover* and thence to *curfew* (French, *couvre-feu*).

Of especial interest are instances in which Kynaston renders terms in such a way as to echo the diction or phrasing of classical poetry. Henryson's remark that Cresseid had been Troilus's "only paramour" (l. 53) Kynaston paraphrases, most appropriately, as "illam solam statuit deperire," thus reminding one of the Plautine and Catullan "aliquam deperire" (to be desperately in love with someone). Even better as an illustration of how he attempts by using Latin to preserve Henryson's meaning from slipping away is his conversion of the disparaging "giglotlike" (for *wantonly*, l. 83) into the Martialian idiom for shamelessness, *fronte perfricata*.[21]

With few exceptions, Kynaston's alterations of his original are minor. Rarely does he omit details, though in the opening stanza he does not endeavor to translate the word "lent" (the liturgical season) but rather provides a curious note in English to explain the meaning of this "antient Saxon word."[22] Occasionally, he makes a slight change because of the constraints of rhyming, as when Diana's "wast [wild] woods & wells" (l. 182) become "montes ... fontes." His most serious departure occurs toward the end of the poem where Henryson presents, first, Cresseid's

"Complaint" and then her confession of guilt and last warning to lovers of women like herself. This latter passage, even though it occurs in all of the Chaucerian editions he could have consulted, Kynaston omits completely from his translation, while he expresses bemusement at the stanzaic structure of the "Complaint." For Henryson, in order to set this speech off as a distinctive and more "elevate" rhetorical unit, had switched in it to an intricate nine-line stanza. Kynaston objects to what he considers its excessive alliteration and also protests that "for the authour his varying of his measure & number of lines in his Stanzes, because I know not how to excuse it, I haue neglected it, keeping my selfe in my translation to the number of Heptenaries, *which* is consonant to all the rest of the workes."[23] In part, this refusal to reproduce the original faithfully can be excused because he did not have access to the genuine Scots text, which prints the stanzas correctly, whereas they are garbled in all the early Chaucerian editions, some stanzas having nine, some eight, one but five, and another, a badly pied one that he does not bother to translate, only six lines.

The effect of these crucial omissions and alterations is not negligible, for they do leave an impression that Kynaston was somewhat less sympathetic toward Cresseid, even at the approach of her death, than was Henryson. Not that the Latin version is without touches which exhibit poetic sensitivity to the pity of her changed condition. Henryson, for instance, objects to the cruel doom of Saturn and asks the melancholy god,

> Of faire Creseid, why hast thou no mercy,
> Which was so sweete, gentile, & amorous?
> Withdraw thy sentence, & be gracious.   (ll. 321–23)

These lines become in Kynaston's manuscript

> Creseidae quare nolles misereri
> Quae adeo dulcis erat at*que* pura?
> Subtrahere iudicium nunc cura....

Pura may be there to rhyme with *cura*; yet it may also be that Kynaston ignores the "amorous" of Henryson in order to stress the pathos of the difference between the lady's earlier beauty and grace and the physical foulness that her impending disease will produce. Again, to intensify the pity of her transformation, he goes his original one better. Where Henryson has Cynthia condemn Cresseid to loss of "heale of body" without hope of cure, the translation makes the punishment include psychological suffering as well:

> En corpus aegrum, maestam tuam mentem
> Reddo non erit morbo tuo medela.   (ll. 334–35)

On the other hand, in the great poetic passage where Troilus rides unknowingly by his now-deformed lady, Kynaston's language reminds one, where there is nothing similar in Henryson's words, of his prefatory allusion to her as a "false unconstant whore":

Yet then her looke into his minde he brought
The sweete visage and amorous blenking
Of faire Creseid, sometime his owne derling.   (ll. 481–83)

Sed eius vultus menti imprimebat
Lascivos gestus frontis impudicae
Creseidae pulchrae, quondam suae amicae.

Granted that *lascivos* can mean simply "playful"; when knitted up with "frontis impudicae," it is clear that Kynaston means the attributive to be taken pejoratively.

Finally, he omits Cresseid's moving confession of unfaithfulness to Troilus (ll. 540–74). Had Kynaston retained these five stanzas, with their speaker's admission of having been "elevait ... in wantones ... fickill and friuolous," and the self-accusing refrain, "O, fals Cresseid! and trew knicht Troilus!" the lady may have emerged in his Latin version, as she does in the original, an even more sympathetic, as well as pathetic, figure. For upon the basis of this passage several modern critics have argued that Henryson probably intended to suggest his heroine's conversion from her earlier selfish "Lustis Lecherous" to charity and, hence, her ultimate redemption.[24] On the other hand, the last three stanzas of her confession admonish male lovers to be wary of whom they choose as paramours, since "Thocht sum be trew, I wait richt few are thay" (l. 572). Possibly Kynaston decided to leave out so ungallant an opinion of womankind; whatever his motives, the omission of this entire passage is his only notorious infidelity as a translator.

How his endeavor to make Henryson's fine poem more accessible to contemporary readers, both at home and abroad, might have succeeded we can never know, since it existed only in the unique manuscript now in the Bodleian collection. Yet it was a highly innovative and most accomplished effort at versifying in a classical tongue, demonstrating the openness of neo-Latin authors to experiment, rather than an unvarying adherence to ancient forms, and their willingness to interact with literature in the modern vernaculars.

Stanford University

Notes

1. As one of his modern editors, H. Harvey Wood, observes, "If any single poem were to be chosen to justify the choice of Henryson as the greatest poet of his age, surely it ought to be 'The Testament of Cresseid'" (*Two Scots Chaucerians*. Writers and Their Work: No. 201 [London, Longmans, Green & Co., 1967], p. 11). Marshall W. Stearns cites a number of twentieth-century critics who have expressed esteem for Henryson's poem, among them Aldous Huxley, H. J. C. Grierson, Geoffrey Tillotson, Marianne Moore, and E. M. W. Tillyard (*Robert Henryson* [New York, Columbia University Press, 1949], pp. 4–6).

2. The oldest separate, and oldest genuinely Scots, text is that published by Henry Charteris (Edinburgh, 1593).

3. "The Testament of Cresseid," ll. 40–42, in *The Poems of Robert Henryson*, ed. G. Gregory Smith (Edinburgh and London, William Blackwood and Sons, 1908-14), III, 4.

4. For an account of Cressida's treatment in literature through the Elizabethan period, see Hyder E. Rollins, "The Troilus–Cressida Story from Chaucer to Shakespeare," *PMLA*, 32 (1917), 383–429.

5. "Heic incipiunt descriptiones omnium quos vidi elegantissimae cum quoad authoris inventionem poeticam tam quoad Mythologiam Saturni & caeterorum planetarum quarum in gratiam fateor me hasce annotationes scripsisse & hoc paruum opusculum ex lingua Scotica in Latinam transtulisse" (Note to Stanza 22, *Poems of Henryson*, I, cl).

6. Ibid., I, ciii. This remark inspired Rollins to comment, somewhat curiously, that "Both Henryson and Kinaston were quite modern in their attitude toward Cressid" (op. cit., p. 397, n. 34).

7. *Musae Querelae de Regis in Scotiam Profectione* (London, Thomas Harper, 1633). Kynaston also published translations of other poems by Johnston in the latter's *Musae Aulicae* (London, Thomas Harper, 1635).

8. *The Constitutions of the Museum Minervae* were printed at London in 1636; they are also preserved in a manuscript in the Bodleian Library, Oxford.

9. "In aggredienda hac versione, duo praecipuè fuerunt in votis, Primò conservatio huius poematum gemmae an interitu & oblivione, quae ferè amissa erat, & a nostratibus vix intellecta, (saltem nemini in deliciis) ob verborum in eâ obsoletorum ignorantiam, quae in desuetudine abiêre. Deinde illius Romano artificio munitae & ornatae tibi dedicatio, quam ob eruditissimi genij tui honorem, & nominis celebritatem, exteris gratiorem & acceptiorem non immeritò autumem" (Geoffrey Chaucer, *Amorum Troili et Creseidae Libri duo priores Anglico-Latini*, transl. Sir Francis Kynaston [Oxford, John Lichfield, 1635], fol. A3ᵛ).

10. Preface "Candido Lectori," ibid., fol. † ʳ⁻ᵛ.

11. Although Smith assumed (*Poems of Henryson*, I, cv, n. 1) that Kynaston used Thynne's edition of Chaucer (1532) as his basic text, Denton Fox has established that he was following the London, 1598 edition by Thomas Speght in preparing his own transcription and translation of the original (Robert Henryson, *Testament of Cresseid*, ed. Denton Fox [Edinburgh, Thomas Nelson and Sons, 1968], pp. 12–13).

12. "Sed peccatum inexpiabile in MANES *Chauceri* admississe me existimarem, si vel minimum Iota in eius scriptis immutassem, quae sacra & intacta in aeternum manere digna sunt" (Preface, 1635, fol. †ᵛ).

13. George Saintsbury, while labeling Kynaston's effort to reproduce Chaucer's rime royal in a Latin translation an "ultra-eccentric enterprise," granted that it was "a venture, in which he at least showed that he had thoroughly saturated himself with the rhythm" (*Minor Poets of the Caroline Period* [Oxford, At the Clarendon Press, 1906], p. 64).

14. "Non me praeterit, quantò facilius mihi fuisset authoris verba & sensus vulgaribus Latinis Hexametris & Pentametris reddidisse: sed cum recorder quod celeberrimi *Torquari*, [*sic*] *Tassi*, atque elegantissimi *Ludovici Ariosti* opera (ut Gallos & Iberos taceam) hoc metri genere verè nobili & Enharmonico sint composita, & quod haec septennaria compositio non tantùm Italis, sed & Anglis, Gallis, immò omnibus sit in deliciis, utpote melos quod aurem mirifico modulamine mulceat & delectet. Tentare mihi visum est, quid Lingua Latina posset, & experiri, num grata forent carmina Idiomate Romano pacta & concinnata, quae in linguis derivatis & modernis, tantam obtinuerunt per tot saecula sequiora existimationem" (Preface, 1635, fols. †ᵛ⁻†2ʳ).

15. Stanza 12, ll. 78–84 (*Poems of Henryson*, I, cxi).

16. Stanza 1, ll. 1–7 (ibid., p. cv). The metrical irregularity does not occur in the final line in the Scots version: "That scantlie fra the cauld I micht defend."

17. An anonymous nineteenth-century critic, in presenting excerpts from Kynaston's volume of 1635, asserted of the Chaucerian translation what also applies to the version of Henryson's poem: "Considering the difficulties of his task, Sir Francis must be allowed to have acquitted himself with much dexterity; and he deserves praise for the fidelity with which he adheres to his original, in spite of the temptations afforded by so ornamental a language as the Latin" (*Retrospective Review*, 12 [1825], 110).

18. Stanza 24 (*Poems of Henryson*, I, cxvii). To the word "Felterd" in the second line of this stanza, Kynaston has a wonderful gloss, explaining that he was constrained to use the paraphrase "Incomptis nodis" since "nullum sit in lingua Latina vocabulum quod genuine eius energiam explicet, tale enim significat capillorum discompositionem, quae maior sit vlla complicatione textura aut connexione." Then he goes on to explain at length how the Scots word is related to *felt*, out of which rough-textured hats are made that are weatherproof, "cum petasi hoc modo elaborati nec ventis nec pluuijs sint penetrabiles" (ibid., p. cli).

19. Stanza 26, l. 4 (ibid., p. cxviii). Smith renders this line in his notes: "With golden borders, or selvages, gilt on every 'gore'" (ibid., p. 47).

20. Kynaston's note to his emendation reads: "*Sicarijs, &c.*: Propter ignorantiam verae significationis Scotici vocabuli *Tullieur* erratum est fere in omnibus impressionibus in quibus perpaerem describitur *Tulsur*. vox haec apud Scotos hominem trucem & efferum significat qualem nos Angli vocamus *a Swaggerer*, & Itali *vno Brauo*" (ibid., p. cliv).

21. The Latin idiom means "having rubbed the face to hide evidence of blushing"; hence, Martial speaks of one who "perfricuit frontem posuitque pudorem" (XI.xxvii.7). Kynaston's manuscript (p. 480) reads "gligotlike" for "giglotlike."

22. "Lent is an antient Saxon word and doth properly signifie that time of the yeare wherein beggers creepe out of their booths, & do lie sunning themselues in the open feilds: hence the Saxons haue an antient prouerbe in their owne tongue, Lent nempt knechten, that is, lent takes vpp seruants. the word is now indifferently vsed for all the time betweene Shrouetide & Ester, which falls out allwayes in the begining of the Spring" (ibid., p. cvi).

23. (Ibid., p. cxxxvi.) By "Heptenaries" Kynaston means his seven-line stanzas.

24. Most notably, E. M. W. Tillyard in *Five Poems, 1470–1870* (London, Chatto & Windus, 1948), and Henryson's editor, Charles Elliott, who looks upon the appearance of Troilus "as the power through which Cresseid achieves spiritual regeneration" (in Robert Henryson, *Poems* [Oxford, At the Clarendon Press, 1974], p. xvi). C. David Benson finds that Cresseid "approaches, if never actually reaches, a Christian understanding" and he makes an interesting contrast between the spiritual dispositions of the two lovers after their encounter ("Troilus and Cresseid in Henryson's *Testament*," *Chaucer Review*, 13 [1979], 263–71).

Bacon's Legal Learning:
Its Influence on His Philosophical Ideas

Roger T. Simonds

Although Francis Bacon is now chiefly remembered as an essayist, philosopher and politician, he was also a distinguished lawyer; yet the influence of his professional training and experience upon the formation and articulation of his ideas has been largely neglected. Certain aspects of the Continental legal tradition, in particular, had special importance to Bacon for reasons to be explored in this paper.

The possibility that Bacon's legal expertise had important effects on his philosophy is the subject of a passing remark in Holdsworth's *History of English Law*,[1] and the thought was developed at some length twenty-eight years ago in an article by Paul Kocher,[2] but with less than satisfactory results. Interpreting Bacon's philosophy as a naive empiricism, Kocher finds a few passages in his legal writings which suggest that Bacon believed that one can derive general rules from particular cases by induction; he then criticizes Bacon for failing to see that the rules might be wrong because the cases might have been wrongly decided. But recent studies have shown that Bacon's epistemological and methodological views are much more complex and sophisticated than they have usually been made to appear, for he unequivocally rejects the naive empiricism and inductivism so often attributed to him by modern critics following Macaulay.[3] And the methodological doctrine of deriving legal rules from judicial decisions, characteristic of modern Anglo-American "legal realism," could hardly have been imagined in Bacon's time, when no official reports of opinions or decisions existed. He was himself, to be sure, among the first to call for the establishment of a reporting system, but he never claimed that it would be the basis for some new doctrine or method in jurisprudence.

Bacon's expertise in the common law was as great as any in his generation. He had the rare distinction of being appointed Reader twice at Gray's Inn. Like many of his colleagues, he was also familiar with certain civil-law and canon-law principles. While he never favored a "reception" of Roman law in England, he was convinced that English law needed reform and codification, and he proposed this idea to Queen Elizabeth in 1593 and 1596 and again to King James in 1614 and 1616.

The codification proposed to James is very specific.[4] It is to have two main parts: a "digest or recompiling of the common laws," inspired by Justinian's Digest but quite different in content, and a similar treatment of recent statutes, inspired by Justinian's Code. The common-law part would have three elements. First, there would be a book *De antiquitatibus juris*, a collection of ancient acts of Parliament, letters patent, commissions, judgments and the like, "to be used for reverend precedents, but not for binding authorities" (XIII.68). The second element, the main bulk of the work, would be a completion and refinement of the series of Year-books from Edward I onwards. The third element would consist of "certain introductive and auxiliary books touching the study of the laws," including Institutions (an introductory survey modelled on Justinian's), a treatise *De regulis juris* modelled on the last title of the Digest (*De diversis regulis juris antiqui*), and finally "a better book *De verborum significationibus*" or legal glossary, modelled on the penultimate title of the Digest.

Thus Bacon visualized first Elizabeth, then James, as an English Justinian, with himself in the role of Tribonian. The dream came to nothing. But the Latin translation and revision of his *Advancement of Learning*, the *De augmentis scientiarum* (1623), contains a new "Example of a Treatise on Universal Justice or the Fountains of Equity, by Aphorisms: one Title of it," which incorporates the substance of his reform proposals and constitutes a sort of micro-treatise on jurisprudence. Many of the details are quoted or paraphrased from Roman law, as noted by the editor of the Latin text (I.803–27), although they are unfortunately not acknowledged in the English translation (V.88–109). This collection of rather cryptic generalizations is the only outcome, published by Bacon himself, of some forty years of intermittent labor on his pet project.

A much more impressive work, *The Maxims of the Law*, was published posthumously in 1630, with a dedication to Queen Elizabeth dated 1596 and with a fascinating Preface, which, as the editor D. C. Heath rightly says, was never intended to go with the text as it now stands (VII.309–87). The work consists of twenty-five legal maxims in Latin, each with a brief explanation in English and with several illustrative cases in English. Bacon says in the Preface that he has collected three hundred of these maxims and, in what appears to be the earliest manuscript of the Preface, that he has decided to publish the first hundred, so as to profit by critical reactions "for the altering of the other two." The later manuscripts and the printed version say only that he decided "to publish some few ... for the altering of the other which remain" (VII.323). The earliest ("Cambridge") manuscript, however, contains only twenty maxims, while all the others have twenty-five. Bacon also says that he decided "not to derogate from the authority of the rules by vouching the authority of the cases, though in mine own copy I had them quoted" (VII.322), which shows that the cases were not merely hypothetical; and in fact most of them are easily located in the Abridgments or the Year-books. But he says further that "for the expositions and distinctions, I have retained the peculiar language of our law," that is, Law-French; which shows that the Preface was not intended to be published with any of the extant versions of the text, as Heath points out (VII.309). One manuscript, at Lincoln's Inn, is unique in having only the first paragraph of the Preface, although it must be later than the "Cambridge" manuscript (as shown by a variation in the dedication to the Queen). The present writer has seen a second Cambridge manuscript in the University Library, not mentioned by Heath, which contains neither Preface nor dedication but is otherwise similar to the other late manuscripts. Neither Bacon's personal copy of this work nor his collection of 300 maxims has ever been found.

Heath's explanation of these facts is not convincing. He assumes that the fragmentary Lincoln's Inn Preface must be earlier than the others, and consequently that the rest of the Preface was written later than the longer version of the main text. But he forgets that the full Preface, with the minor variation already noted, is present in the Cambridge manuscript, which is the earliest according to Heath himself.

Bacon must have formulated his project for a *Corpus Iuris Civilis Anglicum* very early in his career, perhaps shortly after his admission to Gray's Inn in 1575 at the age of fourteen. He kept a commonplace book or books, no doubt, in which he jotted down legal maxims as he came across them, with one or more illustrative cases under each rule. It is not implausible that the number of entries in these books should approach three hundred, if we assume that he was working at them fairly steadily over the next twenty years, a period during which he had no regular employment. In 1593 a speech by the Lord Keeper Puckering gave Bacon reason to think that the time was ripe for publication, and he may have composed the first version of his Preface at this time.[5] But in April of the same year he was suddenly involved in a year-long struggle for the post of Attorney General, and after that a try for Solicitor General; and by then he was desperate for some way to win the Queen's confidence and a job in her government. He decided to obtain a personal interview with the Queen and try to convince her of the importance of his reform project and of his own special contribution to it, the maxims. This was, I believe, the reason why he translated a few of his expositions and cases from Law-French into English: the Queen could then read them herself. At some time during the year 1596, Bacon was ready with twenty translated sets and composed his first dedication to Queen Elizabeth. This sequence of events would account for the (earlier) Cambridge manuscript. It was intended only for presentation to the Queen, not for publication, which was still supposed to be in Law-French. Soon afterward in the same year, Bacon had his interview with the Queen. She expressed interest in the project, and he added a new paragraph to his dedication mentioning this event and ending with a new date, "January 8th 1596" (i.e., 1597), which is what appears in all of the later manuscripts containing the dedication (VII.310).

From now on, however, Bacon was increasingly busy with affairs of state, having accepted as a consolation prize the post of Counsel at Large to the Queen, which brought him into close touch with the activities of the Privy Council and Star Chamber. At the same time he was working on his essays and his philosophical writings. Before long, he must have decided that he would probably never find the time to put all of his first hundred maxims into final shape for publication, settling rather for "some few." Even this proved to be too much. What happened instead was that he added five more sets to those already translated for the Queen, and perhaps he intended to publish those English versions. But in 1603 Queen Elizabeth died, and the plan (if any) had to be dropped. The later manuscripts must have been for private use among Bacon's friends. They could not have been published with the original Preface, nor could they have been presented to King James with the dedication to Elizabeth. Although he pressed the question of legal reform again after becoming Attorney General in 1613, Bacon never rededicated his work to James, and for all we know he never again hoped to publish that work.

Two factors may help to explain this apparent change of heart. One is that the whole question of legal reform was becoming entangled with the political struggle between Crown and Parliament that began immediately after James's accession. The other factor is that Bacon was becoming more and more absorbed in his plans for the reconstruction of inductive reasoning and natural philosophy.

Proposals for law reform inevitably involved comparisons between English and Continental legal systems. At the outset of King James's reign, such comparisons were still quite respectable and proper. Christopher St Germain's popular *Doctor and Student* (1523 and 1530 in Latin, 1532 in English), in which the "Doctor" is a civilian (in effect) and the "Student" is a student of English common law, had shown the way long before. Around the turn of the seventeenth century, treatises or dialogues on comparative law appeared, or were written, by Fulbeck, Ashe, Hake, Ridley, West and Cowell.[6] About the same time, unfortunately, the advocates of civilian learning were being identified as partisans of the Crown and the royal prerogative, which did not endear them to Parliament. Some, like Alberico Gentili, who represented Spanish interests in the English courts, were avowed royal absolutists.[7]

The last straw was the publication in 1607 of a legal dictionary, *The Interpreter*, by Dr John Cowell of Cambridge, a friend of some of the king's intimate advisers and a supporter in this book of the king's own doctrine of absolute royal power. There was a violent reaction in Parliament two years later; the book was condemned and burnt with the king's reluctant consent. Bacon suggested in the Commons that Cowell's offense was "extreme indiscretion," that it was not error but presumption. Mr Holt said that it was "not an Error, Indiscretion, or Presumption; but a contemptuous, seditious, prodigious Opinion."[8] Aside from the offending opinion, however, Cowell had written something else in his Preface, which Bacon must have noticed with chagrin: "I have in some towardnes a tract (de regulis iuris) wherein my intent is, by collating the cases of both lawes, to shewe, that they both be raised of one foundation, and differ more in language and termes than in substance, and therefore were they reduced to one method (as they easily might) to be attained (in a maner) with all one paines."[9] Now this was Bacon's own project, almost to the letter. In the Preface to the *Maxims* (VII.321) he had written that

> whereas some of these rules have a concurrence with the civil Roman law, and some others a diversity, and many times an opposition; such grounds as are common to our law and theirs I have not affected to disguise into other words than the civilians use, to the end they might seem invented by me, and not borrowed or translated from them: no, but I took hold of it as matter of great authority and majesty, to see and consider the concordance between the laws penned and as it were dicted *verbatim* by the same reason.

This worthy aim was now tainted by association with the upstart Dr Cowell's political heresies.

At the same time, the topic of law reform became for Bacon a subordinate part of the general scheme for the reform of all learning which he announced to the world in *The Advancement of Learning* of 1605. And it was not until eighteen years later, in the Latin revision of this work, that legal questions were given anything more than passing reference. Yet in spite of the apparent shift in focus, Bacon's thought did not really abandon his earlier legal interests; for there is evidence that those interests had more than a little to do with his philosophical ideas and his peculiar ways of expressing them.

Two of the more obvious characteristics of Bacon's writing style in the philosophical works, its aphoristic form and its strange uses of traditional terms, are noted and explained by the author himself. In the Preface to the *Maxims* (VII.321) he writes:

> whereas I could have digested these rules into a certain method or order, which ... would have made every particular rule, through his coherence and relation unto other rules, seem more cunning and more deep; yet I have avoided to do so, because this delivering of knowledge in distinct and disjointed aphorisms doth leave the wit of man more free to turn and toss, and to make use of that which is so delivered to more several purposes and applications. For we see all the ancient wisdom and science was wont to be delivered in that form; as may be seen by the parables of Solomon, and by the aphorisms of Hippocrates, and the moral verses of Theognis and Phocylades: but chiefly the precedent of the civil law, which hath taken the same course with their rules, did confirm me in my opinion.

Here Bacon is thinking of the last title of Justinian's Digest, which is a collection of ancient legal maxims. This particular passage refers, of course, to the organization of the legal maxims; but it is quite obvious that the adoption of an aphoristic style in the philosophical works, notably the *Novum Organum*, was inspired by the same rationale, and perhaps for an even better reason. For the purposes of the *Maxims* it was convenient but hardly necessary to "leave the wit of man free to turn and toss," and in fact the organization of Bacon's maxims exemplifies this policy only in the rather weak sense that there is no systematic effort to relate the different maxims to each other or to the general concepts of jurisprudence; but each maxim is carefully explained and illustrated. In the *Novum Organum*, however, Bacon is addressing a general, non-professional audience, and he is very consciously presenting a radical challenge to traditional learning and the educational establishment. Hence it was prudent not to say too clearly just what he had in mind: let the imaginative reader draw his own conclusions and make his own applications.

For similar reasons, and again inspired by his legal training, Bacon quite self-consciously employs traditional philosophical terms in novel ways. This is demonstrated by a passage in *The Advancement of Learning* (Book II), where he explains his peculiar use of the term "metaphysic." Here he states a general policy of retaining ancient terms as far as possible, even though his ideas are new; and he criticizes Aristotle for having taken the opposite course with his own predecessors, translating their terms into his own in order to repudiate their ideas. Then he adds (III.353; bracketed material is my own):

> But to me on the other side that do desire, as much as lieth in my pen, to ground a sociable intercourse between antiquity and proficience, it seemeth best to keep way with antiquity *usque ad aras* ["right up to the altars," i.e., to the fullest extent possible without violating sacred duty], and therefore to retain the ancient terms, though I sometimes alter the uses and definitions; according to the moderate proceeding in civil government, where although there be some alteration, yet that holdeth which Tacitus wisely noteth, *eadem magistratuum vocabula* [the names of the magistrates are the same].

The allusion at the end is to Tacitus, *Annals* I.3, which describes the drastic change in public life after Augustus, hidden under a semblance of domestic tranquillity (Domi res tranquillae, eadem magistratuum vocabula). While citing Tacitus, Bacon might well also be thinking of the sort of change introduced by the Statute of Uses (1536), the topic of one of his Readings at Gray's Inn, whereby the old distinction between legal and equitable interests in land was for most purposes abolished, but without disturbing the traditional terminology of the law. Thus, in a similar way, one might introduce radical novelties into philosophy without revealing them to a casual reader.

It should be no surprise, then, that Bacon permits himself so little by way of cosmological or metaphysical speculation. Moreover, his primary interests are those of a methodologist rather than a speculator, and this fact lends further support to the view that he may have been strongly influenced by his expertise in law. Time after time, we find Bacon using imagery drawn from that source, even where we would not ordinarily expect it. Speaking of philosophical first principles, for example, he says that "with regard to the first notions of the intellect, there is not one of [them] but I hold it for suspected, and in no way established, until it has submitted to a new trial and a fresh judgment has been thereupon pronounced" (IV.26). Concerning the three traditionally recognized cognitive faculties of the mind — reason, imagination, sensation — he writes: "It is true indeed that the imagination performs the office of an agent or messenger or proctor in both provinces, both the judicial and the ministerial. For sense sends all kinds of images over to imagination for reason to judge of; and reason again when it has made its judgment and selection, sends them over to imagination before the decree be put in execution" (IV.405–06). And on his favorite topic, methodology, he says that "no judgment can be rightly formed either of my method or of the discoveries to which it leads, by means of ... the reasoning which is now in use; since I cannot be called on to abide by the sentence of a tribunal which is itself on trial" (IV.52). In connection with one of his own important contributions to methodology, the idea of a co-operative and systematic "natural history," Bacon observes that in the past "men of learning ... have taken for the construction or for the confirmation of their philosophy certain rumours and vague fames or airs of experience, and allowed these the weight of lawful evidence" (IV.94).

This way of expressing philosophical notions in legal or political terms was not an invention of Bacon's; he had the well known precedent of Plato's *Republic*, and the legal-process metaphor occurs also in Seneca.[10] But for Bacon the legal imagery had a more pointed significance, because it reflected his own professional training and experience. This shows quite clearly at the end of the brief "Preparative towards a Natural and Experimental History," where he writes: "I mean (according to the practice in civil causes) in this great Plea or Suit granted by the divine favour and providence (whereby the human race seeks to recover its right over nature), to examine nature herself and the arts upon interrogatories" (IV.263).

This statement is virtually a confession that Bacon's theory of experimental method was inspired by his knowledge of "the practice in civil causes," specifically in Star Chamber and Chancery, where civilian and canon-law procedures were routinely followed. Taking evidence by way of interrogatories was standard practice in the "inquisitorial" trial system which had replaced the ordeals in the ecclesiastical courts, and soon also the civil courts, during the thirteenth century (except in the English common-law courts, where the jury system developed instead).[11] Interrogatories were carefully formulated lists of questions, designed to elicit the relevant facts, which often revealed discrepancies between different statements of the same witness or conflicts between different witnesses. One such list, used by Bacon, is preserved in Spedding (VIII.316ff.). The discrepancies and conflicts might be resolved by further interrogatories or by confrontation in open court. It would not take too much imagination to see that the same interrogatory techniques could be applied to the examination of historical documents, reports of natural phenomena or, more generally, the testimonies of the senses. Bacon repeatedly emphasizes the idea that the senses cannot be trusted; they distort and color the information they provide, and this fault is the first of Bacon's famous "idols" or pitfalls of human thought (IV.53–59). On the other hand, paradoxically, the senses are the only sources of information we have. In this respect, they are exactly like the witnesses in a trial: the court must rely on their testimony, having no other, but it cannot afford to take that testimony uncritically.

Bacon's originality as a methodologist lay in his recognition that the traditional notion of inductive reasoning by what he calls "simple enumeration," that is, generalizing from a number of particular observed instances of some characteristic or process, is inadequate as a foundation for the sciences (IV.70; 97–98). He saw that we need, first of all, a systematic survey of the available information on the topic under investigation; we need a systematic collection of the plausible generalizations (which he calls "conjectures") which are suggested by that information; and we need a method for eliminating false conjectures (a "first vintage"), each of which is consistent with all of our evidence. We then search for more information which will enable us to eliminate some of these remaining conjectures; and so the process repeats until, ideally, we have eliminated all but one (IV.126ff.). This process is essentially what we now call the hypothetico-deductive method in experimental science. If, as I am suggesting, it was largely Bacon's civilian learning and professional experience that led him to an understanding of this method, then we can see clearly how that learning and experience, in spite of the apparent failure of his project for legal reform, still had important effects in his philosophy of the sciences and hence also in the development of modern thought.

The American University
Washington, D. C.

Notes

1. William S. Holdsworth, *A History of English Law* (London, Methuen, Sweet and Maxwell, 1903–66), V, 239.

2. "Francis Bacon on the Science of Jurisprudence," *JHI*, 18 (1957), 3–26. Reprinted in Brian Vickers, *Essential Articles for the Study of Francis Bacon* (Hamden, Conn., Archon Books, 1968).

3. See Margery N. Purver, *The Royal Society: Concept and Creation* (Cambridge, Mass., M.I.T. Press, 1967), chs. 2–3.

4. James Spedding, R. Ellis and D. Heath, *Works of Francis Bacon* (London, 1857–74), XIII, 61–71. This work will be cited hereafter in the text by a Roman-numeral volume number followed by an Arabic-numeral page number, enclosed in parentheses.

5. See Kocher, p. 3, and Holdsworth, V, 486.

6. William Fulbeck, *A Direction or Preparitive to the Study of the Law* (1600); *A Parallele or Conference of the Civill Law, Canon Law, and the Common Law of this Realme of England* (1601); *The Pandectes of the Law of Nations* (1602). Thomas Ashe, *ΕΠΙΕΙΚΕΙΑ* (1607). Edward Hake, Epieikeia. *A Dialogue on Equity in Three Parts* (written about 1600; first edition by D. E. C. Yale, New Haven, Conn., Yale U.P., 1953). Thomas Ridley, *View of the Civil Law* (1607). William West, *Symboleography* (1597). John Cowell, *Institutiones iuris anglicani ad methodum et seriem institutionem imperialium compositae et digestae* (1605).

7. See Ernest Nys, *Le droit romain, le droit des gens, et le collège des docteurs en droit civil* (Brussels, Weissenbruch, 1910), p. 61.

8. *Journals of the House of Commons*, 7 Jac. I ("1609", i.e., 1610), pp. 399–400.

9. Cowell, *The Interpreter*, p. 3 *verso*.

10. In *Republic* II, 368d–e, Socrates propses to use the political structure of an idealized city-state as a model for psychoanalysis. Seneca in *Naturales Quaestiones* often uses judicial process language in dealing with evaluation of conflicting scientific opinions. I am indebted to Professor P. H. Schrijvers of the University of Leyden for calling the latter point to my attention. See his paper, "De mens als toeschouwer: Een cultuur-historische verkenning in de Latijnse literatuur," *Lampas*, 13 (1980), 261–76, esp. pp. 270–71 and note 24.

11. See John H. Langbein, *Prosecuting Crime in the Renaissance: England, Germany, France* (Cambridge, Mass., Harvard U.P., 1974), ch. 6.

"Aut ridenda omnia aut flenda sunt": Heraklit und Demokrit in Schottland

A. M. Stewart

Auf einmalige Art wird in dem schottischen Prosawerk *The Complaynt of Scotland* (ca. 1550)[1] ein neulateinisches Gedicht (ca. 1506) eingeführt, zitiert, einer schottischen Übertragung gegenübergestellt und mit dem passenden Seneca-Zitat resümiert.

Die beiden Gedichte lauten wie folgt:

Ad lectorem

Defle hominum vitam plusquam heraclite solebas,
In lachrimas totos, solue, age nunc oculos:
Concute maiori splenem democrite risu,
Et toto resonans ore cachinus hiet.
Vita fuit mundi post condita secula nuncquam,
Et risu, pariter dignior, & lachrymis.

To the readar.

Gude readar, veip and murne this mortal lyif
As did the vyise philosophour heraclite
And thou sal laucht for scorne recreatyfe
As fast as did the prudent democrite
Ane murnit for pite, the tothir leucht in despite
Quhen thai beheld this varldis vanite
Bot var thai nou on lyue, i mycht veil dyit
That tha vald laucht and veip our misire.
Seneca.
Aut ridenda omnia, aut flenda sunt.

In Minitaschenbuchformat, (ca. 11cm x 8cm) in Paris gedruckt, erschien das Werk anonym. Der vermutliche Autor dieser Klage ist Robert Wedderburn aus Dundee, der den Magistergrad 1530 im St Leonards Kolleg der Universität St Andrews erwarb.[2] *The Complaynt of Scotland* ist ein komplexes Kunstwerk, das

vordergründig eine Zeitklage — eine personifizierte Klage Schottlands — (der Dame
Scotia) — während der englischen Besatzung in den Jahren 1547–50 darstellt.
Diese Klage oder Ständekritik umklammert einen pastoralen enzyklopädischen
Teil, den der Kläger als "Monologue Recreative" bezeichnet, einen Einschub,
der als Materialienheft der Kulturbelange der Mitte des 16ten Jahrhunderts
dienen könnte. Die Klage benutzt den allegorischen Vierer-Dialog-Rahmen von
Alain Chartiers "Quadrilogue Invectif" (1422) übernommen.[3] Für die Füllung
dieses Rahmens bedient sich der schottische Kläger musterhaft im ganzen Selbst-
bedienungsladen der Tradition.

Das patriotische Widerstandsdokument in literarischer Kleidung ist vornehm-
lich "ad morum Scotorum correctionem" gedacht. In ihrer Abrechnung mit den
drei Ständen tritt die allegorische Figur Dame Scotia hervor. In auffallender Hervorhebung werden von der Dame Scotia gegen Ende ihres Arguments in einer
kleinen Abhandlung die beiden Gedichte behandelt.

In der "Rahmenerzählung" mahnt die Dame Scotia die drei Stände mit Hilfe
des Beispieles der beiden Philosophen Heraklit und Demokrit, die hier eine neu-
zeitgeschichtliche Funktion haben. Heutzutage in Schottland würden die beiden
Philosophen auch so reagieren wie damals, denn sie würden genug Gründe vor-
finden. An dieser Stelle fährt die Dame Scotia plötzlich wie folgt fort: "i vil rehers
sex versis in latyn quhilk var conposit be ane knycht of itale M. Antonio philiremo fregoso and syne i sal rehers the exposition of them in our scottis tong
as neir the sentens of the text as i can" ("Ich werde jetzt sechs Zeilen eines lateinischen Gedichtes wiederholen, welche von einem italienischen Adeligen, M.
Antonio Philiremo Fregoso verfaßt wurden. Danach werde ich die Exposition
dieser Verse so sinngemäß wie möglich in unserer schottischen Sprache wieder-
geben"). Es folgen die Gedichte und das "Epimythion."[4] Der Kläger faßt das
Beispiel als "vanitas mundi" Topos auf und erwähnt eine Parallelstelle in der
Bibel (*Ecclesiastes* Kap. 2). Germanisten kennen das ähnliche Alciati-Gedicht und
die deutsche Übersetzung.[5] Die im schottischen Werke abgedruckten Gedichte
haben offensichtlich dieselbe Quelle wie das Alciati-Emblem. Diese gemeinsame
Quelle ist ein Epigram aus der *Anthologia Planudea* (*Liber* I, titulus XIII, Vers II)
wie A. Blankert in seinem kunstgeschichtlichen Artikel darstellt.[6] Der schottische
Kläger hat aber nicht unmittelbar aus der *Griechischen Anthologie*, sondern von der
Titelseite bei Fregoso geborgt.

Die neulateinischen Verse, die angeblich von Fregoso stammen, sind in Wirklichkeit, wie wir auf Fregosos Titelseite selbst lesen, ein Gedicht von einem Freund
Fregosos, Bartolomeo Simonetta aus Mailand. Simonetta hat vermutlich speziell
dieses Gedicht für die Titelseite von Fregosos "Riso di Democrati e pianto d'Era-
clite" gedichtet.[7]

Wir haben also in dem schottischen Rahmenwerk eine kleine "erasmianische"
Abhandlung (Einführung: neulateinisches Gedicht: schottisches Gedicht: Seneca-
Zitat: Kommentar) eine Art Vorform vom Essai.[8]

Das Vorkommen zweier Gedichte in dem sonst ausschließlich in Prosa verfaßten

Werk, ist eine stark betonte Hervorhebung. Eine solche Mischung ist in einer Satire angebracht. Die Gedichte werden mit einer Einführung eingeleitet: die Quelle wird genannt ("auctoritas"): der Sinn des Inhaltes wird kommentiert und hermeneutisch zeitkritisch allgemeingültig angewandt: weiterführende Lektüre, gleichzeitig Beweis für die Richtigkeit der Moral, wird empfohlen. Das Seneca-Zitat hat auch mnemotechnische Funktion.

Der schottische Dichter wählt absichtlich ein lateinisches Gedicht von der Titelseite eines italienischen Werkes und zitiert es in einem schottischen mundartlichen Prosawerk der Mitte des 16ten Jahrhunderts. Warum zitiert er Fregoso / Simonetta? Es ist klar, daß der Kläger Fregoso / Simonetta keineswegs aus Verlegenheit zitiert, denn er kennt die Quellen der Antike.[9] Er zitiert absichtlich auch die Seneca-Formulierung, gewissermaßen als nachträgliche Überschrift. Er zitiert aus mehreren Gründen.

Er zitiert die italienische Quelle aus patriotischen Gründen und weist damit auf den Anschluß der schottischen Literatur an die Weltliteratur hin.

Das Wort "Weltliteratur" erinnert an Goethes Kommentar: "Vielleicht überzeugt man sich bald, daß es keine patriotische Kunst und patriotische Wissenschaft gebe. Beide gehören, wie alles Gute, der ganzen Welt an und können nur durch allgemeine freie Wechselwirkung aller zugleich Lebenden, in steter Rücksicht auf das, was uns vom Vergangenen übrig und bekannt ist, gefördert werden" (*W. A.* I.48, 23). Der Kläger strebt diese Wechselwirkung durch Anschluß an die Weltliteratur an. Wie Hans Pyritz einmal die Goethe-Stelle kommentierte,[10] ist Goethes Meinung deutlich: "Als Jünger Herders leugnet er keineswegs, daß Werke der Kunst und Resultate des Denkens geprägt sind durch das geschichtliche Lebens- und Entwicklungsgesetz nationaler Kulturen. Aber über dieser Vielfalt von biologischen Zusammenhängen erblickt der reife und alte Goethe einen höheren Kosmos der Werte, auf den alle geistige Schöpfung zielt: eine Kultur der Menschheit, für die wir arbeiten." In Schottland im 16ten Jahrhundert hatte der Kläger die sekularisierte Erklärung nicht nötig. Die damalige Geschichtsschreibung diente dem theologischen Gesamtbild. Wie Pyritz bemerkt, sind die Erfahrungen des Daseins, die der Künstler in Symbolen gestaltet und die Fragen, die der Forscher an die Phänomene des Lebens richtet in tausend Formen, doch letztlich immer die gleichen Grunderfahrungen und Grundfragen, die den Menschen seit Adams Zeiten bewegen. Der Kläger empfindet auch diese unterliegende Einheit. Er ist aber Patriot. Die Juxtaposition beider Gedichte ist eine Herausforderung. Die Kritiker sollen die schottische Übertragung mit dem Original vergleichen und beurteilen. Ein gutes anerkanntes gelobtes neulateinisches Modell wird als Original zum Vergleich angeboten. Diese Herausforderung zur Kritik steht im Gegensatz zur Einstellung des Autors / Actors in anderen Teilen des Werkes, worin es vorrangig um die wichtige politische Mahnung geht. Dort wäre rhetorische Spitzfindigkeit eine irrelevante Ablenkung von der wichtigen Botschaft. Dort sind Quellen und Übertragungen getarnt. (Chartier z. B. wird nicht genannt). Hier dagegen ist ein stolzer klarer Verweis auf die patriotische Leistung

des Übersetzers in seinem Beitrag zur Imitatio-Debatte und zur "Deffence et Illustration de la Langue Ecossaise," zur Bereicherung der schottischen Kultur-
bestrebungen, zum schottischen Selbstbewußtsein.

Was man wohl als Binsenwahrheit oder Plattheit abtun könnte im Sinne etwa
des Sprichwortes "'Viele haben den Heraklit auf der Stirn und den Demokrit im
Herzen," d. h. "Thun kläglich äußerlich und lachen im Herzen": oder "Hera-
klit/Demokrit" gleicht "Pessimismus/Optimismus") wird in dem schottischen Werk
als wertvolle Weisheit oder Topos untersucht. Dieses Verfahren ist durchaus
gerechtfertigt.

Eine Rechtfertigung sehe ich erstens in der ganzen damaligen Einstellung zur
Geschichtsschreibung,[11] die Einstellung zur Geschichte als sich erinnernde
Vergegenwärtigung der Ewigen Ideen, zur Tradition als "reminiscentia": wie in
Ciceros Formulierung "historia vero testis temporum / lux veritatis, vita memoriae,
/ magistra vitae, nuntia vetustatis" (De Oratore II.ix.36).

Eine Rechtfertigung sehe ich weiter auch in der Einstellung, die auch von
Erasmus geteilt wird. Erasmus lobt solche Abhandlungen, die das sonst fragmen-
tarsich wirkende Sprichwort zum "Essai" ausbauen. Erasmus lobt solche Arbeit,
da es nicht selten sich herausstellt, daß ein Adagium aus nur zwei Worten bestehend zu Unklarheit führt, wenn es unbemerkt vorbeihuscht, daß es aber ein-
leuchtend wirkt, wenn es von einer Erläuterung begleitet wird: "utpote qui non
ignorarent saepe numero fieri ut duobus verbis comprehensum adagium multum
tenebrarum adferret, si latuisset, plurimum vero lucis, si scite fuisset
explicatum."[12]

Eine Rechtfertigung sehe ich auch gerade in diesem schottischen Werk. Hier
ist die Adagia-Methode durchaus angebracht. Das Werk ruft zur Zusammenarbeit für das Gemeinwohl auf. Gerade in der Frage der Konsensbildung, in der
Frage der sozialen Kohäsion leisten die Baukomponenten der sprichwörtlichen
Redensarten (wie das witzige Wortspiel, einprägsame Sentenzen und Epigramme,
moralisierbare Dicta, lebenskluge Sprichwörter, gescheite Apophthegmata, Exempla, Memorabilia, loci communes, u.s.w.) im Argument einen wichtigen Beitrag.[13]

Das schottische Werk ist eine Art Mosaik. Mosaikartig werden Fragmente,
Steinchen der Weisheit zusammengetragen. Das Fragmentarische hat program-
matischen Aussagewert. Es ist ein methodisches Kennzeichen. Auch bei Erasmus
ist das Fragmentarische ein Merkmal seiner Methode. Erasmus beschreibt einmal die sprichwörtlichen Formulierungen als Edelsteine. Sie besitzen zeitlose
Neuigkeit, sind eine Quelle der Erneuerung der sozialen Kohäsion angesichts der
moralischen Fragmentierung.[14] Im Adagium ist Beweis, ist Glaubwürdigkeit
(fides) inhärent; denn, fragt Erasmus, "was ist wahrscheinlicher als das was keiner
ablehnt noch bestreitet. Wer empfindet sich nicht bei der Zustimmung (consensus)
von so vielen Epochen und Nationen zutiefst gerührt?"[15] Auf Grund des sozialen
Consensus wird jedes Adagium zu einer Verbindung von verba und res.[16]

Eine Rechtfertigung sehe ich ferner in der Methode des Klägers möglichst viele

Autoritäten zu zitieren, um damit seine Analyse allgemeingültig zu machen. Der Kläger sichtet, wie Erasmus[17] nicht nur die "praesidia humana," sondern auch die "praesidia coelestia" der Tradition der Hl. Schriften und sucht eine Synthese. Weisheit oder Plattheit? Hier ist das Seneca-Zitat ein Hinweis. "Aut ridenda omnia aut flenda sunt": keine stark polarisierende Gegenüberstellung! Wie Simonettas neulateinisches Gedicht formuliert: "Et risu pariter dignior et lachrimis." Der Kläger denkt bestimmt an Heraklit und Demokrit in erster Linie im selben Zusammenhang wie sie bei Melanchthon erwähnt werden (in dem Abschnitt "De Humoribus" in seiner Abhandlung "De Anima," II (*CR* XIII, Kol. 83f.).[18] Heraklit und Demokrit werden in der Diskussion der "Melencolia" erwähnt. Wie wir auch aus der Sekundär-Literatur zu Dürers *Melencolia I* wissen, ist die Melencolia mehr als nur ein einfacher Pessimismus. Wie Erasmus auch argumentiert sind Heraklit und Demokrit Sileni-Gestalten.[19] In Erasmus Abhandlung "Sileni Alcibiadis" unterstreicht er wie die beiden Philosophen nur beim ersten Anblick ein augenscheinlich einfaches gegensätzliches Paar bilden. Bei näherer Betrachtung entlarven sie sich als weitaus kompliziertere, ambivalente, rätselhafte, mehrdeutige, ja widersprüchliche Sileni-Figuren.

Der Kläger malt die Analyse nicht weiter aus. Er lädt zu selbständigem Nachdenken ein.

Als letztes Wort seines Werkes jedoch wiederholt er seine Einstellung als inklusiver Denker, der gesunden Menschenverstand vermitteln will, der jedoch dem Einzelnen die persönliche Verantwortung einimpfen will. Autarkie und Freiheit des Willens sind Ziele des weisen Menschen: "Sapiens dominabitur astris": "Felix quem faciunt aliena pericula cautum."[20]

Der Kläger ist wie Thomas Morus von dem Erasmus erzählt: "Keiner wird weniger vom Urteil der Menge angezogen: keiner weicht weniger vom gesunden Menschenverstand ab." Des Klägers Ziel ist es *sapientia* zu erlangen. Der Mensch soll aktiv gegen den Aberglauben kämpfen. Die Veranlagungen, die Heraklit und Demokrit verkörpern, sind für Schottlands Gemeinwohl anwendbar. Blinde Wut ist keine angemessene Lösung. *Ira* ist keine Lösung. *Tranquillitas animi* (*euthymia*) ist keine Faulheit. Die pessimistische Anbetung der Göttin Fortuna ist auch falsch. Stoische *Virtus*, aktiver Widerstand, Zusammenarbeit für das Gemeinwohl (*concordia ordinum*) sind die richtigen Ziele. Der weise Mensch vermeidet *vanitas mundi*; bleibt entschlossen: "Nichil est turpius quam sapientis vitam ex insipientium sermone pendere. Cice. de fini,"[21] ist des Klägers letztes Wort, ganz am Schluß des Werkes. Hier am Schluß dieser Abhandlung über Heraklit und Demokrit ist eine Vorwegnahme der selben Moral.

Heraklit und Demokrit finden unsere weltlichen Geschäfte "vane & detestabil": "Therfor o ȝe my thre sonnis, nobilis clerge and lauberaris, i exort ȝuo to retere fra vanite & til adhere to vertu."[22]

In ihrer neuen Funktion im sechzehnten Jahrhundert kann das sprichwörtliche Sileni-Paar, auferstanden in Ficinos Kreisen in Italien, in den folgenden Jahrhunderten (auf ihre hermetischen, neuplatonischen neupythagoräischen Wurzeln weisend), jederzeit einen Gang durch die Welt unternehmen. Vor dem Hintergrund der Ethik (etwa des Aristoteles, eines Ciceros) kann man die Philosophen (etwa stoisch) interpretieren[23] und die eigene Haltung durchdenken.[24]

University of Aberdeen

Anmerkungen

1. *The Complaynt of Scotland* (ca. 1550) by Mr Robert Wedderburn. Introduction by A. M. Stewart. The Scottish Text Society (Edinburg, 1979). Rezension in *SHR*, 170 (October, 1981), 184–86. A. M. Stewart, "Die Europäische Wissensgemeinschaft um 1550 im Spiegel von Wedderburns 'The Complaynt of Scotland'," in *Geschichtlichkeit und Neuanfang im Sprachlichen Kunstwerk: Studien zur Englischen Philologie zu Ehren von Fritz W. Schulze,* hrsg. von P. Erlebach, W. G. Müller, K. Reuter (Tübingen, 1981), pp. 91–103. A. M. Stewart, "Alain Chartier et l'Ecosse," *Actes du Deuxième Colloque de Langue et de Littérature Ecossaises (Moyen Age et Renaissance)* (Straßburg, 1979), pp. 148–61.

2. *A Compendious Book of Godly and Spiritual Songs Commonly Known As 'The Gude and Godlie Ballatis',* hrsg. A. F. Mitchell, The Scottish Text Society (Edinburgh, 1897). *Acta Facultatis Artium Universitatis St. Andree, 1413–1588,* hrsg. A. I. Dunlop, Scottish History Society, 2 Bde. (Edinburg, 1964), II, 363, 365.

3. Vgl. Anm.1.

4. Bll. 133^v–134^v (STS-Ausg. S. 133–34).

5. In Vitam Hvmanam. / Plus solito humanae nunc defle incomoda uitae / Heraclite, scatet pluribus illa malis. / Tu rursus, si quando alias extolle cachinnum, / Democrite, illa magis ludicra facta fuit. / Interea haec cernens meditor, qua denique tecum. / Fine fleam, aut tecum quomodo splene iocer. /

Vom Menschlichen Leben. / Heraclite du alter greiß / Thu jetzt beweinen mit mehr fleiß / Des Menschlichen Lebens vnglück / Dann steckt es voller böser tück / Du aber widerum erschell / Demokrite dein glechter hell / Dann lecherlicher zu keiner zeit / Gewesen ist als jetzt die geit [= Gier] / Dieweil ich aber dieses sich [= sehe] / Betracht ich bey mir fleissiglich / Ob ichs mit dir beweinen sol / Oder mit dir verlachen wol. /

6. A. Blankert, "Heraclitus en Democritus in het bijzonder in de Nederlandse kunst van de 17de eeuw," *Nederlands Kunsthistorisch Jaarbok*, 18 (1967), 31–125.

7. Antonio Fregoso war der Sohn von Spinetta II Campofregoso aus Genua, der am Sforza-Hof ab etwa 1464 war. Um 1473 ließ er sich in der Nähe von Pavia nieder. Im Jahre 1478 wurde er "cavaliere." Nach 1500 zog er sich zurück, um in der Einsamkeit in einer Villa in Colturano zu leben, weswegen er den Beinamen Filaremo erhielt. Er starb 1532.

Nach Azgelati, *Bibliotheca scriptorum mediolanensium* (Mailand, 1745), Bd. II, Sp. 1394, wurden viele der Verse von Simonetta nur in Anthologien von andern Dichtern abgedruckt: viele blieben ungedruckt. Fregosos Werk erschien erst bei Peter Martyr in Mailand (ca. 1506), dann bei Rusconi in Venedig, 1511, 1514; bei Zanotto da Castione und bei Andrea de Barchis, beide 1515 in Mailand; bei Rusconi in Venedig 1517 und 1522; bei Alessandro und Benedetto Bindoni in Venedig 1520; bei Zoppino in Vendig 1528; bei Bindoni in Venedig noch einmal 1542; also—ein sehr beliebtes Werk! Vgl. *Le ris de Démocrite et le pleur de Héraclite, sur les follies & misères de ce monde: invention de Antonio P. Fregoso, interprétée en ryme Françoise par noble homme Michel d'Amboyse* (Paris, 1547). Vgl. Opuscule III, "Le Pleur d'Héraclite et Le Ris de Démocrite, Philosophes," S. 127-37, in Etienne Forcadel, *Œuvres poétiques, Opuscules, Chants Divers, Encomies et Élégies,* hrsg. F. Joukovsky (Genf, 1977). (Hinweis von T. Thomson, Dundee.)

8. Peter M. Schon, *Vorformen des Essays in Antike und Humanismus: Ein Beitrag zur Entstehungsgeschichte der 'Essais' von Montaigne* (Wiesbaden, 1954).

9. Seneca, *De Tranquillitate Animi,* XV, 2; *De Ira,* II, 10; Juvenalis, *Satyrae,* X, v. 28ff.; *Anth. Planudea,* I, tit. XIII, v. II.

10. Hans Pyritz, *Schriften zur deutschen Literaturgeschichte,* hrsg. Ilse Pyritz (Köln, Graz, 1962), S. 73.

11. Vgl. Anm. 1. (bes. Art. in *FS F. W. Schulze* [1981]). Vgl. W. Brückner, "Historien und Historie. Erzählliteratur des 16. und 17. Jahrhunderts als Forschungsaufgabe," in *Volkserzählung und Reformation,* hrsg. W. Brückner (Berlin, 1974), pp. 13-83.

12. P. S. Allen, ed. *Opus Epistolarum Des. Erasmi Roterodami* (Oxford, 1906-58), I, ep. 126, Z. 106-09.

13. D. Kinney, "Erasmus' Adagia: midwife to the rebirth of learning," *JMRS,* XI, 2 (1981), 193-209.

14. D. Kinney, in *JMRS,* XI, 2 (1981), S. 179, Anm. 24.

15. D. Kinney, ibid., S. 188, Anm. 43: Allen, I, ep. 126, Z. 57-58.

16. D. Kinney, ibid., S. 188.

17. D. Kinney, ibid., S. 182.

18. *Philippi Melanchtonis Opera Quae Supersunt Omnia,* edd. C. G. Bretschneider et H. G. Bindseil (Halle, 1834-52), 28 Bde. [= *Corpus Reformatorum,* Bd. XIII.], *De Anima II,* Kol. 83-87. Vgl. R. Klibansky, E. Panofsky, F. Saxl, *Saturn and Melancholy* (London, 1964).

19. Adagia 2201, in *Opera Omnia Desiderii Erasmi Roterodami, Ordinis Secundi, Tomus Quintus* (Amsterdam, Oxford, 1981), S. 184. Vgl. M. M. Phillips, *Erasmus On His Times* (Cambridge, 1967), SS. 77-97, hier S. 92. Vgl. Erasmus, *Moriae Encomium,* C. 48.

20. A. M. Stewart, "*Sapiens dominabitur astris*: Wedderburn, Abell, Luther," *Aberdeen University Review,* 153 (1975), 55-62. Vgl. L. Forster, *Das Album Amicorum von Dietrich Bevernest* (Amsterdam, Oxford, New York, 1982), S. 14, Bl. 24a, Bl. 81a.

21. *Complaynt,* Bl. 147ᵛ, STS Ausg. SS. xviii-xx.

22. *Complaynt,* Bl. 134ᵛ.

23. Bernard F. Dick, "Seneca and Juvenal 10," *HSCP* 73 (1969), 237-46.

24. Vgl. A. M. Stewart, "What a State," *Aberdeen University Review,* 168 (Autumn, 1982), 253-61. Vgl. Werner Weisbach, "Der sogenannte Geograph von Velasquez und die Darstellungen des Demokrit und Heraklit," *Jahrbuch der preussischen Kunstsammlungen,* 49 (1928), 148-58: Edgar Wind, "The Christian Democritus," *JWI,* I (1937/38), 180-02; E. H. Gombrich, "Botticelli's Mythologies: A Study in the Neoplatonic Symbolism of his Circle," *JWCI,* VIII (1945), 7-60; Liselotte Möller, "Demokrit und Heraklit," *Reallexikon zur deutschen Kunstgeschichte,* Bd. 3 (Stuttgart, 1954), Sp. 1244-51; A. Blankert, Anm. 6 oben; Jean Lebeau, "Le 'Rire de Démocrite' et la Philosophie de l'histoire de Sebastian Franck," *BHR,* 33 (1971), 241-69; G. L. Jones, "Democritus 'versus' Heraclitus: A Note on Satire and Irony in Grimmelshausen and Wieland," *Trivium,* VII (1972), 125-28; Henkel/Schöne, *Emblemata* (Stuttgart, 1976), Nr. 2119, S. clxv; A. Blankert, "Heraclitus en Democritus bij Marsilio Ficino," *SIMIOLUS,* 1 (1966/67), 128-35.

The Latinity of an Oxford College

Christopher A. Upton

John M. Fletcher

During the last two years I have been engaged on a project,[1] together with Dr John Fletcher of Aston University, to transcribe and prepare for publication the internal accounts of Merton College, Oxford for the Tudor period. This paper offers a preliminary attempt to analyse linguistically the evidence from this work. The project stemmed from the realization that until scholars committed themselves to a full scale analysis of such material, our knowledge of the actual practice of a medieval or Renaissance college would remain hopelessly superficial. Statutes and acts do more to indicate the good intentions of founders, benefactors and legislators than what in fact took place. Often they are plainly inaccurate. Until one reads of payments of 10s. "pro lectione graeca" one cannot be certain that royal legislation to provide Greek lectureships was effective. Again, we read much of the consequences of the Reformation upon sixteenth-century Oxford. Those consequences remain problematic until the accounts record wages for one "dealbanti parites chori et fenestras"[2] and "destruenti altaria,"[3] or the purchase of books "novi ordinis precium publicarum"[4] and hence measure the gap between law and enforcement.

The Merton records are not, of course, unique either in their methods or survival. Their procedures have much in common with seignorial rolls. Other colleges kept accounts with similar, but never identical methods. Many of these are extant: "Some made in books, some in long parchment rolls / That were all worm-eaten and full of canker holes." The Mundum Books of King's College, Cambridge, for example, are more complete than at Merton, but detailed comparison is more difficult. It is hoped that by publishing the complete accounts of a college of average size, on the brink of its golden age under Henry Savile,[5] we will be providing a model for future research in this area, and a yardstick for subsequent investigation of other institutions.

Merton College recorded its financial state by means of seven interlocking systems of account. Briefest of all, the Warden accounted annually, recording his stipend and the expenditure at his table. The Master of Wylyot's Exhibition handled the income from, and expenditure on, certain lands in Oxford and London. Stewards logged the purchase of foodstuffs. The Sub-Warden was responsible for all expenses incurred by the chapel and library and other incidental costs. Predominant in this line are repairs to the bells ("reparationes circa campanas"),[6] whose maintenance costs were high, new baudricks, a bell-stock (*truncus*)[7] grease (*adeps*)[8] for the ropes, clappers (*batella*)[9] and the mysterious crustibles. In the library, books had to be secured (*incathenatio librorum*),[10] chains and clasps bought (*catenulae*[11] and *signacula*)[12], the ceiling panelled (*celatura*)[13] and locks on the door replaced (*pro sera et clavi ad ostium*).

However the lynch-pin of the system was the Bursarial account. Here the majority of transactions, be they income from the estates and benefactions or expenditure on the college, are to be found, sometimes amounting to £300 or £400. Three Bursars were elected *per annum* from and by the senior fellows, and each was responsible for a four-month jurisdiction. The archaically named *cista iocalium* (chest of jewels) served as a float to cover the shortfall. Only later did it occur to the college to use the *cista* as a bottomless pit into which to pour its increasing wealth. Initially it simply provided the Bursars with ready cash. This incidentally seems to be the equivalent of the so-called "Tower money" of All Souls[14] and Trinity, Cambridge.

On his roll the Bursar dutifully recorded every item of expenditure incurred during his term of office, from the purchase of a pair of scissors (*forfices*)[15] to that of a new horse. College workmen had to be paid, both stipendiary servants, the warden's butler (*pincerna custodis*)[16] or steward (*promus*),[17] and those contracted for a limited period, the itinerant mole-catcher (*captor talparum*),[18] goldsmith (*aurificus*),[19] coal merchant (*carbonarius*) or tiler (*tegulator*).[20] Robert Maynard, faithful college retainer during the Henrician era, performed a variety of services: *querenti signos* (hunting out the swans), *equitanti signos*, *custos equorum* and *custos orti*.

The purchase of food is recorded, though the Stewards did most of that: pears and wine for visiting celebrities, interminable quantities of salted fish, new and old (*salsamentum*,[21] as it is sometimes called) and then the more unusual items for high table such as *pipiones*[22] (young pigeon or squab), *castrimargius*[23] (woodcock), *ardea*[24] (heron), *dentriculus*[25] (pickerel or young pike), *lupillus*[26] (older pike) and swan.

The bulk of expenditure however was upon running repairs to college property (usually *reparanti* for major alterations and *emendanti* for smaller), or the purchase and replacement of household equipment, everything from a pin (*spinctrum*) to an *ansa* (whose meaning itself extends from a classical door handle to a medieval curtain ring or, by synecdoche, a pot).

The variety and bulk of administrative duties ensured that every fellow, unless he be untimely ripped from office by plague or improper conduct, had the experience or obligation of accounting. By Elizabethan times *socii* were frequently commandeered to collect rents from estates in the south, to attend *curiae*, supervise building operations or accompany a Warden's progress. This area of contact between Merton tenants and their economic and academic overlords is easily overlooked. The sixteenth-century college was no ivory tower. An interesting palaeographical offshoot of this situation is that the jumbled mass of accounts contains specimens of the hands of almost all the scholars that passed through the Merton treasury, for the college employed no Bursar's scribe. Here is a fascinating text-book of palaeographical fashion, charting the emergence, disappearance and revival of humanist and italic, from Warden Chambers (the hand, that, literally, helped to deliver Princess Elizabeth) to Bodley's elegant script.

This rather protracted preamble has, I hope, given some indication of the scope and concerns of the Bursars' accounts. They were all written in Latin and continued to be so until the eighteenth century. This is similarly true of the Lincoln College accounts but was not always the case elsewhere.[27] Those of Trinity College, Cambridge, a foundation of the mid-sixteenth century, were in English from the outset. Nevertheless both in its academic and financial affairs Merton had little cause to meddle with the original plans of its thirteenth-century founder, Walter. But for a disastrous deal in which the college sold off the land upon which Corpus Christi now stands, a mistake for which Warden Rawlyns[28] paid with his job, Merton did not make many errors. The system worked well, and until the decline of the chapel after the Reformation rendered the Sub-Warden's account unnecessary,[29] there was little need to tamper with it. Perhaps for this reason the language of the accounts stuck tightly to this tradition, remaining archaically medieval in terminology throughout our period of study.

Now it has long been acknowledged that Renaissance learning did not one night sweep clean the medieval stables. Similarly it is admitted that fully-fledged Humanism and the English universities did not co-operate at first sight, nor even second sight. However it strikes me as surprising that generation after generation of Merton scholars, Henry Cuff, for example, professor of Greek and later private secretary to the Earl of Essex, John Parkhurst, the poet, Arthur Atie, public orator in the university, Robert Barons, Thomas Symons and John Norrice, all benefactors of Linacre's and Tunstall's scheme to institute salaried lectureships in medicine, whose writings all show the marks of classicism, surprising that each should possess such capacities in back-parlour Latin. Or rather, kitchen Latin would be more appropriate, for that is where the majority of the recondite vocabulary lies.

We are as yet far from the end of the task of editing, and most of the Elizabethan Bursars' accounts remain untranscribed. Yet enough has been done to reveal the breadth and compass of the technical language. There are around thirty terms describing vessels containing or displaying foodstuffs: different types of strainer or colander, half a dozen varieties of basket such as *calathus*,[30] *cophinus*,[31] *corbis*,[32] *fiscina*,[33] *sporta*[34] and *vimen*.[35] There are a multitude of different fish served at table, species now no longer distinguished or recoverable, certainly not usually eaten. They present a wealth of medieval nomenclature on the eve of extinction before a much less colourful resurrected classicism.

Now many of these words may well be synonyms. It is hard to imagine that *patella*[36] and *certago*[37] refer to separate kinds of frying-pan, or that *adeps*,[38] *sevum*[39] and *anxungia*[40] distinguish three varieties of grease. The Merton fellow, in the anxious throes of accounting, might clutch at a variety of straws or cooking utensils to convey his meaning. In desperation, he could even leave the English term untranslated, signifying the presence of an alien word by *ly*, presumably a long-distorted gallicism. There being no convenient Latin for a baldric, we have *ly baudrick*. Parkhurst, unaware perhaps of the traditional term *promptuarium*, wrote *ly larderhouse*.[41] In the 1570s Thomas Bodley, emboldened by a distaste for excessive medievalisms, was far less sparing in anglicisms, preferring *ly shovell* to *vanga* and *ly padlocke* to any other obstruse term — a curious form of assertive classicism.[42]

There are of course occasional signs of conscious classicism; the use of the word *musaeum*[43] for a study, in the odd Graecism, or the replacement of *ecclesia* by *templum*.[44] However these two are often differentiated, *templum* or *aedes* to designate the University church of St Mary's, *ecclesia* the college chapel and parish church of St John's. An awareness of the different functions of the two buildings is reflected here, I think. We stand at a distance at which *copia* (a wide vocabulary) and *cura* (in locating *le mot juste*) are hard to tell apart. *Copia* as advertised in the sixteenth-century vocabulary manuals often seems to be mean little more than ringing the changes and frequently collapsed a medieval or classical distinction.

Let us then examine more closely the words themselves, for I feel that this bilingualism (and I use the word with hesitation) is easier to explain than to accept. When the Renaissance lexicographers of England (Elyot[45] and Cooper, and Veron) stretched a gauze across the mid-sixteenth-century and attempted to trap barbarisms from filtering through into the new purer Latin, they were not entirely successful, as Elyot himself admits.[46] Such words, having been endorsed by Elyot, stubbornly hung on into the seventeenth century. Of this group I would cite from the accounts: *fleu/phlegbotomia*[47] (bloodletting, used of bleeding horses), *chrysis* (unction), *pistura*[48] (in the sense of baking) and *species*[49] (spices).

Thomas Thomas,[50] whose *Dictionary* of 1587 supplanted Cooper's *Thesaurus*, was less squeamish about barbarisms and added much to the Elyot/Cooper corpus from the fifteenth-century glossaries. Of these we might notice *manutergium*[51] (a hand towel) and *pincerna*[52] (a butler).

Secondly, let us look at ecclesiastical terminology: stoups and holy water sprinklers, pulpits and vestments. Of course it was inevitable that a certain amount of post-classical usage would survive in theological writing as long as theology and philosophy remained so central a part of the academic curriculum, and men like Laurence Humphrey condoned this practice. Of the paraphernalia of church ornament, much had been removed as non-classical by Calepinus in his *Dictionarium* of 1502[53] whilst the English lexicographers weeded out the rest, linguistic scruples perhaps disguising politico-religious sensitivity. Such language was an integral part of the Pre-Reformation Sub-Wardens's vocabulary: *amictus*[54] (an amice), *aspergillum* or *aspersorium*[55] (holy water sprinkler — this a word to be found in

Calepinus) and *invitatorium*[56] (antiphon). I might also single out *humectatio*, literally *moistening*, but in the Second Bursar's account of 1507–08 referring to the cleansing of a woman after childbirth.

A third group is those archaic designations of office handed down from one Bursar to another, as indeed much of the format of the documents was dictated by this practice. Of these the most striking is the Graecism *ephippiarius*[57] for a saddler or groom, but also there are *lotrix* (laundress), *senescallus* (steward), *pincerna*[58] (butler) and others. Every college expressed its individuality in the naming of officials. At Merton there is little sign of the *pandaxtor* or brewer (another unclassical profession) seen elsewhere, though there are many references to *brasiatores*.[59]

There remains a whole category of words, some variations upon classical usage, such as *aquaductile*[60] (conduit) or *clipsedra*[61] (not a water clock, but a tap or spigot), others, such as *micatorium*[62] (grater) or *restare*[63] (to rake), decidedly medieval. Nor were fellows averse to spawning their own terms: *cancerulus*[64] (or small crab, or possibly crayfish), *lapidicinus*[65] (quarryman), *damalis*[66] (venison) and *effosura*[67] (digging out).

Much of what remains found currency in the vocabularies and conversation manuals, so popular in the first half of the sixteenth-century, such as the *Promptorium Parvulorum*, *Hortus Vocabulorum* and *Vulgaria* of Stanbridge and Whittinton.[68] These educational tools were frequently sources for later lexicographers, and their continual reprinting alongside the more "correct" *Colloquia* of Erasmus[69] and Corderius[70] is a curious sign of divided loyalties. Their survival, particularly that of Stanbridge's *Vocabula* and *Vulgaria*, is, I think, reflected in the Bursars' extensive technical vocabulary. Here, in the sections headed "Kitchen," "Stables" or "Bakery" are stacked those many pipes and pans and books and candles so evident in the accounts. These two works have always struck me as a trifle eccentric, certainly optimistic in their estimation of a schoolboy's range of experience and expression. At a subsequent stage in the *cursus honorum* the Merton fellow perhaps found a use for this knowledge.

The intention of this paper has been to suggest a corrective to our notion of the abstraction of sixteenth-century Latin in England. Certainly these accounts are a facet of experience that does not seem to accord with our traditional opinion of the academic's life and pursuits. As such, of course, the relevance of the material is not limited to England but to wherever university men handled their own living conditions.

University of Aston

Notes

1. We are pleased to express our thanks to the British Academy, the Social Science Research Council and Merton College for their generous financial support. I would also like to thank the Archivists of Trinity College and King's College, Cambridge, for their help and access to their sixteenth-century records.

2. In the account of the Sub-Warden for the academic year 1549–50, Merton College Record (henceforth noted as M. C. R.) 4043.

3. Sub-Warden 1559–60, M. C. R. 4043.

4. Sub-Warden 1548–49, M. C. R. 4043.

5. Sir Henry Savile, Warden of the College 1585–1621.

6. Sub-Warden 1508–09, M. C. R. 4021. In order to restrict notes to a minimum, only the first occurrence of a word is given. In retrospect it may be possible to record the latest instance, in many ways the more significant of the two dates for lexicographers. Almost all the vocabulary here recorded reappears throught he first half of the century.

7. Sub-Warden 1501–02, M. C. R. 4015.

8. Sub-Warden 1508–09, M. C. R. 4021.

9. Sub-Warden 1491–92, M. C. R. 4010.

10. Sub-Warden 1488–89, M. C. R. 4009.

11. Account of the Third Bursar 1556, M. C. R. 3916.

12. Sub-Warden 1492–93, M. C. R. 4011.

13. Sub-Warden 1502–03, M. C. R. 4016.

14. For a description of the accounting system at All Souls, see *A Dissertation on the Accounts of All Souls College Oxford by Sir William Blackstone*, ed. William R. Anson, Roxburghe Club (London, 1898).

15. Second Bursar 1503–4, M. C. R. 3815.

16. Second Bursar 1486–7, M. C. R. 3812b.

17. ibid.

18. Second Bursar 1500–1, M. C. R. 3842.

19. Sub-Warden 1535–6, M. C. R. 4038.

20. Second Bursar 1486–7, M. C. R. 3812b.

21. Third Bursar 1555, M. C. R. 3913.

22. Accounts recording expenditure on food are seldom dated and are thus referred to by MS number only. M. C. R. 3814.

23. M. C. R. 3842 recording expenditure on the Chapter meal.

24. M. C. R. 3814.

25. M. C. R. 3822.

26. M. C. R. 3833.

27. I am grateful to Dr Vivian Green for information concerning the language of the Lincoln accounts. For their subject matter (having much in common with Merton) see V. A. A. Green, *The Commonwealth of Lincoln College 1427–1977* (Oxford, 1979), especially chapters 2 and 5.

28. Richard Rawlyns, Warden of Merton 1508–21.

29. The Sub-Warden's account was discontinued in 1586. See J. M. Fletcher, *Registrum Annalium Collegii Mertonensis 1567–1603*, Oxford Historical Society (Oxford, 1976), p. 218.

30. Second Bursar 1516–7, M. C. R. 3831.

31. Account of the Master of Wylyot's Exhibition of 1488–9, M. C. R. 4593.

32. First Bursar 1547, M. C. R. 3897.

33. First Bursar 1520, M. C. R. 3835.
34. Second Bursar 1513-4, M. C. R. 3830.
35. Third Bursar 1556, M. C. R. 3896.
36. Second Bursar 1508-9, M. C. R. 3821.
37. Second Bursar 1509-10, M. C. R. 3823.
38. Sub-Warden 1508-9, M. C. R. 4021.
39. Third Bursar 1556, M. C. R. 3916.
40. Sub-Warden 1491-2, M. C. R. 4010.
41. First Bursar 1533, M. C. R. 3856.
42. First Bursar 1568, M. C. R. 3936.
43. Second Bursar 1551-2, M. C. R. 3906.
44. First Bursar 1547, M. C. R. 3897.
45. Thomas Elyot, *Dictionary* (London, 1538); Thomas Cooper, *Thesaurus linguae Romanae & Britannicae* (London, 1565); John Vernon, *Dictionariolum* (London, 1552).
46. "All be it for as muche as partely by negligence at the begynnynge, partly by untrue information of them, whom I trusted, also by to moche trust had in Calepine, some fautes may be founden by dilygent redynge" (Elyot sig. A iii^v).
47. Second Bursar 1501-2, M. C. R. 3813.
48. First Bursar 1521, M. C. R. 3835.
49. M. C. R. 3813 recording expenses for the Chapter meal.
50. Thomas Thomas, *Dictionarium linguae Latinae et Anglicanae* (London, 1587). On the interrelation of these dictionaries, see D. T. Starnes, *Renaissance Dictionaries* (Austin, Texas, 1954).
51. Sub-Warden 1487-8, M. C. R. 4020.
52. Sub-Warden 1522-3, M. C. R. 4027.
53. Ambrosius Calepinus, *Dictionarium* (Reggio, 1502).
54. Sub-Warden 1497-8, M. C. R. 4013.
55. Sub-Warden 1508-9, M. C. R. 4021.
56. ibid.
57. Third Bursar 1547, M. C. R. 3897.
58. These three offices, and a number of others such as *promus*, *mancipius* and *decanus* appear in almost all the Bursars' accounts.
59. Master of Wylyot's Exhibition 1508-9, M. C. R. 4607.
60. Sub-Warden 1505-6, M. C. R. 4019.
61. Second Bursar 1508-9, M. C. R. 3821.
62. Third Bursar 1511, M. C. R. 3824.
63. First Bursar 1511, M. C. R. 3826.
64. M. C. R. 3822.
65. Sub-Warden 1502-3, M. C. R. 4016.
66. First Bursar 1556, no MS number.
67. Second Bursar 1556-7, M. C. R. 3915.
68. The *Promptorium Parvulorum* has a complex manuscript and printing history, but was first printed by Richard Pynson in 1499. *Ortus Vocabulorum* was first printed by Wynkyn de Worde in 1500. The latter printed the *Vulgaria* of both John Stanbridge and Robert Whittinton, in ?1509 and 1520 respectively.
69. Desiderius Erasmus, *Familiarum colloquiorum formulae, et alia quaedam* (Basel, 1518). Subsequently, of course, it was much revised and expanded.
70. Marturinus Corderius, *Colloquiorum scholasticorum libri iv* ... (Leyden, 1564).

The Theory of Climate in the English Renaissance and *Mundus Alter et Idem*

John Wands

I n the second half of the sixteenth century English interest in travel literature and the psychology of behavior (as exemplified by Timothy Bright's
A Treatise of Melancholy [1586]) became allied with the resurgent interest in
the classics. Together these trends explain the upsurge in neo-Latin works like
Jean Bodin's *Methodus ad facilem Historiarum Cognitionem* (1566), Joseph Hall's *Mundus
Alter et Idem* (1605), and John Barclay's *Icon Animorum* (1614) — all of which exploit
the idea that every race possesses innate temperaments, temperaments influenced
by climate and geography.

The earliest instances of this theory go back to the Greeks, but after the classical
period little interest was paid it until the Renaissance. Part of the fascination with
the theory seems to have arisen from its imprecision, its ability to be manipulated
to explain whatever phenomena were under consideration. For example, Aristotle, one of the earliest practitioners of climate theory, uses it in his *Politics* to explain the genius of Greek rule:

> Let us now speak of what ought to be the citizens' natural character. Now
> this one might almost discern by looking at the famous cities of Greece and
> observing how the whole inhabited world is divided among the nations. The
> nations inhabiting the cold places and those of Europe are full of spirit but
> somewhat deficient in intelligence and skill, so that they continue com-
> paratively free, but lacking in political organization and capacity to rule
> their neighbors. The peoples of Asia on the other hand are intelligent and
> skillful in temperament, but lack spirit, so that they are in continuous sub-
> jection and slavery. But the Greek race participates in both characters, just
> as it occupies the middle position geographically, for it is both spirited and
> intelligent; hence it continues to be free and to have very good political in-
> stitutions, and to be capable of ruling all mankind if it attains constitutional
> unity.[1]

For Hippocrates, however, climate explains not political but physical excellence:

> Some physiques resemble wooded, well-watered mountains, others light, dry land, others marshy meadows, others a plain of bare, parched earth. For the seasons which modify a physical frame differ; if the differences be great, the more too are the differences in the shapes.[2]

Hippocrates also notes the effects specific seasons may have on bodily ills, such as dry summers and rainy autumns, which invariably produce winter head-aches and "mortifications of the brain."[3]

With the ability to "explain" such varied phenomena, it is no wonder the Renaissance — with its love of classification and analysis — should seize upon the climate theory of the ancients. Works like Levinus Lemnius's *De Habitu* (1561) and Bodin's *Methodus* (1566) are among the first to attempt a more precise classification by dividing each hemisphere into three climatic regions — torrid, arctic, and temperate — which appear to be rough equivalents of Aristotle's ordering of behavior into excess, defect, and mean. By this reckoning only the inhabitants of middle Europe (the Italians, Germans, and French) enjoy the happy moderation of climate making for a sound body and a sound mind. Countries lying near the border of another climatic zone, of course, share its characteristics. Englishmen, embarrassed by their unfortunate placement, could fall back on a companion theory — Aristotle's reaction of opposites[4] — which would explain the Irishman's lack of husbandry in a perfectly fertile land[5] and the Englishman's intelligence in a climate more suited to blockishness and cruelty.[6]

And if these two conflicting theories still did not allow the writer sufficient latitude to conclude almost anything, they could be modified even further. For example, Barclay notes that every age stamps on mankind "a certaine Genius, which ouer-ruleth the mindes of men, and turneth them to some desires."[7] Eight chapters later he says:

> Besides the Genius of their native Countrey, [there is] something proper to every man: and by a great myracle, ... hath found out for euery man his owne lineaments, that may distinguish the habite of his visage and minde from the likenesse of other mindes and bodies.[8]

Finally, besides the influence of the age and each man's innate desires, there are education and discipline, which

> altereth the vsuall nature, and ordynary conditions of euery Region: for wee see the common sorte and multitude, in behauiour and maners grosse and vnnurtured, wheras the Nobles and Gentlemen ... frame themselues & theirs to a very commendable order, and ciuill behauiour.[9]

Few of the Renaissance writers who uncritically adopt climate theory understand the implications of such uncertain broadness as a guide to predicting behavior. Despite all the qualifications, a writer like Barclay still asserts that "in euery Nation, among all the tides of succeeding ages, which alter the manners

and mindes of men, one certaine quality remaines neuer to bee shaken off."[10]
And so he is led into uncritical stereotyping, such as in his analysis of the British:

> When they salute, or write letters, they scorne to descend to complements
> of feined seruice, which the flattery of these ages haue brought vp, vnlesse
> it be those, which are infected with forreyne behauiour.[11]

Even a cursory reading of Elizabethan and Jacobean commendatory verse will
soon dispel any notion of Barclay's correctness. Only Jean Bodin seems partly
to apprehend the fallaciousness of the theory, for while in one place he claims
that "all, except Jerome, agree on this point—the Gauls are fickle,"[12] several
pages later he acknowledges that "the Hebrews and the Egyptians complain that
the Greeks are fickle; the Italians, the French; and the French, the Germans."[13]

It is in Joseph Hall's dystopian satire *Mundus Alter et Idem* (1605) that the theory
of climate is acknowledged for its imprecision and at the same time fully exploited
for its satiric possibilities.[14] Hall accepts—at least partially—the notion of climate
influencing behavior, but what he prefers is the enhanced satiric power that comes
from using the stereotypes at one point and then ironically undercutting them
somewhere else. The very title of Hall's work reinforces the double vision he expects the reader to adopt, for the vices described as peculiar to "another world"
turn out to be exactly the same as those in the world left behind.

This essay explores the various ways Hall uses climatic theory in the *Mundus*:
first, in his attacks on the pseudo-scientific nature of the theory; secondly, in his
descriptions of the special follies of specific nationalities; and finally, in his descriptions that reinforce the idea of man's general depravity.

Early in *Mundus Alter et Idem* Hall begins his attack on the simplistic notion that
vices are confined to any one people by having Beroaldus, one of the would-be
travellers, say:

> The French are commonly called rash; the Spanish arrogant; the Germans
> drunkards; the English meddling with many things; the Italians unmanly;
> the Swedes timid; the Bohemians inhumane; the Irish barbarous and
> superstitious; but is any man so dull that he supposes no prudent Frenchman
> to have been born, no timid Spaniard, no sober German? They are deceived,
> believe me, who think the makeup of a person's mind and the formation
> of his character to be so totally from the heavens that there remains nothing
> peculiar to his nature, nothing inherited from his parents, and, lastly, nothing
> left to the method of his rearing.[15]

One of Hall's *Epistles* exemplifies his agreement with Beroaldus:

> You shall see, that the soile is not so diuerse, as the inclination of persons:
> vvho, in all Climates, though they differ in particulars, yet still agree too
> well in common falls [i.e., faults].[16]

Having read so many books infected with climate theory, Hall could scarcely have overlooked the contradiction that what one author says is peculiar to the English, a second attributes to the French, and a third to the Dutch. The logical conclusion must be that all vices are peculiar to no one nation, but common to all. His *Characters of Vertues and Vices*, published three years after the *Mundus*, amplify Hall's conviction that vice's "loathsome deformities"[17] pervade the world.

But if Hall does not believe in the climatic theory of behavior, when it suits his purposes he acts as though he does. Thus, the provinces of Pamphagonia and Yvronia (the first a land of gluttons, the second of drunkards) in the *Mundus* are sarcastically said to have the same longitude and latitude "by and large, as our beloved Great Britain (something which should not seem a bad sign to anyone) [and] ... the two Germanies" (p. 19).[18] Or in Moronia Mobilis, the land of inconstant fools, Hall (exemplifying the traits assigned the French by Lemnius)[19] sarcastically suggests that no matter what prolonged navigations the Portuguese may boast of, the French must be given credit for discovering this place,

> since we certainly find vestiges of the French here, whether you consider the names of places, the remains of laws, or the marks on coins. The shape of the land is manifold and uncertain, for what luxuriant pasture you see sacred to Flora this year, expect to see as tilled fields dedicated to Ceres the next; whatever mountains projected to the heavens ages ago now fill an excavated valley and offer themselves to the insolent trampling of travelers. Rivers are often astonished to find themselves in new channels, the former having been closed off.   (p. 73)[20]

In this oblique way Hall is able to ridicule the supposed inconstancy of the French, while at the same time mocking mankind's manic pursuit of change for the sake of change — something that here seems to extend to canal building and crop rotation.

This technique of shading specific criticisms of a people derived from climate theory into general criticism of mankind operates throughout the *Mundus*. For example, the beastly eating habits of the Crapulians, which have earlier been compared to the Britons' gluttony by Hall — who in this criticism agrees with J. C. Scaliger[21] — are later extended to the Germans (who leave cheese to become infested with worms before eating it); to the Venetians (who consider the undigested stomach contents of the game they cook a delicacy); and finally to the Catholics, who supposedly stuff themselves with so much meat on Shrove Tuesday that,

> for nearly 40 days they abstain from meat, during which time they are fed with fish — but cooked in wine and spices at far greater expense — ... so that they may both restore themselves a bit by so many varieties of food and return to meat, so long neglected, with a sharper appetite. (pp. 35–36)[22]

Hall's descriptions, which touch almost every European race, force us to recognize man's pervasive love for his stomach. We are shown a commonwealth where the highest public office is won by the size of one's paunch, where the only library and laboratory comprise a collection of pots and pans, and where the people are forced to eat another meal if, after banqueting, they can squeeze their guts through the same door they entered. Like his *Characters*, these portraits are meant to be sufficiently general to project to the reader a vision of "Vice strip't naked to the open view, and despoiled ... of her ornaments,... whereby the ruder multitude might euen by their sense ... discerne what to detest."[23] If taken seriously, climate theory, by suggesting that some vices are peculiar to certain peoples, not only minimizes the extent of evil, but also subverts the reforming motive of Hall's satire by encouraging readers to accuse others of sin, rather than themselves.

This idea that evil comes from within (man's inherent flaws) and not from without (climatic influence) is sarcastically reinforced by Hall's ridicule of the reaction of opposites, referred to earlier. As stated by Jean Bodin, the theory holds that

> Contraries have opposite traits. So if the southerner is black, the northerner must be white; if the latter is large, the former must be small; the latter robust, the former weak; the latter warm and wet; the former cold and dry;... the latter happy, the former sad; the latter gregarious, the former solitary; the latter reckless; the former timid; the latter given to drinking, the former moderate.[24]

This pseudo-theory helps explain why Hall should joke that Britain's antipodal relationship with Pamphagonia is not a bad sign to anyone (p. 19), since Pamphagonia's gluttony only reinforces England's moderation.

To account for the stupidity of the Moronians, Hall exploits the Aristotelian belief that inhabitants conform to the characteristics of a specific climate, noting that Moronia is:

> situated under the Antarctic Pole itself, exactly like the land of the Pygmies under the Arctic Pole. And, truthfully, now I detect that from one and the same cause, from the most truly intense cold of both regions, has been advanced both the stupidity of the Moronians and the puniness of the Pygmies. Indeed,... that makes it understandable why those who live in the temperate middle zones of the earth are accustomed to be strong both in mind and in body. But that is doubtless the concern of the philosophers. (p. 69)[25]

Yet, a dozen or so pages later he appeals to the opposing explanation, the reaction of opposites, when his needs differ, and he wishes to prove the savageness of the Moronia Asperans stems from the antarctic cold:

> Perhaps even the explorer of lands, an investigator of incredible events, will hesitate and not allow himself to be persuaded (since the ways of the inhabitants are accustomed to conform to the nature of the climate) that this polar region could ever have been the source of so very hot and choleric a race, given its location in the most intense cold. But we philosophers correctly understand that where the climate is more frigid, this phenomenon

may be accomplished by the reaction of opposites; nor will anyone scoff at this who knows that Africa, a most torrid region, produces the coldest serpents.... Now, therefore, supported by philosophy, I hope for and claim your faith in me.   (p. 83)[26]

Hall's self-conscious naming of philosophy as his guide in two contradictory explanations cannot be accidental; he means to call attention to the equivocations of philosophy, which can be exploited to prove anything, and to the self-evident absurdity of any theory that claims heat can be produced from cold. Like Jonathan Swift, Hall has no more toleration for the pride of pseudo-scientists than for the pride of any other group. Here, as elsewhere, Hall's satire operates on several different levels, attacking climate theory, and mankind's ingenuity.

Throughout the *Mundus*, Hall's decision to name and yet — in fact — not to name specific places gives him the freedom to localize his attacks to specific races and at the same time generalize the vice to mankind as a whole. For example, in Moronia Fatua, the stupid Pazzivillani debate how to enhance the beauty of their city, whether by surrounding it with a mountain, or erecting bell towers on every house. Their name, though seemingly Italian, is still imprecise enough to generalize their vices to all Europeans until we discover that their houses "all lack foundations, inasmuch as they say they prefer to dig up stones rather than bury them" (p. 89).[27] Moreover, their houses are inscribed everywhere with the names of their friends and ancestors (p. 90), providing a clear attack not only on ancient Rome's graffiti, but also on Renaissance Rome's interest in archaeology.

But elsewhere in the same chapter Hall spreads his satire on folly to the southern Germans and the Sicilians, who are ridiculed respectively as Baverians and Scioccians. The Scioccians are said to be so blockish that every year "many die from mere starvation and from the cold" (p. 87),[28] inasmuch as they cannot build houses, or "cook food, or produce clothes, or make a bed" (p. 87).[29] The Baverians, illustrating the opposite extreme, value themselves so wise that they constantly "search more deeply into the causes of all things" (p. 87).[30] Their wisdom has taught some of them to go

> naked, so that they spare both the labor and the time of dressing and undressing. Another part prepares shelters for itself, but without walls or partitions, so that the houses may be more open to the air and therefore more healthy."   (p. 87)[31]

Though Hall leaves the result of the Baverians' overexposure unspecified, one cannot help but wonder whether they, in their wisdom, survive the cold any better than the Scioccians. Thus Hall's Ramistic method of dichotomizing into opposing yet complementary pairs succeeds in pillorying each nation's special flaws, while leading us simultaneously to the more general conclusion that human wisdom and folly often have little to distinguish the one from the other.

Likewise, in Moronia Felix, the Lisonicans are a race of quintessential courtiers, fond of long names and said to be so fawning in their behavior that "no Spaniard is as perfect a mimic as these" (p. 92).[32] In keeping with this conceit, most of the names Hall gives them are Spanish. Lisonica derives from *lisonja*, Spanish for "flattery." Their lesser nobles are named Scogidos, from the Spanish *escogido*, for "elect"; their higher nobles are named Sennaladii, from the Spanish *señalado*, "of eminent birth." But Hall's generalizing tendency makes their servants end up with the Italian name Mange-guadagnos, or "earn-your-eats," while the Sennaladians's practice of wiping their mouths and picking their teeth around lunchtime to counterfeit having just eaten (p. 95) is lifted almost verbatim from Hall's earlier satires, *Virgidemiae* (3, 7, 4–6), where this is claimed as the practice of penniless English gallants who stroll about St. Paul's.[33]

Though it *is* true that he does come down harder than normal on Italians and Catholics than on most other races and religions,[34] Hall is generally impartial in his satire, condemning, for example, heretical sects all the way from the second-century Saturnians to a group of so-called Brownists exiled to Canada in 1597.

This tension between the ridicule of vices special to one people or one place (under the guise of climate theory) and the ridicule of man's common depravity continues throughout the *Mundus*, that is until the very end, where the tension is resolved in favor of an image of man's universal error. The Codicians, misers, who take their names from the Spanish *codicia*, "greed,"[35] "walk like quadrupeds, face always downward, so that they don't neglect anything worth picking up; nor do they ever look up at the sky" (p. 116).[36] In their devotion to the world and to Chrysius Deus, the god of money, they exemplify the perverted singlemindedness of most of mankind, which defies national boundaries and mocks climate theory. If such people are influenced by climate, it is a climate that sends its demonic vapors uniformly to the ends of the earth.

Climate theory, by removing from man partial responsibility for his behavior, can in Hall's mind only be a pernicious influence, subverting his amendment. Significantly, Hall follows the *Mundus* with his *Characters of Vertves and Vices*, generalized descriptions of people either good or bad that could never be mistaken as pinpointing any one nationality. These portraits emphasize those virtues or vices common to everyone, and Hall seldom mentions climate theory again, except in passing reference. But he never gives up chastising vice and championing virtue. Nor does he ever cease to emphasize the importance of individual responsibility in opposing vice:

> What if we cannot turn the stream? Yet wee must swim against it: euen without conquest, it is glorious to haue resisted. In this alone, they are enemies, that doe nothing.[37]

Marlborough School, Los Angeles

Notes

1. *Politics*, 1327b; transl. H. Rackham, Loeb (1959), pp. 565–67.

2. "Airs Waters Places," 13; *Hippocrates*, transl. W. H. S. Jones, Loeb (1923), 1, 109–11.

3. "Airs Waters Places," 10; *Hippocrates*, 1, 103.

4. *Meteorologica*, 348b; transl. H. D. P. Lee, Loeb (1952), p. 83: "Now we know that hot and cold have a mutual reaction [ἀντιπερίστασις] on one another (which is the reason why subterranean places are cold in hot weather and warm in frosty weather)."

5. John Barclay, *Icon Animorum* (Londini, Ex officina Nortoniana apud Iohannem Billium, 1614): "Quippe per ignauiam fertiles campos illis colere, ac ferere, pene ignotum. Pabulo, & telluris genio ad armentorum alimenta contenti sunt.... Ita turpi ocio exigunt vitam" (p. 94). *The Mirrovr of Mindes, or, Barclay's Icon animorum*, transl. Thomas May (London, Iohn Norton for Thomas Walkley, 1631): "By reason of their sloth, though their fields are fertile, yet tilling and sowing are things almost vnknowne to them. They are content with that grasse, which the ground yeeldeth of her owne accord for pasture, for their cattell.... Soe in a sordid, and filthy idlenesse, they lead their liues" (pp. 140–41).

6. On the supposed effects of arctic weather on human behavior see Gerhard Mercator, *Atlas sive Cosmographicae Meditationes de Fabrica Mvndi et Fabricati Figvra* (Amsterdam, Henricus Hondius, 1630), p. 42; transl. by William Saltonstall as *Mercator's Atlas* (London, T. Cotes, for Michael Sparke and Samuel Cartwright, 1635), pp. 30–31. Likewise, Levinus Lemnius claims: "Sic qui Aquiloni sunt expositi, tractusque frigidos occupant, ob sanguinem crassiorem, densosque spiritus, animosi conspiciuntur, inhumani, formidabiles, truces, feroces, & qui vultu, voceque minaci hominibus terrorem incutiunt" (*De Habitu et Constitvtione Corporis,... Libri II* [Francofvrdi, Apud Ioannem Wechelum, 1591], p. 15). "They that dwell Northward and in cold regions, by reason of grosse bloud and thick Spirites, are seene to be bolde and full of venturous courage, rude, vnmanerly, terrible, cruell, fierce, and such as with very threatnyng countenaunce, and menacying wordes, make others to stand in feare of them" (transl. of *De Habitu* by Thomas Norton as *The Touchstone of Complexions* [London, Thomas Parsh, 1581], p. 13^r).

7. *The Mirrovr of Mindes*, p. 45; *Icon Animorum*: "Nam omnia saecula genium habent, qui mortalium animos in certa studia solet inflectere" (p. 30).

8. *The Mirrovr of Mindes*, p. 3 [sig. Aa2^r; the book begins renumbering from p. 1 at sig. Aa1^r]; *Icon Animorum*: "Quippe singulis mortalibus praeter patriae suae indolem adhuc proprium aliquid Natura concessit; prorsusque ingenti miraculo, per tot secula, & nomina populorum, vnicuique hominum sua lineamenta inuenit; quae tam frontis quam animi habitum, a reliquorum corporum, mentiumque similitudine distinguerent" (p. 211).

9. Lemnius, *The Touchstone of Complexions*, p. 16^v; *De Habitu*: "Verum ciuiusque regionis conditionem ac naturam, quam imitari populares solent, immutat educatio, institutio, disciplina: sic vt promiscua multitudo incultis motibus conspiciatur, quum viri politici, & qui ex patriciis sunt prognati, immutata victus ratione, relictaque veteri, atque inolita consuetudine optimum viuendi institutum asciscant, ac se suosque ad laudabiles mores componant" (pp. 19–20).

10. *The Mirrovr of Mindes*, p. 55; *Icon Animorum*: "Ita in omni gente per aestus succedentium saeculorum mores animosque mutantium, haeret quaedam vis inconcussa" (p. 37).

11. *The Mirrovr of Mindes*, p. 111; *Icon Animorum*: "Dum salutant, aut scribunt, descendere ad verba imaginariae seruitutis quae istorum seculorum blandicies inuenit, nisi forte externis moribus imbuti, non sustinent" (p. 75).

12. *Method for the Easy Comprehension of History*, transl. Beatrice Reynolds (New York,

Columbia University Press, 1945), p. 123; *Methodus, ad Facilem Historiarvm Cognitionem* (Paris, Apud Martinvm Iuuenem, 1566): "In eo tamen omnes praeter D. Hieronymum, conueniunt, Gallos esse leues" (p. 138).

13. *Method,* p. 127; *Methodus:* "Hebraei & AEgyptij Graecos, Itali Gallos, Galli Germanos leues esse queruntur" (p. 144).

14. The most complete treatment of climate theory in English literature is by Waldemar Zacharasiewicz, *Die Klimatheorie in der englischen Literatur und Literaturkritik von der Mitte des 16. bis zum frühen 18. Jahrhundert* (Vienna, Wilhelm Braumüller, 1977). However, though he does mention Joseph Hall's *Mundus Alter et Idem* in passing (p. 119), he devotes no discussion to it. For periods after Hall see F. W. Hadley, "The Theory of Milieu in English Criticism from 1660 to 1801," diss. University of Chicago, 1925, and Z. S. Fink, "Milton and the Theory of Climatic Influence," *MLQ,* 2 (1941), 67–80. Fink shows the continuing unease Milton had concerning the adverse influence of cold climate on the English, even though other English writers like Thomas Nashe were ready to dismiss the theory, "especially insofar as [it] related to the arts and learning" (p. 70).

15. Joseph Hall, *Another World and Yet the Same, Bishop Joseph Hall's Mundus Alter et Idem,* transl. John Millar Wands (New Haven, Yale University Press, 1981), p. 11. (All subsequent parenthetical references in the text refer to this edition); *Mundus Alter et Idem* (Francofvrti, Apud haeredes Ascanij de Rinialme, n.d. [1605]): "Audiant vulgo Galli temerarij, Hispani arrogantes, bibaces Germani, Britanni πολυπράγμονες, Itali molles, Sueui timidi, Boëmi inhumani, Hyberni barbari ac superstitiosi; quisquamne hominum ita plumbeus est, vt existimet Galliam vix quenquam prudentem, Hispaniam pusillanimum, abstemium Germaniam produxisse? Fallunt, mihi crede, qui animorum compositionem, & efformationem morum ita totam caelo tribuunt, nihil vt propriae cuiusque indoli, nihil semini parentis, nihil denique educationis rationi relinquant" (pp. 4–5).

16. *Epistles, The First Volvme: Containing II. Decads* (London, H. L. for Samuel Macham & E. Edgar, 1608), pp. 85–86.

17. *Characters of Vertves and Vices* (London, Melchior Bradwood for Eleazar Edgar and Samuel Macham, 1608), p. 2. Compare one of his *Epistles,* written about 1608: "Let me be at once (as I vse) bold and plaine: Wanton excesse, excessiue pride, close Atheisme,… greedy couetousnesse, loose prodigalitie, simoniacall sacrilege, vnbridled luxurie, beastly drunkennesse, bloody treachery, cunning fraud, slanderous detraction, enuious vndermin-ings, secret Idolatrie, hypocritical fashionablenesse, haue spred themselues all ouer the world" (*Epistles, The Second Volume: Conteining two Decads* [London, A. H. for Eleazar Edgar & Samuel Macham, 1608], pp. 208–09).

18. *Mundus:* "magna quidem ex parte eiusdem & longitudinis & latitudinis est (quod ominosum nemini videatur) cum nostra Britannia; altera vero cum vtraque Germania" (p. 20).

19. *De Habitu:* "Plerique eorum quibus liberalis deest educatio, ac doctrinae institutio, ingenio sunt mobili, captioso, fallaci, infido, [et] rerum nouarum auido" (p. 22); *The Touchstone of Complexions:* "Many of them which lacke good bringinge vp, and haue not bene trayned in learning and ciuility, are of disposition, wauering, vnconstant, captious, deceitfull, false-hearted, [and] desirous of alterations" (p. 19ʳ).

20. *Mundus:* "Nam certe istic plurima inuenimus Gallorum vestigia; siue locorum nomina, siue legum reliquias, vel denique numismatum spectes monumenta: Facies terrae multiformis est, & dubia; nam quae pascua laeta vides hoc anno Florae sacra, proximo aratrum expectant, Cererique dicantur: quique pridem montes caelo minabantur, nunc cauam replentes vallem, superbum cacumen viatoribus calcandum praebent. Flumina saepe nouos canales mirantur prioribus interclusis" (pp. 123–24).

21. quoted in Peter Heylyn, *ΜΙΚΡΟΚΟΣΜΟΣ. A Little Description of the Great World,* 3rd

ed. rev. (Oxford, I. L. and W. T. for William Turner and Thomas Huggins, 1627):

> Tres sunt convivae, Germanus, Flander, & Anglus:
>   Dic quis edat melius, quis meliusve bibat.
> Non comedis Germane, bibis; tu non bibis Angle,
>   Sed comedis; comedis Flandre, bibisque bene.

> Duch, Flemming, English, are your onely guests
> Which of these three doth drink or eat the best?
> Th'English loue most to eate, the Dutch to swill:
> Only the Flemming eates and drinkes his fill.   (p. 469)

22. *Mundus*: "per dies fere quadraginta carnem fastidiant, & exinde piscibus, sed sumptu longe maiore, vino coctis conditisque ... vescantur;... vt se recreent aliquantulum tanta ferculorum varietate, tum vt eo acriore animo carnem diu neglectam aggrediantur" (p. 51).

23. *Characters of Vertves and Vices*, p. 2 and sig. A5^r-A5^v.

24. *Method*, p. 124; *Methodus*: "Est autem contrariorum contraria disciplina. Igitur si Australis ater est, Septentrionalis candidus: si magnus hic, ille paruus: hic robustus, ille debilis: hic calidus humidus, ille frigidus siccus: hic pilosus, ille glaber: ... hic calorem metuit, ille frigus: hic laetus: ille tristis: hic sociabilis, ille solitarius: hic audax, ille timidus: hic vinosus, ille sobrius" (pp. 139-40).

25. *Mundus*: "Terra sita est sub ipso polo Antarctico (vti contra sub Arctico Pygmaeorum) & sane iam subolet mihi ex vna eademque causa, frigore nimirum vtriusque region[i]s intensissimo, & Pygmaeorum exilitatem, & Moronorum stupiditatem prouenisse; ... quidem ... hoc fidem facit, quod qui sub mediis ac temperatis caeli Zonis habitant, & animo valere soleant & corpore: sed philosophi id curent scilicet" (p. 114).

26. *Mundus*: "Quin & istic forsan haesitabit incredulus rerum indagator, explorator terrarum, neque (cum caeli ingenio soleant incolarum mores conformari) sibi sinet persuaderi, regionem hanc polarem pro loci situ intensissime frigidam, tam plus satis calidae ac cholericae prolis matrem vnquam extitisse. At nouimus, sat bene philosophi, eo verisimilius hoc ex αντιπεριστάσει posse fieri, quo caelum frigidius; neque illud quisquam stupere poterit, qui nouerit Africam regionum torridissimam gelidiss[imas] serpentes generare.... Nunc ergo suffragante philosophia fidem & spero mihi, & arrogo" (pp. 143-44).

27. *Mundus*: "Omnes carent fundamento; quippe aiunt se malle lapides effodere, quam sepelire" (p. 157).

28. *Mundus*: "Multi hic quotannis prae mera inedia ac frigore moriuntur" (p. 151).

29. *Mundus*: "nec cibum coquere, nec vestem concinnare, nec sternere lectum ... norint" (p. 151).

30. *Mundus*: "rerum omnium causas subtilius indagatur" (p. 152).

31. *Mundus*: "Pars nuda incedit, vt induendi & exuendi parcant labori simul & tempori; pars tecta sibi parat, sed absque septo vel pariete, vt aedes eo magis sint perspirabiles, ac proinde salubriores" (p. 152).

32. *Mundus*: "nec quis profecto Hispanorum mimus est, prae istis Lisonicis" (p. 163).

33. *The Poems of Joseph Hall*, ed. Arnold Davenport (Liverpool, Liverpool University Press, 1949; rpt. 1969), p. 41 and note p. 190.

34. Throughout *Quo Vadis?* Hall condemns travel to "the poisonous aire of *Italie* it selfe" (*Quo Vadis? A Ivst Censvre of Travell as it is commonly vndertaken by the Gentlemen of our Nation* [London, Edward Griffin for Henry Fetherstone, 1617], p. 94) because of the popery — "the chaire of pestilence" (*Quo Vadis?*, p. 94) — one is exposed to, and in *Virgidemiae* he constantly attacks the Roman church. His vehemence can be explained as typical of English anti-Catholic attitudes in reaction to Elizabeth's excommunication and the Jesuits' con-

tinued presence in England: "Sure I am that by their tongues Satan labours to inchant the world" (*Quo Vadis?*, p. 73).

35. Hall probably also means Codicia to be derived from *codex, codicis*, in the sense of an "account book" or "ledger," as given by Lewis and Short, *A Latin Dictionary* (Oxford, Clarendon Press, 1969), p. 303, since the word *codex* is transferred intact to every major European language.

36. *Mundus*: "Quadrupedum more prona semper facie incedunt, ne quid inter eundum surreptione dignum praetermittant; neque caelum vnquam suspiciunt" (p. 213).

37. *Epistles, The Second Volume*, p. 214.

Vsque ad aras: Thomas Elyot's Friendship with Thomas More

K. J. Wilson

In a letter to Thomas Cromwell two years after the death of Thomas More, Sir Thomas Elyot requested the Lord Privy Seal "to lay a part the remembraunce of the amity betwene me and sir Thomas More which was but *Vsque ad aras*, as is the proverb, consydering that I was never so moche addict unto hym as I was unto truthe and fidelity toward my soveraigne lorde, as godd is my Juge."[1] This remark has excited controversy on the question of loyalty; and this is as it should be, since loyalty is precisely the subject of Elyot's letter. On the basis of this single comment some of the saint's admirers have regarded Elyot as an abject survivor—at best a flatterer, at worst a traitor to his friendship. It is perhaps not too much to say that Elyot's reputation is poised on his use of this allusion to Gellius and Plutarch. Yet the allusion itself is fraught with ambiguity, and this renders Elyot's comment far more equivocal than has hitherto been recognized. In its equivocation lies its true meaning.

Had he wondered about Elyot's meaning, Cromwell could have found the Latin phrase in the *Adagia* of Erasmus. There Erasmus tells us that "Pericles, when he was asked by a friend to swear a false oath in order to help him, replied: 'It behoves me,' he said, 'to help my friends, but only up to the altars.' Gellius gives this tale. [Erasmus continues:] Plutarch tells it more aptly in a little book Περι Δυσωπίας [in the *Moralia*].... He tells us that it is a proverb by which sometimes when we promote the advantages of our friends and comply with their wishes, it may seem right to depart from a just course of action, but only to the degree that we do violence to the Godhead because of a friend; for in times past those who took oaths touched the altar with their hands."[2]

Thus far Erasmus may be used to explicate Elyot's allusion to Plutarch. Plutarch focuses with great discrimination on the duties of any friendship with one in public life. If Cromwell had consulted the original passage which Erasmus cites, he would have found Plutarch continuing in a vein that not only catches Elyot's dilemma vis-à-vis More but also strikingly articulates More's own dilemma with regard to the King. Plutarch asks:

How will you correct [a friend] when he errs in the affairs of life? How admonish him when he is misguided in the case of some office, *marriage*, or *policy of state*?[3]

And then Plutarch goes on to say,

For my part I cannot even approve Pericles' answer to the friend who asked him to give false testimony under oath, 'As far as the altar I am your friend.' For this was getting much too close.

Yet Elyot tells Cromwell that his amity with More "was but *Vsque ad aras*," that is, that it extended even *beyond* what Plutarch advised.

Erasmus gives us a bit more on the adage. "Moreover," he concludes the entry, "to what degree and to what point we may depart from an honorable course of action for the sake of a friend is copiously and learnedly discussed by Gellius in the first book of *Attic Nights*, chapter three." Thomas More had subjected friendship to precisely the kind of scrupulous attention that Erasmus admired in Gellius when More sternly refused the Duke of Norfolk's entreaty to take an oath against the godhead "for friendship."[4] Gellius raised the very questions More raised, and in alluding to him Elyot hints that he shares those questions. "But what I ask and wish to know," writes Gellius, "is this: when it is that one must act contrary to law and contrary to equity in a friend's behalf, albeit without doing violence to the public liberty and peace; and when it is necessary to turn aside from the path..., in what way and how much, under what circumstances, and to what extent that ought to be done." And, like Plutarch, Gellius cites Pericles's judgment: "'One ought to aid one's friends, but only so far as the gods allow.'"[5] But Gellius's scruples shift the balance slightly. Not "to the altar," but "only so far as the gods allow," that is, so far as one can aid one's friend without violating the laws of the gods or breaking an oath which one has taken in the name of a god.[6]

More, as we know, would not take an oath which, as he saw it, violated divine law. But Elyot, as he says in the letter to Cromwell, could go no further on behalf of his friend than that point where his actions were contrary to law and might do violence to the public liberty and peace. Of course it is hardly to Thomas Cromwell that Elyot can complain of the rupture in his friendship with More. Elyot does not deny the friendship, yet through the proverbial allusion he focuses on the exact limits of that bond. Elsewhere Elyot had written,

he that is a good man, shal do nothing for his frendes sake, that is either against the comon welthe, or els agaynst his othe or fidelite. For the offence is not excusable, to say, thou dyddest it for thy frendes sake.

These words Elyot wrote in a brief and sensitive essay entitled "The Manner to Choose and Cherish a Friend," which was printed after a translation (perhaps Elyot's own) of Plutarch, "How One may Take Profit of his Enemies."[7] Writing to Cromwell in search of advancement, and even a portion of the recently suppressed monastic lands, it is almost as if Elyot was attempting in one letter to find some manner to cherish a friend and still take profit of his enemies.

With the phrase *Vsque ad aras* Elyot clearly indicates that his friendship with More continued up to the time of oath-taking, to the moment when Elyot chose duty to the commonwealth and the king, and took the oath of the Act of Supremacy. Elyot was not alone in believing More to be wrong in choosing pope over king. Here Elyot asserts that his amity with More did not extend to the crime for which he was convicted.

In this assertion we have a clear-headed perception of More's actions as they appeared to the eyes of a friend. Elyot was not in possession of all the information we now have — Rich's perjury, More's letters, and the Tower works — to say nothing of the freedom from personal involvement, which clarifies moral judgment. To Elyot and others in the secondary rank of More's circle and to a larger number of English contemporaries More's intransigent internationalism must have seemed an increasing threat to the national interest and a betrayal of fidelity to the Crown. Thus our view of More as a slaughtered saint may be a far less puzzling and painful one than that of his contemporaries — of a good man carried to an extreme position. Elyot's letter shows us one carefully controlled response to the moral conflict into which More's personal decision threw his patriotic friends. After his death some of his own family chose exile rather than follow him to prison and death. Elyot remained in England.

His trust in the king was of long standing. In 1536 he could still hope that all might be well. *The Governor* of 1531 is the longest of several works devoted to the moral education of the king and the improvement of the English public weal. To him the welfare of the realm held precedence over More's vision of catholic unanimity. His experience at the court of Charles V, where he failed to obtain the emperor's support for Henry's projected divorce, was enough to convince him as early as 1532 of the necessity of making peace with the idea of English independence from Rome. Addict or dependent though he was to the king for patronage, yet he dared to express obliquely his disapproval of the divorce in two satiric dialogues of 1533, *Pasquil the Plain* and *Of the Knowledge Which Maketh a Wise Man*. The king had shown him some marks of favor (though without repaying the debts he had incurred as ambassador) and would soon make available to him the royal library for the compilation of his Latin-English *Dictionary*.

In Cromwell Elyot also had reason to hope. His star now at the zenith, Cromwell had been made Lord Privy Seal on July 2, 1536. Elyot's earliest extant letter to him as Wolsey's secretary (March 25, 1528) is signed "Your Lovyng companyon"; and all of his nine surviving letters to Cromwell are couched in language not merely of respect but of friendship. Strange to say, Elyot seems actually to have tried to befriend Cromwell. It is not for me, but rather for Professor Elton, to speak admiringly of Thomas Cromwell, but he has a precedent in Elyot. I do believe that Cromwell preserved the little batch of Elyot's letters because that gentle-eyed and at times perhaps ingenuous courtier saw in him the capacity for friendship:

"amicorum Praeses," Elyot calls him in a letter written on the flyleaf of a presentation copy of the 1538 edition of the *Dictionary*.[8] The letter we are considering concludes with a proposition aimed at the heart: "by your lordshippes meanes ... what so ever porcion of land that I shall attayne by the kynges gift, I promyse to give to your lordship the first yeres frutes with myn assurid and faithfull hart and servyce."[9]

Throughout their correspondence Elyot builds up the notion that he and Cromwell are bound together by shared intellectual interests, *similitudine studiorum*, which Cicero stresses in the *De Amicitia* and his epistles.[10] Thus Elyot imputes virtue to Cromwell, much as we all do to our friends. Elyot could do this in a particularly compelling way. "May you give me the strength," he writes to Cromwell in Latin, "to be the sort of man whom you ought to consider worthy of your friendship."[11] By directing Cromwell to the phrase *Vsque ad aras* in Plutarch Elyot gives a classical precedent, a moral signpost, for what this powerful statesman must do next. For example, in another reference to Pericles later in the *Moralia* Plutarch says that one must "not be a 'friend as far as the altar' ... but only so far as conforms to any law ... the neglect of which leads to great public injury."[12] More, Elyot might say, went too far, risking "public injury." Now More is gone. But, says Plutarch,

> after [a statesman] has once made the chief public interests safe, out of his abundant resources [he may] ... assist his friends, take his stand beside them, and help them out of their troubles.

Such favor it is now in Cromwell's power to bestow. In referring in the same breath, in the same proverb, both to the limits of loyalty and to the duty of statesmen to reward their friends so far as the gods allow, Elyot for a brief moment yokes together Thomas Cromwell and Thomas More, the king's good servant and God's. If Cromwell failed to appreciate Elyot's oblique comparison between him and More, perhaps, as his own fortunes swiftly revolved towards confiscation of goods, imprisonment, and execution, the phrase *Vsque ad aras* may have taken on tinges of warning and even irony.

New York City

Notes

1. *The Letters of Sir Thomas Elyot*, ed. K. J. Wilson, "Texts and Studies, 1976," *SP*, 73.5 (Chapel Hill, University of North Carolina Press, 1976), p. 31.

2. *Opera omnia*, ed. Jean Leclerc (Leyden, 1703–06), III, II, x, p. 748B–D; my translation, ibid., p. 32, n. 5.

3. *Moralia*, "De vitiose pudore," Loeb (VII, 531C, p. 61); emphasis mine.

4. Actually, Norfolk uses this phrase in Robert Bolt's play *A Man for All Seasons*. Bolt no doubt got the motif from the famous letter signed Margaret Roper but at least co-written by her father, to Alice Alington (as well as to the Court and government circles). It is there (Rogers, *Correspondence*, pp. 521ff.) that More tells a tale of Mr. Cumpany, the odd man out in the jury, to whom his companions say (p. 523, ll. 325ff.): "play the good companion, come furth with us and pass even [i.e., were it only] for good company...." That awkward (to us) "pass" and the "for good company" phrase recur seven or eight times in the next half page, until "good fellowship" is also used, and even "friendship" (p. 524). The readers of that letter (which must have included Cromwell) would refrain from using that argument with the prisoner—whether they had done so earlier, or else Cromwell anticipated they would, since calling him "singular" (or saying to Fisher: "You are but one man," Henry's own words in 1529) came to much the same. (I am grateful to Fr. Marc'hadour for reminding me of this source.)

5. *Attic Nights*, Loeb (I, iii, 19-20).

6. As the Loeb translator, John C. Rolfe, explains in a note.

7. *STC* 20052, sig. Bvi.

8. *Letters*, p. 35.

9. *Letters*, p. 31.

10. See *Letters*, p. 35, n. 5.

11. *Letters*, pp. 36f.

12. "Precepts of Statecraft," 808B.

POLAND

De Joannis Calvini epistula dedicatoria ad Poloniae regem Sigismundum Augustum directa

Andrzej Kempfi

You have a great and splendid Kingdom in which nothing is lacking whatsoever that serves as an ornament and decoration. But, in order to make it fully happy, it is required that it take Christ as a captain and be strengthened with Christ's guardianship." The Kingdom mentioned in the foregoing quotation is sixteenth-century Poland and these are John Calvin's words put in his dedication of the Commentary to Paul's Epistle to the Hebrews (1549). Its addressee was the king of Poland and grand duke of Lithuania Sigismund August, who had just then been raised to the throne.

"The glorious crown of Poland—declares Calvin—does not blemish and the vengeance of Heaven does not claim any bloodshed: on the particular intervention of Providence not even a single drop of blood of those, who are professing the genuine and pure Gospel, was spilled." In ths manner Calvin has done justice to the spirit of toleration of evangelicalism and evangelicals in Poland of those days. And he added immediately: "The father of Your Royal Highness, of blessed memory king Sigismund the Elder, enlightened with mildness and among cruelties raging in numerous Christian countries, he, himself, has kept his hands uncontaminated. And at present in the state of Your Royal Highness the nobility and so many distinguished men not only are ready to accept the truth about Christ, but also rely on it with their whole souls. Yes indeed, I observe that one of the sons of Poland, a person of noble ducal birth, Laski, carried a burning torch of evangelical faith to other countries as well."

In one passage of his letter to Sigismund August, John Calvin states that he does not claim the glory of talent and erudition. But in reality he gave there expression to his talent and erudition in a very significant manner and addressed Sigismund August with splendid apostrophes. Three themes in his letter are placed in the foreground. First we encounter an eloquent exposé on what Calvin describes as a "horrible distortion and profanation of everything that makes up the content of Christian religion," i.e., Calvin demonstrates the corruption of God's word for which the Roman Catholic Church is declared to be responsible. Secondly the

king, Sigismund August, is being called on to undertake the task of repairing ecclesiastical affairs in his country; hence to put himself on the side of the Reformation and to introduce it into Poland.

Thirdly the content of the Epistle to the Hebrews itself is being recommended
to Sigismund August's attention. "The Epistle to the Hebrews—says Calvin—
represents that apostolic letter which is made up from an exposition about the
eternal divinity of Jesus Christ and about Jesus Christ himself as a supreme teacher
and unique priest; therefore it is something that we ought to consider as the essence
of Celestial Wisdom. This letter expresses in a tangible manner the whole power
and ministry of Jesus Christ and should be considered on this account in the
Church of God as an immeasurable treasure."

From what we read further in the dedicatory letter, it follows that the act of
dedication of the Commentary on the Epistle of Paul to the Hebrews was envisaged
by Calvin as a reply: a reply (quite neglected by historians of the Reformation)
to a dedication by Eck in the year 1528 to King Sigismund the Elder—father of
Sigismund August—of a work entitled "On the sacrifice of the mass" (in original:
qui [scil. Eck] suum de sacrificio Missae libellum Sigismundo Regi Maiestati Tuae
patri inscribendo foedam [...] tam illustri regno maculam inussit). And Calvin
assumes that he is going to achieve no little success if he, at least, succeeds through
his act of dedication in expunging what he calls the stain with which Eck, through
his dedication, is said to have soiled the name of Poland: "ego vero si hunc meum
laborem Tuae Maiestati nuncupans ac dicans hoc saltem perfecero, ut a nomine
Polonico eluantur foetidae illae Eccii sordes [...], mihi non parum videbor
consecutus").

Further on refuting the Roman Catholic antagonist of Martin Luther, John
Eck of Ingolstadt, Calvin writes among other things that: "The apostle who composed the Epistle to the Hebrews was quite specially anxious to demonstrate that
this matter which Eck considers as a sacrifice, apparently conflicts with the
priesthood of Christ."

And what can be said about the place of the dedicatory letter to Sigismund
August in the background of Calvin's epistolography as a whole? This letter is
classed by scholars among those writings in which, in a most significant manner,
Calvin has given voice to a consciousness of his mission as a protagonist of the
Reformation, a consciousness reinforced about 1548 by the contemporary successes in the spread of Calvinistic doctrine in various parts of Europe. Apart from
the dedication directed to Sigismund August, writings which reflect Calvin's consciousness as a religious reformer include such prefaces as, firstly, a dedication
in the year 1548 of a commentary on the epistles to Timothy to the contemporary
regent of England Edward Seymour duke of Somerset; secondly, a dedication in
1550 of a commentary on Isaiah to the young sovereign of England Edward VI;
thirdly, dated in the year 1552, a dedication of a commentary on the Acts of the
Apostles in its first redaction to the king of Denmark Christian III.

Illustrious Sovereign! God calls you like a new Esechias or Josias to bring about the restoration of the pure doctrine of the Gospel, a doctrine, which nowadays has become so greatly corrupted all over the world through the insidiousness of evil and human wickedness. And there is no lack of signs indicating that the hope that you will be willing to carry out in Poland this restoration will not be futile. I am not going to speak here about many different virtues, which are known also outside the borders of Poland and which are a great blessing for your Polish subjects. Instead, I would assert that you have always distinguished yourself with a unique piety. And I shall add that there are grounds for maintaining that your mind has been enlightened by the light of the Gospel by Christ himself, who is the sun of justice.

Exhortations to reform the Church like this one, which I have just quoted, are very numerous and I refer interested readers to the original of Calvin's dedicatory letter to the king of Poland. Simultaneously however when he addressed Sigismund August, Calvin was aware of how hard and difficult it is for a sovereign to undertake the task of reform of the established church. "Indeed — confesses Calvin — it is a most difficult enterprise for which even the most courageous may not have enough courage."

It is neither timely nor opportune to discuss here why King Sigismund August did not openly break with the Roman Catholic Church, even though he was well disposed towards the ideas which the Reformers had put forth. In whatever manner one wishes to view this affair, the fact of the matter is that Calvin was not without foundation when he spoke about "indications of the hope that Sigismund August would be willing to renew the Church of Poland in the evangelical spirit." Namely in the year 1548, immediately after he ascended the throne, as well as just before than, while he had been viceroy of Lithuania, he read the evangelical books intensively and was apparently curious about the affairs of reforming the Church. Furthermore in the year of his ascension 1548 he issued a declaration that he was willing to bring about theological discourses and that afterwards he would establish whatever was decided according to Holy Scripture. The news about this evident inclination of the young sovereign toward the Reformation was passed throughout Europe by word of mouth reaching Calvin in Geneva as well.

Calvin's preface of 1549 has until now been rather overlooked by the historians of the Polish and European Reformation movements. More attention has been paid to the two subsequent letters by Calvin to Sigismund August, one written in the year 1554 and the second in 1555. It is interesting to note that this correspondence acknowledges the receipt of an answer on the part of Sigismund August. And although it was not quite satisfactory for him, Calvin still didn't seem to feel that his efforts to persuade the king were completely in vain either. "Your Royal Highness — Calvin addresses Sigismund August — has condescended to send on to me a letter by which it appears that my former zeal has been met with grace and my previous writing with an attempt to propose the best kind of a reform the Church and my suggestion about the most convenient moment was not contemptuously rejected by Your Royal Highness."

There is no doubt that a dedicated copy of Calvin's Commentary to the Epistle to the Hebrews was sent from Geneva to Cracow. Sigismund August did not refuse to accept the gift and it certainly occupied an honourable place in the royal library, a library which just at present is going more and more to absorb the attention of bibliophiles not only in Poland. We have however to deplore that today the copy signed and despatched by Calvin himself is no longer to be found among the preserved and identified items of Sigismund August's collection. There are some indications that like the other non-catholic prints from the theological section of this library it became a victim of some purge undertaken in subsequent times by the heirs to the collection of Sigismund August: a purge aimed at making it obvious that the religious interests of Sigismund August conformed to strict orthodox Catholicism. Polish historians nevertheless know that Sigismund August was not by any means scandalized by that which scandalized others and that in the theological section of his collection there was no lack of non-catholic works. E.g., there was a copy of Martin Luther's Bible-edition, a copy of the Confession of Augsburg, the so-called Bible of Brest with a translation by Protestants of the Holy Writ into Polish, the writings of German, French and Swiss Reformers such as Brenz, Bullinger and Beza.

About the presence of the copy of the Luther Bible in Sigismund August's library there is important evidence which until today has escaped the attention of historians of the Reformation. A note which refers to this copy is preserved in the reports of the Jesuit College in Wilna, to which in subsequent times this library was bequeathed. Here it is in the translation from the Latin: "Luther too has sent to him [scil. to king Sigismund August] his Bible with a dedication. This copy of the Luther Bible — bound in silk and equipped with silver fittings — was to be seen in the library of the Jesuit College and Academy in Wilna up to the time of the Swedish and Moscovite invasion under the reign of King Joannes Casimirus (that is, until the middle of the seventeenth century)." The Latin text runs: "Et Lutherus etiam ipsa sua illi [scil. Sigismundo Augusto] Biblia dedicavit quae videbantur in Bibliotheca Collegii et Academiae Vilnensis Societatis Jesus holoserico et argento compacta usque ad bellum Joannis Casimiri regis cum Suecis et Moschis habitum."

Finally let us mention that the preface of the Epistle to the Hebrews was not the unique literary gift by Calvin to a Pole. In 1560 there appeared a new redaction of a commentary by Calvin on the Acts of the Apostles presented to the voivode of Wilna and chancellor of Lithuania Duke Nicolas Radziwill the Black, a devoted Polish Protestant and patron of the Protestant translation of the Holy Writ into Polish.

University of Warsaw

Monasterij B. Virginis in Ebrac3. A

ꙮ AD INVICTISSI

MVM POLONIAE REGEM SI,
gismundum, de sacrificio Missæ Contra
Lutheranos, libri tres.

Iohanne Eckio authore.

ANNO M D XXVI.
Mense Octobri.

Eckius de Sacrificio Misse

IOANNIS CALVINI COMMEN-
TARII IN EPISTOLAM AD
HEBRAEOS.

POTENTISS. AC SERENISS. PRINCIPI, SIGISMVM-
DO AVGVSTO, DEI GRATIA POLONIAE REGI, MA
GNO DVCI LITHVANIAE, RVSSIAE, PRVSSIAE AC
MAZOVIAE, ETC, DOMINO ET HAEREDI: IOAN-
NES CALVINVS SALVTEM.

V̈M tam multi hodie infulfi homines; paffim ac temerè fcipturi-
endo, imperitos & minus acutos lectores fuis nugis occupent, Cla
riff. Rex, ad hoc vitium alia quoque indignitas accedit, quod dum
Regibus aliifque principibus viris infcribunt fuas ineptias, vt his fucandis,
vel faltem tegendis fplendorem inde mutuentur:non tantum facra alioqui
nomina profanant, fed partem illis quodammodo fui dedecoris afper-

Le poème latin de Jan Kochanowski concernant Wanda (Élégie I.15)

Jerzy Starnawski

L a poésie latine de Kochanowski est principalement lyrique. Les genres littéraires qu'il cultivait en témoignent: des épigrammes, des élégies, des odes. Les odes latines ainsi que les Chants polonais de Kochanowski ont Horace comme modèle, les patrons d'œuvres élégiaques sont des poètes de l'époque d'Auguste: Ovide, Tibulle, Properce. Il est impossible pourtant d'élucider les caractères énigmatiques des poèmes élégiaques de Kochanowski en se fondant seulement sur sa poésie lyrique. L'élégie I.15 concernant Wanda se distingue et mérite d'être considérée comme poème épique.

L'héroïne de ce poème, morte dans les flots de la Vistule, pourrait devenir sujet d'un poème lyrique; ses actions généreuses méritent d'être célébrées par une ode, sa mort peut être chantée dans une élégie. Le poète n'a écrit ni une ode à louange de l'héroïne, ni une élégie lyrique mais il a raconté dans un poème à structure lyrique avec une distance épique.

Est-ce la seule brèche ouverte dans une œuvre élégiaque vers la poésie épique? Point du tout. Ont un caractère épique les narrations de Phèdre et d'Hippolyte (I.2), de l'amour mutuel entre Odatis et Zaradias (III.3, dans un certain degré l'anticipation de la ballade), le souvenir des accidents des voyages d'Odisse (IV.1), bien enchaîné dans la substance élégiaque d'une narration de Paweł Stempowski faisant ses adieux à sa bien-aimée. Sur le fond des œuvres citées le poème de Wanda se détache comme une œuvre le plus formellement épique.[1]

C'est déjà à Rome antique que l'on se servait du distique élégiaque non seulement dans les élégies *sensu stricto*. Ovide—poète qui savait bien manier ce mètre —nous a laissé non seulement les *Tristia* (modèle autant qu'on sache pour notre Janicius), non seulement les lettres de Pontus, très plaintives, non seulement les cycles des poèmes d'amour, mais aussi un poème épique, les *Fasti*, ou des légendes de Rome antique des temps les plus reculés. Kochanowski a lu sans aucun doute le recueil des tables poétiques du sauvetage miraculeux de Romulus et Rémus, de la fondation de Rome, de l'enlèvement des Sabines etc. C'est aussi Properce dont les poèmes épiques racontent l'histoire la plus ancienne de Rome. Rien d'étonnant alors à ce que ce grand humaniste polonais désirât raconter en distiques élégiaques un épisode de l'histoire la plus reculée de la Pologne. Il a choisi une légende concernant la Petite Pologne avec Cracovie, sa capitale si bien connue, une légende que la Chronique du Maître Vincent a insérée dans le canon de l'histoire de la Pologne.

Au temps de Kochanowski il existait déjà le canon de l'histoire de la Pologne élaborée par Jan Dşugosz. Cette œuvre sans être imprimée était cependant connue par tous les historiens polonais du seizième siècle et multipliée avec différentes modifications depuis Miechowita jusqu'à Kromer. Un savant du dix-neuvième siècle conjecturait que le poète s'inspirait sans doute de Długosz mais aussi dans une certaine mesure de Kromer. Mais Kochanowski—contrairement à Długosz—"passe complètement sous silence le jour solennel de l'action de grâce pour la victoire."[2] Cette opinion fut maintenue pendant une durée de soixante-dix ans jusqu'au moment où en 1948 un historien de la littérature, Tadeusz Ulewicz, a discuté l'élégie de Wanda dans une monographie consacrée à la "conscience slave" de Kochanowski et a démontré d'assez grandes différences entre la version de Długosz et celle de Kochanowski que son prédécesseur n'a pas observées. Il a observé justement que la légende de Wanda était déjà du temps de Kochanowski "publica materies," au dire d'Horace. C'est pourquoi la polémique concernant les sources est vaine.

L'élégie I.15 est généralement reconnue comme la plus belle ou au moins la plus intéressante élégie de Kochanowski. Elle est souvent comparée avec une mention de Wanda dans le *Bellum Pruthenum* de Jan de Wiślica (seizième siècle) ainsi qu'avec une épigramme de Janicius (dans les *Vitae regum Polonorum*). Inutile de prouver la supériorité du poète de Czarnolas sur ses prédécesseurs. L'évolution du motif de Wanda dans la poésie latine en Pologne est bien intéressante.

Dès le premier distique du poème de Wanda, dans l'invocation à la Muse, on peut remarquer le caractère épique. On lit les vers:

> Nunc age, quo pacto bellatrix Vanda Polonis
> Praefuerit, solito carmine, Musa, refer (vv. 1–2)

comme écho de l'invocation de Virgile, *Aen.* I.8–11:

> Musa mihi causas memora, quo numine laeso
> Quidve dolens regina deum tot volvere casus
> Insignem pietate virum, tot adire labores
> Impulerit.

Le poème est tout entier une narration, et une narration intéressante. Kochanowski est poète d'une action intéressante, animée par des dialogues (l'énonciation de Rytygier, un dialogue rapide et court de Wanda avec le délégué de Rytygier). L'auteur du *Renvoi des ambassadeurs grecs* a démontré son talent de se servir du dialogue comme d'une ressource artistique.

L'élégie de Wanda est tout imprégnée de lyrisme ainsi que de rhétorique. La harangue de Wanda à la Vistule au moment décisif prend dix distiques sur cinquante trois, formant une cinquième du poème. Durant de longs siècles un monologue du héros précédant l'accomplissement d'un acte était un élément indispensable de chaque œuvre au caractère narratif. On l'appliquait surtout dans des drames. Le monologue de Wilhelm Tell chez Schiller en est un exemple classique. Le monologue est merveilleusement beau mais pas conforme au caractère de Tell présenté par le poète allemand. Tous les deux — Kochanowski et Schiller — mettent en pratique la même convention persistante si longtemps dans notre culture littéraire.

À l'appui de la supposition que les élégies de Properce ainsi que des légendes des *Fasti* d'Ovide pouvaient avoir stimulé l'auteur de "l'élégie" de Wanda, plusieurs *similia* peuvent être cités. Le savant qui discutait ce thème il y a cent ans déjà en a constaté un seul exemple de similitude entre l'Élégie I.15 (v. 29–30) et une élégie de Tibulle (III.6, vv. 27–28).

Multi illam Arctoo iuvenes ex orbe petebant   ... venti temeraria vota
  Quorum vota plagas rapta per arias.   Aeriae et nubes diripienda ferant
               Kochanowski.   Tibullus.

De menus *similia* sautent aux yeux.[3] "Illa ego Wanda" (v. 74), tout comme Ovide dans son autobiographie (*Trist.* IV.10, v. 1). Vers 9:

Unica restabant Craci de sanguine Vanda

c'est l'écho d'un vers de Virgile (*Aen.* IV.230):

Italiam regeret, genus alto a sanguine Teucri.

La tournure "pallenti viola" provient de l'églogue 2.47 de Virgile.

L'on lit chez Kochanowski (v. 70): "orsa loqui est," qui ressemble au: "sic est nurus ausa loqui" chez Ovide (*Fasti* III.206, épisode de l'enlèvement des Sabines).

Il est à noter que "ter revocavit aquis" (v. 100) est un écho de "forte tumebat aquis" d'Ovide (*Fasti* II.390), mais un écho bien éloigné, emprunté d'une œuvre qui a fourni la conception générale. Kochanowski est un grand artiste, il ne suit pas servilement son modèle.

Les *similia* sont bien éloignés. Les textes des poètes de la Rome antique resonnaient dans la pensée d'un humaniste qui comprenait bien la place occupée dans un vers par des mots respectifs (undis, aquis ...) mais qui savait leur donner l'empreinte de son génie.

Des légendes romaines en distiques élégiaques ne sont pas la seuele et unique source où Kochanowski puisait la phraséologie d'Ovide: il se souvenait également des meilleurs hexamètres des *Métamorphoses*, tout spécialement du mythe de Dédale et Icare: Icare périt dans les flots de la mer, Wanda dans ceux de la Vistule ... Le peuple dont Wanda était une souveraine bien aimée "corpus quaesivit in undis" (v. 97). Dédale "pennas aspexit in undis" (*Met.* VIII.233).

Chez Ovide la légende de Dédale et Icare se termine par:

corpus sepulchrum contigit
Et tellus a nomine dicta sepulti.   (*Met.* VIII.234–35)

la légende de Wanda chez Kochanowski par des vers:

Exstat adhuc laeva monumentum hoc nobile ripa,
Qua Mogilam liquidis Vistula lambit aquis. (v. 105–06)

Donner à une localité imaginaire un nom dérivé du nom de Wanda comme le
nom d'Icarie chez Ovide serait pousser la modification trop loin d'une légende
connue généralement. Le fait que Wanda invoque Iupiter à son aide, ou qu'elle
fait ses vœux à Jupiter, peut sembler un peu choquant aux lecteurs du vingtième
siècle. Dans la poétique de Kochanowski c'est tout à fait naturel: écrivant en latin
il introduit à dessein l'Olympe des déités antiques.

L'élégie 15 est une œuvre à peine dépassant cent vers, impeccable quant à la
métrique; les figures de rhétorique n'y sont pas très inventives; la syntaxe est faite
de main de maître dans toutes les œuvres de Kochanowski, y compris l'élégie I.15.
La réitération sert plusieurs fois à rendre le style plus vigoureux: par exemple
les vers:

Vanda potens forma, Vanda potens animo (10)
Hinc odium taede, hinc mentio nulla hymenaei (15)
Hinc irae rabies, hinc ferus urget amor (38)
Des exemples de l'allitération sont:
ante alios instantius ambit (31)
Vanda viri curat virginitatis amans (36)

et de la transposition, brillamment appliqués:

Votum sublatis tale vovens manibus.

La *licentia poetica* est parfois poussée un peu loin. Le messager de Rytygier est
délégué "Vandae" (v. 44) au lieu de "ad Vandam" selon les règles de la grammaire. La tournure "arma virum" (v. 69) n'est pas à rapprocher des premiers
mots de l'*Énéide*: sa fonction est complètement différente, c'est simplement une
contraction de "virorum" en "virum."

C'est déjà vers la fin du seizième siècle que Jan Daniecki, imitateur de Kochanowski, mais de peu de talent, a publié un poème intitulé "Vanda," bientôt tom-
bé en oubli et présenté au public polonais seulement pendant la quatrième dé-
cennie de notre siècle d'après l'unique exemplaire conservé dans une bibliothèque
de Gdańsk. L'adaptation de Daniecki en comparaison de la traduction de Brod-
ziński (première moitié de dix-neuvième siècle) est beaucoup plus indépendante.
Ça se laisse voir en onomastique: p. ex. Mogiła près de Cracovie est nommée
Dłubnia. Daniecki rend hommage à Kochanowski en familiarisant les lecteurs
polonais avec le poème latin de Kochanowski. Il pourrait écrire comme un autre
imitateur de Kochanowski, comme Adam Czahrowski: "Je sais bien que ces vers

ne sont pas de Rej ni de Kochanowski, Ils sont d'un gars militaire, d'Adam Czahrowski." Ce n'est pas de Czahrowski qu'il faut faire mention, plutôt de Jan Białobłocki, rimeur du dix-septième siècle, qui rend hommage à Kochanowski poète historique.

University of Łodz

Notes

1. Voilà en français: Jacques Langlade: *Jean Kochanowski. L'homme, le penseur, le poète lyrique* (Paris, 1932), pp. 236–37; Jean Kochanowski. *Chants.* Traduits du polonais avec une introduction et un commentaire par J. Langlade (Paris, 1932), p. 49.

2. Vide Rafał Löwenfeld: *Johann Kochanowski (Joannes Cochanovius) und seine lateinischen Dichtungen. Ein Beitrag zur Literaturgeschichte der Slawen* (Poznań, 1877), pp. 106–07.

3. Le premier qui a découvert les similia c'est Marceli Ulkowski *De Ioannis Kochanvii elegiis Latinis* (Srem, 1863), pp. V–XI.

The Latin Manuals of Epistolography in Poland in the Fifteenth and Sixteenth Centuries

Lidia Winniczuk

I allowed myself the liberty of suggesting a paper on this subject, because, as far as I know, many scholars are currently taking a keen interest in epistolography and its theory; among others, Professor Emil Polak (New York) has been doing broad research on this subject.

It is, in fact, a crucial issue, as we can observe the remarkable impact of Greek and Roman theories in this domain, too. Moreover, we learn about strong cultural links between many countries in the fifteenth and sixteenth centuries. As far as Poland is concerned, cultural contacts in this domain of Polish scholars with German and Italian ones are clearly noticeable.

It is well known that in, as early as, the Middle Ages letters were written in Latin too, and there existed some manuals — or rather collections of letters — which served as patterns. Latin correspondence, however, confined itself to relations between the Court and the Church.

In the fifteenth century the skill of writing letters ceased to be the medieval domain of the ecclesiastical and court style: the drawing up of rigid formulas for writing letters and documents was given up. Epistolography became a part of the curriculum for teaching style, with emphasis on its literary character. In this way epistolography was elevated to an important position in the school curriculum and was treated on a par with grammar, rhetoric, and stylistics. Not only were court "secretaries" educated in epistolography, but also wide circles of students were taught the principles of correct style; the language of letters acquired colloquial character according to the hints laid down by Cicero: "Epistulas vero cotidianis verbis texere solemus" (*Ad familiares* IX.21.1). It is also remarkable that both in the manuals of foreign Humanists and Polish ones is clearly visible, for example, the principle often repeated after Petrarch, who introduced it by abandoning the medieval habit of using the second person in plural. Instead, he speaks to the addressee in the second person in the singular. This form is recommended by Beroaldo; in Poland Lucas Ruthenus draws attention to this change.

I am going to discuss the manuals which were used in Poland between 1489 and 1538. Why should such time limits be imposed? The reason for it is that the main source of information about manuals of letter-writing is the list of lectures in the Academy of Cracow: *Liber Diligentiarum 1487–1563*. The first lecture of epistolography was delivered by Johannes Sommerfelt-Aesticampianus in 1493. He was preceded, however, by Conradus Celtis, the famous Humanist, who gave a lecture on epistolography; it is attested only by the announcement of the lecture, which must have taken place on 23 July 1489 (Hora XI in aula Hungarorum)—the date assumed to be the starting point of lectures on epistolography in the Academy of Cracow. In this lecture Celtis is thought to have indicated the importance of being aware of the letter-writing principles. This lecture, entitled "Tractatus de condendis epistolis," has been edited with "Epitoma in utramque Ciceronis Rhetoricam cum arte memorativa et modo epistolandi utilissimo" in Ingolstadt in 1492. Conrad Celtis, not having the title of "magister artium," did not have the right to give lectures in the Academy, but he gave some lectures in private colleges; Celtis himself informs in such a way about the purpose of lectures:

> Si quis rhetoricam Ciceronis utramque requirat,
>   Qui latinae linguae dicitur esse parens,
> Si quis epistolica vult vera scribere et arte
>   Et memorativae qui petit artis opus:
> Hic cras octavam dum malleus insonat horam
>   Conradi Celtis candida tecta petat.

The date which closes the period of publishing the manuals of epistolography (1538) derives from the fact that in that year manuals of epistolography, written by Franciscus Niger and Erasmus of Rotterdam, were removed from the syllabus of lectures on the basis of a university injunction. As a replacement, Cicero's original letters were recommended.

During the period in question (1489–1539), the Academy of Cracow boasted about ninety professors who conducted lectures on epistolography. *Liber Diligentiarum* is a valuable source of information for learning about the history of the subject, as each lecturer's name is mentioned beside the manual which he employed for giving his lectures. In this way, we become acquainted with the manuals.

It is noteworthy that "ad usum studiosae iuventutis" collections of letters used to be published, which served as manuals of epistolography, but were also read for moral hints. It is borne out by the very titles, for example in the collection of letters *Fausti Andrelini Foroliviensis Poetae Laureati atque Oratoria clarissimi epistolae proverbiales et morales longe lepidissime nec minus sententiose* (Cracoviae per Mathiam Scharfenberger, Anno MDXXVII), we encounter such themes as: "Non habendum esse cum foemina commercium"; "Labores otio anteponendos"; "Amico reconciliato aut raro aut numquam fidendum."[1]

Our interest, however, covers only typical manuals of letter-writing, namely those which not only comprise general hints, but also, following the pattern of ancient manuals, bear on the division into types of letters, titles, etc.

There were three kinds of manuals of epistolography: (a) collections of hints concerning the style of letters with examples, that is, the necessary expressions, phrases and synonymous expressions. These manuals were entitled "Elegantiae," "Elegantiolae," "Hortulus Elegantiarum" and so on; (b) collections of letters — genuine or fictitious — were supposed to serve as manuals, too, and were designed "Ad usum iuventutis"; (c) the third kind — the most important one — included those manuals which corresponded to their names: they contained the definition of the letter, the theory of writing letters, different kinds or types of letters, title-giving principles, letters — genuine or fictitious — illustrating various kinds of letters according to the ancient theories. The titles varied: "Modus epistolandi," "Ars epistolandi," "Methodus epistolandi," "Manuductio," "Opus de conscribendis epistolis," "De componendis epistolis." On the whole, however, this type of manual was labelled as "'Modi epistolandi." In Poland all the manuals mentioned above were well-known; most often "Modi epistolandi" were used.

One of the earliest foreign manuals was not yet a separate book, but a chapter entitled "De componendi epistolis" in the Latin grammar by Nicolaus Perotti published in 1468.

In Cracow the following epistolographic treatises were published in 1496–1538:

1. Those by foreign Humanists:
   Guillelmus Zaphonensis, 1504; Franciscus Niger, 1503, 1508, 1514, 1521; Filippo Beroaldo, 1512; Rodericus (Raček) Dubravius, 1523, 1524; Erasmus of Rotterdam, 1523, 1527; Nicolaus Perottus, n.d., 1531, 1535, 1544, 1551?; Jacobus Publicius, 1530; Christophorus Hegendorfinus, 1533, 1537, 1538, [1555].

2. Those by Polish Humanists:
   Johannes Sacranus, 1505, 1507, 1512, 1520, 1521.
   Johannes Aesticampianus-Sommerfelt, 1510?, 1513, 1515, 1518?, 1519, 1522.
   Stanislaus Biel-Albinus, 1521.
   Stanislaus de Lowicz, 1522.
   Johannes Baer-Ursinus, 1496?, 1522.
   Matthaeus Legnicensis Franconius, 1534.

The letters in Ursinus's manual are all the more important, as they are the proof of broad interest shown by its author, who brings up serious linguistic and philological subjects and demonstrates a good knowledge of not only Latin writers but Greek ones as well.

In Cracow the first manual of epistolography was published in 1503; thus it can be inferred that up to 1503 lecturers had used manuals written by foreign Humanists, and from 1503 onwards manuals written by Polish and foreign authors were brought out parallelly.

It is worthy of mention that Polish authors often drew on their predecessors' works. For instance Lucas Ruthenus drew upon the manual written by Ursinus, but each of them mentions the names of their contemporaries, for instance:

URSINUS	LUCAS RUTHENUS
Constantiae Ursinae	Barbare Fusce (sic)
Elisbete Regine Poloniae	Bonae Reginae Poloniae
illustrissimae	illustrissimae
Paulo Ursino	Nicolao Herburth
Iohanni Sacrano	Stanislao Biel etc.

Other authors using their predecessors' works are by no means original. Aesticampianus seems to have imitated Niger in his manual, but changes introduced by him — like by the others — concern the change of names. Niger, for instance, in his examples introduces many names from antiquity, Aesticampianus replaces them with authentic Polish names, adjusting them to the Polish situations, e.g.:

NIGER	AESTICAMPIANUS
Commendaticium genus	
Commendetur Caesari Sempronius pro equestri dignitate consequenda.	Commendetur Rector Ursinus doctor Medicinae pro auxilio praestando.
Consolatorium genus.	
Consoletur Ciceronem Lentulus pro exilio quod propter Clodii odium et malivolentiam patitur.	Consoletur mgrm Ioannem Ioannes Ursinus pro exsilio suo quod accusatione cuiusdam nebulonis patitur.
Lamentatorium genus.	
Lamentetur Appius apud Caesarem	Lamentetur magister apud Curionem Vratislaviensem.

Generally, none of the authors of manuals demonstrates originality, but each of them attempted to bring variety into his manual, for example Sacranus drew up the principles of epistolography in the form of tables which were to enable pupils to master them. This was pointed out by Stanislaus from Şowicz, who, preparing Sacranus's manual for publication, added an octastichon ad lectorem just after the preface:

> Omnibus in rebus primum rudimenta docemus
>   Hoc iter ostendit rectus et ordo monet
> Improbus ille labor per quem non tramite recto
>   Itur ad egregias Palladis artis opes.
> Isto rite modo *proprios Sacranus ephebos*
>   *Discipulosque suos instruit et docuit.*
> Erudit doctos blesos prius ante Polonos
>   Oreque facundo verba   diserta loqui.

Ursinus's letters, enclosed as patterns of various types of letters, are of great value, as they include genuine letters written to his contemporaries, reflecting the relations and customs of those times. Several addressees are worth mentioning: Johannes Ursinus Johannis Alberto Regi Polaniae S.p.; Frederico Cardinali ac Archiepiscopo Gnesnensi Episcopoque Cracoviensi S.p.; P. Alberto Brucio Alexandri Magni Ducis Litiphaniae Secretario S.p.; Marco Sultario Romano Pontificii Imperatoriique Iuris Professori S.p.; Philippo Callimacho S.p.

Ursinus refers to contemporary historical events in some letters. The "Epistolas consolatoria" is an imitation of the letter written by Servilius Sulpicius to Cicero after his daughter's death. There are also love letters: "Exemplum epistole erotice siue amatorie." Ursinus's letter to Blanca—the name is probably fictitious, maybe the reference is made to the girl named Margarita Nigra-Schwarz, and her reply in which she expresses her refusal. The description of an excursion to the vicinity of Cracow is of particular interest, as it illustrates the life of Cracovian Humanists and people connected with the Sodalitas Vistulana. Let me quote some fragments of Ursinus's letters which throw some light on the type of Latin used by the author, and on the themes which testify to those times.[2]

1. Capitulum XL. Exemplum epistole historie narrative.
Johannes Ursinus Georgio Montano Equiti Aurato Sa.p.d.

Idibus Maiis Turcorum Imperator ingenti exercitu Mysiam ingressus Kyliam urbem munitissimam obsedit, si hac potitus, fuerit, finitimas regiones ipsamque Poloniam facile dicioni suae posse subicere. Ut autem facilius caperet Kyliam incoleque celerius in eius se potestatem traderent, aditus custodit prohibetque, ne frumentum et alia, que ad victum attinent, in urbem ducerentur. Cum autem nuntiatum esset populo Turcorum classe appparere extensisque velis nauigare ac ad oppugnandam vrbem contendere, tota civitate trepidatur populique clamore cuncta resonant; omnis quoque plebs, que in suburbio erat, cum supellectili vrbem intrat ... Turcus autem colocatis omni ex parte tormentis, que bombarde appellantur, vrbem oppugnat assidueque in loca edificiis frequentiora ingencia saxa machinis torquet ... Dum hec Turcus ageret, ciues robustiores turres murosque conscendentes acerrime se defendunt. Vehementer ibi aliquot dies pugnatum est ... Capta igitur ea [vrbe] arma omniaque bellica instrumenta, quae intus erant, efferunt [scil. Turci], plebem autem dinumerant, matronas pudicissimas stuprant, puellas innuptas viciant et abducunt, pueros virosque robustiores ac sacerdotes vendunt. Habes historiam et eam quidem verissimam, vt res acta est. Vale. Data Cracovie pridie Calendas Quintiles. Anno 1484.[3]

2. Exemplum epistole delatorie siue accusatorie. (XXXIII)
Johannes Ursinus Johanni Alberto Regi Polonie Salutem p.d.

Superioribus diebus, illustrissime Rex, Petrus Fulminius, huius vrbis prefectus maximo impetu in pretorium veniens fores effregit omnesque interfecit lictores ac erarium publicum diripuit, Marcum autem Pontanum

consulem, qui in Diui Francisci monasterium fugerat, inde vi extractum
ense confodit et ante pretorium pertraxit ac in partes minutissimas secuit.
O rem miseram! O rabiem immensam! O scelus non ferendum! Consul,
homo integerrimus et innocentissimus, per summum scelus ac dedecus, per
libidinem et audaciam, per petulentian, temeritatem, crudelitatem a Ful-
minio ad ignominiam et iniuriam consulatus vexatus, verberatus, ex loco
sacro extractus ac crudelissime occisus est.

Violatum ius civium; violatum ius dignitatis, violatum ius religionis,
violatum ius humanitatis, violatam denique reipublicae maiestatem tua
serenitas videt. In quo loco fures tutos esse oportet, in eo ciuis tutus non
fuit ... Quid est aliud statum reipublice retinere, quam perpetuam pacem
in ciuitate conseruare? Ipse vero Fulminius statum reipublice perturbauit,
cum erarium publicum inuasit ac Consulem verberauit et interfecit. Nam
cum esset huius vrbis prefectus, qui ciuitatis iura defendere debuit,
crudelitatem exercuit, consulatus dignitatem et auctoritatem neglexit, ergo
reipublice maiestatem lesit.

... Accuso igitur apud tuam celsitudinem Fulminium ipsum lese maiesta-
tis, rogo oroque, vt huic tanto crimini penam satis idoneam queras, ne
Fulminius in suo tam graui scelere se iactet et vt ceteri metu pene ab iniuria et vi inferenda deterreantur. Nam nisi eiusmodi coercetur violentia, huius
vrbis respublica penitus interibit. Vale, princeps illustrissime.

Date Cracouie tercio Nonas Septembres.[4]

3. Exemplum epistole in genere stomaico. Capitulum XXI.
   Johannes Vrsinus Mathie Dreuicio Salutem p.d.

Nicolaus Lippus et Petrus Barbo mihi familiarissimi cum vxoribus suis
haud illepidis in vnum conuenientes ac satis magna sodalium et amicorum
manu contracta omnibusque ad leticiam dispositis me vna cum vxore in
predium Charamani Medici duxerunt.[5] In quo nullum certe gaudendi, ym-
mo vt verius dicam repuerescendi genus omisimus. Predium est non longe
a fratrum Carmelitarum cenobio, quod amnis quidam circumfluit,
amenissimo loco situm et maxime ad rusticanas voluptates excogitatum;...
traxit nos et vindicauit sibi incredibilis amnis illius amenitas, qui tectus fronde
salignea cristalino alueo viridibus ripis mira placiditate fluebat affatimque
omne genus piscium largiter subministrat; quibus allecti depositis vestibus
et calceis acceptoque reti acerrime piscati sumus. In quo ita lusimus vt pueri,
ita clamauimus vt ebrii, ita concertauimus vt dementes insanique videremur.
Ex amne piscinam ingenti variorum piscium copia refertam intrauimus.

Aderant omnibus vxores nostre ac virgines quedam perpulchre gemmis
auroque decorate ac floreis sertis ornate. Que quamquam pudore impedien-
bantur vna ludere, tamen ita spectabant, vt ea que gerebantur mira festiui-
tate risuque comprobarent. Constantia autem, pro ceteris forme prestantia
pollens, cum vrticis collectis Georgium Turzonem vrere vellet, in profluen-

tem ad vsque venerea decidit; que res non mediocrem risum concitauit. Egressis tandem e flumine piscinaque cena dubia apponitur ex piscibus rostratisque auibus. Exspectasti fortasse vt dicerem: nauibus, sed non ita est, non est; sed aderant aues multe, Vngarica Cretensiaque vina plurima.

Omitto cetera, que cuncta opipare apparate fuerunt. Post cenam vero auide voraciterque, vt laborantibus in aqua euenire consueuit, assumptam deambulatio fuit pedestris inter flauentes segetes et amena vireta ramosque fecunditate fructuum incuruos. Qui longe lateque vagati, cantantes alii, alii cytharam pulsantes, alii iocantes ac uxores puellasque amplectantes ad ipsum amnem reuersi et in prato virenti depositi lacque coagulatum refrigerationis gratia comedentes, agricolas choream ducentes vsque ad solis occasum letissime spectauimus, cum illi potu obruti sepe saltantes in terramque grauissime cadentes ac ceno inuoluti vberem ridendi materiam nobis preberent ...

Moleste autem ferebamus omnes quod nobiscum ire nequisti. Vale et vt me soles ama. Data Cracouie. Quarto Nonas Iulias.

4. Exemplum epistole erotice siue amatorie (XXXVIII):
Johannes Vrsinus Blance virgini formosissime Salutem p.d.

Si Muse ipse, Blanca suauissima, me lactassent vel ingenium Maronis aut eloquentia Marci Ciceronis mihi esset, vix adhuc me tuas egregias et preclaras animi corporisque dotes, quibus te natura insigniuit, persequi posse sperarem ... Ego persepe antehac, iocundissima Blanca, tecum loqui volui, sed copia fandi nunquam mihi dari potuit. Igitur cum tecum coram loqui non possum, litteras ad te scribere cogor.

Ego te, carissima Blanca, ardentissime amo idque tibi mirum videri non debet, siquidem te mihi contemplanti in tam ingenti puellarum cetu sola ante omnes mihi placuisti et Cupidinis telis cor ilico traiecisti. Tu dies noctesque ante oculos meos versaris. Tu spes mea, tu desiderium meum. Tu vnicum vite mee solacium ...

Vestibus preciosis, gemmis ac margaritis te copiosissime decorabo. Da igitur operam, suauissima Blanca, te maioremimmodum (*sic*) rogo id agas, idque effice, vt te conuenire quam primum possem. Si facere volueris, quo loco id commodissime fieri possit et quo die, constitue. Si hoc minus fieri poterit, aut litteris, aut, si faciundum putaueris, nuncio aliquo de tuo in me animo velim me facias cerciorem....

Data Cracouie decimo Calendas Septembres anno a natali Christiano 1485.

5. Exemplum epistole replicatorie / sequitur: Cap. XXXIX/.
Blanca Johanni Ursino Salutem plurimam dicit.

Vellem, Johannes Ursine, omnibus in rebus tue morem gerere voluntati teque, vt petis, amare, permultis enim te muneribus eisdemque preclaris tum Natura insignauit, tum auxit Fortuna quam vocant, ob que quidem dignus es, vt te amarem. Sed id facere mihi minime licet nec profecto in mentem vnquam venit. Desponsata enim sum nuper Marco Leoni Consuli, viro prudentissimo integerrimoque ac mihi charissimo, quem preter amare licet neminem. Tam sancti enim coniugalis thori fidem soluere nephas est. Qui enim eam violant, infames sunt ac diuina humanaque lege plectuntur; qui vero eam caste impolluteque seruant, digni profecto habendi sunt de quibus nulla posteritas conticescat.

Quodsi amare te velle in animo haberem, id tamen perficere minime possem. Tu enim me adire et alloqui non posses, propter difficillimum ad me aditum, cum edes semper, vt scis, sint obseruate. Si domi sum, serui serueque circum me vel ante cubiculum stant, si quoquam exeo, eedem me comitantur. Nec etiam me fugit, quanti periculi est in peregrino versari amore, non igitur me tantis obiciam discriminibus. Multarum preterea me exempla, ne te diligam, mouent, que a suis amatoribus deserte sunt. Nam Iason Medeam deseruit, cuius ope vigilem interemit draconem vellusque aureum asportauit; Theseus autem Ariadnen, cuius auxilio Minotaurum euasit, Eneas vero Didonem, cui peregrinus amore interitum peperit. Quod autem mihi splendidissimos et preciosissimos ornatus polliceris, nihil me mouet istud; si enim huiusmodi delectarer ornamentis eaque deferre vellem, haberem a sponso meo opulentissimo permagnam eorum copiam. Sed ea profecto paruipendo nihilque fide coniugali et amore pudico antiquius duco. Consilium igitur est amori et tuo presertim viam precludere, ne Rhodopeya Phyllis dicar vel altera Sappho. Quamobrem te vehementer etiam atque etiam rogo, ne me vlterius ad te amandum inuites; tuumque in me amorem comprime et extingue, quod enim speras assequi non poteris, nam id ex me queris, quod miihi quam maximo esset dedecori et exicio. Vale.

Data Cracouie Calendis Septembribus anno 1485.

The letters and the composition of the manual of Ursinus are of great value, — therefore the question may arise: why did the manuals of Polish Humanists, if their value is not smaller, not remove, for instance, Niger's manuals from the school curriculum? Why were not Ursinus's and Sacranus's manuals more frequently read during lectures? After all, both of them introduced a wealth of new material; why were those manuals not republished? While other ones, by Hegendorfinus, Dubravius and others, continued to be brought out?

One may venture to say that none of the authors of these manuals had a sufficiently wealthy and influential patron who could take care of the works of his protégé and support the publication of his books. Even if they availed themselves of the protection of the wealthy, it ceased when they completed their studies. Nobody thought of developing and supporting native authors, and the working conditions in the Cracovian Academy were so harsh for the professors that more lucrative posts, such as the position of secretary at wealthy men's courts, were sought for.

Editions of the Manuals of Epistolography
which were used in Poland:

Year	Author	Title	Place	Printer
1492	Celtis		Ingolstadt	
1495	Ursinus	Modus epistolandi	Norymberga	Hochfeder
1496				
1500	Caricinus-Feige	Epistole exemplares	Liptzigk	
1503	Niger	Compendiosa ars de epistolis	Crac.	Hochfeder
1504	Libanius Graecus	Epistolae ed. Sommerfelt	Crac.	Haller
	Zaphonensis	Modus epistolandi	Crac.	Haller(?)
	Niger	De epistolis	Crac.	
	Philelphus	Brev. eleg. Epistolae	Crac.	Haller(?)
1505?	Sacranus			
1507	Sacranus	Modus epistolandi	Crac.	Haller
1508	Niger	Compendiosa ars	Crac.	Haller
1509	Philelphus	Brev. eleg. epistolae	Crac.	Haller
1510?	Esticampianus?	Modus epistolandi		
1511	Dubravus	De componendis epistolis	Viennae	Hier. Victor
1512	Beroaldus	Modus epistolandi	Crac.	Ungler
	Laudinus	Epistolarum Turci Magni ...	Viennae	Singrenius,
	Philelphus	Epistolarum famil. libri XXVI ed. Stan. de Łowicz	Crac.	Haller
	Sacranus	Modus epistolandi	Crac.	Haller
1513	Esticampianus	Modus epistolandi	Crac.	Ungler et Lern
	Laudinus	Epistolae Turci Magni	Crac.	Ungler
	Philelphus	Breves eleg. epistolae	Crac.	Haller
1514	Niger	Compendiosa ars de epist.	Crac.	Haller Ungler et Lern
1515	Esticampianus	Modus epist. et Agricole epistola ad Scharffenberg	Crac.	Ungler (Haller)
	Dubravus	De componendis epistolis	Viennae	Hier. Vietor
1517	Philelphus	Epistolae	Crac.	Haller
1518	Esticampianus	Modus epistolandi	Crac.	Haller
1519	Esticampianus	Modus epistolandi	Crac.	Haller
1520	Albinus-Biel	Exordia epistolarum	Crac.	Florian Ungler
	Sacranus	Modus ep. ed. St. Łowicz	Crac.	Jan Haller
1521	Albinus	Exordia epistol. ed. St. Łowicz	Crac.	
	Niger	De conficiendis epistolis		Vietor et Marc. Scharffenberg
	Sacranus	Modus epistolandi		

1522	Esticampianus	Modus epistolandi	Crac.	Vietor
	Lucas Ruthenus	Compend. in mod. ep. manuduc.	Crac.	Ungler
	Ursinus	Modus epistolandi	Crac.	Haller
1523	Dubravus	De compon. epistolis	Crac.	Vietor
	Erasm Rotherd.	Opus de conscribendis epistolis	Crac.	Vietor
1524	Dubravus	Libellus de compo- nendis epist.	Crac.	Vietor
1527	(Andrelin. Faustus)	Epistolae proverbiales	Crac.	Scharffenberg
	Erasm Rotherd.	Conficiendarum epist. formula	Crac.	Scharffenberg
1528	(Erasm Rotherd.)	Breviores et elegan- tiores epistolae	Crac.	Vietor
1530	Publicius Jacobus	Ars confic. epistolarum	Crac.	
1531	Perottus	Rudimenta gram.	Crac.	Scharffenberg
1533	Hegendorfinus	Compendiosa conscribendarum epistolarum ratio	Crac.	Vietor
1534	Franconius	Elegantiarum praecepta	Crac.	Scharffenberg
1535	Perottus	Rudimenta gram.	Crac.	Vietor
1537	Hegendorfinus	Consc. epistol. ratio	Crac.	Vietor
1538	Hegendorfinus	Consc. epistol. ratio	Crac.	
	Publicius Jacobus	Ars conficiendarum epistolarum	Crac.	
1544	Perottus		Crac.	
1555	Hegendorfinus	Methodus	Crac.	

The greatest number of manuals were published from 1512 to 1524. Cf. Lidia Winniczuk, *Epistolografia* ...

University of Warzaw

Notes

1. Cf. Lidia Winniczuk, *Epistolografia. Łacińskie podręczniki epistolograficzne w Polsce w XV–XVI wieku.* Biblioteka Meandra 19. (Warszawa, 1952), pp. 77 + 2 tabl.

2. Jan Ursyn z Krakowa: *Modus epistolandi cum epistolis exemplaribus et orationibus annexis.* — przełożyła, wstępem i objaśnieniami opatrzyła Lidia Winniczuk. Polska Akademia Nauk., Instytut Badań Literackich, Biblioteka Pisarzów Polskich Seria B nr 7 (Wrocław, MCMLVII), Oss. p. 221.

3. Cf. ibid., Cap. XXII. Exemplum epistole in genere sinthematico, ad Johannem Luprancium: Nudiustercius cum Regi Nostro Casimiro nunciatum esset Turcorum imperatorem ingentibus copiis terra marique Mysiam inuasisse, Belgradum ac Kyliam vrbes

munitissimas intra dies paucos cepisse et citra Danubium et Moldauiam subiugasse omnesque quoque ciuitatis Russiae copiarum magnitudine Turci perterritas iam non in virtute sed in fuga spem habere, Rex trepidus atque de statu rerum solicitus optimates Regni conuocat ineuntque consilium, essetne cum Turco bellum gerendum an ... fedus potius ineundum; consultant, graues atque variae sententie dicuntur. Tamen nihil potius in re fieri decernunt, quam bellum gerere ac eligere probatissimum imperatorem ... Omnibus suffragiis ad tale negocium ydoneus imperator designatur Johannes Albertus Regis filius, qui superiore hyeme ingentem Tartarorum exercitum prostrauit ... Date Cracouie tercio Nonas Maias.

4. Perhaps it is a fictitious letter.

5. Doctor Johannes Charamanus, probably Dr. Johannes Velsz de Posnania, the teacher of the sons of King Casimirus Iagelonenis. Georgius Turzo, a well-known person in Cracow.

M I S C E L L A N E O U S

Engelbert Kaempfer's Account
of the Ordeal by Crocodile in Siam

Robert W. Carrubba

ngelbert Kaempfer, M.D. (1651–1716) devoted an entire decade to cultural and scientific explorations. His travels began with his departure from Sweden in March 1683; they would end with his arrival in Holland in October 1693.[1] The duration and geographical scope of his journey through Russia, Persia, India, the East Indies, Siam, and Japan complemented the breadth and depth of Kaempfer's curiosity and scholarship. He was among the most learned and surely he was the most widely traveled scholar of his era. Perhaps the finest accolade comes from the great Linnaeus who in the *Critica Botanica* said of Kaempfer: "No man deserved better of the Japanese."[2]

Born in Lemgo just three years after the end of the Thirty Years War, Kaempfer spent his early years at the parsonage of Nikolai Lutheran Church where his father Johannes served as pastor. He then enrolled at Danzig and continued his higher education at Cracow and Königsberg (1676–81) with emphasis on language, history, natural science, and medicine: a happy blend of the liberal arts and the sciences, without which Kaempfer's reports and discoveries would not have been possible. Despite a splendid education, Kaempfer's career opportunities in Germany were not promising, while to the north lay Sweden with its university, Uppsala, and a chance to study under the distinguished naturalist, Olaf Rudbeck. Kaempfer's intellectual qualities impressed not only the faculty at Uppsala but King Charles XI of Sweden who offered him the position of court scholar. Kaempfer chose instead to join the embassy of Charles XI to the Shah of Persia in the capacity of secretary.

Before reaching Isfahan in March of 1684, Kaempfer survived a perilous crossing of the Caspian Sea. When the embassy had completed its commercial and political negotiations at Isfahan, Kaempfer faced a second significant decision. He was offered an appointment as court physician in Georgia and he himself considered traveling to Egypt. But Father du Mans, a Capuchin and interpreter for the Persian Court, persuaded Kaempfer to accept employment as a physician with the Dutch East India Company. It was during the period from March 1684 to June

The upper half of Engelbert Kaempfer's illustration depicts the ordeal by fire;
the lower half represents two types of ordeal by crocodile: swimming and diving.
In the lower left corner may be seen an accused making his prayer before an
official prior to the ordeal. To the right, a crocodile observes a man attempting
to swim the river. Above the crocodile, the ordeal by diving is portrayed as two
attendants prepare to press the heads of two persons beneath the surface of the water.

1688 that Kaempfer, while not at work or ill with a protracted fever (probably malaria), compiled observations—first detailed reports—on the electric torpedo fish of the Persian Gulf,[3] Persian mummy or the bituminous liquid thought to be a potent drug and the authentic embalming mummy of ancient Egypt,[4] the Persian dracunculus or worm which infests the human body, and asafetida.[5]

Kaempfer saw Persia for the last time when he set sail from Gamron (Bandar Abbas), which commanded the Strait of Hormuz. Under Vice-Admiral Lykochthon, the Dutch fleet weighed anchor, bound for Batavia, Java, and calling at ports on the Malabar and Coromandel coasts of India. Within a period of one year (August 1688–May 1689) reports were compiled on: Andrum or endemic hydrocele of the scrotum; Perical or madura foot, an infection which greatly enlarges the foot; two supposed antidotes for snake venom: the root of the Mungo plant and snake stone;[6] and the dance of the *Naja Naja*, the hooded cobra of India. In Java Kaempfer continued his studies but his eye was on Siam and beyond to the Dutch factory on the artificial island, Dejima in Nagasaki, where he could collect books, botanicals, and any other Japanese materials. Kaempfer has left us a splendid account of his journey from Batavia, Java, in May 1690 to Siam, of the state of the Court of Siam, and lastly of his departure from Siam in July 1690.[7] From Kaempfer's three years at Java and Japan we have observations on acupuncture, moxibustion,[8] tea and ambergris.

Kaempfer returned to Holland in October 1693, ten years after he had left Stockholm on the mission to Isfahan. He documented some of his observations in ten sections of the dissertation which he presented to the faculty of medicine at the renowned University of Leyden in April 1694.[9] Instead of seeking an academic appointment for which he was eminently qualified, Kaempfer returned in August 1694 to the place of his birth, Lemgo, and to a demanding medical practice which frustrated his intention to rearrange and polish his vast store of materials for immediate publication. On December 16, 1700 he married Maria Sophia Wilstack, but the marriage proved less than harmonious. Maria Kaempfer bore three children, one son and two daughters; all died in their infancy.

It was nineteen years after his return to Europe that Kaempfer saw the publication in 1712 of his first major work: *Amoenitatum exoticarum politico-physico-medicarum fasciculi V, quibus continentur variae relationes, observationes & descriptiones rerum Persicarum & Ulterioris Asiae* (Meyeri, Lemgo). It was to be the last work published during his lifetime. Kaempfer's monumental *History of Japan* (the best account of his era) was published posthumously in 1727. After several attacks of colic Kaempfer died at Lemgo in 1716 at the age of sixty-five. It was during his visits to India and Siam that Kaempfer also witnessed various forms of ordeals. Included in the *Amoenitatum exoticarum* (*The Pleasures of the Exotic*) as observation 12 of fascicle 2 is *Investigatio Innocentiae, per Crocodilos* or *Test of Innocence by Crocodile*, on pages 454–61; the illustration is found on page 458.

Ordeals are commonly classified in five types. The first type depends upon a magical element and the action of some physical object. For example, two individuals would each be furnished with a candle. These were equal in size and lighted at the same time. The person whose candle burned longer won his cause. The second type of ordeal involves a physical test which determines the issue. In this ordeal, a wife might pass through fire in order to prove her fidelity to her husband, or a suspected witch might be thrown into a river whose waters accept the innocent but reject the guilty. In a third type of ordeal, the corpse of the victim is supposed to produce a renewed flow of blood caused by the proximity of the murderer. The fourth type of ordeal relies upon the taking of an oath. The person who swears falsely might be visited with some illness or misfortune. Finally, the ordeal by battle comprises the fifth type, where innocence determined which of the two combatants would emerge victorious.

Having noted five basic types of ordeal, let us now turn to Kaempfer's first detailed report in the ordeal by crocodile, which falls under the second type, the physical test. Kaempfer begins with the form of ordeal he witnessed in India where crocodile worship in many forms was common. The Hindus regarded crocodiles as dedicated to Vishnu, the creator and ruler of the water. As such, the reptile could distinguish right from wrong and innocence from guilt, and thus would not attack an individual whose conscience was clear.[10] Here in translation is Kaempfer's account of the ordeal by crocodile in Malabar:

Ordeal by Crocodile

Malabar

The people of Malabar are a black nation of India, firmly cloaked in the darkness of paganism. Their country, enclosed on the one side by a ridge of mountains and on the other by an ocean, has a damp and low-lying terrain broken by countless streams and inland lakes fed by them. You would be astounded at the places in these waters where hordes of crocodiles have settled. A wicked person could not ford or swim across these waters without exposing himself to the jaws of these most rapacious beasts. The Gentiles believe that crocodiles are avengers of divine justice or what amounts to the same thing, attendants of Jemma, that is, judges in the next world. Or the crocodile may be likened to Charon who ferries the souls of the dead, each according to his merits, either to the elysian fields or Tartarus. The little boats, in which the Siamese transport the dead to their graves (usually a splendid affair), are so constructed as to represent the likeness of a crocodile. Magnificently gilded and ingeniously fashioned, the prow represents the head and the stern represents the tail. Quite frequently you may observe Chinese temples adorned with standards which depict the crocodiles, since with this sign the priests proclaim the triumphs and joys of life in heaven. The bodies of Japanese monks of the Sjodosju sect are also carried to the funeral pyre with this standard leading the way. It is to these avenging crocodiles, I say, that judges, when they are in doubt, expose persons accused to crimes, so that by a just and instant judgment the guilty person may pay the penalty and the innocent person may be absolved. Indeed, often the prisoners themselves appeal to this tribunal, either because they are confident in their innocence or weary of their bonds and extended captivity.

Once a verdict has been rendered, the Brahman priests visit the accused person, they explain the seriousness of the decree, they set forth the dreadful penalties of undergoing the judgment, and they leave no stone unturned in eliciting a confession. When these efforts have failed, on the following day they lead the person amid a throng to the shore of the Rhadamanthine judgment. Again the priests admonish the person at length about repentance but when this is to no avail, they finally order him to undergo the following judgment: to swim to the opposite shore of the river and directly back. If he escapes the crocodiles and accomplishes this task, he is promptly received back with the united applause and congratulations of the whole gathering. Happily he has triumphed over the rocks of suspicion, the forum of the magistrate, and the bonds of prison from which he was unable to be extricated. I believe, however, that just as the guiltless man, who is swallowed up and at once loses his case and his life, will never vindicate his innocence, so the guilty man, who escapes, will never be so demented as to admit his guilt at the cost of his life and reveal that justice has been mocked.

Kaempfer's account, together with the illustration, gives us a precise description of the traditional and now well-attested *Ordeal by Swimming Across or Against a Stream*. You will note that Kaempfer, a practicing Christian and a scientist, placed no faith in this or any other form of ordeal.

Kaempfer's detailed account of the Ordeal by Crocodile in Siam corresponds closely to native descriptions of the Ordeal by Diving which one historian describes as "the most popular and common test of innocence and veracity,"[11] in Siam and the neighboring countries. Let me quote a translation of the seventh article of the Siamese law of ordeal promulgated in A.D. 1356:[12]

Article 7th

When holding an ordeal by water, the Recorder shall read the pledge and the address to the gods. Then the plaintiff and defendant shall bathe and wash their heads; after this let them have a game of cock-fighting (as a preliminary augury).

When both are about to dive under water, let there be stuck two poles (on the bottom), six cubits apart (10 feet); and let a levelling stick be placed over the shoulders of both parties.† The gong having been beaten thrice (as a signal), the necks of both parties are to be pressed down under water simultaneously, and the retaining ropes (tied around the waist) let go. Both parties must then dive at the same time, and reach as far down as the foot of their respective pole. The clepsydras must then be set agoing together.‡

Once the parties have dived, the one appearing first above water shall have the neck surrounded with the Klang collar (as a sign of defeat). Then let the rope be pulled, to draw up the other party still under water.

If at the expiration of six padas neither the plaintiff nor the defendant appears above the water, let the ropes be pulled up, and both parties helped out of the water.*

†I.e., from above the shoulders of one, across to the shoulders of the other, to keep them down at the same level.

‡They generally consist of a brass bowl with a small aperture in the bottom, set afloat in a bucket of water.

*This time, of 36 minutes, seems enormous; but it is to be remembered that native divers are accustomed to remain under water many minutes; and that this figure is given as probably the utmost theoretical limit of a dive, never however reached in practice.

In 1636, Joost Schouten had reported that when Siamese judges were in doubt about a case they would allow the litigants to undergo various tests including "ducking under water," placing their hands in boiling oil, walking barefoot upon hot coals, or eating a "mess of charmed rice." The person who "behaves himself ... with the most courage, is esteemed most innocent and acquitted."[13] The other party would be judged guilty and punished in accordance with the nature of the crime. Other early European visitors to the Orient had also published brief notices of the Ordeal by Diving in Siam. Let us sample two of these. In 1688 Nicolas Gervaise, after citing the ordeal by diving as quite ordinary, gives us this note:[14]

... ils jettent l'accusateur & l'accusé dans la riviere, celuy qui demeure plus long-temps au fond sans se noyer, est tenu pour innocent, & le premier qui revient sur l'eau, est reconnu & puny comme coupable,...

Some years later, Simon de La Loubère reported that the Siamese prepared from youth for the ordeal by fire and by diving:[15]

Tout le monde s'exerce donc de jeunesse en ce païs-là à se familiariser avec le feu, & à demeurer long-temps sous l'eau.

Below is Kaempfer's first detailed report to the Western world:

Siam

The powerful, pious, and simple nation of Siam which shares the beliefs and color of the people of Malabar, also attributes infallibility to the judgment of the crocodile. Accordingly, the Siamese examine the accused in this court of justice so that they might at all events discern the innocent from the guilty, who are to be punished at law according to the gravity of their crime. Although that Rhadamanthine judge rarely visits the rivers here, he exercises his power and judgment in them as if they were his own region. While he does not carry off the guilty themselves, he does nevertheless strike them with such a terror that it is easy for the judges to distinguish them from the innocent.

This is the procedure. The prisoners are sent from the hall of justice to the shore along with men of demonstrated integrity who serve as witnesses to the events. Next two of the accused are led into the river up to their navels and stationed at posts set apart from each other by a modest distance. The men grasp the posts in order to maintain their position and await the orders of the official in charge. Soon two attendants equipped with a long reed pole enter the water. Having placed the pole on the heads of the accused, they await the signal of a gong. At the sound of the gong they forcefully press down the accused at that very place, either by aiming at the neck or the top of the head, provided that the individuals are suddenly and completely submerged. The one of the submerged who is conscious of his guilt will, they say, be so overwhelmed with fear by the Spirit of the river that he abandons his position and leaps violently out of the water to draw a breath. The innocent person, however, having experienced no fear, will calmly emerge into view as the pressure from the pole is relaxed. His face will show no change except from the swiftness or coldness of the current. If there are many accused persons present at the same time, they are ordered successively to submit their necks to this position of examination. When this ceremony has been completed, the accused are led back to the hall of justice so that they may either be set free or receive their just punishment on the basis of the results reported to the judge.

We may now compare the text of the Siamese law with Kaempfer's detailed account of the ordeal by crocodile in Siam. We notice that there are some differences between the Siamese law and the Latin report: (1) Kaempfer stresses the crocodile as the spirit of the river who overwhelms the guilty person with fear, while the Siamese law makes no mention of the crocodile; (2) Kaempfer does not include the clock, safety rope about the waist or collar about the neck; (3) The Siamese law addresses a situation in which plaintiff and defendant are at odds while in Kaempfer it is not at all clear that the immersed persons are competitors or are indeed being examined about the same issue or crime. All in all, however, Kaempfer has once again proven himself a precise observer prepared to notice important cultural practices and eager to report, interpret, and illustrate them for the Western world in first detailed accounts.

Pennsylvania State University

Notes

1. See Karl Meier–Lemgo, *Die Reisetagebücher Engelbert Kaempfers* (Wiesbaden, 1968); and John Z. Bowers, "Engelbert Kaempfer: Physician, Explorer, Scholar, and Author," *Journal of the History of Medicine and Allied Sciences*, 21 (1966), 237–59.

2. Sir Arthur Hort, *The "Critica Botanica" of Linnaeus* (London, 1938), p. 64.

3. See Robert W. Carrubba and John Z. Bowers, "The First Report of the Electric Torpedo Fish of the Persian Gulf," *Journal of the History of Biology*, 15 (1982), 263–74.

4. See Robert W. Carrubba, "The First Detailed Report on Persian Mummy," *Physis*, 23 (1981), 459–71.

5. See Robert W. Carrubba, "The First Report of the Harvesting of Asafetida in Iran," *Agricultural History*, 53 (1979), 451–61.

6. See John Z. Bowers and Robert W. Carrubba, "Exotic Antidotes in Seventeenth-Century Asia," *Clio Medica: Acta Academiae Internationalis Historiae Medicinae*, 14 (1980), 129–40.

7. See Kaempfer's monumental work, *The History of Japan*, transl. J. G. Scheuchzer, 2 vols. (London, 1727). Kaempfer comments, vol. I, p. 4:

> Before I proceed further, I cannot forbear observing in general that the Voyage from Batavia to Siam is attended with no small difficulties and dangers, because of the many small low Islands, Rocks, Shoals and Sands. A careful and prudent Pilot must always keep at a due distance from Land, that is, neither too near it, nor to far off, that in case of strong stormy Winds and Turnado's, which frequently and unawares arise in this Passage, he may have an opportunity of coming to an anchor, and by this means preserve the Ship from running a-ground, or from being cast away too far out of her Course.

8. See Robert W. Carrubba, "Seventeenth-Century Latin Accounts of Acupuncture and Moxibustion," *Acta Orientalia*, 40 (1979), 205–27.

9. See John Z. Bowers and Robert W. Carrubba, "The Doctoral Thesis of Engelbert Kaempfer on Tropical Diseases, Oriental Medicine, and Exotic Natural Phenomena," *Journal of the History of Medicine and Allied Sciences*, 25 (1970), 270–310.

10. A useful survey of the veneration and prosecution of the crocodile can be found in Charles A. W. Guggisberg, *Crocodiles. Their Natural History, Folklore and Conservation* (Harrisburg 1972), pp. 152–73.

11. G. E. Gerini, "Trial by Ordeal in Siâm and the Siâmese Law of Ordeals," *Asiatic Quarterly Review*, 9 (1895), 415–24, at p. 422.

12. G. E. Gerini, "Trial by Ordeal in Siâm and the Siâmese Law of Ordeals," *Asiatic Quarterly Review*, 10 (1895), 156–75, at pp. 168–69.

13. See C. R. Boxer, *A True Description of the Mighty Kingdom of Japan and Siam by François Caron and Joost Schouten. Reprinted from the English edition of 1663 with Introduction, Notes and Appendixes* (London, 1935), p. 101.

14. Nicolas Gervaise, *Histoire naturelle et politique du royaume de Siam* ... (Paris 1688), p. 89.

15. Simon de La Loubère, *Description du royaume de Siam, par Monsr. de La Loubère, envoyé extraordinarie du roy aùprés du roy de Siam en 1687, et 1688*, 2 vols. (Amsterdam, 1700), Vol. I, p. 264.

Literary Criticism in the *Liber Catonianus*

Paul M. Clogan

During most of the Middle Ages poetry was classified and associated with grammar, rhetoric, and logic. This classification, based on the divisions in the trivium and quadrivium, was used at different times for various kinds of knowledge. Each of the three classifications gave rise to distinctive forms of literary criticism and characteristic types of treatise. Of the three classifications the most lasting and traditional was the association of poetry with the grammar curriculum.[1] This paper will examine the distinctive form of literary criticism in the *Liber Catonianus*, one of the characteristic types of treatise that resulted from the association of poetry with grammar in the thirteenth and fourteenth centuries.

The history of the association of medieval poetic with the grammar curriculum can be traced to Dionysius of Thrace and his Greek grammarians who were among the first to make the reading of poetry an important part of grammar,[2] and to Quintilian in Rome who defined grammar as "the science of correct speaking and interpretation of the poets" (*Institutio oratoria* I.iv.2). In Book X of the *Institute* he outlines the most comprehensive formal literary curriculum that has survived from antiquity. Its purpose is to train leaders morally and practically and it includes a course of readings in the works of Greek and Roman authors (Homer, Plato, Sophocles, Demosthenes, Cicero, Livy and Vergil) he considered literary and rhetorical classics who are to be studied for their eloquence and imitated in original compositions. Quintilian's list of authors is the ancestor of the medieval *accessus ad auctores*, the generic title for the tradition of lists of authors featured in a number of treatises beginning in the early eleventh century. Following Quintilian, Marius Victorinus in his *Ars Grammatica* considers grammar as "the science of interpreting the poets and historians and the method of correct speaking and writing."[3] Similar definitions of poetry reflecting the grammatical tradition can be found in Cassiodorus (*Institutiones divinarum et saecularium litterarum* II.i.1) and in John of Salisbury, who argues, "either grammar will contain poetics, or poetics will be excluded from the liberal arts."[4] Thus during the Middle Ages the grammar curriculum was associated with the "reading of the poets" and continued the study of pagan literature, preserving the "canon of classics" or list of certain classical Latin authors as well as the basics of classical criticism. Although the ancient grammar curriculum was simplified in that Latin was taught as a foreign language and there was little room for Greek in the monastic schools, the purpose and emphasis of education were preserved.

Medieval attitudes toward literary criticism were neither those that we find in Aristotle's *Poetics*, which had been completely neglected by medieval writers though it had actually been translated in the thirteenth century, nor those which had been elaborated since the Renaissance. The ancient meaning and classification of tragedy, comedy, epic, elegy, lyric was gradually forgotten; and there was confusion of ancient classifications in the Middle Ages. Dante considered the *Aeneid* a tragedy and his own poem a comedy because his poem ended with happiness in Paradise and was composed in the "middle" style and not in the "noble" style which was reserved for tragedy and epic or in the "humble" style which was reserved for "elegy." Also, the theoretical basis for medieval aesthetics emphasized the intellectual value of poetry and not emotion as does modern aesthetic theory. Indeed the Middle Ages developed literary genres of their own, but without an Aristotle to attempt a definiton or classification of them.

The educators of the twelfth and thirteenth centuries, in particular Conrad of Hirsau, Alexander Neckham, and Eberhard the German developed lists of "curriculum authors" whom they considered to be suitable for study in the schools.[5] They assumed the student had a solid foundation in Latin from the grammar of Donatus, and they compiled lists of classical Latin authors supplemented by Christian authors, on the basis of their educational as well as moral value. The critical interest in these medieval lists of *auctores* lies in the fact that from the beginning they were comparative. In Quintilian's list Greek and Roman authors are subjected to formal rhetorical comparisons. In the medieval canon of classics Latin authors are arranged not by subject — history, literature, philosophy — but according to difficulty of text from easiest to hardest. Although there is some variation in their lists regarding the selection of advanced authors, there was general agreement on the primary texts. The distinctive form of literary criticism in the medieval canon of classics is evidenced by an examination of the thirteenth and fourteenth century manuscripts of the *Liber Catonianus*, one of the characterisitic types of treatise that resulted from the association of poetry with grammar. The manuscripts are as follows.

Cambridge, Peterhouse, MS. 2.1.0 (James 207) (saec. xiii–xiv).
Cambridge, Peterhouse, MS. 2.1.8 (James 215) (saec. xiii).
Lincoln, Cathedral Library, MS. 132 (C.5.8.) (saec. xiii–xiv).
London, British Library, MS. Additional 21213 (saec. xiii).
London, British Library, MS. Royal 15. A. vii (saec. xiii).
Munich, Bayerische Staatsbibliothek, MS. Monacensis 391 (saec. xiv).

Oxford, Bodleian Library, MS. Auct. F. 5. 6 (SC 2195) (saec. xiii).
Oxford, Bodleian Library, MS. Canonici Class. Lat. 72 (an. 1274).
Vatican City, Bibl. Apostolica Vaticana, MS. Barb. lat. 41 (saec. xiii).
Vatican City, Bibl. Apostolica Vaticana, MS. Pal. lat. 1573 (saec. xiv).
Vatican City, Bibl. Apostolica Vaticana, MS. Reg. lat. 1556 (saec. xiii–xiv).
Vatican City, Bibl. Apostolica Vaticana, MS. Vat. lat. 1663 (saec. xiii–xiv).
Worcester, Cathedral Library, MS. F. 147 (saec. xiv).

The history and composition of this textbook, known as the *Liber Catonianus*,[6] was described by Marcus Boas, the author of the standard edition of the *Disticha Catonis*. Since then there has been, as far as I know, no study on the work as a whole. The *Liber Catonianus* became a standard medieval school reader which was used in a curriculum of instruction in grammar in the thirteenth and fourteenth centuries. This textbook originated in the ninth century and comprised only the Distichs of Cato and the Fables of Avianus. By degrees other works were included: the Latin Iliad, the Eclogues of Theodolus, the Elegies of Maximianus, the *Achilleid* of Statius, and the *De Raptu Proserpinae* of Claudian. The additon of Statius and Claudian eventually forced out the Iliad. The final structure, which first appears in the manuscripts of the thirteenth century but may have originated in the twelfth century, comprised Cato, Theodolus, Avianus, Maximianus, Statius and Claudian. These six authors remain standard into the fourteenth century with little change except that sometimes Claudian precedes Statius. The arrangement of the authors is comparative and according to difficulty of text from the easiest to hardest in terms of comprehension, probably the order in which they were taught. In the fifteenth century this group of Latin authors evolved into *Auctores Octo*, which was printed in Lyon, by John de Prato, 31 December 1488.

In the thirteenth- and fourteenth-century manuscripts of the *Liber Catonianus*, which I have so far examined, the texts of the six *auctores* are frequently glossed, some more extensively than others.[7] The standardized glosses and commentaries, some of which originated in the ninth century and grew by accretion, reveal the pedagogic uses of this important textbook. The medieval glosses show the way in which the author was read and studied in the schools. Both what is and is not glossed are significant. What is necessary to point out to students reading Cato, Theodolus, Avianus, Maximianus, Statius and Claudian perhaps for the first time and the way in which it is done tells us something concrete about medieval education and medieval ideas of literary genres. Like their present-day counterparts, the commentaries preserve the transcription of the text of the author and the commentary of the medieval lecturer. When the commentaries came into the possession of university, cathedral, and monastic schools, the nature of the commentary underwent allegorical and exegetical influences. The textual and manuscript traditions of the glosses and commentaries in the *Liber Catonianus* vary, those of Claudian, Statius, and Theodolus have been examined in detail, and the influence of some of the authors has been studied.[8]

Philippe Delhaye has shown how the study of the *artes* as a study of ethics was central to the ethical pedagogy of the twelfth century.[9] At the heart of grammar, the language and literature course seems to have made room for ethical lessons collected by the *grammaticus* in the *auctores*. This combination of grammar and morality was an ancient tradition revived by medieval educators, and applied to pagan poets the technique of allegorical and moral explication to justify the serious study of classical authors. What Delhaye has shown about the pedagogy of the *moralis scientia* of the twelfth century seems, in the light of the thirteenth- and fourteenth-century manuscripts of the *Liber Catonianus* I have studied, to apply to the later period also. This medieval textbook reveals pedagogic use of poetry in the grammar lessons of the *auctores* and the continuity of this teaching technique from the ninth to the fifteenth century. Of the six *auctores*, Cato is, in terms of *grammaticus*, the one whose poetry has the greatest edifying value. The glosses, the *accessus*, and the *Dialogue super auctores* of Conrad of Hirsau invariably remind us to what part of philosophy the *Disticha Catonis* pertain: "Ethice subponitur quia ad utilitatem morum nititur."[10] Cato as an *auctor scholasticus* is in effect a professor of morality.

Composed in the third century by an unknown author,[11] the Distichs of Cato offered easy and practical wisdom in a collection of philosophical maxims put in distichs or couplets. They preached proverbial wisdom — diligence in work, avoidance of quarrels, loyalty to friends, bravery in misfortune, respect of the lessons of book and of life. As a literary genre, of practical ethics, the distichs were an early and safe schoolbook in the educational training of the Middle Ages. From Remigius of Auxerre's glosses in the ninth century to Erasmus's commentary in the sixteenth, the commentaries on Cato developed by degrees. In the thirteenth century the character of the teaching of Cato in the schools is represented in the relatively standardized set of glosses in the manuscript of the *Liber Catonianus*. Richard Hazelton, who has studied these Cato glosses, notes that they "not only Christianized the pagan precepts but also established them within the system referred to as the *moralis scientia*, a system founded on the four cardinal virtues, which the Christian culture of the Middle Ages also inherited from the pagan world and made its own."[12]

In addition to the materials of *rhetorica* and *poetria*, the Cato glosses provide patristic and scriptural quotations and allusions, definitions and classifications of the cardinal virtues, quotations from the Roman poets, and popular proverbs. Moreover, two supplements to Cato are found in some of these manuscripts: the *Facetus* and the *Cato Novus* of Martinus.[13]

The genre of the eclogue is represented by the *Ecloga* of Theodolus, a 344-line pastoral debate written for the most part in hexameters with a simple leonine rime or assonance (leonine hexameters) in the style of Vergil's third Eclogue. The pastoral conventions of the classical eclogue are preserved; the two debaters are shepherds who engage in a singing contest for a prize; a third shepherd acts as judge; and the contest ends with the coming of night. The debate is between Pseutis (or Falsehood) who hails from Athens and Alithia (or Truth) a maiden shepherdess of the lineage of David, with Fronesis (or Prudence) the sister of Alithia as their judge. They conduct their poetical contest in quatrains, concerning the heroes of antique mythology and the Old Testament. Pseutis praises the story of Saturn and the Golden Age, and Alithia the story of Adam and Eve in the Garden of Eden; Pseutis describes Deucalion and Pyrrha and the Flood, and Alithia recounts the history of Noah and his family.

Written in the ninth or tenth century, the poem has occasionally been attributed to Godescalc or Gottschalk of Orbasis.[14] According to this theory the name Theodolus (or Theodulus) is a Greek translation of Gottschalk, slave of God. The commentaries on the *Ecloga* and the biographical dictionaries in the eleventh century assumed Theodolus to be an ancient author who had studied and written his poem in Athens before 529. In the fourteenth century, commentators considered Theodolus to be a pseudonym used by St John Chrysostom for this work. In the sixteenth century Theodolus was associated with the fifth-century author Theodulus of Coelesyrian, and finally in the eighteenth century Theodolus was recognized as medieval Western author.

Bernard of Utrecht wrote his commentary on the *Ecloga* between 1076 and 1099 and dedicated it to Bishop Conard of Utrecht. Bernard of Utrecht is an obscure schoolmaster of the eleventh century and has sometimes been confused with Bernardus Silvestris of Tours. Little is known about the commentator except that he wrote the commentary at the request of his students. It is chiefly concerned with grammatical explanations, understanding the text, and careful narration of the Biblical story or myth.

In the schools of England and Europe in the twelfth and thirteenth centuries the commentary ascribed to Alexander Neckham supplanted Bernard of Utrecht's. It is ascribed to him in two Paris manuscripts (B.N. lat. 1862 and B.N. lat. 2638), and he is identified in nine of the forty-seven manuscripts of this commentary as the source for the amazing definition of a distich. This commentary is known for its euhemeristic interpretations of the pagan myths; Biblical stories are chiefly viewed as prefigurations of Christian doctrine. The commentator defines a distich (*dystigii*) as derived from *dys-* and *stix, -igis* and refers to Ennius's book on the rivers of the underworld.

The genre of the fable is represented by the forty-two Fables[15] in the collection ascribed to Avianus, which were composed around the year A.D. 400. Little is known of the author except that he was a Roman fabulist who dedicated his Fables in elegiac metre to the distinguished grammarian Ambrosius Theodosius Macrobius. His main source was the Greek fabulist Babrius, or probably a Latin prose version of Babrius which Avianus expanded and versified. The style of the Fables is picturesque; Avianus develops his models by expanding the descriptive elements; but his copious employment of Ovidian and Vergilian phrases creates at times a mock-heroic effect. The edifying subject matter and the pretentiousness of the style of the Fables made them immensely popular in medieval schools. They

were introduced into the schools during the Carolingian epoch, perhaps by Al-
cuin, who may have written a commentary upon them. They were imitated, expanded, rendered in prose, translated and accompanied by commentaries and
introductions. The *promythia* or *epimythia*, rhetorical exercises attached to the beginning or end of some of the Fables to point the moral, were composed during the
Middle Ages, although some *epimythia* may have come from Avianus himself. Verse
paraphrases of Avianus were composed by Alexander Neckham who entitled his
work *Novus Avianus*. Most of the 115 manuscripts of Avianus contain some scholia,
indicating the assiduity with which the Fables were studied in the schools.

The fourth genre in the *Liber Catonianus* is represented by the *Elegiae* of Maximian.[16] Written in the sixth century by a man who was of Estruscan origin and
a contemporary of Boethius, the six Latin elegies form a loosely connected cycle
in which the main theme is complaints about old age. The dismal picture of the
painfulness and weakness of old age without the delights of youth painted by an
old man expressing his own disenchantment is not easy to justify as appropriate
reading for a young student. Either the author was developing an elaborate conceit after the manner of the Roman elegiac poets or he was painting his own
depressing portrait. As a cruel *Memento mori* the elegies would indeed seem quite
unsuitable for a school text. In particular the controversial meaning of the third
elegy, in which the young poet is in love with the young girl Aquilina, involves
the role played by Boethius and Maximian's relationship to him. The elegy states
that Boethius tried to corrupt the morals of both Aquilina and the "innocent
Maximian."

Writing around 1200 Alexander de Villedieu in his *Doctrinale* (lines 3–4) objected to Maximian's elegies as trifling verses and as unsuitable as a school text,
but his condemnation was not general. In 1280 Hugo of Trimberg praised the
verses and sentiments of the elegies,[17] and the author of *Accessus ad auctores* noted
that the intention of the elegies was to expose and warn against the foolishness
of old age.[18] The subject, of course, was not new and is found in both Greek and
Roman poetry. Recent studies[19] of the text suggest that the elegies contain many
satirical elements directed against the sensuous character of women, and that the
autobiographical character of the elegies is, apart from a few minor details, far
from being assured. Moreover, the anti-feminist tendency in two of the satires
(second and fifth elegies), which is noted in the glosses to the text in the *Liber
Catonianus*, may account for Maximian's popularity in the medieval schools.

The genre of the epic is exemplified in the medieval textbook by Claudianus
Claudian.[20] Claudian was the last notable representative of the classical tradition of Latin poetry. His unfinished epic, *De Raptu Proserpinae* (3 books) is one
of two examples of that literary genre in the *Liber Catonianus*. His diction and technique bear comparison with the best Silver Age work. His gift of invective, description and epigram are offset by a tendency to over-elaboration. As early as
the ninth century, Claudian was included among school authors, as shown in MS.
Veronensis 163. The circulation of *De Raptu Proserpinae* was given great impetus

from its inclusion in the *Libri Catoniani* in the twelfth and thirteenth century. It probably continued to be studied in the schools in the sixteenth and early seventeenth century. There are more than 130 manuscripts of the poem, and 50 were written before the mid-fourteenth century. The study of *De Raptu Proserpinae* in the schools created the need for a commentary to help the master in his exposition and the student in his comprehension of the poem. This need was supplied by the commentary of Geoffrey of Vitry, written not later than the twelfth century and preserved fully in a thirteenth- or fourteenth-century manuscript (Oxford, Bodl. lat class. c. 12) and in abbreviated form in nine manuscripts from the twelfth to the fourteenth century. Four of these manuscripts are *Libri Catoniani* (Cambridge, Peterhouse, 2.1.8, 13th cent.; Munich, Bayerische Staatsbibliothek 391, 14th cent.; Oxford Bodleian Library ms. Auct. F.5.6, 13th cent.; Vatican City, Barberinianus lat. 41, 13th cent.).

The commentary was composed by Geoffrey, a master at Vitry, probably near Cluny, where there was a strong teaching center in the twelfth century.[21] It begins with the usual classified introduction or *accessus*, comprising a brief biographical sketch of Claudian and general comments on the purpose and subject-matter of the poem (*vita, causa, materia, intentio, utilitas, cui parti philosophiae supponitur, titulus*). Commenting on the poem itself, Geoffrey makes the conventional division into *propositio, invocatio,* and *narratio.* Mythological allusions are fully explained, and quotations from classical authors are abundant.

Geoffrey's treatment of the poem is straightforward and is suited to a poem which was included among primary texts in a school-reader. There is little treatment of philosophical matters and of critical appreciation of the unfinished epic. Claudian's poem is narrated in not-too-difficult Latin and was of appropriate length for a class text. Some of the variant readings in Claudian's text may indeed be simplifications designed to assist the beginning student. Geoffrey's commentary is concerned to please and interest as well as instruct. Together the poem and commentary offer a splendid example of a "school edition" and provide a glimpse into the master's schoolroom and the techniques he employed. Both have special value not only for medieval and classical scholars but for all who are interested in education.

A second example of the genre of an epic in the *Liber Catonianus* is the *Achilleid* of Statius. In the writing of Statius the self-conscious artistry of Silver Latin reached its peak. In many ways he is a typical product of his age and reflects the prevalent literary fashions: excessive use of hyberbole, highly colored and rhetorical episodes, lively descriptive, narrative, and "pathetic" passages. Throughout the Middle Ages, Statius was much admired and was considered as a Christian by Dante, who made him an important character in the *Purgatorio.*

Although Statius planned the *Achilleid* as an epic to cover the entire life of Achilles from his childhood in Scyros through the Trojan War, it remains incomplete, probably cut short in Book two by the poet's death in September 96. One of the striking features of the text of the *Achilleid* as found in the *Liber Catonianus,* and in certain late manuscripts of the poem, is that the incomplete epic is divided into not two but five books, apparently an attempt to make the unfinished epic into a complete work.[22] As the glosses point out, Book I treats the education of Achilles by the Centaur Chiron in his cave in Thessaly; Book II his disguise in feminine garb by his solicitous mother Thetis during his sojourn at the court of Lycomedes in Scyros; Book III his infatuation with Deidameia at Scyros while the Greeks clamored for his valor at Troy; Book IV his detection by Ulysses and Diomedes when he chose armor instead of a feminine gift; and Book V his departure for Troy.

The glosses to the *Achilleid* of Statius appear to be of ancient origin, but are not connected with the commentary of Lactantius Placidus.[23] In addition to grammatical explanations, the Statian glosses also point out the ethical themes of the poem. The *accessus* notes that the author's intention is "non tantum de illis agere que Achilles egit circa Troiam, sed quomodo eum Chiron nutrivit et mater sua Thetis in aula Licomedis eum abscondidit"; *utilitas* of the epic is to know and understand the story of Achilles; and the *moralitas* is to be found in the mother's solicitude for her son and in the son's obedience to his mother.

It is clear from the glosses in the *Liber Catonianus* that the authors were not read for aesthetic reasons. The commentary or gloss in this characteristic type of treatise, which resulted from the association of poetry with the grammar, was not an essay. It usually begins with generalized discussion of the author's life, comments on the style and form of his work, and mainly consists of notes on individual words and lines of the text. Practical in purpose the grammatical gloss defines unusual expressions, explains difficult constructions, notes rhetorical figures, and points out moral lessons and allegorical interpretaions of mythological allusions.

The *Liber Catonianus* was designed and used for more than mere language training. The humanistic technique as found in the selection of and commentaries on the six *auctores*, representing five literary genres, show the combination of grammar and morality, the study of the *artes* as a study of ethics, and the integration of the *ethica* in the *Septennium* of the liberal arts in the thirteenth and fourteenth centuries. The *Liber Catonianus* provided students of this period with not only training in Latin, but also an introduction to ethics. It is reasonable to assume that in this source-book of ethical precepts we have nothing more than the standard authors and literary genres which formed part of the regular course of study in the schools. In the collection of these authors and genres as well as in the type of commentary made on them, we may learn something about the theory and practice of literary criticism in the schools of the thirteenth and fourteenth centuries.

North Texas State University

Notes

1. On the medieval classifications of poetry, see O. B. Hardison, Jr., *The Enduring Monument: A Study of the Idea of Praise in Renaissance Literary Theory and Practice* (Chapel Hill, 1962), pp. 1–23; and C. S. Baldwin, *Medieval Rhetoric and Poetic* (New York, 1928); and J. W. H. Atkins, *English Literary Criticism: The Medieval Phase* (London, 1952).

2. J. W. H. Atkins, *Literary Criticism in Antiquity* (Cambridge, 1934), I, 182–83.

3. Heinrich Keil, ed., *Grammatici Latini* (Leipzig, 1857–80), VI, 50–173.

4. *Metalogicon*, ed. C. I. Webb (Oxford, 1929), I, 43.

5. For the Latin text of the systematic list of Eberhard the German, see his *Laborintus*, ed. Edmond Faral, *Les Arts poétiques du XIIe et du XIIIe siècle* (Paris, 1924), pp. 358–77. On the lists of Conrad of Hirsau, Alexander Neckham, and Hugo of Trimberg as well as a discussion of the "curriculum authors," see Ernst R. Curtius, *European Literature and the Latin Middle Ages* (New York, 1953), pp. 48–54; and M. L. W. Laistner, *Sp*, XXIV (1949), 260ff. On the educational system and texts used in medieval schools, see, for example, Astrik L. Gabriel, "The College System in the Fourteenth Century Universities," in Francis L. Utley, *The Forward Movement of the Fourteenth Century* (Columbus, Ohio State Univ. Press, 1961), pp. 79–124; Louis J. Paetow, *The Arts Course at Medieval Universities with Special Reference to Grammar and Rhetoric* (University of Illinois Studies in Language and Literature, 3) (Urbana, Illinois, 1910), 497–628; Charles H. Haskins, "List of Text-Books from the Close of the Twelfth Century," *Harvard Studies in Classical Philology*, 20 (1909), 76–94; ibid., *The Renaissance of the Twelfth Century* (Cambridge, Mass., 1927); H. J. Thomson, "Lucan, Statius, and Juvenal in the Early Centuries," *Classical Quarterly*, 22 (1928), 24–27; Hastings Rashdall, *The Universities of Europe in the Middle Ages*, eds. F. M. Powicke and A. B. Emden, 3 vols. (Oxford, 1936), passim; H. R. Mead, "Fifteenth Century Schoolbooks," *HLQ*, 3 (1939), 37–42; P. Kibre, *The Nations in the Mediaeval Universities* (Cambridge, Mass., 1948), passim; Pierre Riché, 'Recherches sur l'instruction des laïcs du IXe siècle," *CcMe*, V (1962), 175–82.

6. On the *Liber Catonianus*, see Marcus Boas, "De Librorum Catonianorum historia atque compositione," *Mnemosyne*, 42 (1914), 17–46; Eva M. Sanford, "The Use of Classical Latin Authors in the Libri Manuales," *Transactions of the American Philological Association*, 55 (1924), 190–248; R. Avesani, "Il ritmo per la morte del grammatico Ambrogio e il cosidetto 'Liber Catonianus,'" *SM*, 3rd ser. 6 (1965), 475–85; P. M. Clogan, ed., *The Medieval Achilleid of Statius* (Leiden, E. J. Brill, 1968), pp. 2–17; Y. F. Riou, "Quelques Aspects de la tradition manuscrite des *Carmina* d'Eugène Tolède: du *Liber Catonianus* aux *Auctores Octo Morales*," *RHTe*, Tome Deuxième (1972), 11–44.

7. For a list of the glossed manuscripts of the *Liber Catonianus*, see P. M. Clogan, op. cit., pp. 11–15.

8. See Amy K. Clarke and Harry L. Levy, "Claudius Claudianus," *Translationum et Commentariorum*, Vol. 3 (Washington, 1976), pp. 141–71; ibid., *The Commentary of Geoffrey of Vitry on Claudian's De Raptu Proserpine* (Leiden, E. J. Brill, 1973); J. B. Hall, ed., *De Raptu Proserpinae* (Cambridge, 1969); Betty N. Quinn, "ps. Theodulus," *Catalogus Translationum et Commentariorum*, Vol. 2 (Washington, 1971), pp. 383–408; Arpad P. Orban, "Anonymi Teutonici Commentum in *Theoduli Eclogam* e Codice Utrecht, U. B. 292 editum (1)," *Viv*, 11 (1973), 1–42; (2) *Viv*, 12 (1974); (3) *Viv*, 13 (1975), 77–88; (4) *Viv*, 14 (1976), 50–61; and Christian Schmitt, "Zum Kanon eines bisher unedierten Theodul-Kommentars," *GRM*, Neue Folge, 24 (1974), 1–12; R. A. Pratt, "Chaucer's Claudian," *Sp*, 22 (1947), 419–29; R. Hazelton, "Chaucer and Cato," *Sp*, 35 (1960), 357–80; P. M. Clogan, op. cit., pp. 1–9; "An Argument of Book I of the *Thebaid*," *Man*, 7 (1963), 30–32; "The Manuscripts of the *Achilleid*," *Man*, 8 (1964), 175–79; "Chaucer and the *Thebaid* Scholia," *SP*, 61 (1964),

599–615; "Medieval Glossed Manuscripts of the *Achilleid*," *Man*, 9 (1965), 104–09; "Chaucer's Use of the *Thebaid*," *EM*, 18 (1967), 9–31; "Medieval Glossed Manuscripts of the *Thebaid*," *Man*, 11 (1967), 102–12; "The Manuscripts of Lactantius Placidus' Commentary on the *Thebaid*," *Sc*, 22 (1968), 87–91; "The Latin Commentaries to Statius: A Bibliographic Project," *ACNL Lovaniensis*, eds. J. IJsewijn and E. Kessler (Leuven, Leuven Univ. Press, 1973), pp. 149–57; and A. E. Hartung, "The Non-Comic Merchant's Tale, Maximianus and the Sources," *MedS*, 29 (1967), 1–25.

    9. "L'enseignement de la philosophie morale au XIIe siècle," *Mediaeval Studies*, 11 (1949), 77–99; and Delhaye, "Grammatica et Ethica au XIIe siècle," *RTAM*, 25 (1958), 59–110.

    10. See Delhaye, "Grammatica et Ethica," p. 73.

    11. See Marcus Boas, ed., *Disticha Catonis recensuit et apparatu critico instruit Marcus Boas: Opus post Marci Boas mortem edendum curavit H. J. Botschuyver* (Amsterdam, 1952). On the fiction of "Dionysius Cato," see, in addition to Ferdinand Hauthal, *Catonis Philosophi Liber* (Berlin, 1869), pp. xxii–xxiii, Marcus Boas, "Woher stammt der Name Dionysius Cato?" *Philogische Wochenschrift*, L (1930), no. 21, pp. 649–56, "Nachträgliches zu den Titeln Dionysius Cato und Disticha Catonis," ibid., 53 (1933), 956–60. "Medieval men called the book *Cato*, or *Caton*, or *Liber Catonis* or *ethica Catonis*."

    12. See R. Hazelton, "The Christianization of 'Cato': The *Disticha Catonis* in the Light of Late Medieval Commentaries," *MedS*, 19 (1957), 164–67.

    13. See M. Boas, *Mnemosyne*, N. S. 42 (1914), 43; and Sanford, pp. 230–40.

    14. See Max Manitius, *Geschichte der lateinischen Literatur des Mittelalter*, I (1911), p. 573; J. Osternacher, "Die Überlieferung der Ecloga Theoduli," *Neues Archiv*, 40 (1915), 331ff; Karl Strecker, "Ist Gottschalk der Dichter der Ecloga Theoduli?" *Neues Archiv* 45 (1923), 18; F. J. E. Raby, *A History of Secular Latin Poetry in the Middle Ages* (Oxford, 1957), I, 228; and Quinn, "ps. Theodolos," pp. 383–408.

    15. See A. Guaglianone, ed., *Aviani Fabulae* (*Corpus scriptorum latinorum Paravianum*), Turin, 1958, p. xviii; K. McKenzie and W. A. Oldfather, eds., *Ysopet-Avionnet: The Latin and French Texts* (U. of Illinois Studies In Language and Literature, Vol. 5, No. 4, Urbana, 1921); and Avianus, *Œuvres*, ed. L. Herrmann (Brussels, 1968), pp. 26–29.

    16. Emil Baehrens, *Poetae Latini Minores*, 5 (Teubner, 1883), p. 316; W. Schetter, *Studien zur Überlieferung und Kritik des Elegikers Maximian* (Klassische-Philol. Studien, 36, Wiesbaden, 1970); Maximianus, *Elegie* a cura di T. Agozzino (Bologna: Silva, 1970); Maximianus, *Elegiae*, ed. R. Webster (New York, 1900); and F. Raby, *Secular Latin*, I, 124–25.

    17. *Registrum multorum auctorum*, ed. K. Longosch (Darmstadt, 1942), I, 612.

    18. See R. B. C. Huygens, *Accessus ad auctores, Bernard d'Utrecht, Conrad d'Hirsau, Dialogus super auctores* (Leiden, 1970), p. 25.

    19. See J. Szoverffy, "Maximianus a satirist?" *Harvard Studies in Classical Philology*, 72 (1967), 351–67.

    20. See Alan Cameron, "Claudian," in *Latin Literature of the Fourth Century*, ed. J. W. Binns (London, 1974), pp. 134–59; ibid., *Claudian: Poetry and Propaganda at the Court of Honorius* (Oxford, 1970); Claudian, *De Raptu Proserpinae*, ed. J. B. Hall (Cambridge, 1969); and Clarke and Levy, "Claudius Claudianus," pp. 141–71.

    21. Gaufridus Vitreacensis, *The Commentary of Geoffrey of Vitry on Claudian's De Raptu Proserpine*, ed A. K. Clarke and P. M. Giles (Leiden, E. J. Brill, 1973); and Clarke and Levy, "Claudinus Claudianus," pp. 161–62.

    22. See Clogan, *The Medieval Achilleid of Statius*, pp. 1–17; and "The Manuscripts of the *Achilleid*," pp. 175–79.

    23. See Clogan, "The Manuscripts of Lactantius Placidus' Commentary on the Thebaid," pp. 87–91; and "Medieval Glossed Manuscripts of the *Achilleid*," pp. 104–09.

Ausonius in the Renaissance

Roger Green

This paper is a parergon, containing the partial and provisional results of an investigation which was originally undertaken as an afterthought to a commentary on Ausonius's personal poetry; it is a very brief and incomplete essay on a subject which increases rather than decreases with further research. A thorough approach would demand an acquaintance with the whole of European literature of the period — *magnum opus et arduum*; even the various volumes of *Deliciae* could lose their delights for a myopic nonagenarian. The material utilised here was gathered by ferreting in various works of reference, by burrowing in important authors, and by consulting experts in selected areas. This magpie approach (to change the metaphor) has been most fruitful, but the extent of my debts reminds me of Sosias in Terence's *Andria*, who, only too conscious of kindnesses received, confesses "istaec commemoratio quasi exprobratio est."[1] The topic obviously requires fuller treatment; this paper meanwhile will range over three centuries of Ausonius's *Nachleben* in as many pages and end with a short summary of the principal ways in which his influence made itself felt.

The story begins in the early years of the *trecento*, in the city of Verona; it begins not with a manuscript of Ausonius, but with an extensive marginal addition by Giovanni Mansionario to his *Historia Imperialis*, first brought to light by Roberto Weiss, in which the Veronese Humanist mentions a large number of works which he believed to have been written by Ausonius.[2] A number of these works are not extant or attested elsewhere; while some of them, such as the explanation of Hebrew names, seem hardly authentic, there are others, such as the verses on the later Roman emperors, which cannot be dismissed so easily.[3] The relation of this evidence to the history of Ausonius's text has been elucidated by Michael Reeve, who also suggested that Giovanni was copying an outdated list at the head of a manuscript later received by Politian.[4] After Politian's death its fate is obscure, but there are two extant copies of the manuscript, one of the fourteenth century (P), and one of the late fifteenth (H). The former of these was owned by Petrarch, one of several Italian Humanists to have had Ausonius on their shelves; others were Boccaccio, who quotes him twice in the *Genealogia Deorum* and may well have introduced him to Florence,[5] and Coluccio Salutati, for whom the extant Florentine manuscript known as M was written.[6] This manuscript is one of at least twenty which belong to a single family, usually known as Z, which is independent of the Verona manuscript and very different in content; they are for the most part Italian, but two were copied from a manuscript that was taken to Dalmatia.[7] This family forms the basis of the earliest editions of Ausonius, of which the first was produced at Venice in 1472 by Bartolemeo Girardini; it was followed during the next fifty years by several more Italian editions, which include new material, such as the *Mosella*. The popularity of Ausonius is attested also by clear echoes of his poetry in such poets as Pontano, Mantuan, Navagero, Vida, Molza and Flaminio, and by Peiper's list of imitators of his epigrams, which includes the Strozzi, Marullus, Sannazaro, Crinitus, Navagero, Fracastoro and Alciatus.[8] Politian, as well as Alciatus, is known to have worked on the text, and a life of Ausonius was included in Crinitus's biographies. The editions of Ausonius available to these writers offered rather less than one-half of what was later available; they were well endowed with epigrams (even allowing for various spurious ones),[9] but lacked many of his most interesting compositions. Sannazaro was in fact aware of the manuscript V, which contains the greater part of Ausonius, but after copying various passages he left it in its mediaeval resting-place in the monastery of Ile-Barbe near Lyon. There it remained for fifty more years, during which the fruits of Sannazaro's brief visit had a very limited effect on scholarship.[10] Ironically, however (if that overused word may be allowed in a scholarly publication), it was in the early sixteenth century that the influence of Ausonius (Ausonius *minor*, so to speak) reached its height.

In Northern Europe the earliest writer known to me at the time of writing who shows a familiarity with Ausonius is Conrad Celtes, who mentions him in letters written in the last years of the fifteenth century,[11] and in 1500 published a version of the *Ludus Septem Sapientum*, based on Ugoletus's edition of 1499, along with a similar, spurious, work.[12] In 1515 there appeared another edition of the *Ludus*, at Rostock, and in the same year, at Leipzig, an edition of the entire available Ausonius, prepared by the visiting Englishman Richard Croke. Ausonius's work was well known to Eobanus Hessus, as is very clear from an extensive list of *loci similes* kindly sent to me by Professor Vredeveld, and also to Micyllus. A favourite work was the *Caesares*, which is frequently reprinted during the sixteenth century, along with local imitations. Readers in the second half of the century could consult a very full account of what was known about the poet in Gesner's encyclopaedia, and the new texts became available in editions by Scaliger published at Heidelberg in 1588. A more popular kind of interest is attested by references in *alba amicorum*: Mr. M. Carawan, who has perused the British Library collection, has brought to my notice quotations of four epigrams and one other work of Ausonius, and a few references which indicate that Ausonius was well enough known to have moral tags or other commonplace material credited to him.

To return to the early sixteenth century, Ausonius appears in considerable bulk in Erasmus's *Adages*. He is in fact cited as frequently as Catullus or Augustine, and much more frequently than certain authors now preferred to him, such as Lucretius, Propertius, Lucan or Statius. Mrs. M. Mann Phillips has noted twenty-nine citations altogether;[13] it is clear from the references which she has kindly given me that Erasmus had read very widely in his Ausonius, and that, whether by luck or judgement, he included no spurious material. There are a few misunderstandings on Erasmus's part, and one poor emendation which is also offered by the *Diatribae* of Accursius in 1524; more interesting for the present purpose is the observation that in three places Erasmus seems so intent on Ausonius that he misses the original source of a phrase. In one of these (I.ix.67), when commenting on *Saguntina fames*, Erasmus does not mention the model in Lucan 1. 40 *Perusina fames*; this is perhaps not surprising, since the phrase is not identical in Lucan, who in any case is not one of Erasmus's favourite authors. But when in *Adages* II.x.27 and III.ix.97 Erasmus quotes the phrase *catenatique labores* ("a treadmill of troubles"), he seems unaware, or at least oblivious, that the phrase is borrowed from Martial, a favourite author of Erasmus (1. 15. 7), and it is apparently the case that the phrase was more familiar to him through Ausonius. This evidence of Ausonius's repute is confirmed by a surprising citation by Erasmus's contemporary and compatriot Martin Dorp, in a work entitled *Introductio facilis ... ad Aristotelis libros logice intelligendos utilissima ...* (Paris, 1512): a line of Ausonius's *Technopaignion* is used to elucidate a problem of grammar, and is illustrated by quotations of Vergil, Cicero and Terence, and buttressed ("in case anyone should quibble with Ausonius") by the authority of Buridan.[14]

It is only to be expected that Ausonius would receive a warm welcome in his homeland; his first appearance came at a time when French literature was anxious to assert itself against Italian supremacy, and so an ancient poet of Gallic blood was a valuable symbol of cultural independence. Although closely attached to Bordeaux in his lifetime, Ausonius was known throughout the country in the first half of the sixteenth century, and especially in the capital. Erasmus acknowledged the patriotic connexion in a letter to Alaard of Amsterdam (*Ep.* 676), when he wrote of France's debt to a certain scholar, "that she can now add this new glory to her Hilary, her Ausonius, her Paulinus." A further strong impetus was provided by Jerome Aleander's presence in Paris between 1508 and 1514; his work appears in important editions issued by Badius in 1511 and 1513. A few years later, Ausonius takes his place in the textbook of Ravisius Textor, and it seems that he quickly became a schoolbook; there are commentaries by Franciscus Sylvius on the *Precatio Matutina* and *de Resurrectione Domini* (*alias Versus Paschales*), both of 1518, and on the *Griphus Ternarii Numeri* (1516). This last work, less agreeable to modern taste, was reprinted in 1522, and mentioned by Vivès in his *De Tradendis Disciplinis* of 1531.[15] In that work Ausonius receives a lowly place among curriculum authors, but is praised in the words "ubique argutus et excitans, nec sinit lectorem dormitare." Among those not allowed to fall asleep was François Rabelais; it is noteworthy that when in *Gargantua* he alludes to a scene from Plautus's *Aulularia* he also recalls the reference made to it in Ausonius's preface to the *Griphus*. Other works of Ausonius held attractions for contemporary French poets. Nicolas Bourbon, in his *Nugae* of 1533, likes to recast epigrams, under such titles as "e Graeco Luciani vel potius Ausonii imitatio" (2. 1) or "Exhortatio ad modestiam. E Graeco et Ausonio" (4. 70). The twofold attribution is significant, for part of Ausonius's appeal lay in the fact that he had anticipated the contemporary fashion of translating poems of the *Greek Anthology*. Two longer works form the basis for poems by the vernacular poet Hugues Salel: "de Ambiguitate Eligendae Vitae" and "Cupido Cruciatus."[16] The former poem, which develops a Greek epigram in the style of a Horatian satire, is also treated by Salel with full appreciation of its double origin; the latter, a detailed description of a picture in which various lovelorn heroines in the underworld take their revenge on Cupid, may have appealed to minds attuned to the "querelle des femmes." Both these works of Ausonius appear in the anthology of bucolic poetry produced by Oporinus in 1547 and in the first volume of Duchesne's anthology of epigrams of 1556.

What was the effect of the publication in 1558 of the recently discovered poems of Ausonius? There was naturally the keenest interest among scholars, but evidently rather less enthusiasm elsewhere. The text was scrutinised by Turnèbe and Pithou, and by the Dutchmen Canter and Poelmann, and by others enumerated in Poelmann's edition.[17] Most influential, however, were Élie Vinet of Saintonge and J. J. Scaliger of Agen. Vinet's work, evidently delayed by his wide commitments, was overtaken by that of Scaliger, which eventually appeared also in Germany, as already noted, and in Leyden and Amsterdam, where it inspired several Dutch scholars in the early seventeenth century to work on the text to great effect. But the impact in France seems somewhat muted: Ronsard uses various themes of Ausonius in his works,[18] but a reading of the *Odes* of Dorat has yielded no verbal or other evidence; more significantly, the voluminous *Essays* of Montaigne offer no more than a single epigram, although it is known that Montaigne owned at least two copies of his compatriot's work.[19] Ausonius was very well known to George Buchanan, who could well have seen the new material as a result of his friendship with Élie Vinet, but his extensive verse, mostly written in France in mid-century, has yet to reveal evidence of the expanded Ausonius.

Buchanan is one of the channels, perhaps the principal one—although the process has yet to be traced in detail—by which Ausonius reached Scotland. As has been shown by Professor James Cameron and C. Upton,[20] Ausonius is a strong influence in the work of such Humanists as John Johnstone just after the turn of the century, and later; his geographical and historical works were particular favourites. In England also it is the seventeenth century, rather than the sixteenth, that sees Ausonius's apogee, but the clear influence that he exerted on such poets as George Herbert and Henry Vaughan and (later) Alexander Pope falls outside the limits of this paper (as does the influence of Ausonius in Spain, particularly on Gracián[21]). In England our poet's progress seems to have been slow. Though included in Leland's imposing list of sources for his *Cycnea Cantio*, his "Mosella" is not in fact imitated closely, if at all, in that poem. Baldwin's study of educational practice in the time of Shakespeare produced a single item, and that a spurious one.[22] Ausonius does appear in a work of T. Kendall, *Flowers of Epigrams* (1577), but as an epigrammatist does not share the popularity of Martial or More. At the end of the sixteenth century there is a significant reference in Thomas Meres's *Palladis Tamia*, where Ausonius is mentioned on two counts: firstly, as a translator of epigrams from the Greek, which is true up to a point, and secondly as a writer who "*in libris Fastorum* penned the occurrences of the world from the first creation of it to his time, that is to the raigne of the Emperor Gratian."[23] This notice might be dismissed as largely rubbish, but is significant none the less; it is significant not only because it is rubbish, and because better information was not to hand, but also because there is perhaps a garbled echo of two of the items mentioned in Mansionario's list 300 years earlier, *viz. libri Fastorum cum libris consularibus librum unum. Item cronicam ab initio mundi usque ad tempus suum.* There is no need to suppose that Meres had seen the missing manuscript or even the work of Mansionario, but the information offered by Meres is not derived from Ausonius's text and must come from somewhere. His historical knowledge, incidentally, is more correct than that of the Veronese scholar, who chose a less appropriate emperor.

Ausonius is a poet of enormous variety, and evidently attracted readers, scholars, and poets in diverse ways: but what were the main forms in which his influence showed itself? Firstly, as an epigrammatist; in Charles Estienne's dictionary this is his only claim to fame, and it is the epigrams that occupy much of J. C. Scaliger's attention ("utinam ne scripsisset," thunders the hypercritic).[24] A full catalogue of imitations — unfortunately not undertaken by Hutton in his studies of the *Greek Anthology* in France and Italy[25] — would be vast. Secondly, as a moralist. Here the frequent confusion or conflation of Ausonius with the "Cato" of the *Distichs* is eloquent, and the imaginatively written *Ludus Septem Sapientum* and *de Ambiguitate Eligendae Vitae* are read widely. His occasional indulgence in pornography had an adverse effect on his reputation in some quarters (such as Nosoponus in Erasmus's *Ciceronianus*),[26] but not a fatal one. Thirdly, through his *Caesares*, which were valued not only for their historical information, but also as models for works which, unlike the originals, were written to further nationalistic aims; these are scattered very widely, and are used to trace the royal lines of such diverse nations as Scotland, England, France, Germany, Poland and Turkey.[27]

In addition, the inspiration of Ausonius may be claimed for two common and important kinds of poetic writing. The fashion for *tumuli* or *tombeaux* should not be derived from the sequences of funerary poems under the titles *Parentalia* and *Professores*, which became available later; but a few of the *Epitaphia*, then scattered among the epigrams, were known to earlier writers and in particular seem to have influenced Pontano, with whom *tumulus*-poems may well originate. Ausonius should also be seen as the father of the type of poem best known through Herrick's "Gather ye rosebuds while ye may," but also written by Pontano, Politian, Buchanan, Ronsard, Spenser and Garcilaso, as well as at least two *rhétoriqueurs*, including Lemaire de Belges, who translated the original. The work in question is the "de Rosis nascentibus," generally found in editions only in an appendix, if at all; it is more commonly ascribed to Vergil and lacks any manuscript attribution to Ausonius, but there are good stylistic reasons, as Aleander realised, for supposing that Ausonius was the author and that, like other parts of Ausonius, long restored to him on sound manuscript authority, it was wrongly inserted during the early Middle Ages into the *iuvenalis ludi libellus* credited to the young Vergil.

What may surprise the modern reader is the apparent lack of interest in Ausonius's personality (or *persona*) even after 1558, when the new poems made his self-portrait much clearer. Although he in fact played an important political role in his time, this is hidden in his verse with typical modesty — a trait which may have done his reputation little good — and the personality that emerges is one not likely to appeal to tastes whetted by Plutarch; especially since the Later Roman Empire was not a favoured epoch. It might be expected that Ausonius would have had some appeal as a Christian Humanist, but, although he is sometimes wrongly thought to have been a bishop, there is little sign of this. This is not because of his occasional obscenity; he is no more or less obscene than Buchanan. It is more likely to be due to his opposition to the future saint Paulinus, apparent from their correspondence; whereas a genuine pagan like Socrates or Seneca could be admired, and even made a sort of honorary Christian, a semi-Christian (the term is Erasmus's) who could actually be seen interacting unfavourably with a Christian saint could not. However his argument with Paulinus might be interpreted, in an age of religious polarity Ausonius was bound to come off worse. The erroneous view of Ausonius as a devoted pagan has taken several centuries to evaporate and indeed still exercises its influence; and it was, I suggest, an important if not a crucial factor in his reception in the later Renaissance.

University of St. Andrews

Notes

1. In addition to those mentioned in the text or in other notes, I wish to thank Professors L. W. Forster, J. IJsewijn, A. Jolidon, B. Kytzler, I. D. McFarlane, R. J. Schoeck and P. H. Schrijvers for helpful comments made after the delivery of this paper; I hope nobody has been forgotten. In many cases constraints of time and space have unfortunately prevented me from making full use of their suggestions here.

2. R. Weiss, "Ausonius in the Fourteenth Century," in *Classical Influences on European Culture A.D. 500–1500*, ed. R. R. Bolgar (Cambridge, 1971), pp. 67–72.

3. R. P. H. Green, "Marius Maximus and Ausonius's *Caesares*," *CQ*, 31 (1981), 228ff.

4. M. D. Reeve, "Some Manuscripts of Ausonius," *Prometheus*, 3 (1977), 112–20.

5. Weiss, p. 70f.

6. B. L. Ullmann, *The Humanism of Coluccio Salutati* (Padua, 1963), p. 173, n. 59, pp. 268–69.

7. M. D. Reeve, "The Tilianus of Ausonius," *Rh.Mus.*, n.f. 121 (1978), 362.

8. R. Peiper, "Die Handschriftliche Überlieferung des Ausonius," *Jahrbücher für Klassische Philologie*, Supplementband XI (1880), 251ff.

9. See R. Peiper, *Decimi Magni Ausonii Burdigalensis Opuscula* (Leipzig, 1886), pp. 419ff.

10. R. Peiper (op. cit. n. 8), pp. 344ff.; C. Schenkl, *D. Magni Ausonii Opuscula* (*MGH Auctores Antiquissimi*, Tomus V. 2) (Berlin, 1883), *Prooemium*, XXXIIIff.; Reeve (op. cit. n. 7), p. 364/5.

11. H. Rupprich, ed., *Der Briefwechsel des Konrad Celtis* (Munich 1934), pp. 313 and 322.

12. See K. Adel, ed., *Conradus Celtis Opuscula* (Leipzig, 1966), pp. 73ff.

13. M. M. Phillips, *The Adages of Erasmus* (Cambridge, 1964), p. 395.

14. I owe this reference to Professor J. IJsewijn, and am grateful to Miss J. M. Richardson, Deputy Librarian of Pembroke College, Oxford, for helping me to consult the work.

15. J. L. Vivès, *De Tradendis Disciplinis* (Antwerp, 1531), 3.9.

16. See L.-A. Bergougnioux, *Hugues Salel ... Œuvres Poétiques ...* (Toulouse and Paris, 1929), pp. 74ff.

17. See H. de la Ville de Mirmont, *Le Manuscrit de l'Ile-Barbe* (Bordeaux and Paris, 1917), I, 131.

18. See E. Everat, *De Ausonii operibus et genere dicendi* (Paris, 1885), pp. 120ff., following Corpet. Ronsard may not be imitating Ausonius directly.

19. P. Villey, *Les Sources et L'Évolution des Essais de Montaigne* (Paris, 1908), I, 74–75.

20. See J. K. Cameron, "The Renaissance Tradition in the Reformed Church of Scotland" (Presidential Address), in *Renaissance and Renewal in Church History* (*Studies in Church History*), ed. D. Baker, 14 (Oxford, 1977), 265ff. Mr. C. Upton is preparing a thesis on various aspects of Scottish neo-Latin literature. Johnstone received regrettably short shrift in the spoken version of this paper.

21. E. R. Curtius, *European Literature and the Latin Middle Ages*, transl. Willard R. Trask (Princeton, 1953), pp. 298f.

22. T. W. Baldwin, *Shakespeare's Small Latin and Lesse Greek* (Urbana, 1944), I, 595 and 598.

23. See G. Gregory Smith, ed., *Elizabethan Critical Essays* (Oxford, 1904), II, 317 and 322.

24. J. C. Scaliger, *Poetices Libri Septem* (Lyon, 1561), *Liber* VI (*qui et Hypercriticus*), 318A.

25. J. Hutton, *The Greek Anthology in France and in the Latin Writers of the Netherlands to the Year 1800* (*Cornell Studies in Classical Philology*, 28) (Ithaca, 1946); and *The Greek Anthology in Italy to the Year 1800* (*Cornell Studies in English*, 23) (Ithaca, 1935).

26. *Opera Omnia Desiderii Erasmi Rotterdamensis*, II, 1 (Amsterdam, 1971), 659; a reference I owe to Mrs. B. Sharpe.

27. This information was kindly supplied by Mr. C. Upton, with extra Polish material from Mr. M. Carawan; two former research students who have greatly stimulated my own neo-Latin researches.

Rafael Landívar's *Rusticatio Mexicana* and the Enlightenment in America

Arnold L. Kerson

I n 1781 Rafael Landívar, a Guatemalan Jesuit, published in Modena, Italy, the first edition of the *Rusticatio Mexicana*,[1] a descriptive poem in Latin hexameter verse, in ten books, devoted to various aspects of natural and rural life in New Spain. Because of the favorable reception accorded this work, the author revised the original books, and expanded the poem by adding five new ones, besides an appendix-epilogue. This second version, printed in Bologna in 1782, and consisting of 5,247 lines, was superior to the first, and became the definitive one.[2] It is this second edition that will serve as the basis of my interpretation.

My plan in this brief study is threefold: to explain the circumstances which led Landívar to compose this work; to provide a general view of the poem's content and spirit; and to show how the poem is a manifestation of the eighteenth-century enlightened thought which prevailed in the Spanish-American colonies.

The *Rusticatio Mexicana*, which is considered the most important descriptive poem of Spanish-American eighteenth-century literature in both Latin and Spanish, was virtually unknown in Europe and America until 1924, the year in which two Spanish translations appeared.[3] In a period in which such distinguished naturalists and historians as Buffon, Raynal, De Pauw, and Robertson alluded to the inferiority, not only of the American Indians, but also of the land, climate, plants, and animals of the New World, the *Rusticatio Mexicana* appeared as a proud affirmation of the natural beauty and wealth of rural America, of the abundance and quality of its agricultural products and livestock, and of the industrial skill and intellectual capacity of its inhabitants.

Landívar belongs to the group of Mexican Latinists and humanists of the second half of the eighteenth century, which includes such eminent figures as Francisco Javier Alegre, Diego José Abad, and Francisco Javier Clavijero, who distinguished themselves as teachers, historians, theologians, and men of letters. They were formed intellectually in a period of transition, in which traditional scholastic philosophy was being challenged by modern philosophy and experimentalism, and were familiar with the works of Descartes, Newton, Locke, Leibnitz, Gassendi, and others. The aprioristic physics of the *Principia*, as well as the trend of Newtonian experimentalism, was the modern philosophy that these men defended.

Little is known about Landívar, for whom there are only two main sources of information. One, *Estudios bio-bibliográficos sobre Rafael Landívar*, by J. Antonio Villacorta,[4] provides statistical data on his lineage, and recreates the background and atmosphere of the society of the Guatemala in which he lived. The other source is a very brief biography, which forms part of an unpublished work by Father Félix Sebastián,[5] a contemporary of Landívar, on members of the Company of Jesus exiled to Italy. This second source is invaluable, for it provides an insight into the character of Landívar and the circumstances surrounding the writing of his poem.

Rafael Landívar y Caballero was born in Guatemala City in 1731, of noble lineage. His father, Pedro Landívar, provided him with a solid education in the humanistic tradition. He received degrees from the Colegio de San Francisco de Borja and the Universidad de San Carlos in Guatemala. In 1749 he entered the prestigious Jesuit Colegio Máximo de San Pedro y San Pablo, with the idea of becoming a priest. Ordained in 1755, he later became a teacher of rhetoric and philosophy. Exiled with his fellow Jesuits by the decree of 1767, he went to Bologna, where he served as director of the "Casa de Sapiencia," a Jesuit center of studies. Father Sebastián describes him as studious, intelligent, affectionate, although withdrawn, and at times, morbid. Landívar died on September 27, 1793, of an unidentified illness.

The question often arises as to why Landívar wrote a Creole poem in Latin. Luis Beltranena[6] supposes that Landívar wrote in Latin to show his resentment against the French-dominated rationalist spirit of the times, and thus rejected the idea of writing in a Romance language. This theory has no basis. Indeed, Landívar, to the extent that his religious faith permitted, participated in that very same rationalist spirit. Father Sebastián says that Landívar "wrote in Latin verse, which he handled with great ease, a work which he had published under the title of *Rusticatio Mexicana, seu rariora quaedam ex agris Mexicanis decerpta*, a work much esteemed by the scholars of Italy, whose critics have accorded this work, unique in its class, the praise of which it is worthy. This endeavor took him little time, for he did it to distract his mind...."[7] One must also bear in mind the long tradition of the Jesuits, especially in Italy, of using Latin not only for didactic, but also for more aesthetic types of literature. The most direct model of the *Rusticatio Mexicana* is Vergil's *Georgics*, and after that, the French Jesuit Jacques Vanière's *Praedium Rusticum*.[8] Indeed, in Landívar's time the *Georgics* of the "divine" Vergil was considered the most perfect poem of its class, and Vergil himself, the best poet of all times.

José Mata Gavidia, the Guatemalan critic, believes that Vergil's influence on the *Rusticatio* is limited to linguistic and formal aspects, and sees rather a Theocritean serenity in Landívar's natural and simple descriptions,[9] while John B. Trend suggests that Landívar's inspiration "is not really Vergilian," and that "He is more like Varro that Vergil."[10] The pastoral elements of the *Rusticatio* are mainly found in the deeply moving expressions of the lonely exile, pining for his native land, somewhat reminiscent of the Meliboeus of Vergil's first *Eclogue*. They also occur in scenes of tranquillity which offset the tension produced by scenes of violence or seriousness. I see difficulty in preferring the spirit of Varro's *Res Rusticae*, a long practical manual, over the *Georgics*. Possibly, Trend was referring to the unadorned, straightforward description often found in Landívar.

A comparison of the *Georgics*, as well as the *Aeneid*, with the *Rusticatio Mexicana* reveals that, besides containing many examples of direct linguistic borrowing and imitation the Guatemalan poem is Vergilian in spirit in many aspects. The designation *rusticatio* signifies two distinct things: "country life" and "agriculture." Just as the *Georgics* contains, besides georgic or agricultural material, elements of the pastoral, epic, and mock heroic, the *Rusticatio* includes the georgic, pastoral, epic, mock heroic, in addition to what are more characteristically city scenes, such as bullfights and horse races. Landívar, in effect, combines what is properly agricultural with other aspects of the rural scene: geography, wild animals, mineral wealth, popular games and pastimes. He describes lakes, rivers, waterfalls, birds, domestic livestock, farm workers, the production of dyes, in short, all that might serve as an effective reply to the denigrators of the land, climate, and native people of America. This variety of topics is, we might say, the internal law of the poem's unity. Although distributed over fifteen books and an epilogue, the *Rusticatio*, unlike the *Georgics*, a model of formal perfection, lacks a strict structural organization. It does have a logical evolution or progression of themes.

The dedicatory poem in the elegiac stanza, "Urbi Guatimalae," is a fine example of how the poet adapts the Vergilian expression and spirit to fit his own sentiment. It begins:

> Salve, cara Parens, dulcis Guatimala, salve,
> Delicium vitae: fons, et origo meae:
> Quam juvat, Alma, tuas animo pervolvere dotes,
> Temperiem, fontes, compita, templa, lares.[11]   (p. iii)

These opening lines follow closely this famous set-piece of the *Georgics*:

> Salve, magna parens frugum, Saturnia tellus,
> magna virum: tibi res antiquae laudis et artis
> ingredior sanctos ausus recludere fontes,
> Ascraeumque cano Romana per oppida carmen. (II.173–76)

There is in Vergil a deep sympathy for nature and man. The poet feels an intimacy and fellowship with the creations of nature, and will often attribute human feelings or characteristics to inanimate objects, such as trees, plants, and streams. This device, sometimes referred to as the pathetic fallacy, is frequently used by

Landívar. In Vergil, the use of the pathetic fallacy has been explained as having a kind of relation with primitive animism. In Landívar, its use, along with that of personification, may be attributed to literary tradition, and is almost necessary to enliven the narrative, especially in the case of dry, technical subjects. To read of cochineal worms and how they are processed in technical language would be dull. But because this material is presented in terms of mock-heroic "bloodshed," the process becomes more tolerable, even comic.

As in the *Georgics*, one finds in the *Rusticatio* a certain degree of moralizing. A sense of practical, enlightened "technological age" morality is derived from certain examples which denote that the avoidance of toil or patience in deference to a "labor-saving" scheme results in a material loss. By not taking time to prepare mine borings properly, cave-ins may result; sowing the entire sugar field rather than graduating the plantings results in an uneconomical bumper harvest; by not making the necessary effort to protect the cochineal worms from the cold weather, these insects may perish, with a resulting financial loss.

In preaching salvation through hard work, Vergil shows us the real world with its hardships as well as its joys. He does not shrink from presenting the real and crude facts of life. He openly speaks of manure, the mating of cattle, and the unpleasant details of disease. Landívar, in like manner, approaches matters in a virile fashion. He actually surpasses the Roman poet in the crudeness of detail, reminding one of traditional Spanish realism such as it is seen in the picaresque novel.

There are reminiscences in the *Rusticatio Mexicana* of such classical works as, for example, Lucretius's *De Rerum Natura*, Cato's *De Re Rustica*, Varro's *Res Rusticae*, and Columella's *De Re Rustica*. Also, the *Rusticatio* clearly falls within the tradition of neo-Latin didactic works, particularly those that deal with agriculture and the country. These include Poliziano's *Rusticus*, Pontano's *De Hortis Hesperidum*, Vida's *De Bombycum Cura et Usu*, Rapin's *Hortorum Libri IV*, and Lagomarsini's *De Origine Fontium*. However, Vanière's *Praedium Rusticum*, as I have indicated, is a more direct model of the *Rusticatio*. Vanière idealizes country life, and at the same time presents a realistic picture with factual information. A comparison of the *Rusticatio* with the *Praedium Rusticum* will show similarities in the choice of words, poetic devices, dramatic scenes, and epiclike struggles of humanized animals. The quest for realism in both poets is revealed by their utilization of scientific and historical treatises. Vanière, for example, bases his book on the bees on the observations made by Jacques-Philippe Maraldi, who placed a beehive in a glass enclosure in order to study the bee community. Landívar relies on similar authorities. The aim of Vanière, as well as that of Landívar, in keeping with the ideals of the Enlightenment, is to add to Vergil's excellence of expression an exactness of detail and "modern" scientific and technical knowledge.

For Landívar, nature herself is poetry, and natural sciences and physics are dignified by being expounded in verse. The poet is fascinated by such phenomena as the rainbow, the sources of streams, the weight and condensation of water, the effect of volcanic ash on cultivated land, mine gasses and explosions, to mention a few. His interest in technology is seen in his detailed explanation of the manufacture of sugar, and the precise functioning of the sugar-mill, or *trapetum* ("oil-mill" in classical Latin). He even supplies a very fine labelled illustration, drawn in his own hand. His observations are often supported by footnotes, which include references to authors, an indication of his concern with exactness of detail and truth. The poet defines this aesthetic position at the beginning of his work. He invokes Apollo:

> Tu mihi vera quidem, sed certa rara canenti
> Dexter ades. (I.30–31)

In the "Preface" (*Monitum*),[12] he stresses the absence of fiction in his poem, and, in an enlightened tone, assures us that he ascribes no intelligence or power to the pagan deities that he depicts. He will relate only what he has seen, what trustworthy eye-witnesses have told him, or what can be corroborated by totally reliable sources.

Landívar's enlightened mind, in accord with the scientific spirit of his age, manifests itself in different ways. Many passages involve the discussion of a perplexing or unusual physical phenomenon. For example, the poet seeks out the causes in order to explain a mysterious spring that bubbles up in the midst of beautiful Lake Chalco (I.88–114). An inference is that moisture from condensed air trickles through the ground and eventually forms a spring. It is possible too that the spring is actually filtered seawater. The preferred theory, accepted by Landívar and based on inductive reasoning, is that the spring originates from the melting snows of two nearby mountain peaks. This is one of the many instances of the inquiring mind of the keen and serious observer, and shows a certain kinship with Lucretius.

Another theme related to enlightened thought in the *Rusticatio* is the distastefulness and injustice of political tyranny in the folkloric tale of King Atzcapotzalco (I.140–98). This king forced his subjects to drag to him across Lake Chalco, as tribute, floating gardens called *chinampas*. The poet points out the keenness of mind of these people who penetrated the forests in search of the broom trees from which they fabricated wicker mats for the gardens. The description of the people at work is vigorous, and the pleasure that honest and profitable labor inspires is reminiscent of Vergil's ideal in the *Georgics*. The entire picture of their optimistic activity brings to mind the scene in the *Aeneid*, in which Aeneas contemplates the Tyrians building up a new and magnificent city. Thanks to their foresight and industriousness, the Mexicans not only please the tyrant by complying with his demands, but they also reserve for themselves some of the floating orchards. The implication is that more has been achieved by a rational solution, a kind of compromise based on thoughtfulness, hard work, and ingenuity.

Landívar's respect for science and common sense, and opposition to popular ignorance, is seen in Book II, which describes the earthquake that accompanied the famous eruption of Jorullo, in Michoacán, in 1759. (We are reminded of

Lucretius's discussion of earthquakes and volcanoes in Book VI of the *De Rerum Natura*.) This interesting phenomenon was first analyzed by Alexander von Humboldt,[13] and later became the subject of a book by the Cambridge zoologist, Hans Gadow. Gadow points out that Landívar's description was "the first printed account of the Jorullo volcano," and that this account is "reasonable and matter-of-fact."[14]

Landívar's fine dramatic description of the eruption and earthquake, with a Cassandra-like prophesier whom no one heeds, is Vergilian: The earth rocks crazily, homes totter, huts tumble over, roof-beams creak and sway, and even the marble temple is unsteady. The panic-stricken populace, wailing and weeping, frantically prays, and some place offerings upon the altars of "the Celestial Powers" (*Superum*). Landívar, in the tradition of Father Benito Jerónimo Feijoo, the Spanish encyclopedist, condemns this passive, unenlightened reaction, and has a priest rationally urge the people to cease praying and run. The model for the epic description of the earthquake is clearly the sack of Troy as told by Vergil. But all is not negative. Thanks to Jorullo, the climate is temperate and, although for several years after an eruption the land remains sterile, it eventually produces more than previously. The book on Jorullo is an interesting blend of native Americanism, Lucretian scientific curiosity, and Vergilian epic drama.

One of the most original and refreshing books of the *Rusticatio*, and very revealing of enlightened thought, is the sixth, on the "Beavers" (*Fibri*).[15] Evidence indicates that Landívar took most of his data from the article on the beaver in Valmont de Bomare's *Dictionnaire raisonné universel d'histoire naturelle*. Valmont, in turn, based himself on Buffon's *Histoire naturelle*. The impression that Buffon and Valmont de Bomare give of the beavers is anthropomorphic, and that these animals, just as men, can only function as a community based on love, peace, and altruistic cooperation. It becomes apparent that the poet, through the beavers, is indirectly setting forth his theory of the ideal society.

Landívar sees the beavers as not very attractive physically, but highly intelligent, noble, peace-loving, free from hatred, revenge, and deep concerns, and happy in their labor. They build their "houses" with the precision of engineers, and although they work collectively, each one preserves his individuality, selecting the house that best suits him. They also have an aesthetic sense, which is displayed by the way in which they plaster mud on the walls of the house, and then adorn it artistically with foliage.

Twice the poet employs the term *res publica* to signify the community of beavers, and notes that there exists among them the division of labor and a strong communal spirit. Overtired workers are replaced by solicitous comrades, and the young care for the elderly. In preparation for winter shortages, the beavers store away ample foodstuffs destined for communal use. Landívar emphasizes their idyllic life, in which there is no theft, vengeance, or strife, only love and tranquillity. All, however, comes to a bitter end when the beavers' worst enemy, "brutal man" (*violentus homo*), prompted by a lust for beaver pelts, wreaks havoc with the ideal republic. This admirable utopia ends wretchedly in so many pairs of "elegant boots" (*caligulas subtiles*).

Landívar's authorities, Buffon and Valmont de Bomare, basing themselves on second-hand reports, tend to over-humanize and romanticize the beavers. Landívar, under his rights as a poet, humanizes them even more; one inevitably calls to mind the classical utopias. There is a particular similarity between Book VI of the *Rusticatio* and Campanella's *Civitas Solis*. Of course, the representation of the communal state, with its emphasis on equality, peace, and personal freedom, belongs to that great current of ideas related to the theories of such enlightened thinkers as Rousseau, Voltaire, Montesquieu, Morelly, and Mably.

The most direct literary sources of Book VI appear to be Book XIV (*Apes*) of the *Praedium Rusticum*, and also the fourth *Georgic*, in which Vergil describes the life of the bees, their social organization, and common goal. The political and social theories that Vanière exposes in the *Praedium* are those that the eighteenth-century rationalists propose and develop. In the collective society of Vanière, there is no private wealth and no state authority. Each bee dedicates himself to the task he prefers, and in place of greed and hatred, there is generosity and love, as in the case of Landívar's beavers. In sum, the Utopia of Landívar is that of an imprecisely defined Christian communal society, clearly related to the traditional utopias as well as to the socio-political theories of his time.

Other Enlightenment-related subjects include practical matters concerning the economy, various types of agricultural and production procedures, a classification and description of livestock, and a kind of catalogue of birds and other wildlife. Much of what he deals with concerns the concept of the improvement of society. Often in unfolding these subjects a description will be lively, picturesque, and even humorous. An example is the delightful account of the *cercopithecus*, or long-tailed monkey of Nicaragua, and the means used to trap him. This monkey is homely, yet he has been endowed by nature with a cunning and intelligence unsurpassed by all other beasts. Landívar tells humorously how the monkey, who teases the crocodile by hanging from a branch, and, pretending to fall into the anxious, gaping jaws of his adversary, is merely staging an illusory effect. As the awesome mouth of the crocodile slams shut, our long-tailed friend swings gleefully from a limb, constantly feigning to lose his grip, exasperating the furious reptile until finally, giving up the useless combat, it sinks beneath the waters and repairs to its familiar haunts.

Quite amusing is the explanation of the ingenious trapping of the monkey by means of gourds. Indian hunters hollow out and dry two gourds, making a tiny aperture in each one. They then fill the gourds with small pebbles or grains of corn, so that when rattled, they produce a curious sound. These gourds are left in a vicinity where the monkeys are wont to congregate. Then, in a lively manner, a monkey is shown slipping down a tree, eagerly inspecting the gourds. The monkey proceeds to shake the "rattles," and anxious to find the cause of the noise, struggles to insert his fist into the gourd. Once he succeeds in doing this, he grabs a fistful of pebbles, and attempts to pull out his hand. This is impossible, due to the bulk of the pebbles, and so he thrusts his other fist into the second gourd, and while he struggles to extricate himself, unwilling to leave the mystery unsolved, our simian friend is snatched up by a hunter. A moral note is revealed by the Vergilian line "Tantus amor furti, furtumque notare libido!" (XIV.417). ("Such great love has he for theft, and such passion for contemplating the stolen object!")[16] This episode, with its ethical implication, clearly calls to mind the neoclassic didactic fable, a form of Enlightenment literature.

The *Rusticatio* concludes appropriately with a solemn exhortation to youth. Nature has endowed youth, says the poet, with a great enthusiasm for her mysteries: the sky, the song of birds as they fly through the heavens, the green meadows with their sweet flowers. Landívar the exile, drowning his sorrows and whiling away his idle moments along the banks of the Reno by composing verse, fully appreciates what it means to be young, idealistic, and enthusiastic about life and knowledge. He loves America, and realizes that her future prosperity will be determined by the intellectual paths taken by the new generation of thinkers and leaders:

> Disce tuas magni felices pendere terras,
> Divitiasque agri, praestantia munera coeli,
> Explorare animo, ac longum indagare tuendo.   (*Appendix*, 102–04)

Finally, in keeping with the spirit of his age, Landívar ends with the enlightened thought that is the mark of a modern man:

> Tu tamen interea, magnum cui mentis acumen,
> Antiquos exuta, novos nunc indue sensus,
> Et reserare sagax naturae arcana professa
> Ingenii totas vestigans exere vires,
> Thesaurosque tuos grato recludere labore.   (*Appendix*, 108 12)

These concluding sentiments coincide with those of many of Landívar's comrades-in-exile, who worked for the propagation of modern science and philosophy in Mexico, and opposed certain aspects of traditional Scholasticism. We have seen Landívar's enlightenment particularly in his scientific-rationalist approach, and also, although more indirectly and subtly, in his views on society.

It is not by chance that the *Rusticatio Mexicana* has become a classic of Spanish-American literature. By successfully imitating Vergil's language and assimilating his humanistic spirit, Landívar gave his subject a universal form. American scenic wonders and pictures of farm production and industry have been captured by the eye of the objective observer as well as by the fond recollections of a lonely, nostalgic exile. Alfonso Reyes, thinking both pragmatically and idealistically of Mexico's agrarian problem, suggested that both Vergil's *Georgics* and Landívar's *Rusticatio Mexicana* be read in the agricultural as well as elementary schools of Mexico: "This reading (i.e., of the *Georgics*) could be supplemented by fragments from our own *Georgics*—that is to say, Landívar's *Rusticatio Mexicana* (translated into prose by Loureda and into verse by Escobedo)—to bring home, in tangible fashion, the degree to which the classic spirit is meaningful for us, and even of national utility."[17]

Trinity College, Hartford

Notes

1. *Rusticatio Mexicana, seu rariora quaedam ex agris Mexicanis decerpta, atque in libros decem distributa a Raphaele Landivar* (Mutinae, 1781). Apud Societatem Typographicam. Graciela P. Nemes, "Rafael Landívar and Poetic Echoes of the Enlightenment," in *The Ibero-American Enlightenment*, ed. A. Owen Aldridge (Urbana, Ill., 1971), p. 298, cites the description of this edition in José Toribio Medina, *Noticias bio-bibliográficas de los jesuitas expulsos de América en 1767* (Santiago de Chile, 1914), adding that it is "an edition of 133 pages now merely known through a bibliographical notice." Nevertheless, there exist at least two copies, one in the British Library, and another in the John Carter Brown Library, Providence, Rhode Island. In her article (op. cit., pp. 298–306), Nemes makes some general and useful remarks about the *Rusticatio Mexicana* and its relation to the Enlightenment. My purpose in the present study is to show, by direct reference to the text of the *Rusticatio*, and by the tracing of Landívar's sources, how the poet incorporates elements of Enlightenment thought. I wish to add, at this point, that the translations from Latin and Spanish in this study are mine, with the exception of the one from Vergil, which is by J. W. Mackail, *Virgil's Works* (New York, 1950), and the quote from Harriet de Onis's translation of Alfonso Reyes's "Virgil in America," in *The Position of America and Other Essays* (New York, 1950).

2. *Raphaelis Landivar Rusticatio Mexicana*. Editio altera auctior, et emendatior (Bononiae, 1782). Ex Typographia S. Thomas Aquinitas. In 1950 there appeared in Guatemala a facsimile edition published by the University of San Carlos, with an introduction by José Mata Gavidia.

3. Ignacio Loureda, transl., *Rusticación Mexicana de Rafael Landívar*. Traducción literal y directa de la segunda edición de Bolonia, 1782 (México, 1924).

Two more translations have appeared since 1924: Octaviano Valdés, transl., *Por los campos de México* (México, 1942); segunda edición, primera bilingüe (México, 1965). Graydon Regenos, transl., *Mexican Country Scenes*. In *Philological and Documentary Studies*, vol. I, Middle American Research Institute. Tulane University (New Orleans, 1948), pp. 155–312.

4. Guatelmala, 1931.

5. Father Manuel I. Pérez published this biography in "El Padre Rafael Landívar, S.J.," *Estudios Centroamericanos* (San Salvador), 5, no. 40 (1950), 24–32.

6. "¿Por qué Landívar escribió en latín?," in *Homenaje a los poetas nacionales, Rafael Landívar y Fray Matías de Córdoba, de la O. P.* (Guatelmala, 1932), pp. 89–105.

7. Pérez, "Landívar," p. 30.

8. The *Praedium Rusticum* of Jacques Vanière, 1664–1739, the "French Vergil," is a manifestation of the passion of the eighteenth century for the didactic poem of the countryside. The first version of the *Praedium* appeared in 1707, and the definitive version of

sixteen books, in 1746. On the title-page of both editions of the *Rusticatio*, Landívar quotes
the following two lines from Book I (vv. 21–22) of the *Praedium*:

> Secreti tacita capior dulcedine ruris:
> Quod spectare juvat, placuit deducere versu.

9. "*Rusticatio Mexicana*," copia facsimilar ... op. cit., p. 31.

10. "*Rusticatio Mexicana*," in *Estudios Hispánicos. Homenaje a Archer M. Huntington* (Wellesley,
Mass., 1952), p. 607.

11. All quotes from the *Rusticatio* are from the Bologna edition of 1782.

12. pp. v–vi.

13. See *Cosmos: Sketch of a Physical Description of the Universe* (London, 1859), IV, 290.

14. *Jorullo. The History of the Volcano of Jorullo* ... (Cambridge, 1930), p. 85.

15. For a more complete analysis of Book VI, see my article, "El concepto de Utopía
de Rafael Landívar en la *Rusticatio Mexicana*," *RevIb*, 42, Nos. 96–97 (1976), 363–79.

16. Cf. "tantus amor florum et generandi gloria mellis" (*Georgic* 4.205). ("such is their
love of flowers and their pride in honey-making.")

17. "Virgil in Mexico," p. 153.

François Portus et les Tragiques grecs

Monique Mund-Dopchie*

S ans être un humaniste de premier plan, François Portus se signala à l'attention de ses contemporains et à la nôtre par sa vaste connaissance des littératures grecque et latine, ainsi que par une vie mouvementée, où les problèmes religieux jouèrent un rôle déterminant. A cet égard François Portus est bien un homme de son temps. Tout à la fois érudit et calviniste convaincu, celui que Jacques-Auguste de Thou proclamait "un des plus beaux ornemens de la Grèce" eut beaucoup à souffrir pour concilier les exigences de sa foi et celles d'une carrière commencée pourtant sous les plus heureux auspices.[1]

Né à Réthymnon en 1511, ce Crétois d'origine italienne avait suivi les cours d'Arsénios de Monembasie, savant collaborateur d'Alde Manuce, et il avait très tôt accompagné son maître dans la cité des Doges. Après quelques années dont nous ne savons pas grand-chose, François Portus se vit confier en 1536 la chaire de grec à l'université de Modène et il se lia d'amitié avec Giovanni Grillenzone et avec Ludovico Castelvetro. Il se laissa gagner par les idées de Calvin, ce qui lui valut ses premiers démêlés avec Rome. Obligé de signer un formulaire proposé par le Souverain Pontife, notre humaniste quitta en 1546 Modène pour Ferrare, où il fut protégé par Renée de France, épouse d'Hercule II, laquelle avait des sympathies pour la Réforme. Professeur de grec à l'université de Ferrare, précepteur des filles de la duchesse et membre de l'Académie des *Filareti*, François Portus ne jouit pas longtemps de la tranquillité indispensable à ses travaux et fut contraint par le duc d'Este à s'éloigner en 1554. Au cours de ses errances, il fut arrêté et traduit devant le Saint Office en septembre 1558. Absout de l'accusation d'hérésie, il fut condamné à séjourner deux ans à Venise. François Portus se décida alors à quitter l'Italie. Tandis qu'il s'apprêtait à rejoindre Renée de France, son ancienne protectrice, à Montargis, il reçut en septembre 1561 une lettre de Calvin lui offrant une chaire de grec à l'Académie de Genève et il accepta aussitôt cette proposition opportune. Commence désormais une carrière tout entière vouée à l'enseignement et à la recherche. C'est à la période genevoise que remontent les trois œuvres dont François Portus décida personnellement la publication: une traduction latine de quelques hymnes de Synésios de Cyrène et de Grégoire de Nazianze, imprimée par Henri Estienne en 1568, une édition des traités de rhétorique d'Aphthonios, d'Hermogène et du pseudo-Longin, sortie des presses de Jean Crespin en 1569, enfin, la *Responsio* à Pierre Carpentier, avocat et ancien professeur de droit à l'Académie de Genève, qui fut éditée en 1573 et dont la traduction française parut l'année suivante (il s'agissait d'une œuvre polémique, destinée à défendre la mémoire de Coligny et des autres victimes de la Saint-Barthélemy). Notre humaniste ne refusait pas non plus à cette époque de participer aux travaux d'autrui: c'est ainsi, par exemple, qu'il collabora à l'édition et à la traduction des poètes grecs mineurs, réalisées par Jean Crespin en 1569, et qu'il présenta Homère dans une préface à l'édition de l'*Iliade*, parue chez le même imprimeur en 1570.[2]

C'est toutefois à ses leçons que François Portus consacra l'essentiel de son temps: on sait de source sûre qu'il soumettait ses élèves, parmi lesquels on compte des hommes prestigieux comme Andrew Melville et Isaac Casaubon,[3] à des interrogations fréquentes et à des exercices réguliers d'interprétation personnelle. Il abordait avec eux des pans entiers de la littérature grecque et consignait par écrit le fruit de ses études. Aussi laissa-t-il à sa mort, survenue en 1581, à défaut de publications abondantes, de nombreux travaux inédits. Il n'est donc pas surprenant que son fils Émile, qui hérita d'une partie de ses papiers, ait pu se dire en mesure de faire imprimer des études de son père concernant l'*Iliade* et l'*Odyssée*, Pindare, Euripide, Thucydide, Démosthène, Xénophon, la *Rhétorique* et la *Poétique* d'Aristote, des opuscules de Plutarque, Hermogène, le pseudo-Longin et la poésie épigrammatique. Par ailleurs, il déplorait la disparition de plusieurs documents et comptait bien tout faire pour entrer en leur possession.[4] Parmi ces travaux inédits, acquis par Émile Portus et par d'autres, certains furent publiés à titre posthume entre le seizième et le dix-huitième siècle: un commentaire de la poésie de Pindare (Genève, 1583), une introduction à Sophocle et au περὶ παραπρεσβείας de Démosthène (Morges, 1584), un commentaire de Xénophon (Genève, 1586), une édition de la syntaxe d'Apollonios d'Alexandrie (Francfort, 1590), ainsi que des commentaires de la *Rhétorique* d'Aristote (Spire, 1598), du *Sublime* du pseudo-Longin (Amsterdam, 1733) et des œuvres de Denys d'Halicarnasse (Leipzig, 1774–77). D'autres ouvrages sont demeurés manuscrits; d'autres encore, signalés par Émile Portus, sont provisoirement ou définitivement perdus. Enfin, quelques analyses de François Portus nous ont également été transmises à travers les notes de cours de disciples et d'amis: je songe en particulier au *Parisinus Latinus* 7885, qui contient les *Praelectiones* à l'*Iphigénie à Aulis*, copiées par P. Enoch, et à un manuscrit de Modène, l'*Estense Latinus* 100 (alpha P.9.2), dans lequel Alessandro Sardi a transcrit un commentaire de quelques discours de Démosthène, de l'*Œdipe-roi* et de l'*Antigone* de Sophocle, des deux premiers chants de l'*Iliade* et du premier livre de Thucydide.[5]

Le savant Portus, en qui ses contemporains saluaient un "homo et Latinarum et Graecarum literarum cognitione excellens,"[6] ne pouvait manquer de s'intéresser et d'intéresser ses étudiants à l'œuvre des Tragiques grecs. Il le fit à différentes occasions, comme l'attestent six documents parvenus jusqu'à nous. J'ai déjà cité le manuscrit copié par Sardi, qui contient notamment les commentaires de deux tragédies de Sophocle, datés l'un du 18 novembre 1547, l'autre, du 14 décembre 1548, ce qui nous reporte à l'époque du séjour à Ferrare. Le second document est le volume des *Tragoediae selectae Aeschyli, Sophoclis, Euripidis. Cum duplici interpretatione Latina, una ad verbum, altera carmine*, édité par Henri Estienne en 1567, dans lequel François Portus a revu la traduction en prose de l'*Électre* et de l'*Antigone* de Sophocle réalisée par Vitus Winshemius. Le troisième document est le manuscrit de P. Enoch, dont j'ai déjà parlé, qui se réfère à un cours fait sur l'*Iphigénie à Aulis* d'Euripide à Genève en novembre 1567. Le quatrième et le cinquième document concernent Eschyle: il s'agit d'un exemplaire de l'édition d'Eschyle réalisée par Pier Vettori et parue en 1557, qui a appartenu à François Portus et qui a été annoté par lui, ainsi que d'un manuscrit autographe comportant un commentaire des sept tragédies d'Eschyle: l'un et l'autre sont conservés à la Rijksbibliotheek de l'Université de Leyde (B.P.L. 180 et 756 D 22) et se réfèrent à un travail que la critique interne permet de situer vers les années 1569-73.[7] Enfin, et ce n'est pas l'œuvre la moins intéressante, nous disposons des *Prolegomena in omnes Sophoclis tragoedias*, qui, avec une introduction à Démosthène et six discours prononcés à Modène, constituent l'échantillon qu'Émile Portus livra au public en 1584 en attendant la mise sous presse de l'ensemble de l'œuvre de son père.

Ne pouvant me livrer ici à une étude exhaustive de ces six œuvres, je me contenterai d'en évoquer deux aspects. Je tenterai d'abord de montrer comment François Portus concevait un cours d'auteurs, quels étaient ses centres d'intérêt, ses manies, voire ses lacunes. Me situant ensuite au plan de la critique littéraire, je m'efforcerai de préciser le jugement que cet humaniste portait sur chacun des Tragiques grecs: professeur éminent et apprécié de ses élèves, il devait immanquablement orienter leurs goûts et assumait ainsi une part de responsabilité dans la qualité de la survie qui fut assurée aux trois dramaturges athéniens.

Lorsqu'il explique Eschyle, Sophocle ou Euripide, nous observons d'emblée que François Portus ne cherche pas à traduire fidèlement en latin le texte qu'il étudie; il manifeste, au contraire, une répugnance invincible à l'égard de la version mot-à-mot, comme de la translation littéraire, et préfère paraphraser les vers, les introduire et même les gonfler. Cette démarche lui évite les chausse-trapes d'un texte épineux ou maltraité par la tradition: car il peut se contenter d'en donner le sens global, sans entrer dans les détails; cela lui est assurément fort utile lorsqu'il se trouve devant certains vers d'Eschyle, qui font aujourd'hui encore le désespoir des philologues les plus chevronnés...

Mais il ne faut pas en conclure pour autant que ce goût pour la paraphrase n'est qu'une dérobade devant la difficulté. Tout d'abord, François Portus reconnaît volontiers les obstacles dressés sur la route du traducteur par un texte trop dense ou mal établi et il lui arrive même de s'avouer vaincu. Ainsi, à propos d'un

extrait de l'*Agamemnon* d'Eschyle (vv. 1468 sqq.), où il est question à mots couverts de l'esprit vengeur qui hante la famille des Atrides et la pousse à se détruire
indéfiniment, notre humaniste écrit non sans humour:

> Incidimus iam in aenigmata quae desiderant Oedipodis acumen. Tentabi
> mus tamen pro tenuitate nostrarum virium discutere istius loci tenebras et
> eum illustrare (B.P.L. 180, ff. 183ᵛ⁻ 184ʳ).

De plus, et ceci est essentiel, François Portus s'efforce de donner de chaque passage un commentaire précis. Tantôt il nous explique les nuances de l'un ou l'autre
terme de vocabulaire, opposant, par exemple le substantif ἀστήρ, qui désigne une
étoile isolée, à ἄστρον, qui peut désigner également un ensemble d'étoiles (*Lat.*
7885, f. 2ᵛ; tantôt il rappelle l'origine d'une métaphore, tantôt encore il décrit
une coutume, une institution, un culte, se livrant à ce que nous appelons une
étude de *realia*: je songe, par exemple, à la description de la cérémonie préliminaire
du mariage, nommée προτέλεια, que notre humaniste fait à propos d'Iphigénie
fiancée à Achille (*Lat.* 7885, f. 32ʳ). Il ne craint pas non plus d'aborder occasionnellement un problème de critique textuelle, qu'il résout avec plus ou moins de
bonheur. Enfin, et là malheureusement il se trompe souvent, il propose volontiers l'une ou l'autre étymologie.

Tout concourt donc à nous prouver que l'utilisation de la paraphrase ne représente pas pour Portus une solution de facilité. Elle est, au contraire, un choix
délibéré: François Portus s'efforce, en effet, de donner à son auditoire, non pas
une traduction latine qui pourrait supplanter le modèle grec, mais les éléments
indispensables pour rendre le texte original intelligible à ses lecteurs; il le fait
avec une érudition remarquable, comme en témoignent ses nombreuses références à différents auteurs classiques et aux humanistes qui l'ont précédé, parmi
lesquels Érasme se révèle le plus prestigieux.

A côté de ces explications techniques que ne renierait pas un professeur du
vingtième siècle, François Portus se livre à une étude de style et il s'intéresse à
l'art de l'écrivain. Empruntant aux auteurs des traités de rhétorique qui lui sont
familiers, leurs définitions et leurs critères, il relève régulièrement hyperboles,
polyptotes, prosopopées, périphrases, anacoluthes, amplifications et transitions,
pour ne citer que quelques figures; de même, il se plaît à souligner le caractère
poétique de certains mots utilisés et signale les effets obtenus par différents procédés. Ainsi, il admire pour son élégance la tirade de l'*Agamemnon* décrivant la
chaîne des flambeaux, qui, de Troie en Argolide, annonce la victoire des Grecs
(B.P.L. 180, f. 116ᵛ); il observe que le style familier auquel recourt parfois Euripide ne convient pas au caractère hiératique de la tragédie et que le grand Sophocle évite ce genre d'impair (*Lat.* 7885, f. 11ʳ). Et s'il approuve sans réserves les
plaintes pathétiques de la malheureuse Iphigénie (*Lat.* 7885, ff. 84ᵛ et 86ᵛ), il
dénonce régulièrement l'obscurité du verbe eschyléen, qu'il croit délibérée (B.P.L.
180, ff. 11ʳ, 112ᵛ, 116ᵛ, 117ᵛ, 118ʳ etc.). C'est là, en l'occurrence, un des rares
jugements personnels que François Portus s'autorise à formuler; car il s'abrite

généralement derrière les opinions de ses maîtres à penser, Aristote, Hermogène, le pseudo-Longin et Quintilien, qu'il ne remet jamais en cause.

Il est une autre caractéristique de notre humaniste qui mérite notre attention et qui le distingue de beaucoup de ses confrères: François Portus se préoccupe des problèmes posés par la mise en scène des tragédies; il n'oublie pas que celles-ci sont dotées d'une vie propre et qu'elles ont été jouées devant un vaste public. C'est pourquoi il veille à décrire les va-et-vient des personnages sur scène, les différents décors, les sentiments éprouvés par les spectateurs, et même l'emploi d'une machinerie, si rudimentaire soit-elle. De là cette évocation enthousiaste de la scène initiale de l'*Œdipe-roi*, avec les ornements magnifiques de l'autel et de la statue de Zeus, avec la foule des suppliants agitant des rameaux d'olivier; avec un prêtre majestueux et un Œdipe attirant tous les regards pas ses habits somptueux; de là aussi cette allusion à la terreur que devait susciter la vue des corps meurtris d'Agamemnon et de Cassandre amenés sur la scène au moyen de l'eccyclème, sorté de plateau pivotant. De là encore cette constance à préciser quels sont les personnages qui entrent et qui sortent dans la tragédie d'*Iphigénie à Aulis* et je pourrais multiplier les exemples de ce genre. Par de telles remarques, François Portus prend ses distances vis-à-vis de ces commentateurs qui se bornent à la lettre du texte ou de ces professeurs qui recherchent à tout prix chez les anciens des leçons de morale. C'est pourquoi on regrette amèrement qu'il n'ait pas voulu, du moins dans les œuvres qui sont parvenues jusqu'à nous, regrouper toutes ces remarques judicieuses dans un ensemble cohérent; chez François Portus, la synthèse fait défaut.

Il me reste à présent à considérer, à travers les remarques disséminées dans les écrits de François Portus, l'opinion que celui-ci s'est forgée à propos de chacun des dramaturges athéniens.

Pour aller à l'essentiel, je dirai qu'à ses yeux, Eschyle est le parent pauvre de la tragédie grecque. Sans doute mérite-t-il des éloges pour avoir conçu quelques belles scènes, comme l'arrivée des Océanides sur leur char ailé dans le *Prométhée enchaîné* (B.P.L. 180, f. 207ᵛ), mais il souffre également de faiblesses graves: il recourt à un langage obscur et surtout, il manque de mesure. Toutefois, ce sont des fautes excusables, si on songe qu'Eschyle est un ancêtre, dont l'art mal dégrossi annonce et prépare la perfection d'un Sophocle:

> Quanquam possumus poetam excusare, quia eius temporibus tragoedia erat adhuc rudior et non ita exculta ut eam postea Sophocles eam expolivit (B.P.L. 180, f. 106ʳ).

Sophocle, en revanche, récolte tous les lauriers: il est "semper gravis, semper tragicus, semper sublimis et grandiloquus." De plus, il tempère la hauteur tragique par un sens poétique des plus fins, qui le place sur le même pied qu'Homère (*Prolegomena*, p. 13). Sa mise en scène est généralement excellente, son *Œdipe-roi* représente la tragédie parfaite, qui fait le meilleur usage de tous les artifices dramatiques et qui utilise une élocution remarquable; son *Œdipe à Colone* est une tragédie ingénieuse, qui ménage bien ses effets, tandis que son *Philoctète* est une œuvre d'édification tout à fait réussie.

Quant à Euripide, s'il se révèle légèrement inférieur à son concurrent, il offre cependant un éventail non négligeable de qualités: il est plus simple, plus proche de l'âme populaire et davantage influencé par l'art oratoire; prolixe en lieux communs et en propos sententieux, il n'exploite pas moins admirablement le pathétique des situations et des événements. Il peut être τραγικώτατος, mais aussi composer des drames qui, à l'instar des *Suppliantes*, s'apparentent plutôt à la tragicomédie.

Tout comme les observations sur le style, ces jugements de François Portus s'avèrent, à l'analyse, très peu originaux. Ici aussi l'humaniste se contente de répéter les opinions formulées par les auteurs de traités de rhétorique et il les reproduit sans les critiquer ni les situer dans leur contexte. Ce faisant, il déforme quelque peu la portée de telles remarques et leur confère une valeur absolue que celles-ci ne comportent pas. Prenons, par exemple, le cas d'Eschyle dont Portus et plusieurs érudits font un auteur primitif, voire primaire — une opinion qui prévaudra pendant plus de deux siècles. Il est exact qu'Aristote, dans la *Poétique*, et après lui d'autres écrivains, comme Horace, Quintilien et Hermogène, mentionnent Eschyle presque exclusivement comme fondateur d'un genre tandis qu'ils expriment leur admiration pour Sophocle et pour Euripide en des termes fort semblables à ceux que j'ai rapportés. Mais il ne faut pas oublier que ces traités ont été rédigés après le tournant décisif constitué par le mouvement des sophistes, qui ont privilégié l'éloquence, modifié la conception du théâtre et répandu de nouvelles règles esthétiques. Or les tragédies d'Eschyle sont antérieures à ce mouvement: elles relèvent d'une optique différente et, si elles ne séduisent guère les philosophes des quatrième et troisième siècles, elles ont été fort appréciées par le public contemporain et par une bonne partie de la génération suivante représentée par Aristophane; rappelons à cet égard que ce dernier propose un classement des trois Tragiques radicalement différent de celui d'Aristote. On peut donc légitimement estimer que François Portus, s'il avait eu un peu plus de perspective historique, aurait peut-être apporté quelques correctifs à des opinions trop catégoriques.

Le moment est venu d'établir la synthèse de ces premières investigations. Je le ferai en sachant qu'elles seront partielles et, par conséquent, provisoires. Il ne peut être question ici de prononcer sur l'activité de Portus des avis définitifs en me fondant sur une part aussi réduite de son œuvre.

Ceci étant posé, je ferai observer que François Portus ne se révèle pas inférieur à sa réputation d'expert de la littérature grecque. Son érudition affleure à tout propos: elle se révèle dans ses analyses du vocabulaire et des métaphores, dans ses citations abondantes et dans les descriptions qu'il nous fait des usages, des institutions et de la géographie de la Grèce. Il se distingue également de nombreux commentateurs des Tragiques grecs par ses préoccupations esthétiques: il s'intéresse à la qualité du style, se montre ouvert aux problèmes de la mise en

scène et se garde bien d'étudier la tragédie du cinquième siècle comme du théâtre en chambre. On regrettera seulement qu'il ait en ce domaine manqué d'en-
vergure et de personnalité et qu'il se soit contenté de reproduire, sans les repen-
ser, des présupposés véhiculés par des siècles de critique littéraire. Professeur con-
sciencieux et cultivé, il lui manque un peu cette intuition qui est la marque du
génie et qui survit à l'usure du temps.

Université Catholique de Louvain

Notes

*La documentation dont cet article fait état a été rassemblée grâce à un crédit du Fonds
National de la Recherche Scientifique de Belgique auquel j'exprime ma reconnaissance.
1. Sur la biographie de Portus, on consultera essentiellement: É. Legrand, *Bibliographie
hellénique* (Paris, 1885), t. II, pp. VII–XX; Ch. Borgeaud, *Histoire de l'Université de Genève—
L'Académie de Calvin, 1559-1798* (Genève, 1900), pp. 75-77 et *passim*; J. Sturm, *Beiträge
zur Vita des Humanisten Franciscus Portus* (Würzburg, 1903); F. C. Church, *I Italiani refor-
matori*, trad. D. Cantinori (Florence, 1935), t. II, 89-91, 100-02, 166-68; M. E. Cosenza,
Biographical and Bibliographical Dictionary (Boston, 1962), t. IV, 2497-98 et V, 379, n° 1475.
2. Les œuvres éditées et inédites de F. Portus, dont je dresse ici une liste toute provisoire, sont mentionées le plus souvent dans les ouvrages de É. Legrand, J. Sturm et M.
E. Cosenza, auxquels je renvoie le lecteur. Sur les travaux de Portus publiés par Jean
Crespin, on consultera avantageusement: J.-F. Gilmont, *Bibliographie des éditions de Jean
Crespin 1550-1572* (Verviers, 1981), t. I, 210-11, 217-20, 226-28.
3. Sur les relations de Portus avec Melville et Casaubon, voir Ch. Borgeaud, *Histoire
de l'Université de Genève...*, pp. 110, 210-11, 226-28.
4. Cf. *Francisci Porti Cretensis in omnes Sophoclis tragoedias προλεγόμενα ... His addita
παρασκευὴ ad orationem Demosthenis περὶ παραπρεσβείας, cui accesserunt sex oratiunculae latinae...*,
(Morges, 1584), p. 7; M. Crusius, *Turcograeciae libri octo...*, (Bâle, 1584), p. 534.
5. Cf. P. O. Kristeller, *Iter Italicum* (Leyde, 1963), p. 378.
6. *Catullus et in eum commentarius M. A. Mureti* (Venise, 1554), f. 57ᵛ.
7. Sur ces études d'Eschyle, je renvoie à mon livre, *La survie d'Eschyle à la Renaissance.
Éditions, traductions, commentaires et imitations* (Louvain, 1984).

Freedom of Speech and the Emblem Tradition

Peggy Muñoz Simonds

F reedom of speech as a democratic concept did not find a prominent
Renaissance advocate until John Milton wrote his brilliant *Areopagitica*
in defense of unlicensed publishing. This was a seventeenth-century
phenomenon. However, I have found that popular emblem books written in the
sixteenth century contain a surprising number of bitter complaints about the *lack*
of free speech within the splendid secular courts of the period. In this paper I
shall examine some representative emblems on this theme from the works of Andrea Alciati, Hadrianus Junius, Johannes Sambucus, and the English emblematist
Geffrey Whitney. These emblems, most of which derive from the writings of Erasmus, all comment critically on the difficulties and the dangers of speaking the
truth at court.

The necessity for free speech on the part of counselors to the prince was, of
course, widely recognized throughout Europe, although the problem was usually
discussed obliquely. In the early sixteenth century, Niccolò Machiavelli argued
in Chapter 23 of his *Il Principe*, first, that a prudent ruler should always encourage
trusted advisers to tell him the truth and, second, that he should in turn listen
carefully to what they have to say before making his final decisions. Machiavelli's
third point may seem strange to us in this age of popular opinion polls. He insisted that the prince should not listen to anyone other than his counselors, men
who should have been chosen for their wisdom, or he will fall prey to flatterers
and to the confusion of too many differing opinions. These three major points
are repeated in varying forms by other Humanists writing advice to princes and
to their courtiers for the next one hundred years. For example, in 1528 Baldassare
Castiglione suggested in *Il Libro del Cortegiano* that, since the principal duty of a
courtier is to instruct his prince in virtue, the prince must in turn be willing to
listen to such counsel.[1] Through the *persona* of Lord Octavian, Castiglione firmly
advises the true courtier to leave the service of any tyrant who will not pay attention to sound advice, "lest hee beare the blame of his Lords ill practises, or feel
the hartgriefe that all good men have which serve the wicked."[2] Erasmus of Rotterdam shared similar concerns. In his commentary on the adage "Sapientes tyranni

sapientum congressu" ("Kings grow wise by the society of wise men"), he adds the wry observation that "most of them choose to grow foolish with fools."[3]

Erasmus apparently believed that flattery of princes was the real crux of the problem; therefore, he included an entire chapter entitled "The Prince Must Avoid Flatterers" in his little book on *The Education of a Christian Prince*. Since flattery, or dishonest speech, by some courtiers often interferes with the rights of others to speak truthfully to a prince, Erasmus warns as follows:

> Let no one think that the evil of flatterers (being a sort of minor evil) should be passed over: the most flourishing empires of the greatest kings have been overthrown by the tongues of flatterers. Nowhere do we read of a state which has been oppressed under a great tyranny in which flatterers did not play leading roles in the tragedy.[4]

In addition, Erasmus emphasized the importance of actively encouraging all trusted counselors at court to speak honestly without fear of reprisals:

> the prince should accustom his friends to believe that they will gain favor by giving frank advice. It is the part of those who are closely associated with the prince to give him counsel that is seasonable, appropriate, and friendly.[5]

In other words, the courtier should of course be tactful in his manner of offering advice. But in case he is not, Erasmus further adds that "It will be well for the prince to pardon those whose counsel is crudely given, so that there may be no example to deter his good counselors from their duty."[6] The point is illustrated through an amusing story about Philip of Macedon. Although the Greek king was incensed when a courtier informed him that he did not look graceful "when seated with his cloak pulled up to his knees," he ultimately pardoned the man. "What he did in a trivial matter," argues Erasmus, "should be done much more by a prince for his country during serious events; for example, in undertaking a journey to foreign lands, in revising the laws, in establishing treaties, in beginning war."[7] Not surprisingly, such critical commentators on life at court as Machiavelli, Castiglione, and Erasmus set the stage for the sixteenth-century emblem writers who often quote them.

Among the emblematists, Erasmus's countryman Hadrianus Junius — Dutch physician and historian — was perhaps the most vehement on the need for princes to listen to all sides of any question. He addressed the problem very directly in emblem number 48 of his *Emblemata*, first published by Christopher Plantin in 1565. The motto or *inscriptio* of the emblem states, "Princeps ne cui aures seruas praebeat,"[8] ("Let the Prince not furnish slavish ears to anyone"), and the *pictura* shows the god Jupiter on the back of an eagle hovering over the natural world (Fig. 1). The *subscriptio* or verse offers the following discreet advice to princes:

> A statue of Jove high in the air, lacking an open ear,

>Minoan Crete had dedicated.
>It is characteristic of a Prince, moderating his kingdom
>											with skillful reign,
>Not to lend a slavish ear to anyone.[9]

By couching his advice in negative terms, Junius is tactfully suggesting that in fact most princes do tend to listen only to one side — that which is presented to them by their flatterers. But justice cannot thrive in such an atmosphere. In his commentary on the emblem, Junius is even more forthright in his criticism. First, he explains that the idea comes from Plutarch's *Isis and Osiris* which informs us that

> In Crete there was a statue of Jove without ears: by which symbol the artificer wished to suggest that a prince, or whoever has authority over all, ought not to give his ears in servitude to anyone, that is, to so accommodate the other's wishes as to make his ears seem to be the other's possessions, and to put the latter in a position to abuse their compliance.

Junius, however, is no democrat. Like Machiavelli, he is as much concerned that princes should not listen to the multitude as that they should give ear to both sides of a question. Thus he reminds his readers that only the opinions of the educated, or wise men, must be heard, or the prince will debase himself:

> Nothing is more pernicious than that the prince should leave his ears open to everything: as Marcellinus proclaims in book 16 of his work on Constantine the Great, casting aspersion of turpitude on that great Emperor; against which fault the same author in book 18 cites a famous saying and maxim of Julianus his cousin, who he declares was steadfast in his duties as one who distinguishes the just and the unjust: and he attaches a laudable anecdote by way of example, which is as follows: when Numerius, rector of the province of Narbonne, was accused of embezzling public funds, he easily explained away the basis of the charge by reference to his accounts, but the orator Cephidius bitterly opposed the man's innocence and, deprived of documentary evidence, he exclaimed: "No one would ever be found guilty, if denial were sufficient." Julianus wisely replied, "And who then will be found innocent, if accusation were sufficient?"

Junius then adds that "Alexander of Macedon acted accordingly, when he covered one ear with a hand in order to keep it in reserve for the defendant."[10] We should recall at this point that Alexander claimed descent from Jupiter Ammon, the very god whose earless statue became synonymous with the idea of objective justice in the sixteenth century. Even the English clergyman Stephen Batman, who seems to disapprove of the Renaissance fascination with pagan gods, mentions this peculiar aspect of Jupiter in *The Golden Boke of the Leaden Gods* published in 1577: "His want of Eares declare him to be indifferent unto all, not harkening more to one than to an other."[11]

Most emblem writers, however, attack the problem of free speech a little more indirectly. They complain that courtiers cannot in fact give frank advice to the prince because there are so many false flatterers at court. Junius himself wrote a particularly ferocious warning against such courtly sycophants, although he was certainly as capable of flattery as any man of his time. The elaborate dedication to Queen Elizabeth I of the English translation of his book *The Lyves of Philosophers and Oratours: Written in Greeke by Eunapius* is a case in point.[12] Nevertheless, in emblem number 22 of his *Emblemata* (Fig. 2), Junius uses the blunt *inscriptio* "Adulator Saluti Reip. Grauis" or "The Flatterer is a threat to public health" as a suggestion to princes that they should not tolerate excessive adulation. The *pictura* illustrates a lion eating a monkey, which in this case symbolizes a flatterer or a mere simulation of the true courtier. The *subscriptio* reads:

> As the lion, tormented by the savage power of a hidden sickness,
>   Feels better immediately after devouring a monkey,
> So the king who ejects flatterers and base sychophants from
>   his palace,
> Rids his kingdom of a grievous poison.[13]

The curious information that lions eat monkeys for medicinal purposes derives from such venerable sources as Pliny's *Natural History*, the *Hieroglyphics* of Horapollo, a sermon of St Augustine, and the Latin bestiaries of the Middle Ages.[14] Thus we find the image appearing in a number of sixteenth-century emblem books.

The *pictura* of Johannes Sambucus's version of the emblem shows two men bringing a monkey to the lion (Fig. 3). The Sambucus motto is "Cedendum, sed non adulandum" ("Yield but do not idolize"), suggesting that the courtier be diplomatic but that too much flattery can be dangerous to himself as well as to the prince. The *subscriptio* reads as follows:

> When the lion is hard pressed by serious or fatal ills,
>   A monkey is thrown to him: this is medicine for the sickness.
> You princes afflicted by the envious and base-minded,
>   Why do you not play the same game and relieve your distress
>   with little simians?
> He simulates and imitates all this, he begins to play the game,
>   Who is sick with the same disease and experiences the
>   same hunger.
> And indeed one must take care not to strive to please beyond
>   all measure;
>   The flatterer is a pest and can expect to come to a bad end.
> While you follow the life at court, be you as low in rank
>   As you may, yet be of good simplicity.[15]

But, of course, one generally went to court precisely in order to advance in rank and to win golden chains and badges of office from the prince. This, say the emblematists, is indeed a precarious game for the courtier.

Andrea Alciati points out the practical impossibility of free speech for courtiers in his *Emblemata* of 1534. The *pictura* of "In aulicos" ("On courtiers") depicts a well-dressed bearded man wearing his golden chain of office but sitting in stocks in a palace courtyard (Fig. 4). The verse informs us bitterly yet succinctly that "Palace vassals, produced by vainglorious courts, / are said to be fettered in golden shackles."[16] Thus, although the first prerequisite of good counsel is the liberty to give it without fear of reprisals, Alciati indicates that courtiers do not in fact have such freedom. On the contrary, they are prisoners of the ruler and of their own greed for gold. Why else would they be at court? Alciati's emblem derives from the Erasmian adage "Aureae compedes" or "Golden fetters."[17] This is turn was partly inspired by Diogenes's cynical remark that Aristippus in golden chains at a royal court could not fly away even if he wanted to. One of the earliest classical sources of this "golden fetters" *topos* was Theophrastus, who scolded the philosopher Aristotle for remaining so long at the court of Philip of Macedon as Alexander's well-paid tutor. Julius Held has discussed Rembrandt's deliberate irony when he painted Aristotle hung with golden chains while contemplating the bust of blind Homer.[18] The emblem also recalls Thomas More's *Utopia*, in which the Anemolian Ambassadors are considered slaves by the natives because they arrive wearing chains of gold like those used in Utopia to symbolize disgrace and slavery.[19]

The later Plantin woodcut for the Alciati edition of 1577 of the courtier as a young man in stocks (Fig. 5) reached non-Latinists in England in the year 1586 when Geffrey Whitney published *A Choice of Emblemes*. This popular book was dedicated to Queen Elizabeth's favorite courtier, Robert Dudley, the Earl of Leicester. Whitney uses the Erasmian adage "Aureae compedes" as his *inscriptio* for the courtier emblem. His verse, which is considerably longer than Alciati's brief indictment of the despised "palace vassals," reads as follows:

> It better is (wee say) a cotage poore to houlde,
>   Then for to lye in prison stronge, with fetters made of goulde.
> Which shewes, that bondage is the prison of the minde:
> And libertie the happie life, that is to man assign'de,
> And thoughe that some preferre their bondage, for their gaines:
> And richely are adorn'd in silkes, and preste with massie chaines.
> Yet manie others liue, that are accompted wise:
> Who libertie doe chiefely choose, thoughe clad in gounes of frise,
> And waigh not POMPEYS porte, nor yet LVCVLLVS fare:
> And for to liue with CODRYS cates; a roote, and barly bonne.
> Where freedom they inioye, and vncontrolled liue:
> Then with the chiefest fare of all, attendance for to geue.
> And, if I should bee ask'd, which life doth please mee beste:
> I like the goulden libertie, let goulden bondage reste.[20]

Whitney directly quotes here a well-known proverb by the rhetorician Dionysius

Longinus that "Bondage is the prison of the mind," a significant point for a professional rhetorician to make. Clearly, Whitney interprets both Erasmus's adage and Alciati's emblem "In aulicos" as references to the courtier's real lack of free speech when asked for wise counsel. Whitney understands that wisdom itself cannot flourish without freedom of expression.

Perhaps the most moving cry of the emblematists for freedom of speech can be found in their use of "the bird in the cage" *topos*. The tradition began with Aesop, who was concerned not with free speech but with false reasoning. His fable pertained to "A Nightingale and a Bat":

> As a nightingale was singing in a cage at a window, up comes a bat to her, and asks her why she did not sing in the day, as well as in the night. Why (says the nightingale) I was catch'd singing in the day, and so I took it for a warning. You should have thought of this then, says t'other, before you were taken; for as the case stands now, y'are in no danger to be snapt singing again.

Aesop's moral was simply that "A wrong reason for the doing of a thing is worse than no reason at all."[21] Later, during the Christian era, the bird came to symbolize the soul imprisoned in the body, and Guillaume de la Perrière's emblem 38 in *Le Theatre des Bons Engins* stated that "The Bird Sings in Captivity" because it comforts him to do so.[22] But when we come to the *Emblemata* of 1565 by Junius, we find the picture of a caged bird now used to support an impassioned plea for freedom of speech (Fig. 6). One wonders if the emblem grew out of the personal experiences in scholarship of Junius himself, who by then was living in Haarlem and held the appointment of "historian of the states of Holland."[23]

The *inscriptio* of Junius's emblem 56 is the previously mentioned proverb by Dionysius Longinus, "Animi scrinium seruitus" or "Bondage is the prison of the mind." The *subscriptio* states

> The nightingale, messenger of spring,
> Falls silent when confined in a cage.
> Bondage is the cage of the spirit,
> And it shackles the tongue with a fetter.[24]

The succeeding commentary by Junius is an extraordinary plea for freedom in both oratory and in scholarship. He argues that the condition of bondage to a prince in intellectual matters is

> a halter on the spirit, which does not allow us to speak out freely and express what we have conceived in our mind, bound to the service of magnates or indeed prohibited by their tyranny, as if muzzled by a bridle; while liberty is the nurse and parent of eloquence. That [false eloquence] no doubt became rooted among tyrants from ancient times, and was adopted by princes, willing that their shameful deeds should be covered with the cloak of virtue, and that perfidy should be colored to look like good faith. That custom of

favoring vices, established by use and received into fashion, so corrupted
the character of writing by base servitude that nothing could be made healthy
in it; the sacrosanct confidence in historical truth utterly perished, and we
have nearly equated the infamous Busires with portents from the heavens.
Thence was thought out that ingenious punishment and reproach, by which
books were ordered to be committed to the flames by a Senatus-consultum
to please the Emperors (I shall not say scourges of the Earth); as Seneca
records concerning the writings of Labienus, or Tacitus concerning [the
writings of] Cremutius Cordus. The emblem is derived from Philostratus'
portrait of the sophist Scopelianus who, importuned by the Clazomenians
to conduct an exercise at home, replied, "The nightingale is to sing in his
cage." The picture speaks for itself, showing the nightingale enclosed in a
cage, but sitting idly and not flying.[25]

Significantly, Junius has shifted his metaphor from "not singing" to "not flying"
by the end of his impassioned commentary. The suggestion is that one may indeed have to write words of some kind when in bondage as a courtier to a prince,
but those words will not reach the spiritual heights of which the writer is capable.

Whitney's English version of "Animi scrinium seruitus" employs the same Plantin
woodcut of the caged bird and is followed by an even more critical *subscriptio* than
that of Junius:

> The Prouerbe saith, the bounde must still obey,
>   And bondage bringes, the freest man in awe:
> Who serues must please, and heare what other saye,
> And learne to keepe Harpocrates his lawe:
>   Then bondage is the Prison of the minde:
>   And makes them mute, where wisedome is by kind.
>
> The Nightingall, that chaunteth all the springe,
> Whose warblinge notes, throughout the wooddes are harde,
> Beinge kepte in cage, she ceaseth for to sing,
> And mournes bicause her libertie is barde:
>   Oh bondage vile, the worthie mans deface,
>   Bee farre from those, that learning doe imbrace.[26]

Thus the orator or scholar is advised in England to follow Harpocrates, the Egyp-
tian god of silence, and to say nothing at all when at court. Clearly the time is
now ripe for John Milton.

Whitney concludes his bitter emblem with the prayer, "Oh bondage vile, the
worthie mans deface, / Bee farre from those that learning doe embrace." To this
prayer, all of us gathered here to practice free speech at a far from silent scholarly
conference can surely add a resounding "Amen."[27]

Montgomery College, MD

Notes

My thanks to my friend and teacher Virginia W. Callahan, who introduced me to emblem literature. She is responsible for the English translations of the Latin texts given in notes 8 and 9; the others are by Roger T. Simonds (except n. 16).

1. Baldassare Castiglione, *The Book of the Courtier*, transl. Sir Thomas Hoby (1928; rpt. London and New York, Everyman's Library, 1966), p. 297.

2. ibid., pp. 300–01.

3. III.V.xcvii. Cited and translated by Margaret Mann Phillips, in *The 'Adages' of Erasmus: A Study With Translations* (Cambridge Univ. Press, 1964), p. 110.

4. Desiderius Erasmus, *The Education of a Christian Prince*, transl. Lester K. Born (New York, Columbia Univ. Press, 1936), p. 193.

5. ibid., p. 203.

6. ibid.

7. ibid., pp. 203–04.

8. Hadrianus Junius, *Emblemata* (Antwerp, Christopher Plantin, 1565), p. 54.

9. ibid.

> Sublimem aere Iouis statua, patula aure carente,
> Sacarat Minoia Creta.
> Principis est, regnum destra moderatis habena,
> Seruam ne cui commodet aurem.

10. ibid., pp. 139–40. The entire passage reads as follows in Latin: cc Desumptum est ex Plutarcho, libro de Iside saepius anteacitato, vbi sic ait. In Creta Iouis fuit statua, auribus mutila: quo symbolo innuere voluit artifex, principem & qui ius in omnes habeat, non debere alicui aures suas mancipio dare, hoc est, ita accomodare ut ab illo possessae videantur, ut que illarum osequio abuti queat. Nihil perniciosius est quàm quòd aures in omne patentes princeps habeat: id quod Marcellinus lib. 16. de Constantino Caesare praedicat, turpem tanto Imperatori maculam adspergens; contrà quàm praeclarum acroama & elogium Iuliano lib. 18. idem tribuit illius patrueli, quo praedicat eum personarum indeclinabilem iusti iniustique fuisse distinctorem: addito & documenti vice exemplo laudabili, quod huiusmodi est: nam cùm Numerius prouinciae Narbonensis rector, peculatus insimulatus, rationibus crimen obiectum facilè dilueret, ac Cephidius orator hominis innocentiam acerrimè oppugnaret, inopśque documentorum exclamaret: Neminem quenquam nocentem fore, si infitiari sufficeret: Iulianus sapienter ex tempore subecit, Ecquis tandem innocens erit, si accusasse sufficiet? Non alienum hinc est Alexandri Macedonis factum, altera manu opposita aurem obstruentis, ut reo seruaretur integra."

11. Stephen Batman, *The Golden Boke of the Leaden Gods* (London, 1577; rpt. New York and London, Garland Publishing, Inc., 1976), pp. 1–2.

12. Hadrianus Junius, transl. [into Latin], *The Lyves of Philosophers and Oratours: Written in Greeke, by Eunapius*, transl. into English by Richard Johnes (London, 1579).

13. Junius, *Emblemata*, p. 28. *Inscriptio* and *subscriptio*

> Vt Leo, quem cacci vis lancinat effera morbi,
> Sentit opem, si Simium edat, citam:
> Palponem et dirum sycophantam qui eiicit aula,
> Rex viru regnum vacuat graui.

14. See source listing in Arthur Henkel and Albrecht Schöne, *Emblemata* (Stuttgart, J. B. Metzlersche Verlagsbuchhandlung, 1967), p. 396, and T. H. White, *The Bestiary* (New York, C. P. Putnam's Sons, 1960), pp. 10–11.

15. Reprinted in Henkel and Schöne, p. 397:

Fatali, et grauibus premitur quando leo morbis,
Simia proijcitur: haec medicina mali est.
Inuidia afflictos, scelerata et mente Tyrannos,
Cur non sic ludas, simiolaque leues?
Haec simulat cuncta, atque imitatur, ludere nouit,
Hoc morbo aegrotis conuenit ista fames.
Sed tamen his vltra metam placuisse caueto,
Pestis adulator, morsque inimica siet.
Aulas dum sequeris ne te peruertat abusus,
Sit tenuisque licet, sed bona simplicitas."

16. Andrea Alciati, *Emblemata* (Paris, Christian Wechel, 1534), p. 117. Motto and verse translated by Virginia W. Callahan and William S. Heckscher:

Vana palatinos quos educat aula clientes
Dicitur auratis nectere compedibus.

17. II.III.XXV (531A).

18. Julius Held, *Rembrandt's Aristotle* (Princeton, Princeton Univ. Press, 1969), p. 35.

19. See Sir Thomas More, *Utopia*, eds. Edward Surtz, S. J. and J. H. Hexter (New Haven, Yale Univ. Press, 1965), pp. 155–56.

20. Geffrey Whitney, *A Choice of Emblems*, ed. Henry Green (London, 1886; rpt. New York, Benjamin Blom, Inc., 1967), p. 202.

21. Aesop, *Fables of Aesop According to Sir Roger L'Estrange* (New York, Dover Publications, Inc., 1967), p. 5.

22. Guillaume de la Perrière, *Le Theatre des Bons Engins* (Paris, Denys Janot, 1539), emblem 38.

23. Henry Green, ed., "Essay III" in *A Choice of Emblemes* by Geffrey Whitney, op. cit., p. 283.

24. Junius, *Emblemata*, p. 62:

Luscinia veris nuncia,
Mutescit inclusa cauea.
Est seruitus scrinium animi,
Linguam que vinclo praepedit.

25. ibid., pp. 146–47: "quòd ea sit animi retinaculum, neque sinat libero nos ore eloqui, & liberaliter expromere, quae animo concepimus, addicti magnatum servitio, vel saltem eorum tyrannide prohibiti, velut iniecto ori freno, cum libertas eloquentiae nutrix sit ac parens. Nimirum ea tyrannis ab antiquissimus temporibus inolevit a principibus usurpata, volentibus flagitia sua virtutum velaminibus tegi, perfidiam specioso fidei fuco induci. Ea favendi vitiis consuetudo, usu stabilita, atque in mores recepta, ingenia scribētium seruitute degeneri ita corrupit, ut nihil sit ab hac parte sani, ut sacrosancta illa historiarum fides penitus interierit, ut illaudatos Busires & portenta caelestibus propè aequemus. Inde excogitata fuit ingeniosa illa poena et animadversio, qua libri incēdio absumi iussi sunt Senatuscōsulto in Imperatorum, ne dicam orbis pestium, gratiam; quod de Labieni scriptis memorat Seneca, de Cremutij Cordi Tacitus. Emblema petitū est ex Philostrato in Scopeliani sophistae imagine, qui deprecatus operam à Clazomeniis imperatam, qua domi ludum aperiret, respondet, Lusciniam in cavea cantillare. Pictura per se evidens, lusciniam caveae inclusam, postulat, sed desidem, non volucrem."

26. Whitney, p. 101.

27. This essay is an offshoot of work I did on emblems (and their relation to Shakespeare's *Cymbeline*) in 1982, when I held a Fellowship for College Teachers awarded by the National Endowment for the Humanities.

Figure 2: Hadrianus Junius, *Emblemata*
(Antwerp, 1565), emblem 22 (By permission
of the Folger Shakespeare Library: PN 6349 J8).

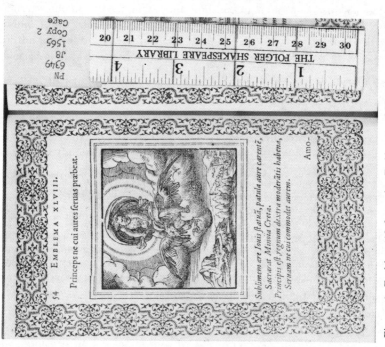

Figure 1: Emblem 48 from the *Emblemata* of Hadrianus Junius
published in Antwerp by Plantin in 1565
(By permission of the Folger Shakespeare Library: PN 6349 J8).

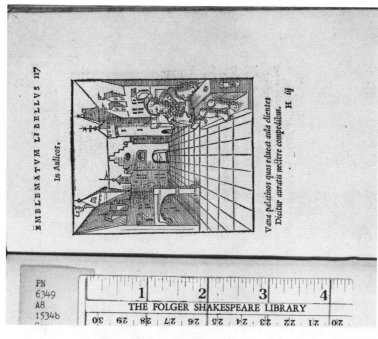

Figure 4: Andrea Alciati, *Emblemata* (Augsburg, 1534), p. 117 (By permission of the Folger Shakespeare Library: PN 6349 A8 1534b).

Figure 3: Johannes Sambucus, *Emblemata, et Aliqvot*, 4th ed. (Antwerp, 1576), p. 178 (By permission of the Folger Shakespeare Library: PN 6349 S2).

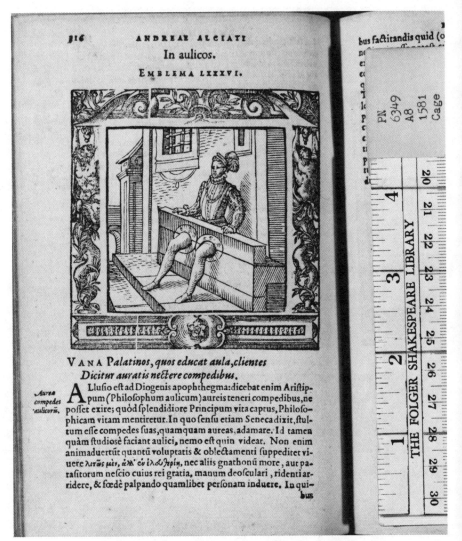

ANDREAE ALCIATI

In aulicos.

EMBLEMA LXXXVI.

VANA *Palatinos, quos educat aula, clientes*
Dicitur auratis nectere compedibus.

Aurea
compedes
aulicorū.

ALlufio eft ad Diogenis apophthegma: dicebat enim Ariftip-
pum (Philofophum aulicum) aureis teneri compedibus, ne
poffet exire; quòd fplendidiore Principum vita captus, Philofo-
phicam vitam mentiretur. In quo fenfu etiam Seneca dixit, ftul-
tum effe compedes fuas, quamquam aureas, adamare. Id tamen
quàm ftudiosè faciant aulici, nemo eft quin videat. Non enim
animaduertūt quantū voluptatis & oblectamenti fuppeditet vi-
uere λιτῶς μὲν, ἀλλ' ἐν ἐλϑϑ9ερίη, nec aliis gnathonū more, aut pa-
rafitorum nefcio cuius rei gratia, manum deofculari, ridenti ar-
ridere, & fœdè palpando quamlibet perfonam induere. In qui-
                                                                              bus

Figure 5: Andrea Alciati, *Emblemata* (Antwerp, 1577), p. 316
(By permission of the Folger Shakespeare Library: PN 6349 A8).

Poetic Digression and the Interpretation of Medieval Literary Texts

Marjorie Curry Woods

In medieval commentaries, glosses on specific words in the text frequently turn into digressions in which the commentator (often a teacher) introduces self-contained and often irrelevant bits of information and units of knowledge; then, without relating this new material to the word being glossed, he moves on to gloss another word. In a mid-thirteenth-century commentary on Geoffrey of Vinsauf's *Poetria nova* (written c. 1215), this kind of digression is specifically associated with the works of poets. The commentator says that the poet, "interrupting the subject, treats something else that comes up by chance, like the description of a place, or the nature of some thing, or some expression of praise and the like, and after this he returns to the subject he had dropped."[1] In an earlier article, I noted the pedagogical utility of this kind of digression in commentaries;[2] here I would like to extend my discussion of these digressions to examine the implications of associating them with poetry, implications that suggest that we may need to reconsider some of our notions of medieval poetry. Specifically, we may find that those digressions apparently leading nowhere (except away from the subject), which have heretofore seemed interruptive, disruptive, and confusing, should be seen by us, as I believe they were by their original audiences, as provocative, evocative, and even liberating.

Before examining this thirteenth-century commentary in more detail, let us review the description of digression in the *Poetria nova* itself and note some of the statements about it in other commentaries. Digression is treated in the *Poetria nova* as one of the kinds of amplification. First, Geoffrey says,

> If it is desirable to amplify the treatise yet more fully, go outside the bounds of the subject and withdraw from it a little; let the pen digress, but not so widely that it will be difficult to find the way back. This technique demands a talent marked by restraint, lest the bypath be longer than decorum allows.[3]
>
> (ll. 527–31)

Then he adds,

A kind of digression is made when I turn aside from the material at hand,
bringing in first what is actually remote and altering the natural order. For
sometimes, as I advance along the way, I leave the middle of the road, and
with a kind of leap I fly off to the side, as it were; then I return to the point
whence I had digressed.[4]   (ll. 532–36)

Thus Geoffrey notes first that one may lengthen the treatment of a subject by
moving away from it to another subject; the potential pitfall of this kind of digression is that one may wander too far away from the original topic. He then adds
that interrupting the natural order of the subject matter, inserting earlier something
that actually occurs later in the narrative, is another kind of digression.[5] This
second kind of digression is marked by an abrupt jump away from the subject,
rather than the gradual moving into a new area which characterizes the first kind.

   That there are two kinds of digression is noted by various commentators on
the text. For example, Guizzardo of Bologna, writing early in the fourteenth century, says that the first kind of digression "is the same thing as leaving the subject
for something useful to that subject."[6] One Cornutus Graftis makes a similar
remark, as we read in a manuscript dated 1424: this first kind of digression is
"leaving the subject for something which is outside it but nevertheless contributes
to it."[7] A fifteenth-century manuscript of the commentary by Bartholomew of
Pisa, who died in 1347, notes that the first kind of digression is accomplished
"by describing occasions, places, things that come in between, and the like."[8]

   As for the second kind of digression, bringing in a remote part of the same
subject, Guizzardo simply says that "it is the same thing as artificial order."[9] A
fifteenth-century manuscript of the commentary by Pace of Ferrara notes that
"the second kind is not properly digression but a certain inversion of the discourse."[10] Cornutus Graftis explains more fully that this second kind of digression occurs "when the rhetor has material of several parts, and after beginning
one part he moves from that first part and puts in something not of that part."[11]
Bartholomew of Pisa says that the second kind of digression "is when I leave some
things out and pass over them and afterwards return to those things which have
been left out"; he adds that "This kind doesn't really seem to amplify the material,
but the author gives it so that no one will think that the only kind of digression
is that which amplifies."[12]

   In some manuscripts the two kinds of digression are called *digressio propinqua*
and *digressio remota*, *digressio propinqua* being the introduction of a related (*propinqua*) but different subject, *digressio remota* the introduction of a remote part of the
same subject.[13] Two manuscripts also mention a distinction between *digressio utilis*
(or appropriate, useful digression) and *digressio inutilis* (that digression which does
not further the author's purpose). One of these manuscripts discusses *digressio utilis*
in terms of the works of *oratores*,[14] the other in the works of *dictatores*;[15] both, however, note that *digressio inutilis* is used by *insapientes*, and is condemned by Horace.
A number of commentators also note that Geoffrey first defines digression and

then gives examples, and that he tells both what should be done and what should be avoided in composing digressions.

The commentary quoted at the beginning, however, is the only one that I have found so far that, by redefining the second kind of digression, interprets Geoffrey's two kinds of digression as embodying different, complementary approaches to the new material introduced in the digression. In the first kind, the poet moves into a new subject that arises, which is then abandoned in his return to the original subject; in the second kind, an abrupt jump is made to what seems to be an unrelated topic that is then integrated into the original subject. The first creates a diagonal path away from the original subject, the second a diagonal path into it. Here is the full quotation:

> 527. IF ONE WISHES TO EXTEND FURTHER. He treats the sixth step, in which he says that the material is lengthened if a digression is made from the work that is begun. Such a digression, as he says, is made in two ways. It is made in one way when the poet, interrupting the subject, treats something else that comes up by chance, like the description of a place, or the nature of some thing, or some expression of praise and the like, and after this he returns to the subject he had dropped. The other way digression is made is when the subject is interrupted and another topic introduced which is far off, but in the end is applied to the subject.[16]

The commentator goes on to say that Geoffrey gives an example of the second kind, "but he gives no example of the first kind because it is common not only in the works of poets, but also in the works of historians," or, in another manuscript, "in the works of philosophers."[17] It is thus the first kind of digression, in which the *poeta* moves away from the subject and then jumps abruptly back to it, that is especially frequent *apud poetas*. The second kind is expressed in the passive voice, without a named agent, and is not specifically associated with the works of poets.

The commentator discusses further the distinction between the two kinds of digression, noting that in the first, which we have seen associated with poetry, the new subject seems closely related to the original one but is finally quite far removed, since it is abandoned. Rather than subtly integrating new material with the original subject, the kind of digression that one finds in poetry abandons the new subject in a crude and obvious way. In the second kind, what is introduced seems far removed at first but is made relevant later:

> These two kinds of digression differ in this, that in the former the idea which is introduced is at first more closely related to the subject which it interrupts, as was said; in the end, however, it is far removed, because it is left without being applied to the subject. In the other kind, however, what is introduced at first seems way off from the subject, but in the end it is appropriate because it is applied to the subject.[18]

A similar distinction can be seen in the commentator's earlier discussion of overt and hidden comparison, in which obvious, overt comparison, rather than the subtle, hidden kind, is associated with the works of poets. Geoffrey of Vinsauf discusses comparison as the third kind of amplification:

> A third step is comparison, made in accord with one of two laws — either in a hidden or in an overt manner. Notice that some things are joined deftly enough, but certain signs reveal the point of juncture. A comparison which is made overtly presents a resemblance which signs explicitly point out. These signs are three: the words *more*, *less*, *equally*. A comparison that is made in a hidden way is introduced with no sign to point it out. It is introduced not under its own aspect with dissembled mien, as if there were no comparison there at all, but the taking on, one might say, of a new form marvelously engrafted, where the new element fits as securely into the context as if it were born of the theme.[19]   (ll. 241–51)

Geoffrey develops the concept of hidden comparison at some length. The commentator, in moving through the text of the *Poetria nova*, also devotes more attention to hidden comparison, but relates the overt kind specifically to poetry:

> 241. A THIRD STEP IS. Next is the third, in which comparison is discussed. There are two kinds, overt comparison and hidden. Overt comparison is when a poet, wishing to evoke a quality of what he treats, turns it into something similar, so that he indicates the less familiar by means of the familiar. And he draws his vehicle from something similar, as in the *Alexandreis*, where the courage which Alexander had in his youth described. An overt comparison is introduced thus: "As if a young lion should see in the Hyrcanian fields / the stags with raised antlers," etc. This kind of comparison is found sufficiently in the works of all the poets, and particularly in these because they are clearly indicated by certain signposts.[20]

One manuscript reads "classical authors"[21] for "poets," and two state that this kind of comparison is found "particularly in the works of Statius."[22] The commentator goes on to say that hidden comparison is "when a different idea, taken from elsewhere, is inserted skillfully into the material, as if it seems to be from that material, even though it is not."[23] In this discussion of comparison, as in that of digression, a poet is named as the agent of the more obvious of two methods of expression, and the more obvious method is described as found in the works of poets.[24]

This early commentary is a particularly important one: it has survived in four mid-thirteenth-century manuscripts (in one copied as a separate text), and another partial copy was made a century later; there are more manuscripts of it than of any other thirteenth-century commentary on the *Poetria nova*, and more than of any other anonymous commentary on this work. Its statements about digression and comparison suggest that we may want to look again at some of our notions about medieval poetry. But first we must acknowledge that this association of certain techniques with poetry is based on non-evaluative observation: if a poet wants to write something, these are some of the ways he goes about it; if one wants to see examples of certain techniques, one looks in poetry. Thus poetry is the repository of obvious rather than subtle technique. The modern endowment of poetry and "the poetic" with numinous qualities is inappropriate here.[25] (Indeed, two manuscripts of the commentary note that hidden comparison is more artistic than the overt kind found in the works of poets.)[26] Subtlety may be more appropriate in the interpretation of poetry, in reading rather than in writing verse. For example, we might now see Dante's *Divina Commedia* as a simple and obvious work, the "Epistola a Can Grande" as a subtle interpretation of it.[27]

The emphasis on returning to the same subject and integrating new ideas into it, which the commentary associates with the second kind of digression, is valued highly as an aesthetic subtlety when found in prose, as in the admiring description by Peter, Prior of Holy Trinity, Aldgate, of a sermon by Gilbert Foliot: "It ran backwards and forwards on its path from its starting point back to the same starting point."[28] But the kind of digression often found in medieval poetry does not integrate new subjects, gathering them and making them relevant; rather, these digressions move away, out into new subjects that are then abandoned, not incorporated into the original subject. The emphasis is centrifugal, rather than, as with Gilbert Foliot, centripetal.

As modern readers, we are often resistant to this movement in poetry away from the subject and hesitant to confer aesthetic merit on disruptive structural elements. But during the last decade, the Post-Structuralists have called into question our desire for integration, unity, and hermeneutic circularity. And so perhaps now we can see the appropriateness of and power in moving *out*, in introducing excursions for their own sakes.[29] To do this, we shall have to educate ourselves fully in rhetorical poetics, in the attitudes toward and approaches to language that were taught during the Middle Ages. An appreciation of breaking out of the confines of a single subject in poetry is one result of medieval rhetorical training, which emphasized the polysemousness of words, the infinite flexibility of language, and the ability of the poet to use both for his own ends.

That the statements about digression on which I have based my argument are found in all of the manuscripts of this particular commentary (which manuscripts do not always agree in other matters of interpretation) and that the association of obvious technique with poetry is the same in the commentator's treatment of digression and comparison indicate that the extrapolation of a consistent argument from this evidence is appropriate. But the applicability of this interpretation of poetic digression and technique will have to be tested on a number of medieval poems before we can judge its universality. I suspect, however, that its importance does not lie in helping us to appreciate medieval digressions (we do that anyway), although it may help us to express our appreciation more positively and appropriately. The primary value of this directional view of digression

may be to enable us to see as digressions movements in works that heretofore
have been interpreted quite differently and then to appreciate their implications.

In conclusion, therefore, I would like to suggest an application of this argument to two of the most controversial passages in Middle English literature, the
conclusions of Chaucer's *Troilus and Criseyde* and the *Canterbury Tales*. Rather than
reinforcing his original subject at the end of each work, Chaucer moves away
from his subject, creating the kind of digression from which there is no possible
return to the original subject. For example, in *Troilus and Criseyde*, the stated subject is

> The double sorwe of Troilus to tellen,
> that was the kyng Priamus sone of Troye,
> In lovynge, how his aventures fellen
> Fro wo to wele, and after out of joye
> My purpose is, ere that I parte fro ye.   (I.1-5)

But at the end, first Troilus moves away from his own story to a perspective from
which no one would want to return, to "This litel spot of erthe ..., / This wrecch-
ed world" (V.1815-17).[30] Then the narrator, too, distances himself from the story
in which he has been so involved, with his acknowledgment of the "fyn" that "hath
false worldes brotlenesse" (1832). Finally, the author himself addresses his readers,
young lovers who might still be involved with the original subject of the woes
of love; he exhorts them to move with him,

> To thilke God that after his ymage
> You made, and thynketh al nys but a faire
> This world, that passeth soone as floures faire.   (V.1839-41)

At the beginning of the *Canterbury Tales*, we learn that it is to be a collection
of stories:

> This is the poynt, to speken short and pleyn,
> That ech of you, to shorte with oure weye,
> In this viage shal telle tales tweye
> To Caunterbury-ward, I mene it so,
> And homward he shal tellen othere two,
> Of aventures that whilom han bifalle.   (I [A] 790-85)

But at the end of the *Tales*, Chaucer moves as he has before to prose, this time
with the Parson, "To knitte up al this feeste, and make an ende" (X [I].47). As
Howard has pointed out, all the tales in the last fragment urge us toward a rejection of stories, of "telling" in any form.[31] When the author speaks at the end of
this work, it is from the place and perspective to which the Parson's tale has led
him. In his "Retraction," as at the end of the *Troilus and Criseyde*, Chaucer urges
his readers to pray, but here for him rather than for themselves, so that he "may
be oon of hem at the day of doom that shulle be saved" (X [I].1091). (If I am

correct in interpreting these endings as digressions in the medieval sense, then it is appropriate that Chaucer end both in his own voice. Two manuscripts of the commentary I have been discussing add a short introduction to the different kinds of amplification in which digression is called an act of speaking: *digressio* is an *exercicium loquendi* and an *actum dicendi*.[32] We may then, it seems to me, under certain circumstances associate digression with what in more modern terms we would refer to as the narrator's or authorial voice.)

In the conclusions of these two works, we move from the perspective of character to narrator to author, and from narrative subject to a place where narrative and subjects no longer have value and meaning. Chaucer journeys into areas that are related to the original subjects but are very different from them and lack final integration into the originally stated plans for the works. And these digressions break down the symmetrical structures implied by the stated subjects: the "double sorwe" of Troilus and the "tales tweye" and "othere two" by the Canterbury pilgrims. Chaucer digresses from these topics to new subjects which cannot be abandoned for a return to the original ones. The narratives of *Troilus and Criseyde* and of the *Canterbury Tales* are not reinterpreted at the end, but left behind.[33]

University of Rochester

Notes

1. The full quotation and manuscript references are found below in note 16.

2. See Marjorie C. Woods, "Literary Criticism in an Early Commentary on Geoffrey of Vinsauf's *Poetria nova*," *ACNL Bononiensis*, ed. Richard J. Schoeck (Binghamton, 1985), pp. 667–73.

3. "Si velit ulterius tractatus linea tendi, / Materie fines exi paulumque recede / Et diverte stylum; sed nec divertere longe / Unde gravet revocare gradum: modus iste modesto / Indiget ingenio, ne sit longior aequo," *Les Arts poétiques du xiie et du xiiie siècle*, ed. Edmond Faral (Paris, 1924; reprinted Paris, 1962), p. 213; Faral has classicized the spelling. The translation quoted is by Margaret F. Nims, *"Poetria Nova" of Geoffrey of Vinsauf* (Toronto, 1967), p. 35.

4. "Est etiam quaedam digressio quando propinqua / Transeo, quod procul est praemittens ordine verso. / Progressurus enim medium quandoque relinquo / Et saltu quodam quasi transvolo; deinde revertor / Unde prius digressus eram...." (Faral, p. 213; Nims, p. 35).

Geoffrey gives similar definitions, but in the opposite order, in his *Documentum de modo et arte dictandi et versificandi* (II.2; Faral, p. 274). One manuscript of the *Poetria nova* (Cambridge, Trinity College MS R. 14. 22, f. 13^v) gives the definition of digression from the *Documentum* as a gloss on part of the treatment of digression in the *Poetria nova*.

5. The treatment of amplification follows a section on natural and artistic order, in which the latter has been highly praised.

6. "idem est quod exitus materie ad quedam utila illi materie," Vatican Library, MS Ottob. lat. 3291, f. 6^r. This and the quotations that follow are short excerpts from longer

glosses on digression. Guizzardo taught at Bologna from 1289–1319 and wrote a commentary on, among other works, the "Epistola a Can Grande." See Bruno Nardi, "Osservazioni sul medievale 'Accessus ad Auctores' in rapporto all'Epistola a Can Grande," *Studi e problemi di critica testuale* ... (Bologna, 1961), pp. 273–305, especially 289–93.

7. "exitus a themate ad aliquod quod est extra materiam, conferens tamen aliquot propositum materie," Vienna, Nationalbibliothek MS 5001, f. 24ᵛ.

8. "describendo tempora, loca, res intervenientes, et huiusmodi," Rome, Biblioteca Casanatense MS 311, f. 23ʳ. On Bartholomew of Pisa, see Giuseppe Manacorda, "Fra Bartolomeo da S. Concordio Grammatico e la fortuna di Gaufredo di Vinesauf in Italia," *Raccolta di studi di storia e critica letteraria dedicata a Frances Flamini da'suoi discepuli* (Pisa, 1918), pp. 139–53; and Dom André Wilmart, "L'Art Poétique de Geoffroi de Vinsauf et les commentaires de Barthélemy de Pise," *RB*, 41 (1929), 271–75.

9. "idem est quod ordo artificialis," Vatican Library, MS Ottob. lat. 3291, f. 6ʳ.

10. "secundus non est proprie digressio sed quedam orationis preposteratio," London, British Library Additional MS 10095, f. 124ʳ. Pace was a professor of grammar and logic in Padua during the early fourteenth century; for further information about him, see Philip A. Stadter, "Planudes, Plutarch, and Pace of Ferrara," *IMU*, 16 (1973), 137–62. Pace's commentary is an important one that has survived in several manuscripts.

11. "quando rethor habet aliquam materiam habentem duas uel tres partes, et post quam posuit unam partem, tunc digreditur a principali materia inserenda aliqua que non sunt...," Vienna, Nationalbibliothek MS 5001, f. 24ᵛ.

12. "Altero vero est quando aliqua omitto et pertranseo, et postea redeo ad omissa," Rome, Biblioteca Casanatense MS 311, f. 23ʳ; "Sed iste modus non uidetur ampliare materiam. Unde potest dici quod auctor non posuit ipsum quasi ampliaret, sed ne forte crederetur esse unus solus modus digressionis, scilicet qui ampliat, posuit eciam istum quod pervertit," f. 23ᵛ.

Nicholaus Dybinus of Prague also wrote an important commentary on the *Poetria nova* that has survived in a number of manuscripts; it is being edited by Professor Hans Szklenar of the University of Heidelberg. For information on Dybinus, see Samuel Peter Jaffe's introduction to his edition of *Nicholaus Dybinus' "Declaracio Oracionis de Beata Dorothea"*: *Studies and Documents in the History of Late Medieval Rhetoric* (Wiesbaden, 1974).

Many other commentaries on the *Poetria nova* have survived, most anonymous and found in a single manuscript. A preliminary summary of the numbers of extant manuscripts may be found in Woods, "Literary Criticism"; I am preparing a bibliographical study of these commentaries for publication.

13. e.g., Paris, Bibliothèque Nationale MSS lat. 8171, f. 10ᵛ, and 15135, f. 169ᵛ.

14. Princeton, Robert Garrett Library collection MS 121, f. 26ʳ.

15. London, British Library Additional MS 18153, f. 14ᵛ.

16. "SI VELIT ULTERIUS. Agit de sexto gradu in quo dicit prolongari materiam, si fiat digressio ab incepto opere. Hec autem digressio, sicut ipse dicit, fit dupliciter: vno modo fit quando poeta, intermissa materia, de alia re agit que forte incidit, sicut de situ alicuius loci uel de natura alicuius rei, uel de laude aliqua et de similibus, et post hec redit ad materiam quam reliquerat. Alio modo fit digressio quando relicta materia aliud inducitur, quod longe remotum est, sed in fine adaptatur" (Munich, Bayerische Staatsbibliothek Clm 4603, f. 132ʳ).

This anonymous commentary has survived in five manuscripts, four from the thirteenth and one from the fourteenth century: (M) Munich, Clm 4603, s. XIII, f. 130ʳ–36ʳ; (V) Vienna, Nationalbibliothek MS 526, s. XIII, f. 95ᵛ–111ᵛ; (P) Vienna, Nationalbibliothek MS 2513, s. XIII, f. 34ʳ–62ᵛ; (G) Wolfenbüttel, Herzog August Bibliothek cod. Guelf. 124 Gud. lat., s. XIII, f. 1ʳ–22ʳ; (O) Vienna, Nationalbibliothek MS 1365, s. XIV, f.

65^v-75^r; unfortunately, MS O is incomplete and the commentary ends at l. 270. A sixth manuscript, Metz, Bibliothèque Municipale MS 516, s. XIV, was destroyed during World War II.

An edition of MSS M, V, P, and O is available in Woods, "The *In principio huius libri* Type A Commentary on Geoffrey of Vinsauf's *Poetria nova*: Analysis and Text" (Diss. Toronto, 1977); my edition of all the manuscripts and a translation of the commentary will be published by Garland Publishing, Inc. The choice of M as base manuscript and the method of editing are discussed in Woods, "Editing Medieval Commentaries: Problems and a Proposed Solution," *TEXT*, 1 (1984 for 1981), 133–45.

17. "De priori autem non dat exemplum quia frequens est non solum apud poetas uerum etiam apud hystoriographos" (M, f. 132^r); "... philosophos" (V, f. 99^v; the other manuscripts have M's reading).

18. "Differunt autem ille digressiones in hoc, quod in priori res que inducitur in principio melius conuenit materie ⟨quam⟩ incidet, sicut dictum est; in fine autem remota est quia relinquitur sine adaptatione. In altera autem res que inducitur in principio penitus remota est a materia sed in fine conuenit quia adaptatur" (M, f. 132^r, with G), corrected by P. V is more succinct: the digressions differ "in hoc, quod prima non ⟨ad⟩ aptatur, secunda vero adaptatur" (f. 99^v).

19. "Tertius est graduum collatio, facta biformi / Lege: vel occulte, vel aperte. — Respice quaedam / Juncta satis lepide; sed quaedam signa revelant / Nodum juncturae: collatio quae fit aperte / Se gerit in specie simili, quam signa revelant / Expresse. Tria sunt haec signa: magis, minus, aeque. / — Quae fit in occulto, nullo venit indice signo; / Non venit in vultu proprio, sed dissimulatio, / Et quasi non sit ibi collatio, sed nova quaedam / Insita mirifice transsumptio, res ubi caute / Sic sedet in serie quasi sit de themate nata" (Faral, p. 204; Nims, p. 25).

20. "TERCIUS EST GRADUS. Sequitur tercius in quo agitur de comparatione que duplex est, comparatio manifesta et oculta. Manifesta comparatio est quando poeta uolens demonstrare qualitatem rei de qua agit conuertitur ad rem similem, ut per partem notam partem minus notam ⟨demonstret⟩. Et trahat argumentum a simili, sicut in Alexandro ⟨ubi⟩ describatur animositas Alexandri quam habuit in pueritia. Inducitur comparatio manifesta sic: 'Qualiter Hircanis si forte leunculus aruis / Cornibus ⟨elatos⟩,' et cetera. Huiusmodi comparatio aput omnes poetas sufficienter inuenitur et precipue in istis quia quibusdam signis manifestantur" (M, f. 131^v, with G; corrected from P and O). V's gloss is different; it states that comparison "fit quando, per magnum notum uel eque notum, res minus nota demonstratur, uel quando trahitur argumentum a simili uel a maiori uel a minori; comparatio enim est rei ad rem collatio et fit per hec signa: ⟨246⟩ 'magis, minus, eque'; unde in Alexandro ..." Manuscripts V, P, G, and O quote Walter of Châtillon at great length, and V's gloss ends with the quotation. Note that the fourteenth-century manuscript O contains this section of the commentary.

21. "auctores" (O, f. 75^r).

22. "precipue apud Stacium" (P, f. 39^v, with GO). There are a number of small variants that I have not quoted here.

23. "Quando aliqua res aliunde assumpta ita subtiliter inseritur materie, quasi uideatur esse de ipsa materia, cum tamen non sit" (M, f. 131^v, with PGO).

24. It is possible, however, that the change from active to passive voice is simply rhetorical variation. And, of course, hidden comparison is found in poetry, too: the commentator goes on to illustrate hidden comparison with a quotation from Ovid.

25. See Judson B. Allen, "Commentary as Criticism: Formal Cause, Discursive Form, and the Late Medieval Accessus," *ACNL Lovaniensis*, ed. J. IJsewijn and E. Kessler (Louvain, 1973), p. 29.

26. It is hidden comparison which is accomplished "skillfully" ("subtiliter") in the quotation above; P notes several times that Geoffrey recommends hidden comparison; and at l. 261, P and O state that "hidden comparison involves more art than overt comparison" ("Habet ergo oculta comparatio magis artis quam manifesta").

27. In his life of Dante, Boccaccio praises poetry as "more obvious," *piu ... apparente*, than philosophy (*Trattatello in laude di Dante*, 1st version, ed. Pier Giorgio Ricci, in *Tutte le opere di Giovanni Boccaccio*, ed. Vittore Branca, Vol. 3 [Milan, 1974], par. 125, p. 468). This medieval distinction between poetry and prose discourse may have provided a pattern for those who followed. For example, Milton described poetry as "less subtle and fine, but more simple, sensuous, and passionate," *Milton on Education: The Tractate "Of Education"* ... , ed. Oliver M. Ainsworth (New Haven, 1928), p. 60. Merritt Hughes notes that "Milton is not defining the sublime art of poetry which had had its classical definition in Horace's *Art of Poetry* and Aristotle's *Poetics*; he is simply distinguishing poetry from rhetoric as *more simple, sensuous, and passionate* than any of the varieties of prose composition," John Milton, *Complete Poems and Major Prose* (Indianapolis, 1957), p. 637, n. 75.

28. "a principio per tramites suos ad idem principium decurrebat et recurrebat," R. W. Hunt, "English Learning in the Twelfth Century," *Essays in Medieval History*, ed. R. W. Southern (New York, 1968), pp. 120 (trans.) and 126, ll. 83–84 (Latin). (And, of course, the circularity in such poems as the *Pearl* show that such an effect was used effectively in medieval poems.)

29. See Paul Zumthor's discussion of the technique of the "sortie du poète hors du poème ou du poème hors du poète," in the gothic poem (" 'Roman' et 'gothique': Deux aspects de la poésie médiévale," *Studi in onore di Italo Siciliano* [Florence, 1966], II, 1233); and Robert Levine's application of this concept to Wolfram von Eschenbach's *Parzival*: "Zumthor ... assigns a technique to the gothic mode that manifests itself relentlessly in *Parzival*: the *sortie*. In its attempt to shatter the closed and potentially constricting universe of the fictional world of the poem, the gothic poem tries to break through to the world of actual life, resorting to the *sortie* to separate the poet deliberately from his poem. Consequently, we may expect to find the poet 'leaving' his poem, and the poem in a sense 'leaving' the poet; and in fact we do find such a process going on constantly in *Parzival*, as Wolfram continually breaks into and out of his poem ..." ("Wolfram von Eschenbach: Dialectical 'Homo ludens,' " *Viator*, 13 [1982], p. 187).

30. All quotations from Chaucer are taken from *The Works of Geoffrey Chaucer*, ed. F. N. Robinson (Boston, 1961).

31. Donald R. Howard, *The Idea of the Canterbury Tales* (Berkeley, 1976), p. 304.

32. In contrast to description, which is called an *exercicium* and an *actum operandi*; I am not sure of the meaning of *operandi* here (MSS P, f. 38A^r, and O, f. 74^r).

33. I am grateful to the American Council of Learned Societies and the National Endowment for the Humanities for a grant-in-aid which allowed the purchase of microfilms of commentaries on the *Poetria nova*. Those who heard versions of this paper at the Medieval Academy meeting at Kalamazoo, Michigan, in May, 1982, and at the Medieval Forum at Plymouth, New Hampshire, in April, 1983, as well as at the I.A.N.L.S. conference at St. Andrews, made many valuable suggestions; Professors Paula Backscheider and Mary Maleski read and criticized earlier drafts; Reid Barbour, Thomas Hahn, and Mary Nyquist suggested references.

Ernst Robert Curtius and Aby M. Warburg

Dieter Wuttke

You might think it unsuitable that I am going to talk about "Ernst Robert Curtius and Aby M. Warburg" at a congress on neo-Latin. The title of Curtius's philological main work runs: *European Literature and the Latin Middle Ages*. But I may recall that the term "Middle Ages" following Curtius's definition covers the period from the decline of the Roman Empire in the fourth century A.D. to the age of Goethe (about 1800). In addition to that his work is—without question—looked upon as one of the most important fundamental works of our subject, the neo-Latin studies, with regard to its topical as well as methodical qualities.

My contribution deals with a special topic of the history of Middle and neo-Latin Studies. It wants to clear up the background to the fact that Ernst Robert Curtius dedicated his famous book on *European Literature and the Latin Middle Ages* not only to Gustav Gröber, the well-known Romance philologist, but also to the art and cultural historian Aby M. Warburg.

The dedication of Curtius's book, first published in 1948 with a second, revised edition in 1954, reads: "Gustav Gröber (1844–1911) und Aby Warburg (1866–1929) in memoriam." One of the ten mottoes preceding the book is taken out of the *Grundriß der romanischen Philologie* (I, 1883, 3) by Gustav Gröber. At the end of Curtius's book the reader learns that Gröber has been Curtius's teacher who brought the tradition of strict philological research near to him, something that to continue and develop further has been one of the most important tasks of the author. From a footnote we learn that Curtius published a longer essay on "Gustav Gröber und die romanische Philologie." What kind of relation Curtius and *Warburg* had, we, however, do not learn. This is reflected in an interesting way in the various reviews of Curtius's book: while you come across the name of Gröber again and again the name of Warburg as the second person the book is dedicated to is consequently not mentioned. Who wants to know why the book is not only dedicated to Gröber but to Aby M. Warburg too, has to find the answer himself with the help of three different passages of the book: first he learns to know Warburg as a man who — like Curtius — advocates interdisciplinary research in humanities (p. 23). The other two passages deal with Warburg's teaching his students the saying "Der liebe Gott steckt im Detail" (God dwells in minutiae) thus rendering the strict method of historical-philological research (pp. 45, 386). As in the same context Gröber is mentioned and the reader recalls his motto adapted by Curtius he concludes that the accordance with Gröber and Curtius in the methodology of interdisciplinary historical and philological research has brought Warburg the honour of the dedication.

In 1945 shortly after the end of the war Curtius published the first version of his preface in the magazine *Die Wandlung* at Heidelberg. Here he talks very freely about the politico-cultural and above all the personal background of his book. Relating to cultural policy it is the answer to the new humanism Curtius required in his polemic treatise *Deutscher Geist in Gefahr* (German Genius in Danger) published in 1932. This new humanism should be a medievalism. Personally Curtius's book results from an inescapable necessity to change the field of research or, as he also says, to go back to archaic layers of consciousness. It results from his deeply felt experience in Rome which let the Roman Empire become for him a "Wunschraum" and "zeitlose Wirklichkeit." Furthermore the book results personally from his being deeply rooted in the areas of the upper and middle parts of the Rhine during his childhood, youth, and in the later years. Gröber appears in this first version of his preface as the great philological teacher who has given his pupil the preconditions which were necessary to rediscover the Middle Latin literature as an important aim of research. Aby M. Warburg's name does not appear here.

At another opportunity, however, Curtius forms a connecting link. It is in his Festschrift-article "Classical Pathos Formulas in Medieval Literature" (Antike Pathosformeln in der Literatur des Mittelalters), published in 1950. The term "Pathos-formula" has been invented and first used by Warburg. He understood it as formula born in classical antiquity to express extreme psychic and/or physical agitation or to express pathetic inner as well as outer tranquillity. Curtius's short essay can be looked upon as an attempt to prove in the study of literature the fertility of the Warburgian art historical initiative.

Several times Curtius hints at the interrelation between his politico-cultural prelude, his polemic treatise "German Genius in Danger" of 1932 and the learned accomplishment of his new humanism — programme in the following years which gets shape in his great book of 1948. This fact encourages us to look for traces of Warburg in the polemic treatise — with success, as we shall see. When defining characteristic features of the German intellectual situation of the time Curtius recognizes "a new deeply rooted general view of man" as the outstanding field of research worked at differently in the various disciplines like philosophy, medicine, psychoanalysis, pre- and early history and comparative cultural history (p. 29). As one of the scholars who has influenced this tendency decisively Warburg is mentioned. Curtius writes that "if the results of the lifework of Aby Warburg, who died too early, are collected, we will get a deep insight in the struggle between the magic-demonic and the rational conception of the world." Later, when expounding the sociologism of the time, he comes back to this important German contribution to the humanities and calls — among others — art history and the new cultural history one of the most important supporters of this new course of research (p. 83). That Curtius refers mainly to Warburg's research and the research he has stimulated in respect to art and cultural history is indubitable.

At the end of his treatise, when delineating his new humanism concept, Curtius defines humanism as "enthusiasm of love" (p. 107); he calls it "an intoxicating discovery of a beloved archetype." In this context Curtius recalls Warburg's pathos formulas, which entered the art of the Renaissance because of this power of the soul. So we see that Curtius as early as the end of 1931, when writing his polemic treatise, was well acquainted with very important aspects of Warburg's research. Warburg's complete works had not yet been published at that time. When thinking of the remarks of 1932 the dedication of 1948 seems to be more understandable: we get the idea of a more deeply rooted respect and an intellectual and mental mutuality than Curtius's remarks on Warburg's strictness in methodical questions since 1948 make us think. The uncommented 1948 dedication to Warburg can now — temporarily — be explained as the result of a matter-of-fact relationship.

With what was printed by Curtius on the relationship Curtius–Warburg we have come to an end now. In this situation we are glad to have other sources which Peter Dronke and I could use at the Warburg Institute. I am talking about the more than seventy letters and postcards still extant which Curtius and sometimes his wife Ilse and Gertrud Bing, Warburg's former assistant, as well as Fritz Saxl and Ernst Hans Gombrich exchanged, most of which were exchanged between Curtius and Gertrud Bing. From this correspondence we learn the following: Curtius met Warburg in Rome during the winter 1928/29. They seem to have met more than once to talk to each other and Curtius, as a different source says, was present when Warburg delivered his famous lecture on his Mnemosyne-Atlas at the Biblioteca Hertziana on 19 January 1929. The guestbook of the Biblioteca with Curtius's entry does still exist. These meetings impressed Curtius deeply. Since that winter in Rome he called himself one of the "Warburg people" (letter of 24 May 1936), "he always thinks of Warburg full of gratitude" (letter of 26 May 1948), and he continuously underlines his being highly interested in a close connection with Gertrud Bing and the Warburg Institute. Moreover we learn that Bing, Curtius and his wife met several times in neighboring foreign countries during their holidays. Expressions of deep love and longing attachment run like a leitmotiv through the correspondence in which finally also the question of the dedication was touched upon by Curtius in 1947/48.

In winter 1928/29 Curtius thus started to study the publications of Warburg and the circle around the Warburg Library. This was done steadily and intensively. By September 1934 he had worked through Warburg's complete works, published in 1932. The first volume of the *Bibliography of the Survival of the Classics*

Curtius welcomed enthusiastically and recognized in Edgar Wind's introduction the confirmation, clarification and continuation of his own thoughts. He read Panofsky's *Idea* and the until today too little known excellent book of Ernst Kris and Otto Kurz on *The Legend of the Artist* (Die Legende vom Künstler). Since 1937 he subscribed to the *Journal of the Warburg and Courtauld Institutes*. Curtius confesses that his main field of research is now the survival of the classics and that he has more than once used the same sources as Panofsky and Liebeschütz did.

When in 1946 the connection was reestablished through Bing's intiative, Curtius at once kept up again the former possibilities. Book presents partly important for his great book were gratefully accepted. Even a regular lending service developed. And he called the Institute in 1948 "the only open door to the cosmopolis of research." Along with and prior to the book-lending there was a constant wish for information including even certain iconographic items. Thus he got throughout the years many useful hints which were of benefit to the essays preparing his book.

Between 1934 and 1936 he enthusiastically drew his students' and some colleagues' attention to the Warburg Institute, including the philosophers Jacques Maritain and Erich Rothacker and the historian Arnold Toynbee. Rothacker spontaneously asked him to write an article on Warburg and his Institute in the *Deutsche Vierteljahresschrift für Literaturwissenschaft und Geistesgeschichte*. As the anti-jewish pressure increased in Germany in 1936 this article was not written. It is remarkable that Curtius interpreted the Botticelli pictures "Spring" and the "Birth of Venus" in his lectures in the winter of 1934/35 exactly following Warburg's dissertation.

For the development of our train of thought three important questions, however, remain still unanswered: first, we do not learn, *what* has brought about the close relationship with Warburg in the winter of 1928/29 personally as well as professionally. Secondly, it is not quite understandable that Curtius speaks about the enormous influence Rome has had on him (in his 1945 preface) but that he leaves out the above-mentioned encounters with Warburg. If we believe his letters—and why shouldn't we?—his relationship with Warburg can be compared to the same magic which attached him to the remains of ancient Rome becoming for him a "Wunschraum" and "zeitlose Wirklichkeit" (endless in respect to space and time). These two expressions he quotes without doubt from the famous essay by Alfred Doren on "Wunschräume und Wunschzeiten" which had been inspired and published by the "Kulturwissenschaftliche Bibliothek Warburg." Thirdly, having in mind the close connections with Warburg, Bing, and the Warburg Institute and the advantages Curtius had from Warburg's and the Institute's fundamentally art-historical studies his well-known attack on the history and theory of art, its global condemnation and the strict separation of art and literature cannot be comprehended. As Curtius himself asked Bing about this, Ernst H. Gombrich—asked by Bing to do so—wrote a detailed comment on Curtius's corresponding discours. This discourse refers to a preprint in the magazine *Merkur* (1947). Curtius could have changed his attitude in the book; but he did less than this. He let Gombrich send a hearty thank-you and still in 1951 he insisted proudly on his rigid remarks in his book-diary published in the *Tat* at Zürich. At the beginning of 1952 this strange wish of keeping his distance undergoes a sudden change. He is now interested in cave painting and tells Bing about his latest discoveries. His thoughts run like this: "In the beginning there was not the thought but the picture, or better to say, making pictures was thinking. Very similar thoughts have been taught by Konrad Fiedler." It is difficult to imagine Bing's reaction on Curtius's ideas, for—as Curtius should have known—it belongs to Warburg's fundamental findings that mankind has not yet overcome the primeval symbiosis of picture and thinking up to our days. That is why Warburg thought his institute of such importance and why he opened the way for the theory and history of art to a comprehensive iconology. And only because of Warburg's opening the way to interdisciplinary and comparative studies Curtius as a historian of literature could take advantage of Warburg's publications and of those who were near to him. In other words: in this respect something irrational must have been involved.

Let us finally go back to the first question as to what the close relationship with Warburg in personal as well as in professional respect has brought about. A kind of guessing is necessary but it is not totally unjustified. From sources of the Warburg remains we learn what problems Warburg tried to solve during the winter of 1928/29 in Rome. The fact that Curtius was deeply impressed by Warburg's ideas and kept them well in mind can be read from an essay on the occasion of the tenth anniversary of Curtius's death by his former student Gustav René Hocke in the magazine *Merkur* in 1966. With respect to Warburg two things are remarkable in this essay: first, Hocke gives the impression that Curtius and Warburg were good friends whereas in respect to Curtius this relationship was one of a deeply psychic kind as well. Secondly, Hocke states that Curtius was grateful for Warburg's motif-research and that the subject of one of their conversations in Rome was Manet's "Déjeuner sur l'herbe." Manet's source Warburg proved to be a Renaissance engraving. Hocke goes on to say that at the end of October 1929 while staying at a hotel at Mannheim and learning there by telegram that Warburg had died Curtius's glance fell on a copy of this engraving that happened to hang there and he understood it as a greeting from his dead friend.

Probably a kind of myth is involved here which keeps the truth under cover.

Let us now see with what subject Warburg was occupied in Rome and what was the content of his Hertziana lecture. At that time he tried to complete his Mnemosyne-Atlas which was to complete his lifework. The somewhat complicated German subtitle runs in English translation: "Series of pictures to examine the function of classical forms of expression when depicting inner and outer movement in the art of the European Renaissance" (*Bildreihe zur Untersuchung der Funktion vorgeprägter antiker Ausdruckswerte bei der Darstellung bewegten Lebens in der Kunst der europäischen Renaissance*). The classical forms of expression include the abovementioned pathos formulas. Warburg first defined them as forms of expression to delineate limits of utmost psychic and physical agitation. In the Hertziana lecture he presented his Mnemosyne-Atlas to an audience for the first time. Whether now or a little bit later cannot be said for sure, but during that time he expanded the term pathos formula to a form of expression to delineate pathetic psychic and physical tranquillity as well. This extension had become necessary to him as a result of his research on Manet's "Déjeuner sur l'herbe." This piece of art, displayed at Paris in 1863, belongs to those which mark the beginning of modern painting. This painting, however, proves to be in a striking way influenced by tradition. Warburg is able to trace the central group of three persons back to antiquity; it can be discovered for the first time on a Roman sarcophagus which shows the judgement of Paris, then on an engraving by Marcantonio Raimondi made in Rome between 1510 and 1524 after a lost work of art by Raffael, and finally on a copy of the Raimondi engraving of the seventeenth century. Thus Warburg discovered the continuity of a form of expression to delineate pathetic tranquillity from antiquity to Manet (Gombrich, *Aby Warburg*, pp. 273–77). This corresponds in the field of the theory of art with what Curtius later called a topos or cliché in the study of literature (Curtius, *Europ. Lit.*, p. 79).

Warburg was not satisfied with following the continuity of topoi diachronically as Curtius did — as you know, a fact that caused quite a few and in a way justified criticisms of Curtius. On the contrary Warburg was from the beginning concerned with finding out what kind of change the forms of expression undergo, what function they have in the piece of art that realizes them, of what importance they are for the works of art as well as for the artist in respect to style and content. To come back to our example very briefly, it means: from antiquity to the seventeenth century the resting group has always been connected to the judgement of Paris. On the Roman relief the group is deeply rooted in the mythical event: the observation of the returning of the gods to Olympus. A fourth person, a nymph, makes frightful, defending gestures. In Raimondi's engraving one of the sitting women turns to the onlooker as if she were fishing for compliments on her beauty, she obviously is not interested anymore in the return of the gods, the river-god on the right side seems to rebuke her because of her inattentiveness in spite of his classical apathy; in the seventeenth century the return of the gods to Olympus is replaced by a herd of cattle crossing a river; thus the group is suddenly embedded in a pastoral scenery. According to Warburg this transition made it possible for Manet to remove the group completely from the frame of the Paris-Judgement and to make it a symbol of a new, in a way revolutionary discovery of light in painting or, as Warburg himself said, a symbol of Manet's fight for the human rights of the eye ("die Menschenrechte des Auges": Gombrich, p. 274).

Beyond that Warburg strives to find a theory which explains the origin of the forms of expression and their adaptation. In his opinion they have had their origin specially in the Dionysos cult within orgiastic mass excitement and have implanted themselves in the collective memory of European mankind as engrams of passionate experience. As artists — social organs according to Warburg (*Ausgewählte Schriften*, p. 602) — have special access to the collective memory they use these formulas when they want to express the limits of agitation or tranquillity. With his Mnemosyne-Atlas Warburg wanted to publish his collection of forms of expression derived from antiquity in order to prove the existence of a collective memory and at the same time to give insight into its way of functioning (Gombrich, pp. 283–306; *Ausgewählte Schriften*, pp. 307–09). This is much more than what Curtius has ever tried to do with the literary topoi.

By the way, in 1965 Gertrud Bing, in 1970 Arthur R. Evans, Jr., in 1978 Peter Burke, in 1980 Götz Pochat, and in 1981 Jan Białostocki have already underlined that Warburg founded the topos research for the theory and history of art.

About 1930, according to his own words, Curtius felt himself compelled to change his previous field of work. If I am not mistaken Curtius found in Warburg his stimulator and guide during the winter of 1928/29 in Rome. In his memoirs, the famous British art historian Kenneth Clark calls Warburg's Hertziana-lecture "a lecture that changed my life." For Curtius as well, this lecture and the following conversations with Warburg have obviously been a lecture that changed his life. This seems to be the real personal meaning which the experience with the reproduction of Raimondi's engraving, when receiving the news of Warburg's death, he expresses: at that moment of deep emotion Curtius had the feeling as if the dead master once more showed him the flag he had to follow in his own study of literature in the future.

In this context it is worth mentioning that by 1936, moreover, he had come to know the above-mentioned book by Kris and Kurz on "The Legend of the Artist" the theme of which was already the literary topos research in Curtius's sense. Saxl had drawn Curtius's attention to this book.

If Curtius had had the chance to write his memoirs—like Kenneth Clark—he would surely have paid tribute to Warburg and the Warburg-Institute in a deserved way. As matters stand it is true that he erected a monument for Warburg in 1948 on one hand but on the other he effaced the traces of Warburg's true importance in a way. The irrational attack on the theory and history of art can probably be understood as an attempt by the subconscious to free himself from the deep relationship with Warburg and especially the realization of not having reached his example. It is a striking fact that the amazing circulation of Curtius's book did not contribute practically to a Warburg renaissance in the years after the war. If Curtius had displayed Warburg's true importance he would not have presented himself as the pioneer the way he did and the way he was looked at by his readers: an unsolvable predicament.

Let us sum up the results: one of the many merits of Aby M. Warburg is probably the fact that he inspired one of the most important humanistic works of our century. But that is not half enough: he anticipated the essential criticism of future critics without one of these critics recognizing this fact. In other words: Warburg had run rings round Curtius in methodical questions, when Curtius had not yet started his preparatory studies. This remark is not intended to diminish

Curtius's great merits, but to convey the knowledge that Warburg has deserved the dedication in a much wider sense than the reading of the book makes us think.[1]

Note

1. My research on "Ernst Robert Curtius and Aby M. Warburg" has been supported by The Warburg Institute, especially by Miss Anne Maria Meyer, and by the "Hamburgische Wissenschaftliche Stiftung." Mrs Ilse Curtius, Bonn, kindly permitted me to quote from Ernst Robert Curtius's letters.

Bibliography

1. A. Warburg, *Gesammelte Schriften*. Herausgegeben von der Bibliothek Warburg. Band I/II. Unter Mitarbeit von Fritz Rougemont herausgegeben von Gertrud Bing: *Die Erneuerung der heidnischen Antike*. Kulturwissenschaftliche Beiträge zur Geschichte der europäischen Renaissance. Mit einem Anhang unveröffentlichter Zusätze (Leipzig–Berlin, 1932. Nendeln,[2] 1969). (Out of print.)

2. Aby Warburg, *La rinascità del paganesimo antico. Contributi alla storia della cultura*. Raccolti di Gertrud Bing. Traduzione di Emma Cantimori. Firenze 1966. (Italian Translation of most parts of No. 1, introduced by G. Bing, cf. No. 4.)

3. Aby M. Warburg, *Ausgewählte Schriften und Würdigungen*. Herausgegeben von Dieter Wuttke. In Verbindung mit Carl Georg Heise (Baden–Baden, [2]1980).

4. Gertrud Bing, "A. M. Warburg," in *JWCI*, 28 (1965), 229–313. (Italian translation in No. 2, German in No. 3.)

5. E. H. Gombrich, *Aby Warburg. An Intellectual Biography*. With a Memoir on the history of the Library by F. Saxl (London, 1970). (German translation Frankfurt/M., 1981. German translation of Saxl's Memoir also in No. 3.)

6. Dieter Wuttke, *Aby M. Warburgs Methode als Anregung und Aufgabe*. Dritte, um einen Briefwechsel zum Kunstverständnis erweiterte Auflage (Göttingen, 1979).

7. *Mnemosyne*. Beiträge zum 50. Todestag von Aby M. Warburg. Herausgegeben von Stephan Füssel (Göttingen, 1979). (p. 47ff. Kenneth Clark "A lecture that Changed my Life.")

8. Ernst Robert Curtius, *Deutscher Geist in Gefahr* (Stuttgart–Berlin, 1932, [3]1933).

9. Ernst Robert Curtius, *Europäische Literatur und lateinisches Mittelalter* (Bern, 1948. Zweite, durchgesehene Auflage 1954. [9]1978). (English translation 1953, Spanish 1955, French 1956, Portugese 1957, Italian 1963.)

10. Ernst Robert Curtius, *Kritische Essays zur europäischen Literatur* (Bern, 1950). (pp. 429–35 reprint of the 1945 introduction of No. 9.)

11. Ernst Robert Curtius, *Gesammelte Aufsätze zur romanischen Philologie* (Bern und München, 1960). (pp. 23–27 "Antike Pathosformeln in der Literatur des Mittelalters.")

12. Gustav René Hocke, "Begegnungen mit Ernst Robert Curtius." In: *Merkur*, 20 (1966) 690–97.

13. Arthur R. Evans, Jr., "Ernst Robert Curtius," in *On Four Modern Humanists. Hofmannthal, Gundolf, Curtius, Kantorowicz.* Ed. Arthur R. Evans, Jr. (Princeton, N.J., 1970), pp. 85–145.

14. Peter Dronke, "Curtius as a Medievalist and Modernist." In: *TLS*, October 3, 1980, pp. 1103–06.

15. Peter Burke, *Popular Culture in Early Modern Europe* (London, 1978). (German translation, Stuttgart, 1981, see p. 160.)

16. Götz Pochat, "Kunstgeschichte als europäische Erziehung," in Lars Olof Larsson-Götz Pochat, *Kunstgeschichtliche Studien zur Florentiner Renaissance* (Stockholm, 1980), pp. 1–33 (p. 5ff).

17. Jan Białostocki, "Aby M. Warburgs Botschaft: Kunstgeschichte oder Kulturgeschichte?" in *Vorträge und Aufsätze*, hg. vom Verein für Hamburgische Geschichte, Heft 23 (Hamburg, 1981), pp. 25–41 (pp. 26, 36ff.).

18. Dieter Wuttke, "Warburg, Curtius und Latein für Europa," in *Deutsche Tagespost*. Sonderbeilage Latein, 23/24 Dezember, 1982, p. VI.

19. Dieter Wuttke, "Die Emigration der Kulturwissenschaftlichen Bibliothek Warburg," in *Berichte zur Wissenschaftgeschichte*, 7 (1984), pp. 179–94.

20. Dieter Wuttke, "Ernst Robert Curtius und Aby M. Warburg," *Arcadia*, 21 (1986). (Extended version of the above printed lecture with edition of parts of the correspondence between Curtius and The Warburg Institute.)

21. Martin Jesinghausen-Lauster, *Die Suche nach der symbolischen Form. Der Kreis um die Kulturwissenschaftliche Bibliothek Warburg* (Baden-Baden, 1985). (With additional observations on the relationship between Curtius and Warburg.)

Report on the Seminar "Varieties of Nominalism from Cusa to Montaigne"

Robert Ginsberg

The work of the seminar springs from three contributions on nominalism in Montaigne, Nizolio, and Hobbes. The challenge posed by the organizer P. G. Kuntz was to see if a consistent nominalism unites these contributions or if instead there is an array of different nominalisms. The latter result triumphed.

Kuntz views Montaigne as an eclectic without a care for the cosmos that includes humanity. Whereas Ockham was schooled in logic and makes a commitment to God as principle, Montaigne uses grammar as his tool and makes his commitment to humanity, discoverable in the individual. Hence, Montaigne is a humanistic nominalist who chooses to be an artist as essayist. Kuntz argues Montaigne's thought stands or falls on the question of a consistent human nature.

C. Vasoli characterizes Nizolio's nominalism as that of a grammarian offering a critique of philosophy. The philosophers have reified terms, producing barbaric absurdity and useless falsity. Thus, universals were taken to be real substances in themselves. Rhetoric and grammar are more dependable and truthful than metaphysics because they reveal the realities of language. One really defines names not things. So linguistic analysis is the remedy to philosophical dogmatism. Hence, there is a closeness between the linguistic critique in philosophical nominalism and the linguistic attitude in philosophical humanism.

P. A. Redpath portrays Hobbes as schooled in speech rather than grammar, and his nominalism is voluntaristic rather than rationalistic. Hobbes deduces the world from clear and distinct sensations rightfully defined in speech. And speech is a social invention, dependent, as is the very Leviathan, on agreement of human wills. Nonetheless, Redpath will not accept Hobbes's reduction of all knowledge to human will.

Thus, whereas Nizolio's nominalism is a grammatical critique of systematic philosophy, Hobbes's nominalism is a systematic construction of philosophy based on a theory of speech that arises from human analysis. Montaigne too starts with self-study of the human — the individual — but he refrains from building systems.

J. J. Supple defends Montaigne as a shatterer of all categories pressed down upon him, for Montaigne thrives on contradiction. Though eclectic, Montaigne did have a critique of language, and his nominalism is intended as an attack on contemporary humanist pedagogy rather than on realist metaphysics.

I. J. Winter inquires just what portion of Montaigne's eclecticism is nominalism. A. S. McGrade adds that while nominalism is often looked at as suspicion of system, true eclecticism must also be looked at in that light. Perhaps nominalism is more systematically against system.

McGrade and Kuntz suggest that Montaigne and Hobbes are both sensationalists or radical empiricists. Winter and Kuntz recall that Montaigne's nominalism is related to his celebrated skepticism. Kuntz proposes that Hobbes be called a naturalistic nominalist. Messrs. Kuntz, McGrade, Supple, and Redpath conclude the seminar with investigation of the relationship of nominalism to scientific method.

At adjournment for tea, thirty-two senses of nominalism had been discussed, evidence that the participants had not treated nominalism in name only but had penetrated its variegated intellectual substance.

Index

Time, space and the need for easy reference make this index less comprehensive than it could have been: thus deliberate omissions have been decided. Only proper names are included; but mythological names are not taken into account, nor are those of fictitious characters (unless they are deemed to have autobiographical significance). Modern historians or critics are excluded, unless they form the subject of a paper (e.g. Curtius). Where lists of names occur, mainly for illustrative purposes or as examples of a trend, period or group, only the most important references — e.g. names dealt with in more detail in the relevant paper(s) — are mentioned. Names in footnotes are omitted: they could increase the text immeasurably; the more important ones are usually dealt with in the relevant main text. With contributors coming from so many countries, complete standardisation of names has not always been possible (e.g. Vergil/Virgil). It is doubtless more important that further delay in publication is avoided.